O9-BRY-451

lar recipe stage; subsequent cooking will usually compensate for any differences in wattage. **Note: *Always check food for doneness after minimum microwave time.***

~~~~~~Whenever specific tests for doneness are given, they are essential to the success of the recipe.

~~~~~~Whenever ingredient list includes another recipe by name (Jiffy Tomato Sauce, for example), its cooking time is not added to that of the recipe in which it's included.

~~~~~~Whenever two preparations can be performed simultaneously–chopping the onions, for example, while the sauce cooks 5 minutes–5 minutes only are added to the total prep time.

~~~~~~Whenever two cooking jobs are performed simultaneously, as when pasta boils top-stove while you microwave the sauce, the two individual times are not added together. Only the longer time is factored into the total.

~~~~~~Whenever a food is allowed to stand while you microwave the next stage of a recipe, that standing time is written thus at the top of the recipe: None.*

POWER LEVELS

HIGH = 100% power
MEDIUM-HIGH = 70% power
MEDIUM = 50% power
MEDIUM-LOW = 30% power
LOW = 10% power

Note: *All recipes in this book were developed for mid- and full-size microwave ovens in the 600-to-700-watt range. In ovens of less than 600 watts, increase cooking times about 10–15%.*

NUTRITIVE COUNTS

~~~~~~Figures per average-size serving are set down to the nearest round number (148 calories instead of 147.79, 5 milligrams [mg] cholesterol instead of 4.86, and 83 grams [g] carbohydrate instead of 82.91). *But whenever portions are small–a tablespoon of sauce or jam, for example, one hors d'oeuvre or canapé, one brownie or piece of fudge–the nutritive counts are quite specific.* There's good reason for this: You'll rarely confine yourself to a single tablespoon of sauce or jam, or to a single brownie, and the fractions, sacrificed for the sake of round numbers in larger meal-size portions, quickly add up. For example, if a piece of candy contains 40.5 milligrams of cholesterol, a second piece will increase the total amount by a full milligram.

~~~~~~Whenever recipes yield a variable number of servings (e.g., 4–6), the first and higher number represents 4 servings; the second and lower number, 6.

~~~~~~*Unless otherwise indicated, all nutritive counts are based upon recipe ingredients and do not include such suggested accompaniments as rice or sauce.*

~~~~~~*Abbreviations used:* C (calorie), P (protein), F (fat), CARB (carbohydrate), S (sodium), CH (cholesterol): also, g = gram and mg = milligram.

Note: *If you are on a low-sodium diet, use only low-sodium or salt-free prepared foods such as canned broths, vegetables, and sauces.*

(Continued on Back End Papers)

Also by Jean Anderson and Elaine Hanna

THE DOUBLEDAY COOKBOOK*

THE NEW DOUBLEDAY COOKBOOK

Also by Jean Anderson

THE ART OF AMERICAN INDIAN COOKING
(with Yeffe Kimball)

FOOD IS MORE THAN COOKING

HENRY THE NAVIGATOR, PRINCE OF PORTUGAL

THE HAUNTING OF AMERICA

THE FAMILY CIRCLE COOKBOOK
(with the Food Editors of *Family Circle*)

RECIPES FROM AMERICA'S RESTORED VILLAGES

THE GREEN THUMB PRESERVING GUIDE

THE GRASS ROOTS COOKBOOK

JEAN ANDERSON'S PROCESSOR COOKING

HALF A CAN OF TOMATO PASTE & OTHER CULINARY DILEMMAS†
(with Ruth Buchan)

JEAN ANDERSON COOKS

UNFORBIDDEN SWEETS

JEAN ANDERSON'S *NEW* PROCESSOR COOKING

THE FOOD OF PORTUGAL‡

* *Winner of the R. T. French Tastemaker Award, Best Cookbook of the Year (1975)*
† *Winner of the R. T. French Tastemaker Award, Best Specialty Cookbook of the Year (1980)*
‡ *Winner of the Seagram/International Association of Cooking Professionals Award, Best Foreign Cookbook of the Year (1986)*

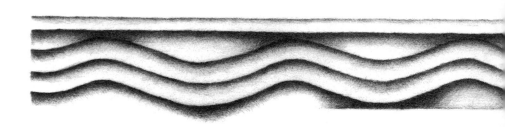

PHOTOGRAPHY BY RUDY MULLER
ILLUSTRATION BY LAUREN JARRETT

DOUBLEDAY BOOK & MUSIC CLUBS, INC.
GARDEN CITY, NEW YORK

MICRO WAYS

EVERY
COOK'S
GUIDE
TO
SUCCESSFUL
MICROWAVING

JEAN ANDERSON &
ELAINE HANNA

PUBLISHED BY DOUBLEDAY
a division of
Bantam Doubleday Dell Publishing Group, Inc.
666 Fifth Avenue, New York, New York 10103

and

GuildAmerica Books™, an imprint of Doubleday
Book & Music Clubs, Inc., 501 Franklin Avenue,
Garden City, New York 11530

DOUBLEDAY and the portrayal of an anchor
with a dolphin are trademarks of Doubleday,
a division of Bantam Doubleday Dell Publishing
Group, Inc.

GuildAmerica Books™ is a trademark registration
pending on behalf of Doubleday Book & Music
Clubs, Inc.

"Micro Ways" is used with the permission of *Newsday*.

Library of Congress Cataloging-in-Publication Data

Anderson, Jean
    Micro ways: every cook's guide to successful microwaving / by Jean Anderson and Elaine Hanna.—
    1st ed.
        p.   cm.
        Includes index.
        1. Microwave cookery.   I. Hanna, Elaine. II. Title.
TX832.A52   1990   89-1421
641.5'882—dc20   CIP

ISBN 0-385-24300-6
Copyright © 1990 by Doubleday, a division of Bantam Doubleday Dell
Publishing Group, Inc.

All Rights Reserved
Printed in the United States of America

First Edition
FFG

Quality printing and binding by:
Arcata Graphics/Fairfield
100 North Miller Street
Fairfield, Pa. 17320
U.S.A.

ACKNOWLEDGMENTS

We are greatly indebted to the following firms for providing microwave cookware and accessories to use in developing recipes for this book: Corning Glass Works, Corning, New York; Regal Ware, Inc., Kewaskum, Wisconsin; Revere Ware, Inc., Clinton, Illinois; and Rubbermaid, Inc., Wooster, Ohio.

We should also like to thank the following individuals and companies for so graciously supplying valuable information: Amana Refrigeration, Inc., Microwave Oven Dept.; American Dairy Association; American Egg Board; Anchor Hocking Corp.; Caloric-Modern Maid Co.; Joy Daniels, Sharp Electronics Corp.; Alan F. Donnelly, Corning Glass Works; Dow Chemical Co.; Frigidaire Co.; General Electric Co.; Hitachi Sales Corp. of America; R. Carl Hoseney, Ph.D., Dept. of Grain Science and Industry, Kansas State University; Jenn-Air Co.; Patricia Kendall, Ph.D., Food Science and Human Nutrition, Cooperative Extension, Colorado State University; KitchenAid, Inc.; Robert C. LaGasse, International Microwave Power Institute; Nancy Boyle Levene, Sharp Electronics Corp.; Litton Microwave Cooking Products; Litton Systems, Inc.; Magic Chef, Inc.; National Live Stock and Meat Board; Nordic Ware, Northland Aluminum Products, Inc.; Neal O'Donnell, Corning Glass Works; Panasonic and Quasar, both Matsushita Electric Corp. of America; Republic Molding Corp.; Reynolds Metals Co.; Sanyo Electric, Inc.; Sears, Roebuck & Co.; Tappan; Thermador Waste King Co.; Toshiba America, Inc.; Union Carbide Corp.; United Fresh Fruit and Vegetable Association; Whirlpool Corp.; White-Westinghouse Appliance Co.

We also wish to thank our valiant friends, neighbors, and relatives who, ever willing to serve as guinea pigs, helped "proof the pudding" during the five years that we were developing recipes for this book.

CONTENTS

INTRODUCTION

With more than 60 million microwave ovens now in use across America and 12 million more being bought every year, it's scarcely surprising that there's been an avalanche of microwave cookbooks.

And yet relatives, friends, and neighbors continue to tell us they're intimidated by their microwave ovens—afraid of them, even—and don't know how to use them properly. Well, they're not alone. Nearly 80% of all microwave owners use their ovens for little more than thawing frozen foods, heating TV dinners, and popping the occasional batch of corn.

In our experience, the microwave cookbooks that concentrate on recipes tend to short-change techniques. And those that zero in on the mechanics of microwaving provide lackluster recipes, for the most part quickies tossed together out of instants and mixes.

Where's the one big book that gets it all together? That demystifies the mumbo-jumbo of microwaving? That makes that sleek box with all the electronic touch pads, beeps, bings, and programmed cooking modes user-friendly? To many of us the microwave oven is some sort of space-age alien to be treated with fear and trembling instead of a kitchen appliance of remarkable versatility.

Microwave ovens needn't, for example, always cook at near-supersonic speed. They make dandy *slow* cookers. And there's no reason on earth not to involve yourself with food as it microwaves, to touch, taste, poke, prod, and stir just as you do when cooking the old-fashioned way. You're the cook, and the microwave oven, if you'll only let it, is there to serve you.

In this book we've tried to do the following: We're "up front" about what microwave ovens can do and, maybe more important, *can't* do. The temptation, whenever a new appliance catches the public fancy, is to use it exclusively, to make it perform jobs it was never intended to do. As amazing as microwave ovens are, they can't do everything and are, in fact, abysmal flops when it comes to baking yeast breads, sponge cakes, and crisp meringues.

We tell you how to use your microwave oven in tandem with your stovetop, conventional oven, and broiler, as well as how to use it solo. You don't throw your kitchen range away when you buy a microwave oven. You learn to use the two in concert.

We discuss in detail the kinds of microwave ovens available, review the mountain of microwave cookware and accessories, and explain which materials work best for which cooking procedures.

We decipher the language of microwaving (often more baffling than computereze) with a no-nonsense dictionary of microwave terms and techniques.

We think we've given you a genuinely broad recipe repertoire, with enough basics to launch the beginner in high style, enough dinners in a dish and a dash to accommodate the busy working mother, and enough shortcut classics to challenge the pro. A French pâté, for example. A Portuguese cataplana. An Italian osso buco or German sauerbraten. An Oriental skillet scramble or barbecue of ribs.

We hope we've succeeded in covering everything you need to know to use your microwave oven with confidence and creativity. We've devoted the better part of five years to the project (not counting, of course, the thirty-odd years we've worked as food editors and writers).

Here, then, are just some of the features that we hope make this microwave cookbook different:

More than 800 recipes especially created for the microwave oven, a discriminating collection, tested and retested until fail-safe, that uses the microwave both solo and in tandem with the stovetop, oven, and/or broiler.

Recipes that include every specific: preparation times . . . precise microwave times, together with standing times and descriptions of what a particular recipe should look, taste, or feel like when "done" . . . microwave powers for each recipe stage . . . pan, casserole, or mold sizes whenever size is critical to the recipe's success. And, lest you mistake a natural microwave phenomenon for failure, you're alerted to any surprises you may encounter in the course of preparing a particular recipe.

Recipes for singles and doubles as well as for four, six, and eight.

Party recipes, family recipes, international classics, and all-American favorites, each reworked especially for the microwave.

Recipes that can be prepared in stages, refrigerated or frozen, and then quickly finished by microwave.

Recipes keyed whenever they are low-calorie, low-cost, or particularly quick and easy.

Per-serving calorie, protein, fat, carbohydrate, cholesterol, and sodium counts for virtually every recipe.

Tips on adapting your own recipe favorites for the microwave.

Dozens of easy-to-read charts for thawing, reheating, and cooking all kinds of food by microwave.

This book's purpose, quite simply, is to assemble between two covers the most complete, up-to-date information available about microwaving; to answer the cook's most troubling questions, no matter how basic (Do microwave ovens leak radiation? How can you give microwaved quick breads a nice brown crust? Can you roast a turkey by microwave?).

We aim to teach the *whys* of microwaving as well as the *hows,* the fun as well as the fundamentals. In short, to show the cook—*every cook*—how to use this extraordinary oven to best advantage and to the hilt. It is, after all, not just a nifty new appliance. It's a whole new method of cooking.

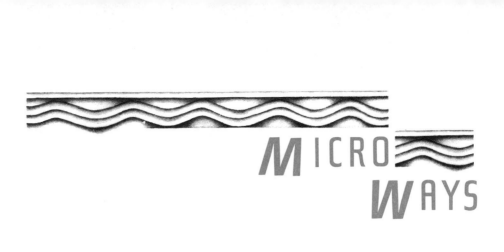

PART ONE

$\underline{\underline{1}}$

The Microwave and How It Works

*R*emember when food processors were the hot new kitchen ''toy'' and we tried to make them do *everything?* We soon learned that they did a lousy job of mashing potatoes and that blenders were better at buzzing up frothy drinks.

*N*ow comes the microwave, and miraculous as it is, it can't cook everything to perfection. Nor should we expect it to. The microwave was never meant to replace the stovetop or conventional oven, but was intended merely to be used in conjunction with them. Each is a specialist and each performs certain jobs better than the others. We'll discuss what the microwave does and doesn't do well later on in this chapter, but first:

WHAT ARE MICROWAVES AND HOW DO THEY COOK FOOD?

*L*est we turn you off at the start, we'll keep this as untechnical as possible. As a friend said, ''I don't need to know *everything* about a telephone to use it.'' Quite so. Still, microwave cooking differs so radically from conventional methods it's good to have some notion of what microwaves are all about.

*L*ike radio and television broadcast waves, they are electromagnetic waves transmitted through air instead of through wires like electricity. As wavelengths go, they're very short (less than five inches), hence their name—*micro*waves. They're also of high frequency, *cycling 2,450 million times every second* (with normal household current, it's just 60 times).

*A*bout fifty years ago, scientists discovered that microwaves could make water boil (the scientific explanation, vastly simplified, is that they set the water molecules in such frenzied motion that they generate considerable heat). Because most food is largely water, would food, bombarded with microwaves, also heat—and perhaps *cook?* It would, and the era of microwave cooking was off to a slow, shaky start.

There were many riddles to unravel, many problems to solve, before microwave cooking could come into everyday use. First of all, microwaves reacted in three different, sometimes startling ways, depending upon the material with which they made contact. *They might be:*

1. **REFLECTED:** Microwaves bounce off metal like Ping-Pong balls off a hard surface. Thus metal pots and pans are useless for microwave cooking because microwaves cannot penetrate them to reach the food inside. For this very reason, foil strips effectively shield skinny areas of food (poultry wings, drumstick tips, and the like) from microwaves and prevent their drying and/or burning while the thicker portions finish cooking.

2. **TRANSMITTED:** Microwaves pass straight through glass, porcelain, paper, and certain plastics without heating or changing them in any way. It's almost as if they weren't there. These are therefore the materials of choice for microwave cookware (for details, see Chapter 3).

3. **ABSORBED:** Only substances that absorb microwaves will heat—or *cook.* For the sake of simplicity, let's just say that foods containing water and/ or fat and/or sugar microwave best. *Microwaved foods do not, as has been written, cook from the inside out.* They cook from the outside in— by microwaves for the first 1" to 1½", and by conduction thereafter. Strangely, foods being microwaved will often seem cooler on the surface than in the interior. There's an easy explanation for this. The air inside a microwave oven remains cold, and any surface heat on the food quickly dissipates in that air.

WHAT DETERMINES MICROWAVE COOKING TIMES?

What early researchers discovered—and what every microwave cook today should know—is that different foods absorb microwave energy at different rates and heat at different speeds. Water, for example, heats quickly, but ice does not; its molecules, quite literally frozen in place, can't budge. Only when molecules can move freely, crashing into one another and causing considerable friction, is heat generated.

Then, too, some substances naturally absorb more microwave energy than others and thus take longer to heat. Liken it, if you will, to a porous sponge and a piece of paper toweling. Which will hold more water? And which will take longer to saturate? The sponge, on both counts. Here, therefore, in addition to wattage, are major factors that determine how—and how fast—foods heat in the microwave:

NATURE OF FOOD: Fats and oils, syrups and sugary mixtures all heat faster than water. Thus the jelly in a jelly doughnut will be blistering by the time the doughnut itself is warm. And thus a fatty piece of meat will cook faster than a lean one. Bones, by the way, absorb microwaves poorly, so boneless cuts microwave more quickly than bone-in ones. Also, porous items such as cake heat more quickly than dense or compact ones such as meat.

SIZE OF FOOD: Food cut into uniform pieces of 2" or less will microwave much more quickly and evenly than single large chunks.

SHAPE OF FOOD: Smooth, compact foods such as a boned and rolled pot roast will microwave more evenly than irregularly shaped ones (whole fish or fowl). Whenever there are skinny ends, as there often are with fish fillets, equalize the thickness by folding thin ends underneath. Finally, naturally round foods—meatballs, apples, beets, and the like—will cook the most evenly of all.

QUANTITY OF FOOD: Because there are only so many micro-waves to go around within the oven, small quantities will cook faster than large ones. One potato, for example, may bake in 4 minutes. But 8 potatoes, which must share the same amount of energy, may need 20 minutes.

TEMPERATURE OF FOOD: Refrigerator-cold foods require longer to cook than room-temperature ones. Frozen foods require longest of all.

Note: All recipes in this book were developed using foods at their natural storage temperatures.

〜〜〜 **ARRANGEMENT OF FOOD:** For best results, spread pieces of food out so that all surfaces are exposed. Always place thickest portions toward the outside, thinner ones in the middle. Drumsticks, asparagus, and other stalked foods fare best when arranged spoke fashion; chopped or minced foods, custard cups, and unshucked clams, oysters, or mussels, when arranged in a ring or doughnut shape around the edge of the container. All recipes in this book are specific about how each food should be arranged to ensure uniform cooking.

〜〜〜 **SHAPE OF CONTAINER:** Round or ring-shaped containers are better than square or oblong ones because there are no sharp corners to overcook.

〜〜〜 **PLACEMENT IN OVEN:** The nearer foods are to the microwave source (usually the top of the oven), the faster they will cook. When foods are fairly flat and of uniform thickness, they will cook evenly. But if they are tall or irregularly shaped, the cook must turn them over as they microwave and/or rearrange or stir them so that all areas are done at the same time.

A LOOK INSIDE A MICROWAVE OVEN

A. MAGNETRON: What transforms household current into microwaves.

B. WAVE GUIDE: The tunnel through which microwaves flow into the microwave oven proper.

C. MODE STIRRERS OR ROTATING ANTENNAS: Once microwaves are funneled into the cooking cavity of a microwave oven, they must be distributed evenly. The two most effective means of doing so are mode stirrers, little fans with blades especially designed to spread microwaves uniformly, and rotating antennas, which keep microwaves rotating in a regular pattern throughout the oven.

D. BUILT-IN TURNTABLE: Once standard equipment in many microwave ovens. Newest models boast such improved methods of microwave distribution that turntables are no longer necessary. Their original function was to move food steadily through the microwave field so it would cook more evenly.

E. RAISED OVEN FLOOR OR GLASS TRAY: Slightly higher than the oven floor, this special surface, whether built in or removable, reflects microwaves back into the bottom of food to help ensure uniform cooking.

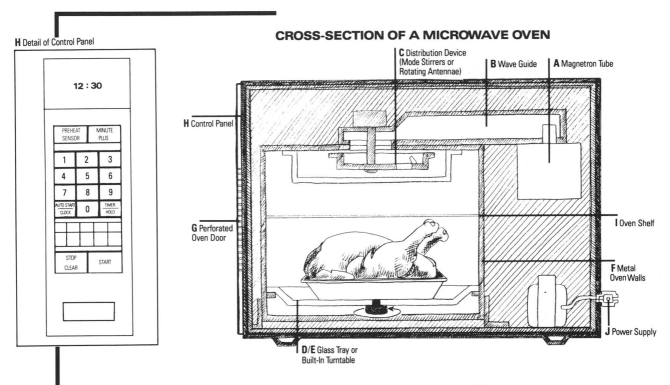

CROSS-SECTION OF A MICROWAVE OVEN

H Detail of Control Panel

12:30

PREHEAT SENSOR	MINUTE PLUS
1	2	3
4	5	6
7	8	9
AUTO START CLOCK	0	TIMER HOLD
STOP CLEAR	START

C Distribution Device (Mode Stirrers or Rotating Antennae)

B Wave Guide

A Magnetron Tube

H Control Panel

G Perforated Oven Door

I Oven Shelf

F Metal Oven Walls

J Power Supply

D/E Glass Tray or Built-In Turntable

F. METAL OVEN WALLS: Metal, remember, bounces microwaves back into the air. And so it is with metal oven walls, redirecting the microwave energy into the food. If there is no food in the oven, microwaves bounce around and can build up to such an extent that they damage the oven. So never, ever, turn an empty microwave oven on.

G. PERFORATED OVEN DOOR: Microwaves cannot pass through this finely perforated screen. In most models, it's sandwiched between glass or

7

plastic to simplify cleanup. Every oven door, moreover, is now fitted with two safety interlocks, which shut the oven off the instant the door is opened. ***Note:*** *Whenever you buy a microwave oven, always check carefully around the door to see if the seal has been damaged in shipment. If so, return the oven at once and get a replacement.*

H. CONTROL PANEL: These panels lie near the oven door and usually contain a clock as well as electronic "pads" for punching in the different power levels. Older ovens may have mechanical dials, buttons, or switches, which because of their inevitable "play," or give, aren't as precise as the electronic pads. Because they protrude and are quick to catch dirt and grime, they're also peskier to clean than smooth, flat electronic panels.

I. OVEN SHELF: Only larger, more expensive models come equipped with oven shelves. Usually they're made of plastic or metal (there's no danger of arcing because grids are small and also spaced so that microwaves pass through the shelves evenly and unobstructed). Their advantage, quite obviously, is that they allow you to cook or reheat more items at once.

J. POWER SUPPLY.

THE PROS AND CONS OF MICROWAVING

PROS

SPEED: For small to moderate amounts of food, microwave ovens cook 30%–50% faster than conventional ovens or stovetops.

COOLNESS: The air in microwave ovens remains cool no matter how long the oven is on. And in many instances, so does the container in which food is cooked. When containers are covered, however, steam buildup can heat them enough to give you a nasty burn.

EASE AND SAFETY: Microwave ovens are easy enough for children to use, and because they remain cool, shut off automatically, and accept paper containers (which also remain cool), they're altogether safe *IF* the children are old enough to operate them responsibly. **Note:** *If children will be using your microwave oven, make sure it's placed low enough for easy, safe access. Shoulder height is the best level.*

ENERGY EFFICIENCY: Microwave ovens consume about 50% less power than conventional ovens because they needn't be preheated and cooking times are short.

VITAMIN RETENTION: Because most foods simmer in their own juices or steam in their own vapor in a microwave oven, there's little liquid to leach out soluble vitamins and minerals. And because cooking's so quick, there's less chance of heat-sensitive nutrients being destroyed.

ADAPTABILITY: You can use dozens of different containers in the microwave (see Chapter 3)—heat soup in the cup in which it's to be served, prepare oatmeal in cereal bowls, crisp chips and crackers in paper toweling, warm leftovers directly on dinner plates *if* they're microwave-safe. *To determine if a container is microwave-safe:* Place ½ cup cold water in a 1-cup ovenware glass measure and set in the microwave oven. Set the container to be tested beside—but not touching—the cup. Microwave on high (100% power) 1 minute. The water should be very warm, even hot. Now touch the container being tested. If it's cool or only slightly warm, it's microwave-safe. *If it's hot, it's not.*

QUICK-TO-CLEAN DESIGN: Because spatters don't "bake on" in a microwave oven as they do in a conventional oven, the most that's needed daily is a light sponging with mild detergent and warm water.

MOBILITY: Many microwave ovens are completely portable and can be moved from kitchen to patio to camper to boat. The only requirements: a grounded, three-prong outlet and a circuit that's not carrying another heavy-duty appliance, especially one that switches on and off, such as a refrigerator or air conditioner. The microwave oven won't operate to fullest capacity while the other appliance is on, and you may blow a fuse or trip a circuit breaker.

CONS

～～～ Pastries and piecrusts don't crisp.

～～～ Baked goods don't brown, so you must build in color by adding whole grain flours, using brown sugar instead of white, or adding a colorful topping to camouflage the anemic exterior.

～～～ Small quantities of meat or poultry don't brown.

～～～ Food may cook unevenly; this is especially true of meat, fish, and fowl where there's some fat, some lean, some flesh, some bone.

～～～ Meats often develop "steamed" rather than roasted or sautéed flavor.

～～～ Large quantities of food cook even more slowly in the microwave than they do by stovetop or conventional oven.

～～～ Food can quickly overcook. In a microwave, the difference between success and failure can often be counted in *seconds.*

NEVER USE THE MICROWAVE FOR:

BISCUITS: They go pale and soggy.
PANCAKES: They remain doughy.
PIECRUSTS OR OTHER FLAKY PASTRIES: They taste raw.
CHOUX PASTRY: It never puffs or browns.
POPOVERS OR YORKSHIRE PUDDING: They never "pop" or brown.
ANGEL OR CHIFFON CAKES: They toughen and never achieve full volume.
DESSERT OR VEGETABLE SOUFFLÉS: They fail to rise properly.
POPCORN: Unless it's commercially packaged for the microwave, it will scarcely pop. And never, ever, try to microwave regular popcorn in a brown paper grocery bag: it may catch fire.
BREADED OR BATTER-DIPPED FOODS: They won't crispen or brown

unless microwaved on active microwave cookware;* commercial foods are packaged in special "microwave susceptor" materials that promote browning. For the same reason, frozen french fries fare poorly in the microwave.

OR FOR

COOKING EGGS IN THE SHELL: They'll burst.

DEEP-FAT OR SHALLOW FRYING: It's dangerous to fry in deep—or even shallow fat—in the microwave because fats can ignite. The flash point ranges from 380° to 625°F., depending on the composition of the fat or oil. And the lower of these temperatures can quickly be reached in the microwave.

PROCESSING HOME-CANNED FOODS: The sealed jars can explode.

MELTING PARAFFIN: Microwaves pass right through it, leaving it as cold and hard as ever.

ABOUT VARIABLE POWER LEVELS

Ever questing for the "perfect microwave oven," engineers constantly add new features and refinements. The most important to date is the introduction of variable power levels, which give you as much control and flexibility as conventional ranges do. If, for example, a sauce should bubble furiously on HIGH (100% power), you need only reduce the power level to MEDIUM-HIGH (70%). Or if a stew should drop below a simmer on MEDIUM (50% power), you need only raise the power level to 60% or 70%.

What determines the different power levels is how often the microwaves cycle on and off and how long they remain on at a time. On HIGH (100% power) there is no interruption in the flow of microwave energy. On MEDIUM (50% power) the microwaves pulse on and off at regular intervals, so that periods of rest (no power) alternate equally with those of full power. At lower power levels the off periods outlast the on, and at higher power levels it's just the reverse. These on/off cycles mean that such heat-sensitive foods as meats, eggs, and creams can cook far more evenly because the heat inside them has a chance to spread slowly and equalize during each off period.

Top-of-the-line microwave ovens offer ten variable power levels; simplest ovens, only HIGH (100% power) and DEFROST (usually 30% power, but it varies from manufacturer to manufacturer). Older ovens may also label 70% power as MEDIUM and 40% power as LOW, so it may be necessary to test your microwave oven to determine just what its power levels are.

HOW TO TEST MICROWAVE OVEN POWER LEVELS

1. Mix 1 cup cold water and 8 ice cubes in a 1-quart measure. Stir for 1 minute exactly (time carefully).

2. Pour 1 cup of this ice-cooled water into a 1-cup measure, discard remaining water and ice cubes.

3. Microwave water, uncovered, on HIGH (100% power) until it comes to a full rolling boil. This should take 3–4 minutes. Jot down the exact time it takes in your microwave oven. Discard the water and let the measure come to room temperature.

4. Repeat steps 1 and 2. Then microwave water, uncovered, on MEDIUM until the water comes to a full boil. Again jot down the time it takes. If it takes the water exactly twice as long to boil on MEDIUM as it does on HIGH, then the MEDIUM power level on your microwave oven is indeed 50% power. If the water boils in less than twice the time, your MEDIUM power setting is higher than 50%.

5. Again repeat steps 1, 2, and 3, but use a power setting lower than MEDIUM. Once you determine which setting on your oven actually represents 50% power, you can then calculate which settings correspond to LOW, MEDIUM-LOW, and MEDIUM-HIGH. Make a record of each and post as a handy reference. **Note:** *Power levels can fluctuate according to local electricity consumption, so at times of peak usage your microwave oven may not be operating at full capacity.*

VARIABLE POWER LEVELS USED THROUGHOUT THIS BOOK

We use the following terms and power levels standardized by the International Microwave Power Institute:

Power Level Setting	Amount of Power
HIGH	100%
MEDIUM-HIGH	70%
MEDIUM	50%
MEDIUM-LOW	30%
LOW	10%

ABOUT MICROWAVING AT HIGH ALTITUDES

As everyone who's tried to cook at high altitudes knows, vegetables take forever to cook because water may boil at temperatures below 200° F. Meats dry because of excessive evaporation. And cakes and quick breads may overflow their pans because of the low atmospheric pressure. So it's only logical to wonder if microwaving at high altitudes presents similar problems. The answer, sadly, is yes.

Because problems vary from one altitude to the next, the best advice we can offer is to contact your county home extension agent or utility company home economist, who will know precisely what adjustments must be made in your area.

ABOUT MICROWAVE SAFETY

In the beginning, people thought that using microwave ovens could make you "sterile" or give you cancer. There were also rumors that microwaved foods were radioactive and that the ovens themselves leaked X rays.

Nonsense! We now know better, but it took almost a quarter of a century for Americans to overcome their fear of microwave ovens. And lest you harbor any residual qualms, here are the facts:

~~~~~~ Unlike X rays, microwaves are nonionizing and thus not radioactive.

~~~~~~ There is no retention of microwaves in a microwave oven after the power is snapped off. The flow of energy stops just as it does when electric lights are switched off.

~~~~~~ The U.S. Government strictly limits how much nonionizing radiation home microwave ovens may safely emit (for new ovens, it's 1 milliwatt per square centimeter at a distance of 2 inches, and for pre-1971 ovens, 5 milliwatts per square centimeter). These exposure levels are thousands of times lower than those at which harm might actually be done. As you move away from the oven, the drop-off increases dramatically. At 2 feet, for example, the microwave energy is 100 times less than it is at 2 inches. If you're a "nervous Nellie," however, you can buy a *power density meter* to monitor microwave leakage (it can cost anywhere from about $200 to $800).

~~~~~~ The U.S. Government also approves all microwave oven designs and requires, further, that each oven door be fitted with two independent interlocks that shut power off the instant the door is opened. There's even further safety backup—a monitor that cuts power should both interlocks fail.

~~~~~~ The only injuries so far reported from microwave use are the sorts of burns that routinely occur with more conventional methods of cooking.

SOME TIPS FOR USING A MICROWAVE OVEN SAFELY

~~~~~~ Read your oven's instruction manual carefully before using the oven, and always follow its recommendations.

~~~~~~ Always install a microwave oven exactly as the manufacturer instructs, allotting it its own electrical circuit, if possible. If the oven is a

countertop model, make sure there's sufficient clearance all around for proper ventilation.

～～～ Avoid using an extension cord with a microwave oven, *but if you must, make sure it's a heavy-duty one with a grounded, UL-approved, three-prong plug.*

～～～ Never plug a microwave oven into a stove outlet, and make sure its cord is well away from burner heat, which can damage the oven's fragile electronics.

～～～ Never operate a microwave oven if the door is dented, warped, or damaged in any way, if it doesn't close snugly, or if anything is caught in it.

～～～ Never stick anything through the door's grid or around the seal.

～～～ Check door hinges and seal from time to time, and if they show signs of wear, call a qualified repairman.

～～～ Never turn an empty microwave oven on. You may seriously damage it.

～～～ If there are small children about, leave a 1-cup glass ovenware measure filled with water in the microwave oven at all times lest small fingers accidentally push the ON button.

～～～ Never leave a temperature probe in the oven if it isn't being used. As for the oven shelf, store it outside the oven and slide it into place when needed.

～～～ If your oven has no temperature probe, use only those thermometers that are safe for microwave use.

～～～ Use only microwave-safe cookware and coverings (for details, see Chapter 3), never metal utensils (except for those that are especially designed for microwave use). Ordinary metal pots and pans can cause arcing (sparking that can damage the oven; see Arcing, in "The Terms and Techniques of Microwaving," Chapter 3). And never microwave Melamine tableware; it chips and cracks.

〜〜〜 Always remove all metal clamps from food or wrappers before they go into the microwave. And never use twist-ties (they contain metal) or metal skewers lest they cause arcing.

〜〜〜 If your oven should begin to arc, turn it off at once.

〜〜〜 Don't heat partially filled jars of food (especially baby food) in a microwave oven; they may crack. And never warm bottles of baby formula by microwave; they'll heat unevenly and may burn the baby.

〜〜〜 Never microwave food in closed jars or narrow-necked bottles. Pressure can build, causing boilovers or, worse, explosions.

〜〜〜 When heating soup, tea, or coffee by the cup or mug, always stir at halftime to keep them from boiling over.

〜〜〜 Never reach in with bare hands to pull a dish from the microwave oven. Containers, particularly covered ones, can become very hot because of steam buildup; they also absorb heat from the food cooked in them. So always have potholders at the ready.

〜〜〜 Always vent plastic food wrap when using it as a covering, otherwise steam will build up and burst the plastic (for the same reason, plastic cooking pouches should be slit or pierced). **Note:** *The easiest way to vent plastic wrap is to fold back a corner.*

〜〜〜 When removing lids or plastic food wrap from hot dishes, always do so carefully, using the lid or wrap to direct any steam away from you.

〜〜〜 If you must cook pasta by microwave, never add oil to the cooking water. It will film over the water, then "pop" and sputter dangerously.

~~~~~ Always prick tight-skinned whole fruits and vegetables (potatoes, plums, squash, eggplants, and the like) to keep them from bursting. For the same reason, sausages and chicken livers must also be pricked.

~~~~~ Always prick egg yolk membranes *gently* with a toothpick before microwaving the eggs; unpricked yolks will burst. *And never, ever, microwave eggs in the shell—they'll explode.*

~~~~~ Keep the microwave oven clean and dry, wiping it with paper toweling after each use and with mild detergent and warm water if there are grease spatters. Never use scouring pads or abrasive powders that can mar the interior surfaces (for details on cleaning your microwave oven, see Chapter 2).

~~~~~ If food should catch fire in the oven, keep the door tightly shut, then turn the oven off or unplug it. The fire will soon burn itself out.

~~~~~ Don't turn your microwave oven into a "catchall" by piling books or other items on top. And never use the oven cavity for storage. You may inadvertently snap the oven on and set things ablaze.

~~~~~ Never use your microwave to dry clothes—they might ignite. And never try to soften nail polish in the oven. It, too, can catch fire.

HOW TO CONVERT FAVORITE RECIPES FOR MICROWAVE USE

First of all, wait until you feel at home with your microwave oven before you try to adapt conventional recipes for it. Certain types of dishes lend themselves to adaptation: soups, stews, casseroles, and recipes whose principal ingredients are such high-moisture foods as fish, fowl, and vegetables. Others are more difficult: cakes, cookies, quick breads. Needless to add, you should never try to convert recipes that microwave poorly in the first place: pastries, yeast breads, fried foods, or any foods with crisp crusts.

Here, then, are the basic guidelines to follow when adapting conventional recipes for microwave use:

1. Find a microwave recipe similar to the one you want to convert that serves no more than 8. Read the recipe carefully, then use the method of preparation it recommends, the container size, type of covering, power level, and cooking and standing times. Also rearrange foods and/or rotate the container as this recipe directs.

2. Reduce amount of fat or oil in casseroles, soups, stews, and braised dishes by about half. And use *ungreased* containers; microwaved foods rarely stick.

3. Reduce liquid called for in casseroles, sauces, soups, and stews by about a fourth. Foods microwave so fast there's little time for liquid to reduce or evaporate.

4. Reduce herbs by about half, peppers and strong spices by two thirds or three fourths; microwaving intensifies all seasonings.

5. Unless salt is mixed with the cooking liquid, don't add it until after the food comes from the microwave oven.

6. Cut food in smallish pieces of uniform size and shape (large or irregularly shaped pieces will cook unevenly in a microwave oven).

7. Microwave any heat-sensitive foods such as eggs and cheese on 50% power or less. This is good practice, too, for layered casseroles.

8. Halve cooking time for soups and stews and other dishes containing solid chunks of food.

9. Reduce cooking times for liquid or "soft" mixtures by a fourth to a third.

10. Check all recipes for doneness *after minimum cooking time,* then every 30 seconds or so thereafter, lest they overcook. Remember that all microwaved foods continue to cook during the standing period.

11. Whenever a conventional recipe calls for browning food, do so on top of the stove, then transfer to the microwave to finish cooking. Or if the recipe is one that profits from a last-minute crisping or browning,

microwave it, then transfer to a preheated broiler for a few final minutes.

12. Study the following sample recipe. It shows what major adjustments to make when adapting conventional recipes for microwave use.

Grandma's Chili

SERVES 6

2   medium-size yellow onions, peeled and ~~coarsely chopped~~ *minced*

1 ~~2~~   cloves garlic, peeled and crushed

2 ~~4~~   tablespoons vegetable oil

1½ teaspoons crumbled dried oregano

1   pound ground beef *(lean)*

3 ~~4~~   tablespoons chili powder

⅛ ~~¼~~   teaspoon red pepper flakes

1 ~~2~~   teaspoons salt

1   can (1 pound) crushed tomatoes

2   cans (1 pound, 3 ounces each) kidney beans (do not drain)

Microwave ~~Sauté~~ onions and garlic in oil in ~~heavy kettle,~~ *uncovered 4-quart microwave-safe casserole on HIGH 5-5½ minutes* stirring occasionally, ~~10 minutes,~~ until golden. Add oregano and meat and ~~sauté 10 minutes,~~ *microwave, uncovered, on HIGH 5-6 minutes* until meat is no longer pink. Add remaining ingredients, ~~and simmer, uncovered~~ *cover with wax paper and microwave on MEDIUM-HIGH, 18-20 minutes,* and stirring occasionally. ~~1½ hours.~~

ABOUT DOUBLING AND HALVING MICROWAVE RECIPES

Don't double a recipe unless it serves no more than 6 to 8 *after* it's doubled. As we've already pointed out, large amounts of food microwave unevenly and, in some instances, cook much more slowly than they would on top of the stove or in the oven. To ensure even cooking of doubled recipes, use a container of larger diameter—*but the same depth*—as that originally called for. Also, instead of doubling the amount of liquid, multiply it by 1⅓ to 1½. Increase microwave time by about half, and test often for doneness.

Halving recipes presents fewer problems than doubling them, but lest the food boil dry or overcook, you must make sure that its level in the container is the same as in the full recipe (use a casserole of identical depth but smaller diameter). As for the microwave time, reduce it by about a third.

2

WHICH MICROWAVE OVEN IS BEST FOR YOU?

*B*efore you buy a microwave oven, which can cost anywhere from $100 for a pint-size portable to $1,000 or more for a top-of-the-line, state-of-the-art built-in piggybacked above a conventional oven, talk to friends, neighbors, and relatives about *their* microwave ovens. Find out what they like about them and—maybe more important—*don't* like.

Then ask yourself these questions. And answer them honestly. Why do you want a microwave oven? How do you plan to use it? Do you merely want to defrost frozen foods quickly? Warm up TV dinners? Do you like to entertain? Cook from scratch? Do you have the time and patience to learn to use a microwave oven to fullest advantage? How big is your family? Your budget? The space where you plan to install the microwave oven?

There's no point in buying a fancy model to heat TV dinners. If, on the other hand, you're determined to cook the microwave way, don't waste money on a small low-wattage oven that's little more than a food warmer.

ABOUT OVEN WATTAGES

Generally speaking, the higher a microwave oven's wattage, the faster it will cook. Indeed, the 1,000-watt models of a few years ago have been phased out because they cooked so fast they gave the cook no control. The microwave ovens now being manufactured range from 350 to 750 watts, but the most popular are in the 500-to-700-watt category.

Which wattage is best for you depends on how you'll use the oven. If you'll only be baking the occasional potato or brewing a quick cup of soup or cereal, an inexpensive, low-wattage model will do. But if you intend to cook by microwave, choose an oven of at least 600–725 watts (the best wattages for all-round cooking, also those at which the majority of magazine and cookbook microwave recipes are tested). **Note:** *Foods that cook in 1 hour in a 725-watt oven will need an extra 24 minutes in a 500-watt oven. A 500-watter may be okay for simple cooking, but it's a poor choice for family-size recipes or long-simmering dishes.*

You should know, moreover, that the wattage listed for your particular oven may not be the wattage actually delivered. Microwaves operate at top efficiency only when the voltage is between 115 and 120 (lower voltages mean slower cooking). In many areas during hours of peak electrical use, voltage dips, and *for each volt lost there's also a drop of 10 watts.* Overloading a household circuit causes a similar power drain, so you should allot your microwave oven its own 15-to-20-amp line.

If you're buying a microwave for a boat or recreational vehicle, make sure its generator produces 120 volts AC (DC won't work, although converters are available; better check with the oven manufacturer, however, as to which converter is best).

FACTORS AFFECTING HOW FAST AND EVENLY MICROWAVE OVENS COOK

WATTAGE, as we've just seen.

THE SIZE AND SHAPE OF THE OVEN CAVITY. Usually microwaves are distributed more uniformly inside small cubes than inside large rectangles.

THE WAY MICROWAVES ARE CHANNELED INTO AND DIS- TRIBUTED INSIDE THE OVEN. Do they come from a single source or several? How are they distributed? By rotating "wave guides," rotating antennas, stirrers? And how good a job do these do? The more quickly and evenly microwaves fill an oven, the more efficient it will be (especially with family-size quantities of food), which explains why a 500-watt oven with swift, uniform microwave distribution may sometimes actually cook faster than an inefficient 700-watter.

THE MAGNETRON'S EFFICIENCY. This key component is what converts household electricity into microwaves. Its power, together with that of the transformer, determines how effective—and how efficient—each microwave oven will be.

HOW TO DETERMINE YOUR MICROWAVE OVEN'S WATTAGE

If you don't know the wattage of your oven and can't get the information from the dealer or manufacturer, here's how to figure it out on your own:

1. Place 1 cup tap water in a small bowl.
2. If you have a thermometer that will register as low as 75° F., take the temperature of the water, then add ice or hot water as needed to bring the water temperature to 75° F. Now pour exactly 1 cup of this water into a 1-cup glass ovenware measure. *Note: If you don't have a thermometer, simply let 1 cup water stand on the counter overnight.*
3. Microwave the 1 cup water, uncovered, on HIGH (100%) until bubbles rise to the surface and break. Using a watch or clock with a second hand, time exactly how long it takes the water to boil.
4. Using the following graph, compute the wattage of your oven.

MICROWAVE WATTAGE GRAPH

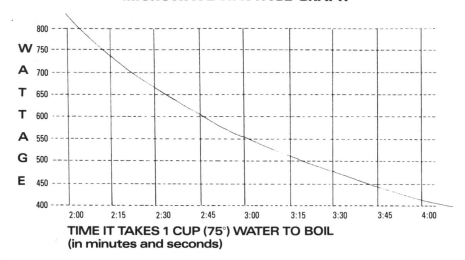

W A T T A G E (vertical axis)

800, 750, 700, 650, 600, 550, 500, 450, 400

TIME IT TAKES 1 CUP (75°) WATER TO BOIL
(in minutes and seconds)

2:00 2:15 2:30 2:45 3:00 3:15 3:30 3:45 4:00

Thus, if it takes water between 2¼ and 2½ minutes to boil in your oven, the oven's wattage is 700.

A SECOND WAY TO COMPUTE WATTAGE: Place 2 cups tap water in a 2-cup glass ovenware measure, take the water temperature, and jot that figure down. Now microwave the water, uncovered, on HIGH 1 minute exactly. Again take the water temperature. Subtract the first temperature reading from the second and multiply the difference by 18.5. You'll have the approximate wattage of your oven.

HOW TO CHECK POWER LEVELS

As we've already pointed out in Chapter 1, the International Microwave Power Institute has standardized microwave oven power levels (HIGH = 100% power; MEDIUM-HIGH = 70%; MEDIUM = 50%; MEDIUM-LOW = 30%; and LOW = 10%). *And these are the ones we use in recipes throughout this book.* Unfortunately, not all microwave manufacturers use these approved power levels, so you may need to determine what HIGH, MEDIUM, and LOW—or the various numbered settings—mean on your microwave oven (see "How to Test Microwave Oven Power Levels" in Chapter 1).

ABOUT OVEN SIZES AND SHAPES

Here, too, you must consider the kind of microwaving you plan to do. Would you, for example, be likely to roast a turkey? Bake large casseroles? If so, you'll need an oven large enough to accommodate them (it's a good idea, by the way, to take along a favorite casserole when you go microwave shopping to see if it will fit into the oven you like best). Here are the four oven categories as defined by the International Microwave Power Institute:

Category	Usable Cubic Feet
Full-size	1.0 or more
Mid-size	0.8 to 1.0
Compact	0.6 to 0.7
Subcompact	0.5 or less

Usually full-size ovens are blessed with the highest wattages (600–750), mid-sizes average 600–650 watts, and compacts and subcompacts average 500 watts or less, although the latest trend is for more powerful small ovens.

ABOUT OVEN TYPES

Here's yet another factor to consider. Do you have room for a countertop model? Do you need a slim space saver that can be slid into the slot now occupied by a range hood? Would you prefer a new free-standing range with an over-the-cooktop microwave oven? How about replacing an existing wall oven with a new "hi-low" cooking center that boasts an eye-level microwave oven and, just underneath it, a conventional oven? Or does one of the new combination convection-microwave ovens appeal? Or a multi-use model that amounts to three or four ovens in one—microwave, convection, conventional, broiler or broiler-toaster oven? Your kitchen space, your cooking style, and your budget should dictate.

To date, *countertop microwave ovens,* available in a full range of wattages and sizes, are the most popular, because of their versatility and portability.

The *combination microwave-convection* ovens have so far failed to catch on. They cook more slowly than microwaves alone, yet faster than conventional ovens, meaning that most microwave recipes can't be used in them successfully without major adjustments. What these hybrids do best is long-cooking dishes that must also be browned or crisped. Most cooks find it simpler just to brown foods on the stovetop, then transfer them to the microwave, or to give microwaved recipes a fast brown finish in the broiler.

As for microwave ovens with browning elements (called in the trade *micro-browners* or *micro-toasters),* they do brown food, thanks to electric coils mounted top and/or bottom. But these appropriate precious oven space and complicate cleaning, and the ovens are frankly too small and limited for serious cooking.

SPECIAL FEATURES AND OPTIONAL EXTRAS

The options offered by the many different brands of microwave oven today simply boggle the mind, and more gadgetry is on the way. Here are the major items now available:

TURNTABLES (CAROUSELS): Standard equipment on some ovens (the best of them can be removed), these rotate food constantly as it microwaves to ensure even cooking. They eliminate the need to turn food by hand. Still, you must be vigilant because pans of food can shift on carousels and may require recentering. Rectangular containers, moreover, may scrape the oven walls. The biggest disadvantage of turntables is that they reduce overall oven capacity. With the improved microwave distribution now featured in many second-generation ovens, turntables are becoming less important. Besides, if you need one, you can always buy an inexpensive portable windup or battery-run model at almost any good housewares store.

AUTOMATIC TEMPERATURE PROBES: Many ovens are equipped with probes, others offer them as an extra; and they're a valuable accessory, especially when it comes to cooking meats, fish, and poultry. Probes are programmed to monitor the temperature of food as it cooks, then shut the oven off the instant the desired temperature (or degree of doneness) is reached. But unless two thirds of the probe is buried in the food, its exposed parts will overheat and send false readings to the probe's thermostat, and the oven will turn off prematurely. Like meat thermometers, probes must be inserted carefully for accurate readings. In meat, fish, and poultry, this means that the probe's tip must be in the middle of the largest lean muscle, touching neither fat nor bone. Always use probe as manufacturer directs.

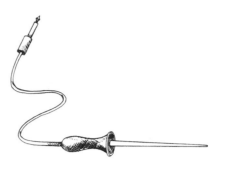

ELECTRONIC CONTROL PANELS: The greatest advantages of these smooth glass panels with electronic touch pads are that they're far more precise about cooking times than mechanical dials or switches and that they're a breeze to clean. As a bonus, many incorporate digital clocks. ***Note: Make sure the touch pad's numbers are large and legible (not all are), also that they're arranged in an orderly, easy-to-use sequence. Some oven manufacturers arrange the numbers with which you set power levels and cooking times like the buttons on a Touch-tone telephone. Others line them up vertically.***

REMOVABLE SHELF: A shelf allows you to microwave more than one dish at a time, or as many as six ears of corn or a whole meal. But the more food you put into a microwave oven, the more slowly and unevenly it will cook. When using oven shelves, you must stagger the food so that the microwaves move as freely and uniformly as possible. You must also place the slower-cooking items nearest the power source (usually the top) and the faster-cooking ones on the bottom. Never store the shelf in the oven; it affects the way foods cook.

BROWNING ELEMENTS: As we've already said, these may not be as practical as they seem (see About Oven Types). Most cooks find it easier to use their stovetop, conventional oven, or broiler in tandem with their microwave ovens than to adjust microwave cooking times for these hybrids.

VARIABLE POWER LEVELS: Sophisticated microwave models give the cook almost as much control as conventional ranges. What makes this possible is variable power levels, which cycle on and off with varying intervals of time at full power and at rest (for details, see About Variable

Power Levels, in Chapter 1) so that you can boil soups, sauces, and stews actively or "bake" cakes and/or casseroles slowly. State-of-the-art ovens offer ten different power levels, but four or five afford the cook all the flexibility needed.

AUTOMATIC DEFROST: Microwaves melt ice slowly, but scientists discovered early on that by letting frozen foods rest between successive "blasts" of energy, they would thaw quickly and evenly. Defrost cycles switch the power on and off automatically, then alert you when the thawing is complete.

DELAYED STARTS: We've always been able to use timers to turn conventional ovens on and off, and the delayed start performs the same function on a microwave. It sounds like a good idea but isn't altogether practical. First, it's risky to leave raw food at room temperature for long periods of time. Second, microwaving requires more attention—rearranging, stirring, and the like—than conventional cooking. Wonderful as it is, a microwave oven can't relieve you of *all* responsibility. Nor should you expect it to.

PROGRAMMED COOKING: This feature is designed to eliminate guesswork by allowing you to punch in on your microwave's control panel such factors as the type of food to be cooked, its weight, and the desired degree of doneness. The oven then automatically sets the necessary cooking time and power levels. Some ovens monitor the cooking progress via humidity or steam sensors, some use weight sensors (to calculate food weight loss during cooking), and others use infrared "eyes" to measure heat given off by food. In each case, the oven "knows" when the food is perfectly cooked and shuts itself off. But again, you must keep an eye on the doings and prod, turn, rearrange, or stir the food as needed. No microwave can yet perform these necessary functions.

MULTISTAGE COOKING: With this feature, sometimes called "memory levels," you can program the oven to cook at different power levels and in specified sequences. For example, you may want to start a casserole on HIGH, then after 5 minutes reduce the power level to MEDIUM for the duration of cooking. Or you may want to instruct the oven to keep something warm after it's done. It's good to have such capability; still, you must tend the food yourself and stir or rearrange as needed for perfect results.

PROGRAMMED RECIPES: Supersophisticated ovens enable you to program specific recipes electronically via numbered codes or magnetized bar codes much like those at supermarket checkout counters. The oven sets the proper cooking times and power levels and, it goes without saying, turns itself off when the recipe is done.

THE VALUE OF OVEN MANUALS

The most valuable piece of microwave literature available is the user's manual that accompanies your oven. Study it carefully *before* you use your oven because here's where the manufacturer spells out all the features and functions of your particular model. To get you started in fine style, it may also include an appetizing collection of recipes, and these are the best place to begin. Whatever you do, don't lose your oven manual; it's your microwave bible. But if for some reason your manual should disappear, don't despair. Contact the dealer from whom you bought your oven and ask for the phone number and address of the manufacturer. Many manufacturers will gladly send a new manual for free; others may charge a small fee.

ABOUT WARRANTIES

Always read an oven manufacturer's statement of warranty—*preferably before buying*—to learn what it does and doesn't cover (damage caused by improper oven use, to name one exception). There are two basic types of warranty:

FULL WARRANTY: The manufacturer agrees to repair or replace a defective oven within a specified period of time (most often one year) although the warranty may last longer for such key parts as magnetrons (these are sometimes covered for from two to ten years). The repairman, moreover, will usually come to your home.

LIMITED WARRANTY: Only certain oven parts may be repaired or replaced within a given length of time. It's routine for rubber gaskets to be excluded, also interior and exterior surfaces, oven trays, shelves, and temperature probes. And, alas, repairs are more likely to be done at the shop than in your kitchen (reason enough, if you have a built-in model, to buy an in-house warranty).

ABOUT MICROWAVE OVEN MAINTENANCE

Good news! It's a whale of a lot easier to keep a microwave oven spanking-clean than a conventional one because oven walls, floor, and ceiling don't heat and spatters can't bake on. Always read your user's manual, then clean the oven as the manufacturer directs. He knows best, but here are some general tips that may help:

TO CLEAN THE INSIDE OF THE OVEN

Boil a cup of water (or 1 cup warm water mixed with 2 tablespoons lemon juice or baking soda) for a few minutes in the microwave to "steam-clean" the interior and loosen any bits of food or splatters (most ovens are lined with quick-to-clean stainless steel or enameled metal). Then wipe with damp paper toweling or cloth. For more stubborn grime, use warm water and a mild detergent, or a lemon or soda solution (2 tablespoons lemon juice or baking soda per cup warm water; this deodorizes the oven, too).

Never use cleaners containing ammonia; the smell lingers and can be absorbed by food.

Never use scouring pads, abrasive, or harsh detergents that may scratch or damage the oven surface.

If your oven has a glass or ceramic tray on the oven floor that can be removed, wash gently in hot sudsy water or put through a dishwasher. **Note:** *Always let the tray cool to room temperature before you wash it.*

Never remove the cover protecting the stirrer blades or antennas unless the manufacturer recommends doing so. Simply wipe the cover clean with a damp cloth.

Refresh the oven interior by mixing 1 cup warm water with 2 teaspoons of ground allspice, cinnamon, dried thyme, sage, or mint, then microwaving, uncovered, on HIGH (100% power) for 1 minute.

TO CLEAN THE OUTSIDE OF THE OVEN

Using a soft cloth or paper toweling, wipe the case with warm, mild, soapy water, then wipe dry.

Wipe the glass door and any chrome trim with a damp cloth, or use a chrome or glass cleaner as directed.

Wipe the control panel gently with a damp cloth and then dry with a clean cloth; to keep from turning the oven on, leave the door open.

Clean any vents with a damp cloth, making certain that no water seeps down into them.

TO CLEAN OVEN ACCESSORIES

Many spots will sponge right off oven shelves. If not, gently scrub with a soft nylon brush and mild soapy water, then rub any recalcitrant spots with baking soda sprinkled onto a damp sponge. Never use steel wool or scouring powders, which may permanently scratch the shelves.

Sponge temperature probes with warm sudsy water, applying a scouring pad to stubborn bits of soil. Rinse well, then dry carefully. Never immerse the plug or wires in water. And never wash the probe in a dishwasher.

Scrub browning dishes and trays with a half-and-half mixture of baking soda and water; rinse well and dry.

To remove stale odors from popcorn poppers, bring a weak soda solution (about 1 tablespoon baking soda to 1 quart water) to a boil in the popper; rinse well and dry.

3

MAKING THE MOST OF YOUR MICROWAVE

We'll deal here with the mumbo-jumbo of microwaving (like computerese, it's a language unto itself). We'll also survey in some detail the different kinds of microwave cookware available, then include a handy section on "Shortcut Cooking" to show what a breeze it is to melt butter by microwave, soften cheese or chocolate, toast nuts, plump dried fruit, even caramelize sugar.

THE TERMS AND TECHNIQUES OF MICROWAVING

If you're the last on your block to own a microwave oven, you may find microwave-savvy friends and neighbors lapsing now and then into foreign tongues. The following quick dictionary of important microwave terms and techniques will help you translate the mysterious words and phrases.

ACTIVE COOKWARE: Containers especially designed to attract microwaves so that they heat enough to crisp and/or brown food. The best examples of these are *browning dishes and grills* (see Active Microwave Cookware, in the Microwave Utensil Chart that follows), also the new materials (microwave susceptors) used to package such crisp-crusted frozen foods as pizza. One shortcoming of browning dishes and grills is that they must be preheated each time food is to be browned, often several times within a single recipe. Frequently it's faster and easier to brown food in a skillet on top of the stove.

ARCING: Sparks or electric flashes crackling and popping inside a microwave oven. They produce such intense heat that the oven—and the containers put into it—can be seriously damaged. There's also danger of fire. What causes arcing, and how can it be prevented? It occurs when metal containers are used, also metal skewers, metal clamps (the sort found on poultry), even twist-ties that contain metal. To prevent arcing, use only microwave-safe cookware (for details, see the Microwave Utensil Chart that follows). *Note: Small strips of foil may safely be used to shield areas of food that are cooking too fast, and small foil containers can be used provided they're lightweight, no more than ¾" deep, and at least three-quarters full of food.*

ARRANGE: To place two or more pieces of food in a specific pattern so that they will microwave evenly—in a circle, for example, or side by side.

BOIL: To microwave liquid until bubbles break actively on the surface, not just until they rise to the top. Some liquids will froth and foam, making it difficult to tell if the liquid is actively boiling in the center as well as around the edges. Always push the froth aside and have a look.

BRAISE: To brown food, then to cook it in a covered container with a small amount of liquid or at least in the company of fruits or vegetables that give off considerable steam. When it comes to braising in a microwave oven, the best plan is simply to brown foods on top of the stove the old-fashioned way in a casserole that's both microwave-safe and rugged enough to take direct heat (see the Microwave Utensil Chart that follows).

BROWN: To sear food until brown. In a microwave oven, the only way to brown most quick-cooking foods—certainly small steaks and chops—is in a browning dish or grill (see Active Cookware, above). Large roasts and birds *will* turn golden in a microwave because they cook for considerable lengths of time and contain enough surface fat to encourage browning.

BROWNING AGENTS: Because chops, chicken parts, and other small cuts rarely brown attractively in a microwave oven, they're often colored cosmetically with browning agents, either commercial preparations or bastes you can mix yourself. The most popular are half-and-half mixtures of water and liquid gravy browner, soy sauce, or Worcestershire sauce. For best results, brush food with the browner before microwaving, then again at halftime.

BROWNING DISH OR GRILL: See Active Cookware, above, also the

Microwave Utensil Chart that follows.

BROWNING ELEMENT: Some microwave ovens come equipped with browning elements or electric coils mounted on the top or on both the top and bottom. Units with top-mounted coils (*micro-browners*) are being phased out in favor of the more efficient ovens with coils top and bottom (*micro-toasters*), which can simulate both conventional baking and broiling.

CAROUSEL (TURNTABLE): Lazy Susan–type discs that rotate food slowly as it microwaves to ensure even cooking (for pros and cons, see Special Features and Optional Extras, in Chapter 2).

CARRYOVER COOKING: Foods don't finish cooking the instant you take them from a microwave oven. Indeed, they continue to cook for some minutes thereafter during the standing time (which see), and this is what's known as "carryover cooking."

CHOKE SEAL: The tight seal around microwave oven doors that prevents microwave leakage.

COMBINATION COOKING: Using a microwave oven in tandem with the stovetop, oven, or broiler. The object is to use each appliance for what it does best—browning, in the case of the stovetop or broiler, zip-quick cooking in the case of the microwave. Combination cooking—or *complementary cooking,* as it's sometimes called—is particularly useful for stews and braised meats that must first be browned to develop rich brown color and mellow flavor, then simmered until meltingly tender. Microwave ovens were never intended to replace conventional ranges, merely to supplement them and speed things up.

COMBINATION OVEN: Two or more different cooking modes combined in a single oven (microwave, convection, conventional, broiler and/or toaster) that may cook first one way, then another, or sometimes in two different modes at once, e.g., convection (forced hot air) *plus* microwaves. The advantage is that foods brown and dry on the surface, not true when microwaves alone are used. The disadvantage is that these ovens cook at different speeds and power levels than do microwave ovens; thus microwave recipes cannot be used in them without major adjustment.

CONDENSATION: As foods microwave, they generate clouds of steam. If they are covered, the steam condenses on the lid into beads of water that drop back into the food and water it down. Not a problem, perhaps, for soups and stews, but more critical for fragile sauces and custards whose thickening depends upon precise ratios of egg or flour to liquid. **Note:** *Accumulated moisture on oven walls and floors slows overall cooking, so always wipe oven dry after each batch of food is done before adding the next.*

CONDUCTION: Microwaves penetrate food only 1" to 1½", so areas in the heart of a roast, say, cook more slowly via conduction—that is, by a gentle spreading of the heat inward.

COMPOSITION: The content and structure of a food—the amount of fat and/or sugar it contains, for example (both speed microwave cooking). Protein-rich eggs must be treated with TLC in a microwave lest they toughen or curdle. And bone-in meats must often receive special attention because bone absorbs microwaves poorly. **Note:** *Our recipes carefully spell out each technique so that you will learn as you cook.*

CONVECTION: Cooking via forced hot air (see Combination Oven, above).

COOKING BAG: Plastic pouches designed especially for cooking food in a microwave oven (see the Microwave Utensil Chart that follows).

COOKING PATTERNS: The distribution of microwaves (i.e., the cooking pattern) at oven floor level will be different from that a few inches higher. Thus flat foods placed on the oven floor won't cook the same way as taller items or those elevated on an oven shelf. The problem with tall items is that the top often cooks faster than the bottom. All foods, moreover, cook more quickly on the outside than on the inside. To equalize the microwave cooking patterns, it's often necessary to use special containers (ring molds, for example). It's also important to rotate containers during microwaving, to turn foods over, or to stir and/or rearrange them. **Note:** *For this reason, our recipes provide all the specifics.*

COVER: To cover food while it microwaves or stands. Some foods require a lid or vented plastic food wrap to seal in all steam (certain vegetables); some call for wax paper (usually fatty items that can spatter fiercely in a microwave oven) and others for paper toweling when it's desirable for some—but not all—of the steam to escape (breads, chips, and crackers are often warmed and/or crisped in paper toweling).

DEFROST: To thaw frozen food. Many microwave ovens offer automatic defrost cycles that eliminate all guesswork.

DENSITY: The solidity or porousness of food. Light, porous foods cook faster than heavy, dense (nonporous) ones.

DISH TEST: A test to determine a container's microwavability (see How to Tell if a Container Is Microwave-safe in the microwave utensil discussion that follows).

DOUGHNUT FASHION: Refers to arranging food in a ring around the edge of a container to ensure faster, more uniform cooking.

ELEVATE: To raise food above the floor of a microwave oven by placing it on a shelf, rack, or turned-upside-down bowl. The purpose is to permit microwaves to reach the slower-cooking bottom, especially the center bottom.

HALFTIME: A term used in recipes throughout this book to indicate the midpoint of cooking—or of a specific stage of cooking.

HIGH: The full-power (100%) setting on a microwave oven.

HOLDING PERIOD: The length of time covered or wrapped food will stay hot after the standing period. The term also applies to the "keep warm" setting on microwave ovens.

HOT SPOTS: In nearly every microwave oven there are locations where foods cook faster than in others. These are called hot spots, and it's important not to position such delicate foods as custards or egg-thickened sauces in these areas. Turntables, rotating antennas, and stirrer fans all help distribute microwaves more evenly and minimize hot spots. Still, nearly every oven has them. *To test your oven for hot spots:* Cover the oven floor with slices of bread, allowing the crusts to touch. Microwave, uncovered, on HIGH (100% power) 5–7 minutes, until the bread begins to toast. Wherever the bread is brownest, you have a hot spot.

INSTANT-REGISTER THERMOMETER: These microwave-safe thermometers must be inserted at least 2″ into the food if they are to register accurately. To prevent arcing, make sure no part of the thermometer touches oven walls, door, or floor.

INTERLOCK: The safety locks installed on microwave oven doors that shut the oven off the instant the door is opened. By law, all microwave ovens must now contain two independent interlocks, and some models, to be absolutely fail-safe, feature a third backup.

INVERT: To turn food upside down (or right side up), usually after it has microwaved for a certain period of time, so that it will cook more evenly.

LOAD: The amount or volume of food to be microwaved at one time. The bigger the load, the more slowly the food will cook. One potato, for instance, will bake in 4–5 minutes, but 8 will require 20–24 minutes.

LOW: The slowest power setting (10%) on a microwave oven that can be used for cooking. "Keep warm" settings may be even lower.

MAGNETRON: Probably the single most important part of a microwave oven, the magnetron converts household current into microwaves. It's generally located at the top of the oven and funnels microwaves into the oven via a wave guide.

MEDIUM: Half, or 50%, microwave power (good for keeping foods at a simmer).

MEDIUM-HIGH: A moderately high microwave power level (70%). It's best for foods that should bubble gently.

MEDIUM-LOW: A moderately low microwave power level (30%). Use it for delicate foods that should never actively boil or cook too fast.

MEGAHERTZ: The unit used to measure the frequency of microwaves; for most microwave ovens it is 2,450 megahertz or 2,450 million cycles per second.

MICROWAVABLE, MICROWAVE-SAFE: Terms used to describe containers, coverings, and accessories that are safe for microwave use. Most manufacturers mark their products in some way to indicate that they're microwave-safe, and they include makers of paper toweling and plastic food wraps as well as of cookware.

MICROWAVE: To cook in a microwave oven.

MICROWAVES: Short, high-frequency, electromagnetic waves similar to radio and television broadcast waves that are transmitted through air (to learn how they cook food, see Chapter 1).

MODE STIRRER, STIRRER FAN: A little fan that literally stirs the microwaves to distribute them evenly throughout the interior of a microwave oven.

MULTIPLE POWER LEVELS: See Variable Power Levels, below.

OVENABLE PAPERBOARD: Heat-resistant, plastic-coated cardboard used to make disposable, microwave-safe containers. It's now being used more often than aluminum to package frozen TV dinners and side dishes.

PIERCE: To jab food with a sharp-pronged fork or skewer so that it won't burst as it microwaves. Tight-skinned, moisture-laden whole vegetables such as potatoes, eggplants, and summer and winter squash should all be pierced before they go into the microwave oven.

POACH: To simmer food gently in liquid. In the microwave, it's rarely necessary to immerse food in liquid because microwaving is such a moist method of cooking, although long-cooked foods may need to be turned over to keep them juicy. Among the items that poach to supreme succulence in the microwave are chicken and suprêmes of chicken, those boneless, skinless breasts that often become dry as a chip when cooked by conventional means.

POSITION: A synonym for "arrange," which means simply to place food in a microwave oven in a specific pattern or manner to equalize the cooking. *Note: All recipes in this book are quite specific about how food should be arranged for best results.*

PRICK: A gentler technique than to pierce (which see). Egg yolks, chicken livers, sausages, and other foods covered with fragile membranes must be lightly pricked with a toothpick or pin before they are cooked, otherwise steam will build inside them, rupture their membranes, and splatter them all over the inside of the oven.

RAISE (INCREASE) POWER: To move from a lower microwave power setting to a higher one. For example, to reduce liquid or evaporate excess moisture from, say, a shredded or sliced vegetable, you can up the power level from MEDIUM (50% power) to HIGH (100%) for a few fast seconds. This is usually done at the end of cooking.

REARRANGE: One of the most important microwave techniques because it helps ensure uniform cooking. Because items around the edge of a container microwave faster than those in the middle, it's necessary to rearrange them, usually at halftime, by moving the less-cooked items in the center toward the outside, and vice versa.

REDUCE (LOWER) POWER: To switch the power level from a higher setting to a lower one, as from HIGH (100% power) to MEDIUM (50%). Often a soup, stew, or casserole is begun on HIGH; then, after the liquid comes to a full boil, the power is reduced to MEDIUM or maybe MEDIUM-LOW (30%) so that the food simmers slowly, gaining succulence and savor.

REFLECTIVE: An adjective used to describe materials that reflect micro-waves rather than absorb them. Metals are reflective, and it's because microwaves bounce off them that they shouldn't be used in the microwave oven. They not only keep food from cooking properly but may also cause the oven to arc dangerously (see Arcing, above). *Note: Smooth strips of foil can be used to deflect microwaves from turkey wings, drumsticks, or other skinny areas of food in danger of cooking too fast. And aluminum foil pans can safely be used in a microwave oven provided they're lightweight, no more than ¾" deep, and at least three-quarters full of food.*

REST: See Stand.

ROTATE: When foods cannot be stirred or rearranged—custards and coffee cakes, for instance—it's imperative that you rotate their containers now and then as they microwave. Usually the rotating is done at halftime, and usually the containers are rotated 180° or given a half-turn. But sometimes they may be rotated more often and given a 90° (quarter) turn each time. *Note: All recipes in this book specify when a container should be turned, how often, and to what degree.*

ROTATING ANTENNAS: Wands that spin slowly to distribute microwave energy equally throughout the cooking cavity of a microwave oven.

RUNAWAY: A term used to describe food that's cooking much faster in one area than in another. For example, if you heat a jelly doughnut in a microwave oven, the sugar-rich jelly center will bubble ferociously before the doughnut itself is hot. Similarly, liquefied portions of frozen food will boil vigorously while still-icy portions remain inert. The automatic defrost cycles available today on microwave ovens vary and/or pulse the power on and off, allowing heat to spread via conduction from thawed portions to frozen ones so that, in the end, all areas are defrosted at the same time.

SENSOR: A device used in automatic or programmed microwaving to gauge doneness of food. Most sensors measure either the amount of weight lost by food as it cooks or the amount of heat or moisture given off (see Programmed Cooking in the Special Features and Optional Extras section of Chapter 2).

SEQUENTIAL COOKING: An umbrella term that can mean one of three things: (1) choreographing meal preparation so that the longest-to-microwave items cook first and the zip-quick ones last; (2) programming an oven to change power levels automatically in the course of preparing a recipe; and (3) combining microwaving with convection cooking and/or browning in a multipurpose oven.

SHAPE: The conformation of food or utensil, which affects cooking time. Irregularly shaped whole birds and fish require special attention to keep them from overcooking in thin areas before the fleshy ones are done (usually it's a simple matter of shielding the food—see Shield, below). As for utensils, round shapes and rings help ensure uniform cooking; squares and rectangles don't.

SHIELD: To cover areas of food that are browning too fast with smooth, thin strips of foil to deflect the microwaves and to slow cooking. *Examples:* the wingtips and drumsticks of whole birds, the heads and tails of whole fish. It's essential that the foil strips be no more than 2″ wide, also that they be smoothed around the food, not just draped on top. Crinkled foil can make

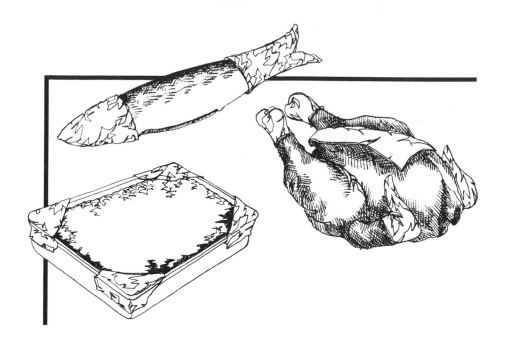

the oven arc (see Arcing, above), as can letting the foil touch oven walls, floor, or door.

SIMMER: To let food cook just below the boil (bubbles rise to the top but do not break). In microwave cookery, the items most apt to be simmered are soups, stews, and dried bean dishes. MEDIUM (50% power) is usually sufficient to keep them at a simmer, but in ovens of 700 watts or more, MEDIUM-LOW (30% power) may be all that's needed.

SIZE: Small, uniform pieces of food microwave faster and more evenly than large, irregularly shaped ones.

SPOKE FASHION: Refers to arranging long, slim, or irregularly shaped pieces of food—drumsticks, asparagus or broccoli spears, carrots, zucchini, etc.—in a container like the spokes of a wheel. Their thickest parts should be placed toward the rim of the dish, their tender tips or thinner portions toward the center.

STAGGER: When using the oven shelf, to arrange foods so that they are not directly above one another. Staggered, they will cook more uniformly.

STAND: To allow microwave foods to stand flat on a heat-resistant surface for a specified period of time after they come from the oven. Many foods actually finish cooking, firm up, and develop flavor during this all-important rest period. Baked potatoes, when first taken from the microwave oven, will seem as hard as stones, but they will soften nicely as they stand. Custards, on the other hand, will still be a bit soft in the center at the end of microwaving but will set completely on standing.

STANDING TIME: The amount of time that a microwaved food must stand before it is served. *Note: All recipes in this book are quite specific about standing times. Indeed, at the top of every recipe, the necessary standing time is listed along with the preparation time. Whenever a recipe is partially prepared and then left to stand WHILE you proceed with another stage of preparation, the standing time at the top of the recipe is written thus: None*.*

STARTING TEMPERATURE: The temperature of food before it goes into the microwave oven. Refrigerator-cold items will take longer to cook than room-temperature ones, and frozen foods longest of all.

STEAM: To cook food in a covered container with minimal liquid so that steam swirls around it. Because microwaving is such a moist method of cooking, moisture-laden vegetables, fish, and shellfish often need no liquid.

STIR: To bring the outer, more cooked portions of a soup, stew, sauce, or other stirrable food in toward the center and the less-cooked middle portions outward so that the cooking is equalized.

STIR-COOKING: Stir-*frying*, for which foods must constantly be tossed and turned over high heat, makes no sense for a microwave. But stir-*cooking* does. First of all, stir-cooked dishes don't require nonstop attention. Second, they can be cooked in a minimum of oil—sometimes with no oil at all—and that's good news for dieters. Finally, vegetables, whether cooked solo or in tandem with meats or seafood, remain crisp and colorful, with most of their vitamins intact.

TEMPER: To partially heat or thaw a food before it is cooked.

TEMPERATURE PROBE: An oven accessory that can be programmed to monitor the internal temperature of foods as they cook; it turns the oven off when the desired (preset) temperature is reached. For details, see Automatic Temperature Probes in the Special Features and Optional Extras section of Chapter 2.

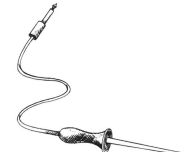

TURN OVER: To invert food or reverse its present position so that it will cook more evenly. Whole birds are often begun breast side down in a microwave oven, for example, then turned over and finished breast side up.

TURNTABLE: See Carousel.

UNIFORMLY HOT: In a microwave oven, foods may bubble or steam around the edges while still tepid in the center. Stirring, of course, helps spread the heat. But it's also important to test food for doneness in several spots to make sure that it is uniformly hot.

VARIABLE POWER LEVELS: Many microwave ovens, through their system of variable power levels, allow you to cook on HIGH (100% power), MEDIUM-HIGH (70% power), MEDIUM (50%), MEDIUM-LOW (30%), and LOW (10%); sophisticated models offer even more power options, but these five are the ones that matter most. To learn how they work and how much control they give the microwave cook, see under Special Features and Optional Extras in Chapter 2.

VENT: To provide a steam vent by piercing a plastic cooking bag or, in the case of plastic food wrap, by folding back one corner of it. If plastic food wrap is not properly vented, steam can build to the point that the plastic bursts, shrivels, and falls into the food. ***Note:*** *Don't try to vent plastic food wrap by puncturing or slitting it. During steam buildup, a small slit or hole can become a mighty tear. Needless to add, you should use microwave-safe food wrap only.*

VENTED PLASTIC FOOD WRAP: Wrap folded back at one corner so that steam can escape.

VOLUME: See Load.

WATER TEST: A simple test used to determine oven wattage (for details, see "How to Determine Your Microwave Oven's Wattage," in Chapter 2).

WAVE GUIDE: The channel through which micro-waves are fed from the magnetron into the cooking cavity of a microwave oven.

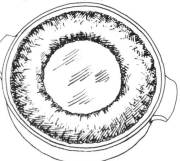

WREATHE: To place food in a ring around the edge of a container or, as the arrangement is also called, *doughnut* fashion.

ABOUT MICROWAVE UTENSILS

Buying a microwave oven needn't mean reequipping your kitchen. Far from it, although clearly you can't use conventional metal pots and pans in a microwave oven because microwaves can't penetrate them and reach the food inside.

But requirements aren't as strict as they once were, thanks to the new generation of microwave ovens with vastly improved systems of microwave distribution, which all but eliminate "hot" and "cold" spots.

In the beginning, microwave cookware had to be round or, better yet, ring-shaped if foods were to cook evenly. In the new and improved mid- and full-size microwave ovens, rectangular and square pans *can* be used—provided their corners are rounded. So can aluminum foil pans—*if* they're lightweight, are no more than ¾" deep, *and* are three-quarters full.

As for the utensils found in most kitchen cupboards, these criteria determine their microwavability. They should:

Allow microwaves to pass through them easily and into the food.

45

~~~~ Be able to withstand high temperatures (fat- and sugar-rich foods, in particular, may reach temperatures of 375°–400° F.).

~~~~ Be nonporous and nonflammable.

~~~~ Have straight rather than sloping sides.

~~~~ Be made of a material that the Food and Drug Administration (FDA) has approved for use with food. It should not give off chemical odors or flavors or absorb them, either.

Those kitchen standbys most likely to meet these requirements, the ones generally considered to be microwave-safe (or *microwavable,* as the industry prefers to call it), include:

GLASS OVENWARE casseroles, baking dishes, pie plates, ramekins, and measuring cups. Although these can withstand conventional oven heat, they shouldn't be set on a burner or in a broiler, something to consider whenever food is to be browned either before or after it's microwaved.

GLASS CERAMIC CONTAINERS, which can move from stovetop to microwave to broiler to table—or from freezer to microwave to broiler. These include Corning's opaque white and "Visions" (transparent brown).

POTTERY, TERRA-COTTA, CLAY, AND EARTHENWARE COOKWARE, but test first to make sure they're microwavable (see How to Tell If a Container Is Microwave-safe, below). The composition of both the ware and the glaze determines. Those containing metallic elements may not be microwavable.

STONEWARE devoid of metal parts or trim.

CHINA DINNERWARE free of metal trim or metallic glazes. Again, test.

GLASS JARS, but only the wide-mouth, heatproof canning variety.

NATURAL SCALLOP SHELLS, but for short-term heating or cooking only.

STRAW BASKETS, but only if they're devoid of metal trim or cleats and then for brief periods only.

THE "UNMICROWAVABLES"

These include *conventional metal pots and pans; lacquerware* (it will crack and buckle); *wooden bowls* (they'll warp and split); *metal-trimmed items,* which can cause arcing in the microwave; *Melamine dinnerware* (it can char and turn brittle); *Styrofoam* (it may melt); *plastic storage containers* (except those made especially for microwave use; see the Microwave Utensil Chart); *foil-lined cartons* (food never heats in them); *cups, mugs, or jugs with glued-on handles* (the glue may melt). By no means use plastic deli containers or the tubs in which butter, margarine, and dessert toppings are packaged; they may break down chemically into compounds hazardous to your health.

With microwave ovens now operating in millions of American homes cross-country, it's scarcely surprising that utensil manufacturers are flooding the market with a mesmerizing array of microwave cookware and accessories. Here's a quick "what's what."

MICROWAVE UTENSIL CHART

Note: *Follow each manufacturer's "Use and Care" instructions to the letter.*

Glass Ceramic Cookware

Available in many shapes and sizes, these sturdy lidded and unlidded containers are truly multipurpose. Although Anchor Hocking warns not to heat Creative Cuisine items above 400° F., you can brown food either by stovetop or broiler in Corning Ware, also in Corning's French White and Visions; you can microwave a wide variety of recipes in them; you can freeze food in them—indeed, transfer them directly from freezer to microwave to table (meaning one "pot" to clean instead of three).
Advantages: Glass ceramic utensils are dishwasher-proof, nonporous, and wholly inert, meaning they react in no way to the foods put into them and neither impart nor absorb flavors and aromas.
Disadvantages: Only one: *Weight.* These containers *are* heavy and may be cumbersome, especially for the elderly or infirm.

Heat-resistant or Oven-tempered Glass (Glass Ovenware)

Advantages: Sleek, nonporous lidded and unlidded containers, racks, and trivets in a wide variety of sizes and shapes that can be used in both conventional ovens or microwaves. Anchor Hocking recommends that its Oven Basics and Kitchen Classics not be heated beyond 400° F. and its Glass Microwave items beyond 450° F. Corning posts no such limits for Microwave Plus, Corelle, or Pyrex. Like glass ceramic containers, these are utterly inert and dishwasher-safe. And here's a new development from the Glass Packaging Institute: An immediately identifiable symbol—an open jar with microwaves passing through it—that will be used by food processors to show which glass jars are microwave-safe.

Disadvantages: Weight; inability to take burner or broiler heat.

Permanent Plastic Dual-purpose Cookware

"Dual-purpose" means that the cookware can be used in both conventional ovens—within reason—and microwaves (but not on the stovetop or in the broiler). Mosts items are made of *thermoset polyester* (fiberglass–reinforced plastic).

Advantages: The number of sizes and shapes available; rigidity, multipurpose versatility; ability to withstand machine dishwashing.

Disadvantages: Tendency to chip and crack, to stain, and to make foods "stick"; inability to take oven heat of more than 400°–420° F. (Tupperware's Ultra 21 can withstand temperatures up to 500° F.).

Permanent Plastic Cookware for Microwaves Only

Here the picture becomes more complex because several different thermoplastics are used: *polycarbonate, polypropylene, polymethylpentene* (TPX), and *polysulfone* (UDEL). Their greatest advantage is that they remain cool during cooking and are thus quick to clean. But their properties differ, so we discuss them one by one. When buying new permanent plastic cookware, always read the fine print to determine just which thermoplastic was used to make it.

Polycarbonate:

Advantages: Durability; stain-resistance; dishwasherability; availability in clear plastic (the better to monitor cooking) as well as opaque.

Disadvantages: Can't be used with high-fat or high-sugar foods; should not be used at temperatures above 350° F.

Polypropylene:
  Advantages: Sturdiness, resistance to stains and sticking.
  Disadvantages: Can't be used in conventional ovens.

Polymethylpentene (TPX):
  Advantages: Lack of heft; dishwasherability; stain-resistance; availability in clear plastic as well as opaque.
  Disadvantages: Absorbs food odors; softens when heated; can't be used in conventional ovens.

Polysulfone (UDEL):
  Advantages: Sturdiness; dishwasherability; imperviousness to food odors; availability in clear plastic as well as opaque.
  Disadvantages: Can't be used in conventional ovens at temperatures higher than 300° F.

Microwavable Plastic Storage Containers

Most of these are made of *polypropylene* or *polycarbonate* (see their advantages and disadvantages listed earlier); a few are manufactured of the more durable thermoset (fiberglass–reinforced) polyester.
Advantages: Availability, convenience, versatility.
Disadvantages: Few items can withstand temperatures higher than 350° F. and some can't tolerate those above 290° F. (read manufacturer's instructions carefully). Some containers stain easily; others absorb and impart odors.

Reusable Plastic and Paperboard Microwave Ware

Advantages: Lightweight, cheap, readily available.
Disadvantages: Most can't be used at temperatures above 400° F.; many stain and absorb food odors; few are dishwasher-safe; most are difficult to clean and don't last long.

Paper Plates, Cups, and Bowls

Use only plastic-coated, pale or uncolored, undecorated containers *not made of recycled paper.*
Advantages: Quick and cheap to use for reheating hot drinks, soups, appetizers, individual portions of stews; handy for cooking small amounts of bacon.
Disadvantages: Esthetically displeasing.

Metal Microwave Cookware

Some bantamweight shallow foil containers can be used in the microwave and some cookware is now rimmed with stainless steel to prevent food from overcooking around the edges. Innovative manufacturers have developed metal (or part-metal) roasters that brown meat effectively in the microwave, even a metal fryer that can safely move from stovetop to microwave. But consumers remain wary and they have not proved popular. Indeed, Revere Ware's revolutionary MicroMetal-Fryer has been discontinued. Too bad.

Coverings and Lids

LIDS: The most useful are transparent ones that allow you to follow the progress of food as it microwaves. Casserole lids are quick to remove and replace when it's time to stir or rearrange food, and they're particularly appropriate for long-simmering soups, stews, and pot roasts, also for fat- or sugar-rich foods that reach high temperatures. *Tip: When opening a casserole, always use the lid as a shield to deflect the steam away from you.*

PLASTIC FOOD WRAPS: Use only those recommended for microwaving (most are *polyvinylidene* or *polyethylene*) because they won't soften or deform. Plastic wraps are best for covering foods that are to be kept moist or steamed briefly—vegetables and seafoods, for example. To prevent steam buildup, always vent the wrap by rolling it back slightly at one side.

OVEN COOKING BAGS: These are the same heat-resistant nylon bags that we've been using in conventional ovens. They're best, we find, for pork roasts, which must be cooked until well done. Cooking bags promote even microwave distribution and keep meat moist and succulent. But it's a messy job to get the finished roast out of the bag. Use these bags only as the manufacturer directs.

OTHER PLASTIC BAGS: Use only those recommended for microwave ovens and for *brief* periods only. Never use plastic food storage bags (or their twist-ties, which can causing arcing), and never, ever, use the tear-off fresh produce bags offered as a customer convenience by many supermarkets.

WAX PAPER: Handiest for reheating cooked foods, and for cooking fruits and poultry. Wax paper speeds cooking by evening heat distribution. It also absorbs spatters, which makes it the perfect choice for fatty foods, and finally, it helps keep foods moist.

PAPER TOWELING AND NAPKINS: Use unprinted, uncolored ones *not* made of recycled paper; the latter may contain harmful chemicals or even bits of metal, which can ignite. Because paper towels are porous, they allow steam to escape and are just the wrapper to use when crisping crackers and chips or when reheating sandwiches, pita breads, rolls, and tortillas. They also absorb fat and spatters and thus make handy covers when cooking bacon.

ALUMINUM FOIL: In the microwave oven, small strips (2″ maximum) are used *not* to cover food but to deflect microwaves from (shield) areas that are cooking or browning too fast. Foil coverings help keep foods hot as they stand (it's during this final resting period that many microwaved foods develop the proper flavor and texture or consistency).

Active Microwave Cookware

With the exception of aluminum foil, which deflects microwaves, everything discussed thus far can be classified as *passive microwave cookware,* meaning that it holds or covers the food being microwaved, nothing more. *Active microwave cookware,* on the other hand, can redirect or shield the microwaves for more attractive, more palatable food. For example, the single biggest complaint lodged against microwave ovens is that they neither brown nor crisp foods properly.

To overcome these shortcomings, scientists have developed a variety of nonstick browning dishes and skillets, trays and grills, which when properly preheated in the microwave will indeed brown food. Preheating times vary according to the food that's to be browned (less time is needed for cheese sandwiches than for meat) and the size of the browning unit (the larger it is, the longer it will take to heat). ***Note: Always use browning utensils as the manufacturer suggests. Never overheat; you risk breaking the clear glass shelf that's standard equipment on the floor of many microwave ovens.*** Scientists have also created special browner-crispers, some with metal heating plates, on which pies and pizzas can microwave without going limp. Also included in the category of *active microwave cookware:* popcorn poppers, coffee makers, steamers, and egg poachers. It's a competitive field with new items constantly coming onto the market.

Microwave Accessories

TURNTABLES: Battery-powered or spring-wound, these lazy Susans, whether portable or standard oven equipment, rotate food continuously so that it microwaves evenly without your having to do the job yourself. *Note: Some turntables are noisy, so check the decibel level before buying.* Many of the second-generation oven models, with their improved distribution of microwaves, are making turntables obsolete.

ROAST AND BACON RACKS: Deeply ridged to elevate meat and drain away fat and juices, these fit inside microwave casseroles and roasting "pans."

SHELVES: Handy to have when you want to cook more than one item—or a whole meal—at a time.

TEMPERATURE PROBES: See the discussion under Automatic Temperature Probes in Chapter 2.

MICROWAVE SCALES: These compute the cooking times and power levels needed to cook specific foods of a given weight.

TIPS ON CHOOSING AND USING MICROWAVE UTENSILS

WHEN BUYING MICROWAVE WARE

Many factors determine how you should equip yourself for microwave cooking. How will you use the microwave? Mainly for thawing and reheating? For simple cooking? For sophisticated cooking? How much cupboard space do you have? How much money do you want to spend? How large is your family? Will you be cooking in small quantities or large? Here, then, are a few points to consider:

ITEMS ON HAND: Inventory your kitchen cupboards and determine which items can be used in a microwave. Then concentrate on filling in the gaps.

VERSATILITY: Multipurpose cookware that can be used on the stovetop and in conventional ovens and broilers as well as in the microwave will prove particularly useful. Most have their own microwave-safe lids—a decided plus.

DURABILITY: Fragile cookware will soon have to be replaced.

SHAPE AND DESIGN: For most microwave recipes, round or oval containers are better than square or rectangular, and rings are better yet for foods that cannot be stirred as they cook (many quick breads and cakes, most pâtés). So give these shapes top priority when adding to your inventory of microwave cookware. Also check the design of each item. Is it smooth and clean of line with no ridges or grooves to catch and harbor cooked-on foods? (A major drawback of bacon racks, roast racks, and some browning grills is that coagulated meat juices are difficult to remove.) Are the container sides straight or sloping? (Straight is more microwave-efficient.) Are there handles that can be easily gripped with potholders? (Because of steam build-up, many containers get blisteringly hot in the microwave.) Are the containers shallow enough to allow maximum microwave exposure?

SIZE: How large is your microwave oven? Choose cookware that will fit into it easily without touching sides or top. Also select sizes that meet your specific family needs.

WEIGHT: Heavy containers may be difficult to handle within the small confines of a microwave oven, especially if it's set high above the stovetop.

STACKABILITY: If cupboard space is precious, choose items that stack neatly and compactly.

USE: What are you most likely to cook by microwave? Casseroles? Quick breads and cakes? Pot roasts? Soups and stews? Candies? Plan carefully and buy accordingly.

PRICE: Some microwave utensils are cheap but short-lived. Are they a better bargain than more expensive items that will last a lifetime?

UPKEEP: Can the utensils be put through the dishwasher? Do they have nonstick finishes that simplify cleanup?

USING MICROWAVE COOKWARE

How and how long food is to be cooked determines what container should be used. So does the food itself and the quantity of it. Always use the container a recipe specifies or a close approximation. Here are a few guidelines:

Choose containers that approximate the size and the shape of the food to be cooked, but, for even microwave penetration, never crowd the food. *Note: Often the diameter and depth of a container are critical to a recipe's success. Our recipes provide these dimensions whenever necessary.*

Use only containers that fit into your microwave oven comfortably without touching walls, door, or top.

When cooking soups and other liquids, allow plenty of head room at the top of the container so that the mixtures don't boil over. This is especially important for milk- or cream-rich mixtures and certain cereals; they boil up fast and furiously.

When cooking candies, jams, or preserves, use glass ceramic containers, glass ovenware, or thermoset plastics that can withstand intense heat. These recipes will need plenty of head room, too.

If food is to be browned on the stovetop before cooking or in the broiler afterward, use a microwave-safe container that can also take burner or broiler heat.

When preparing stews, pot roasts, or other long-simmering recipes, use lidded casseroles that not only hold in moisture, but also simplify the stirring and rearranging. If the lids are transparent, so much the better. You can often monitor a recipe's progress without opening the oven door.

When reheating frozen or refrigerated foods, use multipurpose cookware that can go from freezer or fridge to microwave.

~~~ Unless recipes direct otherwise, use Bundt or ring molds for uniform cooking of cakes, quick breads, delicate pâtés, and other foods that can't be stirred.

~~~ If children use your microwave oven, identify all microwave cookware with an indelible marker so they're quickly recognizable to young cooks.

~~~ If a container seems to have no back or front, mark an indelible dot or slash on one side so you'll know at a glance when you've rotated it 90° or 180° during microwaving.

HOW TO TELL IF A CONTAINER IS MICROWAVE-SAFE

Place ½ cup cold water in a 1-cup ovenware glass measure and set in the microwave oven. Set the container to be tested beside—but not touching—the cup. Microwave on HIGH (100% power) 1 minute. The water should be very warm, even hot. Now touch the container being tested. If it's cool or only slightly warm, it's microwave-safe.

ABOUT IMPROVISING MICROWAVE-SAFE CONTAINERS

As sometimes happens when you're stranded mid-recipe minus a key ingredient, you may find yourself without the proper microwave container. Not to worry. Here are some quick substitutions that work nicely.

RING MOLD OR BUNDT PAN: Stand a glass ovenware custard cup, water glass, or preserving jar in the center of a microwave-safe round casserole of the proper diameter.

MUFFIN PAN OR CUPCAKER: Use microwavable custard cups or ramekins and arrange them in the microwave in a ring.

COMPARTMENTALIZED CONTAINERS: Heat each menu item in its own

55

microwave-safe bowl (cereal bowls and small mixing bowls are just right).

REUSABLE PLASTIC OR PAPERBOARD MICROWAVE COOKWARE: For quick heatings or reheatings, use any microwave-safe plate or pie plate, even a plastic-coated, undecorated paper plate *not* made of recycled paper.

SOME ADDITIONAL TIPS: Two items that we find indispensable are standard preserving jars and glass ovenware or microwavable plastic measuring cups, which come in 1-cup, 2-cup, 1-quart, 6-cup, even 2-quart sizes. You can store sauces, gravies, and soups in tightly capped preserving jars in the refrigerator. Come serving time, uncap them and set in the microwave; the contents will come to serving temperature in almost no time at all. Measuring cups are handy for brewing quick beverages, soups, sauces, and gravies. *For stirring,* wood, microwavable plastic, even metal (but not pewter, silver, or gold alloy) spoons may safely be left in foods containing more than 1 cup of liquid, but for *brief heatings only.* Wood and plastic are better choices because they remain cool.

SOME QUICK MICROWAVE TIPS

Here are a few handy tricks we've learned in the course of writing this book that may serve you well:

ALWAYS CODE or key each piece of microwave-safe cookware—with an indelible *M,* for example—so that each family member and visiting fireman will instantly know what's okay to use in the microwave oven.

PAINT A SMALL DOT of indelible ink on the center rim of each piece of microwave cookware. Then always set the container in the microwave oven with the dot at twelve o'clock so that whenever a recipe calls for rotating a container, you can see at a glance when you've given it a half (180°) or quarter (90°) turn.

TO AVOID BOILOVERS of soups, sauces, syrups, and other sugar-rich mixtures, always use a container two to three times the volume of the ingredients put into it.

To keep microwave oven fans from blowing wax paper covers off food during microwaving, crumple the paper slightly.

Use dental floss to tie microwave cooking bags, never twist-ties, which contain metal and can cause the oven to arc (see Arcing, in The Terms and Techniques of Microwaving, earlier in this chapter).

When food must be stirred often, leave a wooden spoon (or other microwave-safe one) in the food as it cooks—it saves taking the spoon in and out every time you stir.

If your microwave is equipped with pause control, use it to remind you to stir, rearrange, or rotate food.

SHORTCUT COOKING

One of the microwave's great bonuses is that it simplifies so many once tedious cooking jobs—the softening of brick-hard brown sugar, for example . . . the making of chocolate curls . . . the toasting of nuts and seeds. And these are just the beginning. It's even a zip-quick way to dry fresh flowers and make hot compresses.

BREAD, CHIPS, CRACKERS, CROUTONS, AND CRUMBS

TO CRISP STALE CRACKERS: Arrange 25–30 crackers in single layer on microwave-safe baking sheet and microwave, uncovered, on HIGH (100% power) 30 seconds, until barely warm. Cool and store airtight.

TO CRISP CHIPS AND PRETZELS: Line microwave-safe basket or colander with paper toweling, add 2–3 cups chips or pretzels, and microwave, uncovered, on HIGH (100% power) 30–60 seconds, until warm, tossing once or twice. Cool and store airtight. *Note: Popcorn and breakfast cereals can be crisped this way.*

TO MAKE MUFFINS WITHOUT PANS: Stack crinkly paper cup liners 4 deep, half fill the top liner in each stack with batter, then microwave as recipe directs. The three outer liners support muffins as they bake, and can be reused again and again.

TO RAISE (PROOF) YEAST DOUGH: Pour 3 cups hottest tap water into 1-quart measure and set, uncovered, in oven beside, but not touching, uncovered bowl containing enough dough for two (9″ × 5″ × 3″) loaves. Microwave on LOW (10% power) 15–20 minutes, rotating bowl 90° every 5 minutes, until doubled in bulk. Stick two fingers into dough; if ½″ depression remains, dough is properly risen (batter bread and soft doughs will look puffed and spongy). This same technique can be used to raise shaped loaves, but watch carefully—the second rising usually goes faster. **Note:** *Never use a power level higher than 10% (you'll kill the yeast). And never bake the bread by microwave. It will be drab, crustless, and alternately dry and doughy.*

TO MAKE MELBA TOAST: Trim crusts from 4 thin (⅛″) slices bread, halve diagonally, and arrange on double-thickness paper toweling on oven floor. Microwave, uncovered, on HIGH (100% power) 2¾–3 minutes, rearranging slices at halftime, until crisp. Cool and store airtight.

TO MAKE RUSKS: Spread 6 (3″ × ½″) strips firm-textured white bread on double-thickness paper toweling on oven floor. Microwave, uncovered, on HIGH (100% power) 1¾–2½ minutes, rearranging strips at halftime, until crisp and pale golden. Cool and store airtight.

TO MAKE CROUTONS: Spread 1 quart ½″ stale crustless bread cubes in single layer in shallow 3-quart casserole. Microwave, uncovered, on HIGH (100% power) 4–5 minutes, stirring every 2 minutes, until dry. Cool and store airtight. **Note:** *Time will vary according to staleness and type of bread (white, whole wheat, rye, etc.).*

TO MAKE GARLIC CROUTONS: Mix 2 tablespoons soft butter or margarine with 1 crushed clove garlic, spread lightly on bread before cubing, then microwave, uncovered, on HIGH (100% power) 3½–4½ minutes, stirring every 2 minutes, until dry. Cool and store airtight.

V A R I A T I O N S

HERB CROUTONS: Prepare as directed, mixing butter with ¼ teaspoon each minced fresh chives, parsley, and basil instead of garlic.

ITALIAN CROUTONS: Mix 2 tablespoons each olive oil and grated Parmesan with ¼ teaspoon each crushed garlic, dried basil, and dried oregano. Spread on bread, cube, and microwave as directed.

TO DRY BREAD CRUMBS (Makes 1 cup): Arrange 4 slices day-old or stale bread on paper toweling on oven floor and microwave, uncovered, on HIGH (100% power) 3½–4½ minutes, until dry. Cool, then buzz 5–6 seconds in food processor for coarse crumbs, 15–20 seconds for fine. Or place Croutons in plastic bag and crush with rolling pin. Or simply buzz cooled Croutons to crumbs (1 cup Croutons = 1 cup crumbs). Store airtight.

V A R I A T I O N

SEASONED BREAD CRUMBS: Buzz cooled Garlic, Herb, or Italian Croutons to crumbs as directed above. Store airtight.

CHOCOLATE

TO MELT CHOCOLATE: For 1–2 (1-ounce) squares chocolate, unwrap and place in bone-dry ramekin; for 3 or more, arrange in triangle, square, or ring in dry pie plate. **Note:** *Never melt chocolate in wet container and never cover; it will streak.* Microwave, uncovered, on MEDIUM (50% power), allowing 2–2½ minutes for the first ounce and 30 seconds for each additional ounce (unsweetened chocolate may need 10–20 seconds more per ounce). Stir at halftime and again at end until smooth and glossy (unstirred chocolate will hold its shape, even when melted). **Note:** *If chocolate is melted along with butter, shortening, cream, or other ingredient, you can use HIGH (100% power).*

TO MELT SEMISWEET CHOCOLATE BITS: Arrange 1–2 cups chocolate bits doughnut fashion in 9" pie plate and microwave, uncovered, on MEDIUM (50% power), allowing 2–2½ minutes for 1 cup and 3–4 minutes for 2 cups, until bits are glossy (they'll hold their shape). Let stand, uncovered, 1 minute and stir.

TO MAKE CHOCOLATE CURLS: Unwrap 1-ounce square chocolate (any type), place on plate, and microwave, uncovered, on MEDIUM (50% power) 15–20 seconds, until just warm. Using swivel-bladed vegetable peeler, shave off curls. If chocolate hardens, rewarm.

DAIRY:

TO SCALD MILK: Microwave 1–2 cups milk in uncovered 1-quart measure on MEDIUM-HIGH (70% power) until tiny bubbles form around edge, allowing 2½–3 minutes for 1 cup and 3½–4 minutes for 2 cups. *Note: If you have temperature probe, set at 175° F. and insert in center of milk.*

TO SOFTEN BRICK-HARD ICE CREAM: Set unopened container in oven and microwave on LOW (10% power) 1½–1¾ minutes for ½ gallon, 50–60 seconds for 1 quart, and 30–40 seconds for 1 pint. Let stand 2–3 minutes before serving.

TO MELT BUTTER: Place refrigerator-cold butter in suitable container (ramekins are perfect for small amounts, 1-cup measures for larger ones), cover with wax paper, and microwave on HIGH (100% power) as follows:

1–1½ tablespoons	25–30 seconds
2 tablespoons	35–45 seconds
3 tablespoons	45–55 seconds
4 tablespoons (¼ cup)	55–65 seconds
⅓ cup	65–75 seconds
½ cup	1¼–1½ minutes

Note: Because margarine contains polyunsaturated fats, it melts 5–10 seconds faster than butter.

TO SOFTEN BUTTER FOR SPREADING: Microwave refrigerator-cold butter on butter plate (if microwave-safe), uncovered, on MEDIUM-LOW (30% power), allowing 10 seconds for ½ stick (¼ cup) and 15–25 seconds for 1 stick (½ cup) and rotating plate 180° at halftime. Let stand 10–15 seconds, then serve.

TO SOFTEN CREAM CHEESE: Unwrap cheese, place on plate, and microwave, uncovered, on HIGH (100% power), allowing 30–45 seconds for 3 ounces and 1–1½ minutes for 8 ounces and rotating plate 180° at halftime. *Note: Cheese holds its shape as it softens, so test after minimum time.*

TO SOFTEN CHEESE SPREADS: Microwave in uncapped jar, allowing 1–2 minutes for each cup cheese. If container is not microwave-safe, transfer to ovenware glass measure.

TO "RIPEN" SOFT CHEESES: See Chapter 6, "Appetizers, Snacks, and Sandwiches."

TO TEMPER REFRIGERATOR-COLD CHEESES: See Chapter 6, "Appetizers, Snacks, and Sandwiches."

FRUITS AND VEGETABLES

TO PEEL TOMATOES, APRICOTS, PEACHES, NECTARINES: Bring 1 cup hottest tap water to boiling by microwaving in uncovered 1-quart measure on HIGH (100% power) 1¾–2 minutes. Add 1 tomato or fruit and microwave, uncovered, on HIGH (100% power) 30 seconds. Plunge into ice water and peel. *Note: When peeling more than 4 tomatoes or fruits, do it the old-fashioned way.*

TO REHYDRATE SUN-DRIED TOMATOES: Place 1 ounce (about 20 pieces) sun-dried tomatoes and ¾ cup hot tap water in 2-cup measure, cover with vented plastic food wrap, and microwave on HIGH (100% power) 50–60 seconds, until boiling. Stir, re-cover, and microwave on MEDIUM (50% power) 1 minute. Let stand 5 minutes, drain, and pat dry on paper toweling (save liquid for soup or sauce).

TO PEEL PEPPERS: Halve, core, and seed 1 sweet or hot pepper and place in plastic bag, twisting end and folding under (do not use twist-tie). Microwave on HIGH (100% power), allowing 2¼–2½ minutes for red or yellow pepper and 3–3½ minutes for green, rotating bag 180° at halftime. Let green pepper stand in bag 3–4 minutes (no standing needed for red or yellow). Cool pepper under cold running water, then peel.

TO INCREASE JUICE OF CITRUS FRUITS: Microwave whole refrigerator-cold fruit, uncovered, on HIGH (100% power) just until warm, allowing 40 seconds for 1 fruit, 60 seconds for 2, and 1½–2 minutes for 4. *Note: Halve times for room-temperature fruit.* Roll fruit on counter with palm, then cut and squeeze. **Note: *This technique also makes citrus fruits easier to peel.***

TO DRY CITRUS RIND:
Finely grate rind of 3 large oranges, 4 medium-size lemons or limes, or 3 medium-size grapefruits onto wax paper and spread evenly. Set paper of rind in oven and microwave, uncovered, on HIGH (100% power) 3½–4½ minutes, forking every minute until dry. Let stand, uncovered, to complete drying. Stored airtight, rind will keep 8 weeks. Use in recipes, substituting ½ teaspoon dried rind for 2 teaspoons fresh.

TO CANDY CITRUS RIND:
Peel 3 large navel oranges or 2 medium-size grapefruits and cut in 3″ × ½″ strips. If white pith is extra thick, remove excess. Place rind and 2 cups hot water in 3-quart casserole, cover with lid or vented plastic food wrap, and microwave on HIGH (100% power) 5–6 minutes, until boiling. Drain and repeat (mixture may take 1 minute less to boil this time). Drain rind, rinse in strainer under cold running water, and blot dry on paper toweling. In same casserole, mix 1 cup sugar and ¼ cup hot tap water, add rind, and microwave, uncovered, on HIGH (100% power) 9–10 minutes, stirring every 3 minutes, until rind is translucent. Mix 1 teaspoon unflavored gelatin with 1 tablespoon cold water, stir into casserole, and microwave, uncovered, on HIGH (100% power) 1 minute. Let rind stand in syrup, uncovered, 5 minutes. With slotted spoon, lift out rind, letting excess syrup drain off, then roll in ⅔ cup sugar. **Note: *Toothpicks are handy for this messy job.*** Dry rind on wire rack and store airtight.

TO THAW FROZEN FRUIT JUICE CONCENTRATES:
Open can and microwave, uncovered, on MEDIUM (50% power) allowing 2–2½ minutes for 6-ounce can, 4–4½ minutes for 12-ounce. Stir well. Juice liquefies but doesn't heat.

TO PLUMP DRIED FRUITS:
Spread 1 pound dried fruit in pie plate, sprinkle with 3 tablespoons water, cover with vented plastic food wrap, and microwave on HIGH (100% power) 2½–3 minutes, stirring at halftime. Let stand, covered, 2 minutes to plump fully. Drain or not as recipes direct.

TO PLUMP RAISINS AND DRIED CURRANTS:
Spread 1 pound seedless raisins or currants in casserole at least 10″ across, sprinkle with 2 tablespoons water, fruit juice, brandy, or rum, cover with vented plastic food wrap, and microwave on HIGH (100% power) 2–2½ minutes. Let stand, covered, 2 minutes to plump fully. Drain before using in baked goods.

TO MACERATE CANDIED FRUIT ZIP-QUICK: Microwave ¼ cup brandy, Grand Marnier, or other fruit liqueur in uncovered 1-quart bowl 30 seconds on HIGH (100% power). Stir in 1 cup finely diced candied fruit (or dried currants or raisins) and microwave, uncovered, on HIGH (100% power) 2 minutes. Let stand, uncovered, until all liquid is absorbed. Use as directed in fruit cakes or steamed puddings.

TO SOFTEN UNDERRIPE AVOCADOS: Pierce avocado once or twice, place on upside-down saucer, and microwave, uncovered, on HIGH (100% power) 30–60 seconds, turning over and rotating 180° at halftime, until warm; cool and peel.

GELATIN

TO DISSOLVE UNFLAVORED GELATIN: Mix 1 envelope unflavored gelatin and ¼ cup cold water in ramekin and microwave, uncovered, on HIGH (100% power) 40–50 seconds, until dissolved. Stir and use as recipes direct.

TO MELT TOO STIFF FRUIT OR VEGETABLE GELATIN: Microwave, uncovered, on MEDIUM (50% power) 1–2 minutes per cup gelatin, stirring every 30 seconds, until syrupy.

HERBS AND FLOWERS

TO DRY FRESH HERBS: Wash 2 cups loosely packed, freshly picked herb leaves and pat dry; spread evenly on double-thickness paper toweling on oven floor, and microwave, uncovered, on HIGH (100% power) 3½–4½ minutes, until crumbly. Pack whole in airtight jars or crush by rolling between sheets of wax paper, then pack airtight. ***Note:*** *Celery leaves can be dried the same way but will take about 5 minutes to dry completely.*

TO DRY FRESH FLOWERS: Cut all but 1″ stems from small blossoms (button or pompon mums, marigolds, sweetheart roses, etc.), then arrange 1 layer deep in shallow ramekin. Cover with silica gel (available at florists) and place in microwave oven. Set ½ cup water beside ramekin and micro-wave, uncovered, on HIGH (100% power) 3–7 minutes, until blossoms are dry. Let gel-covered blossoms stand overnight. Carefully lift flowers from

63

gel, gently shaking off excess, attach to floral wire with floral tape, then "fix" with acrylic spray.

NUTS AND SEEDS

TO SHELL NUTS: Place 1 pound almonds, Brazil nuts, filberts, pecans, or walnuts in 3-quart casserole, add 2 cups hot water, cover with lid or vented plastic food wrap, and microwave on HIGH (100% power) 4–5 minutes, until boiling. Let stand, covered, 1 minute. Drain, dry on paper toweling, cool, and crack—nuts will be easy to extract. *Note: Shell nuts over bowl; some may contain water.* Spread shelled nuts on paper toweling and dry overnight.

TO BLANCH ALMONDS: Bring 1 cup hot tap water to boiling in uncovered 1-quart casserole by microwaving on HIGH (100% power) 1½–2 minutes. Add 1 cup shelled, unblanched almonds and microwave, uncovered, on HIGH (100% power) 1 minute. Drain, cool slightly, slip off skins, and spread on paper toweling to dry.

TO TOAST NUTS: Spread ½–2 cups nuts (any kind, blanched or unblanched, whole or cut up) in 9"–11" pie plate, depending on amount. Microwave, uncovered, on HIGH (100% power), allowing 3–3½ minutes for ½ cup and 4–5½ for 1–2 cups (size and type of nut determine time), stirring once or twice, until *lightly* browned. Let stand, uncovered, 2–3 minutes. *Note: Nuts will continue browning as they stand, so don't overcook.*

TO BUTTER-BROWN NUTS: Melt 1 tablespoon butter or margarine in wax-paper-covered 9" pie plate by microwaving on HIGH (100% power) 25–30 seconds. Stir in ½ cup nuts and toast as directed above. *Note: For 1 cup nuts use larger pie plate and 2 tablespoons butter and microwave 35–45 seconds to melt; for 2 cups nuts use 4 tablespoons butter and microwave 55–65 seconds to melt.*

TO TOAST COCONUT: Spread ½–1 cup flaked coconut evenly, doughnut fashion, in 9" pie plate or paper plate, then, for best results, set on turntable. Microwave, uncovered, on MEDIUM (50% power), allowing 2½–3½ minutes for ½ cup and 3½–4 minutes for 1 cup. Toss with fork every minute, until lightly browned, watching carefully toward end lest coconut scorch in spots. Toss again, cool, and store airtight.

TO DRY FRESH COCONUT: Spread ½–1 cup coarsely grated fresh coconut evenly, doughnut fashion, on paper toweling in 9″ pie plate or paper plate. Microwave, uncovered, on MEDIUM-HIGH (70% power), allowing 2½–3½ minutes for ½ cup and 4–5 minutes for 1 cup. Stir and toss with fork every minute, until dry. Lift paper of coconut to wire rack, cool, and store airtight.

TO TOAST SESAME, PUMPKIN, OR SUNFLOWER SEEDS: Melt 1 tablespoon butter or margarine in wax-paper-covered 9″ pie plate by microwaving on HIGH (100% power) 25–30 seconds. Stir in ½ cup seeds, spread doughnut fashion, and microwave, uncovered, on HIGH (100% power) 3–4 minutes, stirring every minute, until golden. **Note:** *Seeds will continue browning outside oven.* Drain on paper toweling and store airtight. *To Toast Seeds Without Butter:* Microwave as directed but for 2½–3½ minutes only.

PASTA

TO DRY HOMEMADE PASTA: Spread ½ pound uniformly cut pasta on microwave-safe tray or baking sheet lined with double-thickness paper toweling and microwave, uncovered, on MEDIUM-LOW (30% power) 5–7 minutes, until dry, rearranging every 3 minutes. Lift to wire rack, toweling and all, and cool. **Note:** *Don't try to dry more than ½ pound pasta at a time; it won't dry evenly.*

SPIRITS

TO FLAME LIQUOR: Microwave ¼ cup brandy, Cognac, or light or dark rum in uncovered 1-cup measure on HIGH (100% power) 15–20 seconds, until warm. Remove from oven, blaze with match, and spoon, flaming, over dessert. Or pour warm spirits over dessert and *then* flame.

SUGARS AND SYRUPS

TO SOFTEN BRICK-HARD BROWN SUGAR: Place sugar and a peeled apple slice in bowl, cover with vented plastic food wrap, and microwave on HIGH (100% power) until soft, allowing 30 seconds for each cup sugar. Break up sugar with fork after each 30-second increment.

TO CARAMELIZE SUGAR: Mix ½ cup each sugar and water in 1-pint measure and microwave, uncovered, on HIGH (100% power) 8–10 minutes, without stirring, until amber. Let stand ½–1 minute, until rich caramel brown. *Note: Mixture will continue to darken on standing, so don't overcook.*

TO CLEAR CRYSTALLIZED HONEY OR PRESERVES: Uncap jar, and if more than half-full or in plastic container, empty into bowl twice the volume of honey or preserves. Microwave, uncovered, on HIGH (100% power), allowing 1–1½ minutes per cup and stirring or rotating container 180° at halftime until sugar crystals dissolve. Cool and use within 1–2 days.

TO WARM PANCAKE SYRUP: Place ½ cup syrup or honey in 1-cup measure (or microwave-safe jug) and microwave, uncovered, on HIGH (100% power) 30 seconds. For 1 cup syrup, use 2-cup measure and microwave 45–55 seconds.

MISCELLANEOUS

TO SCENT HOT TEA TOWELS: Sprinkle each of 4–6 damp washcloths with several drops lemon oil or 1 tablespoon lemon juice, fold in half, and roll up. Set side by side on microwave-safe tray and microwave, uncovered, on HIGH (100% power) 1–1½ minutes. Or omit lemon oil and tuck several sprigs lemon or rose geranium, lemon verbena, lemon grass, or lavender into towels before rolling. Pass at meal's end, using tongs (towels may be too hot to handle).

TO MAKE HOT COMPRESSES: Fold damp hand towel in half, then in half again. Microwave, uncovered, on HIGH (100% power) 30–40 seconds. Wonderful for sore muscles! And what a nifty way to avoid steamy cauldrons of water.

ABOUT PLANNING MEALS FOR THE MICROWAVE

If you intend to prepare whole meals by microwave, consider this: the more you load into the oven, the more slowly it will cook and the more often you must poke and prod, stir and rearrange. Scarcely efficient.

So unless you're serving only one or two persons, the best way to microwave entire meals is to choose foods and recipes that can be microwaved at different times. For example, you might pick a stew or casserole that can be prepared well ahead of time, then reheated shortly before serving. And you might select a dessert that can be microwaved a day or two early, then served cold or at room temperature.

It's also possible to microwave meals sequentially, that is, to include a vegetable that can cook *while* the meat stands, a bread that can be warmed *while* the meat is carved, and a dessert that can be microwaved *while* the main course is being served.

Easiest of all, perhaps, is the meal that uses the microwave oven as an adjunct to the stovetop, conventional oven, and/or broiler. It takes a bit of choreography, to be sure. But once you learn to program the various cooking jobs efficiently, you'll discover that nothing speeds dinner like using the microwave oven to supplement conventional cooking methods.

However you use the microwave oven for preparing meals, do observe this basic rule of planning: jot down several days' worth of menus at a time so you can vary the food, make it both attractive and nutritious, and, not least, stick to the budget.

67

4

THE MICROWAVE AS
WARMING OVEN/DEFROSTER

Despite all the cooking jobs a microwave can perform to perfection, millions of people still limit their use of this revolutionary new oven to defrosting and warming food. Friends, neighbors, and relatives constantly ask us how long it takes to thaw this or reheat that. Defrosting and reheating, to be sure, remain important functions of every microwave oven, regardless of its size. Who wouldn't want to defrost and cook (or reheat) a brick-hard bird or casserole in minutes instead of hours?

And yet most cookbooks give such specifics short shrift. We don't. In fact, we devote this entire chapter to the subject, covering the do's and don'ts in detail as well as telling you how to freeze food for the microwave.

ABOUT FREEZING FOOD FOR THE MICROWAVE

Whenever you freeze food that will later be microwaved, here's how to prepare, pack, and wrap it so that it will defrost, cook, and reheat with all of its flavor, texture and good looks intact.

GENERAL TIPS

Choose only foods that freeze well. *These don't:* Avocados, bananas, cabbage (or sauerkraut), celery, any cheese *other than* cream cheese or hard types, milk and cream (except for whipped cream), cucumbers, cream- or custard-filled pies or pastries (except for commercial ones, which have stabilizers added to keep them from separating), unshelled eggs, hard-cooked egg whites, egg- or cream-thickened soups, sauces, and salad dressings, gelatins, salad greens, long-grain rice, potatoes (except for mashed), and raw tomatoes. *In addition, the following foods defrost poorly by microwave:* Butter, margarine, lard, whole eggs, egg yolks and whites.

~~~~~ **U**nderseason recipes slightly. Some seasonings fade, others gain strength in the freezer, and most are intensified by microwaving.

~~~~~ **U**ndercook food slightly, especially pasta and rice. They'll finish cooking as they defrost and reheat.

WRAPPING AND PACKAGING TIPS

~~~~~ **U**se only microwave-safe containers or materials that are also recommended for long-term freezing (the best are both moisture- and vaporproof). Never use aluminum foil or pans. Lightweight foil freezer "trays" can be used *if* they are no more than ¾″ deep.

~~~~~ **A**lways suit the packaging to the food being frozen:
Plastic Food Wrap—for irregularly shaped soft foods.
Plastic Bags, Pouches—for all but sharp or extra-large items. To Quick-fill with Soups, Stews, or Sauces: Spoon food into wide-mouth jar, invert bag or pouch on top, then turn jar upside down.
Laminated Papers—for large roasts, birds, and fish. Use butcher paper only for overwrapping and reinforcing large packages first wrapped in laminated paper.
Freezer Jars—for soups, stews, sauces, or juicy foods.
Individual-size Containers—for leftovers. These include freezer jars, plastic containers, and reusable microwave convenience food dishes.
Compartmentalized Containers—for homemade TV dinners, also leftovers.

~~~~~ **A**lways date and label all foods to be frozen. Also include such specifics as weight, thickness, quantity, etc., that will prove helpful later when it's time to defrost or reheat the food by microwave.

TIPS FOR FREEZING MEAT

Use top-quality meat only. Although raw meat may tenderize in the freezer thanks to the cutting action of ice crystals, its overall quality will not improve.

Always freeze meat as soon after purchasing as possible.

Trim excess fat from meat before freezing.

When freezing 1–1½ pounds ground meat in bulk, shape into circle 1"–1½" high and make a depression in the center to speed thawing.

When preparing meat loaves (either cooked or raw), shape in ring-shaped molds. Freeze, remove from mold, and wrap snugly in plastic food wrap.

Shape hamburgers before freezing. Stack patties, no more than 4 high, slipping dividers of plastic food wrap or wax paper between them so they can be separated easily during early stages of defrosting. **Note:** *Scaloppine, also thin steaks and chops can be stacked and frozen this way, too.*

Shape meatballs before freezing; also fill peppers or cabbage rolls. Freeze on baking sheet, then pack in freezer bags.

TIPS FOR FREEZING POULTRY

Choose top-quality birds only.

Always freeze poultry as soon after purchase as possible.

Pull all loose fat from body cavities. Remove giblets, wash, and pack separately in plastic food wrap or small plastic freezer bags.

When freezing poultry parts, cut wings from breasts and drumsticks from thighs. Wash parts, spread on baking sheet, freeze, then transfer to freezer bags.

~~~~~ Never stuff birds before freezing them.

TIPS FOR FREEZING FISH AND SHELLFISH

~~~~~ Freeze absolutely fresh seafood only and freeze as soon as possible.

~~~~~ For best results, do not freeze watery fish (they turn mushy) or oily ones (their fishy flavors intensify during freezing and microwaving).

~~~~~ Always clean and scale fish before freezing. Leave whole, if you like, fillet, or cut into steaks. Whole fish and large fillets fare best when glazed with ice.

To GLAZE FISH WITH ICE: Lay fish on baking sheet, freeze until firm, dip in ice water, and refreeze. Repeat 2–3 times, until ice coating is about ⅛" thick. Wrap fish or fillets in plastic food wrap or plastic bags. *Note: Smaller amounts can be glazed simply by freezing in plastic bags along with 2–3 tablespoons water.*

~~~~~ When freezing thin steaks or fillets, stack no more than 4 high, slipping dividers of plastic food wrap or wax paper between them so they can be separated easily during early stages of defrosting.

~~~~~ Before storing commercially frozen blocks of fish, overwrap original package with foil, but remove foil before defrosting. *Note: These fillets cannot be separated until after defrosting and standing time.*

~~~~~ Shell and devein shrimp before freezing but do not cook; spread on baking sheet and freeze until firm; transfer to airtight bag.

~~~~~ When freezing crab or lobster meat, cook shellfish whole, remove meat, cool to room temperature, then pack airtight. If shells are needed, scrub, wrap snugly, and freeze separately.

Freeze shucked oysters or clams only and cover with their own liquor; if liquor is insufficient, add brine (1 tablespoon salt to each 1 cup cold water) until oysters or clams are submerged. **Note:** *To speed thawing, pack oysters and clams in 1-pint containers no more than 3"–4" deep.*

Freeze shucked scallops only, and to each 1 pound add ⅓ cup brine (1 teaspoon salt mixed with ⅓ cup cold water).

TIPS FOR FREEZING VEGETABLES

These need only be trimmed and divided into pieces of uniformly small size, then blanched. The microwave oven makes a dandy vegetable blancher (see About Blanching Vegetables in the Microwave, in Chapter 11).

TIPS FOR FREEZING PARTIALLY OR FULLY COOKED FOOD

Freeze only those foods that freeze well. *These don't:* Whole, sliced, or cubed potatoes (they turn mushy), cheese and crumb toppings (they go rubbery or limp), cornstarch-thickened mixtures (these break down; use flour instead to thicken liquid, or rethicken it when hot by mixing in, for each 1 cup liquid, 1 teaspoon cornstarch blended with 1 teaspoon cold water).

If freezer space is limited, omit bulky rice and pasta from casseroles; cook these separately while casserole reheats and add shortly before serving.

Quick-chill all hot food before packaging it for the freezer.

Always spread food evenly in casseroles, leaving 1" head room at the top. Also push chunks of food underneath gravy, sauce, or other liquid.

Whenever possible, freeze stews and casseroles in freezer-to-microwave-to-table containers. Better yet, foil-line the containers, add food, and freeze. When brick-hard, remove solid block of food, wrap airtight, and return to freezer. Before thawing, unwrap and refit into original container.

When stacking sliced meats, always slip dividers of plastic food wrap or wax paper between the slices so they can be separated easily.

When freezing individual portions of sliced meats, poultry, or meat loaves, overlap slices slightly on plastic-coated plates. Spoon gravy or sauce on top, if you like, then wrap snugly in plastic food wrap.

TIPS FOR FREEZING PARTIALLY OR FULLY COOKED PLATE DINNERS

Use plastic-coated plates or lightweight aluminum "trays" no more than ¾" deep.

Always arrange thick, chunky, or dense foods around edge of plate or tray (meat, for example, poultry, mashed potatoes, stuffing).

Place porous or delicate foods in the center of the plate or tray (small pieces of vegetable, seafood, cheese-filled food, rice, or pasta).

When arranging food on plates, spread low for an even profile.

When there are baked beans or mashed potatoes on a plate dinner, always make a depression in the center.

Overwrap all plate dinners snugly with plastic food wrap, then with foil. Label, date, and freeze.

TIPS FOR FREEZING SANDWICHES

Avoid fillings that do not freeze well: egg, chicken, meat, or fish salads; jams, jellies. Also omit all lettuce.

To prevent sogginess, spread both sides of bread with butter or margarine, not with mayonnaise or salad dressing, which break down when frozen.

Wrap all sandwiches airtight and freeze on tray, away from freezer walls, top, or bottom. Direct contact can cause ice crystals to form inside sandwich, which will make bread soggy.

TIPS FOR FREEZING SWEET BREADS, CAKES, AND PIES

~~~~~ Freeze frosted cakes, coffee cakes, sweet breads, open-face pies, or other sticky food *unwrapped.* When brick-hard, wrap airtight in plastic food wrap and overwrap with foil.

~~~~~ Freeze pies whole or cut in wedges. ***Note:*** *Two-crust pies frozen raw may have soggy bottom crusts when baked.*

~~~~~ For a quick pie topping, freeze small mounds or rosettes of whipped cream, then drop on top of warmed piece of pie just before serving. To make, pipe rosettes or mounds onto foil-lined baking sheet, freeze hard, then bundle in plastic bag and seal airtight.

ABOUT DEFROSTING AND REHEATING FOOD BY MICROWAVE

Inevitably, some foods thaw and heat unevenly. Sometimes a frozen food will defrost in one spot but not in another because ice absorbs microwaves slowly and the melted portions scavenge all available energy. These factors also affect the speed with which foods defrost and heat:

~~~~~ **DENSITY:** Dense foods such as meat and mashed potatoes always take longer to thaw or heat than porous ones such as rice or bread.

~~~~~ **SUGAR AND/OR FAT CONTENT:** Sugar- and fat-rich foods often heat much more rapidly than expected because in a microwave oven fats and oils, syrups and sugary mixtures bubble or boil with near-supersonic speed.

~~~~~ **PACKAGING:** Improperly packaged foods defrost and heat unevenly, as do those frozen in too large quantities. If a container is too deep or too shallow, the food will be spread too thick or thin and microwaves will fail to penetrate it uniformly.

Fortunately, microwave manufacturers have learned to overcome some of these problems. Most important, perhaps, is that on newer models they've reduced the "defrost" power level to 30% (on older ovens it may be 50% or even higher). In both instances, however, the power pulses on and off at regular intervals to allow heat to spread naturally (via conduction) from warm areas to icy ones.

What every microwave owner must learn is never to rush the thawing or reheating of food by blasting it full time—with HIGH (100% power). Using lower power levels—or a combination of HIGH or MEDIUM and LOW—almost always produces better results.

SOME GENERAL TIPS FOR DEFROSTING FROZEN FOOD BY MICROWAVE

First study your oven manufacturer's manual for its recommendations on defrosting; read, too, about any automatic defrosting programs that may be built into your particular oven model.

Whenever you defrost commercially frozen food, follow package directions to the letter. **Note:** *Do not microwave frozen food or TV dinners in aluminum trays that are more than ¾" deep; you may cause your oven to arc.*

Stir or break up and redistribute frozen food as soon as possible during defrosting, moving icier pieces to the outside, turning large items over, and flexing frozen pouches or bags. **Note:** *Our defrosting charts tell, food by food, exactly what should be done and when.*

Shield vulnerable areas of food with small foil strips as charts direct: edges of roasts, for example, poultry wings and drumsticks, fish heads and tails. Also shield any areas that feel warm or show subtle changes of color—sure signs that they are beginning to cook. Finally, shield any casserole corners that start to bubble before the center thaws.

To equalize thawing of dense casseroles containing pasta, defrost them in a browning casserole but do not preheat it. Its special coating transmits heat up from the bottom of the casserole so that the food will defrost from the bottom as well as from the top and sides.

Always test food after the minimum defrosting time recommended by our charts. You should be able to insert a skewer easily into the center of large roasts or pierce smaller items with a fork. Liquid ingredients, it goes without saying, should be soft. **Note:** *Ice crystals may still be clearly visible in many defrosted foods, but these will melt on standing.*

Always allow defrosted food to stand, after it comes from the microwave, as our charts direct. It's during this period that any remaining ice crystals melt and food thaws uniformly.

For future reference, record the defrost times of your favorite foods and recipes.

ABOUT DEFROSTING FROZEN MEAT BY MICROWAVE

The shape of a cut, as well as its weight, determines overall defrosting time. Because of the way microwaves circulate and penetrate food, irregularly shaped cuts will thaw unevenly. For best results—and this is particularly important for such large cuts as roasts—make sure they are as compact and uniformly shaped as possible.

Must a roast be thawed before it's roasted in the microwave? We say yes. Trying to cook a solidly frozen roast by microwave is a waste of an expensive piece of meat. The roast will toughen and cook unevenly. Its microwave time, moreover, will be about the same as for a roast that's both defrosted *and* cooked by microwave. For best results when defrosting meat by microwave, follow these guidelines:

Begin defrosting the meat in its original wrapper, but as soon as you can easily remove it, do so. Also remove any paper liners, which attract

77

microwaves away from the meat, or Styrofoam trays (these trap heat and cause the meat to begin cooking). **Note:** *Because it's so thinly sliced, bacon can be defrosted in its original package.*

After meat has been defrosted in a microwave *(but before it stands)*, it should look moist, soft, and glossy and its fat will be white. Although juices may have begun to run, ice crystals will be clearly visible.

Touch the meat as soon as it comes from the microwave oven. If any areas feel warm, the meat has begun to cook and you must finish the job at once lest the meat spoil. **Note:** *If you intend to cook meat some hours after defrosting it, microwave for the minimum time only (see chart).*

In order for meats to defrost properly (until a skewer can be inserted in the center of large cuts or a fork into small ones), *they must stand at room temperature, after microwaving, as chart directs.*

MICROWAVE DEFROST CHART FOR MEAT

Use the defrost times in this chart as a guide only. The internal temperature of frozen meat can vary by several degrees depending upon the freezer temperature (not all maintain the recommended 0° F.). Test meat after minimum defrost time and, if not properly defrosted, continue microwaving on MEDIUM-LOW (30% power) in increments of 1 minute for each pound of meat.

Burgers (Uncooked)

Number of Burgers	Time on MEDIUM-LOW (30% Power)	Minutes Standing Time
1	50–60 sec.	3
2	1¾–2 min.	4
3	2–2½ min.	5
4	2½–3 min.	5
5	3–3½ min.	5
6	3½–4 min.	5

Microwave on plate or platter, removing wrapper as soon as possible. Separate burgers, arrange 2 side by side, 3 in triangle, 4 or more in circle, and cover with wax paper; if defrosting more than 2, rearrange at halftime.

Ground Beef, Veal, Lamb, or Pork (Uncooked)

Minutes per Pound on MEDIUM-LOW (30% Power)	Minutes Standing Time
5–7	5

Begin defrosting in shallow casserole and unwrap as soon as possible; cover with wax paper. At halftime, break up frozen block with fork and spread meat in doughnut shape. *Note: If thawing more than 2 pounds, scrape off and remove defrosted meat every 3–4 minutes; also break up frozen block as soon as possible.* At halftime, rearrange chunks, placing thinner ones toward center.

Note: To defrost and cook 1-pound block of frozen ground beef in one step, microwave in wax-paper-covered 2-quart casserole on HIGH (100% power) 10–12 minutes, breaking up meat after 5 minutes and stirring after 8. Meat may be pink in spots; let stand, covered, 1–3 minutes, until pink disappears. Use meat in casseroles, chilis, or sauces or mix with leftovers for a quick lunch.

Roasts (Bone-in or Boneless; Uncooked) (Beef, Veal, Lamb, or Pork)

Minutes per Pound on MEDIUM-LOW (30% Power)	Minutes Standing Time
10–13	30

Microwave on platter just until roast can be unwrapped, place on rack in shallow casserole, and cover with wax paper. At halftime check edges and shield* warm areas with foil strips; also turn roast over and rotate casserole 180°. *Note: Roasts of more than 6 pounds should be microwaved only 7½–9¾ minutes per pound, then further defrosted 45–60 minutes in refrigerator. Omit standing time at room temperature.*

Spareribs, Short Ribs (Uncooked)

Minutes per Pound on MEDIUM-LOW (30% Power)	Minutes Standing Time
4–8	15

Microwave on platter just until ribs can be unwrapped, then cover with wax paper. At halftime separate ribs, turn over, moving icy pieces toward edge, and rotate platter 180°.

Steaks and Chops (Bone-in or Boneless, Uncooked) (Beef, Veal, Lamb, or Pork)

Size and Weight per Piece	Minutes per Pound on MEDIUM-LOW (30% Power)	Minutes Standing Time
Small (2–8 oz., ½"–1" thick)	5–7	5
Large, Thin (9 oz. up, ½"–1" thick)	4–5	5
Large, Thick (9 oz. up):		
1" thick	7–9	5
1½" thick	8–10	10
2" thick	11–13	10
Scaloppine (Beef, Veal)	5–7	5

Begin defrosting in shallow casserole and unwrap as soon as possible. Also separate pieces as soon as possible, place on rack in casserole, and cover with wax paper. *Scaloppine, small steaks, and chops:* Rearrange at halftime, moving thickest parts to edge, bony ones to center. *Large, thick steaks:* Turn over at halftime, and if more than one is being defrosted, rearrange.

Chunks, Strips, Stew Meat (Uncooked) (Beef, Veal, Lamb, or Pork)

Minutes per Pound on MEDIUM-LOW (30% Power)	Minutes Standing Time
6–9	5

Begin defrosting in shallow casserole and unwrap as soon as possible; cover with wax paper. At halftime separate pieces and spread out (remove any thawed pieces). After ¾ defrosting time, rearrange pieces and again remove thawed ones.

Kidneys, Sliced Liver (Uncooked)

Minutes per Pound on MEDIUM-LOW (30% Power)	Minutes Standing Time
6–8	5

Begin defrosting in shallow casserole and unwrap as soon as possible; arrange on rack in casserole and cover with wax paper. At halftime separate pieces and arrange doughnut fashion. If thick, turn pieces over after ¾ defrosting time. **Note:** *Remove kidneys as they thaw.*

80

Sausages

Type	Minutes per Pound on MEDIUM-LOW (30% Power)	Minutes Standing Time
Links (raw, precooked)	4–5	3
Patties (raw)	4–5	2
Bulk, Roll (raw)	4–6	5
Frankfurters (raw, precooked)	3–5	None
Kielbasa, Knockwurst, Brat-wurst, Italian (raw, pre-cooked)	5–7	5

Begin microwaving on platter, unwrap as soon as possible, and cover with wax paper. *Links, patties, frankfurters:* At halftime separate sausages; arrange links spoke fashion, patties in circle around edge of platter. *Large sausages:* Turn over after ¾ defrosting time. *Bulk sausage:* Turn over at halftime.

Bacon (Uncooked)

Minutes per Pound on MEDIUM-LOW (30% Power)	Minutes Standing Time
4–5	5

Defrost in package; at halftime remove thawed strips, turn package over, and rotate 180°.

ABOUT DEFROSTING FROZEN POULTRY BY MICROWAVE

Begin defrosting in wrapper or bag (remove twist-tie); then, as soon as wrapper loosens, unwrap and proceed as chart directs.

After defrosting—but before standing time—break apart disjointed birds; ice crystals will still be visible.

When completely defrosted, chicken will be soft, moist, and cold to the touch; juices may run slightly.

To defrost wild duck or goose, follow directions for farm-raised duckling or goose.

To defrost farm-raised pheasant, follow directions for whole broiler-fryer chicken.

To defrost small game birds (woodcock, snipe, quail, doves), follow directions for chicken, but allow 1 minute less per pound. Also shield* tiny legs, wings, and breastbone carefully with foil strips. Turn birds frequently and microwave minimum amount of time—small game birds thaw fast.

MICROWAVE DEFROST CHART FOR POULTRY

Use the defrost times in this chart as a guide only. The internal temperature of frozen birds can vary by several degrees depending upon the freezer temperature (not all maintain the recommended 0° F.). Test bird after minimum defrost time and, if not properly defrosted, continue microwaving on MEDIUM-LOW (30% power) in increments of 1 minute for each pound of bird.

Whole Turkey (Uncooked)

Bird Size	Minutes per Pound on MEDIUM (50% Power)	Minutes per Pound on MEDIUM-LOW (30% Power)	Minutes Standing Time
6–12 lbs.	3	2–3	30

Begin defrosting on MEDIUM (50% power) in large shallow casserole, unwrap bird as soon as possible, place breast down on rack in casserole, cover with wax paper, and time as directed. At halftime pour off juices, turn bird breast up, shield* as needed with foil strips, and re-cover with wax paper. _Note: If any areas feel warm, shield these, too._ After turkey has stood 30 minutes, run cool water into body cavity until giblets can be removed. Refrigerate these and finish thawing turkey by submerging in cool water 1–2 hours or, if bird is large, by letting stand overnight in refrigerator.

Turkey Breast (Uncooked)

Breast Type and Size	Minutes per Pound on MEDIUM-LOW (30% Power)	Minutes Standing Time
Bone-in (4–6 lbs.)	5–7	10
Boneless (2–4 lbs.)	7–9	10

Begin microwaving in shallow casserole. Remove wrapper as soon as possible, lay breast skin down on rack in casserole and cover with wax paper. At halftime turn breast over, pour off juices and, if breastbone feels warm, shield.*

Turkey Legs, Thighs, Wings (Uncooked)

Minutes per Pound on MEDIUM-LOW (30% Power)	Minutes Standing Time
7–9	10

Begin microwaving in shallow casserole, removing wrapper as soon as possible. Arrange on rack in casserole with thickest parts toward edge and cover with wax paper. At halftime rearrange and pour off juices; also shield* as needed.

Turkey Cutlets, Breast Slices, Tenderloin Steaks (Uncooked)

Minutes per Pound on MEDIUM-LOW (30% Power)	Minutes Standing Time
5–7	5

Begin microwaving in shallow casserole, removing wrapper and separating pieces with table knife as soon as possible. Cover with wax paper and rearrange at halftime.

Whole Turkey Tenderloins (Uncooked)

Minutes per Pound on MEDIUM-LOW (30% Power)	Minutes Standing Time
6–8	10

Begin microwaving in shallow casserole, removing wrapper as soon as possible. Arrange on rack in casserole and cover with wax paper. At halftime turn tenderloin over and rotate casserole 180°. Also shield* ends, if needed.

Ground Turkey Meat (Uncooked)

Minutes per Pound on MEDIUM-LOW (30% Power)	Minutes Standing Time
5–7	5

Begin microwaving in shallow casserole, removing wrapper as soon as possible; cover with wax paper. At halftime break up with fork; check frequently thereafter, removing thawed portions with fork.

THE MICROWAVE AS WARMING OVEN/DEFROSTER

Whole Capon (Uncooked)

Bird Size	Minutes per Pound on MEDIUM (50% Power)	Minutes per Pound on MEDIUM-LOW (30% Power)	Minutes Standing Time
6–9 lbs.	3	2–3	30

Defrost as directed for Whole Turkey (Uncooked).

Whole Chicken (Uncooked)

Bird Type and Size	Minutes per Pound on MEDIUM-LOW (30% Power)	Minutes Standing Time
Roaster (4–8 lbs.)	6–8	10–20
Broiler-Fryer (3–4 lbs.)	6–7	10

Begin microwaving in shallow casserole, removing wrapper as soon as possible. Arrange breast down on rack in casserole and cover with wax paper. At halftime turn bird breast up, shield* as needed, and pour off any juices. After standing time, run cool water into body cavity and remove giblets.

Chicken Parts (Uncooked)

Bird Part	Minutes per Pound on MEDIUM-LOW (30% Power)	Minutes Standing Time
Broiler-Fryer		
Halves, Quarters, Legs, Thighs, Wings	5–6	5
Broiler-Fryer Boneless		
Breasts (whole or halves)	4–5	5
Sliced Boneless Breast		
(Roasting Chicken)	3–5	5

Unwrap parts and place on rack in shallow casserole. Cover with wax paper and microwave just until parts can be separated. Arrange with thickest parts toward edge of casserole, wings in center. At halftime turn parts over and rearrange; also pour off juice. **Note:** In combination packages, bony wings and neck (also giblet bag) thaw faster than meaty parts; remove these as they thaw.

Whole Rock Cornish Hens (Uncooked)

Bird Size	Minutes per Pound on MEDIUM-LOW (30% Power)	Minutes Standing Time
1–2 lbs.	6–7	10

Begin microwaving in shallow casserole and unwrap as soon as possible; place breast down, 1″ apart, on rack in casserole and cover with wax paper. If defrosting more than 2 hens, use oven shelf and stagger casseroles. At halftime turn birds breast up and shield* wings, breastbone, and "knees" as needed with foil strips; also pour off juices.

Whole Duckling (Uncooked)

Bird Size	Minutes per Pound on MEDIUM-LOW (30% Power)	Minutes Standing Time
4–5 lbs.	7–8	10

Defrost as directed for Whole Chicken (Uncooked)—Roaster.

Whole Goose (Uncooked)

Bird Size	Minutes per Pound on MEDIUM (50% Power)	Minutes per Pound on MEDIUM-LOW (30% Power)	Minutes Standing Time
4–12 lbs.	3	3–4	20–30

Defrost as directed for Whole Turkey (Uncooked).

Chicken Livers (Uncooked)

Minutes per Pound on MEDIUM-LOW (30% Power)	Minutes Standing Time
4–6	5

Begin microwaving in shallow casserole, removing wrapper as soon as possible. Arrange on rack in casserole and cover with wax paper. At halftime gently separate livers, placing icy pieces around edges, and pour off juices. Before standing time, rinse livers in cool water to melt ice crystals, then let stand as directed.

ABOUT DEFROSTING FROZEN FISH AND SHELLFISH BY MICROWAVE

~~~~~~ Always give fish and shellfish an extra helping of TLC—they're fragile, are unusually perishable, and defrost rapidly.

~~~~~~ Remember that shape, as well as weight, determines overall defrosting time, and this is especially true of fish. Thus a short, chunky whole fish may take longer to thaw than a long, skinny one of equal weight. And pound for pound, frozen blocks of fish or thick fillets will require longer on defrost than slim ones.

~~~~~~ Begin defrosting fish and shellfish in the package in a shallow casserole to catch the liquid. Once the seafood is unwrapped, elevate it on a rack above the liquid, which slows defrosting and so should be poured off as it accumulates.

~~~~~~ Always defrost seafood for the minimum recommended time at first. When properly thawed, it will be just slightly icy but pliable.

~~~~~~ To complete the defrosting, always let seafood stand, covered, as accompanying chart recommends.

~~~~~~ Never try to thaw and cook seafood in a single step by blasting it with HIGH (100% power). It will toughen and dry and taste like wood chips.

MICROWAVE DEFROST CHART FOR FISH AND SHELLFISH

Use the defrost times in this chart as a guide only. The internal temperature of frozen fish and shellfish can vary by several degrees depending upon the freezer temperature (not all maintain the recommended 0° F.). Test after minimum defrost time and, if not properly defrosted, continue microwaving on MEDIUM-LOW (30% power) in increments of 1 minute for each pound of fish or shellfish.

Whole Fish (Uncooked)

Fish Size	Minutes per Pound on MEDIUM-LOW (30% Power)	Minutes Standing Time
1 lb. or less	5–6	5
1½–3 lbs.	7–8	10

Begin microwaving in shallow casserole and unwrap as soon as possible. Place fish on rack in casserole and cover with wax paper. At halftime separate and rearrange small fish. Shield* head and tail of large fish with foil, turn fish over, rotate casserole 180°, and pour off liquid.

Fish Fillets, Steaks, Chunks (Uncooked)

Type and Thickness	Minutes per Pound on MEDIUM-LOW (30% Power)	Minutes Standing Time
Fillets (¼"–½") in Block	5–6	5
Ice-glazed* Fillets (¾"–1")	6–8	5
Steaks, Chunks (1"–1½")	7–9	5

Begin microwaving in shallow casserole and unwrap as soon as possible. *Fillets in Block:* Cover with wax paper and at halftime check corners of block; remove any warm pieces. After block stands 5 minutes, separate fillets under cool running water. **Note:** *Thin packages of fillets should be separated as soon as possible during defrosting, thick packages only after standing. Glazed Fillets:* Place on rack in casserole and cover with wax paper. At halftime rearrange fillets. *Steaks and Chunks:* Place on rack in casserole and cover with wax paper. At halftime, rearrange steaks or chunks and also turn them over.

Clams (Shucked and Uncooked)

Quantity	Minutes per Pound on MEDIUM-LOW (30% Power)	Minutes Standing Time
1 pint	6–8	3

Begin microwaving in container, but transfer to shallow casserole as soon as possible and cover with wax paper. At halftime gently break frozen clumps apart with table knife and stir clams.

THE MICROWAVE AS WARMING OVEN/DEFROSTER

Crab and Crab Meat

Type and/ or Size	Minutes per Pound on MEDIUM-LOW (30% Power)	Minutes Standing Time
Whole Crabs in the Shell (cooked and uncooked)	8–10	10

Unwrap and arrange belly up in shallow casserole. Cover with vented plastic food wrap and at halftime turn crabs over and rotate casserole 180°.

Alaska King Crab Legs (uncooked; 8–10 oz.)	6–8	3

Begin microwaving in shallow casserole and unwrap and separate as soon as possible. Arrange legs with thickest parts to outside and cover with vented plastic food wrap. Rearrange legs at halftime.

Crab Meat (cooked)		
6-oz. package	4–5	3
1-lb. block	10–12	5

Begin microwaving in shallow casserole and unwrap as soon as possible; cover with wax paper. At halftime break crab up with fork and arrange doughnut fashion in casserole; stir 1-pound block after 8 minutes' defrosting.

Lobsters and Lobster Meat

Type and/ or Size	Minutes per Pound on MEDIUM-LOW (30% Power)	Minutes Standing Time
Whole Lobsters in the Shell (cooked and uncooked)	8–10	10

Unwrap and arrange belly up in shallow casserole. Cover with vented plastic food wrap and at halftime turn lobsters over and rotate casserole 180°.

Lobsters and Lobster Meat, continued

Type and/ or Size	Minutes per Pound on MEDIUM-LOW (30% Power)	Minutes Standing Time
Lobster Meat (cooked; 1-lb. block)	10–12	5

Begin microwaving in shallow casserole and unwrap as soon as possible; cover with wax paper. At halftime break lobster apart with fork and arrange doughnut fashion in casserole; stir after 8 minutes' defrosting.

Rock Lobster Tails (Uncooked)

Number of 8–10-oz. Tails	Total Time on MEDIUM-LOW (30% Power)	Minutes Standing Time
2	6–8 minutes	3
4	10–14 minutes	3
6	15–18 minutes	3

Begin microwaving in shallow casserole and unwrap as soon as possible. Arrange belly up, spoke fashion, in casserole with thickest parts to outside. At halftime turn tails over and shield* any warm areas with foil.

Oysters (Shucked and Uncooked)

Quantity	Minutes per Pound on MEDIUM-LOW (30% Power)	Minutes Standing Time
12-oz. container	6–8	3
1 pint	7–9	3

Begin microwaving in container, but transfer to shallow casserole as soon as possible and cover with wax paper. At halftime gently break frozen clumps apart with table knife and stir oysters.

Scallops (Shucked and Uncooked)

Type	Minutes per Pound on MEDIUM-LOW (30% Power)	Minutes Standing Time
Bay Scallops	4–5	5
Sea Scallops	5–7	5

Begin microwaving in shallow casserole and unwrap as soon as possible; place on rack in casserole and cover with wax paper. Break up block with table knife as soon as possible and thaw scallops only until slightly soft but still icy. Rinse under cold water to melt remaining ice, separate scallops, and let stand.

Shelled and Deveined Shrimp (Uncooked)

Size	Minutes per Pound on MEDIUM-LOW (30% Power)	Minutes Standing Time
Small to medium	4–5	3
Jumbo to colossal	5–7	5

Begin microwaving in shallow casserole and unwrap and separate as soon as possible. Spread shrimp doughnut fashion in single layer in casserole and cover with wax paper. Rearrange at halftime and thaw only until slightly pliable but still translucent. Rinse under cold running water, then let stand.

ABOUT DEFROSTING FROZEN FRUITS BY MICROWAVE

Microwave fruits in their freezer containers or plastic pouches.

Never try to rush defrosting of fruits by microwaving on HIGH (100% power)—they'll turn to mush.

Always allow fruits to stand, after they come from the microwave oven, as chart directs; it's during this critical period that fruits finish thawing.

Quantity of Fruit	Total Time on MEDIUM-LOW (30% Power)	Minutes Standing Time
1 cup	1½–2 minutes	5
1 pint	2½–3 minutes	5
1 quart	4–5 minutes	5

Place unopened package or container in shallow casserole. At halftime turn pouch or container over and rotate 180°; also flex pouch. After microwaving, fruit will be icy here and there; only after standing can it be separated.

ABOUT DEFROSTING FROZEN BAKED GOODS BY MICROWAVE

Never hurry defrosting of breads, cakes, or pies by microwaving on HIGH (100% power); by the time outside is soft, centers will still be frozen.

Allow baked goods to stand as chart recommends so that they will finish defrosting without drying out.

MICROWAVE DEFROST CHART FOR BAKED GOODS

Breads

Type and Size or Amount	Total Time on MEDIUM-LOW (30% Power)	Minutes Standing Time
1-lb. loaf	3–4 minutes	5
2-lb. loaf	5–7 minutes	7
2 slices	40 seconds	1

Defrost in original wrapper but remove metal twist-ties; wrap slices individually in paper toweling.

91

Breads, continued

Type and Size or Amount	Total Time on MEDIUM-LOW (30% Power)	Minutes Standing Time
1 Coffee Cake or Ring	3–5	1

Remove foil packaging or "tray" (cardboard "tray" can be left in place) and cover with wax paper.

Large Rolls		
1	30–40 seconds	1
2	1–1¼ minutes	1
4	1¾–2 minutes	1
6	2–2¼ minutes	1
4–6 Small Rolls	1–1½ minutes	1

Remove from metal trays and bundle in paper toweling.

----

1 Doughnut or Sweet Roll	45–60 seconds	1

Place on paper toweling and microwave, uncovered.

----

1 English Muffin (whole)	30–40 seconds	1

Wrap in paper toweling.

Cakes

Type and Size or Amount	Total Time on MEDIUM-LOW (30% Power)	Minutes Standing Time
1 (2-layer) Cake (frosted)	1½–3 minutes	10
1 (14–16-oz.) Pound Cake	1½–2 minutes	5
1 (16–19-oz.) Cheesecake	3–4 minutes	10

Unwrap, place on plate, and do not cover. After 1 minute, rotate plate 180°. Watch frosted cake carefully and remove at once if edge begins to soften. After standing time, test cakes in center with toothpick; it should slide in easily.

Cakes, continued

Type	Time per Cupcake on MEDIUM-LOW (30% Power)	Minutes Standing Time
Cupcakes (frosted and unfrosted)	30–50 seconds	1

Arrange 2 side by side, 3 in triangle, and 4 or more in circle on plate and, if unfrosted, cover with paper toweling. If microwaving more than 3, rearrange at halftime.

Pies

Type and Size	Total Time on MEDIUM-LOW (30% Power)	Minutes Standing Time
Commercial Cream or Custard Pie (14 oz.)	1–2 minutes	5
Uncooked Fruit Pie (8"–9")	6–8 minutes	5

Transfer pie from metal pan to glass ovenware pie plate; do not cover. At halftime rotate pie 180°; also check edges and, if warm, cover with 1" foil circle. Let stand as directed or until toothpick can be inserted easily into center of pie. *Note: Recut steam vents in top crust of fruit pie, then bake pie in conventional oven.*

ABOUT REHEATING FROZEN COOKED FOOD

Casseroles . . . one-dish dinners . . . soups and stews . . . pasta and rice combos. All can be reheated by microwave, often from the solidly frozen state, often on HIGH (100% power), and yet emerge, minutes later, tasting for all the world as if they'd just been cooked. Best of all, most thaw and heat with little danger of burning, sticking to the "pot," or drying. All you need do is stir them now and then or give the container a turn.

As a general rule, any stirrable, porous food that doesn't contain eggs, cheese, fish, or other delicate ingredients can be warmed on HIGH (100% power) from start to finish. Layered casseroles such as lasagne, on the other hand, require lower power levels if they're to heat evenly without overcooking around the edges.

Still other foods—Old-fashioned Minestrone, for example, Braised Short Ribs, and anything in large quantities (about 3 quarts)—can be begun on HIGH (100% power), but should then be finished on MEDIUM (50% power) or even lower so that the edges don't dry and crust over by the time the middle is uniformly bubbly. Overall reheat times, needless to say, will depend upon a recipe's ingredients and a particular food's composition. Dense combinations—thick meaty stews, for example, and such layered casseroles as lasagne and pastitsio—always take longer to heat than mostly liquid soups or sauces.

Thanks to new developments, many late-model microwave ovens feature automatic, sequential defrost/heat programs that virtually eliminate guess-work as well as "keep warm" settings to keep foods uniformly hot until you're ready to serve them. Read your oven user's manual to learn what your own oven's capabilities are, then follow the directions in the accompanying chart. But first, a few guidelines:

SOME GENERAL TIPS FOR REHEATING FROZEN COOKED FOOD

Never overload the microwave oven by trying to heat too much frozen food at once. You'll merely slow things in the long run. And you'll also find yourself constantly probing, prodding, and testing each individual item for doneness—scarcely efficient. *Note: A 3-quart casserole is all a full-size oven can thaw and reheat properly at one time. If you must warm more food, do so in batches, keeping the first casserole warm in the conventional oven while the second one microwaves.*

Whenever food has been frozen in a plastic container, microwave just until it loosens around the edges, then ease the frozen block into a microwave-safe casserole twice its volume (to give you plenty of stirring room).

If your oven has an automatic temperature probe, insert it after the food begins to soften.

To speed reheating, cover the food.

To equalize the heating of TV dinners, whether homemade or store-bought, use a turntable.

If a favorite freezer-to-table recipe doesn't seem to reheat properly, remove it from the oven at halftime and let stand on the counter 5 minutes. Then return it to the microwave and finish reheating. This technique is particularly effective with stews, sauced foods, layered casseroles, and any dishes containing thin, bony pieces of meat or poultry.

Always allow food to stand after it comes from the microwave, as our charts direct. It's during this all-important step that the heat distributes itself uniformly throughout the food. *Note: Sometimes our chart calls for a particular food to stand partway through microwaving instead of at the end, for good reason. It's sometimes necessary to let heat spread naturally (via conduction) to inner parts of food before microwaving continues lest the outer portions overcook.*

Remember that young children are often sensitive to heat and don't like their food as hot as adults do.

MICROWAVE CHART FOR REHEATING
FROZEN COOKED FOOD

Power Levels: HIGH (100%), MEDIUM-HIGH (70%), MEDIUM (50%), MEDIUM-LOW (30%), and LOW (10%).

Layered Casseroles, Seafood, Cheese, and Bean Casseroles

Quantity	Power Level	Minutes Microwaving	Minutes Standing
1 quart	MEDIUM	20–30	None
2 quarts	MEDIUM	40–50	None

Cover with lid or vented plastic food wrap and, if desired, insert temperature probe set at 160° F. when mixture softens. Rotate 2-quart casseroles 90° every 10 minutes, 1-quart casseroles 180° at halftime.

Stirrable Casseroles, Stews, Thick Meat and Vegetable Soups, Pasta Sauces

Quantity	Power Level	Minutes Microwaving	Minutes Standing
1 pint	HIGH	6–10	None
1 quart	HIGH	10–15	None
2 quarts	HIGH	20–25	3–5
3 quarts	HIGH	15	—
	and then		
	MEDIUM	30–40	None

Cover with lid or vented plastic food wrap and microwave ⅓ of time; break up with fork and, if desired, insert temperature probe set at 160° F. Stir several times as mixture heats.

Meats and Poultry

Type and Quantity	Power Level	Minutes Microwaving	Minutes Standing
Meat Loaf	MEDIUM-LOW	10	—
(9″ × 5″ × 3″ loaf	and then		
or 8″–9″ ring)	HIGH	4–5	5

Place in casserole and cover with wax paper. After time on MEDIUM-LOW, rotate casserole 180° and turn loaf over. **Note:** *If rectangular loaf is dense, halve crosswise, rearrange so centers are at edge of casserole, and continue heating. Ring may require only 8 minutes on MEDIUM-LOW before being microwaved on HIGH. If loaf is sliced, separate slices as soon as possible and arrange doughnut fashion in casserole, overlapping slices slightly.*

Meatballs			
12 (½″–1″) balls	HIGH	6–8	None
12 (1½″–2″) balls	MEDIUM-LOW	10	—
	and then		
	HIGH	2–4	3

Separate balls as soon as possible and arrange doughnut fashion in casserole; cover with wax paper. After time on MEDIUM-LOW, rotate casserole 180°.

---

1 Chicken Breast	MEDIUM-LOW	2	—
	and then		
	HIGH	2	None
2 Chicken Breasts	MEDIUM-LOW	3	—
	and then		
	HIGH	3	None

Separate breasts as soon as possible and arrange spoke fashion in casserole with thick parts toward edge; cover with wax paper. After time on MEDIUM-LOW, rotate casserole 180°.

Thin Soups, Stocks, Eggless Sauces, and Gravies

Quantity	Power Level	Minutes Microwaving	Minutes Standing
1 cup	HIGH	4–5	None
1 pint	HIGH	6–8	None
1 quart	HIGH	10–12	None

Beginning microwaving in freezer container but transfer to cup, measure, or casserole as soon as possible. Cover with vented plastic food wrap. When mixture softens slightly, break up with fork. Also stir often during reheating.

Leftovers

Type and Quantity	Power Level	Minutes Microwaving	Minutes Standing
1 TV Dinner	HIGH	4	1
(entrée + 2	and then		
vegetables)	MEDIUM	4–5	None

Cover with vented plastic food wrap or wax paper, tucking ends under plate. After standing and before microwaving on MEDIUM, rotate plate 180°. Before serving, feel underside of plate—it should be hot. ***Note:*** *If only food at edge of plate is hot, cover edge with 1" foil circle and continue microwaving on MEDIUM in 1-minute increments.*

Thinly Sliced Poultry,	HIGH	2	1
Meat, or Meat Loaf	and then		
(3–4 oz.) with Gravy	MEDIUM	1–2	None

Overlap slices slightly on plate, top with gravy, and cover with wax paper. Or cut slit in plastic bag and place on plate.

Braised Chops,	MEDIUM-LOW	15	5
Swiss Steak	and then		
(1½–2 lbs.)	HIGH	7–8	None

Cover with wax paper; as soon as possible, separate chops and arrange with bone toward center of casserole. After standing and before microwaving on HIGH, rotate casserole 180° and turn chops or steak over.

Leftovers, continued

Type and Quantity	Power Level	Minutes Microwaving	Minutes Standing
Vegetables			
1 cup	HIGH	1–1½	None
1 pint	HIGH	2–2½	None

Cover with vented plastic food wrap; as soon as possible, break up with fork. Also stir often.

Rice and Pasta			
1 cup	HIGH	2–3	None
1 pint	HIGH	3–4	3
1 quart	HIGH	6–7	3

Cover with vented plastic food wrap; as soon as possible, break up with fork and spread out in casserole. Also stir often.

ABOUT REHEATING REFRIGERATED AND ROOM-TEMPERATURE FOOD (COOKED)

Use the following guidelines whenever you reheat cooked foods from their normal storage temperatures:

Always use microwave-safe containers.

To speed the reheating of food, cover it.

If your oven has an automatic temperature probe, set it at 160° F. and use it when reheating soups, stews, casseroles, and meat loaves.

When reheating convenience foods (also soups, cereals and such that require no refrigeration), always follow package directions.

99

Because room and refrigerator temperatures fluctuate dramatically, check foods frequently as they reheat. The point is to bring them just to serving temperature, not to cook them any further.

Always stir and taste food before serving it or feel the center bottom of the container. Just because food is bubbling around the edges doesn't mean it's uniformly hot throughout.

Remember that young children like their food less hot than adults do.

MICROWAVE CHART FOR REHEATING REFRIGERATED AND ROOM-TEMPERATURE FOOD (COOKED)

Power Levels: HIGH (100%), MEDIUM-HIGH (70%), MEDIUM (50%), MEDIUM-LOW (30%), and LOW (10%).

Appetizers

Type and Quantity	Power Level	Minutes Microwaving	Minutes Standing Time
12 Meatballs	HIGH	2–4	None

Arrange doughnut fashion on plate and cover with wax paper. Rotate plate 180° at halftime. *Note: Meatballs larger than 1"–1½" may take somewhat longer.*

Type and Quantity	Power Level	Minutes Microwaving	Minutes Standing Time
12 Bite-size Hors d'Oeuvre	HIGH	1½–2½	1
12 Bite-size Hors d'Oeuvre with Cheese	MEDIUM	2–3	1

Arrange doughnut fashion on plate and cover with wax paper. Rotate plate 180° at half time.

Layered Casseroles; Seafood, Cheese, and Bean Casseroles

Quantity	Power Level	Minutes Microwaving	Minutes Standing
1 quart	HIGH	5	—
	and then		
	MEDIUM	12–15	3–5
2 quarts	HIGH	9	—
	and then		
	MEDIUM	20–25	10

If desired, insert temperature probe set at 160° F. and cover with lid or vented plastic food wrap. Rotate casserole 180° after time on HIGH and again halfway through time on MEDIUM. When food is uniformly hot, center bottom of casserole will feel hot. *Note: to speed heating of food, use a browning casserole but do not preheat it.*

Stirrable Casseroles, Stews, Thick Meat and Vegetable Soups, Pasta Sauces

Quantity	Power Level	Minutes Microwaving	Minutes Standing
1 cup	HIGH	2½–3	None
1 pint	HIGH	3–5	None
1 quart	HIGH	6–8	None
2 quarts	HIGH	10–13	3–5

If desired, insert temperature probe set at 160° F., then cover with lid or vented plastic food wrap. Stir several times as mixture heats, moving large or thick pieces of food to edges of casserole.

Thin and Water-based Soups, Canned Cream Soups, Stocks, Eggless Sauces and Gravies

Power Level	Minutes Microwaving per Cup	Minutes Standing
HIGH	1½–2	None

Use container twice volume of item being reheated; cover, using lid or vented plastic food wrap for soups, stocks, and gravies but wax paper for sauces (so they aren't diluted by drops of condensation). Stir mixtures often during reheating and, if desired, use automatic temperature probe, set to 150°–160° F.

101

Egg-thickened Soups and Sauces

Power Level	Minutes Microwaving per Cup	Minutes Standing
MEDIUM-LOW	2½–3½	None

Use container 3 times volume of soup or sauce being reheated; do not cover. Stir every minute and heat only until warm, not hot (if desired, use automatic temperature probe set at 130°–140° F.). Never heat more than 1 quart at a time or mixture may curdle.

Meats and Poultry

Type and Quantity	Power Level	Minutes Microwaving per Portion	Minutes Standing
2 (½") Slices Meat Loaf	HIGH	1½–2	None

Arrange slices, not touching, on plate and cover with wax paper. Rotate 180° at halftime. *Note: If microwaving more than 2 slices, arrange in circle, overlapping slices slightly.*

Type and Quantity	Power Level	Minutes Microwaving per Portion	Minutes Standing
3–4 Thin Slices Meat			
Rare	MEDIUM-HIGH	1–1½	None
Medium	MEDIUM-HIGH	1½–2½	None
3–4 Thin Slices Poultry	MEDIUM-HIGH	1–1½	None

Overlap slices slightly. If meat is rare, arrange in center of plate and do not cover. If meat is medium or well done, arrange around edge of plate and cover with wax paper.

Type and Quantity	Power Level	Minutes Microwaving per Portion	Minutes Standing
6–8 oz. Thick Slices Meat, Steaks, Chops, Ribs	MEDIUM-HIGH	2–3	1

Arrange, not touching, on plate and cover with wax paper; if in more than 1 piece, rearrange at halftime.

Meats and Poultry, continued

Type and Quantity	Power Level	Minutes Microwaving per Portion	Minutes Standing
1 burger	MEDIUM-HIGH	1–2	None

Place burger on plate and cover with wax paper.

Type and Quantity	Power Level	Minutes Microwaving per Portion	Minutes Standing
1 frankfurter (in bun)	MEDIUM-HIGH	1–2	None

Wrap in paper toweling and place on oven floor or plate.

Type and Quantity	Power Level	Minutes Microwaving per Portion	Minutes Standing
½ Chicken Breast or 1 Leg and Thigh	MEDIUM-HIGH	1–2	None

Place chicken on plate and cover with wax paper.

Leftover Plate Dinners (2 Slices Meat, 1 Cup Mashed Potatoes, ½ Cup Vegetables)

Type and Quantity	Power Level	Minutes Microwaving per Portion	Minutes Standing
1 plate	MEDIUM-HIGH	2½–3½	1
2 plates	MEDIUM-HIGH	4–5	1

Arrange dense or chunky food around edge of plate (meat, poultry, stuffing, mashed potatoes) and porous, delicate, or quick-to-heat items in center (small pieces of vegetable, seafood, cheese-filled food, rice, or pasta). Spread food for low, even profile and make deep depression in middle of mashed potatoes or baked beans to form ring shapes. Cover plate with vented plastic food wrap or wax paper and rotate 180° at halftime. When dinner is properly heated, center bottom of plate will feel hot. **Note:** *When heating 2 plates at once, place first on oven floor, second on oven shelf, staggering positions; at halftime, reverse positions of plates and rotate each 180°.*

Vegetables

Power Level	Minutes Microwaving per ½ Cup	Minutes Standing
HIGH	¾–1	None

Cover with vented plastic food wrap and stir at halftime.

Rice and Pasta

Power Level	Minutes Microwaving per Cup	Minutes Standing
HIGH	1–1½	None

Cover with vented plastic food wrap and stir at halftime.

Breads
(Hamburger and Hot Dog Buns, Dinner Rolls, Muffins, Biscuits)

Quantity	Power Level	Microwaving Time	Minutes Standing
1	MEDIUM	15–20 seconds	None
2	MEDIUM	30–40 seconds	None
4	MEDIUM	50–60 seconds	None
6	MEDIUM	1¼–1½ minutes	None

Wrap in paper toweling; turn over and rotate 180° at halftime. *Note: Rolls, muffins, and biscuits can be wrapped in napkin and heated in straw basket.*

Pita Bread, Pancakes, Waffles, Crepes, Tortillas, French Toast

Quantity	Power Level	Microwaving Time	Minutes Standing
1	MEDIUM	20–30 seconds	None
2	MEDIUM	35–45 seconds	None
4	MEDIUM	50–70 seconds	None
6	MEDIUM	1¼–1½ minutes	None

Wrap in paper toweling; turn over and rotate 180° at halftime.

----

6 Breadsticks	MEDIUM	30 seconds	None

Wrap in paper toweling; turn over and rotate 180° at halftime.

----

1 (9″) Coffee Cake	MEDIUM-LOW	3–4 minutes	1

Remove foil, aluminum, or twist-ties from store-bought coffee cake. Wrap in paper toweling, turn over, and rotate 180° at halftime.

MICRO WAYS

Sweet Rolls, Doughnuts, Coffee Cake Wedges

Quantity	Power Level	Microwaving Time	Minutes Standing
1	MEDIUM-LOW	30–45 seconds	None
2	MEDIUM-LOW	1–1½ minutes	None
4	MEDIUM-LOW	1½–2 minutes	None
6	MEDIUM-LOW	2–2½ minutes	None

Remove foil, aluminum, or twist-ties from store-bought food. Wrap in paper toweling; turn over and rotate 180° at halftime. *Note: Filling in sweet rolls may get blisteringly hot.*

Desserts
Stewed Fruit

Power Level	Minutes Microwaving per Cup	Minutes Standing
MEDIUM-HIGH	1–2	None

Cover with vented plastic food wrap and stir at halftime.

Puddings and Pies

Type and Quantity	Power Level	Minutes Microwaving	Minutes Standing
1 Steamed Pudding	HIGH	2–3	1

Wrap in plastic food wrap. After 1 minute, turn pudding over and rotate 180°.

Type and Quantity	Power Level	Minutes Microwaving	Minutes Standing
8"–9" Open-face Pie	MEDIUM-HIGH	4–5	None
8"–9" Two-crust Pie	MEDIUM-HIGH	5–7	5
1 Portion (⅛ pie)	HIGH	½–1	None

If necessary, transfer pie from metal pie pan to microwave-safe pie plate; do not cover. At halftime rotate pie plate 180°. *Note: Sugar fillings will become very hot although pastry remains cool.*

THE MICROWAVE AS WARMING OVEN/DEFROSTER

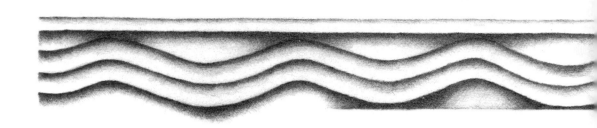

PART TWO

5

BEVERAGES, SOUPS, AND SAUCES

Microwave ovens heat (and reheat) liquids zip-quick. A minute is about all it takes to brew a cup of instant coffee, tea, or bouillon, and in seven minutes you can mull enough wine for four. Because beverages, soups, and sauces use many of the same microwave techniques, we cover them all here.

ABOUT MICROWAVING BEVERAGES

Use your microwave for a quick cup of coffee, cocoa, tea, or bouillon, but not for large amounts—the stovetop heats them faster. Milk-based drinks won't burn or stick to the microwave container, but they will foam up alarmingly because microwaves exaggerate boiling. For best results when microwaving beverages, follow these guidelines:

Never heat drinks in Styrofoam cups (they may melt), mugs with glued-on handles (the glue may melt), or those with decorative metal trim, which can cause arcing.

Never heat or defrost liquid in a bottle or can; it may explode.

Never heat milk-based beverages on HIGH (100% power)—they'll boil over. And always use a container at least twice the volume of the ingredients put into it. To minimize further the risk of boilovers, microwave milk-based drinks for the minimum recommended time. Also watch them closely. **Note:** *Water-based drinks can be microwaved on HIGH—they're less likely to boil over.*

Use an automatic temperature probe, if you have one, for microwave beverages. Following the manufacturer's directions, set the desired temperature (see the Beverage Heating Chart that follows) and the probe will turn the oven off *before* the drink boils over. The probe's "hold" setting (150°–160° F.) will keep drinks properly hot (and no, alcoholic drinks won't lose their "punch").

When cooking four or more milk-based drinks at once, arrange them in a circle and rearrange once or twice during microwaving.

To avoid curdling, heat egg-based beverages on MEDIUM (50% power) or MEDIUM-LOW (30% power).

BEVERAGE HEATING CHART

Water, Broth, Bouillon, and Other Water-based Beverages

If you use hottest tap water at the start, reduce microwave times 50–60 seconds for 1 cup and 1¼–1½ minutes for 2 cups. If you use room-temperature liquids, reduce microwave times by 15–20 seconds per cup. **Note:** *All times given here are for cold water drawn from the tap.*

| Minutes on HIGH (100% Power) | | Desired |
1 (8-oz.) Cup	2 (8-oz.) Cups	Temperature
1–1¼	1¾–2	125°–130° F. (warm to drink)
1½–1¾	2¾–3	140°–150° F. (hot)
2¼–2½	3¾–4¼	170°–180° F. (steaming hot)
3–3¼	5½–6	212° F. (boiling)

Milk and Milk-based Beverages

Note: *All times given are for refrigerator-cold milk.*

| Minutes on MEDIUM-HIGH (70% Power) | | Desired |
1 (8-oz.) Cup	2 (8-oz.) Cups	Temperature
1¾–2	3¼–3½	125°–130° F. (warm to drink)
2¼–2½	4½–5	140°–150° F. (hot)
3–3¼	6–6½	170°–180° F. (steaming hot)
4¼–4¾	7–8	212° F. (boiling)

To save cleanup, heat water-based beverages right in the cup or mug—provided it's microwave-safe.

Speed the "brewing" of coffee or tea by using hottest tap water. Just be sure to leave a microwave-safe spoon in the water as it microwaves, also to stir it occasionally to prevent superheated bubbles from forming below the surface. These can erupt and cause nasty burns when you go to stir in instant coffee or tea. Or even when you move the container of water.

Stir all beverages before serving to distribute heat uniformly.

To reheat cooled beverages, microwave each cup, uncovered, on HIGH (100% power), in 30-second increments.

HOT SPICED TEA

PREP TIME: | 1 MINUTE | COOKING TIME: | 6-7 MINUTES | STANDING TIME: | NONE

SERVES 4

3 cups hottest tap water

1 stick cinnamon

6 whole cloves

6 whole allspice

2 strips (2" × ½" each) lemon zest

4 teaspoons tea or 4 tea bags

4 thin slices lemon

Honey

Microwave water, spices, and lemon zest in uncovered 1-quart measure on HIGH (100% power) 5–6 minutes, until boiling, then boil 1 full minute. Pour over tea in teapot, cover, and steep 2–3 minutes. Serve with lemon and honey. *Note: Tea can be added to boiling water in measure, covered, steeped, then strained before serving.*
PER SERVING: 7 C 0 g P 0 g F 3 g CARB 8 mg S 0 mg CH

V A R I A T I O N

 ICED SPICED TEA: Prepare as directed, increasing tea to 5 teaspoons (or 5 tea bags), cool, and serve with plenty of ice. Insert a cinnamon stick stirrer in each glass.
PER SERVING: 8 C 0 g P 0 g F 3 g CARB 10 mg S 0 mg CH

111

LEMONADE MIX

PREP TIME: | 3 MINUTES | COOKING TIME: | 6½–7 MINUTES | STANDING TIME: | NONE

This handy mix will keep several weeks in the refrigerator. Just add ice and water and stir. What could be easier? Or more welcome on a sultry summer day?

¢

MAKES 5 CUPS, ENOUGH FOR 20 GLASSES

2 cups sugar

2 cups hottest tap water

Zest of 1 lemon, cut into 2" × ½" strips

2 cups lemon juice

Microwave sugar, water, and lemon zest in uncovered 2-quart measure on HIGH (100% power) 5½–6 minutes, stirring at halftime, until boiling, then boil 1 full minute. Mix in lemon juice, cool, strain, and store in tightly covered jar in refrigerator. *To serve:* Shake well, pour ¼ cup mix into 12-ounce glass, add ice, ¾ cup water or club soda, and stir well. When making lemonade in quantity, allow ¼ cup mix for each 1 cup water.

PER SERVING: 82 C 0 g P 0 g F 22 g CARB 5 mg S 0 mg CH

V A R I A T I O N S

¢ LIMEADE MIX: Prepare as directed, using lime zest and juice; also increase sugar to 2¼ cups and, if desired, tint mix pale green.

PER SERVING: 92 C 0 g P 0 g F 24 g CARB 4 mg S 0 mg CH

¢ ORANGEADE MIX: (Makes 3½ cups, enough for 14 glasses): Prepare as directed but use zest of ½ orange, 2 cups orange juice, and 1 cup each sugar and water.

PER SERVING: 71 C 0 g P 0 g F 18 g CARB 0 mg S 0 mg CH

Mulled wine

SERVES 4

1   bottle (750 ml) red Burgundy, Bordeaux, or other dry red wine

1   cup water

¼–⅓ cup sugar (depending on tartness of wine)

1   stick cinnamon tied in cheesecloth with 4 whole cloves, 4 whole allspice, and ½ thinly sliced lemon

Mix wine, water, and sugar in 2-quart measure or bowl, drop in spice bag and microwave, uncovered, on HIGH (100% power) 4½–5 minutes until simmering, stirring at halftime; do not boil. Reduce power to LOW (10% power) and microwave, uncovered, 2 minutes. Remove spice bag and ladle wine into heatproof mugs.

PER SERVING: 134 C 0 g P 0 g F 19 g CARB 10 mg S 0 mg CH

VARIATIONS

MULLED WHITE WINE: Substitute 1 bottle (750 ml) dry white wine (Vouvray and Gewürztraminer are especially good but any white jug wine will also do provided it's not too acidic) for red wine; also substitute orange slices for lemon and add 1 cracked whole nutmeg. Otherwise, prepare and serve as directed.

PER SERVING: 134 C 0 g P 0 g F 19 g CARB 10 mg S 0 mg CH

¢ **MULLED CIDER:** Substitute 1 quart apple cider for wine and water and brown sugar for granulated; omit cloves and proceed as directed. Pour into mugs, add cinnamon-stick stirrers, and serve.

PER SERVING: 180 C 0 g P 0 g F 46 g CARB 13 mg S 0 mg CH

WASSAIL BOWL (HOT CHRISTMAS PUNCH)

PREP TIME: [1 MINUTE] COOKING TIME: [11–12 MINUTES] STANDING TIME: [NONE]

Wassail, the "loving cup" of good cheer, health, and happiness, always contains beer or ale.

SERVES 12

- **6 cups apple cider or juice**
- **2 cans (12 ounces each) beer or ale**
- **6 tablespoons honey**
- **12 whole cloves**
- **2 cups brandy**
- **1 small orange, sliced thin**
- **1 small lemon, sliced thin**
- **2 tablespoons seedless raisins**

Mix cider, beer, honey, and cloves in 3-quart bowl and microwave, uncovered, on HIGH (100% power) 11–12 minutes, stirring at halftime, until mixture steams but does not boil. Pour into heat-resistant punch bowl, mix in brandy, orange and lemon slices, and raisins, and serve in mugs or heatproof punch cups, making sure each person gets a few raisins.

PER SERVING: 215 C   0 g P   0 g F   28 g CARB   8 mg S 0 mg CH

V A R I A T I O N

GLÖGG (Serves 12–14): Mix 2 (750 ml) bottles dry port or red Bordeaux wine, 2 (750 ml) bottles aquavit or vodka, 2 cups water and 1 cup sugar in 4-quart bowl. Tie the cloves in cheescloth with 2 cracked cinnamon sticks and 1 tablespoon cracked cardamom seeds and drop into bowl. Microwave, uncovered, as recipe directs, stirring at halftime, and adding 1 cup whole blanched almonds along with the raisins. When mixture steams, pour into heat-resistant punch bowl and float orange and lemon slices on top. Ladle into heatproof punch cups or mugs, making sure each person gets plenty of almonds and a few raisins.

PER SERVING: 640–549 C   5–4 g P   8–7 g F   28–24 g CARB 4–3 mg S 0–0 mg CH

OLD-FASHIONED HOT CHOCOLATE

PREP TIME: | 1 MINUTE | COOKING TIME: | 9–10 MINUTES | STANDING TIME: | NONE |

To avoid boilover, heat on MEDIUM-HIGH (70% power) or use an automatic temperature probe set at 180° F.

SERVES 6

2   squares (1 ounce each) unsweetened chocolate

1   quart milk

¼–⅓   cup sugar

½   teaspoon vanilla

⅓   cup heavy cream, whipped to soft peaks (optional)

Microwave chocolate, milk, and sugar in uncovered 2-quart measure on MEDIUM-HIGH (70% power) 9–10 minutes, whisking every 3 minutes, until chocolate melts and mixture is blended (do not boil). Whisk in vanilla and top, if you like, with whipped cream.

PER SERVING: 278 C   10 g P   16 g F   30 g CARB   120 mg S 34 mg CH

V A R I A T I O N

MEXICAN HOT CHOCOLATE: Prepare as directed, but increase chocolate to 3 ounces and microwave an extra 30–40 seconds (again, do not boil). Mix in ½–¾ teaspoon ground cinnamon along with vanilla and beat with rotary beater or electric mixer until frothy. Serve at once.

PER SERVING: 315 C   10 g P   19 g F   329 CARB   121 mg S 34 mg CH

115

HOT SPICED CRANBERRY PUNCH

PREP TIME: | 2 MINUTES | COOKING TIME: | 7¼–8 MINUTES | STANDING TIME: | NONE

SERVES 4–6

1 cup hottest tap water

2 tea bags

4½ cups cranberry juice cocktail

1 cup orange juice

½ cup firmly packed light brown sugar

2 sticks cinnamon

6 whole cloves

6 thin slices orange (garnish)

Microwave water and tea bags in uncovered 2-quart measure or bowl on HIGH (100% power) 2¾–3 minutes until boiling. Stir, remove tea bags, add all remaining ingredients (except garnish) and microwave, uncovered, on HIGH (100% power) 4½–5 minutes, stirring at halftime, until steaming but not boiling. Ladle into mugs and garnish each serving with an orange slice.

PER SERVING: 295–197 C   0 g P   0 g F   75–50 g CARB   18–12 mg S   0 mg CH

EASY EGGNOG

PREP TIME: | 1 MINUTE | COOKING TIME: | 2½–3 MINUTES | STANDING TIME: | NONE

MAKES 24 (4-OUNCE) SERVINGS

½ gallon vanilla ice cream

3 eggs plus 2 egg whites

2½ cups milk

2 cups light rum

2 tablespoons light corn syrup

¼ teaspoon freshly grated nutmeg

Microwave ice cream in uncovered 4-quart casserole on MEDIUM (50% power) 1 minute. Cut into 8 pieces, separate slightly, and microwave on MEDIUM (50% power) 1½–2 minutes, stirring after 1 minute, until very soft—almost liquid. Meanwhile, beat eggs and egg whites at highest mixer speed 30 seconds. Mix milk, rum, and corn syrup into ice cream, then fold in eggs with a wire whisk. Ladle into punch bowl and sprinkle with nutmeg.

PER SERVING: 164 C   3 g P   6 g F   13 g CARB   65 mg S   58 mg CH

ABOUT MAKING STOCK IN A MICROWAVE OVEN

When it comes to making stock, the microwave becomes a "slow cooker," enabling mixtures to bubble lazily, almost unattended, gathering flavor. Why, you may wonder, use the microwave oven for stocks if you can't make them either zip-quick or in large quantities? Good question. One distinct advantage is that the microwave puts the stock-making out of the way, "behind closed doors," so to speak, freeing the stovetop for other uses. But before you set out to microwave a cauldron of stock, read this checklist to see if your oven is large enough to handle the job and whether or not the microwave method is easier and more efficient for you than the old-fashioned one. It may not be.

Measure the inside of your microwave oven. Will a 4-quart casserole fit into it without touching the sides or top? You must use a deep casserole at least two and a half times the volume of the ingredients put into it to avoid boilover during cooking, preferably one with a lid that's easy to take on and off. You can also use a double thickness of plastic food wrap.

Don't prepare more stock at a time than the following recipes recommend. Larger amounts are difficult and dangerous to lift from the microwave.

To reduce cooking time 10–15 minutes, begin stocks with boiling water (or very hot tap water) instead of cold water.

Always use potholders. The casseroles in which you microwave stocks will become blisteringly hot. Also, to avoid nasty steam burns, uncover the casseroles carefully, using the lid to shield yourself from the considerable steam that will have built up during the slow simmering.

If your oven has a temperature probe, set it at SIMMER (180° F.) to keep stocks at just the right temperature. Insert the probe in the center of the mixture, making sure that its tip rests on the casserole bottom and not on bones. **Note:** Don't use the temperature probe for Beef Stock or All-purpose Stock, where large bones may give false temperature readings.

117

ALL-PURPOSE STOCK

PREP TIME: 7-8 MINUTES   COOKING TIME: 85-90 MINUTES   STANDING TIME: NONE

An ideal base for soups and stews, this stock is the perfect way to use up leftover vegetables, celery tops, mushroom stems, woody asparagus or broccoli stalks, tomato peelings, carrot parings, and other vegetable trimmings. It does take time to make in the microwave, but it needs very little attention.

MAKES ABOUT 5½ CUPS

2–3   cups finely chopped mixed leftover lean meat and vegetables

1   pound beef, veal, lamb, or poultry bones

1   medium-size yellow onion, peeled and coarsely chopped

1   medium-size carrot, peeled and coarsely chopped

1   medium-size stalk celery, coarsely chopped (include some leaves)

1   teaspoon salt, or to taste

6   peppercorns

2   sprigs parsley or 1 bay leaf and 1 sprig each parsley and thyme, tied in cheesecloth (bouquet garni)

6   cups cold water

Place all ingredients in 4- or 5-quart casserole, cover with lid or *double*-thickness vented plastic food wrap, and microwave on HIGH (100% power) 25–30 minutes, stirring at halftime, until mixture boils; skim off all froth. Re-cover and microwave on MEDIUM-LOW (30% power) 1 hour, rotating casserole 180° at halftime. Remove casserole from oven and let cool, covered, to room temperature. Adjust seasoning, strain stock through fine sieve, chill, and lift off surface fat. Stock is now ready to use. Store in refrigerator or freezer.

PER CUP: 29 C   1 g P   1 g F   5 g CARB   423 mg S   0 mg CH

V A R I A T I O N S

BEEF STOCK: Prepare as directed, substituting 1 pound each cracked beef shin and marrow bones for combined meat and vegetables.

PER CUP: 29 C   1 g P   1 g F   5 g CARB   423 mg S   0 mg CH

CHICKEN STOCK: Prepare as directed, substituting 2 pounds chicken backs and wings for combined meat and vegetables. After straining stock, discard skin, remove meat from bones, mince, and use for sandwich fillings or salads.
PER CUP: 49 C 1 g P 2 g F 7 g CARB 419 mg S 0 mg CH

TURKEY STOCK: Prepare as directed, substituting 2 pounds turkey neck, back, wings, or legs for combined meat and vegetables. After straining stock, discard skin, remove meat from bones, mince, and use for sandwich fillings or salads.
PER CUP: 49 C 1 g P 2 g F 7 g CARB 419 mg S 0 mg CH

FISH STOCK

PREP TIME: 7–8 MINUTES COOKING TIME: 85–90 MINUTES STANDING TIME: NONE

Use for making soups and sauces, mousses and terrines.

MAKES ABOUT 5½ CUPS

1½ **pounds fish bones, heads, and trimmings**

¼ **cup lemon juice**

1 **teaspoon salt, or to taste**

6 **peppercorns**

2 **sprigs parsley or 1 bay leaf and 1 sprig each parsley and thyme, tied in cheesecloth (bouquet garni)**

6 **cups cold water or a half-and-half mix of water and dry white wine**

Place all ingredients in 4- or 5-quart casserole, cover with lid or *double*-thickness vented plastic food wrap, and microwave on HIGH (100% power) 25–30 minutes, stirring at halftime, until mixture boils; skim off all froth. Re-cover and microwave on MEDIUM-LOW (30% power) 1 hour, rotating casserole 180° at halftime. Remove casserole from oven and let cool, covered, to room temperature. Adjust seasoning and strain stock through fine sieve. Stock is now ready to use. Store in refrigerator or freezer.
PER CUP: 26 C 4 g P 1 g F 1 g CARB 420 mg S 12 mg CH

119

GIBLET STOCK FROM SMALL BIRDS

PREP TIME: [7–8 MINUTES]   COOKING TIME: [37–38 MINUTES]   STANDING TIME: [NONE]

Use for making poultry gravies and sauces. Mince the giblets, if you like, along with any neck meat, and add to the gravy or sauce. Or use in any recipes calling for cooked chicken meat.

⚖ ¢

MAKES ABOUT 1¾ CUPS

Giblets and neck from 1 chicken, duckling, Rock Cornish hen, squab, pheasant, or other small bird, washed

1   **small yellow onion, peeled and minced**

½   **small carrot, peeled and minced**

½   **small stalk celery, minced**

½   **teaspoon salt, or to taste**

2   **peppercorns**

½   **small bay leaf, crumbled**

1   **sprig parsley**

2   **cups cold water**

Place all ingredients in 2-quart casserole, cover with lid or vented plastic food wrap, and microwave on HIGH (100% power) 7–8 minutes, until mixture boils. Stir, re-cover, and microwave on MEDIUM-LOW (30% power) 30 minutes. Remove casserole from oven and let cool, covered, to room temperature. Adjust seasoning and strain stock through fine sieve; chill, then lift off surface fat. Stock is now ready to use. Store in refrigerator or freezer.

PER CUP: 66 C 9 g P 2 g F 2 g CARB 667 mg S 127 mg CH

———————————— V A R I A T I O N

⚖ ¢ GIBLET STOCK FROM LARGE BIRDS (Makes 3⅔ cups): Prepare as directed, using goose or turkey giblets and neck, doubling all other ingredients, and increasing microwaving times as follows: 11–12 minutes on HIGH (100% power) and 45 minutes on MEDIUM-LOW (30% power). Strain, chill, and remove fat as directed.

PER CUP: 65 C 9 g P 2 g F 2 g CARB 645 mg S 131 mg CH

ABOUT MICROWAVING SOUPS

You won't save much time making soups in a microwave oven, but you *will* reduce the risk of boilovers and burned pots. Additional pluses: Starch- or egg-thickened soups needn't be stirred constantly as indeed they must be on top of the stove, and any soup can be prepared right in its serving tureen (provided it's microwave-safe). **Note:** *To heat commercially prepared soups, see Reheating Refrigerated and Room-temperature Food in Chapter 4; to adapt conventional recipes for microwave preparation, see How to Convert Favorite Recipes for Microwave Use in Chapter 1.*

SOME GENERAL TIPS FOR MAKING BETTER SOUPS

Whenever a recipe calls for a tight cover (to prevent evaporation), use the container lid (glass, ceramic, or other microwave-safe material). Such lids are handier to remove than plastic food wrap—a decided advantage when soups must be stirred frequently.

Don't try to shortcut cooking times by using HIGH (100% power) when recipes call for MEDIUM-LOW (30% power) or even LOW (10% power). And don't skip the standing times. For many soups, the lower microwave powers and/or standing times are essential to develop and mellow flavors.

To enrich the flavor of microwave soups, prepare them a day or two ahead of time, then reheat (see Reheating Refrigerated and Room-temperature Food in Chapter 4).

To keep soups hot, use the temperature probe set at 170° F., and follow manufacturer's directions.

When there are soup leftovers, freeze what you can't eat within a day or two in individual-size containers that can be reheated in a jiffy for one, two, three, or even four persons (see Some General Tips for Reheating Frozen Cooked Food in Chapter 4).

HOMEMADE CHICKEN SOUP

PREP TIME: | 10 MINUTES | COOKING TIME: | 45–57 MINUTES | STANDING TIME: | 30 MINUTES

SERVES 4–6

- 1 **broiler-fryer (2½–3 pounds), disjointed, or 2½–3 pounds chicken parts**
- 1 **small yellow onion, peeled and minced**
- 1 **large carrot, peeled and cut into ¼" dice**
- 1 **stalk celery, cut into ¼" dice**
- 1 **teaspoon salt, or to taste**
- 6 **cups water**
- 6 **peppercorns, 1 bay leaf, and 2 sprigs parsley, tied in cheesecloth (bouquet garni)**

Pepper to taste

- 1 **tablespoon minced parsley (optional)**

Arrange chicken skin side up in single layer in 4-quart casserole with thick portions toward outside and wings in center. Scatter vegetables evenly over chicken. Dissolve salt in water and add to casserole along with cheesecloth bag of seasonings. Cover with lid or double-thickness vented plastic food wrap and microwave on HIGH (100% power) 35–45 minutes, rearranging chicken at halftime, until tender. Let covered casserole stand until chicken is cool enough to handle—about 30 minutes. Discard cheesecloth bag, strain broth, reserving vegetables, if you like, chill, and skim off fat. Skin chicken, strip meat from bones and cut into bite-size pieces. Pour broth into 3-quart casserole, add 1–1½ cups chicken meat (save balance for sandwiches), strained-out vegetables, if you like, cover with lid or vented plastic food wrap, and bring to simmering by microwaving on HIGH (100% power) 10–12 minutes. Taste for salt and pepper and adjust as needed. Sprinkle, if you like, with parsley and serve.

PER SERVING: 195–130 C   32–22 g P   5–3 g F   4–3 g CARB   681–454 mg S   105–70 mg CH

─────────────────────────────── V A R I A T I O N S

CHICKEN-NOODLE SOUP: Bring 5 cups chicken broth to a boil in covered 3-quart casserole (use lid or vented plastic food wrap) by microwaving on HIGH (100% power) 12–14 minutes. Add 1 cup each fine egg noodles and diced cooked chicken, re-cover, and microwave on HIGH (100% power) 2½–3 minutes just until noodles are tender. Adjust seasoning, sprinkle with parsley, and serve.

PER SERVING: 178–118 C   15–10 g P   6–4 g F   16–10 g CARB   1148–765 mg S   48–32 mg CH

122

CHICKEN-RICE SOUP: Prepare Chicken-Noodle Soup as directed, substituting ⅓ cup uncooked converted rice for noodles and increasing final microwaving time on HIGH (100% power) to 4½–5 minutes, stirring at halftime, until rice is tender. Adjust seasoning, sprinkle with parsley, and serve.

PER SERVING: 164–109 C   14–9 g P   5–4 g F   15–10 g CARB   1149–766 mg S   31–21 mg CH

ITALIAN CHICKEN-ESCAROLE SOUP: Bring 5 cups chicken broth to a boil as directed for Chicken-Noodle Soup. Add 2 cups finely shredded escarole along with chicken, cover with lid or vented plastic food wrap, and microwave on HIGH (100% power) 2½–3 minutes. Stir in 2 tablespoons freshly grated Parmesan cheese, adjust seasoning, and serve.

PER SERVING: 60–40 C   4–3 g P   4–2 g F   4–2 g CARB   1173–786 mg S   2–2 mg CH

PENNSYLVANIA DUTCH CHICKEN-CORN SOUP

PREP TIME: | 10 MINUTES | COOKING TIME: | 19½–22 MINUTES | STANDING TIME: | 2–3 MINUTES

SERVES 6

5   cups chicken broth

½   cup minced yellow onion

½   cup minced celery

1   clove garlic, peeled and minced

1   cup fresh or frozen whole-kernel corn (do not thaw)

Pinch saffron strands, crushed

1   cup diced cooked chicken

¾   cup wide egg noodles

¼   cup minced parsley

1   hard-cooked egg, peeled and minced

Salt and pepper to taste

Bring broth, onion, celery, and garlic to a boil in covered 3-quart casserole (use lid or vented plastic food wrap) by microwaving on HIGH (100% power) 12–14 minutes. Add corn and saffron, re-cover, and microwave on HIGH (100% power) 4 minutes. Add chicken, noodles, and parsley, re-cover, and microwave on HIGH (100% power) 3½–4 minutes, stirring at halftime, just until noodles are tender. Let covered casserole stand 2–3 minutes to mellow flavors. Stir in chopped egg, salt and pepper, and serve.

PER SERVING: 150 C   12 g P   5 g F   15 g CARB   883 mg S   75 mg CH

AUTUMN VEGETABLE SOUP

PREP TIME: [10 MINUTES] COOKING TIME: [38–43 MINUTES] STANDING TIME: [NONE]

This soup and its variations not only taste better if made a day ahead of time but also freeze well. **Note:** *For best results, cut the carrot, turnip, celery, and potato into ¼" dice.*

⚖ ¢

SERVES 4

1 **medium-size yellow onion, peeled and minced**

½ **cup finely diced carrot**

½ **cup finely diced turnip, rutabaga, or celery root**

½ **cup finely diced celery**

1 **bay leaf and 1 sprig each parsley and thyme, tied in cheesecloth (bouquet garni)**

¼ **teaspoon pepper, or to taste**

½ **teaspoon salt, or to taste**

1 **quart beef or chicken broth**

½ **cup fresh or frozen green peas (or snapped green or wax beans)**

½ **cup fresh or frozen whole-kernel corn or baby lima beans or ½ cup finely diced all-purpose potato**

1 **cup peeled, cored, seeded, and coarsely chopped tomatoes or 1 can (8 ounces) tomatoes, chopped (do not drain)**

2 **tablespoons minced parsley**

Mix onion, carrot, turnip, and celery in 4-quart casserole, add bouquet garni, pepper, and combined salt and broth. Top with lid and microwave on HIGH (100% power) 18–20 minutes, stirring at halftime, until mixture boils. Stir, add all remaining ingredients except parsley, re-cover, and microwave on HIGH (100% power) 20–23 minutes, stirring at halftime, until vegetables are just tender. Remove bouquet garni, adjust seasoning, sprinkle with parsley, and serve.

PER SERVING: 87 C 5 g P 2 g F 15 g CARB 1138 mg S 0 mg CH

VARIATIONS

⚖ ¢ **HEARTY MEAT AND VEGETABLE SOUP** (Serves 6): Prepare as directed, using beef broth and adding 1½ cups cooked lean beef or lamb cut into ¼" cubes along with peas, corn, and tomatoes. Proceed as directed, increasing final microwaving time to 28–30 minutes.

PER SERVING: 136 C 14 g P 5 g F 10 g CARB 782 mg S 32 mg CH

OLD-FASHIONED MEATBALL SOUP (Serves 6): Prepare as directed, using beef broth and omitting peas and corn; add tomatoes, cover, and microwave on HIGH (100% power) 14–16 minutes. Meanwhile, prepare meatballs: Combine ½ pound lean ground beef; ⅔ cup soft bread crumbs; 1 tablespoon each milk, grated yellow onion, and minced parsley; ½ teaspoon salt; ⅛ teaspoon each grated nutmeg and pepper; and ½ lightly beaten egg. Shape into ¾" balls, and when vegetables are tender, add to soup. Cover and microwave on MEDIUM-LOW (30% power) 5–6 minutes, stirring at halftime and rotating casserole 180°. Test meatballs for doneness, and if not done, continue microwaving on MEDIUM-LOW (30% power) in 1-minute increments (do not overcook; pinkish traces in center will disappear during standing). Adjust seasoning, then let stand, covered, 2–3 minutes. Sprinkle with parsley and serve.
PER SERVING: 159 C   10 g P   9 g F   8 g CARB   997 mg S   52 mg CH

TURKEY-VEGETABLE SOUP (Serves 6): Prepare as directed, using turkey or chicken broth instead of beef broth and adding 1½ cups cooked turkey (or chicken), cut in ¼" cubes, along with peas, corn and tomatoes. Proceed as directed, increasing final microwave time to 28–30 minutes. Serve in deep bowls topped with Herb Croutons, if you like, or pass chunks of hot crusty French or Italian bread.
PER SERVING: 219 C   19 g P   10 g F   15 g CARB   1142 mg S   41 mg CH

SZECHUAN HOT AND SOUR SOUP

PREP TIME: | 15 MINUTES | COOKING TIME: | 14½–16½ MINUTES | STANDING TIME: | NONE

To make pork easier to slice, set in freezer 20 minutes. Dried Chinese mushrooms, tiger lily stems, and chili oil are available at most Oriental groceries.

SERVES 6

4–5	**large dried black mushrooms (½ ounce)**
4–5	**dried tree ear mushrooms**
6	**dried tiger lily stems**
½	**cup very hot water**
2	**tablespoons Oriental sesame oil or peanut oil**
¼	**pound boneless pork loin, trimmed of fat and cut into matchstick strips about 2" long and ⅛" thick**
2	**scallions, thinly sliced (keep green and white parts separate)**
⅓	**cup bamboo shoots, cut into julienne strips**
2	**tablespoons soy sauce**
1	**quart chicken broth**
3	**tablespoons red wine vinegar**
⅛–¼	**teaspoon chili oil**
3	**tablespoons cornstarch blended with 3 tablespoons cold water**
3	**ounces tofu, drained well and cut into ½" cubes**
2	**tablespoons minced fresh coriander (cilantro)**

Soak mushrooms and tiger lily stems in hot water 20 minutes; drain, thinly slice mushrooms, discarding stems and any hard bits. Cut tiger lily stems into ½" pieces. Heat sesame oil in paper-toweling-covered 3-quart casserole by micro-waving on HIGH (100% power) 1½ minutes. Toss pork in oil, cover with paper toweling, and microwave on HIGH (100% power) 3½–4 minutes, stirring at halftime and adding white part of scallions. Add mushrooms, tiger lily stems, bamboo shoots, and soy sauce, cover with paper toweling, and microwave on HIGH (100% power) 1 minute. Add broth, vinegar, and chili oil, cover with lid, and bring to a boil by microwaving on HIGH (100% power) 6–7 minutes. Blend in cornstarch mixture, re-cover, and microwave on HIGH (100% power) 2½–3 minutes, until thickened. Gently stir in tofu, sprinkle with green part of scallions and coriander. Adjust seasoning and serve hot.

PER SERVING: 140 C   8 g P   8 g F   10 g CARB   1028 mg S 12 mg CH

OLD-FASHIONED MINESTRONE

PREP TIME: [5 MINUTES] COOKING TIME: [76–80 MINUTES] STANDING TIME: [10 MINUTES]

This minestrone doesn't cook with the speed of light, but it's easy and requires almost no attention.

SERVES 6

- ⅔ **cup dried navy, pea, or red kidney beans, washed**
- 1 **pint cold water**
- 1 **small yellow onion, peeled and minced**
- 1 **small carrot, peeled and minced**
- 1 **small stalk celery, minced**
- 1 **clove garlic, peeled and minced**
- 1 **tablespoon bacon drippings**
- ¼ **teaspoon pepper**
- 2 **cups hot water**
- 2 **cups beef broth (about)**
- ¼ **cup tomato paste**
- 1 **medium-size all-purpose potato, peeled and diced**
- 1 **cup finely shredded cabbage**
- 1 **small carrot, peeled and diced**
- ⅓ **cup ditalini**
- 1 **tablespoon minced parsley**
- ½ **teaspoon crumbled dried thyme**
- ¼ **teaspoon crumbled dried basil**
- ½ **teaspoon salt (about)**
- 3 **tablespoons grated Parmesan cheese**

Quick-soak* beans in cold water or soak overnight in 3-quart casserole. Add onion, carrot, celery, garlic, drippings, pepper, and hot water. Cover casserole with tight lid and bring to a boil by microwaving on HIGH (100% power) 8–10 minutes. Reduce power to MEDIUM (50%) and microwave 50 minutes, stirring at halftime, until beans are tender but not mushy. If after 50 minutes beans are not tender, continue microwaving in 5-minute increments. Let stand, covered, 10 minutes. Drain beans, measure liquid, and add enough beef broth to total 1 quart. Pour into 3½-quart casserole, mix in tomato paste, beans, potato, cabbage, diced carrot, ditalini, and seasonings. Cover and microwave on HIGH (100% power) 18–20 minutes, until pasta and vegetables are tender. Stir in Parmesan, adjust seasoning, and serve.

PER SERVING: 183 C   9 g P   3 g F   30 g CARB   619 mg S   4 mg CH

FRENCH ONION SOUP

PREP TIME: 3 MINUTES   **COOKING TIME:** 24–28 MINUTES   **STANDING TIME:** NONE

Instead of browning nicely in the microwave, onions turn bitter and rubbery. You can overcome the problem, however, by mixing a little sugar and gravy browner into the onions.

SERVES 4

- 2 **tablespoons butter or margarine**
- 1 **teaspoon liquid gravy browner**
- 1 **teaspoon sugar**
- ½ **pound Spanish or yellow onions, peeled and sliced tissue-thin**
- 1 **quart beef broth**
- ⅛ **teaspoon pepper**
- **Salt to taste**

Melt butter in wax-paper-covered 2½-quart casserole by microwaving on HIGH (100% power) 35–45 seconds. Mix in liquid gravy browner and sugar, add onions, and toss with butter mixture. Cover with wax paper and microwave on HIGH (100% power) 9–10 minutes, until onions are almost tender. Add broth and pepper, cover with lid, and microwave on HIGH (100% power) 9–10 minutes, stirring at halftime, until mixture boils. Stir again and develop flavors by microwaving on MEDIUM (50% power) 5–7 minutes. Taste for salt and add, if needed. Ladle into bowls and serve with French bread.

PER SERVING: 96C 3gP 7gF 6gCARB 895mgS 16mgCH

V A R I A T I O N S

¢ FRENCH ONION SOUP AU GRATIN: Prepare soup as directed, and while it simmers, toast 4 (⅜") slices French bread. Ladle soup into 4 marmites or individual casseroles, float a toast slice in each, and sprinkle each with ¼ cup grated mozzarella cheese. Microwave, uncovered, on MEDIUM (50% power) 1½–2 minutes, rearranging marmites after 1 minute, until cheese melts. *Note: If your microwave oven can't accommodate 4 marmites, microwave them 2 at a time, allowing about 1 minute for the cheese to melt.* If you prefer browned cheese, set marmites instead in preheated broiler, 4" from heat, and broil about 1 minute until cheese melts and is tipped with brown.

PER SERVING: 214 C 10 g P 13 g F 14 g CARB 1078 mg S 38 mg CH

MADEIRA ONION SOUP: Prepare soup as directed, substituting 1 tablespoon each olive oil and unsalted butter for butter and adding 2 tablespoons golden seedless raisins, ½ teaspoon paprika, and ⅛ teaspoon ground cloves along with broth. Just before serving, whisk 1 egg yolk with ¼ cup dry Madeira wine, whisk in about ½ cup hot broth, stir back into casserole and microwave, uncovered, on MEDIUM-LOW (30% power) 1 minute. Stir and serve.

PER SERVING: 154 C   4 g P   9 g F   12 g CARB   841 mg S   76 mg CH

*S*OPA DE GRÃO COM ESPINAFRES
(PORTUGUESE CHICK-PEA–SPINACH SOUP)

PREP TIME: | 10 MINUTES | COOKING TIME: | 32–44 MINUTES | STANDING TIME: | NONE

¢

SERVES 6

1   **medium-size yellow onion, peeled and minced**

2   **cloves garlic, peeled and minced**

3   **tablespoons olive oil**

3   **cups cooked or canned chick-peas, drained**

1   **medium-size all-purpose potato, peeled and cut into ¼" dice**

1   **tablespoon minced parsley**

1   **tablespoon minced fresh coriander (cilantro)**

½   **teaspoon crumbled dried marjoram**

½   **teaspoon salt, or to taste**

¼   **teaspoon pepper**

3   **cups chicken broth**

2   **cups finely shredded spinach**

1   **tablespoon cider vinegar**

Microwave onion, garlic, and 2 tablespoons of the oil in wax-paper-covered 4-quart casserole on HIGH (100% power) 3½–4 minutes, until glassy. Add chick-peas, potato, seasonings, and broth. Cover with lid and microwave on HIGH (100% power) 20–30 minutes, stirring at halftime, until peas are very soft. Purée 2 cups peas with ½ cup cooking liquid and return to casserole. Heat remaining oil in wax-paper-covered 1-quart casserole by microwaving on HIGH (100% power) 1½ minutes. Add spinach, toss, and microwave, uncovered, on HIGH (100% power) 2½–3 minutes, stirring at halftime, until wilted. Mix into peas, cover with lid, and microwave on MEDIUM-LOW (30% power) 4–5 minutes to blend flavors. Stir in vinegar, adjust salt as needed, and serve.

PER SERVING: 244 C   10 g P   10 g F   31 g CARB   707 mg S   0 mg CH

NEW ENGLAND CLAM CHOWDER

PREP TIME: [10 MINUTES] COOKING TIME: [22–25 MINUTES] STANDING TIME: [NONE]

This soup will have richer flavor if you make it ahead of time, then reheat it slowly (see Chart for Reheating Refrigerated and Room-temperature Foods—Soups, in Chapter 4). **Note:** For best results, the salt pork should be rind-free and cut into ⅛″ dice, the potatoes into ¼″ dice.

SERVES 6

⅓ **cup finely diced salt pork**

1 **medium-size yellow onion, peeled and minced**

2 **cups moderately finely diced all-purpose potatoes**

1 **pint minced fresh or canned clams, drained (reserve liquid)**

Drained clam liquid plus enough bottled clam juice to total 1 pint

1 **cup milk**

1 **cup light cream**

¼ **teaspoon salt (about)**

⅛ **teaspoon white pepper**

⅛ **teaspoon paprika**

Lightly brown salt pork in wax-paper-covered 3½-quart casserole by microwaving on HIGH (100% power) 3–3½ minutes, stirring at halftime. Remove pork to paper toweling to drain with slotted spoon. Toss onion with casserole drippings, cover with wax paper, and microwave on HIGH (100% power) 3–3½ minutes, until glassy. Add potatoes and 1½ cups clam liquid. Cover casserole with lid and microwave on HIGH (100% power) 7–8 minutes, stirring at halftime, until potatoes are nearly tender. Add reserved salt pork, remaining clam liquid, and all remaining ingredients except paprika. Re-cover and microwave on HIGH (100% power) 4½–5 minutes, stirring at halftime, until hot but not boiling (soup will curdle if it boils). Stir again, re-cover, and microwave on MEDIUM-LOW (30% power) 4½–5 minutes to mellow flavors. Taste for salt and adjust as needed. Ladle into hot bowls and dust with paprika.

PER SERVING: 263 C   14 g P   16 g F   15 g CARB   413 mg S 65 mg CH

FISH CHOWDER: Cook onion in 2 table-spoons bacon drippings, butter, or margarine as directed; add potatoes and 1½ cups Fish Stock (or ¾ cup each bottled clam juice and water), cover and microwave as directed until potatoes are nearly tender. Lay 1 pound haddock or cod fillets on potatoes, tucking skinny ends underneath so they won't dry. Re-cover and micro-wave on MEDIUM (50% power) 6–9 minutes, until fish flakes. *Note: If fillets are thick, turn them over at halftime.* Add ½ cup Fish Stock, also milk, cream, and seasonings called for, mixing gently with fish. Cover and microwave on MEDIUM (50% power) 4½–5 minutes, until soup steams but does not boil. Stir gently, then microwave, uncovered, on LOW (10% power) 3–4 minutes, to mellow flavors. Ladle into hot bowls and dust with paprika.

PER SERVING: 244 C 18 g P 13 g F 13 g CARB 288 mg S 78 mg CH

MANHATTAN CLAM CHOWDER: Micro-wave onion in 2 tablespoons butter or margarine as directed. Add 1 cup moderately finely diced potatoes, ½ cup each finely diced carrots and celery and 2 cups coarsely chopped canned tomatoes, with their juice. Cover and microwave on HIGH (100% power) 9–10 minutes, stirring at halftime, until vegetables are almost tender. Add clams, clam liquid, ½ cup water, ½ teaspoon salt, and ⅛ teaspoon pepper. Re-cover and microwave on HIGH (100% power) 4½–5 min-utes, until mixture steams but does not boil. Stir again, re-cover, and microwave on MEDIUM-LOW (30% power) 4½–5 minutes, to mellow flavors. Sprinkle with parsley and serve.

PER SERVING: 137 C 11 g P 5 g F 12 g CARB 537 mg S 36 mg CH

CORN CHOWDER

PREP TIME: | 10 MINUTES | COOKING TIME: | 23–27 MINUTES | STANDING TIME: | NONE

¢

SERVES 4

3 **slices bacon, cut crosswise into julienne strips**

1 **large yellow onion, peeled and minced**

1 **medium-size sweet green or red pepper, cored, seeded, and moderately finely diced**

2 **cups fresh or frozen whole-kernel corn**

2½ **cups milk**

⅛ **teaspoon pepper**

Pinch ground nutmeg

1 **teaspoon salt (about)**

Lightly brown bacon in paper-toweling-covered 3-quart casserole by microwaving on HIGH (100% power) 3–3½ minutes. Remove bacon to paper toweling to drain with slotted spoon. Toss onion and green pepper with drippings, cover with wax paper, and microwave on HIGH (100% power) 3½–4 minutes, until onion is glassy. Add corn and milk, cover with lid, and microwave on HIGH (100% power) 9–10 minutes, stirring at halftime, until corn is tender. *Note: Watch soup carefully at end to avoid boilover; if necessary, reduce power to MEDIUM-LOW (30%).* Stir in pepper, nutmeg, and salt to taste, re-cover, and mellow flavors by microwaving on LOW (10% power) 7–9 minutes. Top with bacon and serve.

PER SERVING: 272 C 10 g P 16 g F 26 g CARB 754 mg S 33 mg CH

VARIATIONS

CLAM AND CORN CHOWDER: Prepare soup as directed, using 1 cup whole-kernel corn and 1½ cups minced fresh or canned clams; reduce salt to ½ teaspoon and use drained clam liquid for part of the milk.
PER SERVING: 272 C 9 g P 15 g F 25 g CARB 754 mg S 32 mg CH

CORN AND HAM CHOWDER: Prepare as directed, using 1 cup whole-kernel corn and 1½ cups diced cooked ham; reduce salt to ½ teaspoon.
PER SERVING: 335 C 21 g P 20 g F 18 g CARB 1184 mg S 65 mg CH

CORN AND CHICKEN OR TURKEY CHOWDER: Prepare as directed, using 1 cup whole-kernel corn and 1½ cups diced cooked chicken or turkey.
PER SERVING: 339 C 24 g P 19 g F 18 g CARB 794 mg S 79 mg CH

132

OYSTER STEW

PREP TIME: | 1 MINUTE | COOKING TIME: | 12½–14 MINUTES | STANDING TIME: | NONE

So that the oysters will cook evenly, choose those that are uniformly medium-size. Also use the very freshest cream to prevent curdling.

SERVES 4

2 tablespoons butter or margarine

1 pint shucked oysters, drained (reserve liquid)

1 cup milk

1 cup light cream

¼ teaspoon salt

¼ teaspoon celery salt

Pinch white pepper

Pinch paprika

Melt butter in wax-paper-covered 2-quart casserole by microwaving on HIGH (100% power) 35–45 seconds. Add oysters, cover with wax paper, and microwave on MEDIUM (50% power) 4½–5 minutes, stirring at halftime, just until oysters begin to ruffle. Let stand, covered, while you proceed. Pour milk, cream, and oyster liquid into 2-quart casserole and microwave, uncovered, on HIGH (100% power) 4½–5 minutes, until mixture steams but does not boil. Stir in oyster mixture and all remaining ingredients, cover with wax paper, and bring to serving temperature by microwaving on MEDIUM-LOW (30% power) 3–3½ minutes (do not boil or mixture may curdle).

PER SERVING: 292 C   13 g P   22 g F   10 g CARB   477 mg S 133 mg CH

V A R I A T I O N

SCALLOP STEW: Prepare as directed, substituting 1 pound quartered or, if large, diced sea scallops for oysters and cooking just until scallops turn milky.

PER SERVING: 305 C   23 g P   20 g F   8 g CARB   519 mg S 101 mg CH

133

CHEDDAR CHEESE SOUP

PREP TIME: 6 MINUTES   COOKING TIME: 13½–15 MINUTES   STANDING TIME: NONE

SERVES 4

2	tablespoons butter or margarine
⅓	cup minced yellow onion
⅓	cup minced celery
1	clove garlic, peeled and minced
2	tablespoons flour
1½	cups milk
1	cup chicken broth or ½ cup each chicken broth and dry white wine
2½	cups grated sharp Cheddar cheese
¼	teaspoon dry mustard

Pinch rubbed sage

⅛	teaspoon white pepper

Salt to taste

Melt butter in wax-paper-covered 3-quart casserole by microwaving on HIGH (100% power) 35–45 seconds. Toss onion, celery, and garlic with butter, cover with wax paper, and microwave on HIGH (100% power) 3½–4 minutes, until glassy. Blend in flour and microwave, uncovered, on HIGH (100% power) 30 seconds, until foamy. Gradually whisk in milk and broth and microwave, uncovered, on HIGH (100% power) 6–7 minutes, whisking vigorously at halftime, until mixture boils and thickens. Mix in cheese and seasonings and simmer, uncovered, to melt cheese and mellow flavors by microwaving on MEDIUM-LOW (30% power) 3 minutes (do not boil or cheese will "string"). Serve at once.

PER SERVING: 423 C   22 g P   33 g F   10 g CARB   803 mg S   103 mg CH

VARIATION

CHÈVRE SOUP: Prepare as directed, using milk and chicken broth and substituting ½ pound any very fresh, mild, semisoft goat cheese for Cheddar. Top with minced chives. *Note: This soup is especially refreshing if sieved and served cold on a hot day; thin, if needed, with a little milk or buttermilk.*

PER SERVING: 343 C   15 g P   26 g F   13 g CARB   713 mg S   81 mg CH

SOME TIPS FOR MAKING BETTER CREAMED VEGETABLE SOUPS

~~~~~ Always use *deep* casseroles or measures at least three times the volume of the combined soup ingredients to prevent boilover (milk mixtures foam furiously in the microwave), also to provide plenty of room for the stirring or whisking needed to keep soups smooth as they thicken.

~~~~~ Microwave creamed soups uncovered; lids merely trap steam, which condenses, drops into the soup, and thins it.

~~~~~ To shortcut cooking time by about 5 minutes, add only half the liquid called for to the roux (fat-flour mixture); once that mixture is thickened and smooth, add the remaining liquid. Adding the full amount of liquid to the roux nearly doubles the initial cooking time and may also mean an incompletely cooked roux that tastes of raw starch.

~~~~~ When halving a recipe, use a 1½-quart casserole and reduce cooking times by one half to two thirds. Do be sure no raw floury taste remains, however, and that the soup is brought to the proper serving temperature (170° F.).

~~~~~ For better flavor, make soups ahead of time and refrigerate overnight; if the soup is to be served hot, bring to serving temperature in the microwave.

~~~~~ For silky-smooth soups, rub them through a fine sieve, then bring to serving temperature in the microwave or chill as directed.

~~~~~ To thicken thawed, frozen creamed soups (they will have turned watery), blend 1 teaspoon cornstarch with 1 tablespoon milk, combine with 1 cup reheated soup and microwave, stirring every minute, until mixture boils.

~~~~~ To take the guesswork out of cooking and heating creamed soups, use an automatic temperature probe, following the manufacturer's directions.

135

BASIC CREAMED VEGETABLE SOUPS

PREP TIME (for all soups): 15–30 minutes if using fresh vegetables, 2–3 minutes if using cooked vegetables

COOKING TIME (for all soups): 9–10 minutes

STANDING TIME (for all soups): 3–4 minutes

SERVES 6

Artichoke (Globe and Jerusalem), Asparagus, Celery, or Fennel

Cooked Vegetable Purée	Butter or Margarine	Flour	Liquid	Basic Seasoning	Optional Extras
2½ C	3 T	3 T	1 C each milk and light cream + 2 C chicken or vegetable broth	1 t salt, ⅛ t white pepper, 2 T grated onion, pinch dried thyme	¼ t celery salt, pinch grated nutmeg, ¼ C dry white wine

Beans (Green or Wax) or Beets

2 C	3 T	3 T	2 C each milk and chicken or vegetable broth	1 t salt, ⅛ t white pepper, 1 t prepared horseradish	*For Beans:* 4 T grated Parmesan *For Beets:* 2 T grated onion, pinch ground mace

Broccoli, Cabbage, Cauliflower, Kale, Leek, Onion, Sweet Red or Green Pepper

2 C	3 T	3 T	1 C each milk and light cream + 2 C beef or vegetable broth	1 t salt, ⅛ t white pepper, pinch each ground cardamom and mace	1 t Dijon mustard, ¼ C grated mild Cheddar or Gruyère cheese

Cooked Vegetable Purée	Butter or Margarine	Flour	Liquid	Basic Seasoning	Optional Extras

Carrot or Green Pea

Cooked Vegetable Purée	Butter or Margarine	Flour	Liquid	Basic Seasoning	Optional Extras
2 C	2 T	2 T	1 C each milk and light cream + 2 C chicken or vegetable broth	1 t salt, ⅛ t white pepper, 1 T minced fresh tarragon or chervil or 1 t dried	1 t grated orange rind + pinch dried thyme, savory, or rosemary

Celery Root, Parsnip, Rutabaga, Turnip

2 C	2 T	2 T	1 C each milk and light cream + 2 C chicken or beef broth	1 t salt, ⅛ t white pepper, pinch dry mustard	Pinch each ground cinnamon, allspice, and ginger

Mushroom

2 C	3 T	3 T	1 C each milk and light cream + 2 C beef or vegetable broth	1 t salt, ⅛ t pepper, 1 T Worcestershire sauce	2 T grated onion + ¼ C dry sherry or Madeira

Potato (Parmentier)

2 C + ¾ C scallions (white part)	2 T	1 T	2 C each milk and chicken broth	1 t salt, ⅛ t white pepper, 2 T minced parsley	2 T grated onion, 1 T minced fresh mint or dill

Cooked Vegetable Purée	Butter or Margarine	Flour	Liquid	Basic Seasoning	Optional Extras
Pumpkin, Sweet Potato, or Winter Squash					
2 C	2 T	1 T	1 C each milk and light cream + 2 C chicken broth	1 t salt, ⅛ t pepper, ¼ t each ground cinnamon and cloves	¼ C each orange juice and honey, ¼ t ground ginger
Sorrel, Spinach, or Watercress					
2½ C	3 T	3 T	2 C each milk and chicken broth	1 t salt, ⅛ t pepper, 2 T each grated onion and lemon juice	1 crushed clove garlic or ½ t curry powder
Tomato					
2 C	2 T	2 T	2 C each milk and chicken or beef broth	1 t salt, ⅛ t pepper, ¼ t each dried basil, oregano, and sugar	¼ t each dried chervil and celery salt, 1 crushed clove garlic
Zucchini, Yellow Squash, or Cucumber					
3 C	3 T	3 T	1 C each milk and light cream + 2 C chicken broth	1 t salt, ⅛ t pepper, 2 T grated onion, ½ t dill weed	2 T minced watercress or ¼ C minced green chilies

BASIC METHOD FOR MAKING CREAMED VEGETABLE SOUPS

Melt butter in wax-paper-covered 3-quart casserole by microwaving on HIGH (100% power) allowing 35–45 seconds for 2 tablespoons, 10 seconds longer for 3 tablespoons. Blend in flour and microwave, uncovered, on HIGH (100% power) 30 seconds, until foamy. Slowly stir in half the liquid and microwave, uncovered, on HIGH (100% power) 3–4 minutes, whisking briskly at halftime, until mixture boils and thickens; whisk briskly again. Smooth in remaining liquid, vegetable purée and seasonings and microwave, uncovered, on HIGH (100% power) 4½–5 minutes, stirring at halftime, until mixture steams but does not boil. **Note:** *Do not allow Creamed Sorrel Soup to boil at any time after adding purée; it will curdle instantly.* Cover with foil and let stand 3 or 4 minutes to mellow flavors. Serve hot or chill and serve cold. **Note:** *Recipes too flexible for meaningful nutritive counts.*

V A R I A T I O N S

POTAGE DUBARRY (Serves 6): Prepare Creamed Cauliflower Soup as directed, reducing flour to 2 tablespoons and adding ½ cup mashed potatoes along with cauliflower purée. Omit cardamom and mace and add 1 tablespoon minced fresh chervil (or 1 teaspoon dried) along with salt and pepper. Top with croutons.
PER SERVING: 197 C 4 g P 16 g F 10 g CARB 793 mg S 48 mg CH

VICHYSSOISE (Serves 6): Prepare Creamed Potato Soup as directed, reducing milk to 1 cup and substituting 1½ cups puréed cooked leeks for scallions; omit parsley. Stir 1 cup heavy cream into finished soup and chill well. Sprinkle with minced chives and serve.
PER SERVING: 264 C 4 g P 21 g F 17 g CARB 781 mg S 70 mg CH

WILD MUSHROOM SOUP (Serves 6): Prepare Creamed Mushroom Soup as directed using puréed cooked cèpes, chanterelles, or morels and, for liquid, 3 cups beef broth and 1 cup heavy cream. Omit Worcestershire sauce and add ¼ cup tawny Port or Verdelho Madeira.
PER SERVING: 215 C 3 g P 19 g F 8 g CARB 469 mg S 65 mg CH

139

CREAM OF JALAPEÑO SOUP (Serves 6): Wrap 6 cored and seeded jalapeño peppers in plastic food wrap and steam until soft by microwaving on HIGH (100% power) about 3 minutes. Purée and mix with 2 cups puréed sweet green peppers. Proceed as directed for Creamed Sweet Green Pepper Soup, omitting cardamom and mace. Just before serving, mix in ⅓ cup coarsely grated Monterey Jack or mild Cheddar and microwave, uncovered, on HIGH (100% power) 30 seconds to melt cheese. Stir well, top with diced pimiento, and serve.
PER SERVING: 213 C 6 g P 17 g F 10 g CARB 772 mg S 53 mg CH

¢ POTAGE CRÉCY (Serves 6): Prepare Creamed Carrot Soup as directed, reducing flour to 1 tablespoon and puréeing ½ cup cooked rice and 1 extra cup chicken broth with carrot purée. Omit tarragon, add 2 tablespoons finely grated yellow onion, and bring to serving temperature as directed. Serve with croutons.
PER SERVING: 201 C 5 g P 14 g F 15 g CARB 611 mg S 42 mg CH

⚖ TOMATO-ORANGE SOUP (Serves 6): Prepare Creamed Tomato Soup as directed, omitting oregano and adding 2 teaspoons finely grated orange rind and 3 tablespoons finely grated yellow onion along with tomato purée.
¢ **PER SERVING: 141 C 5 g P 7 g F 15 g CARB 797 mg S 22 mg CH**

¢ CHILLED CUCUMBER-YOGURT SOUP (Serves 6): Prepare Creamed Cucumber Soup as directed, increasing minced dill to 2 tablespoons. Chill soup, mix in 1 cup plain yogurt, taste for seasoning and adjust as needed.
PER SERVING: 219 C 6 g P 16 g F 14 g CARB 826 mg S 50 mg CH

SOME TIPS FOR MAKING BETTER BISQUES AND VELOUTÉS

Don't make more than 5 cups soup at a time because it may curdle around the edges before it's heated through.

To monitor the cooking of these fragile cream- and/or egg-yolk-thickened soups and to facilitate frequent stirring, use a lidded glass ovenware casserole.

For better flavor, make bisques and veloutés ahead of time, then reheat slowly in the microwave (see Reheating Refrigerated and Room-temperature Food in Chapter 4).

Don't freeze bisques or veloutés; they'll separate.

SHELLFISH BISQUE

PREP TIME: [6 MINUTES] COOKING TIME: [20–23 MINUTES] STANDING TIME: [10 MINUTES]

A true bisque is thickened with cooked rice, which won't overpower the delicacy of the shellfish. Leftover rice does the job perfectly.

SERVES 4

2   tablespoons butter or margarine

¼   cup minced yellow onion

¼   cup minced carrot

1½   cups (about ¾ pound) very finely minced cooked shrimp, lobster, crab, clams, or mussels

¼   cup cooked rice

1½   cups Fish Stock or a half-and-half mix of bottled clam juice and water

1   bay leaf and 1 sprig each parsley and thyme, tied in cheesecloth (bouquet garni)

1½   cups heavy cream

2–3 tablespoons medium-dry sherry or brandy

¼   teaspoon salt (about)

⅛   teaspoon white pepper

Melt butter in wax-paper-covered 3-quart casserole by microwaving on HIGH (100% power) 35–45 seconds. Toss onion and carrot in butter, cover with wax paper, and microwave on HIGH (100% power) 3½–4 minutes, until onion is glassy. Add shellfish, rice, 1 cup of the Fish Stock, and bouquet garni, cover with lid, and microwave on HIGH (100% power) 4½–5 minutes, until mixture boils. Stir well, re-cover, and microwave on MEDIUM (50% power) 4½–5 minutes. Let mixture stand, still covered, 10 minutes to blend flavors. Remove bouquet garni, then purée mixture. Add remaining Fish Stock, cream, and sherry, return bisque to casserole, cover, and bring to serving temperature by microwaving on MEDIUM (50% power) 7–8 minutes, stirring well every 3 minutes and paying particular attention to edges where mixture cooks first and is apt to curdle. Add salt and pepper, taste and adjust as needed. Serve hot or cold. *Note: For a pretty garnish, buy an extra ounce or two of shellfish and reserve a few choice pieces to top each portion.*

PER SERVING: 470 C   20 g P   40 g F   9 g CARB   519 mg S   304 mg CH

V A R I A T I O N

FRESH SALMON BISQUE: Prepare as directed, substituting 1½ cups finely minced, poached, boned, and skinned fresh salmon for shellfish and dry white

141

wine for sherry. Serve hot or cold and garnish each serving with thin lemon or lime slice or twist of lemon or lime rind.

PER SERVING: 503 C   19 g P   44 g F   8 g CARB   365 mg S   185 mg CH

CHICKEN OR TURKEY VELOUTÉ

PREP TIME: 3 MINUTES   COOKING TIME: 22–27 MINUTES   STANDING TIME: 10 MINUTES

Leftover light-meat scraps of Rock Cornish hen, squab, pheasant, or other game birds also make a delicious velouté.

SERVES 4

¼ cup (½ stick) butter or margarine

¼ cup unsifted flour

3 cups chicken broth

¾ cup heavy cream

1 cup very finely minced cooked chicken or turkey breast

¼ teaspoon salt (about)

Pinch white pepper

Pinch ground nutmeg or mace

3 egg yolks, lightly beaten

1 tablespoon minced parsley or chives

Melt butter in wax-paper-covered 3-quart casserole by microwaving on HIGH (100% power) 55–65 seconds. Blend in flour and microwave, uncovered, on HIGH (100% power) 30 seconds until foamy. Stir in broth, a little at a time, and microwave, uncovered, on HIGH (100% power) 7–9 minutes, whisking briskly every 3 minutes, until mixture boils and thickens. Stir in cream and chicken, cover with lid, and microwave on MEDIUM (50% power) 5–6 minutes. Let casserole stand, still covered, 10 minutes, to mellow flavors. Put mixture through fine sieve, extracting as much liquid as possible. Return soup to casserole, mix in salt, pepper, and nutmeg, re-cover with wax paper, and bring to a simmer by microwaving on HIGH (100% power) 2–3 minutes. Blend ½ cup hot soup into egg yolks, stir back into casserole, re-cover, and microwave on MEDIUM-LOW (30% power) 6–7 minutes, whisking every 3 minutes, until no raw egg taste remains. *Note: Whisk most vigorously around edge where mixture cooks first.* If soup tastes eggy after 7 minutes, microwave in 1-minute increments until raw egg taste is gone (do not let soup boil or it may curdle). Serve hot or cold sprinkled with parsley.

PER SERVING: 423 C 16 g P 37 g F 9 g CARB 1059 mg S 328 mg CH

V A R I A T I O N S

SHRIMP, CRAB, OR LOBSTER VELOUTÉ: Prepare as directed, substituting 3 cups Fish Stock (or a half-and-half mix of clam juice and water) for chicken broth and 1 cup finely minced cooked shrimp, crab, or lobster for chicken. Serve hot or cold and top each portion, if you like, with 2 tablespoons minced cooked shellfish.

PER SERVING: 369 C   12 g P   33 g F   7 g CARB   549 mg S   366 mg CH

HOME-STYLE CREAM OF CHICKEN OR TURKEY SOUP: Prepare as directed, substituting light cream for heavy cream and diced chicken or turkey for the minced. Do not strain soup. Serve hot, garnishing as directed.

PER SERVING: 357 C   16 g P   29 g F   9 g CARB   1060 mg S   296 mg CH

SENEGALESE SOUP: Melt butter as directed, add 4 minced shallots or scallions; 1 peeled, cored, and minced tart green apple; 1½ teaspoons curry powder; and ⅛ teaspoon chili powder, cover with wax paper, and microwave on HIGH (100% power) 3½–4 minutes, until shallots are soft. Blend in flour and proceed as recipe directs. Serve hot or cold, sprinkled with a little ground hot red pepper.

PER SERVING: 450 C   16 g P   37 g F   16 g CARB   1061 mg S   328 mg CH

ABOUT MICROWAVING SAUCES AND GRAVIES

Here's where the microwave truly excels. You can prepare as much as a quart of sauce or gravy faster and easier in a microwave oven than you can on top of the stove. Better yet, you don't have to stir nonstop. Or worry about scorching. Indeed, making starch-thickened sauces and gravies by microwave is almost foolproof if you follow these guidelines (for directions on reheating sauces or gravies, see Chart for Reheating Refrigerated and Room-temperature Food in Chapter 4; for tips on adapting conventional sauce recipes for the microwave, see How to Convert Favorite Recipes for Microwave Use in Chapter 1). *Note: When nutritive counts are given per tablespoon, figures are precise instead of rounded off to the nearest whole number. Rare is the person who'd use one tablespoon sauce, and amounts can add up.*

SOME GENERAL TIPS

Use measures with handles or "eared" round casseroles twice the volume of the ingredients put into them to allow room for beating and boiling (the recipes that follow all specify container size).

To distribute the heat evenly, stir every 1–1½ minutes unless recipes direct otherwise.

Whenever a sauce must boil, make sure that it bubbles *throughout,* not merely around the edges (monitor progress through the oven door). *Note: The temperature of the liquid used in making a sauce, i.e., room temperature versus refrigerator-cold, determines how quickly a sauce will boil.*

If a sauce is too thin, thicken as follows: For each cup sauce, blend 1 teaspoon flour or ½ teaspoon cornstarch with 1 tablespoon cold water, mix into hot sauce, and microwave on HIGH (100% power) in 30-second increments, until mixture boils and thickens. *Note: You can't reduce (thicken) sauces as quickly by microwave as you can on top of the stove.* If a sauce is too thick, simply thin with a little additional liquid (the same one called for in the recipe).

SOME TIPS FOR MAKING BETTER STARCH-THICKENED SAUCES AND GRAVIES

The principal starch thickeners are flour and cornstarch, but arrowroot and potato flour also work well. Each has about twice the thickening power of flour, but is trickier to use because an arrowroot or potato-starch sauce will thin out if allowed to boil after it has thickened.

For maximum thickening, blend the fat and flour to a smooth paste, then microwave on HIGH (100% power) for 30 seconds before adding any liquid.

Cook starch-thickened sauces *uncovered* to concentrate flavors and speed thickening (covers trap steam, which can condense and thin a sauce).

To ensure smoothness and even heat distribution, whisk sauces and gravies vigorously every 1½ minutes and once again at the end of cooking.

To develop the flavors of some sauces, mellow for a few minutes by microwaving on MEDIUM-LOW (30% power) at the end of cooking or allowing sauces to stand before serving (recipes specify when either method is necessary).

Do not taste sauces or gravies for seasoning until after they have mellowed, for only then will their flavors have developed fully.

If, despite all precautions, a starch-thickened sauce should lump, simply put through a moderately fine sieve.

If a starch-thickened sauce must be held for more than 5 minutes on LOW (10% power), cool it and reheat—it may thin during prolonged holding.

145

SOME TIPS FOR MAKING BETTER EGG-THICKENED SAUCES

〜〜〜 Cook uncovered to concentrate flavors and ensure proper thickening.

〜〜〜 Before adding eggs to a hot sauce, always whisk a little of the hot sauce into the eggs, which will raise their temperature gradually and help prevent curdling.

〜〜〜 Microwave on MEDIUM-LOW (30% power) after the eggs have been added to reduce the risk of curdling. If a sauce should curdle, no matter how careful you were, it can be rescued (see To Salvage Curdled Hollandaise; the technique is the same).

ABOUT BUTTERS AND BUTTER SAUCES

Softened, melted, and clarified butters, whether flavored or plain, are indispensable to the creative cook. Luckily, the microwave does most of them to perfection and even makes it possible to melt butter right in the sauceboat in which it's to be served. *Note: One butter that's easier to prepare the old-fashioned way is Beurre Blanc, for which the butter must be incorporated drop by drop. It can be prepared in the microwave, but it's ridiculous to try because you spend all of your time opening and closing the oven door.*

TO SOFTEN BUTTER (½ cup): Microwave ½ cup (1 stick) refrigerator-cold butter, uncovered, on microwave-safe butter dish or plate on MEDIUM-LOW (30% power) 15–25 seconds, until almost soft enough to spread (test by touching). Let stand 10–15 seconds to complete the softening. For *Jiffy Garlic Butter,* simply mix in 1 crushed clove garlic. And for *Jiffy Herb Butter,* mix in 1 tablespoon minced fresh basil, tarragon, or dill, or 1 teaspoon crumbled dried basil or tarragon or dillweed.

TO MELT BUTTER (½ cup): Place ½ cup (1 stick) refrigerator-cold butter in 1-pint measure, cover with wax paper, and microwave on HIGH (100% power) 1¼–1½ minutes, until melted. For *Seasoned Butter,* simply stir in 1 teaspoon salt and ¼ teaspoon pepper. *Note: Room-temperature butter will obviously melt faster than cold butter (so will margarine because it's made from polyunsaturates). The best plan in melting butter or margarine is to micro-wave the shortest suggested time, then continue microwaving in 5-second increments, following the progress through the oven door and removing the butter or margarine from the oven as soon as it liquefies.*

TO MELT SMALL QUANTITIES

Place butter in a custard cup or ramekin, then microwave, using the following times as a guide:

1–1½ tablespoons butter	25–30 seconds
2 tablespoons butter	35–45 seconds
3 tablespoons butter	45–55 seconds
¼ cup (½ stick) butter	55–65 seconds

TO CLARIFY BUTTER (½ cup): Melt butter as directed, then let stand, uncovered, 2–3 minutes until solids settle. Skim off clear liquid butter and discard white milk solids.

SOME EASY BUTTER SAUCES

ALMOND BUTTER SAUCE (¾ cup): To ½ cup melted butter add ¼ cup toasted slivered almonds.* Serve over broiled fish, steamed broccoli, or asparagus.
PER TABLESPOON: 84 C 0.7 g P 9 g F 0.6 g CARB 78.4 mg S 20.7 mg CH

BEURRE NOIR (BLACK BUTTER) (½ cup): Melt ½ cup (1 stick) butter in 6-cup *clear* measure as directed, then continue to microwave, uncovered, on HIGH (100% power) 3½–4½ minutes until nut-brown; watch carefully after 3 minutes to avoid overbrowning. *Note: Butter will foam as it begins to brown and foam will look several shades lighter than butter actually is, so be careful about overbrowning.* Stir in 1 tablespoon each minced parsley, capers, and cider vinegar. Delicious with fish, sweetbreads, broccoli, spinach, and asparagus.
PER TABLESPOON: 102 C 0.1 g P 11.5 g F 0.1 g CARB 144.7 mg S 31 mg CH

BEURRE NOISETTE (½ cup): Brown butter as directed for Beurre Noir, omit parsley, capers, and vinegar, and add 3 tablespoons lemon juice. Serve with fish or green vegetables.

PER TABLESPOON: 103 C 0.14 g P 11.5 g F 0.4 g CARB 118 mg S 31 mg CH

LEMON BUTTER SAUCE (½ cup): To ½ cup melted butter add 2 tablespoons lemon juice, a pinch pepper, and, if you like, 2–3 tablespoons minced parsley. Stir well, cover with wax paper, and microwave on LOW (10% power) 2–3 minutes. Serve with fish or vegetables.

PER TABLESPOON: 103 C 0.13 g P 11.5 g F 0.3 g CARB 118 mg S 31 mg CH

HERB BUTTER SAUCE (½ cup): To ½ cup Lemon Butter Sauce add any of the following: 2 tablespoons minced chives, shallots, or scallions (terrific with steaks, chops, and fish); 3 tablespoons snipped fresh dill (great with asparagus, carrots, broccoli, salmon, and lean white fish); ½ teaspoon each minced fresh marjoram and thyme or rosemary (perfect for corn on the cob, peas, and lamb); 1 tablespoon each minced fresh tarragon and tarragon vinegar (superb with meat, fish, poultry, carrots, and asparagus).

PER TABLESPOON: 103 C 0.2 g P 11.5 g F 0.3 g CARB 118 mg S 31 mg CH

CHILI BUTTER SAUCE (½ cup): Prepare Lemon Butter Sauce as directed, adding 1 teaspoon chili powder at outset and omitting parsley. Use to baste broiled tomatoes, meat, fish, or poultry. Great, too, on corn on the cob.

PER TABLESPOON: 103 C 0.16 g P 11.5 g F 0.4 g CARB 121 mg S 31 mg CH

CURRY BUTTER SAUCE (½ cup): Prepare Lemon Butter Sauce as directed, adding 1 teaspoon curry powder at the outset and omitting parsley. Serve with broiled meat, fish, or poultry; also delicious with steamed broccoli, cabbage, or cauliflower.

PER TABLESPOON: 103 C 0.2 g P 11.5 g F 0.4 g CARB 118 mg S 31 mg CH

GARLIC BUTTER SAUCE (½ cup): Combine ½ cup melted butter with 2 crushed cloves garlic, ¼ teaspoon salt, and ⅛ teaspoon pepper. Cover with wax paper and microwave on LOW (10% power) 2–3 minutes. Strain, if you like, and use for making garlic bread or for basting broiled steaks, chops, and fish.

PER TABLESPOON: 103 C 0.2 g P 11.5 g F 0.3 g CARB 184.7 mg S 31 mg CH

DRAWN BUTTER SAUCE

PREP TIME: [1 MINUTES] **COOKING TIME:** [4¼–5 MINUTES] **STANDING TIME:** [1 MINUTE]

MAKES 1 CUP

¼   cup clarified butter*
2   tablespoons flour
1   cup Fish Stock, vegetable cooking water, or water
½   teaspoon salt
⅛   teaspoon paprika
½–1 teaspoon lemon juice

Melt butter by microwaving in wax-paper-covered 1-quart measure on HIGH (100% power) 55–65 seconds. Blend in flour and microwave, uncovered, on HIGH (100% power) 30 seconds until foamy. Gradually mix in stock, add salt and paprika, and microwave, uncovered, on HIGH (100% power) 2¾–3½ minutes, whisking every 1½ minutes to ensure smoothness, until sauce bubbles and thickens. Blend in lemon juice to taste and let stand 1 minute, stirring now and then. Serve with broiled fish or steamed green vegetables.

PER TABLESPOON: 32 C   0.1 g P   3.2 g F   0.8 g CARB 84.5 mg S   8.3 mg CH

BASIC WHITE SAUCE

PREP TIME: [1 MINUTES]   COOKING TIME: [3½–5 MINUTES]   STANDING TIME: [1 MINUTE]

MAKES 1 CUP

Sauce Type	Fat (Butter, Margarine, or Drippings)	Flour	Milk	Seasonings	Use
Very thin	1 tablespoon	½ table-spoon	1 cup	¼ teaspoon salt, pinch pepper	For thickening thin cream soups
Thin	1 tablespoon	1 table-spoon	1 cup	¼ teaspoon salt, pinch pepper	For thickening standard cream soups
Medium	2 tablespoons	2 table-spoons	1 cup	¼ teaspoon salt, pinch pepper	As a base for sauces and creamed dishes
Thick	3 tablespoons	3 table-spoons	1 cup	¼ teaspoon salt, pinch pepper	For binding casserole ingredients
Very Thick	¼ cup	¼ cup	1 cup	¼ teaspoon salt, pinch pepper	For binding croquettes

Melt fat by microwaving in wax-paper-covered 1-quart measure on HIGH (100% power) as follows: 25–30 seconds for 1 tablespoon fat, 35–45 for 2 tablespoons, 45–55 for 3 tablespoons, and 55–65 for ¼ cup. *Note: Margarine, because of its polyunsaturated fats, usually melts about 10 seconds faster than butter.* Blend in flour, then microwave, uncovered, on HIGH (100% power) as follows: 20 seconds for ½–1 tablespoon flour and 30 seconds for 2–4 tablespoons (¼ cup), or until foamy. Gradually mix in milk and add salt and pepper. **Note:** *Don't panic if sauce looks curdled when milk is first added; it will smooth out as it cooks.* Microwave, uncovered, on HIGH (100% power) 2¾–3½ minutes, whisking every 1½ minutes, until sauce boils and thickens; whisk again at end of cooking. Let sauce stand 1 minute, stirring now and then. **Note:** *If sauce must be held a short while before it's served, stir occasionally or set circle of wax paper flat on surface to prevent skin from forming. To reheat, cover with wax paper and microwave on MEDIUM (50% power) 1–1½ minutes, stirring at halftime. Or cover with wax paper as directed, cool, and refrigerate until ready to proceed (for reheating sauces see Chart for Reheating Refrigerated and Room-temperature Food in Chapter 4).*

PER TABLESPOON:

VERY THIN WHITE SAUCE: 17 C   0.5 g P   1.2 g F   0.9 g CARB   48.5 mg S   4 mg CH

THIN WHITE SAUCE: 17 C   0.6 g P   1.2 g F   1 g CARB   48.5 mg S   4 mg CH

MEDIUM WHITE SAUCE: 26 C   0.6 g P   1.9 g F   1.5 g CARB   55.9 mg S   6 mg CH

THICK WHITE SAUCE: 34 C   0.7 g P   2.7 g F   1.8 g CARB   63.2 mg S   8 mg CH

VERY THICK WHITE SAUCE: 42 C   0.7 g P   3.4 g F   2 g CARB   70.5 mg S   9.9 mg CH

To make 1 Pint Very Thin, Thin, or Medium White Sauce: Double quantities called for in Basic White Sauce chart and using 6-cup measure, microwave butter and flour as directed. After adding milk, increase microwave time on HIGH (100% power) to 4½–5½ minutes, beating well every 1½ minutes, until sauce boils and thickens. Let stand as directed.

V A R I A T I O N S

▨ **MUSTARD SAUCE** (1¼ cups): To each 1 cup Medium White Sauce add ¼ cup prepared mild yellow or spicy brown mustard and 1 teaspoon cider vinegar. Good with ham, frankfurters, tongue, broccoli, and green beans.
PER TABLESPOON: 23 C 0.6 g P 1.7 g F 1.4 g CARB 83.8 mg S 4.8 mg CH

▨ **CHOPPED EGG SAUCE** (1¼ cups): To each 1 cup Medium White Sauce add 1 minced hard-cooked egg and 1 teaspoon minced parsley. Good with poached fish.
PER TABLESPOON: 24 C 0.8 g P 1.8 g F 1.2 g CARB 48.2 mg S 18.5 mg CH

▨ **PARSLEY SAUCE** (1–2 cups): Prepare 1 cup or 1 pint Medium White Sauce as directed, adding 2–4 tablespoons minced parsley along with other seasonings. Good with fish, boiled potatoes, and carrots.
PER TABLESPOON: 26 C 0.6 g P 1.9 g F 1.5 g CARB 56 mg S 6 mg CH

151

⧖ CHEESE SAUCE (1½ cups): To 1 cup Medium White Sauce add ¾ cup coarsely grated sharp Cheddar or Swiss cheese; 1 teaspoon each Worcestershire sauce and finely grated onion; and a pinch each dry mustard, ground nutmeg, and hot red pepper. Microwave, uncovered, on MEDIUM (50% power) 1–1½ minutes, stirring at halftime, until cheese melts and sauce is smooth. Thin, if necessary, with milk. *To Make 1½ Pints Cheese Sauce:* Double all ingredients, use 6-cup measure, and microwave on MEDIUM (50% power) 2–2½ minutes.

PER TABLESPOON: 32 C   1.3 g P   2.5 g F   1 g CARB   61.5 mg S   7.7 mg CH

SHRIMP SAUCE (2 cups): Prepare 1 cup Medium White Sauce as directed, adding 2 teaspoons tomato paste along with other seasonings. To finished sauce, add 1 cup coarsely chopped cooked shrimp (or lobster or crab) and 2 tablespoons medium-dry sherry or water. Stir well, cover with wax paper, and microwave on MEDIUM (50% power) 2 minutes to blend flavors.

PER TABLESPOON: 18 C   1.2 g P   1 g F   0.9 g CARB   40.6 mg S   11.6 mg CH

ONION SAUCE (1½ cups): Microwave 1 coarsely chopped large yellow onion with ¼ cup water in covered 1-quart casserole on HIGH (100% power) 4½–6 minutes until very soft. Mix into 1 cup Medium White Sauce, cover with wax paper, and microwave on MEDIUM-LOW (30% power) 2–3 minutes to blend flavors.

PER TABLESPOON: 19 C   0.5 g P   1.3 g F   1.5 g CARB   37.4 mg S   4 mg CH

MUSHROOM SAUCE

PREP TIME: | 5 MINUTES | COOKING TIME: | 8½–10 MINUTES | STANDING TIME: | NONE

MAKES 2½ CUPS

- **2 cups coarsely chopped mushrooms**
- **¼ cup (½ stick) butter or margarine**
- **¼ cup unsifted flour**
- **2 cups milk**
- **½ teaspoon salt**
- **Pinch pepper**

Microwave mushrooms in butter in paper-toweling-covered 2-quart casserole on HIGH (100% power) 3½–4 minutes, stirring at halftime, until limp. Blend in flour and microwave, uncovered, on HIGH (100% power) 30 seconds. Mix in milk, salt, and pepper and microwave, uncovered, on HIGH (100% power) 4½–5½ minutes, stirring at halftime, until sauce boils and thickens; stir again.

PER TABLESPOON: 21 C   0.6 g P   1.6 g F   1.3 g CARB   45.2 mg S   4.8 mg CH

SHERRIED MUSHROOM SAUCE: Prepare Mushroom Sauce as directed, adding ¼ teaspoon ground nutmeg or mace along with the other seasonings and stirring in 2–3 tablespoons dry sherry or white wine just before serving.

PER TABLESPOON: 22 C   0.5 g P   1.5 g F   1.4 g CARB   43 mg S   4.6 mg CH

BÉCHAMEL SAUCE

PREP TIME: | 2 MINUTES | COOKING TIME: | 11–12½ MINUTES | STANDING TIME: | NONE

Popular opinion to the contrary, classic French sauces *can* be successfully prepared in the microwave. In fact, microwaving them is often easier than making them the old-fashioned way. This subtly flavored Béchamel needs no double boiler when cooked in the microwave and the reduction of it needed for Mornay Sauce (see the variation that follows) requires almost no attention.

MAKES 1⅔ CUPS

¼ cup (½ stick) butter (no substitute)

2 tablespoons minced yellow onion

¼ cup unsifted flour

2 cups milk or 1 cup each milk and chicken broth, Fish Stock, or vegetable cooking water

½ teaspoon salt (about)

⅛ teaspoon white pepper

1 small sprig fresh thyme or a pinch crumbled dried thyme

¼ bay leaf (do not crumble)

Pinch ground nutmeg

Microwave butter and onion in wax-paper-covered 6-cup measure on HIGH (100% power) 1¼–1½ minutes, until glassy. Blend in flour and microwave, uncovered, on HIGH (100% power) 30 seconds until foamy. Gradually stir in milk, add remaining ingredients, and microwave, uncovered, on HIGH (100% power) 4½–5½ minutes, whisking after 2 minutes, until sauce boils and thickens; whisk again. Cover with wax paper and microwave on LOW (10% power) 5 minutes, whisking at halftime. Strain sauce, adjust salt, if needed. Serve hot.

PER TABLESPOON: 32 C 0.7 g P 2.4 g F 1.8 g CARB 69.3 mg S 7.4 mg CH

153

MORNAY SAUCE (2½ cups): This delicate cheese sauce is superb with fish, fowl, eggs, or vegetables (which you're preparing will determine the kind of stock you use). Prepare Béchamel as directed, mix in ½ cup more stock and microwave, uncovered, on HIGH (100% power) 9–10 minutes, until sauce reduces to 2 cups. *Note: Wipe condensation from microwave oven before proceeding.* Mix in ⅓ cup grated Gruyère and ¼ cup grated Parmesan cheese, cover with wax paper, and microwave, uncovered, on MEDIUM (50% power) 1 minute. Thin, if needed, with a little milk or stock.

PER TABLESPOON: 24 C   0.9 g P   1.9 g F   1 g CARB   92 mg S   5.4 mg CH

CAPER SAUCE (2 cups): Prepare Béchamel as directed, using milk and Fish Stock; omit salt, and just before serving, mix in ⅓ cup coarsely chopped capers and 1 tablespoon lemon juice. Serve with fish.

PER TABLESPOON: 21 C   0.4 g P   1.7 g F   1.2 g CARB   62.8 mg S   4.9 mg CH

HORSERADISH SAUCE (2 cups): Prepare Béchamel as directed, mix in ¼–⅓ cup well-drained prepared horseradish and 1 teaspoon prepared mustard. Cover with wax paper and microwave on LOW (10% power) 2 minutes. Serve with corned beef or boiled beef.

PER TABLESPOON: 27 C   0.6 g P   1.9 g F   1.7 g CARB   60.4 mg S   6 mg CH

PAN GRAVY

PREP TIME: | 2 MINUTES | COOKING TIME: | 12–17 MINUTES | STANDING TIME: | NONE |

The time to make gravy is while the roast is standing. The foundation of this recipe is a brown roux, which the microwave does to perfection.

MAKES 2 CUPS

¼ cup pan drippings (or pan drippings plus enough bacon drippings, melted butter, or vegetable oil to total ¼ cup)

Microwave drippings in wax-paper-covered 6-cup measure on HIGH (100% power) 40–50 seconds. Blend in flour and microwave, uncovered, on HIGH (100% power) 7–10 minutes, stirring every 3 minutes, until light brown. **Note:**

¼ cup unsifted flour

2 cups hot water, vegetable cooking water, or a half-and-half mix of the two

Liquid gravy browner (optional)

Salt and pepper to taste

In 600–725-watt ovens, roux will be light brown after 7–8 minutes; for darker gravy, microwave 2–3 minutes longer but watch carefully to prevent overbrowning. Mixture will look grainy but will smooth out once liquid is added. While roux browns, pour water into drained roasting pan and scrape up brown bits. When roux is brown, whisk in water slowly and carefully (hot roux may sputter). Microwave, uncovered, on HIGH (100% power) 3½–4 minutes, whisking at halftime, until gravy thickens and boils. Microwave, uncovered, on MEDIUM-LOW (30% power) 1–2 minutes to mellow; mix in gravy browner, if desired, and salt and pepper to taste.

PER TABLESPOON: 18 C 0.1 g P 1.5 g F 0.7 g CARB 5.53 mg S 1.4 mg CH

~~~ V A R I A T I O N S

RICH GRAVY: Prepare as directed, substituting rich beef broth for water.
PER TABLESPOON: 19 C   0.3 g P   1.6 g F   0.8 g CARB   51.6 mg S   1.4 mg CH

SOUR CREAM GRAVY (3 cups): Prepare as directed, but before microwaving on MEDIUM-LOW (30% power), smooth in 1 cup sour cream. Proceed as directed, but increase cooking time to 2–3 minutes; do not boil or gravy will curdle.
PER TABLESPOON: 22 C   0.2 g P   2 g F   0.7 g CARB   2.5 mg S   3 mg CH

RAISIN SAUCE (2½ cups): Prepare as directed, but before microwaving on MEDIUM-LOW (30% power), add ⅓ cup seedless raisins and ¼ cup medium-dry Madeira, sherry, or port. Proceed as directed, but increase cooking time to 4–5 minutes, or until raisins are plump. Serve with ham or tongue.
PER TABLESPOON: 18 C   0.1 g P   1.2 g F   1.7 g CARB   0.3 mg S   1 mg CH

MUSHROOM GRAVY (2½ cups): Microwave 2 cups coarsely chopped mushrooms and ¼ cup minced yellow onion with 3 tablespoons butter in paper-toweling-covered 1-quart casserole on HIGH (100% power) 3½–4 minutes, stirring at halftime, until limp. Remove from oven and reserve. Prepare Pan Gravy as directed, but before microwaving on MEDIUM-LOW (30% power), stir in mushroom mixture. Proceed as directed, but increase cooking time to 4–6 minutes, stirring at halftime, until flavors are blended. Taste and adjust seasonings.

PER TABLESPOON: 23 C   0.2 g P   2.1 g F   0.8 g CARB   8.9 mg S   3.4 mg CH

ONION GRAVY (2½ cups): Microwave 2 thinly sliced medium-size yellow onions in ¼ cup pan drippings in wax-paper-covered 2-quart casserole on HIGH (100% power) 4–6 minutes, stirring at halftime, until glassy. Blend in flour and microwave, uncovered, on HIGH (100% power) 2 minutes. *Note: Do not microwave longer to brown flour because onions will turn bitter.* Add liquid and proceed as Pan Gravy recipe directs.

PER TABLESPOON: 15 C   0.2 g P   1.2 g F   0.9 g CARB   0.1 mg S   1.1 mg CH

CHICKEN OR TURKEY GRAVY: Prepare Pan Gravy as directed, but substitute rich chicken or turkey broth for water.

PER TABLESPOON: 7 C   0.3 g P   0.2 g F   0.9 g CARB   62.8 mg S   0.1 mg CH

CHICKEN OR TURKEY CREAM GRAVY: Prepare Chicken or Turkey Gravy as directed, using 1½ cups broth and ½ cup light cream.

PER TABLESPOON: 14 C   0.4 g P   0.9 g F   1 g CARB   48.6 mg S   2.5 mg CH

MILK GRAVY: Prepare Chicken or Turkey Gravy as directed, using 1 cup each rich chicken or turkey broth and milk in place of water. Omit gravy browner.

PER TABLESPOON: 10 C   0.5 g P   0.4 g F   1.2 g CARB   35.1 mg S   1.1 mg CH

WINE GRAVY: Prepare Pan Gravy or Chicken or Turkey Gravy as directed, but use 1 cup each dry red wine and beef broth for beef or lamb and 1 cup each dry white wine and chicken broth for poultry.

PER TABLESPOON (Pan Gravy): 19 C   0.2 g P   1.6 g F   0.9 g CARB   26.2 mg S   1.4 mg CH

PER TABLESPOON (Chicken or Turkey Gravy): 6 C   0.3 g P   0.1 g F   0.9 g CARB   31.7 mg S   0.1 mg CH

GIBLET GRAVY: (Makes 2½ cups): Prepare Chicken or Turkey Gravy as directed, but substitute Giblet Stock for water; mix in minced cooked giblets and neck meat and serve.

PER TABLESPOON: 8 C   0.6 g P   0.3 g F   0.7 g CARB   51.7 mg S   5 mg CH

HERB GRAVY: Prepare any of the gravies, adding herbs as follows along with liquid: ½ teaspoon crumbled dried savory, thyme, or marjoram (for beef), 1 teaspoon crumbled dried tarragon or mint, or ¼ teaspoon crumbled dried rosemary (for lamb or veal), and ½ teaspoon crumbled dried sage and/or thyme (for pork or poultry). *Recipe too flexible for meaningful nutritive counts.*

THIN GRAVY: Prepare Pan Gravy or Chicken or Turkey Gravy as directed, but reduce fat and flour to 2 tablespoons each; also reduce browning time on HIGH (100% power) to 4–5 minutes.

PER TABLESPOON (Pan Gravy): 9 C   0.1 g P   0.8 g F   0.4 g CARB   0 mg S   0.7 mg CH

PER TABLESPOON (Chicken or Turkey Gravy): 4 C   0.2 g P   0.2 g F   0.5 g CARB   62.8 mg S   0 mg CH

THICK GRAVY: Prepare Pan Gravy or Chicken or Turkey Gravy as directed, but increase fat and flour to 5–6 tablespoons each; if needed, increase browning time on HIGH (100% power) to 8–11 minutes.

PER TABLESPOON (Pan Gravy): 21 C   0.2 g P   1.7 g F   1 g CARB   0 mg S   1.6 mg CH

PER TABLESPOON (Chicken or Turkey Gravy): 8 C   0.4 g P   0.2 g F   1.2 g CARB   62.8 mg S   0.1 mg CH

LOW-CALORIE GRAVY: When preparing Pan Gravy, Chicken or Turkey Gravy, drain all but 1 tablespoon clear drippings from roasting pan, add liquid, scrape up brown bits, pour into measure, and microwave, uncovered, on HIGH (100% power) 3½–4 minutes, until small bubbles begin to appear at edge of liquid. Slowly whisk in ¼ cup flour blended with ¼ cup cold water. Microwave, uncovered, on HIGH (100% power) 1½–2 minutes, whisking well after 1 minute, until gravy boils and thickens; beat well again. Microwave, uncovered, on MEDIUM-LOW (30% power) 1–2 minutes to mellow. Color, if you like, with gravy browner and season to taste. *Note: For richer flavor, dissolve 1–2 beef bouillon cubes in the hot liquid.*

PER TABLESPOON (Pan Gravy): 7 C   0.1 g P   0.4 g F   0.7 g CARB   0 mg S   1.3 mg CH

PER TABLESPOON (Chicken or Turkey Gravy): 6 C   0.3 g P   0.1 g F   0.9 g CARB   62.8 mg S   0 mg CH

AU JUS GRAVY: Prepare low-calorie variation of Pan Gravy as directed, but omit flour paste; microwave on HIGH (100% power) until mixture boils, then microwave, uncovered, on MEDIUM-LOW (30% power) 2 minutes to mellow. Color, if you like, with gravy browner and season to taste with dry red wine, salt, and pepper.

PER TABLESPOON: 4 C   0 g P   0.4 g F   0 g CARB   0 mg S   0.3 mg CH

WHITE CLAM SAUCE

PREP TIME: | 1 MINUTE | COOKING TIME: | 10-12 MINUTES | STANDING TIME: | NONE

MAKES ABOUT 3 CUPS, ENOUGH TO DRESS 1½ POUNDS LINGUINE, OR 6 SERVINGS

2   **cloves garlic, peeled and minced**

¼   **cup olive or vegetable oil**

2   **tablespoons flour**

2   **cups clam juice (use liquid drained from clams, rounding out measure as needed with bottled clam juice)**

1½ **cups finely chopped raw clams or 3 cans (6½ ounces each) minced clams, drained (reserve liquid)**

1   **tablespoon minced parsley**

⅛   **teaspoon pepper**

1   **tablespoon unsalted butter or margarine, cut into small pieces**

Microwave garlic in oil in uncovered 2-quart casserole on HIGH (100% power) 1¾–2 minutes, until golden. Blend in flour and microwave, uncovered, on HIGH (100% power) 30 seconds, until foamy. Gradually mix in clam juice and microwave, uncovered, on HIGH (100% power) 4½–5½ minutes, whisking well at halftime, until sauce boils, is smooth, and lightly thickened. Add all remaining ingredients except butter, cover with wax paper, and microwave on MEDIUM-LOW (30% power) 3½–4 minutes, stirring at halftime, to develop flavors. Stir in butter and serve over hot pasta, sprinkling, if you like, with additional parsley.

PER CUP: 303 C 16 g P 23 g 8 g CARB 409 mg S 49 mg CH

LEMON SAUCE

MAKES 2 CUPS

- 1 **cup milk**
- 1 **cup chicken broth, Fish Stock, or All-Purpose Stock**
- ¼ **cup (½ stick) butter or margarine**
- ¼ **teaspoon finely grated lemon rind**
- 2 **tablespoons cornstarch blended with 2 tablespoons cold water**
- 1 **egg yolk, lightly beaten**
- 2 **tablespoons lemon juice**
- ½ **teaspoon salt, or to taste**

Pinch white pepper

- 1 **teaspoon minced parsley (optional)**

Microwave milk, broth, butter, and lemon rind in wax-paper-covered 2-quart casserole on HIGH (100% power) 4–5 minutes, until almost boiling. Whisk in cornstarch mixture and microwave, uncovered, on HIGH (100% power) 3–4 minutes, whisking after 2 minutes, until sauce boils and thickens. *Note: Watch sauce carefully toward end of cooking to avoid boilover.* Blend a little hot sauce into egg yolk, stir back into casserole, and microwave, uncovered, on MEDIUM-LOW (30% power) 1 minute (do not boil or sauce may curdle). Mix in lemon juice, salt, pepper, and, if desired, parsley. Serve hot with Pâté di Mare, poached chicken breasts, or fish fillets. Or serve with boiled or steamed asparagus, carrots, broccoli, cauliflower, Brussels sprouts, or green beans.

PER TABLESPOON: 22 C   0.4 g P   1.9 g F   0.9 g CARB   84.4 mg S   13.5 mg CH

HOLLANDAISE SAUCE

PREP TIME: [2 MINUTES]   COOKING TIME: [3¼–4½ MINUTES]   STANDING TIME: [NONE]

Hollandaise is less apt to curdle if you microwave it on MEDIUM-LOW (30% power) once it begins to thicken. If, despite every precaution, your Hollandaise does curdle, all is not lost (see To Salvage Curdled Hollandaise below).

MAKES 1⅓ CUPS

4   **egg yolks**
1   **tablespoon cold water**
½   **cup (1 stick) butter (no substitute)**
2   **tablespoons lemon juice**
¼   **teaspoon salt**
Pinch white pepper

Beat egg yolks until color and consistency of mayonnaise, then mix in water. Microwave butter in wax-paper-covered 1-quart casserole on HIGH (100% power) 1–1½ minutes until just melted, *not hot.* Whisking briskly, add butter to yolks in slow, steady stream. Return to casserole and microwave, uncovered, on MEDIUM (50% power) 1¼–1½ minutes, whisking vigorously every 30 seconds, until mixture *begins* to thicken at edge of casserole (it will resemble soft custard). Reduce power to MEDIUM-LOW (30% power) and microwave, uncovered, 1–1½ minutes in 30-second increments, beating after each, *just* until sauce thickens enough to coat a metal spoon. Remove sauce from oven the *instant* it thickens, beat well, mix in lemon juice, salt, and pepper, and pour at once into cold sauceboat to prevent further cooking. Stir again and serve warm, not hot, with vegetables or seafood.

PER TABLESPOON: 51 C   0.6 g P   5.4 g F   0.1 g CARB
72.2 mg S   63.7 mg CH

To Salvage Curdled Hollandaise: Add 2 tablespoons boiling water to sauce and beat briskly until smooth. Or set in an ice bath and whisk until smooth, then warm gently by microwaving, uncovered, on MEDIUM-LOW (30% power) about 2 minutes in 30-second increments, beating after

160

each, *just* until sauce reaches serving temperature.

To Make Hollandaise Ahead: Prepare sauce as directed, pour into 1-pint microwave-safe serving bowl, place wax paper flat on sauce to prevent skin from forming, and refrigerate. About 3 minutes before serving, microwave sauce, uncovered, on MEDIUM-LOW (30% power) 2–3 minutes, stirring every 30 seconds, until warm, not hot. If sauce seems thick, whisk in 1–2 tablespoons hot water.

VARIATIONS

BÉARNAISE SAUCE (1⅓ cups): Place ¼ cup each dry white wine and white wine vinegar, 1 tablespoon each minced fresh tarragon and chervil (or 1 teaspoon each dried), 1 tablespoon minced shallots or scallions, ⅛ teaspoon salt, and a pinch white pepper in 1-pint shallow casserole. Microwave, uncovered, on HIGH (100% power) 5–6 minutes, until liquid reduces to 2 tablespoons. *Note: Check frequently as mixture boils rapidly.* Wipe condensation from oven before proceeding. Strain liquid and cool to room temperature, then prepare Hollandaise as directed, substituting reduced liquid for lemon juice. Just before serving, mix in ½ teaspoon each minced fresh tarragon and chervil and a pinch ground hot red pepper. Superb with grilled steaks, chops, salmon, swordfish, and tuna. *Note: For Cilantro Béarnaise: Substitute freshly chopped fresh coriander (cilantro) for tarragon and chervil.*
PER TABLESPOON: 52 C   0.6 g P   5.4 g F   0.3 g CARB   85.6 mg S   63.7 mg CH

MUSTARD HOLLANDAISE (1⅓ cups): Prepare Hollandaise as directed, but blend 1–2 teaspoons Dijon mustard with lemon juice before adding to sauce. Superb with steamed green vegetables, also steamed, poached, or grilled fish.
PER TABLESPOON: 51 C   0.6 g P   5.4 g F   0.1 g CARB   82.9 mg S   63.7 mg CH

FIGARO SAUCE (1⅔ cups): Prepare Hollandaise as directed, but blend in ⅓ cup lukewarm tomato purée and 1 teaspoon minced parsley along with lemon juice. Especially good over broiled salmon, swordfish, or tuna.
PER TABLESPOON: 43 C   0.5 g P   4.4 g F   0.4 g CARB   80 mg S   51.4 mg CH

CHANTILLY SAUCE (2 cups): Prepare Hollandaise as directed, then fold in ½ cup heavy cream, beaten to soft peaks, and additional salt and pepper as needed. Serve with fish, shellfish, green vegetables, carrots, or cauliflower.
PER TABLESPOON: 46 C   0.4 g P   4.9 g F   0.2 g CARB   48.8 mg S   46.9 mg CH

161

COOKED SALAD DRESSING

PREP TIME: | 2 MINUTES | COOKING TIME: | 4¼–5 MINUTES | STANDING TIME: | NONE |

Old-fashioned dressings contain three times as many egg yolks as this one, meaning they're loaded with cholesterol. This dressing can also be made with water instead of milk— good news for those allergic to lactose.

MAKES 1¼ CUPS

2 **tablespoons flour**

2 **tablespoons sugar**

1 **teaspoon dry mustard**

½ **teaspoon salt**

Pinch ground hot red pepper

½ **cup milk combined with ¼ cup cold water or ¾ cup cold water**

2 **egg yolks, lightly beaten**

¼ **cup lemon juice or white wine vinegar**

2 **tablespoons vegetable oil**

1 **teaspoon celery seeds (optional)**

Combine flour, sugar, mustard, salt, pepper, and milk mixture in 6-cup measure and microwave, uncovered, on HIGH (100% power) 2½–3 minutes, whisking well at halftime, until mixture boils and thickens. Combine egg yolks and lemon juice, blend in ¼ cup hot mixture, then stir back into measure. Microwave, uncovered, on MEDIUM-LOW (30% power) 1¾–2 minutes, whisking at halftime, until no raw egg taste remains—do not allow to boil or dressing may curdle. Whisk dressing well, then beat in oil, 1 tablespoon at a time. Mix in celery seeds, if you like. Place wax paper flat on dressing, cool to room temperature, then store tightly covered in refrigerator. Stir well before using. If dressing seems thick, thin with 1–2 tablespoons water or milk.

PER TABLESPOON: 31 C 0.6 g P 2 g F 2.3 g CARB 59 mg S 28 mg CH

V A R I A T I O N

FRUIT SALAD DRESSING (1¼ cups): Prepare as directed, but substitute 1 tablespoon cornstarch for flour and ½ cup orange juice and ¼ cup pineapple juice for milk mixture. Also reduce lemon juice to 2 tablespoons and add ¼ teaspoon bruised caraway seeds in place of celery seeds. If you like, fold ½ cup heavy cream, whipped to soft peaks, into cooled dressing. Use to dress any fruit salad.
PER TABLESPOON: 30 C 0.3 g P 1.9 g F 2.8 g CARB 55.9 mg S 27.2 mg CH

FRENCH MAYONNAISE

Serve warm with hot meat, poultry, fish, and green vegetables.

MAKES 1⅓ CUPS

- **1 cup mayonnaise**
- **⅓ cup French dressing**
- **1 teaspoon finely grated yellow onion**
- **½ clove garlic, peeled and crushed**

Combine all ingredients in 1-quart measure and microwave, uncovered, on MEDIUM-LOW (30% power) 3½–4½ minutes, stirring every 2 minutes, until warm—*do not boil or the sauce may curdle.*

PER TABLESPOON: 92 C 0.1 g P 9.9 g F 1 g CARB 113.4 mg S 6.2 mg CH

VARIATIONS

HOT MUSTARD MAYONNAISE (1¼ cups): Blend 1 cup mayonnaise with ¼ cup milk, 3 tablespoons Dijon mustard, and 1 tablespoon cider vinegar. Microwave as directed and serve with ham, tongue, boiled beef, or hot green vegetables.

PER TABLESPOON: 84 C 0.2 g P 8.9 g F 0.8 g CARB 131.5 mg S 6.9 mg CH

WARM AIOLI SAUCE (1 cup): Blend 1 cup mayonnaise with 4 crushed garlic cloves and pinch each sugar and ground hot red pepper. Microwave as directed, serve with seafood (especially seafood stews), poultry, and vegetables.

PER TABLESPOON: 100 C 0.2 g P 10.9 g F 0.6 g CARB 78.3 mg S 8.1 mg CH

WARM RÉMOULADE SAUCE (1¼ cups): Blend 1 cup mayonnaise with 1 tablespoon each minced capers and gherkins, 1½ teaspoons each anchovy paste and Dijon mustard, and 1 teaspoon each minced parsley and fresh chervil. Microwave as directed; serve with steamed fish, shellfish, or warm vegetable salads.

PER TABLESPOON: 81 C 0.2 g P 8.8 g F 0.6 g CARB 101.2 mg S 6.7 mg CH

HORSERADISH–SOUR CREAM SAUCE

PREP TIME: | 1 MINUTE | COOKING TIME: | 3½–4½ MINUTES | STANDING TIME: | NONE

Warm sour cream sauces (not to mention their low-calorie yogurt counterparts) quickly jazz up everything from poultry to baked potatoes. Try this one with boiled meats or beets or almost any steamed fish.

MAKES 1¼ CUPS

1 cup sour cream or plain low-fat yogurt

2 tablespoons prepared horseradish

2 tablespoons cider vinegar

Blend all ingredients in 1-pint casserole, cover with wax paper, and microwave on MEDIUM-LOW (30% power) 3½–4½ minutes, stirring every minute, until warm, not boiling. *Note: Mixture heats quickly toward end so watch carefully; it must not boil, even at the edges, or sauce will thin.*

PER TABLESPOON (with sour cream):
25 C 0.4 g P 2.4 g F 0.7 g CARB 7.5 mg S 5 mg CH

PER TABLESPOON (with yogurt):
8 C 0.6 g P 0.2 g F 1 g CARB 9.4 mg S 0.7 mg CH

V A R I A T I O N S

ANCHOVY–SOUR CREAM SAUCE (1¼ cups): Blend 1 cup sour cream with 3 tablespoons each milk and anchovy paste and 1 tablespoon lemon juice, then microwave as directed. Serve with broiled, poached, or steamed fish.

PER TABLESPOON (with sour cream):
30 C 1 g P 2.7 g F 0.6 g CARB 73.4 mg S 6.4 mg CH

PER TABLESPOON (with yogurt):
13 C 1.2 g P 0.4 g F 0.9 g CARB 75.2 mg S 2 mg CH

MUSTARD–SOUR CREAM SAUCE (1 cup): Blend 1 cup sour cream with 2–3 tablespoons any prepared mustard and 1 tablespoon cider vinegar, then microwave as directed. Serve with beef, ham, pork, green beans, Brussels sprouts, carrots, or boiled, peeled new potatoes.

PER TABLESPOON (with sour cream):
33 C   0.6 g P   3.1 g F   0.8 g CARB   38.2 mg S   6.3 mg CH

PER TABLESPOON (with yogurt):
11 C   0.9 g P   0.3 g F   1.2 g CARB   40.5 mg S   0.9 mg CH

BLUE CHEESE–SOUR CREAM SAUCE (2 cups): Soften 1 package (3 ounces) cream cheese by microwaving, uncovered, in 1-quart casserole on MEDIUM (50% power) 50–60 seconds. Blend in 1 cup sour cream, ½ cup crumbled blue cheese, and 3 tablespoons milk. Microwave as recipe directs, increasing overall time by 30 seconds, or until sauce is warm, *not boiling*. Serve with green vegetables or as a topper for burgers or baked potatoes.

PER TABLESPOON (with sour cream):
33 C 0.9 g P 3.1 g F 0.5 g CARB 41.8 mg S 7.9 mg CH

PER TABLESPOON (with yogurt):
22 C 1.1 g P 1.7 g F 0.7 g CARB 43 mg S 5 mg CH

CHIVE SOUR CREAM SAUCE: Blend 1 cup sour cream with 3–4 tablespoons minced chives and 1 small crushed clove garlic and microwave as directed. Serve with baked potatoes, carrots, or seafood.

PER TABLESPOON: 25.4 C   0.4 g P   2.4 g F   0.7 g CARB   7.5 mg S   5.1 mg CH

CURRY SOUR CREAM SAUCE (Makes 1 cup): Blend 1 cup sour cream with 1 tablespoon finely grated onion and 1 teaspoon curry powder, then microwave as directed. Serve with broiled chicken breasts or lamb chops.

PER TABLESPOON: 25.4 C   0.4 g P   2.4 g F   0.7 g CARB   7.5 mg S   5.1 mg CH

DILL SOUR CREAM SAUCE: Blend 1 cup sour cream with 2 tablespoons each minced fresh dill and parsley and microwave as directed. Serve with seafood.

PER TABLESPOON: 25.4 C   0.4 g P   2.4 g F   0.7 g CARB   7.5 mg S   5.1 mg CH

JIFFY TOMATO SAUCE

PREP TIME: [1 MINUTE] COOKING TIME: [17½–20 MINUTES] STANDING TIME: [NONE]

This easy sauce is just the ticket for spaghetti. Preparing it in a large casserole and covering with wax paper keeps the sauce from spattering the microwave oven. If fresh tomatoes are in season, try Fresh Tomato Sauce.

MAKES ABOUT 1 QUART

2	**cloves garlic, peeled and minced**
¼	**cup olive oil**
1	**can (1 pound, 13 ounces) tomato purée**
½	**cup hot water**
1–1½	**teaspoons salt**
1	**teaspoon sugar**
1	**teaspoon crumbled dried basil**
1	**teaspoon crumbled dried oregano**
⅛	**teaspoon red pepper flakes**

Microwave garlic in oil in uncovered 2-quart casserole on HIGH (100% power) 1¾–2 minutes, until golden. Add remaining ingredients, cover with wax paper, and microwave on HIGH (100% power) 7–8 minutes, stirring at halftime, until bubbly. Stir again, re-cover and microwave on MEDIUM (50% power) 9–10 minutes, stirring at halftime, until flavors mellow. Adjust salt as needed and serve.

PER CUP: 212 C   4 g P   14 g F   23 g CARB   1506 mg S   0 mg CH

VARIATIONS

MUSHROOM-TOMATO SAUCE (5 cups): Microwave 2 cups coarsely chopped or thinly sliced mushrooms with oil and garlic in paper-toweling-covered casserole on HIGH (100% power) 3½–4 minutes, stirring at halftime, until mushrooms are limp. Add remaining ingredients and proceed as recipe directs.

PER CUP: 177 C   4 g P   11 g F   19 g CARB   1206 mg S   0 mg CH

BOLOGNESE TOMATO SAUCE (with meat) (5 cups): Spread ½ pound lean ground beef evenly in casserole, add 1 tablespoon olive oil, the garlic, and ¼ cup minced yellow onion, and microwave, uncovered, on HIGH (100% power) 2¾–3 minutes, stirring after 2 minutes to break up beef, until no trace of pink remains. Add remaining ingredients and proceed as recipe directs.

PER CUP: 316 C   11 g P   23 g F   19 g CARB   1236 mg S   34 mg CH

166

¢ BEEF AND SAUSAGE SAUCE (5 cups): Prepare as directed for Bolognese Tomato Sauce, using ¼ pound each lean ground beef and sweet or hot Italian sausage, removed from its casings.

PER CUP: 335 C   10 g P   26 g F   19 g CARB   1386 mg S   34 mg CH

RED CLAM SAUCE (6 cups): Prepare Jiffy Tomato Sauce as directed, substituting liquid drained from 2 cans (6½ ounces each) minced clams for water. Microwave until sauce bubbles, add clams, then proceed as recipe directs.

PER CUP: 173 C   7 g P   10 g F   17 g CARB   1354 mg S   20 mg CH

*F*RESH *T*OMATO *S*AUCE

PREP TIME: **10 MINUTES**   COOKING TIME: **22–30 MINUTES**   STANDING TIME: **NONE**

Overall cooking time will vary according to the type of tomatoes you use—meaty ones may take as long as 30 minutes to cook down to the proper consistency. Use potholders—casserole will be blisteringly hot.

MAKES ABOUT 3 CUPS

¼	*cup olive oil*
2	*cloves garlic, peeled and minced*
1	*small yellow onion, peeled and minced*
3	*pounds fully ripe tomatoes, peeled, cored, seeded, and coarsely chopped*
1–1½	*teaspoons salt*
1	*teaspoon sugar*
1	*tablespoon minced fresh basil or 1 teaspoon crumbled dried basil*
1	*tablespoon minced fresh oregano or 1 teaspoon crumbled dried oregano*
⅛	*teaspoon red pepper flakes*

Combine oil, garlic, and onion in 4- or 5-quart casserole and microwave, uncovered, on HIGH (100% power) 1¾–2 minutes, until glassy. Add remaining ingredients and microwave, uncovered, on HIGH (100% power) 18–25 minutes, stirring every 7–8 minutes, until sauce is very thick. Taste for salt and adjust as needed. *Note: If you prefer smooth sauce, cook 10 minutes, then purée. Return sauce to casserole, cover with wax paper, and microwave on MEDIUM (50% power) 2–3 minutes until bubbly.*

PER CUP: 254 C   4 g P   19 g F   22 g CARB   948 mg S   0 mg CH

167

ALL-PURPOSE BARBECUE SAUCE

PREP TIME: | 3 MINUTES | COOKING TIME: | 8–9½ MINUTES | STANDING TIME: | NONE

A good sauce to have on hand whether you're barbecuing meats in the microwave, conventional oven, or on an outdoor grill. The Cajun variation is plenty hot, but you can reduce the amount of red pepper to suit your taste.

MAKES 1¾ CUPS

- **1 small yellow onion, peeled and minced**
- **1 clove garlic, peeled and minced**
- **1 tablespoon vegetable oil**
- **¾ cup ketchup**
- **¼ cup cider vinegar**
- **⅓ cup hot water**
- **¼ cup light corn syrup**
- **1 tablespoon prepared mild yellow mustard**
- **2 tablespoons bottled steak sauce or Worcestershire sauce**
- **1 teaspoon salt**
- **¼ teaspoon pepper**
- **¼ teaspoon chili powder**

Microwave onion and garlic in oil in uncovered 6-cup measure on HIGH (100% power) 3–3½ minutes, until very soft. Mix in all remaining ingredients, cover with vented plastic food wrap, and microwave on HIGH (100% power) 1½–2 minutes, until bubbling. Stir, re-cover and microwave on MEDIUM (50% power) 3½–4 minutes, stirring at halftime, until flavors mellow. *Note: Stored tightly covered in refrigerator, sauce will keep about 3 weeks.*

PER TABLESPOON: 23 C   0.1 g P   0.5 g F   4.4 g CARB   184.6 mg S   0 mg CH

VARIATIONS

CAJUN HOT BARBECUE SAUCE: Add ½ minced sweet green pepper to onion-garlic-oil mixture and microwave as directed. Add all remaining ingredients, substituting red wine vinegar for cider vinegar and ¼ cup firmly packed dark brown sugar for corn syrup. Also reduce chili powder to ⅛ teaspoon and add ⅛ teaspoon each ground hot red pepper, paprika, and liquid hot red pepper seasoning. Proceed as recipe directs.

PER TABLESPOON: 22 C   0.2 g P   0.5 g F   4.3 g CARB   182.7 mg S   0 mg CH

CALIFORNIA GINGER-BARBECUE SAUCE: Add 1 tablespoon crushed fresh ginger to onion-garlic-oil mixture and microwave as directed. Add remaining ingredients, substituting ¼ cup frozen orange juice concentrate for vinegar, honey for light corn syrup, and omitting chili powder. Proceed as recipe directs.

PER TABLESPOON: 27.3 C   0.1 g P   0.5 g F   5.4 g CARB   184.6 mg S   0 mg CH

KEYS BARBECUE SAUCE: Add ½ minced sweet red pepper to onion-garlic-oil mixture and microwave as directed. Stir in remaining ingredients, substituting light brown sugar for corn syrup, increasing chili powder to ½ teaspoon, and adding ¼ cup lime or lemon marmalade. Proceed as recipe directs. This barbecue sauce is superb on grilled red snapper, pompano, tuna, swordfish and salmon.

PER TABLESPOON: 26 C   0.1 g P   0.5 g F   5 g CARB   184.6 mg S   0 mg CH

CHINESE BARBECUE SAUCE

PREP TIME: | 4 MINUTES | COOKING TIME: | 3–4 MINUTES | STANDING TIME: | NONE

Make this sauce ahead of time and store in the refrigerator (if tightly covered, it will keep one to two weeks). Use to baste poultry, spareribs, pork loin, lamb shanks or chops, beef kebabs, shrimp, salmon, swordfish, tuna, or bluefish.

MAKES 1 CUP

1⅓ *cups firmly packed dark brown sugar*

¼ *cup soy sauce*

¼ *cup cider vinegar*

2 *cloves garlic, peeled and minced very fine*

2 *cubes (½" each) fresh ginger, peeled and minced very fine*

Combine all ingredients in 1-quart measure, cover with wax paper, and microwave on MEDIUM (50% power) 3–4 minutes, stirring at halftime, until gently bubbly. Cool before using.

PER TABLESPOON: 72 C   0.3 g P   0 g F   18.4 g CARB   262.8 mg S   0 mg CH

169

SWEET RED PEPPER SAUCE

PREP TIME: 5 MINUTES   COOKING TIME: 11–13½ MINUTES   STANDING TIME: NONE

This unusual sauce is superb on poached chicken breasts or white fish fillets.

MAKES 1¼ CUPS

- 2 **large sweet red peppers, cored and seeded**
- 1 **large clove garlic (do not peel)**
- 1 **tablespoon butter or margarine**
- 1 **small carrot, peeled and minced**
- 2 **tablespoons minced shallots or scallions**
- 1 **tablespoon minced fresh tarragon or 1 teaspoon crumbled dried tarragon**
- 1 **tablespoon minced parsley**
- ½ **cup dry white wine**
- ½ **teaspoon salt**
- ⅛ **teaspoon white pepper**
- ⅓ **cup sour cream**

Microwave peppers and garlic in tightly closed plastic bag on HIGH (100% power) 5–6 minutes, rotating bag 180° and turning it over at halftime, until peppers are soft. Cool peppers under cold running water, peel, seed, and pat dry. Squeeze garlic from skin into food processor, add peppers, and churn 1 minute. Place butter, carrot, shallots, tarragon, parsley, wine, salt, and pepper in 1-quart casserole, cover with vented plastic food wrap, and microwave on HIGH (100% power) 4½–5½ minutes, stirring at halftime, until carrots are tender. Strain liquid, pressing vegetables lightly to extract more flavor, then mix ⅓ cup liquid with pepper purée and sour cream. Transfer sauce to 1-quart measure, cover with wax paper, and microwave on MEDIUM (50% power) 1½–2 minutes until warm, not boiling.

PER TABLESPOON: 19 C   0.3 g P   1.4 g F   1.3 g CARB   64.4 mg S   3.2 mg CH

Pineapple sweet-sour sauce

PREP TIME:	COOKING TIME:	STANDING TIME:
3 MINUTES	7½–8 MINUTES	NONE

Serve warm with roast pork, baked ham, braised spareribs, broiled shrimp or chicken. This sauce is also delicious with meat loaf or used as a dipping sauce for bite-size meatballs, cocktail sausages, or broiled chicken wings.

MAKES 2½ CUPS

- 1 **cup pineapple juice (including pineapple can liquid below)**
- ½ **cup pineapple jam**
- ¼ **cup firmly packed light brown sugar**
- ¼ **cup cider vinegar**
- 1 **tablespoon soy sauce**
- ½ **clove garlic, peeled and crushed**
- ¼ **teaspoon prepared spicy brown mustard**
- ⅛ **teaspoon ground ginger**
- 2 **tablespoons cornstarch blended with 2 tablespoons cold water**
- 1 **can (8 ounces) crushed pineapple, drained (reserve liquid)**

Mix all but last two ingredients in 6-cup measure and microwave, uncovered, on HIGH (100% power) 4½–5 minutes, stirring at halftime, until boiling. Blend in cornstarch mixture and microwave, uncovered, on HIGH (100% power) 1 minute, stirring at halftime, until mixture boils and thickens. Add pineapple and microwave, uncovered, on MEDIUM-LOW (30% power) 2 minutes, until flavors mellow.

PER TABLESPOON: 24 C   0.1 g P   0 g F   6 g CARB   27 mg S 0 mg CH

V A R I A T I O N

PINEAPPLE-ORANGE SWEET-SOUR SAUCE: Prepare as directed, using half-and-half mixture of orange and pineapple juice and substituting orange marmalade for pineapple jam. For a tarter sauce, use lemon marmalade.

PER TABLESPOON: 25 C   0.1 g P   0 g F   6.6 g CARB   27 mg S 0 mg CH

SPICY SULTANA SAUCE

PREP TIME: 3 MINUTES COOKING TIME: 15½–20½ MINUTES STANDING TIME: 5 MINUTES

This glistening raisin sauce is delicious with boiled tongue, baked ham, roast duck or goose, also with any grilled or roasted game or game birds.

MAKES 2½ CUPS

¼ **cup butter, margarine, or vegetable oil**

¼ **cup unsifted flour**

1 **cup beef broth or water**

1 **cup apple cider or juice**

1 **tablespoon red wine vinegar**

2 **tablespoons light brown sugar**

1 **stick cinnamon, broken**

1 **whole nutmeg, cracked**

3 **cloves**

3 **whole allspice**

2 **strips (about 2" × ½" each) orange zest (colored part of rind)**

2 **strips (about 2" × ½" each) lemon zest (colored part of rind)**

⅓ **cup golden seedless raisins**

Salt and pepper to taste

Microwave butter in wax-paper-covered 6-cup measure on HIGH (100% power) 55–65 seconds. Blend in flour and microwave, uncovered, on HIGH (100% power) 7–10 minutes, stirring every 3 minutes, until light brown. *Note: In 600–700-watt ovens, roux will be light brown after 7–8 minutes; for darker sauce, microwave 2–3 minutes longer but watch carefully to prevent over-browning. Mixture will look grainy but will smooth out once liquid is added.* When roux is brown, slowly and carefully whisk in broth and cider (hot roux may sputter). Microwave, uncovered, on HIGH (100% power) 4–4½ minutes, whisking at half time, until sauce thickens and boils. Add all remaining ingredients except raisins, salt and pepper, and microwave, uncovered, on LOW (10% power) 3–4 minutes. Cover and let stand 5 minutes to intensify flavors. Strain, return to measure, add raisins and microwave, uncovered, on MODERATELY HIGH (70% power) for 1 minute until raisins plump and sauce simmers. Season to taste with salt and pepper.

PER TABLESPOON: 24.2 C   0.1 g P   1.2 g F   2.2 g CARB 20.5 mg S   1.4 mg CH

CRANBERRY SAUCE

PREP TIME: | 5 MINUTES | **COOKING TIME:** | 6–7 MINUTES | **STANDING TIME:** | NONE

MAKES 2 CUPS

1 **package (12 ounces) fresh or frozen cranberries, stemmed**

1 **cup sugar**

¼ **cup water**

Mix all ingredients in 2-quart casserole, cover with vented plastic food wrap, and microwave on HIGH (100% power) 6–7 minutes, stirring at halftime, until cranberry skins pop. *Note: Frozen cranberries will take 2–3 minutes longer to cook and should be stirred twice.* Stir again and cool, covered, to room temperature. Stir and serve, or chill before serving.

PER TABLESPOON: 29 C   0 g P   0 g F   7.6 g CARB   0.2 mg S 0 mg CH

VARIATIONS

SPICY CRANBERRY SAUCE: Prepare as directed, but mix ¼ teaspoon each ground cinnamon, ginger, and cloves with sugar.

PER TABLESPOON: 29 C   0 g P   0 g F   7.6 g CARB   0.2 mg S 0 mg CH

ORANGE-CRANBERRY SAUCE: Prepare as directed, substituting firmly packed light brown sugar for granulated sugar, orange juice for water, and adding finely grated rind of 1 orange.

PER TABLESPOON: 32 C   0 g P   0 g F   8.2 g CARB   2.2 mg S 0 mg CH

6

APPETIZERS, SNACKS, AND SANDWICHES

*H*ere's where a microwave truly excels as many savvy hostesses have already discovered. Nothing beats it for keeping the hot hors d'oeuvre coming at an open house or cocktail party (it's a snap to prepare a variety of hors d'oeuvre in advance, then heat them in batches as the party progresses). The microwave can crispen crackers, melbas, and chips in minutes, "ripen" cheeses, temper dips and spreads to the perfect dipping or spreading consistency. As for snacks and sandwiches, they can be prepared well ahead of time, refrigerated until needed, then heated in a jiffy. Nothing could be quicker. Nothing could be easier.

SOME GENERAL TIPS

When cooking for a crowd, warm hors d'oeuvre in small batches, which will microwave to serving temperature in almost no time at all. Larger quantities will require a disproportionately longer time to heat, so if you're feeding an army, it's more efficient to warm appetizers in a conventional oven.

Whenever possible, cook or heat hors d'oeuvre in the containers in which you'll serve them (paper plates and bowls can go straight from microwave to patio or pool, then be pitched out at party's end; no dishwashing needed).

When microwaving commercially frozen or packaged appetizers and snacks, follow the microwave directions on the label for best results. For more information on defrosting and heating precooked appetizers, snacks, and sandwiches, see About Defrosting and Reheating Food by Microwave in Chapter 4.

SOME MICROWAVING SPECIFICS

TO CRISP LIMP CRACKERS AND MELBAS: Arrange 25–30 crackers or melbas in a single layer on a baking sheet or platter, then microwave, uncovered, on HIGH (100% power) 30 seconds, until warm. Cool and serve at once or store airtight.

TO CRISP PRETZELS; POTATO, CORN, AND TORTILLA CHIPS; AND POPCORN: Line a basket or colander with paper toweling, add 2–3 cups snacks, and microwave, uncovered, on HIGH (100% power) 30–60 seconds, tossing snacks once or twice, until warm. Cool and serve at once or store airtight. *Note: The technique for refreshing breakfast cereals is just the same.*

TO SOFTEN CREAM CHEESE: Unwrap, place on a plate or pie plate, and microwave, uncovered, on HIGH (100% power) allowing 1–1½ minutes for 8 ounces, 30–45 seconds for 3 ounces and rotating plate 180° at halftime. *Note: Cream cheese holds its shape as it softens, so test after minimum microwaving time.*

TO TEMPER REFRIGERATOR-COLD CHEESES (FIRM AND SEMISOFT): Cheeses are not only easier to slice and spread at room temperature but a little warmth also intensifies and balances their flavors. The microwave brings cheese to room temperature in seconds. Unwrap cheese, place on a serving dish, then microwave, uncovered, on MEDIUM (50% power) allowing 50–60 seconds for ½ pound and 1¼–1½ minutes for 1 pound, until just slightly warm; at halftime turn cheese over and rotate platter 180°. Let cheese stand 5 minutes before serving.

TO ''RIPEN'' SOFT CHEESES: If the Brie, chèvre, or Camembert you've bought is disappointingly firm, a microwave can perform the miracle of ripening. Unwrap cheese, place ½ pound of it on a serving dish, then microwave, uncovered, on MEDIUM (50% power) 1 minute, rotating platter 180° at halftime, until center begins to soften. Let cheese stand 2 minutes before serving.

SOME TIPS FOR MICROWAVING DIPS AND SPREADS

Note: If your microwave oven has a temperature probe, you'll find it especially helpful in warming dips and spreads to the proper serving temperature (it can even be set to keep dips and spreads warm if guests are late). Simply insert the probe's tip in the middle of the dip or spread, then gather plastic food wrap loosely around the probe to allow venting, or cover the dip or spread with wax paper, allowing about 1" overhang, and insert the probe by piercing the paper. What serving temperatures are best? It varies according to the dip, but you won't go wrong setting the temperature probe at 90° F. for sour cream dips (no chance of their curdling) and 140°–150° F. for dips or spreads containing seafood, meat, or cheese.

HOT SOUR CREAM DIPS: Place in a bowl, cover with vented plastic food wrap, and microwave on LOW (10% power) 3½–4 minutes per cup (8 ounces) of dip, stirring at halftime, until the consistency of mayonnaise; stir dip again at end of microwaving.

HOT CHEESE DIPS AND SPREADS: Place in a bowl, cover with wax paper, and microwave on MEDIUM (50% power) 2¾–3½ minutes per cup (8 ounces) of dip, stirring dip or rotating bowl 180° at halftime, until a good dipping or spreading consistency; stir dip again at end of microwaving. *Note: If a hot cheese dip or spread should cool and harden during the course of a party, you can soften it exactly the same way; simply reduce the microwave time to about 1½ minutes per cup (8 ounces).* As for commercial cheese dips and spreads, you can soften them directly in their glass jars—with lids removed— by microwaving on MEDIUM (50% power) 1–2 minutes per cup (8 ounces). *Note: Any dips or spreads packed in plastic containers should be transferred to bowls before they go into the microwave oven.*

HOT MEAT OR SEAFOOD DIPS AND SPREADS: Place in a bowl, cover with wax paper, and microwave on MEDIUM (50% power) 3–4 minutes per cup (8 ounces) of dip, stirring dip or rotating bowl 180° at halftime, until a good dipping or spreading consistency; stir dip again at end.

ABOUT MICROWAVING CANAPÉS

Decorative open-face sandwiches, whether made with bread, melba toast, crackers, pastry, or chips, can be heated zip-quick via microwave no matter what the topping—cheese, for example, minced cooked seafood, meat, poultry, or vegetables bound with a savory sauce or mayonnaise. Use these tips as a guide.

TO KEEP BREAD-BASED CANAPÉS FROM GOING LIMP: Toast the bread cutouts before spreading, or brown in butter on top of the stove. For best results, use firm-textured, thinly sliced loaves (baguettes are perfect). When ready to microwave finished canapés, arrange on paper-toweling-lined plates (the toweling will absorb excess moisture). *Note: All crackers, chips, and pastries will remain crisper if microwaved on paper-towel- or napkin-lined plates.*

TO ENSURE EVEN COOKING: Arrange canapés in concentric circles with space in the center—no need to rearrange them at halftime, but *do* rotate plate 180° unless you use a turntable. Heating times will vary according to the canapé topping, but these times can be used as a guide:

SEAFOOD, MEAT, AND POULTRY CANAPÉS: Microwave, uncovered, on HIGH (100% power), allowing 1–1½ minutes for 12 canapés, 1¾–2½ minutes for 24; to complete cooking, let plate of canapés stand 1–2 minutes before serving. *Note: If the topping is mayonnaise-based, microwave canapés on MEDIUM (50% power) and increase heating time by 30 seconds.*

CHEESE CANAPÉS: Microwave, uncovered, on MEDIUM (50% power), allowing 1½–2 minutes for 12 canapés and 2½–3 minutes for 24; remove from oven as soon as cheese *begins* to melt and to complete the cooking, let canapés stand 1–2 minutes before serving. *Note: Using MEDIUM power (rather than HIGH) melts cheese slowly without turning it to rubber; it also allows the canapés nearer the center of the plate to warm before those around the edge overcook.*

Hot Spiced Cranberry Punch (p.116)

Old-Fashion Minestrone (p. 127)

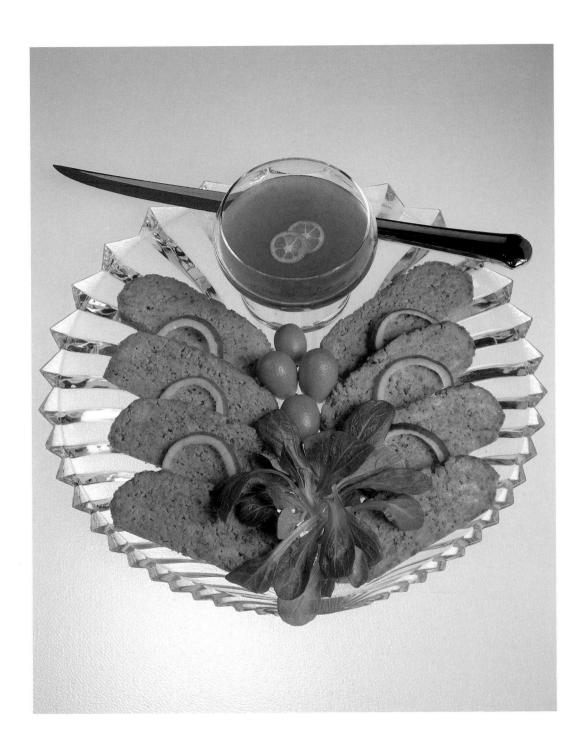

Pineapple-Glazed Ham and Veal Loaf (p.343) with Pineapple Sweet-Sour Sauce (p.171)

Fusilli, Tomato and Roasted Green Peppers with Basil Aioli (p.245)

Hot Turkey, Tomato, and Cheese Monte Carlo (p.204) • *Hot Seafood-Stuffed Avocados (p.398)*
Indonesian Snow Peas and Red Pepper in Peanut Sauce (p.485)

Soufflé Omelet (p.236) filled with sautéed mushrooms on Sweet Red Pepper Sauce (p.170)

Ratatouille (Provençal Eggplant, Zucchini and Tomato Stew) (p.454)

Peach and Ginger Jam (p.266) • *Orange and Lemon Marmalade (p.270)*

Fresh Strawberry Preserves (p.267)

ABOUT MICROWAVING STUFFED VEGETABLES

Hollowed-out tender baby pattypan squash, cherry tomatoes, tiny parboiled new potatoes still in their jackets, or peeled small silverskin onions, not to mention snow pea pods, bite-size zucchini, or cucumber boats can all be stuffed with a variety of savory fillings and heated in the microwave as easily as canapés. The technique is the same, the microwaving times, too (use those given for the different canapés—cheese, for example, meat, fish, or poultry). **Note:** *Any of the mushroom-stuffing recipes included in this chapter can be used to stuff cherry tomatoes or small zucchini or yellow squash "boats." And do try filling snow pea pods with Kedgeree or Crab Norfolk.*

ABOUT MICROWAVING NUTS

The microwave speed-blanches and toasts nuts. Always watch them closely lest they burn; they'll continue browning a bit as they stand.

TO BLANCH ALMONDS, PEANUTS, PISTACHIOS, AND FILBERTS: Heat 1 cup very hot tap water, uncovered, in a 1-quart casserole on HIGH (100% power) 1½–2 minutes until boiling. Add 1 cup shelled, raw, whole nuts and microwave, uncovered, on HIGH (100% power) 1 minute. Drain, cool slightly, then slip off the skins. Dry nuts on paper toweling.

TO TOAST NUTS WITHOUT BUTTER: Spread ½–2 cups (2–8 ounces) blanched or unblanched whole, chopped, or slivered nuts (any kind) in a pie plate and microwave, uncovered, on HIGH (100% power), stirring once or twice, until lightly browned—3–3½ minutes for ½ cup nuts, about 4 minutes for 1 cup, and 5–5½ minutes for 2 cups. Remove from oven and let stand 2–3 minutes.

TO BROWN NUTS IN BUTTER: Melt 1 tablespoon butter or margarine in a pie plate by microwaving, uncovered, on HIGH (100% power) 25–30 seconds. Add ½ cup blanched or unblanched nuts (any kind) and microwave, uncovered, on HIGH (100% power) 3–3½ minutes, stirring once or twice, until *pale* brown. remove from oven and let stand 2–3 minutes.

179

PÂTÉ DE CAMPAGNE _(COUNTRY PÂTÉ)_

PREP TIME: | 10 MINUTES | COOKING TIME: | 26–30 MINUTES | STANDING TIME: | 30 MINUTES

To keep classic pâtés from drying, chefs mix in considerable fat and do the baking in a water bath. This moist, low-fat microwave version needs no messy water bath and effectively trims both calories and cholesterol. It freezes well and if tightly wrapped, will keep for about a week in the refrigerator.

SERVES 12

¼ **pound cooked ham or tongue, cut into ¼" cubes**

2 **tablespoons brandy**

¾ **pound ground lean pork shoulder**

¾ **pound ground veal shoulder**

¼ **pound thickly sliced bacon, cut into 1" pieces**

2 **tablespoons bacon drippings, butter, or margarine**

2 **small white onions, peeled and minced**

2 **shallots, peeled and minced (optional)**

1 **clove garlic, peeled and minced**

¼ **pound chicken livers, halved at the natural separation and pricked well with a fork**

¼ **pound mushrooms, wiped clean and coarsely chopped**

¼ **cup fine dry bread crumbs**

Marinate ham in brandy. Meanwhile, put pork, veal, and bacon through the finest blade of a meat grinder or pulse 6–8 times in food processor. _Note: Bacon will be easier to grind if partially frozen._ Melt drippings in wax-paper-covered 2-quart casserole by microwaving on HIGH (100% power) 40–50 seconds. Add onions, shallots, if desired, and garlic, and microwave, uncovered, on HIGH (100% power) 4 minutes, stirring at halftime. Add chicken livers and mushrooms, re-cover with wax paper, and microwave on ME-DIUM (50% power) 3½–4 minutes, stirring at halftime, until livers are just firm and no longer pink. Remove livers and coarsely chop; mix into ground meats along with mushroom mixture and all remaining ingredients except bay leaves. Gently mix in ham and brandy. Spoon mixture into ungreased 9" × 5" × 3" loaf pan and shape into loaf 1" smaller all around than pan (to keep pâté from looking "steamed"); round ends and smooth top (for even cooking), and lay bay leaves on top. Insert temperature probe in middle of pâté, if you like.

1   **egg, lightly beaten**

1   **teaspoon salt**

¼   **teaspoon pepper**

½   **teaspoon crumbled dried thyme**

¼   **teaspoon rubbed sage**

¼   **teaspoon ground allspice**

2   **large bay leaves (do not crumble)**

Microwave, uncovered, on HIGH (100% power) 18–21 minutes, or until instant-register meat thermometer reads 170° F. when inserted in three different places. As pâté bakes, give pan a quarter-turn every 5 minutes; cover pâté with wax paper after 15 minutes and shield ends with 2"-wide foil strips to prevent overcooking. *Note: If drippings sputter, remove with bulb baster—accumulated fat will make bottom cook faster than top.*

Remove pâté from oven, cover tightly with foil, and let stand 30 minutes. Weight pâté with 1 or 2 heavy cans and refrigerate in pan overnight. To serve: Remove bay leaves, scrape off fat and congealed juices, slice pâté thin, and accompany with black bread or French bread, cornichons, or mustard.

PER SERVING: 212 C   17 g P   14 g F   4 g CARB   472 mg S   117 mg CH

V A R I A T I O N S

TRUFFLED PÂTÉ DE CAMPAGNE: Prepare as directed, spoon half the pâté mixture into pan, arrange 2 or 3 thinly sliced truffles upright in a decorative pattern the length of the pâté, top with remaining pâté mixture and cook as directed.

PER SERVING: 212 C   17 g P   14 g F   4 g CARB   472 mg S   117 mg CH

PÂTÉ IN ASPIC: Prepare, chill, and unmold pâté, scrape off all fat and congealed juices. Make clear aspic by mixing 1 envelope unflavored gelatin with ¼ cup cold water and microwaving, uncovered, on HIGH (100% power) 40–50 seconds until gelatin dissolves. Stir in 3 cups beef broth and pour ⅔ cup gelatin mixture into an 8½" x 4½" x 2⅜" loaf pan and chill until tacky. *Note: If remaining aspic begins to set, liquefy by microwaving, uncovered, on HIGH (100% power) 1–1½ minutes.* Arrange truffle, radish and/or lemon rind cutouts, parsley, or tarragon sprigs in decorative design on aspic, spoon a little warm aspic on top, and chill until tacky. Fit pâté into pan, fill to brim with aspic, and chill until firm. Also chill any remaining aspic. Unmold pâté, chop extra chilled aspic, and wreathe around pâté. Garnish with watercress and radishes.

PER SERVING: 211 C   18 g P   13 g F   4 g CARB   673 mg S   116 mg CH

181

BRANDIED CHICKEN LIVER PÂTÉ

PREP TIME: 4 MINUTES   COOKING TIME: 9–11 MINUTES   STANDING TIME: NONE

The bits of fat and air pockets underneath the outer membrane of chicken livers sometimes make them explode in the microwave oven. You can prevent this by pricking the livers well with a sharp-tined fork and cooking them on MEDIUM (50% power) or even MEDIUM-LOW (30% power) in ovens of 700 watts or more.

MAKES ABOUT 2 CUPS

2 slices bacon, finely diced

3 scallions, minced (white part only)

¾ pound chicken livers, halved at the natural separation and pricked well with a fork

2 tablespoons brandy

2 hard-cooked eggs, peeled and quartered

¼ teaspoon salt (about)

⅛ teaspoon pepper

⅛ teaspoon ground nutmeg

½ cup (1 stick) butter or margarine, softened to room temperature

Microwave bacon in wax-paper-covered 1-quart casserole on HIGH (100% power) 2 minutes, stirring at halftime. Add scallions and chicken livers, re-cover with wax paper, and microwave on MEDIUM (50% power) 7–9 minutes, stirring every 3 minutes, until livers are just firm and no longer pink. *Note: If you must reduce power to MEDIUM-LOW (30% power) to avoid sputtering, you may need to cook livers 1–2 minutes longer.* Cool mixture to room temperature; drain, reserving liquid; churn solids with ¼ cup reserved liquid and all remaining ingredients except butter in food processor 20–30 seconds, until smooth. Add butter and pulse to incorporate; adjust salt as needed. Spoon pâté into 2-cup serving bowl, cross-hatch surface with fork tines, cover, and chill 2–3 hours. Serve with hot buttered toast, melbas, or crackers.

PER TABLESPOON: 52 C   2.5 g P   4.4 g F   0.5 g CARB   68.6 mg S   72.5 mg CH

V A R I A T I O N S

GLAZED BRANDIED CHICKEN LIVER PÂTÉ: Prepare pâté as directed. While pâté chills, mix ¼ cup canned madrilène or beef broth with 1 teaspoon unflavored gelatin in a custard cup and microwave, uncovered, on HIGH (100% power) 30 seconds, until gelatin dissolves. Combine with 1 cup madrilène or beef broth, chill until consistency of unbeaten egg white, then spoon thin layer of gelatin mixture on top of pâté; chill until tacky. Decorate with truffle and pimiento cutouts and parsley or tarragon sprigs, seal in design with remaining aspic, and chill until firm.

PER TABLESPOON: 55 C   2.7 g P   4.4 g F   0.8 g CARB   103 mg S   72.5 mg CH

CHICKEN LIVER PÂTÉ WITH PISTACHIOS: Prepare pâté mixture as directed, adding ⅓ cup minced blanched pistachios. Just before serving, sprinkle pâté with 1 tablespoon minced blanched pistachios. *Note: You can substitute ⅓ cup minced blanched almonds or ¼ cup crisp bacon crumbles for pistachios.*

PER TABLESPOON: 61 C   2.8 g P   5.2 g F   0.8 g CARB   68.7 mg S   72.5 mg CH

PÂTÉ DI MARE (SEAFOOD PÂTÉ)

PREP TIME:
| 5 MINUTES |

COOKING TIME:
| 11½–14 MINUTES |

STANDING TIME:
| 30 MINUTES |

This delicately flavored, feather-light pâté makes an elegant appetizer. Serve it warm or cold.

SERVES 12

½ **pound delicate white fish fillets (cod, haddock, flounder, etc.), cut into 1″ chunks**

½ **pound cooked shrimp, crab meat, or lobster, well picked over for bits of shell or cartilage**

2 **egg whites**

½ **cup mayonnaise**

¼ **cup soft white bread crumbs**

⅔ **cup heavy cream**

½ **teaspoon salt**

Pinch white pepper

Churn fish and shellfish in food processor 15–20 seconds, until very fine. Add egg whites and churn 10 seconds; add all remaining ingredients except gelatin and water and churn 4–5 seconds, just to blend. Mix gelatin and water in custard cup and microwave, uncovered, on HIGH (100% power) 40–50 seconds, until gelatin dissolves. Add to fish mixture and churn 2–3 seconds to blend. Spoon into well-oiled 1½-quart ring mold, smooth surface, and rap lightly on counter to expel air bubbles. Cover with wax paper and microwave on HIGH (100% power) 4 minutes, turning mold 180° after 2 minutes. Reduce power to MEDIUM-LOW (30% power) and microwave, covered, 7–9 minutes, turning mold 90° every 3 minutes, until pâté is almost firm but still slightly

Pinch ground nutmeg or mace

1 envelope unflavored gelatin

¼ cup cold water

<u>*Herb Mayonnaise*</u>

1½ cups mayonnaise

*1½ teaspoons each minced
fresh tarragon, chervil,
chives, and parsley*

moist. Cover with foil and let stand 30 minutes. Chill several hours or overnight. Meanwhile, prepare Herb Mayonnaise by mixing all ingredients; cover and refrigerate until ready to serve.

To Serve Cold: Loosen pâté with spatula and invert on platter. **Note:** *If pâté sticks, dip mold briefly in hot water.* Slice and accompany with Herb Mayonnaise or serve as a spread for crackers.

To Serve Warm: Unmold on platter, cover with wax paper, and microwave on MEDIUM (50% power) 5–6 minutes, until lukewarm, turning platter 180° at halftime. **Note:** *Do not overheat or pâté will "weep" (ooze liquid).* Accompany with warm Lemon Sauce.

PER SERVING: 350 C   9 g P   34 g F   2 g CARB   371 mg S 85 mg CH

~~~~~~~~~ V A R I A T I O N

SALMON AND SCALLOP PÂTÉ: Prepare as directed, substituting ½ pound salmon fillets for white fish and ½ pound uncooked bay or sea scallops for shrimp.

PER SERVING: 360 C   9 g P   35 g F   2 g CARB   357 mg S 57 mg CH

ARTICHOKE AND LIMA BEAN PÂTÉ

PREP TIME: 4 MINUTES **COOKING TIME:** 16–18 MINUTES **STANDING TIME:** 30 MINUTES

A terrific vegetarian spread.

MAKES 3 CUPS

- 1 **package (10 ounces) frozen lima beans**
- ¼ **cup water**
- 2 **tablespoons margarine**
- 3 **scallions, minced (include green tops)**
- 1 **clove garlic, peeled and crushed**
- 1 **can (14 ounces) artichoke hearts, drained**
- ¼ **cup milk**
- 1 **cup soft white bread crumbs**
- 1 **egg, lightly beaten**
- ⅓ **cup finely grated Parmesan cheese**
- 1 **teaspoon salt**
- ¼ **teaspoon pepper**
- ¼ **cup minced fresh parsley or ⅓ cup minced pecans or walnuts**

Cook lima beans in covered 1-quart casserole with water, butter, scallions, and garlic by microwaving on HIGH (100% power) 7–8 minutes, until very tender; stir beans well at halftime. Purée casserole mixture and artichokes in food processor by churning 15–20 seconds. Mix in all remaining ingredients except parsley or nuts and pack into well oiled 1-quart bowl. Cover with wax paper and microwave on MEDIUM (50% power) 9–10 minutes, rotating 180° at halftime, until slightly puffed. *Note: Mixture will still be quite soft but will firm up as it cools.* Let stand, covered, 30 minutes, then carefully unmold, sprinkle with parsley, and serve with crackers. Or, chill pâté several hours, unmold, and roll in chopped nuts before serving.

PER TABLESPOON: 21 C 1 g P 0.9 g F 2.3 g CARB 76.3 mg S 7.8 mg CH

V A R I A T I O N

ARTICHOKE AND CHESTNUT PÂTÉ: Substitute ½ pound shelled, peeled, cooked chestnuts for limas, reduce bread crumbs to ½ cup, then proceed as recipe directs. *Note: Frozen, peeled Italian chestnuts are available in many specialty food shops. To cook: Microwave unthawed nuts on HIGH (100% power) 10–12 minutes until very soft.*

PER TABLESPOON: 20 C 0.8 g P 0.9 g F 2.2 g CARB 71.8 mg S 7.7 mg CH

185

MOZZARELLA MUSHROOM CAPS AL PESTO

PREP TIME: 10 MINUTES COOKING TIME: 7–9½ MINUTES STANDING TIME: NONE

MAKES 1 DOZEN

- 12 medium-size mushrooms (about ½ pound), wiped clean
- 3 tablespoons olive oil
- ¼ cup minced yellow onion
- ¼ cup minced celery
- 1 small clove garlic, peeled and minced
- 1 tablespoon minced fresh basil or 1 teaspoon crumbled dried basil
- ⅓ cup fine dry bread crumbs
- ⅓ cup coarsely grated mozzarella cheese
- ¼ cup minced piñon nuts
- 1 tablespoon milk
- ⅛ teaspoon salt
- ⅛ teaspoon pepper

Carefully remove mushroom stems from caps, chop fine, and place in 1½-quart casserole with olive oil, onion, celery, and garlic. Cover with wax paper and microwave on HIGH (100% power) 3½–4 minutes, stirring at halftime, until onion is glassy. Mix in remaining ingredients and stuff mushroom caps, mounding mixture in center. Arrange caps in 12″ round, shallow serving dish. *Note: If you arrange caps in single ring around edge of dish, they'll cook more evenly—without rearranging.* Microwave, uncovered, on HIGH (100% power) 3½–5½ minutes, turning dish 180° at halftime and rearranging caps if not in single circle, until mushrooms are crisp-tender and stuffing is hot. Serve at once. *Note: You can stuff mushrooms ahead of time, refrigerate, then microwave as directed, increasing cooking time by about 2 minutes.*

PER MUSHROOM: 72 C 2 g P 5.8 g F 3.9 g CARB 58.7 mg S 2.7 mg CH

GENE'S MUSHROOMS CASINO

PREP TIME: [10 MINUTES] COOKING TIME: [7–9½ MINUTES] STANDING TIME: [NONE]

We've taken the recipe of a friend who loves to cook and adapted it for the microwave with superb results.

MAKES 1 DOZEN

- 12 *medium-size mushrooms (about ½ pound), wiped clean*
- 3 *tablespoons butter or margarine*
- ¼ *cup minced yellow onion*
- 1 *tablespoon minced parsley*
- ⅓ *cup fine dry bread crumbs*
- ½ *cup minced clams*
- ¼ *cup crisp bacon crumbles*
- 2 *tablespoons minced pimiento*
- 1 *tablespoon light cream*
- ¼ *teaspoon liquid hot red pepper seasoning*
- ⅛ *teaspoon salt*
- ⅛ *teaspoon pepper*

Carefully remove mushroom stems from caps, chop fine, and place in 1½-quart casserole with butter and onion. Cover with wax paper and microwave on HIGH (100% power) 3½–4 minutes, stirring at halftime, until onion is glassy. Mix in all remaining ingredients and stuff mushroom caps, mounding mixture in center. Arrange caps in 12" round, shallow serving dish. *Note: If you arrange caps in single ring around edge of dish, they'll cook more evenly—without rearranging.* Microwave, uncovered, on HIGH (100% power) 3½–5½ minutes, turning dish 180° at halftime and rearranging caps if they are not in single circle, until mushrooms are crisp-tender and stuffing is hot. Serve at once. *Note: If you like, stuff mushrooms ahead of time, refrigerate, then microwave as directed, increasing cooking time by about 2 minutes.*

PER MUSHROOM: 66 C 2.7 g P 4.6 g F 3.6 g CARB 120 mg S 13.9 mg CH

STUFFED CLAMS

PREP TIME: | 5 MINUTES | COOKING TIME: | 10½–11 MINUTES | STANDING TIME: | NONE

SERVES 4

6 **tablespoons butter or margarine**

1 **small yellow onion, peeled and minced**

1 **small clove garlic, peeled and crushed**

2 **cans (6½ ounces each) minced clams, drained (reserve liquid)**

2 **cups soft white bread crumbs**

1 **tablespoon steak sauce**

1 **tablespoon minced parsley**

1 **tablespoon lemon juice**

¼ **teaspoon salt (about)**

⅛ **teaspoon pepper**

12 **large clam shells or small scallop shells, well buttered**

2 **tablespoons finely grated Parmesan cheese**

Melt butter in a wax-paper-covered 1-quart casserole by microwaving on HIGH (100% power) 55–65 seconds. Measure out and reserve 2 tablespoons melted butter. Add onion and garlic to casserole, re-cover, and microwave on HIGH (100% power) 2½–3 minutes, stirring at halftime, until glassy. Mix in clams, ⅓ cup reserved clam liquid, bread crumbs, and all seasonings; adjust salt as needed and spoon mixture into clam shells. Sprinkle remaining butter over clams and top each with ½ teaspoon Parmesan. Arrange shells 1" apart on large platter, anchoring as needed with wax paper crumples. Cover with paper toweling and microwave on HIGH (100% power) 4 minutes, rotating platter 180° at halftime. Rearrange shells, re-cover, and microwave on MEDIUM (50% power) 3 minutes, until hot. *Note: Cheese will color only slightly. If you prefer bubbly brown tops, transfer shells to baking sheet, anchoring in crumpled foil, and broil 5" from heat of preheated broiler about 1 minute.*

PER SERVING: 310 C 11 g P 23 g F 16 g CARB 1104 mg S 87 mg CH

SHRIMP DIJON

PREP TIME: 5 MINUTES COOKING TIME: 3–5 MINUTES STANDING TIME: 1 MINUTE

SERVES 4–6

1 recipe Steamed Shelled Shrimp (use medium-size shrimp)

⅓ cup heavy cream

⅓ cup mayonnaise

1½ tablespoons prepared horseradish

1 tablespoon Dijon mustard

Pinch ground hot red pepper

Prepare Steamed Shelled Shrimp as recipe directs and drain well. Meanwhile, combine cream, mayonnaise, horseradish, mustard, and pepper. Place shrimp in a large bowl, add cream mixture, and toss well. Cover, cool to room temperature, and serve with toothpicks as an hors d'oeuvre.

PER SERVING: 325–217 C   24–16 g P   24–16 g F
3–2 g CARB   397–264 mg S   210–140 mg CH

SWEDISH MEATBALLS

PREP TIME: 8 MINUTES COOKING TIME: 6–7½ MINUTES STANDING TIME: 30 SECONDS

Hors d'oeuvre meatballs are easier to eat if they have no sauce. If they're to be served from a chafing dish, however, you may want to keep them warm—and moist—in Sour Cream Gravy (with gravy, they're also a snap to reheat).

**MAKES 2½ DOZEN (1")
MEATBALLS**

1 small yellow onion, peeled and minced

1 tablespoon butter, margarine, or vegetable oil

½ pound ground beef chuck

½ pound ground veal shoulder

½ cup fine dry bread crumbs

Microwave onion and butter in a wax-paper-covered 1½-quart casserole on HIGH (100% power) 2½–3 minutes, until glassy. Mix in remaining ingredients and shape into 1" balls. Arrange on roasting rack, cover with wax paper, and microwave on HIGH (100% power) 3½–4½ minutes, rearranging meatballs at halftime, until no longer pink in center. Let stand, uncovered, 30 seconds (standing improves appearance and texture of meatballs because it allows excess

189

1   *egg, lightly beaten*
1   *tablespoon cold water*
1   *teaspoon salt*
⅛   *teaspoon pepper*
Pinch ground nutmeg

moisture to evaporate). Serve warm with mustard or chutney for dipping.

PER MEATBALL: 41 C   3.3 g P   2.4 g F   1.3 g CARB   97.7 mg S   20.3 mg CH

CHILI MEATBALLS: Prepare as directed, substituting 1 pound ground beef for beef-veal mixture and adding 1 tablespoon chili powder and 2 tablespoons chili sauce. Microwave as directed; serve with Mexican salsa for dipping.
PER MEATBALL: 45 C   3.2 g P   2.7 g F   1.7 g CARB   115.8 mg S   19 mg CH

SPICY BEEF BALLS: Prepare as directed, substituting 1 pound ground beef for beef-veal mixture and adding 2 tablespoons each steak sauce and minced parsley. Microwave as directed; serve with spicy mustard or any suitable dipping sauce or gravy.
PER MEATBALL: 44 C   3.1 g P   2.7 g F   1.5 g CARB   116.5 mg S   19 mg CH

MEATBALLS AS AN ENTRÉE (Serves 4): Shape any of the meatball mixtures into 18 balls that are 1½" in diameter. Microwave as directed on HIGH (100% power) 4½–5½ minutes, turning meatballs over and rearranging at halftime, until no longer pink in center. *Note: If your microwave roasting rack is large enough, arrange meatballs in circle around perimeter of rack; they'll cook more evenly and you won't have to rearrange them.*
PER SERVING (Swedish Meatballs): 310 C   25 g P   18 g F   10 g CARB   733 mg S   153 mg CH

*I*TALIAN MEATBALLS

PREP TIME: | 8 MINUTES | COOKING TIME: | 10½–13 MINUTES | STANDING TIME: | 30 SECONDS

Also delicious over spaghetti with hot Jiffy Tomato Sauce or with Fresh Tomato Sauce for dipping.

**MAKES 2½ DOZEN (1")
MEATBALLS**

½   *pound hot or sweet Italian sausage*
½   *pound ground beef chuck*

Remove sausage from casing and cut into 1" chunks; arrange on roasting rack, cover with paper toweling, and microwave on HIGH (100% power) 4½–5½ minutes, rearranging pieces at halftime, until no longer pink. Cool sausage briefly, mince fine, and mix with beef. Microwave

190

1 **small yellow onion, peeled and minced**

1 **clove garlic, peeled and minced**

1 **tablespoon butter, margarine, or vegetable oil**

½ **cup toasted seasoned bread crumbs**

1 **egg, lightly beaten**

2 **tablespoons cold water**

2 **tablespoons finely grated Parmesan cheese**

¾ **teaspoon salt**

⅛ **teaspoon pepper**

onion, garlic, and butter in wax-paper-covered 1½-quart casserole on HIGH (100% power) 2½–3 minutes, until glassy. Mix in meat mixture and all remaining ingredients and shape into 1" balls. Arrange on roasting rack, cover with wax paper, and microwave on HIGH (100% power) 3½–4½ minutes, rearranging meatballs at halftime, until no longer pink in center. Let stand, uncovered, 30 seconds (standing time improves appearance and texture of meatballs by allowing excess moisture to evaporate). Serve hot.

PER MEATBALL: 49C 3.1gP 3.2gF 1.6gCARB 175.8mgS 19.3 mg CH

HUNAN-STYLE CHICKEN WINGS

PREP TIME: | 7 MINUTES | COOKING TIME: | 9½–12 MINUTES | STANDING TIME: | 2 MINUTES

Here are adaptations of two spicy seasoning sauces that we enjoyed recently in Hong Kong, which with its six thousand restaurants, floating sampans, and street stalls, is the ideal place to sample the many cuisines of China. Increase or decrease the amount of chili oil depending upon how "hot" you like things.

MAKES 20

10 **chicken wings (about 1¾ pounds), separated at the joints (save wing tips for soup)**

⅓ **cup hoisin (fermented bean) sauce**

2 **cloves garlic, peeled and crushed**

1 **tablespoon soy sauce**

¼ **cup water**

Arrange chicken wings 1 layer deep in shallow 2-quart casserole; combine remaining ingredients, pour over chicken, cover, and refrigerate 10 hours or overnight, turning chicken in marinade now and then. Drain chicken, reserving marinade, and arrange on 11" or 12" roasting rack with smaller pieces in center. Cover with wax paper and microwave on HIGH (100% power) 9–11 minutes, until tender, turning rack 90° every 3 minutes. At halftime, turn wings over, rearrange, and baste with marinade. When done, cover with foil and let stand 2 minutes.

191

1   **teaspoon sugar**
2   **(½") cubes fresh ginger, peeled and minced**
¼–½ **teaspoon chili oil (Oriental hot pepper oil available in specialty groceries)**

Meanwhile, microwave remaining marinade in 1-cup measure, covered with vented plastic food wrap, on HIGH (100% power) 30–60 seconds; pour over wings or pass separately. *Note: For crisp chicken skin, transfer wings to broiler rack and broil 4" from heat of preheated broiler 3–4 minutes, turning wings over at halftime. Or grill 4" from coals of moderate charcoal fire 3–4 minutes, turning often and basting with marinade.*

PER PIECE: 52 C   4.2 g P   3 g F   1.6 g CARB   198.4 mg S   12.6 mg CH

V A R I A T I O N S

HUNAN-STYLE SPARERIBS (6 appetizer servings): Marinate 2 pounds spareribs, cut into 3" × 1" pieces, as directed for chicken wings. Drain, reserving marinade, arrange ribs 1 layer deep in shallow 3-quart casserole, cover with wax paper, and microwave on HIGH (100% power) 5 minutes. Reduce power to MEDIUM (50%) and microwave 35–45 minutes, until well done. At halftime, remove drippings and rearrange ribs. When ribs are done, cover with foil and let stand 5 minutes. Crisp as directed for chicken wings above.

PER SERVING: 263 C   18 g P   18 g F   5 g CARB   675 mg S   71 mg CH

¢ CANTONESE-STYLE CHICKEN WINGS: In 1-quart measure combine ½ cup firmly packed light brown sugar, ¼ cup ketchup, 3 tablespoons soy sauce, 2 tablespoons each Worcestershire sauce and cider vinegar, 1 teaspoon prepared mustard, and 1 peeled and crushed clove garlic. Microwave, uncovered, on HIGH (100% power) 2 minutes, pour over chicken wings, then marinate and microwave as directed for Hunan-Style Chicken Wings.

PER PIECE: 71 C   4.3 g P   2.9 g F   6.8 g CARB   224 mg S   12.6 mg CH

CANTONESE-STYLE SPARERIBS (6 appetizer servings): Prepare marinade for Cantonese-Style Chicken Wings, pour over 2 pounds spareribs, cut into 3" × 1" pieces; marinate and microwave as directed for Hunan-Style Spareribs.

PER SERVING: 326 C   18 g P   18 g F   23 g CARB   761 mg S   71 mg CH

BARBECUED CHICKEN WINGS: Marinate chicken wings in 1½ cups All-Purpose, Chinese, or Cajun Hot Barbecue Sauce, then microwave as directed.

PER PIECE: 57 C   4.1 g P   3.2 g F   2.6 g CARB   123 mg S   12.6 mg CH

MALAY BEEF OR LAMB SATAY

PREP TIME: **20 MINUTES** COOKING TIME: **8½–10¼ MINUTES** STANDING TIME: **NONE**

Often called the national dish of Malaysia, satay (or *saté*) is popular throughout Indonesia. It may be made with beef, lamb, pork, or poultry—every cook has a pet recipe. Most contain galangal, a pungent root of the ginger family, as well as fresh ginger (we make do with extra ginger). These can also be served as an entrée—just allow 4 to 5 skewers per person. **Note:** *The meat some supermarkets package as "meat for stir-fry" can be used for satay.*

SERVES 6–8

¾ **pound boneless sirloin, top round or leg of lamb, cut into 4" × ¼" × ¼" strips**

Marinade

½ **teaspoon cuminseed, well bruised**

½ **teaspoon aniseed, well bruised**

1 **small red onion, peeled and minced**

1 **clove garlic, peeled and crushed**

1 **tablespoon lemon juice**

2 **tablespoons soy sauce**

¼ **cup Oriental sesame oil (available in better supermarkets and specialty groceries)**

1 **teaspoon sugar**

½ **teaspoon ground coriander**

1 **(½") cube fresh ginger, peeled and minced**

⅛ **teaspoon red pepper flakes**

Place meat in bowl; combine marinade ingredients and knead into meat thoroughly. Cover and chill overnight, turning meat several times in marinade.

Meanwhile, prepare Dipping Sauce: Place onion, garlic, and oil in 1-quart container; cover with wax paper, and microwave on HIGH (100% power) 2½–3 minutes, until onion is glassy. Add remaining sauce ingredients except coconut milk, re-cover, and microwave on MEDIUM (50% power) 2 minutes, stirring at halftime. Beat in coconut milk and refrigerate until ready to proceed.

Loosely weave 3 strips meat on each of 15 (4"–5") bamboo skewers (tightly pleated meat won't cook evenly). Lay skewers across top of shallow 3-quart casserole and microwave, uncovered, on HIGH (100% power) 3–3½ minutes for rare and 3½–4 minutes for medium, turning satays over at halftime and rotating casserole 180°; also rearrange satays, bringing ones on outside toward center and vice versa. Watch satays carefully because they cook fast; some may need to be removed before others are done.

193

Dipping Sauce

- ¼ cup minced red onion
- 1 small clove garlic, peeled and crushed
- 2 tablespoons peanut or Oriental sesame oil
- ⅓ cup peanut butter (creamy or crunchy)
- 1 tablespoon lime or lemon juice
- 1 teaspoon minced fresh ginger
- 1 teaspoon sugar

Pinch red pepper flakes

Pinch ground coriander

- 1 small stem fresh lemongrass, minced, or 2 (2 × ½") strips lemon zest
- 6 tablespoons coconut milk or ¼ cup water plus 2 tablespoons low-fat milk

Note: To cook satays on browning grill, heat ungreased large grill on HIGH (100% power) as manufacturer directs, lay satays directly on hot surface, and microwave, uncovered, on HIGH (100% power) about 3 minutes for rare and 3½ for medium, turning satays over at halftime. Cooking times will vary, so read the chart *Active Microwave Cookware* in Chapter 3. When satays are done, warm dipping sauce by microwaving in wax-paper-covered container on MEDIUM (50% power) 1–1¼ minutes, stirring at halftime.

PER SERVING (Beef Satay):
341–256 C   15–11 g P   30–22 g F   5–4 g CARB   266–200 mg S
36–27 mg CH

PER SERVING (Lamb Satay):
315–237 C   15–11 g P   27–20 g F   5–4 g CARB   266–200 mg S
39–29 mg CH

V A R I A T I O N S

PORK, CHICKEN, OR TURKEY SATAY: Substitute ¾ pound boneless pork loin, chicken or turkey breast, cut into 4" × ¼" × ¼" strips, for beef and marinate as directed; also prepare Dipping Sauce. Weave on skewers and microwave, uncovered, on HIGH (100% power) as directed, allowing 5–5½ minutes for well-done pork and 4½–5 minutes for tender chicken or turkey.

PER SERVING (Pork Satay):
326-244 C   15–11 g P   28–21 g F   5–4 g CARB   266–200 mg S   36–27 mg CH

PER SERVING (Chicken Satay):
266–199 C   18–13 g P   20–15 g F   5–4 g CARB   278–208 mg S   33–25 mg CH

PER SERVING (Turkey Satay):
268–201 C   18–13 g P   20–15 g F   5–4 g CARB   279–209 mg S   35–26 mg CH

TERIYAKI BEEF HORS D'OEUVRE: Marinate beef strips in mixture of ⅓ cup Japanese soy sauce; 2 tablespoons mirin (sweet rice wine), sake, or medium dry sherry; 1 tablespoon sugar; and 2 teaspoons finely grated fresh ginger instead of marinade called for. Marinate, skewer, and microwave as directed for Beef Satay. Serve remaining marinade as a dipping sauce.

PER SERVING: 167–125 C   11–8 g P   10–8 g F   5–4 g CARB   931–698 mg S   36–27 mg CH

Y<small>AKITORI HORS D'OEUVRE</small>: Marinate ¾ pound chicken or turkey breast, cut into 4" × ¼" × ¼" strips, as directed for Teriyaki and weave onto bamboo skewers. Microwave, uncovered, on HIGH (100% power) 4½–5 minutes. Sprinkle, if you like, with Seven Spice Pepper (available in Japanese food shops) and use remaining marinade for dipping. Serve as an hors d'oeuvre or entrée with fluffy boiled rice, allowing about 4 yakitori per person.

PER SERVING (Chicken):

92–69 C	14–10 g P	0.7–0.5 g F	5–4 g CARB	942–707 mg S	33–25 mg CH

PER SERVING (Turkey):

95–71 C	14–10 g P	0.9–0.7 g F	5–4 g CARB	943–708 mg S	35–26 mg CH

R UMAKIS

PREP TIME: 20 MINUTES   COOKING TIME: 6–8½ MINUTES   STANDING TIME: 30 SECONDS

You can prepare these bite-size hors d'oeuvre ahead of time, then do the final microwaving 5 minutes before serving. Although chicken livers usually rupture if microwaved on HIGH, these *can be* because their bacon wrappers insulate them.

MAKES 2 DOZEN

6 **chicken livers (about ½ pound), quartered**

¼ **cup soy sauce**

1 **tablespoon sake or medium dry sherry**

½ **clove garlic, peeled and crushed**

1 **(½") cube fresh ginger, peeled and crushed**

12 **slices bacon (about ½ pound), each halved crosswise**

8 **water chestnuts, each cut into 3 thin slivers**

¼ **cup firmly packed light brown sugar**

Marinate chicken livers in refrigerator in mixture of soy sauce, sake, garlic, and ginger 2 hours. Arrange bacon on 3 paper-toweling-lined paper plates, cover with paper toweling, and microwave, 1 plate at a time, on HIGH (100% power) 2½–3½ minutes, rotating plate 180° at halftime, until bacon is pale golden but still limp. Make slit in each piece of chicken liver, insert water chestnut sliver, roll lightly in brown sugar, wrap in bacon, and secure with toothpicks. Marinate in soy mixture 2 hours or overnight, drain well, and arrange in circle on 2 paper-toweling-lined paper plates. Cover with paper toweling and microwave, 1 plate at a time, on HIGH (100% power) 3½–5 minutes, rotating plate 180° at halftime and turning rumakis over, until bacon is slightly crisp. *Note: Watch bacon toward end of cooking; crisping time will vary according to how thick and fat bacon is. Remember, too, that bacon will continue to cook during standing time.* Let rumakis stand, still covered, 30 seconds. Serve warm.

PER RUMAKI: 40 C   2.6 g P   1.7 g F   3.4 g CARB   140 mg S 43.8 mg CH

V A R I A T I O N S

BACON-WRAPPED SCALLOPS: Microwave bacon as directed, wrap 12 halved sea scallops, and secure with toothpicks. Omit brown sugar but marinate bacon rolls in soy mixture 1 hour. Microwave as directed. *Note: Use lean bacon for this recipe because scallops should just be cooked about 3 minutes.*

PER SCALLOP: 25 C 2.5 g P 1.4 g F 0.4 g CARB 146.6 mg S 5.4 mg CH

BACON-WRAPPED WATER CHESTNUTS: Microwave bacon as directed; roll 12 halved water chestnuts in brown sugar, wrap with bacon, and secure with toothpicks. Marinate in soy mixture 1 hour. Microwave as directed.

PER CHESTNUT: 27 C   0.9 g P   1.3 g F   2.8 g CARB 132.4 mg   S 2.2 mg CH

BACON-WRAPPED PINEAPPLE: Prepare Bacon-wrapped Water Chestnuts as directed, but substitute 24 (¾") chunks pineapple for water chestnuts.

PER PIECE: 28 C   0.9 g P   1.3 g F   3.2 g CARB   132 mg S 2.2 mg CH

CHEESE NACHOS

PREP TIME: [5 MINUTES] COOKING TIME: [1½ MINUTES] STANDING TIME: [30 SECONDS]

Because melted cheese sticks to uncoated paper plates, you should microwave nachos on plastic- or wax-coated paper plates. In a pinch, however, you can line uncoated paper plates with wax paper.

MAKES 12

12 large tortilla chips

1 cup coarsely grated Monterey Jack or sharp Cheddar cheese

1 can (4 ounces) green chili peppers, drained, seeded and minced

Spread tortilla chips on 10½" or 11" plastic- or wax-coated paper plate; sprinkle evenly with cheese and chilies. Microwave, uncovered, on MEDIUM (50% power) about 1½ minutes, turning plate 180° at halftime, until cheese *begins* to melt. Remove from oven and let stand, uncovered, 30 seconds, until cheese melts completely. Serve at once accompanied, if you like, by taco sauce. *Note: Don't crowd more chips onto plate than amount specified above or cheese will melt unevenly; for more nachos, cook in batches.*

PER SERVING: 52 C   3 g P   4 g F   3 g CARB   135 mg S   8 mg CH

— V A R I A T I O N

BEAN, BACON, AND CHEESE NACHOS: Arrange chips on paper plate as directed; top each with 1 teaspoon room-temperature baked or refried beans, sprinkle with a few crisp bacon crumbles, then with the cheese and chilies. Microwave as directed, but increase cooking time by 30–50 seconds.

PER SERVING: 65 C   3 g P   4 g F   4 g CARB   176 mg S   9 mg CH

CHILI CON QUESO DIP

PREP TIME: 10 MINUTES COOKING TIME: 9½–10½ MINUTES STANDING TIME: NONE

Serve warm with tortilla chips or crisp raw vegetables. Good, too, as a topping for hamburgers, hot dogs, or baked potatoes. Use processed cheese only for this recipe; only it will melt to satin smoothness in the microwave oven.

MAKES 3 CUPS

1	pound processed American cheese, cut into 1" cubes
1	can (4 ounces) green chili peppers, drained, seeded and minced
½	cup mild taco sauce or a half-and-half mix of mild and hot taco sauce
1	tablespoon grated yellow onion
¼–½	teaspoon liquid hot red pepper seasoning
1	medium-size ripe tomato, peeled, seeded, and coarsely chopped

Melt cheese in wax-paper-covered 2-quart casserole by microwaving on HIGH (100% power) 3½–4½ minutes. Mix in all remaining ingredients except tomato, re-cover, and microwave on MEDIUM-LOW (30% power) 6 minutes; stir well after 3 minutes and mix in tomato. *Note: If dip cools and thickens too much during serving, reheat (see Some Tips for Microwaving Dips and Spreads above).*

PER TABLESPOON: 38 C 2 g P 3 g F 0.7 g CARB
169.2 mg S 8.9 mg CH

VARIATION

JALAPEÑO CHILI CON QUESO DIP: Prepare as directed, but omit liquid hot red pepper seasoning, add 2 minced, seeded, canned jalapeño peppers and substitute 2 coarsely chopped canned pimientos for the tomato.

PER TABLESPOON: 38 C 2 g P 3 g F 0.7 g CARB
177.5 mg S 8.9 mg CH

WARM BLUE CHEESE DIP

PREP TIME: [3 MINUTES] COOKING TIME: [5½–6 MINUTES] STANDING TIME: [NONE]

Serve warm with crisp apple or pear slices, vegetable sticks, or crackers. Or serve at room temperature as a spread.

MAKES 1¼ CUPS

- ¼ **pound blue cheese (Roquefort, Danish, Stilton, Gorgonzola, Maytag, etc.)**
- 1 **package (3 ounces) cream cheese**
- 1 **small clove garlic, peeled and crushed**
- 2 **scallions, minced (include some green tops)**
- ⅓ **cup sour cream**
- 1 **tablespoon bourbon or medium dry sherry**

Microwave both cheeses in wax-paper-covered 1-quart casserole on MEDIUM (50% power) 2 minutes; stir until smooth. Add all remaining ingredients, re-cover, and microwave on MEDIUM-LOW (30% power) 3½–4 minutes, stirring at halftime, until warm.

PER TABLESPOON: 44 C   1.7 g P   3.9 g F   0.5 g CARB   93.8 mg S   10.6 mg CH

V A R I A T I O N

BLUE CHEESE–PECAN DIP: Prepare recipe as directed, and just before serving, stir in ¼–⅓ cup coarsely chopped pecans.

PER TABLESPOON: 45 C   1.5 g P   4 g F   0.6 g CARB   78.2 mg S   8.8 mg CH

HOT SEAFOOD DIP

PREP TIME: 2 MINUTES   COOKING TIME: 4½–5½ MINUTES   STANDING TIME: NONE

Also delicious spread cold on crackers, canapés, and sandwiches.

MAKES ABOUT 2⅓ CUPS

- **1 package (8 ounces) cream cheese**
- **⅓ cup mayonnaise**
- **2 tablespoon minced sweet pickle relish**
- **1 tablespoon ketchup**
- **1½ teaspoons grated yellow onion**
- **1 teaspoon prepared horseradish**
- **1 teaspoon white or red wine vinegar**
- **½ teaspoon Dijon mustard**
- **½ pound finely chopped, cooked, shelled and deveined shrimp, crab meat, lobster, or well-drained minced clams**

Soften cheese by microwaving in uncovered 1-quart casserole on HIGH (100% power) 1–1½ minutes. Blend in all remaining ingredients except seafood, then fold in seafood. Cover with wax paper and microwave on MEDIUM (50% power) 3½–4 minutes, until hot, stirring at halftime. Serve warm as a dip for raw vegetables or crackers. *Note: This dip will have better flavor if made 12–24 hours ahead of time. To reheat, cover casserole with wax paper and microwave on MEDIUM (50% power) 2–3 minutes, stirring at halftime.*

PER TABLESPOON: 43 C   1.8 g P   3.7 g F   0.6 g CARB   55.9 mg S   19.9 mg CH

TRAIL MIX

PREP TIME: 3 MINUTES   COOKING TIME: 6–7 MINUTES   STANDING TIME: NONE

¢

MAKES ABOUT 7 CUPS

- **3** **cups mixed ready-to-eat high-fiber cereals**
- **1** **cup shelled, unblanched peanuts**
- **½** **cup dry-roasted cashews or whole unblanched almonds**
- **1** **cup dry-roasted soybean nuts**
- **½** **cup pepitas (Mexican pumpkin seeds)**
- **1½** **cups thin pretzel sticks**
- **¼** **cup (½ stick) butter or margarine**
- **1** **large clove garlic, peeled and crushed**
- **2** **tablespoons Worcestershire sauce**
- **1** **tablespoon soy sauce**
- **⅛** **teaspoon ground celery seeds**
- **1** **cup seedless raisins**

Mix cereals, nuts, pepitas, and pretzels in large bowl. Combine remaining ingredients except raisins in 1-pint measure, cover with wax paper, and microwave on HIGH (100% power) 1 minute. Drizzle evenly over dry mixture, toss well, and spread evenly on 13″ × 8″ tray or 12″ platter lined with double-thickness paper toweling. Microwave, uncovered, on HIGH (100% power) 5–6 minutes, stirring after 3 minutes, until nuts are lightly toasted. *Note: Watch center for over-browning—mix continues to brown as it stands.* Cool to room temperature, stirring now and then for first 5 minutes. Mix in raisins and store airtight.

PER ½ CUP: 247 C   8 g P   13 g F   29 g CARB   322 mg S   9 mg CH

ABOUT MICROWAVING SANDWICHES

Open-face meat or poultry sandwiches, cheese melts, stuffed rolls, heroes, and hoboes all microwave superbly. But grilled sandwiches fare better on the stovetop and filled croissants in a regular oven because microwaving makes them soggy. For best results when microwaving sandwiches, following these tips:

Always wrap closed sandwiches in paper toweling or napkins so that excess moisture is absorbed.

Never overheat bread; it will toughen and dry.

Layer deli-style heroes, subs, and hoboes so cheese is in the middle where it's less apt to overcook and "string." If you have an automatic temperature probe, insert it horizontally one third of the way into filling, making sure it's midway between top and bottom of filling; set temperature to 110° F. After microwaving roll with temperature probe, let stand, covered, 2 minutes before serving so inner portions have a chance to heat properly.

When making hot corned beef or pastrami sandwiches, it's best to heat sliced meat alone (see About Reheating Refrigerated and Room-temperature Food in Chapter 4), then make the sandwiches.

When preparing a soup-and-sandwich meal, microwave soup just until it comes to a simmer, place sandwich alongside soup, and microwave as sandwich recipe directs. The soup and sandwich will be ready to serve at the same time and the soup won't overcook.

HOT ITALIAN SAUSAGE, ONION, AND PEPPER HEROES

PREP TIME: | 5 MINUTES | COOKING TIME: | 9½–12 MINUTES | STANDING TIME: | NONE |

SERVES 2

½ **pound sweet or hot Italian sausages**

1 **medium-size sweet green pepper, cored, seeded, and sliced thin**

1 **small yellow onion, peeled and minced**

2 **(6"–7") Italian rolls, split, or a 12" section Italian bread, halved crosswise and split**

Separate sausage links (or halve coiled sausage), prick well, and arrange around edge of 8" or 9" casserole; pile pepper and onion in middle. Cover with wax paper and microwave on HIGH (100% power) 8–10 minutes, until sausages are well done. At halftime, rotate casserole 180°, stir pepper and onion, turn sausages over, and drain off all fat. Drain again, slice sausage ⅜" thick, pile on bottom halves of rolls, cover evenly with pepper and onion, then add tops of rolls. Wrap in paper toweling, leaving ends open, place on oven floor, and microwave on HIGH (100% power) 1½–2 minutes, turning rolls over and rotating 180° at halftime, until heated through.

PER SERVING: 740 C   28 g P   37 g F   72 g CARB
1533 mg S   88 mg CH

VARIATION

HOT KIELBASA AND KRAUT HEROES: Arrange ½ pound kielbasa, halved crosswise, around edge of casserole and place 1 cup well-drained sauerkraut in middle. Cover with vented plastic food wrap and microwave on HIGH (100% power) 3 minutes. Slice kielbasa, re-cover, and microwave on HIGH (100% power) 1 minute. Spread rolls with Dijon mustard, fill with sausages and kraut, and serve.

PER SERVING: 731 C   27 g P   35 g F   74 g CARB
2418 mg S   81 mg CH

HOT OPEN-FACE ROAST BEEF SANDWICH

PREP TIME: [1 MINUTE] **COOKING TIME:** [2–2½ MINUTES] **STANDING TIME:** [NONE]

⧗

SERVES 2

4 **slices firm-textured white or whole-grain bread, trimmed of crusts**

½ **pound thinly sliced cooked roast beef (cooked to desired doneness)**

½ **cup beef gravy**

Lay 2 slices bread, barely touching, on each of 2 (10″) microwave-safe plates. Cover evenly with beef. Microwave gravy in wax-paper-covered 1-pint measure on HIGH (100% power) 30 seconds and spoon over beef. Cover each plate with wax paper, place one on oven floor and second on oven rack. Microwave on MEDIUM (50% power) 1½–2 minutes, reversing plate positions and rotating each 180° at halftime, until uniformly hot. *Note: If you have no oven rack, microwave one plate at a time 1–1¼ minutes, rotating 180° after 30 seconds.*

PER SERVING: 358 C   37 g P   12 g F   24 g CARB   304 mg S 95 mg CH

VARIATIONS

⧗ HOT OPEN-FACE TURKEY OR CHICKEN SANDWICH: Prepare as directed, but use thinly sliced cooked turkey or chicken breast and chicken gravy.
PER SERVING: 320 C   38 g P   7 g F   24 g CARB   374 mg S 89 mg CH

⧗ HOT TURKEY, TOMATO, AND CHEESE MONTE CARLO: Lay 2 (½″) slices toasted French bread on each of 2 plates and cover each with 2 ounces (⅛″) slices roast turkey, then 2 (¼″) slices tomato, and ½ cup warm Cheese Sauce. Microwave, uncovered, on MEDIUM-

HIGH (70% power) 2½–3 minutes, rotating plates 180° and repositioning at halftime, until uniformly hot and cheese bubbles gently. Top each sandwich with a crumbled crisp bacon slice.

PER SERVING: 592 C   36 g P   28 g F   48 g CARB   1043 mg S   113 mg CH

ZIP-QUICK PIZZAS

PREP TIME: [3 MINUTES]   COOKING TIME: [1½–2 MINUTES]   STANDING TIME: [NONE]

¢ ⊠

SERVES 2

⅓ **cup tomato purée or spaghetti sauce**

¼ **teaspoon crumbled dried oregano**

¼ **teaspoon crumbled dried basil**

¼ **teaspoon olive oil**

1 **small clove garlic, peeled and crushed**

Pinch sugar

Pinch red pepper flakes

2 **English muffins, split, or 4 (½") slices Italian bread, toasted**

¾ **cup coarsely grated mozzarella cheese**

Mix all but last two ingredients. Arrange muffin halves in circle on paper-toweling-lined 10" plate or on bake/roast rack. Spread evenly with sauce and sprinkle with cheese, dividing amount equally. Microwave, uncovered, on MEDIUM-HIGH (70% power) 1½–2 minutes, rotating plate 180° at halftime, until cheese melts. Serve as a snack or quarter each pizza and serve as an appetizer.

PER SERVING: 275 C   13 g P   11 g F   32 g CARB   614 mg S   33 mg CH

V A R I A T I O N

¢ PEPPERONI OR SAUSAGE PIZZAS: Prepare as directed, but before microwaving, ⊠ top with 3–4 thin slices pepperoni or cooked hot or sweet Italian sausage, overlapping slices slightly.

PER SERVING: 310 C   15 g P   14 g F   32 g CARB   758 mg S   39 mg CH

205

Melted cheese sandwich

PREP TIME: [3 MINUTES] COOKING TIME: [30–40 SECONDS] STANDING TIME: [NONE]

Don't use china plates; they trap moisture and make bread soggy. The type of bread and cheese both affect cooking time—processed cheese melts fastest; firm breads protect cheese best.

SERVES 1

2 slices firm-textured white, rye, or whole-grain bread, toasted

1 tablespoon butter, margarine, or mayonnaise (optional)

2 slices (1 ounce each) Cheddar, Swiss, Muenster, Gruyère, or processed cheese

Spread bread on one side with butter, if desired, then sandwich together with cheese. Wrap in paper toweling, place on paper plate on oven floor, and microwave on HIGH (100% power) 30–40 seconds, until cheese melts. Serve at once.

PER SERVING: 360 C 18 g P 20 g F 25 g CARB 599 mg S 61 mg CH

V A R I A T I O N S

DEVILED CHEESE, BACON, AND TOMATO MUFFINS (Serves 2): Spread 2 split and toasted English muffins with following mixture: 2 tablespoons mayonnaise, 1 teaspoon Dijon mustard, ½ teaspoon Worcestershire sauce, and pinch ground hot red pepper. Top each muffin half with 1 slice tomato, 1 thick slice sharp Cheddar, and 1 crumbled slice crisp bacon. Place muffins on paper-toweling-lined paper plate and microwave, uncovered, on MEDIUM-HIGH (70% power) 1–2 minutes, rotating plate 180° at half-time, until cheese melts.

PER SERVING: 539 C 22 g P 37 g F 29 g CARB 1012 mg S 78 mg CH

206

CALIFORNIA BRIE AND SUN-DRIED TO-MATO MUFFINS (Serves 2): Spread 2 split and toasted English muffins with 4 ounces ripe Brie, top with 8–10 slivered rehydrated sun-dried tomatoes* and 2 minced scallions, dividing amounts evenly. Microwave as directed 45–60 seconds, just until cheese begins to melt.

PER SERVING: 706 C 19 g P 54 g F 42 g CARB 3235 mg S 57 mg CH

BOSTON BOATS

PREP TIME: | 6 MINUTES | COOKING TIME: | 4½–5½ MINUTES | STANDING TIME: | NONE

SERVES 4

½ **pound coarsely chopped cooked lobster or crab meat, shrimp, or bay scallops**

1 **hard-cooked egg, peeled and coarsely chopped**

½ **cup mayonnaise**

2 **tablespoons finely minced Bermuda onion**

⅓ **cup finely minced celery**

1 **tablespoon minced capers or dill pickle**

2 **teaspoons minced parsley**

1 **teaspoon lemon juice**

¼ **teaspoon salt (about)**

⅛ **teaspoon pepper**

4 **large firm-textured rolls, halved**

4 **teaspoons soft butter or margarine**

Mix all but last two ingredients. Hollow out roll bottoms leaving 1″ shells; spread tops with butter and set aside. Fill bottoms evenly with shellfish mixture, wrap each in paper toweling, leaving ends open, and arrange, not touching, on oven floor. Microwave on MEDIUM (50% power) 3–3½ minutes, rearranging after 2 minutes. Unwrap, add roll tops, re-wrap, and lay upside down in oven. Microwave on HIGH (100% power) 1½–2 minutes, until uniformly hot and serve.

For ¼ Recipe (Serves 1): Quarter ingredients; microwave 1 minute on MEDIUM (50% power) and 40–60 seconds on HIGH (100% power).

For ½ Recipe (Serves 2): Halve ingredients; microwave 2 minutes on MEDIUM (50% power) and 1 minute on HIGH (100% power).

PER SERVING: 466 C 19 g P 29 g F 32 g CARB 940 mg S 137 mg CH

CHICK-PEA AND SPINACH PITA POCKETS

PREP TIME: [8 MINUTES] COOKING TIME: [5–5½ MINUTES] STANDING TIME: [NONE]

Microwaving restores pita bread to its original soft texture.

SERVES 4

1   small yellow onion, peeled and minced

1   medium-size clove garlic, peeled and minced

1   tablespoon olive oil

1   can (1 pound) chick-peas, drained (reserve liquid)

2   tablespoons creamy or chunky peanut butter

1   tablespoon minced parsley

½   teaspoon salt

¼   teaspoon pepper

Pinch crumbled dried thyme

1½   cups finely shredded fresh spinach

2   tablespoons French dressing

2   pita pockets

Mix onion, garlic, and oil in 1-quart casserole, cover with wax paper and microwave on HIGH (100% power) 2½–3 minutes until glassy. Purée ⅓ cup chick-peas with 2 tablespoons reserved liquid in food processor; set aside. Pulse remaining peas 5 to 6 times to chop moderately fine and stir into casserole mixture along with pea purée, peanut butter, parsley, salt, pepper, and thyme. Cover with vented plastic food wrap and microwave on HIGH (100% power) 2 minutes, stirring at half time, until uniformly hot. Let stand, covered. Meanwhile, wrap each pita pocket in paper toweling, lay on oven floor and microwave on HIGH (100% power) 30–35 seconds just until warm. Halve each pita crosswise, spoon in half of chick-pea mixture and spinach, then remaining chick-pea mixture and spinach. Sprinkle with French dressing and serve.

PER SERVING: 343 C   11 g P   12 g F   48 g CARB   956 mg S   0 mg CH

V A R I A T I O N

GREEK SALATA PITA POCKETS: Mix 6 ounces crumbled well-drained feta cheese, ½ cup coarsely chopped pitted Greek or ripe olives, 1 coarsely chopped medium-size tomato, ¼ cup thinly sliced radishes, 1½ teaspoons mashed anchovy fillets, 1 tablespoon minced fresh oregano (or 1 teaspoon minced fresh mint), and ⅛ teaspoon pepper and use to fill warm pita pockets. Or, if you prefer, warm feta mixture slightly in wax-paper-covered casserole by microwaving on MEDIUM (50% power) 1–1½ minutes, stirring at halftime; then fill warm pita pockets.

PER SERVING: 271 C   10 g P   16 g F   23 g CARB   1307 mg S   39 mg CH

ABOUT MICROWAVING POPCORN

Never microwave popcorn unless you use a special microwave popper or corn especially packaged for the microwave. Trying to microwave regular popcorn in a brown paper bag can cause an oven fire. When microwaving popcorn, always follow package directions to the letter. Also:

Never allow small children to microwave popcorn unsupervised.

Never exceed recommended microwave time because popcorn will scorch. There will always be "old maids" (unpopped kernels), but forcing them to pop by microwaving longer will surely burn the rest and possibly start a fire.

Read your oven user's manual carefully; corn will not pop in many low-wattage models.

Always open bags of popped corn carefully lest you scald yourself with the steam sealed inside.

To refresh popped corn, place in paper-toweling-lined, microwave-safe colander (or on a tray) and microwave, uncovered, on HIGH (100% power) 30–60 seconds per quart, tossing once or twice, until warm and crisp.

SPICY LOUISIANA POPCORN

PREP TIME: [2 MINUTES] COOKING TIME: [1½ MINUTES] STANDING TIME: [NONE]

Louisiana hot sauce is more flavorful and less fiery than liquid hot red pepper seasoning.

MAKES 2 QUARTS

2 **quarts unseasoned freshly popped popcorn**

3 **tablespoons butter or margarine**

2 **large cloves garlic, peeled and crushed**

½ **teaspoon Louisiana hot sauce or ¼ teaspoon liquid hot red pepper seasoning**

1 **teaspoon Worcestershire sauce**

¼ **teaspoon chili powder**

¼ **teaspoon ground celery seeds**

Pinch ground hot red pepper

Place popcorn in large bowl. Combine remaining ingredients in 1-pint measure, cover with wax paper, and microwave on HIGH (100% power) 1 minute. Reduce power to MEDIUM (50%) and microwave ½ minute. Pour evenly over popcorn and toss well to mix. Serve at once.

PER ½ CUP: 32 C   0.4 g P   2.3 g F   2.6 g CARB   30 mg S 5.8 mg CH

V A R I A T I O N S

 CURRIED POPCORN: Omit Louisiana hot sauce and celery seeds, substitute 1 teaspoon curry powder for the chili powder, and microwave seasoning mixture as recipe directs. Pour evenly over popcorn, toss well, and serve.

PER ½ Cup: 32 C   0.4 g P   2.3 g F   2.6 g CARB   30 mg S 5.8 mg CH

 BARBECUED POPCORN: Omit Louisiana hot sauce and celery seeds, add 2 tablespoons bottled barbecue sauce, and microwave seasoning mixture as recipe directs. Pour mixture evenly over popcorn, toss well, and serve.

PER ½ Cup: 32 C   0.4 g P   2.3 g F   2.6 g CARB   30 mg S 5.8 mg CH

HERBED PARMESAN POPCORN

PREP TIME: **2 MINUTES** COOKING TIME: **1½ MINUTES** STANDING TIME: **NONE**

¢ ⊠

MAKES 2 QUARTS

- **2 quarts unseasoned freshly popped popcorn**
- **¼ cup (½ stick) butter or margarine**
- **1 teaspoon vegetable oil**
- **2 teaspoons minced fresh basil or 1 teaspoon crumbled dried basil**
- **2 teaspoons minced fresh oregano or 1 teaspoon crumbled dried oregano**
- **1 large clove garlic, peeled and crushed**
- **½ cup finely grated Parmesan cheese**

Place popcorn in large bowl. Combine all remaining ingredients except cheese in 1-pint measure, cover with wax paper, and microwave on HIGH (100% power) 1 minute. Reduce power to MEDIUM (50%) and microwave 30 seconds. Stir in cheese, pour evenly over popcorn, and toss well to mix. Serve at once.

PER ½ CUP: 54 C 1.7 g P 4.2 g F 2.6 g CARB 86.2 mg S 10.2 mg CH

V A R I A T I O N

⊠ PEANUT BUTTER POPCORN: Omit all herbs and cheese, reduce butter to 2 tablespoons, and combine in 1-pint measure with ⅓ cup crunchy peanut butter and the 1 teaspoon vegetable oil and 1 peeled and crushed clove garlic called for. Cover and microwave on HIGH (100% power) as recipe directs or until peanut butter is very soft. Stir well, pour over popcorn, and toss thoroughly to mix.

PER ½ CUP: 69 C 1.3 g P 2.8 g F 3.6 g CARB 61.2 mg S 4 mg CH

7

BREAKFASTS, BRUNCHES, AND LUNCHES

The microwave makes breakfast a breeze. Lunch and brunch, too. Take eggs, for example. They microwave to perfection fifteen different ways— and faster than you would have dreamed possible. Bacon, moreover, browns and crisps with no messy spattering.

With a microwave you can bake a batch of muffins in 2½ minutes flat (and a coffee cake or tea bread *almost* as fast). You can stir up a hot cereal with no danger of its scorching or sticking, even bubble up a few jars of fresh fruit preserves *without* having to stand over a steamy kettle and stir.

Some people insist that you can't make a decent soufflé in the microwave. We beg to differ and have just the recipes to prove them wrong. As for quiches, you've never tasted silkier ones than those we've created especially for the microwave. Or more feathery steamed breads. Imagine a loaf of Boston Brown Bread in just six minutes!

Miraculous as the microwave is, however, it can't prepare all breakfast, brunch, or lunch foods. It fails resoundingly when it comes to baking yeast breads. These never brown or develop a crust or bake to the fine uniform texture we expect. There are, inevitably, dry patches and doughy spots all in the same loaf. Any attempts to crumb-coat yeast loaves to impart a bit of color fail, too, because the crumbs splotch and/or drop off during the second rising.

What we concentrate on in this chapter are those breakfast, brunch, and lunch favorites at which the microwave does excel. We also pass along all the tips and techniques you'll need to microwave eggs, bacon, sausage, and cheese-rich casseroles just the way you like them.

ABOUT MICROWAVING CEREALS

Oatmeal, farina, cream of wheat, cream of rice, even the Southerner's choice, grits, are cooked much the same way in the microwave—the only variable is the ratio of cereal to liquid. Most cereals, especially the quick-cooking varieties, cook fast enough on the stovetop, so what's the point of microwaving them? Your chances of lumping or scorching the cereal are reduced almost to zero. You needn't stir so often or resort to the double boiler to keep cereals smooth and creamy. Best of all, you save messy pot scrubbing because cereals can be microwaved right in their serving bowls. It's such a snap the children may want to fix their own breakfast cereal.

SOME TIPS FOR PREPARING CEREALS BY MICROWAVE

Always use the bowl or casserole size specified. To prevent boilovers, it must be twice the volume of the ingredients put into it. For each individual serving, use a deep 1-pint bowl. Cover or not as recipes direct. Cooking cereals uncovered reduces the risk of boilover; covering them keeps a crust from forming.

To speed cooking time, use hot tap water instead of cold.

Always follow the microwaving directions on a cereal package. If there are none, use the chart and directions that follow.

If at the end of suggested cooking time, a cereal tests—and tastes—done but seems soupy, microwave in 15-second increments (for 1 serving) and in 1-minute increments (for 4 servings) until the mixture thickens properly. If, on the other hand, the cereal cooks dry before it's done, add a little hot water and microwave as directed for thickening the mixture.

Cereal bowls and casseroles get intensely hot in a microwave oven, so be forewarned and use potholders. Also, cool cereals slightly before tasting lest you scald your tongue.

214

CHART FOR MICROWAVING CEREALS

For 1 Serving	Oatmeal	Farina or Cream of Wheat or Rice	Grits
Bowl Size	1 pint	1 pint	1 pint
Cereal	⅓ C	2 T	3 T
Hot Water	⅔ C	⅔ C	⅔ C
Salt (optional)	⅛ t	⅛ t	⅛ t
Optional Extras (add at outset of cooling time)	1 T maple sugar, sprinkling cinnamon or allspice	1 T brown sugar, sprinkling nutmeg or mace	1 T butter or 3 T gravy (especially ham gravy)
Cook Covered?	No	No	No
Cooking Time	3½–4 minutes	1¾—2 minutes	2–2½ minutes
Cooling Time	30 seconds	30 seconds	30 seconds

For 2 Servings: Microwave single portions in 2 bowls for 5½–6 minutes.

For 4 Servings	Oatmeal	Farina or Cream of Wheat or Rice	Grits
Bowl Size	3 quarts	3 quarts	3 quarts
Cereal	1⅓ C	⅔ C	1 C
Hot Water	2⅔ C	3 C	3½ C
Salt (optional)	½ t	½ t	½ t
Optional Extras (add at outset of cooling time)	4 T maple sugar, sprinkling cinnamon or allspice	4 T brown sugar, sprinkling nutmeg or mace	4 T butter or ¾ cup gravy (especially ham gravy)
Cook Covered?	No	No	Yes (with vented plastic wrap)
Cooking Time	9–10 minutes	8–9 minutes	9–10 minutes
Cooling Time	1–2 minutes	1–2 minutes	1–2 minutes

For 4 Individual Servings: Microwave single portions in 4 bowls, placed 1″ apart and staggering 2 on oven shelf, 9–10 minutes.

Method: Combine cereal, water, and if you like, salt in bowl. Cover or not as directed and microwave on HIGH (100% power) as chart recommends, stirring at halftime, until all liquid is absorbed and cereal thickens. Stir again, add optional extras, if you like, and cool as directed on heat-resistant surface. Serve at once.

PER SERVING:

Oatmeal: 103 C   4 g P   2 g F   18 g CARB   1 mg S   0 mg CH

Farina: 81 C   2 g P   0 g F   17 g CARB   1 mg S   0 mg CH

Cream of Wheat: 80C   2 g P   0 g F   17 g CARB   2 mg S   0 mg CH

Cream of Rice: 80 C   1 g P   0 g F   18 g CARB   1 mg S   0 mg CH

Grits: 109 C   3 g P   0 g F   23 g CARB   0 mg S   0 mg CH

V A R I A T I O N S

TO MAKE WITH MILK: Prepare as directed, substituting milk for ¼ of the water (no more or cereal will not cook properly) and using a casserole at least 3 times the volume of the combined ingredients (milk mixtures bubble up dramatically in the microwave). After stirring at halftime, reduce power level to MEDIUM (50%) and microwave 2 minutes longer for 1 serving, 3 minutes longer for 4. Cool as directed.

TO MAKE WITH QUICK-COOKING CEREAL: Prepare as directed, reducing total cooking time by half.

SOME QUICK WAYS TO JAZZ UP COOKED CEREALS

Add any of the following to each portion of cooked cereal, then cool briefly as directed:

1–2 teaspoons light brown or maple sugar plus a sprinkling of ground cinnamon, nutmeg, mace, or allspice

1–1½ tablespoons seedless raisins, diced dates, prunes, dried figs, apples, peaches, or apricots

~~~~~1 tablespoon honey and/or wheat germ

Just before serving:

~~~~~Top oatmeal, farina, cream of wheat, or cream of rice with jam, jelly, or preserves; any sliced or diced fresh fruit; or whole ripe berries. A dollop of sour cream adds a finishing touch.

For grits only:

~~~~~Do as Southerners do and fry some country ham to accompany the grits. Then make "red-eye gravy" by splashing a little hot water and breakfast coffee into the empty ham skillet. Set over moderate heat and cook, scraping up browned bits ("red eyes") from the skillet bottom, 2–3 minutes. Ladle the gravy over the grits.

~~~~~Cook grits in chicken or beef broth instead of water, then serve in place of potatoes.

ABOUT MICROWAVING BACON

Microwaving times for bacon vary because of differences in thickness and fattiness (not to mention in the amount of salt and sugar used in curing). *Note: It takes longer to microwave large amounts of bacon (more than 8 slices) than to fry them in a skillet, so either use the old-fashioned method or microwave in batches of 8 slices. The advantages to microwaving bacon: it's less greasy (dieters, take note), it's neater (less spattering), and it needn't be turned more than once as it cooks.* For best results, follow these guidelines:

~~~~~Choose slices of uniform thickness to ensure even cooking.

~~~~~For crisp bacon, microwave small amounts (4 slices or less) between several thicknesses of paper toweling instead of on a bake/roast rack. *Note: This method doesn't work as well for larger quantities because the toweling becomes grease-soaked and must be changed often.*

217

~~~~ If bacon is very lean, allow a little extra microwaving time (it's the fat in bacon that attracts microwaves).

~~~~ To separate slices of refrigerator-cold bacon easily, microwave on HIGH (100% power) 15–20 seconds. Or if you're in a hurry, microwave *unseparated* slices for one third of total cooking time, separate, and proceed as directed in Bacon Microwave Chart that follows.

~~~~ To separate frozen bacon slices, microwave 1-pound package at MEDIUM-LOW (30% power) 5–6 minutes, rotating package 180° and turning it over at halftime. Do not refreeze, simply wrap and refrigerate what you don't use.

~~~~ If you're planning a bacon and egg breakfast, the time to microwave the eggs is while the bacon is standing.

ABOUT MICROWAVING HAM

Ready-to-eat ham steaks and thinly sliced canned hams both microwave beautifully. You can glaze them or not, even "fry" them—*without* the added calories. Two points to remember: Allow 5–6 ounces ham per serving and to ensure even cooking, make sure steaks and slices are of uniform thickness.

V A R I A T I O N S

"FRIED" HAM STEAK OR SLICES: Prepare ham steak or slices for cooking as directed in Ham Microwave Chart (p. 220) and preheat browning skillet or grill as manufacturer recommends. *Note: Brushing ham steaks or slices lightly with vegetable oil on both sides before placing in browning skillet will heighten browning.* After adding ham to skillet, press lightly with spatula for close contact with heated surface. Microwave, *uncovered,* as manufacturer directs, rotating dish 180° when turning ham; brown second side the same way.

GLAZED HAM STEAK: Microwave as directed; at halftime, drain steak, turn and spread with any suitable glaze (Pineapple Sweet-Sour Sauce, for example), cover with wax paper, and finish cooking as directed.

JIFFY FRUIT-GLAZED HAM: Blend ⅓ cup plum, pineapple, peach, apricot, or cherry preserves or orange marmalade with 2 tablespoons each maple syrup and light or dark corn syrup and 1 tablespoon spicy brown mustard. Spread on sliced whole ham or ham steak at halftime if overall cooking time is less than 10 minues, on ham for final 5 minutes if cooking time is longer.

BACON MICROWAVE CHART

Thin Bacon = 30 slices per pound
Regular Bacon = 16–20 slices per pound
Thick Bacon = 12–16 slices per pound

Bacon Type	No. of Slices	Minutes on HIGH (100% power)	Minutes Standing	Prep Tips
Thin	2	1–1¼	1	For 2–4 slices: Separate and arrange between several sheets paper toweling; microwave on plate or coated paper plate. For 6–8 slices: Arrange, not over-lapping, on bake/roast rack or rack in bake/roast pan; cover with paper toweling. Microwave all bacon, regardless of thick-ness, until fat is translucent and bubbly; bacon will be limp; it will crisp and brown during standing; rearrange bacon on rack at halftime, moving less-done center slices to outside.
	4	1½–2	2	
	6	3–3½	3	
	8	4½–5	3	
Regular	2	1½–2	1	
	4	3–3½	2	
	6	4½–5	3	
	8	5½–6¼	3	
Thick	2	2–2½	1	
	4	3½–4	2	
	6	5–6	3	
	8	7–8	3	
Canadian Bacon	2	1–1½*	None	Arrange in pie plate, overlap-ping 4 or more slices in circle; cover with wax paper; turn ba-con over at halftime.
	4	2–2½*	None	
	6	3–3½*	None	

* Thick Canadian bacon may need 30%–50% more cooking time, depending on quantity.

HAM MICROWAVE CHART

Ham Type and Size	Minutes on MEDIUM (50% power)	Minutes Standing	Prep Tips
Ready-to-Eat Ham Steak			Remove rind, trim fat covering to ⅛", and slash every 1" to prevent curling. Lay ham steak on bake/roast pan, cover with vented plastic food wrap, and turn steak over at halftime. When done, drain and let stand, still covered, as chart directs.
¼" thick (about 10½ oz.)	9–10	1	
½" thick (about 1¼ lbs.)	10½–11½	2	
1" thick (about 2 pounds)	12–14	2	
2" thick (about 3½ lbs.)	20–25	3	

Note: For 1 serving, microwave 5 ounces ¼" ham steak as directed but reduce cooking time to 3–4 minutes.

Ham Type and Size	Minutes on MEDIUM (50% power)	Minutes Standing	Prep Tips
Sliced Canned Ham			Line up slices, side by side and slightly overlapping, in shallow casserole or pie plate. Add 2 tablespoons water and cover with plastic food wrap; rearrange slices at halftime. Serve at once.
2 (¼") slices (2–3 oz.)	1½–1¾	None	
4 (¼") slices (about 5 oz.)	2¼–2½	None	
6 (¼") slices (about ½ lb.)	3–3½	None	
8 (¼") slices (about ¾ lb.)	4–4½	None	

Ham Type and Size	Minutes on HIGH (100% power)	Minutes Standing	Prep Tips
Ready-to-Eat Whole Ham			Slice ¼' thick, overlap in 12" × 8" × 2" bake/roast pan; add ¼ cup water, apple, pineapple, or orange juice and cover with vented plastic food wrap; rotate 180° at halftime; drain and let stand, still covered, as chart directs.
1½–2 lbs.	10–12	5	
3 lbs	20–22	5	

Sausages, whether fully cooked (frankfurters, knackwurst, bratwurst, kielbasa, etc.) or fresh, microwave easily, superbly. For best results, read these tips:

Because sausages vary dramatically as to size, composition, and fat content, check for doneness after minimum recommended cooking time. Fully cooked sausages only need be heated. But fresh (raw) sausages, particularly pork sausages, *must be fully cooked*—until no pink remains in the center; if they are not done after minimum recommended cooking time, microwave in 1-minute increments thereafter, testing often. **Note:** *What affects overall cooking time more than the number of sausages being microwaved is their combined weight. The best way to determine doneness: cut a sausage in half.*

Prick or slash sausages as directed to keep them from bursting.

Ignore whistling/popping noises as sausages microwave; it's just air expanding and escaping.

If you need hot dogs for a crowd, cook in batches of 10 (larger batches won't heat evenly).

When adding franks to casseroles, cut in thirds and bury them in the casserole mixture so they won't overcook or heat unevenly.

To give sausages rich brown color, brush with *Browning Glaze* (½ cup each liquid gravy browner and water plus 1 teaspoon sugar). *Or* transfer cooked sausages to a preheated broiler and brown quickly. *Or* use a browning skillet as its manufacturer directs. Avoid overbrowning sausages; they'll toughen. **Note:** *Browning skillets are not recommended for large fresh sausages because the pork may not cook fully by the time the sausages brown.*

To grill or barbecue knackwurst, bratwurst, or kielbasa, microwave as directed, place on a grill over a moderate fire, and broil, turning often, until evenly browned. Brush often, if you like, with a favorite barbecue sauce. Or serve whole, Polish style, on a bed of sauerkraut.

SAUSAGE MICROWAVE CHART

Frankfurters (regular size, 9–10 per pound):

Method 1: Prick with fork or slash diagonally 4 or 5 times. Arrange on plate or coated paper plate, cover with wax paper, and microwave as follows, rearranging at halftime if cooking more than 2 franks (ends overcook quickly, so watch carefully):

Number of Franks	Time on HIGH (100% power)	Number of Franks	Time on HIGH (100% power)
1	30–35 sec.	6	2–2½ min.
2	45–55 sec.	8	3–3½ min.
4	1¼–1½ min.	10	4½–5½ min.

Method 2 (in buns): Prick with fork, slip into buns, wrap individually in paper toweling or napkins, and microwave as follows, turning over at halftime if cooking more than 2 franks:

Number of Franks	Time on HIGH (100% power)	Number of Franks	Time on HIGH (100% power)
1	40 sec.	6	3–3½ min.
2	1–1¼ min.	8	4½–5½ min.
4	1½–2½ min.	10	6–7 min.

V A R I A T I O N S

CHILI DOGS: Cook in buns as directed, then smother with any favorite chili. *Recipe too flexible for a meaningful nutritive count.*

KRAUT 'N' DOGS: Place franks in buns, top each with scant ¼ cup sauerkraut, wrap, and microwave as directed, allowing an extra 5 seconds per frank.
PER SERVING: 269 C 9 g P 16 g F 23 g CARB 819 mg S 25 mg CH

¢ CHEESE DOGS: Split franks lengthwise, but not clear through, tuck rolled slice American or sharp Cheddar cheese spread with mild yellow mustard into each, place in buns, wrap, and microwave as directed until cheese melts.

PER SERVING: 348 C 13 g P 22 g F 23 g CARB 1080 mg S 45 mg CH

¢ PIZZA DOGS: Split franks lengthwise, but not clear through, spread each with 1–2 tablespoons tomato sauce and top with 2 tablespoons each chopped pepperoni and coarsely grated mozzarella. Place in buns, wrap, and microwave as directed until cheese melts.

PER SERVING: 366 C 14 g P 23 g F 25 g CARB 1126 mg S 45 mg CH

SAUSAGE MICROWAVE CHART

Method 3 (in water): A good way to cook franks in quantity. Prick franks and place in casserole large enough to hold them in single layer, add ½ cup hot water, cover with vented plastic food wrap, and microwave as follows, rotating casserole 180° and rearranging franks at halftime if cooking more than 4:

Number of Franks	Time on HIGH (100% power)	Number of Franks	Time on HIGH (100% power)
4	2–3 min.	8	4–5 min.
6	3–4 min.	10	6–7 min.

V A R I A T I O N S

¢ FRANK 'N' BEAN POT (Serves 6): In 2-quart casserole mix 2 cans (1 pound each) baked beans, 2 tablespoons each molasses and ketchup, and 1 tablespoon spicy brown mustard. Bury 1 pound cold frankfurters, cut into thirds, in beans (to prevent overcooking), cover with wax paper, and microwave on HIGH (100% power) 10–12 minutes, stirring at halftime and again pushing franks underneath beans, until bubbly. Stir again before serving.

PER SERVING: 409 C 16 g P 23 g F 39 g CARB 1534 mg S 38 mg CH

¢ FRANK 'N' KRAUT CASSEROLE (Serves 4): In 2-quart casserole mix 1 can (1 pound) drained sauerkraut, ¼ cup minced yellow onion (or 2 tablespoons onion flakes), and 1 tablespoon caraway or dill seeds. Bury 1 pound cold frankfurters, cut into thirds, in kraut (to prevent overcooking), cover with vented plastic food wrap, and microwave on HIGH (100% power) 8–10 minutes, stirring at halftime and making sure franks are still buried. Stir again before serving.

PER SERVING: 383 C 14 g P 33 g F 7 g CARB 1526 mg S 57 mg CH

223

SAUSAGE MICROWAVE CHART

Knackwurst (6 per pound): Prick sausages with fork or slash diagonally 4 or 5 times, then wrap 1–2 at a time in wax paper and microwave as follows, rearranging at halftime if cooking more than 2:

Number of Sausages	Time on HIGH (100% power)	Number of Sausages	Time on HIGH (100% power)
1	40–50 sec.	4	2–2½ min.
2	1¼–1½ min.	6	3–3½ min.

Note: Knackwurst can also be steamed; follow directions for Fresh Bratwurst below, but reduce microwave times by half.

Fresh Bratwurst (6 per pound): Prick sausages with fork and arrange 1 layer deep in 1½-quart casserole. Add 1 cup water or beer, cover with vented plastic food wrap, and microwave as follows, rearranging and turning wurst over at halftime:

Number of Sausages	Time on HIGH (100% power)	Number of Sausages	Time on HIGH (100% power)
1	2–2½ min.	4	3½–4 min.
2	2½–3 min.	6	4–5 min.

Precooked or Packaged Bratwurst (6 per pound): Prick with fork or slash diagonally 4 or 5 times, wrap 1–2 at a time in wax paper, and microwave as follows, rearranging at halftime if cooking more than 2:

Number of Sausages	Time on HIGH (100% power)	Number of Sausages	Time on HIGH (100% power)
1	50–60 sec.	4	2½–3 min.
2	1½–2 min.	6	3–3½ min.

Weisswurst (6 per pound): Do not prick or slash. Arrange 1 layer deep in 1½-quart casserole. Add 1½ hot cups water, cover with vented plastic food wrap, and microwave as follows, rearranging and turning wurst at halftime. *Note: These delicate veal sausages should never boil, so reduce power level, if necessary.*

Number of Sausages	Time on MEDIUM (50% power)	Number of Sausages	Time on MEDIUM (50% power)
1	2–2½ min.	4	3½–4 min.
2	2½–3 min.	6	4–5 min.

Kielbasa (1–1½ pounds apiece; allow ⅓ pound per person): Prick kielbasa with fork, wrap in wax paper, place in shallow casserole, and microwave on HIGH (100% power) allowing 4–5 minutes for 1 pound; rotate casserole 180° and turn sausage over at halftime.

FRESH PORK SAUSAGE

Large Links (8 per pound): Separate links, prick each 3 or 4 times, and brush, if you like, with Browning Glaze. Arrange sausages, not touching, on rack in bake/roast pan, cover with wax paper, and microwave as follows until no pink shows in center; turn sausages every 2 minutes (at halftime if cooking time is less than 4 minutes) and uncover for last 2 minutes; at this point, drain excess drippings from pan.

Number of Sausages	Time on HIGH (100% power)	Number of Sausages	Time on HIGH (100% power)
2	2½–3 min.	6	5–5½ min.
4	4–4½ min.	8	6–6½ min.

Note: Omit Browning Glaze, if you like, transfer cooked sausages to preheated broiler, and broil 4"–5" from heat 3–4 minutes, turning as needed to brown evenly. Do not overbrown or sausages will toughen.

Small Links (12–14 per pound): Microwave as directed for large links, timing as follows:

Number of Sausages	Time on HIGH (100% power)	Number of Sausages	Time on HIGH (100% power)
2–4	1½–2 min.	8–10	4–4½ min.
4–6	2–3 min.	10–12	4½–5 min.
6–8	3–4 min.	12–14	5–5½ min.

Note: To brown, use browning skillet as manufacturer recommends.

Italian Sweet or Hot Sausages (about 4 per pound): Microwave as directed for large links, but use following *lower* power level and cooking times. Also pour off fat as it accumulates.

Number of Sausages	Time on MEDIUM-HIGH (70% power)	Number of Sausages	Time on MEDIUM-HIGH (70% power)
2	5–6 min.	4	9–10 min.

Note: If you like, transfer cooked sausages to preheated broiler and broil 4" from heat 3 minutes, turning as needed to brown lightly and evenly.

Fresh Pork Sausage, continued

Brown 'n' Serve Links (10 per 8-ounce package): Thaw, do not prick, and microwave on rack as directed for large links, timing as follows and turning at halftime:

Number of Sausages	Time on HIGH (100% power)	Number of Sausages	Time on HIGH (100% power)
2–4	1–1½ min.	6–8	2–2½ min.
4–6	1½–2 min.	8–10	2½–3 min.

Note: To brown, use browning skillet as manufacturer recommends.

Patties: Slice sausage roll ½" thick or shape bulk sausage into patties ½" thick and 2½" across. Place, not touching, on bake/roast rack, brush, if you like, with Browning Glaze, cover with wax paper, and microwave as follows, turning every 2 minutes until no pink remains in center. Uncover for final 2 minutes and at this point, drain off excess drippings.

Number of Patties	Time on HIGH (100% power)	Number of Patties	Time on HIGH (100% power)
2	3–4 min.	6	4½–5 min.
4	4–4½ min.	8	5½–6 min.

Note: Patties may be microwaved in browning dish as directed for Small Links.

Brown 'n' Serve Patties (8 per 12-ounce package): Thaw, place, not touching, on bake/roast pan rack and brush, if you like, with Browning Glaze. Cover with wax paper and microwave as follows, turning patties at halftime, until no pink shows in center. Uncover for last 2 minutes and drain off drippings.

Number of Patties	Time on HIGH (100% power)	Number of Patties	Time on HIGH (100% power)
2	1–1½ min.	6	2½–3 min.
4	2–2½ min.	8	3–4 min.

Note: To brown, use browning skillet as manufacturer recommends.

ABOUT MICROWAVING EGGS

Cooking times are based on *refrigerator-cold, large eggs* unless recipes indicate otherwise. Obviously warmer, larger, or smaller eggs will microwave more quickly or slowly. For best results, follow recipes explicitly and abide by the guidelines below. **Note:** *For single eggs, yolks and whites, we give precise nutritive counts instead of taking them to the nearest round number.*

SOME GENERAL TIPS

Never microwave eggs in the shell unless you have a special microwave egg cooker and use it only as manufacturer directs.

Never reheat whole hard-cooked eggs in the microwave; they may explode.

For best results, use turntable when cooking eggs or egg mixtures.

TIPS FOR POACHING EGGS

Don't poach more than two eggs in the same dish; they won't cook evenly. **Note:** *Poachers for microwaving 4 eggs at a time are available in many housewares stores. Use only as manufacturer instructs.*

Because egg whites and yolks cook at different speeds in the microwave, it's a bit tricky to poach or shirr whole eggs. Adding a little water helps equalize the cooking times as does using MEDIUM (50% power) and allowing the eggs to stand after cooking. Properly handled, however, whole eggs can be shirred or poached to the exact degree of doneness you want—until whites are just set, for example, and yolks still runny. **Note:** *Scrambling the eggs narrows the margin in yolk and white cooking times and makes it possible to microwave eggs on HIGH (100% power) without toughening them.*

Never salt and pepper eggs until after they're cooked, lest yolks look spotty.

〰〰 Always cover eggs to hold in steam and speed cooking of whites (being fatty, yolks attract microwaves and cook faster than whites). **Note:** *Adding a little vinegar to cooking water will make whites set faster.*

〰〰 Always remove eggs from microwave when a thin ring of uncooked egg white still surrounds yolk; it will finish cooking on standing. **Note:** *Examine each egg after minimum recommended cooking time; some eggs may cook faster than others, so remove as soon as they are done. Microwave remaining eggs in 10-second increments.*

TO HARD-COOK EGGS

WHOLE EGGS (ideal for sandwich spreads, salads, casseroles, garnishes):
1 EGG: Break egg into greased custard cup and puncture yolk membrane with toothpick. Cover with wax paper and microwave on MEDIUM (50% power) 1¾– 2 minutes, until yolk is almost firm. Let stand, still covered, 1 minute to complete cooking, then chop and chill.

2 EGGS: Break each egg into greased custard cup, puncture yolk membranes with toothpick, cover with wax paper, and microwave on MEDIUM (50% power) 2½–3 minutes. Let stand, still covered, 1 minute; chop and refrigerate.

4 EGGS: Break eggs into greased round 1-pint casserole, cover with wax paper, and microwave on MEDIUM (50% power) 3½–4¼ minutes, stirring gently at halftime. Let stand, still covered, 1 minute; chop and refrigerate.
PER EGG: 87 C   6 g P   6.5 g F   0.6 g CARB   80 mg S   274 mg CH

EGG WHITES (ideal for sandwiches, salads, garnishes):
Place 1–2 egg whites in greased custard cup, cover with vented plastic food wrap, and microwave on MEDIUM (50% power) 1¾–2¼ minutes, until almost firm; stir once or twice. Let stand, still covered, 2 minutes; chop and chill.
PER WHITE: 25 C   3.4 g P   0.9 g F   0.4 G CARB   61 mg S   0 mg CH

EGG YOLKS (use for sandwich spreads, salads, garnishes):
1–2 YOLKS: Place in greased custard cup, stir with fork, cover with wax paper, and microwave on MEDIUM (50% power) 35–50 seconds, until nearly firm. Stir and let stand, still covered, 1 minute to complete cooking; mince and chill.

3—4 YOLKS: Microwave as directed, increasing cooking time to 1–1½ minutes.
PER YOLK: 71 C   2.8 g P   6.5 g F   0 g CARB   19.3 mg S   272.3 mg CH

TO POACH EGGS

METHOD 1: Pour 1 cup hottest tap water into 1-pint round casserole and mix in 1 teaspoon vinegar. Microwave, uncovered, on HIGH (100% power) 2 minutes, until water boils vigorously. Meanwhile, break 1 egg into each of 2 small dishes and pierce yolk membranes with toothpick to prevent bursting. Swirl water in casserole into whirlpool and slide egg into it; repeat with remaining egg. Cover with vented plastic food wrap and microwave on MEDIUM (50% power) 1½–1¾ minutes, rotating casserole 180° at halftime, until whites are nearly set. Let stand, still covered, ½–1 minute to complete poaching. Lift eggs out with slotted spoon and serve.

METHOD 2: Place 2 tablespoons hottest tap water and ¼ teaspoon vinegar in each custard cup. Arrange cups 1" apart in oven, placing 2 side by side, 3 in triangle and 4 in circle on tray or platter. Microwave, uncovered, on HIGH (100% power) 30–35 seconds per cup, until water boils. Break 1 egg into each cup, pierce yolk membranes with toothpick, cover with vented plastic food wrap, and microwave on MEDIUM (50% power) allowing 1–1¼ minutes for 1 egg, 1½–1¾ minutes for 2, 2–2¼ for 3, and 2½–3 for 4 eggs, rotating cups or tray 180° at halftime, until whites are almost set. Let stand, still covered, ½–1 minute, until whites are as done as you like. Lift eggs out with slotted spoon and serve.
Note: *If slotted spoon is too big to fit into custard cup, simply ease egg onto it. Or drain liquid through vent in plastic wrap.*
PER EGG: 79 C   6 g P   5.5 g F   0.6 g CARB   69 mg S   272.5 mg CH

V A R I A T I O N S

BROTH- OR MILK-POACHED EGGS: Poach eggs as directed, but substitute chicken broth or milk for water and vinegar. ***Note:*** *Watch milk carefully lest it boil over.*
PER EGG (BROTH): 81 C   6.2 g P   5.7 g F   0.7 g CARB   131.8 mg S   274 mg CH
PER EGG (MILK): 88 C   6.6 g P   6 g F   1.3 g CARB   76.5 mg S   276 mg CH

229

SHIRRED EGGS: Break eggs into separate buttered custard cups, pierce yolk membranes with toothpick, and top each, if you like, with 1 tablespoon light cream. Cover with vented plastic food wrap and microwave as directed in Method 2, reducing microwaving time on MEDIUM (50% power) by 10 seconds for each egg.

PER EGG: 87 C   6 g P   6.5 g F   0.6 g CARB   78.6 mg S   276.5 mg CH
PER EGG (WITH CREAM): 117 C   6.5 g P   9.4 g F   1 g CARB   84.6 mg S   286.4 mg CH

EGGS, BACON, TOMATO, AND CHEESE MUFFINS (Serves 4): Top each half of 2 hot toasted and buttered English muffins with 1 tomato slice, 2 strips crisp bacon, and 1 poached egg. Cover each egg with 1 slice provolone, Swiss, Gruyère, or Cheddar cheese and microwave, uncovered, on MEDIUM (50% power) about 1 minute, until cheese begins to melt.

PER SERVING: 294 C   17 g P   18 g F   15 g CARB   603 mg S   299 mg CH

EGGS BENEDICT (Serves 4): Prepare 1 recipe Hollandaise Sauce, set container in bowl of hot, not boiling, water and keep warm. Arrange 4 thin slices boiled ham or Canadian bacon in single layer in shallow 8" casserole, dot with 1 tablespoon butter or margarine, cover with wax paper, and microwave on HIGH (100% power) 1–1¼ minutes, until warm. Top each half of 2 hot toasted and buttered English muffins with ham, trimming to fit. Center 1 poached egg on each ham slice and add a ladling of Hollandaise and sprinkling of paprika.

PER SERVING: 521 C   18 g P   44 g F   14 g CARB   1087 mg S   643 mg CH

EGGS FLORENTINE (Serves 4): Prepare 1 recipe Mornay Sauce, set container in bowl of hot, not boiling, water and keep warm. Spoon ⅓ cup hot, well-drained spinach into each of 4 buttered custard cups, make depression in center of each, and arrange cups in circle on tray. Slide 1 poached egg into each depression, cover completely with Mornay Sauce, and sprinkle with 1 tablespoon finely grated Parmesan. Cover with wax paper and microwave on MEDIUM (50% power) 1½–2 minutes, until warm. Or, if you prefer, set in preheated broiler and broil 5" from heat 15–20 seconds, until touched with brown.

PER SERVING: 372 C   19 g P   27 g F   13 g CARB   1156 mg S   335 mg CH

EGGS SARDOU (Serves 4): Prepare 1 recipe Hollandaise Sauce, set container in bowl of hot, not boiling, water and keep warm; also prepare 1 recipe Creamed Spinach. Spoon ⅓ cup hot spinach into each of 4 buttered individual au gratin dishes or shallow ramekins, top with 1 cooked* or canned artichoke bottom, hollow side up, a poached egg, and several spoonfuls of hot Hollandaise. Cover with wax paper and microwave on MEDIUM-LOW (30% power) 2¾–3 minutes, until warm.

PER SERVING: 481 C   15 g P   42 g F   15 g CARB   776 mg S   629 mg CH

TO FRY EGGS

We frankly find it faster, more efficient and reliable to fry eggs the old-fashioned way in a skillet on top of the stove.

SCRAMBLED EGGS

PREP TIME: | 15 SECONDS | COOKING TIME: | 3¼–4½ MINUTES | STANDING TIME: | 1–2 MINUTES

Microwave-scrambled eggs can be the fluffiest imaginable, but overcooking—even by seconds—will make them rubbery. If you're dieting, eliminate butter; eggs don't stick to microwave ''pans'' the way they do to a stovetop skillet. Always use the container size recommended—scrambled eggs foam in the microwave.

SERVES 4

2 **tablespoons butter or margarine**

6 **eggs**

¼ **cup water, milk, or light cream**

½ **teaspoon salt (about)**

⅛ **teaspoon pepper**

Melt butter in wax-paper-covered 1-quart measure by microwaving on HIGH (100% power) 35–45 seconds. Break eggs into measure, add water, and beat just to combine yolks and whites. Microwave, uncovered, on HIGH (100% power) 1½ minutes. With fork, stir eggs from edges toward center, and microwave, uncovered, on HIGH (100% power) 1¾–2¼ minutes, stirring at halftime, until creamy-firm but still moist. Stir in salt and pepper and let stand, covered, 1–2 minutes, until eggs reach desired degree of doneness. Stir, adjust salt as needed, and serve.

To Scramble Eggs for 1: Prepare as directed, using 1-pint measure, 1 tablespoon each butter and water, and 2 eggs. Allow 25–30 seconds to melt butter and 1¼–1½ minutes to microwave eggs, stirring them twice.

To Scramble Eggs for 2: Prepare as directed, using 1-pint measure, 2 tablespoons each butter, and water and 3 eggs. Allow 35–45 seconds to melt butter and 1¾–2¼ minutes to microwave eggs, stirring them twice.

PER SERVING: 170 C   9 g P   14 g F   1 g CARB   162 mg S   427 mg CH

SOME SUGGESTED SEASONINGS FOR SCRAMBLED EGGS

Prepare scrambled eggs for 2 or 4 as directed, then 30 seconds before eggs are done, mix in ¼–⅓ cup of any of the following:

Minced cooked sausages, frankfurters, ham, tongue, or salami

Minced cooked chicken or turkey

Minced cooked chicken livers

Minced crisply cooked bacon

Minced cooked fish or shellfish

Minced steamed asparagus, broccoli, or cauliflower

Butter-sautéed sliced or chopped mushrooms; onions; sweet red, green, and/or yellow peppers

Coarsely chopped peeled, cored, and seeded ripe tomatoes

Coarsely grated sharp Cheddar, Swiss, Gruyère, or crumbled mild blue cheese

Coarsely grated Monterey Jack cheese *plus* 2–3 tablespoons minced, drained, canned jalapeño peppers

OR

Mix in 1–2 tablespoons minced fresh basil, chervil, chives, coriander (cilantro), dill, marjoram, parsley, or tarragon.

PLAIN OR FRENCH OMELET

PREP TIME: | 10 SECONDS | COOKING TIME: | 1¾–2 MINUTES | STANDING TIME: | NONE

Moist, creamy omelets can be made in the microwave if you follow these directions to the letter. The best omelets are two-egg ones (one serving) or four-egg ones (two servings). Larger ones are difficult to handle and won't cook evenly. Don't salt an omelet before you cook it because you'll toughen the eggs. The best containers for microwaving omelets are glass ovenware or glass ceramic skillets. **Note:** *Omelets do not brown in the microwave, so a colorful topping will be welcome. Browning dishes aren't practical for omelets.*

SERVES 1

2 eggs (at room temperature)
1 tablespoon butter or margarine
Scant ¼ teaspoon salt
Pinch white pepper

Beat eggs briskly with fork until frothy. Melt butter in wax-paper-covered 5½" glass ovenware or glass ceramic skillet by microwaving on HIGH (100% power) 25–30 seconds; tilt skillet to coat bottom evenly. Pour egg mixture into skillet and microwave, uncovered, on HIGH (100% power) 1 minute. With rubber spatula, draw partially set edges toward center and tilt pan so uncooked portion flows underneath. Microwave on HIGH (100% power) 25–30 seconds, until just set and top is creamy. Sprinkle with salt and pepper, loosen omelet with spatula, and let fold over as you turn onto warm plate. Top with one of the following sauces: Mushroom, Cheese, Shrimp, or Fresh Tomato.

PER SERVING: 260 C   12 g P   23 g F   1 g CARB   795 mg S 579 mg CH

To Fill Omelet: Spoon filling (see Some Suggested Fillings for Savory Omelets also) over half of omelet just before folding.

233

Omelet FOR 2: Prepare Plain Omelet as directed, using 4 eggs and 1 tablespoon butter in 8" skillet. Microwave 2½–3 minutes as recipe directs, drawing edges toward center every minute. Sprinkle with ¼ teaspoon salt and ⅛ teaspoon pepper before filling and folding. **Note:** *A turntable will help this large omelet cook more evenly.*

PER SERVING: 209 C   12 g P   17 g F   1 g CARB   467 mg S   564 mg CH

Fines herbes OMELET (Serves 1): Add ½ teaspoon minced fresh chives, ¼ teaspoon minced fresh chervil, and ⅛ teaspoon minced fresh tarragon (or pinch of each dried herb) to melted butter before adding 2 beaten eggs. Microwave as directed. **Note:** *For a 4-egg omelet, double quantity of herbs.*

PER SERVING: 261 C   12 g P   23 g F   1 g CARB   795 mg S   579 mg CH

Spanish OMELET (Serves 2): In 1-pint measure mix 1 tablespoon olive oil; 1 slivered pimiento; 1 peeled, cored, seeded, and coarsely chopped tomato; 1 crushed clove garlic. Cover with wax paper and microwave on HIGH (100% power) 2 minutes, stirring at halftime. Add 1 tablespoon minced parsley, re-cover, and let stand while you prepare Omelet for 2 as directed. Fill omelet with tomato mixture, fold, and serve.

PER SERVING: 288 C   13 g P   24 g F   6 g CARB   477 mg S   564 mg CH

Cheese OMELET (Serves 2): Prepare Omelet for 2 as directed, and 15 seconds before it is done, sprinkle with ⅓ cup coarsely grated sharp Cheddar or Gruyère cheese and complete microwaving. *Other cheese choices:* 2–3 ounces soft ripened cheese such as Boursin, Brie, chèvre, mascarpone, or semisoft cheese such as crumbled feta, grated Muenster, or mozzarella.

PER SERVING: 285 C   17 g P   23 g F   2 g CARB   583 mg S   583 mg CH

Sonoma BRUNCH EGGS (Serves 2): Two hours before preparing omelet, mash 1 medium-size ripe avocado with 2 teaspoons lemon juice; 1 teaspoon each grated yellow onion and olive oil; ⅛ teaspoon each ground cumin, salt, and red pepper flakes. Place plastic food wrap flat on guacamole and refrigerate. Prepare Omelet for 2 as directed; just before turning out, top evenly with guacamole and ⅓ cup coarsely grated Sonoma or Monterey Jack cheese, fold, and serve.

PER SERVING: 463 C   19 g P   40 g F   9 g CARB   717 mg S   580 mg CH

SOME SUGGESTED FILLINGS FOR SAVORY OMELETS

For each 2-egg omelet, use ⅓ cup of any of the following. **Note: *Except for cheese, refrigerator-cold fillings should be warmed. Place in small bowl, cover with vented plastic wrap, and microwave on HIGH (100% power) 45–60 seconds.***

~~~~~~ Cottage, ricotta, or cream cheese (either flavored or plain)

~~~~~~ Boned and flaked cooked fish or shellfish, particularly smoked salmon, haddock, and trout

~~~~~~ Any minced cooked meat or sausage

~~~~~~ Crumbled crisp bacon

~~~~~~ Cooked vegetables such as chopped spinach; sautéed mushrooms, onions, or sweet red, yellow, or green peppers; diced boiled potatoes; steamed asparagus tips, cauliflower or broccoli florets, summer squash, green peas, or carrots

~~~~~~ Raw vegetables such as minced sweet red, yellow, or green peppers; minced red or Spanish onion; shredded zucchini; shredded carrot

~~~~~~ Grated Monterey Jack cheese *plus* 2 tablespoons each sour cream, minced scallions, and minced, canned jalapeño peppers (this is a variation of the splendid Durango Omelet served at Cafe Pasqual's in Santa Fe, New Mexico).

SOUFFLÉ OMELET

PREP TIME: [2 MINUTES] COOKING TIME: [4½–5 MINUTES] STANDING TIME: [NONE]

A fluffy five-minute miracle that won't collapse when you cut into it. **Note:** *A turntable will make the omelet rise more evenly.*

⚖ ¢

SERVES 2

4 eggs, separated (at room temperature)

2 tablespoons cold water

½ teaspoon salt

⅛ teaspoon white pepper

⅛ teaspoon cream of tartar

1 tablespoon butter or margarine

Beat egg yolks and water briskly with fork; set aside. Beat whites until frothy, add salt, pepper, and cream of tartar and beat to soft peaks; fold gently into yolk mixture. Melt butter in wax-paper-covered 1½-quart round casserole about 2″ deep by microwaving on HIGH (100% power) 25–30 seconds; tilt casserole to coat sides with butter. Pour egg mixture into casserole, smooth top lightly, and microwave, uncovered, on MEDIUM (50% power) 4–4½ minutes, until puffed and just set, rotating omelet 180° at halftime if you do not use turntable. Loosen omelet with spatula, divide in half using two forks, and ease onto warmed plates.

To Fill Omelet: Before turning out, crease center of omelet with spatula, top half with filling (see Some Suggested Fillings for Savory Omelets above), fold, lift from pan, and divide in two. *Note: Since folded puffy omelets do not hold much filling, you may prefer to spread omelet with filling, then halve it.*

PER SERVING: 209 C   12 g P   17 g F   1 g CARB   743 mg S 564 mg CH

236

PIPERADE

PREP TIME: 7 MINUTES COOKING TIME: 14½–16 MINUTES STANDING TIME: NONE

The success of this showy Basque omelet depends upon the cooking containers. Use only the sizes and types specified.

SERVES 4

- 1 **medium-size yellow onion, peeled and minced**
- 1 **small sweet green pepper, cored, seeded, and chopped fine**
- 1 **small sweet red pepper, cored, seeded, and chopped fine**
- 2 **tablespoons olive or vegetable oil**
- 2 **medium-size ripe tomatoes, peeled, cored, seeded, and coarsely chopped**
- 1 **clove garlic, peeled and crushed**
- 1 **teaspoon minced fresh basil or ¼ teaspoon crumbled dried basil**
- ½ **teaspoon salt**
- ⅛ **teaspoon pepper**
- ½ **cup cooked ham strips about 2″ long and ¼″ wide**
- 2 **tablespoons butter or margarine**
- 6 **eggs, lightly beaten**

Mix onion, green and red peppers, and oil in shallow 9″ casserole about 2″ deep (this permits maximum evaporation of vegetable juices). Cover with wax paper and microwave on HIGH (100% power) 6 minutes, stirring at halftime. Add tomatoes and garlic and microwave, uncovered, on HIGH (100% power) 4½–5½ minutes, stirring at halftime, until most liquid has boiled away. *Note: If tomatoes are extra juicy, tightly cover casserole with vented plastic wrap and drain.* Mix in basil, salt, pepper, and ham, cover with foil, and set aside.

Melt butter in wax-paper-covered 8″ round glass ovenware casserole about 2″ deep by microwaving on HIGH (100% power) 35–45 seconds; tilt casserole to coat sides with butter. Add eggs and microwave, uncovered, on HIGH (100% power) 3½–4 minutes, drawing partially cooked edges toward center at halftime. When eggs are just set or creamy-firm throughout, spread lightly and evenly with ham mixture. Cut into wedges and serve with crusty French bread.

PER SERVING: 288 C 14 g P 23 g F 7 g CARB 708 mg S 437 mg CH

QUICHE LORRAINE

PREP TIME: | 5 MINUTES | COOKING TIME: | 14½–17 MINUTES | STANDING TIME: | 10 MINUTES

Because pastries don't bake well in a microwave oven, we call here for a conventionally baked pie shell. A turntable will help quiche microwave evenly, and using MEDIUM (50% power) allows the filling to cook gently and set smoothly. If you want to serve quiche as an appetizer, cut into slimmer wedges.

SERVES 6

8   slices crisply cooked bacon, crumbled

1⅓ cups coarsely grated Gruyère or Swiss cheese

1   (9") baked pie shell in a pie plate

1½ cups light cream

4   eggs, lightly beaten

½   teaspoon salt

⅛   teaspoon white pepper

⅛   teaspoon ground nutmeg

Pinch ground hot red pepper

Scatter bacon and cheese evenly over pie shell. Microwave cream in wax-paper-covered 1-quart measure on HIGH (100% power) 2¾–3 minutes until steaming; do not boil. Slowly mix cream into eggs, blend in seasonings and pour into pie shell; place on turntable and center on oven shelf. *Note: If you have neither turntable nor shelf, elevate pie on shallow bowl and rotate quiche 90° every 4 minutes.* Microwave, uncovered, on MEDIUM (50% power) 12–14 minutes, until knife inserted 1" from center of quiche comes out clean. *Note: The soft 1" circle in center will set on standing.* Tent quiche with foil and let stand 10 minutes. Cut into wedges and serve warm.

To Reheat Refrigerator-cold Quiche: Microwave, uncovered, on turntable or flat on oven floor on MEDIUM (50% power) 6–8 minutes, until warm (if not using turntable, rotate quiche 180° at halftime). *To Reheat Room-temperature Quiche:* Reheat as directed, reducing microwave time to 4–5 minutes.

PER SERVING: 473 C   18 g P   38 g F   16 g CARB   655 mg S   257 mg CH

Sʜᴇʟʟғɪsʜ ǫᴜɪᴄʜᴇ: Prepare as directed, but substitute 1 cup minced cooked shrimp, lobster, crab meat, or well-drained clams for bacon and use ⅔ cup each heavy cream and clam juice instead of light cream.
PER SERVING: 423 C   19 g P   32 g F   14 g CARB   617 mg S   293 mg CH

Jᴀʟᴀᴘᴇ̃ɴᴏ, ᴄᴏʀɴ, ᴀɴᴅ ʙᴀᴄᴏɴ ǫᴜɪᴄʜᴇ: Sprinkle baked pie shell evenly with 4 slices crumbled cooked bacon; the cheese; 2–3 minced, cored, seeded, very well-drained canned jalapeño peppers; and ½ cup very well-drained cooked whole-kernel corn; set aside. Microwave 1 tablespoon butter and 1 minced small yellow onion in wax-papered-covered 1-quart casserole on HIGH (100% power) 2½–3 minutes, until glassy, stirring at halftime. Add 1⅓ cups cream, re-cover with wax paper, and microwave until steaming as recipe directs. Mix cream mixture with eggs and all seasonings, pour over corn, cheese, and bacon, spreading onion evenly. Microwave and let stand as directed.
PER SERVING: 367 C   9 g P   28 g F   20 g CARB   614 mg S   227 mg CH

Sᴘɪɴᴀᴄʜ ǫᴜɪᴄʜᴇ: Omit bacon and sprinkle pie shell with 1 cup cheese. Top with 1 cup minced cooked spinach wrung dry in clean dish towel. Microwave 1 tablespoon butter and ½ cup minced yellow onion in wax-paper-covered 1-quart casserole on HIGH (100% power) 3½–4 minutes, until glassy, stirring at halftime. Add 1⅓ cups cream, re-cover with wax paper, and microwave until steaming as recipe directs. Mix cream mixture with eggs and all seasonings, pour over spinach, spreading onion evenly. Microwave and let stand as directed.
PER SERVING: 413 C   14 g P   32 g F   18 g CARB   537 mg S   244 mg CH

SOME OTHER QUICHE FILLINGS

Prepare Quiche Lorraine as directed, but substitute 1 cup of any of the following for the bacon:

Minced, well-drained, cooked artichoke hearts or bottoms
Minced cooked ham, tongue, pork, or Italian sausage
Minced smoked salmon
Minced, well-drained, cooked broccoli or Swiss chard
Sliced, well-drained, butter-sautéed mushrooms
Steamed asparagus tips
Slivered, steamed, peeled, cored, and seeded sweet red and/or green peppers

239

BREAKFASTS, BRUNCHES, & LUNCHES

LOW COUNTRY EGG PIE

PREP TIME: 5 MINUTES COOKING TIME: 18–21 MINUTES STANDING TIME: 5–7 MINUTES

¢

SERVES 4

- **4** **slices firm-textured white bread, trimmed of crusts**
- **1** **cup milk**
- **⅔** **cup half-and-half cream**
- **1** **cup coarsely grated sharp Cheddar cheese**
- **¼** **cup finely grated Parmesan cheese**
- **2** **tablespoons finely grated yellow onion**
- **3** **eggs, lightly beaten**
- **2** **tablespoons Dijon mustard**
- **½** **teaspoon salt**
- **¼** **teaspoon ground hot red pepper**
- **⅛** **teaspoon white pepper**
- **2** **hard-cooked eggs, peeled and coarsely chopped**
- **Paprika (garnish)**

Soak bread in milk and cream 5 minutes, then mix in remaining ingredients, folding in hard-cooked eggs last. Spoon into 9″ round 1½-quart casserole, sprinkle with paprika, and microwave, uncovered, on MEDIUM (50% power) 18–21 minutes, rotating casserole 90° every 4 minutes, until just set. *Note: The tiny moist area in pie's center will dry on standing. To test for doneness, insert knife midway between rim and center; if it comes out clean, pie is done.* Cover with foil and let stand 5–7 minutes. Cut in wedges and serve. *Note: To reheat seconds, cover with wax paper and microwave on MEDIUM-LOW (30% power) in 1-minute increments; don't overheat or pie will separate and weep.*

PER SERVING: 403 C 22 g P 26 g F 19 g CARB 1035 mg S 401 mg CH

FLAMICHE *(BURGUNDIAN LEEK PIE)*

PREP TIME: 10 MINUTES | COOKING TIME: 28–32 MINUTES | STANDING TIME: 10 MINUTES

This delicate one-crust version of the traditional two-crust French pie microwaves beautifully and makes a lovely luncheon entrée.

SERVES 6

1½ *pounds leeks (each about 1″ in diameter), trimmed, washed well, and sliced ¼″ thick*

1 *tablespoon butter (no substitute)*

1¼ *cups coarsely grated Gruyère cheese*

1 *(9″) baked pie shell in a pie plate*

1 *cup light cream*

3 *eggs, lightly beaten*

½ *teaspoon salt*

⅛ *teaspoon white pepper*

Place leeks in 2-quart casserole, dot with butter, cover with vented plastic food wrap, and microwave on HIGH (100% power) 9–10 minutes, stirring at halftime, until soft but not mushy. *Note: If liquid hasn't evaporated, drain leeks well.* Toss cheese with leeks and spread evenly in pie shell. Microwave cream in wax-paper-covered 1-quart measure on HIGH (100% power) 2¾–3 minutes, until steaming; do not boil. Slowly mix cream into eggs, blend in salt and pepper, and pour into pie shell; place on turntable and center on oven shelf. *Note: If you have neither turntable nor shelf, elevate pie on shallow bowl and rotate pie 90° every 4 minutes.* Microwave, uncovered, on MEDIUM (50% power) 16–19 minutes, until knife inserted 1″ from center of pie comes out clean. *Note: The soft 1″ circle in center will set on standing.* Tent pie with foil and let stand 10 minutes. Serve warm. *Note: Reheat as directed for Quiche Lorraine above.*

PER SERVING: 413 C 14 g P 30 g F 22 g CARB 525 mg S 195 mg CH

241

WELSH RAREBIT

PREP TIME: **3 MINUTES** COOKING TIME: **3½–4 MINUTES** STANDING TIME: **NONE**

¢ ⌛

SERVES 4

- **1 tablespoon butter or margarine**
- **1 tablespoon Worcestershire sauce**
- **½ cup beer, ale, or milk**
- **½ teaspoon dry mustard**
- **Pinch ground hot red pepper**
- **¾ pound Cheshire or well-aged sharp Cheddar cheese, coarsely grated**
- **8 slices firm-textured white bread, toasted and crusts removed**

Microwave all ingredients except cheese and bread in uncovered 1-quart measure on HIGH (100% power) 1¾–2 minutes, until bubbly. Add cheese by handfuls, stirring after each addition, then microwave, uncovered, on MEDIUM (50% power) 1¾–2 minutes, until cheese melts completely and mixture is smooth and thick. Spoon over toast and serve.

PER SERVING: 508 C   26 g P   33 g F   27 g CARB   843 mg S   99 mg CH

~~~~~~~ V A R I A T I O N S

⌛ ROQUEFORT RAREBIT: Prepare as directed, using ¼ pound crumbled Roquefort and ½ pound sharp Cheddar. Garnish with snipped chives.

PER SERVING: 498 C   25 g P   32 g F   27 g CARB   1181 mg S   94 mg CH

¢ ⌛ CALIFORNIA RAREBIT: Microwave butter, uncovered, with ¼ cup each minced yellow onion and sweet green pepper on HIGH (100% power) 3–3½ minutes, until glassy. Add Worcestershire, milk, and mustard along with 1 peeled, seeded, and coarsely chopped medium-size tomato; 2 minced canned jalapeño peppers; and ⅛ teaspoon red pepper flakes. Microwave, uncovered, on HIGH (100% power) 2¾–3 minutes, until bubbly. Add cheese and finish as directed. Serve over toasted sourdough bread or English muffins.

PER SERVING: 534 C   27 g P   34 g F   30 g CARB   969 mg S   103 mg CH

MACARONI AND CHEESE

PREP TIME: 4 MINUTES | COOKING TIME: 13–15½ MINUTES | STANDING TIME: 2–3 MINUTES

Because the saltiness of Cheddar varies, taste the macaroni mixture before you microwave it, increasing the amount of salt as needed. A crushed cornflake topping adds color and crunch, but if you prefer a more traditional brown top, run the macaroni and cheese in and out of the broiler after microwaving.

SERVES 4

½   **pound elbow macaroni**

¼   **cup (½ stick) butter or margarine**

1   **tablespoon finely grated yellow onion**

¼   **cup unsifted flour**

2½ **cups milk**

1   **tablespoon Worcestershire sauce**

1   **tablespoon prepared spicy brown mustard**

½   **teaspoon salt (about)**

⅛   **teaspoon white pepper**

2½ **cups coarsely grated sharp Cheddar cheese**

¼   **cup crushed cornflakes (optional topping)**

Begin cooking macaroni by package directions. Meanwhile, microwave butter and onion in wax-paper-covered 2½-quart casserole about 3" deep on HIGH (100% power) 55–65 seconds, until butter melts. Blend in flour and microwave, uncovered, on HIGH (100% power) 30 seconds, until foamy. Gradually mix in milk, add Worcestershire, mustard, salt, and pepper and microwave, uncovered, on HIGH (100% power) 4½–5½ minutes, beating every 1½ minutes, until sauce boils and thickens. Mix in 2 cups cheese and microwave, uncovered, on MEDIUM (50% power) 2–2½ minutes, until completely melted. The instant macaroni is done, drain well and fold into cheese mixture, spreading evenly in casserole. Cover with lid or vented plastic food wrap and microwave on MEDIUM (50% power) 5–6 minutes, stirring at halftime, until hot. Sprinkle with remaining cheese, cover with wax paper, and let stand 2–3 minutes to melt cheese. Sprinkle with crushed cornflakes, if you like, and serve. Or if casserole is flameproof, omit cornflakes, increase cheese topping to ¾ cup, transfer to preheated broiler, and broil 3" from heat 2–3 minutes, until touched with brown.

To Cook in Individual Casseroles: Spoon macaroni mixture into 4 or 5 individual 1½-cup au

243

gratin dishes, arrange in oven not touching oven walls or one another, and microwave 6–7 minutes, rearranging at halftime.

PER SERVING: 727 C 31 g P 41 g F 58 g CARB 985 mg S 127 mg CH

THREE CHEESE–ZITI RING

PREP TIME: | 15 MINUTES | COOKING TIME: | 13½–15½ MINUTES | STANDING TIME: | 10 MINUTES

¢

SERVES 6–8

½ **pound ziti, cooked and drained by package directions**

2 **cups soft whole wheat bread crumbs**

1 **cup coarsely grated Cheddar cheese**

1 **cup coarsely grated Swiss cheese**

½ **cup finely grated Parmesan cheese**

¼ **cup moderately finely diced pimiento**

2 **tablespoons minced parsley**

3 **eggs, lightly beaten**

1½ **teaspoons salt**

¼ **teaspoon pepper**

½ **cup minced scallions (include tops)**

1¾ **cups milk**

Mix ziti with all ingredients except scallions and milk; set aside. Place scallions and milk in 1-quart measure and microwave, uncovered, on HIGH (100% power) 4½–5½ minutes, until small bubbles appear around edge. Stir into ziti-cheese mixture. Spoon into 2-quart ring mold, cover with vented plastic food wrap, and microwave on MEDIUM (50% power) 9–10 minutes, rotating mold 180° at halftime, until just firm. *Note: The small soft area midway between edge and center will set on standing.* Cover with foil and let stand 10 minutes. Invert on platter and gently ease cheese ring out of mold. Accompany, if you like, with hot Jiffy Tomato Sauce or Mushroom Sauce.

To Reheat: Cover with vented plastic food wrap and microwave on MEDIUM (50% power) 4–5 minutes, rotating platter 180° at halftime.

PER SERVING: 441–331 C 25–19 g P 20–15 g F 41–31 g CARB 991–744 mg S 190–142 mg CH

FUSILLI, TOMATOES, AND ROASTED GREEN PEPPERS WITH BASIL AIOLI

PREP TIME: [2 MINUTES] COOKING TIME: [6–8 MINUTES] STANDING TIME: [5 MINUTES]

SERVES 4 AS AN ENTRÉE, 6 AS A SIDE DISH

- 1 **pound fusilli, cooked and drained by package directions**
- 2 **tablespoons olive oil**
- 2 **large sweet green peppers**
- 4 **large cloves garlic (do not peel)**
- 1 **cup mayonnaise**
- 3 **tablespoons minced fresh basil**

Pinch sugar

Pinch ground hot red pepper

- 1 **teaspoon salt (about)**
- ¼ **teaspoon black pepper**
- 12 **cherry tomatoes, halved or quartered**

Toss pasta with olive oil in large serving bowl and set aside. Place green peppers in plastic bag, twist ends and knot, place on oven floor, and microwave on HIGH (100% power) 3–4 minutes. Turn bag over and rotate 180°. Wrap garlic in paper toweling and place in oven beside peppers. Microwave on HIGH (100% power) 3–4 minutes, until peppers are slightly soft and garlic very soft. Let bag of peppers and wrapped garlic stand 5 minutes. Cool peppers under cold tap, peel, seed, pat dry on paper toweling, and dice. Squeeze garlic from skins into food processor, add mayonnaise, basil, sugar, and red pepper and pulse 6–8 times, until creamy; add ¾ cup to pasta along with, diced peppers, salt, and black pepper; toss well. Adjust salt as needed, add tomatoes and toss gently. If pasta seems dry, add remaining basil mixture and toss lightly. Serve at once or cover and mellow 30 minutes at room temperature before serving.

PER SERVING: 900–600 C 16–11 g P 52–35 g F 93–62 g CARB
870–580 mg S 32–22 mg CH

GREEN SHELLS WITH GORGONZOLA CREAM

PREP TIME: 2 MINUTES | **COOKING TIME:** 4¾–6¼ MINUTES | **STANDING TIME:** NONE

For efficiency's sake, set the pasta on to cook a couple of minutes before you begin microwaving the sauce so that both will be ready at the same time.

SERVES 4

¾ **pound small green seashell pasta**

1 **large clove garlic (do not peel)**

½ **pound Gorgonzola cheese**

¾ **cup light cream**

Freshly ground black pepper

Optional Extras (choose one)

2 **tablespoons finely shaved white or black truffles**

⅓ **cup toasted piñon nuts**

¼ **cup diced, pitted, oil-cured black olives**

½ **cup diced pimiento**

Begin cooking pasta by package directions. Meanwhile, wrap garlic in paper toweling and microwave on HIGH (100% power) 1–1½ minutes, until soft; remove from oven. Crumble cheese into ½" chunks, place in 1-quart measure, cover with wax paper, and microwave on MEDIUM (50% power) 2–2½ minutes to soften. Squeeze garlic from skin into cheese, blend in cream, re-cover with wax paper, and microwave on HIGH (100% power) 1¾–2¼ minutes, stirring well at halftime, until sauce is hot, not boiling. The instant pasta is *al dente,* drain well and return to kettle. Pour cheese sauce on top, add one of the optional extras, if you like, and toss well. Top with plenty of freshly ground black pepper and serve.

PER SERVING: 629 C 26 g P 31 g F 63 g CARB 1049 mg S 161 mg CH

PENNE WITH LIMAS AND JALAPEÑO-TOMATO SAUCE

PREP TIME: [6 MINUTES] COOKING TIME: [17–19 MINUTES] STANDING TIME: [NONE]

There used to be a wonderful vegetarian restaurant in Santa Fe, New Mexico, called the Desert Cafe, and this recipe is a microwave version of one of Chef Larry Vito's inspired offerings.

SERVES 6

- 2 **tablespoons olive oil**
- 1 **small yellow onion, peeled and minced**
- 1 **small sweet green pepper, cored, seeded, and minced**
- 2 **cloves garlic, peeled and minced**
- 2 **small canned jalapeño peppers, cored, seeded, and minced**
- 2 **cups tomato purée**
- ⅓ **cup hot water**
- 1 **teaspoon salt**
- ¼ **teaspoon sugar**
- ⅛ **teaspoon pepper**
- 1 **package (10 ounces) frozen baby lima beans**

Pasta

- 1 **pound penne**
- 1 **tablespoon olive oil**

Topping

- 1 **cup sour cream (at room temperature)**
- ½ **cup thinly sliced scallions**

Microwave oil, onion, green pepper, and garlic in wax-paper-covered 2½-quart casserole on HIGH (100% power) 4½–5½ minutes, until onion is glassy. Add jalapeños, tomato purée, water, salt, sugar, and pepper; cover with lid or vented plastic food wrap and microwave on HIGH (100% power) 3–3½ minutes, until steaming. Add limas, re-cover, and microwave on HIGH (100% power) 5½–6¼ minutes, breaking up frozen chunks at halftime, until limas are almost tender. Stir, re-cover, and microwave on MEDIUM (50% power) 4 minutes to mellow flavors. As sauce nears doneness, cook penne by package directions, drain, return to kettle, add oil, and toss well. Divide pasta among 6 heated plates, top with sauce, a dollop of sour cream, and sprinkling of scallions.

PER SERVING: 528 C 16 g P 16 g F 81 g CARB 820 mg S 17 mg CH

ABOUT MICROWAVING SOUFFLÉS

Popular opinion to the contrary, soufflés *can* be cooked successfully in the microwave. They won't rise as stratospherically as soufflés baked in conventional ovens, but they *will* puff about ¾" above the rim of the soufflé dish when made just as these recipes instruct. The microwave soufflés included here are even more stable than standard ones, meaning they won't collapse within minutes of being taken from the oven. Their main drawback is that they don't brown. A small problem, really, because you've only to top a soufflé with a compatible sauce. For perfect microwave soufflés, read and abide by these guidelines:

Follow each recipe to the letter. Do not substitute one major ingredient for another and do not use a soufflé dish larger or smaller than the one specified. The only adjustments that can be made safely are such minor ones as using one herb in place of another. What must never change are the basic proportions of butter, flour, liquid, egg, and principal flavoring (cheese, fish, chicken, etc.).

For a slightly more stable soufflé of firmer texture, use evaporated milk in place of light cream. ***Note: This is a good trick for beginners.***

Always beat the egg whites with a bit of cream of tartar. It not only makes them climb to greater heights but also stabilizes them so that they're less likely to deflate.

When baking a soufflé in the microwave, always use an *ungreased* straight-sided, microwave-safe soufflé dish in the size recommended. It will help the soufflé rise and cook more evenly.

To ensure even cooking and rising, smooth the surface of the soufflé batter lightly; peaks will only dry out during microwaving. Also use a turntable, which eliminates the need to rotate the soufflé dish frequently and gives the finished soufflé an evenly risen, professional look. ***Note: The turntable can sometimes speed cooking time by 2–3 minutes.***

For maximum rising, always microwave a soufflé *uncovered* (the lack of a cover will dry the surface of the soufflé faster, too—a decided advantage).

~~~ To allow a soufflé to rise slowly and evenly and to keep its edges from overcooking before the center is done, microwave on MEDIUM-LOW (30% power) or on DEFROST.

~~~ Check the soufflé's progress often by peering through the oven door window. You'll note that the soufflé batter seems to rise and fall as it cooks—almost as if breathing. As the soufflé nears doneness, the "breathing" will slow noticeably—your clue that it's time to begin testing for doneness.

~~~ To test a soufflé for doneness: Touch the top of the soufflé lightly. It will be dry, but stick to your finger, revealing a dry interior except for a moist—but not runny—center. **Note:** *Soufflés require no standing time.*

~~~ HERBED CHEESE SOUFFLÉ

PREP TIME: COOKING TIME: STANDING TIME:

PREP TIME: **4 MINUTES** COOKING TIME: **27–32 MINUTES** STANDING TIME: **NONE**

Evaporated milk makes for a denser soufflé that beginners may find easier to prepare. For an evenly risen, professional-looking soufflé, use a turntable.

SERVES 4

¼ cup (½ *stick*) *butter or margarine*

¼ cup *sifted flour*

1 cup *light cream or evaporated milk*

1 cup *coarsely grated sharp Cheddar or Swiss cheese*

4 *eggs, at room temperature, separated*

Melt butter in wax-paper-covered 6-cup measure by microwaving on HIGH (100% power) 55–65 seconds. Stir in flour and microwave, uncovered, on HIGH (100% power) 30 seconds, until foamy. Gradually blend in cream and microwave, uncovered, on HIGH (100% power) 3–3½ minutes, until sauce boils and thickens, beating well at halftime (sauce will be very thick). Add cheese and stir until melted; cool 1 minute. Blend a little hot sauce into egg yolks, stir back into measure, and microwave, uncovered, on

249

1   **tablespoon minced fresh
    basil, oregano, marjoram,
    cilantro, or parsley**
½   **teaspoon salt**
⅛   **teaspoon white pepper**
1   **teaspoon Dijon mustard**
⅛   **teaspoon cream of tartar**

MEDIUM (50% power) 30 seconds. Beat well, then stir in basil, salt, pepper, and mustard.

Beat egg whites with cream of tartar until stiff, not dry. Stir about ¼ cup beaten whites into sauce, then fold in remaining whites. Spoon into 6-cup soufflé dish, lightly smooth top, and microwave, uncovered, on MEDIUM-LOW (30% power) 22–26 minutes, until soufflé rises about ¾" above rim of dish. *Note: If not using turntable, rotate dish 90° every 5 minutes.* As soufflé cooks, it will rise and fall, almost as if breathing. Toward end of cooking, "breathing" will slow, meaning soufflé is almost done. Watch carefully. To test soufflé for doneness, touch lightly. Except for moist dime-size area in middle, surface will be dry and stick to your finger, revealing a dry interior. Serve soufflé at once—no standing time needed. Accompany, if you like, with Sweet Red Pepper Sauce or a favorite cheese or tomato sauce.

To Make the Soufflé for 2: Prepare sauce as directed, using 2 tablespoons each butter and flour and ½ cup light cream. Microwave sauce on HIGH (100% power) as directed for 2 minutes only; add ½ cup grated cheese and 2 egg yolks; do not heat sauce once yolks are added. Mix in 1½ teaspoons minced fresh herb, ¼ teaspoon salt, a pinch white pepper, and ½ teaspoon Dijon mustard. Fold in 2 egg whites beaten stiff with pinch cream of tartar. Spoon mixture into 3– 3½-cup soufflé dish and microwave, uncovered, on MEDIUM-LOW (30% power) 9–10½ minutes.

PER SERVING: 441 C   16 g P   38 g F   9 g CARB   697 mg S   374 mg CH

V A R I A T I O N S

LEMONY SALMON SOUFFLÉ: Prepare sauce as directed, substituting 1 cup finely flaked, boned, skinned cooked salmon (or well-drained canned salmon or any finely flaked, cooked delicate white fish) for cheese. Add 1 tablespoon minced parsley and 1 teaspoon finely grated lemon rind along with salt and pepper; omit mustard and proceed as directed. Serve with Caper Sauce.

PER SERVING: 382 C   17 g P   31 g F   9 g CARB   679 mg S   360 mg CH

DILLED SHRIMP SOUFFLÉ: Prepare sauce as directed, substituting 1 cup finely minced cooked shrimp, lobster, crab, or well-drained clams for cheese. Add 1 tablespoon each minced fresh dill and parsley along with salt and pepper; omit mustard and proceed as directed. Serve with Shrimp or Parsley Sauce.

PER SERVING: 382 C   21 g P   29 g F   9 g CARB   612 mg S   455 mg CH

DEVILED HAM SOUFFLÉ: Prepare sauce as directed, substituting 1 cup ground cooked ham for cheese. Omit herbs but add 1 teaspoon Worcestershire sauce and ⅛ teaspoon ground hot red pepper along with mustard, salt, and white pepper; proceed as directed. Serve with Mustard or Cheese Sauce.

PER SERVING: 391 C   17 g P   32 g F   9 g CARB   1075 mg S   366 mg CH

¢ CURRIED CHICKEN OR TURKEY SOUFFLÉ: Melt butter as directed, blend in flour and 1 tablespoon each curry powder and finely grated yellow onion, then proceed as directed, substituting 1 cup finely ground cooked chicken or turkey (white meat is preferable) for cheese. Increase salt to 1 teaspoon and omit mustard. Serve with chutney and, if you like, Mushroom Sauce.

PER SERVING: 397 C   19 g P   32 g F   10 g CARB   791 mg S   376 mg CH

ABOUT MICROWAVING QUICK BREADS

Not all quick breads microwave well. Biscuits fare poorly, drying—but not browning—on top and bottom while remaining doughy inside. Popovers refuse to pop, crispen, or brown, as does Yorkshire pudding. So bake these three in a standard oven. We focus here on the quick breads that *do* microwave well (muffins, coffee cakes, tea breads, steamed breads) and show how to solve the problems inherent in this moist method of "baking." As for adapting family favorites for the microwave, see "How to Convert Favorite Recipes for Microwave Use" in Chapter 1. Many oven manufacturers include quick-bread recipes in their manuals; read these carefully for useful tips about making quick breads in your particular oven. When it comes to microwaving packaged mixes, do exactly as the label instructs.

MICROWAVE ADVANTAGES

SPEED: You can bake half a dozen muffins in about 2½ minutes, a coffee cake or loaf of tea bread 66 percent faster than you can in a conventional oven. You can even steam a loaf of brown bread in 5½–6 minutes. Pretty impressive.

UNIFORM TEXTURE AND GREATER VOLUME: Because breads baked in a microwave oven do not develop a crust, they rise to greater heights and develop a more uniform texture than those baked the old-fashioned way. They are also supremely moist and tender.

251

PROBLEMS, PREVENTIVES, AND SOLUTIONS

FAILURE TO BROWN: Microwaved quick breads seem anemic unless you build a little color into the batter. Our recipes, for example, often use whole-grain flours instead of the highly refined (this means more fiber, too), brown sugar instead of white, and plenty of spices either alone or in tandem with fruits and nuts (muffins, especially, are handsomer when made with bran, wheat berries, yellow cornmeal, dried fruits, or nuts). Another trick is to apply a colorful topper to a pale bread. Sprinklings of wheat germ, crumbs, or streusel (crumbs mixed with sugar and spice) all make nifty cover-ups.

FAILURE TO DEVELOP A CRUST: This is both a blessing (greater volume, more uniform texture, moister bread) and a problem, albeit a cosmetic one. Who doesn't like the crusty "heel" of a conventionally baked loaf? Of a crisp brown muffin? You can simulate crusts for microwave breads by coating the baking dishes with fine crumbs (graham cracker and gingersnap are especially effective; minced nuts *aren't*—they absorb moisture and turn rubbery, and white flour's a disaster, producing an ugly film). **Note:** *If your "crust" is to be properly impressive, you must grease the baking dish evenly with vegetable shortening, unsalted butter, or margarine (crumbs don't stick as well to oiled surfaces), then coat the dish completely and uniformly with crumbs.*

FRUITS OR NUTS SINKING TO THE BOTTOM OF A LOAF: Because batters thin considerably during the early stage of microwaving, dried fruits and nuts must sometimes be minced if they're to stay afloat.

THE NEED TO BAKE LOAVES IN UNCONVENTIONAL SHAPES: When it comes to microwaving, round is better than square or rectangular, and rings are best of all. For traditionalists who like brick-shaped loaves or square tea breads that can be cut into bars like brownies, it's something of a jolt to see these breads emerge as Frisbees or giant doughnuts. It *is* possible to use a square baking dish for some breads (we include one such), but you must shield the corners with foil strips, for the initial microwaving, at least, lest the corners of the bread overcook (see Shield in The Terms and Techniques of Microwaving, Chapter 3). **Note:** *When preparing recipes in this book, always use the size and shape of dish or mold called for.*

If a recipe specifies a ring mold and you have none, all is not lost. Simply improvise one as follows:

HOW TO IMPROVISE A RING MOLD: Stand a greased 5- or 6-ounce custard cup right side up in the middle of a greased round casserole. To determine the capacity of the improvised ring mold, subtract the volume of the cup from the volume of the casserole.

FAILURE TO COOK EVENLY: Breads baked in a microwave oven tend to cook unevenly because of the way the microwaves are distributed (most ovens have "hot spots"). Using round or ring-shaped "pans" helps overcome the problem, but there are other solutions too:

Always spread batter as evenly as possible in a baking dish so that it is of equal depth throughout.

Use a turntable and center it on the oven shelf (the bread should be as near the middle of the oven as possible). *Note: If you have no shelf, elevate the turntable on an upside-down shallow bowl. If you have no turntable or shelf, elevate the baking dish and rotate it during microwaving as individual recipes specify.*

Follow the recommended two-stage microwaving procedure, first on MEDIUM (50% power) to allow gases to expand slowly, leavening the bread evenly, followed by a period on HIGH (100%). To permit maximum escape of steam, microwave quick breads *uncovered.*

To complete cooking of quick breads *after* microwaving, let them *stand flat on a heat-resistant surface* (the handiest is the floor of the turned-off oven). This will conduct heat back into the breads, especially the bottoms, which are the last to cook. This standing period also allows the tops of loaves to air-dry. Our recipes are quite specific about standing times and techniques; they vary from bread to bread, so follow instructions carefully.

UNUSUAL MOISTNESS OR STICKINESS: Most microwaved quick breads are singularly tender because they have no crust. Always cool them as directed before cutting or turning out. To keep their moist tops from sticking to cooling racks, turn loaves right side up on serving plates at once.

253

FAILURE TO REMAIN MOIST: Because they are crustless, microwaved quick breads dry out very quickly. They should be covered loosely with clean dish towels (or paper toweling) while they cool, then wrapped airtight without delay.

HOW TO TEST QUICK BREADS FOR DONENESS

Begin testing for doneness as soon as the minimum microwaving time has elapsed. Here's how:

1. Insert a toothpick or cake tester in the center of the bread; it should come out clean. **Note:** *Test tall breads right to the bottom of the baking dish.*

2. Touch the top of a loaf gently. Despite a few moist spots, it should feel springy. Touch the moist spots, too; the bread underneath should look dry and cooked. **Note:** *Never microwave a bread until all surface spots dry; you'll overcook it. These moist spots will disappear as the bread cools.*

3. If a bread is not done after the maximum cooking time, continue microwaving on the same power level in 30-second increments, testing for doneness after each.

BASIC MICROWAVE MUFFINS

PREP TIME: | 2 MINUTES | COOKING TIME: | 2–2½ MINUTES | STANDING TIME: | 2 MINUTES |

This recipe contains slightly more oil and sugar than the standard muffin recipe, but produces muffins of uniform texture and tender crumb. To give the muffins extra support as they microwave and to ensure even rising, line each muffin pan cup with 2 crinkly paper liners. Because plain, fruit-, or nut-filled muffins do not brown, a topping will make them more attractive (see Some Muffin Toppings). **Note:** *If tightly* *covered, plain muffin batter will keep 4–5 days in the refrigerator. Add fruit, nuts, bacon, etc. just before baking and allow 15–30 seconds longer for the chilled batter to cook.*

¢

MAKES 1 DOZEN

2 cups unsifted flour

⅓ cup sugar

2 teaspoons baking powder

Pinch salt

⅓ cup vegetable oil

⅔ cup milk

2 eggs, lightly beaten

1 teaspoon vanilla (optional)

Topping

¼ cup sugar mixed with 1 teaspoon ground cinnamon or use another topping (see Some Muffin Toppings)

Sift flour, sugar, baking powder and salt together into mixing bowl. Combine oil, milk, eggs, and if you like, vanilla. Make well in dry ingredients, add egg mixture, and stir lightly just to mix— batter should be lumpy. Line each cup of 6-cup muffin pan or cupcaker with 2 crinkly paper liners, half-fill each and sprinkle evenly with 1 teaspoon topping. Microwave, uncovered, on HIGH (100% power) 2–2½ minutes. *Note: No need to rotate pan because cooking time is short; still, if your oven has severe hot spots, muffins will be better if set on a turntable or rotated 180° at halftime.* Test for doneness after 2 minutes by inserting toothpick in center of each muffin; it should come out clean (any moist spots on surface will dry on standing). Remove outer liners at once and transfer muffins (in single liners) to wire rack so they don't go soggy. Let stand 2 minutes and serve. Microwave remaining batter as directed. *Note: If you plan to microwave fewer muffins at a time, allow 45–55 seconds for 1 muffin, 1¼–1½ minutes for 2, and 1½–2 minutes for 4.*

PER MUFFIN: 188 C   4 g P   8 g F   26 g CARB   101 mg S   48 mg CH

V A R I A T I O N S

¢ CURRANT, RAISIN, FIG, OR DATE MUFFINS: Toss 1 teaspoon finely grated lemon rind and ¾ cup dried currants, seedless raisins, or moderately finely chopped figs or pitted dates with dry ingredients and proceed as directed.

PER MUFFIN: 214 C   4 g P   8 g F   33 g CARB   102 mg S   48 mg CH

¢ NUT MUFFINS: Toss ¾ cup minced nuts (any kind but toasted nuts are especially good) with dry ingredients and proceed as directed.

PER MUFFIN: 237 C   5 g P   12 g F   28 g CARB   102 mg S   48 mg CH

255

¢ HONEYED WHEAT GERM—BACON MUFFINS: Toss ⅓ cup minced crisply cooked bacon with dry ingredients and proceed as directed. Before microwaving, top each muffin with 1½ teaspoons honey-flavored wheat germ. Microwave as directed.

PER MUFFIN: 222 C   6 g P   9 g F   28 g CARB   151 mg S   50 mg CH

¢ ORANGE STREUSEL MUFFINS: Toss finely grated rind of 1 orange with dry ingredients. Combine oil and eggs with ⅓ cup each orange juice and milk, add to dry ingredients, and proceed as directed. Before microwaving, top each muffin with scant tablespoon of following mixture: ¼ cup each graham cracker crumbs and firmly packed dark brown sugar, 2 tablespoons softened butter, and ¼ teaspoon ground cinnamon. Microwave as directed.

PER MUFFIN: 216 C   4 g P   9 g F   29 g CARB   133 mg S   52 mg CH

¢ BLUEBERRY MUFFINS: Toss ¾ cup well-dried blueberries with dry ingredients, combine liquid ingredients using 1 egg only, add to dry ingredients, and proceed as directed.

PER MUFFIN: 187 C   3 g P   7 g F   28 g CARB   96 mg S   25 mg CH

TO MICROWAVE MUFFINS IN CUSTARD CUPS: Line 1–6 custard cups (5-ounce size) with double thickness of crinkly paper liners. Half-fill with muffin batter and bake as directed, arranging cups 1" apart, 3 in triangle and 4 or more in circle. ***Note:*** *Set 3 or more cups on plate to make lifting in and out of oven easy, also rotating or rearranging.*

TO REHEAT MUFFINS (FROM ROOM TEMPERATURE): Wrap in paper toweling and microwave on MEDIUM (50% power) 15–20 seconds per muffin.

SOME MUFFIN TOPPINGS

Sugar:
  Light or dark brown
  Granulated maple sugar

Crumbs:
  Graham cracker
  Cookie (vanilla, orange,
    lemon, or ginger)
  Melba toast

Grains:
  Crushed dry cereal
  Wheat germ

Nuts:
  Chopped pecans, walnuts,
    almonds, or peanuts
  Lightly toasted shredded coconut

Other:
  Crisp bacon crumbles

Before microwaving, sprinkle about 1 teaspoon of any of the suggested toppings over each muffin and microwave as recipes direct.

CORN MUFFINS

PREP TIME: 5 MINUTES   COOKING TIME: 1¾–2¼ MINUTES   STANDING TIME: 2 MINUTES

These muffins will cook more evenly if you use a turntable.

MAKES 10

- 1 cup sifted flour
- 1 cup sifted yellow cornmeal (not stone-ground)
- 2 teaspoons baking powder
- 3 tablespoons sugar
- ¼ teaspoon salt
- 1 egg, lightly beaten
- ¼ cup vegetable oil, melted vegetable shortening, or bacon drippings
- ⅔ cup milk

Sift flour, cornmeal, baking powder, sugar and salt together into mixing bowl and make a well in center. Combine egg, oil, and milk, dump into well in dry ingredients, and stir lightly just to mix—batter should be lumpy. Line each cup of 6-cup muffin pan or cupcaker with 2 crinkly paper liners and half fill each. Microwave, uncovered, on HIGH (100% power) 1¾–2¼ minutes, rotating pan 180° at halftime if you are not using turntable. Test for doneness after 1¾ minutes by inserting toothpick in center of each muffin; it should come out clean (moist spots on muffin surfaces will dry on standing). Remove outer liners at once, transfer muffins (in single liners) to wire rack, let stand 2 minutes, and serve warm with plenty of butter. Microwave remaining batter as directed (there will be 4 muffins), reducing cooking time to 1½–2 minutes.

PER MUFFIN: 173 C   3 g P   7 g F   24 g CARB   155 mg S   30 mg CH

V A R I A T I O N

CHEESE AND GREEN CHILI MUFFINS (Makes 1 dozen): Prepare batter as directed, increasing baking powder to 2¼ teaspoons, then stir in ¾ cup coarsely grated Monterey Jack or sharp Cheddar cheese and ¼ cup finely minced, very well-drained canned green chilies or jalapeño peppers. Microwave each batch of 6 muffins as recipe directs for 2–2½ minutes.

PER MUFFIN: 171 C   5 g P   8 g F   20 g CARB   193 mg S   31 mg CH

257

APRICOT-BRAN MUFFINS

PREP TIME: **7 MINUTES** COOKING TIME: **2–2½ MINUTES** STANDING TIME: **2 MINUTES**

Bran cereals vary, so don't be surprised if these muffins take 10–15 seconds longer to bake.

¢

MAKES 1 DOZEN

- **1 cup ready-to-eat whole bran cereal**
- **⅔ cup milk**
- **1 cup sifted flour**
- **⅓ cup sugar**
- **1 tablespoon baking powder**
- **Pinch salt**
- **⅔ cup finely chopped dried apricots**
- **⅓ cup vegetable oil**
- **2 eggs, lightly beaten**

Soak bran in milk 2 minutes. Sift flour, sugar, baking powder, and salt together into mixing bowl, add apricots, and toss to dredge; make well in dry ingredients. Beat oil and eggs together, stir into bran mixture, then dump into well in dry ingredients and stir lightly just to mix—batter should be lumpy. Line each cup of 6-cup muffin pan or cupcaker with 2 crinkly paper liners and half fill each. Microwave, uncovered, on HIGH (100% power) 2–2½ minutes. Test for doneness after 2 minutes by inserting toothpick in center of each muffin; it should come out clean (moist spots on surface of muffins will dry on standing). Remove outer liners at once, transfer muffins (in single liners) to wire rack, let stand 2 minutes, and serve. Microwave remaining batter as directed.

PER MUFFIN: 166 C   4 g P   8 g F   24 g CARB   202 mg S   48 mg CH

V A R I A T I O N S

¢ RAISIN-BRAN MUFFINS: Prepare as directed, substituting seedless raisins (no need to chop) or dried currants for apricots.

PER MUFFIN: 173 C   4 g P   8 g F   26 g CARB   202 mg S   48 mg CH

NUT-BRAN MUFFINS: Prepare as directed, substituting ⅔ cup minced nuts (any kind) for apricots.

PER MUFFIN: 192 C   4 g P   12 g F   20 g CARB   202 mg S   48 mg CH

NUT-APRICOT-BRAN MUFFINS: Prepare as directed, using ⅓ cup each minced nuts and chopped apricots (or seedless raisins or dried currants).

PER MUFFIN: 178 C   4 g P   10 g F   22 g CARB   202 mg S   48 mg CH

*B*UTTERMILK–WHEAT BERRY MUFFINS

PREP TIME: | 4 MINUTES | COOKING TIME: | 3–3½ MINUTES | STANDING TIME: | 2 MINUTES

Most health food stores carry wheat berries.

MAKES 1 DOZEN

¼ cup wheat berries

¼ cup boiling water

1 cup sifted all-purpose flour

1 teaspoon baking soda

Pinch salt

¾ cup unsifted whole wheat flour (not stone-ground)

¼ cup vegetable oil

⅔ cup buttermilk

⅓ cup honey

2 eggs, lightly beaten

Place wheat berries and water in custard cup, cover with vented plastic food wrap, and microwave on HIGH (100% power) 1 minute. Let cool, covered, 10 minutes, then drain well. Sift all-purpose flour, baking soda, and salt together into mixing bowl; add whole wheat flour and wheat berries and toss well; make well in dry ingredients. Combine oil, buttermilk, honey, and eggs; dump into dry ingredients and stir lightly just to mix—batter should be lumpy. Line each cup of 6-cup muffin pan or cupcaker with 2 crinkly paper liners and half fill each. Microwave, uncovered, on HIGH (100% power) 2–2½ minutes. Test for doneness after 2 minutes by inserting toothpick in center of each muffin; it should come out clean (moist spots on surface of muffins will dry on standing). Remove outer liners at once, transfer muffins (in single liners) to wire rack, let stand 2 minutes, and serve. Microwave remaining batter as directed.

PER MUFFIN: 159 C   4 g P   6 g F   23 g CARB   107 mg S   46 mg CH

259

ORANGE-PECAN COFFEE CAKE

PREP TIME: 5 MINUTES   COOKING TIME: 10–11½ MINUTES   STANDING TIME: 10 MINUTES

Instant coffee powder tints the batter amber and eliminates the usual need for a topping to mask the coffee cake's wan exterior.

MAKES 1 (8½") ROUND LOAF, 12 SERVINGS

1½ **cups buttermilk biscuit mix**

⅓ **cup sugar**

⅓ **cup coarsely chopped pecans**

1 **teaspoon instant coffee powder**

¼ **cup milk**

¼ **cup orange juice**

¼ **cup vegetable oil**

1 **egg, lightly beaten**

1 **tablespoon finely grated orange rind**

Sifted confectioners' sugar

Mix biscuit mix with sugar and pecans. Stir instant coffee powder with milk until well dissolved, then combine with orange juice, vegetable oil, egg, and orange rind; mix into dry ingredients and beat by hand 30 seconds. Spread batter evenly in well-greased 8½" round, 1½-quart, straight-sided casserole about 2" deep. Center casserole on oven shelf or elevate on upside-down shallow bowl. Microwave, uncovered, on MEDIUM (50% power) 8 minutes, rotating casserole 180° at halftime. Rotate casserole 180° again and microwave on MEDIUM-HIGH (70% power) 2–3½ minutes, or until cake tests done. *Note: A 2" area in center may seem moist, but cake will be dry underneath; using a toothpick, test for doneness in two other areas— it should come out clean.* Let coffee cake stand 10 minutes to complete cooking, loosen carefully, invert on wire rack, then immediately turn right side up on serving plate. Dust with confectioners' sugar, cut into slim wedges, and serve warm or cover loosely with clean dish towel and cool to room temperature. Wrap airtight.

PER SERVING: 153 C   2 g P   9 g F   16 g CARB   183 mg S 24 mg CH

BLUEBERRY–SOUR CREAM COFFEE CAKE

PREP TIME: **15** MINUTES COOKING TIME: **11½–13** MINUTES STANDING TIME: **30** MINUTES

You can microwave this coffee cake in a conventional square dish, but you must shield the corners with foil to prevent overcooking. If you prefer, cook in an 8½″ round dish (no foil needed) and cut into slim wedges.

MAKES 1 (8″) SQUARE LOAF, 16 (2″) SQUARES

1¼ **cups sifted flour**

1¼ **teaspoons baking powder**

Pinch salt

½ **cup (1 stick) butter or margarine**

½ **cup sugar**

1 **egg plus 1 egg white**

1 **teaspoon vanilla**

½ **cup sour cream**

1 **cup blueberries, washed and patted dry on paper toweling**

Topping

¼ **cup graham cracker crumbs**

¼ **firmly packed light brown sugar**

½ **teaspoon ground cinnamon**

½ **teaspoon ground allspice**

Sift flour, baking powder and salt together into mixing bowl. Cream butter and sugar until light, beat in egg and egg white, then vanilla. Add flour mixture, a few spoonfuls at a time, alternately with sour cream, beginning and ending with flour and beating after each addition only enough to incorporate. Stir in blueberries and spread batter evenly in 8″ × 8″ × 2″ glass ovenware dish.

Combine topping ingredients and sprinkle evenly over batter. Wrap corners of dish smoothly with 2″ foil strips, then center dish on oven shelf or elevate on upside-down shallow bowl. Microwave, uncovered, on MEDIUM (50% power) 8 minutes, rotating dish 180° at halftime. Remove foil and microwave on MEDIUM-HIGH (70% power) 3½–5¼ minutes, again rotating 180° at halftime. Test for doneness after 3½ minutes by inserting toothpick in center of cake; it should come out clean. Cake should be springy to the touch; it may have a few moist spots on surface, but these will dry as cake cools. Let stand 30 minutes before cutting into squares.

PER SQUARE: 156 C 2 g P 8 g F 20 g CARB 124 mg S 36 mg CH

BUTTERSCOTCH-GLAZED CINNAMON-RAISIN COFFEE CAKE: Prepare as directed, sifting 1 teaspoon ground cinnamon with dry ingredients and substituting 1 cup coarsely chopped seedless raisins for blueberries (or ½ cup each chopped raisins and nuts). Omit cinnamon from topping, then proceed as recipe directs. When coffee cake is cool, drizzle Butterscotch-Maple Frosting on top.

PER SQUARE: 229 C   2 g P   11 g F   32 g CARB   155 mg S   44 mg CH

*A*LMOND-APRICOT BUNDT BREAD

PREP TIME: **8 MINUTES**   COOKING TIME: **9-10 MINUTES**   STANDING TIME: **15 MINUTES**

MAKES 1 (9″) BUNDT OR RING LOAF, 12 SERVINGS

¼ **cup graham cracker crumbs**

2 **cups sifted flour**

2 **teaspoons baking powder**

¼ **teaspoon salt**

½ **cup firmly packed light brown sugar**

⅓ **cup coarsely chopped toasted blanched almonds***

½ **cup finely chopped dried apricots**

⅔ **cup milk**

⅓ **cup vegetable oil**

1 **egg, lightly beaten**

1 **teaspoon almond extract**

Grease 9″ (8- to 10-cup) Bundt pan or ring mold well, then coat evenly with graham cracker crumbs. Sift flour, baking powder, and salt together into mixing bowl, add brown sugar, and rub between fingers to break up lumps. Add almonds and apricots and toss to dredge; make well in center of dry ingredients. Combine milk, oil, egg, and almond extract, dump into dry ingredients, and mix well. Spoon into pan, spreading batter evenly and taking care not to dislodge crumbs. Center pan on oven shelf or elevate on upside-down shallow bowl. Microwave, uncovered, on MEDIUM (50% power) 8 minutes, rotating pan 180° at halftime. Rotate pan 180° again and microwave on MEDIUM-HIGH (70% power) 1–2¼ minutes, or until bread pulls slightly from sides of pan, is springy to touch, and toothpick inserted in bread comes out clean. Let stand 15 minutes, loosen carefully, and invert on serving plate. Cover loosely with clean dish towel, cool to room temperature, then slice and serve with butter or whipped cream cheese.

PER SERVING: 220 C   4 g P   9 g F   30 g CARB   148 mg S 25 mg CH

FIG AND FILBERT BRUNCH BREAD: Prepare as directed, substituting toasted, blanched filberts for almonds and dried figs for apricots.

PER SERVING: 225 C   4 g P   9 g F   32 g CARB   148 mg S   25 mg CH

*G*LAZED SPICY LEMON TEA BREAD

PREP TIME: | 5 MINUTES | COOKING TIME: | 9¼–10½ MINUTES | STANDING TIME: | 10 MINUTES

MAKES A (9″) TUBE LOAF, 16 SERVINGS

¼	**cup fine gingersnap crumbs**
2¼	**cups sifted flour**
2	**teaspoons baking powder**
¼	**teaspoon salt**
½	**cup sugar**
1	**teaspoon ground cinnamon**
½	**teaspoon ground nutmeg**
½	**teaspoon ground ginger**
½	**cup melted butter or margarine**
⅔	**cup milk**
2	**eggs, lightly beaten**
2	**teaspoons finely grated lemon rind**

Lemon Glaze

| 2 | **teaspoons lemon juice** |
| 1 | **cup sifted confectioners' sugar** |

Grease 9″ (8-cup) ring mold well and coat evenly with crumbs. Sift flour, baking powder, salt, sugar, cinnamon, nutmeg, and ginger together into mixing bowl and make well in center. Combine butter, milk, eggs, and lemon rind; dump into dry ingredients and mix well. Spoon into mold, spreading batter evenly and taking care not to dislodge crumbs. Center mold on oven shelf or elevate on upside-down shallow bowl. Microwave, uncovered, on MEDIUM (50% power) 8 minutes, rotating mold 180° at halftime. Rotate mold 180° again and microwave on HIGH (100% power) 1–2¼ minutes, until bread pulls slightly from sides of mold, is springy to touch, and toothpick inserted in bread comes out clean. Let stand 10 minutes, loosen carefully and invert on serving plate. Cover loosely with clean dish towel and cool to room temperature.

For the Glaze: Microwave lemon juice in uncovered 1-cup measure on HIGH (100% power) 20 seconds, just until warm. Sprinkle confectioners' sugar slowly into lemon juice and blend until smooth. Drizzle glaze over bread, letting it run down sides, then cool several minutes until glaze hardens.

PER SERVING: 182 C   3 g P   7 g F   27 g CARB   169 mg S 52 mg CH

263

BOSTON BROWN BREAD

PREP TIME: 5 MINUTES COOKING TIME: 5½–6 MINUTES STANDING TIME: 5 MINUTES

Old-fashioned brown bread takes about an hour to steam, but a loaf of this speedy microwave version is done in just 6 minutes! New Englanders eat brown bread with baked beans, but it's equally delicious spread with cream cheese.

MAKES 2 SMALL LOAVES (6 SLICES EACH)

⅔ **cup sifted all-purpose flour**

¼ **teaspoon salt**

½ **teaspoon baking powder**

½ **teaspoon baking soda**

½ **cups unsifted whole wheat flour (not stone-ground)**

⅓ **cup yellow cornmeal (not stone-ground)**

⅓ **cup dark molasses**

1 **cup buttermilk**

½ **cup seedless raisins**

Sift all-purpose flour with salt, baking powder, and soda into mixing bowl. Add all remaining ingredients except raisins and beat with electric mixer 30 seconds, until well blended; stir in raisins. Spoon half of mixture into lightly greased 1-pint measure. Cover with vented plastic food wrap and microwave on MEDIUM (50% power) 5½–6 minutes, rotating measure 180° at half-time, until toothpick inserted in center of bread comes out clean. **Note:** *Do not use turntable; it will make loaf "mushroom" as it cooks.* Uncover and let stand 5 minutes to complete cooking. Invert and ease loaf onto platter. Cool 5 minutes. Meanwhile, microwave remaining batter the same way. Slice loaves ½" thick and serve slightly warm. **Note:** *The easiest way to cut this tender bread is using fine, strong thread in a see-saw motion. The bread will firm up after a day or so and can be cut more easily and thinly.*

PER SLICE: 199 C 5 g P 1 g F 44 g CARB 256 mg S 2 mg CH

To Reheat Brown Bread: Wrap loaf loosely in plastic food wrap and microwave on MEDIUM (50% power) 2 minutes until warm, rotating loaf 180° and turning it over at halftime.

ABOUT SHAPING AND CRISPING TORTILLAS

With a microwave, you can shape and crisp tortillas in seconds. Best of all, you can do the job well ahead of time, then store the crisp tortillas in airtight containers to use as edible bowls for chili and salad. The microwave can also soften less than fresh store-bought tortillas that are too stiff or brittle to shape without tearing or shattering. *Note: When it comes to shaping and crisping tortillas, most microwave ovens can't accommodate more than three at a time. If you have more tortillas to shape, do them in batches of three.*

TO SOFTEN STALE TORTILLAS: Unwrap tortillas, rewrap in stacks of three in paper toweling, and microwave, one at a time, on HIGH (100% power) 30–40 seconds.

TO SHAPE AND CRISP TORTILLAS: Gently press a soft and pliable 8″ flour tortilla into each of 3 shallow (10-ounce) glass ovenware ramekins or microwave-safe cereal bowls or small casseroles, letting edges ruffle and extend above ramekins. Microwave, uncovered, on HIGH (100% power) 3½– 4 minutes, rearranging ramekins and rotating them 180° at halftime, until tortillas are dry and lightly browned. Carefully remove tortillas from ramekins and cool upside down. *Note: A small area on bottom of each tortilla may be damp, but it will dry on standing.* Store shaped, crisped tortillas airtight.

ABOUT MICROWAVING JAMS AND PRESERVES

When spring and summer fill produce stands with rich fruity promise, the urge to make jams and preserves is almost irresistible. But who wants to slave over a steamy kettle most of the morning? The good news is that you don't have to. Microwave ovens make dandy preserving kettles that can shortcut cooking times as much as 30 percent. No old-timey method, moreover, can touch the microwave for producing jewel-bright jams with just-picked flavor. Best of all, you needn't stir the whole enduring time (only now and then) because microwave jams and preserves don't scorch. For best results, note these guidelines:

Follow recipes to the letter. Do not substitute one fruit for another and never, ever, use one type of pectin in place of another. They are not interchangeable. We call for the new "light" powdered pectin (it's available at supermarkets), which not only "sets up" fast but also lets you pare calories by using one-third less sugar (it does not contain artificial sweeteners).

Do not double or triple recipes, great as the temptation may be. If you want more jam or preserves, simply cook up another batch. It's a breeze with the microwave.

Chop fruit uniformly; even cooking of jams and preserves depends on it. Use a food processor only if you're adept at controlling it. Otherwise, the fruit may be unevenly chopped or churned to mush.

Always use casserole size recommended. It should be at least four times the volume of the ingredients put into it and about 4" deep.

As jams and preserves microwave, monitor progress through the oven door. Sugar molecules attract microwaves, so there's always some risk of boilover.

PEACH AND GINGER JAM

PREP TIME: | 30 MINUTES | COOKING TIME: | 19-23 MINUTES | STANDING TIME: | NONE

MAKES 6 HALF-PINTS

5   **cups finely chopped, peeled fully ripe peaches (about 3½ pounds)**

¼   **pound crystallized ginger, finely chopped (discard loose sugar)**

2   **tablespoons lemon juice**

3½ **cups sugar**

Mix peaches, ginger, and lemon juice in 5-quart casserole at least 4" deep. Combine ¼ cup sugar with pectin and stir into fruit. Microwave, uncovered, on HIGH (100% power) 9–11 minutes, until boiling, stirring at halftime. Mix in remaining sugar and microwave, uncovered, on HIGH (100% power) 9–11 minutes, stirring every 4 minutes, until mixture reaches full rolling boil that foams up in casserole. **Note:** *Toward end of cooking,*

266

1   package (1¾ ounces)
    powdered "light" fruit
    pectin (for jams and jellies
    with less sugar)

monitor progress through oven door. A small area in center of jam may be too obscured by foam to show boiling, but balance should roll like ocean waves. Maintain full boil by micro-waving 1 minute longer on HIGH (100% power). Using thick potholders, remove to heat-resistant surface. With large metal spoon, quickly skim off foam, stirring jam occasionally. Ladle jam at once into hot, sterilized half-pint preserving jars, filling to within ⅛" of tops. Wipe jar rims and seal jars. Cool, check seals, then label and store in cool, dark, dry place. Allow jam to mellow several weeks before opening.

PER TABLESPOON: 41 C 0.1 g P 0 g F 10.5 g CARB 0.9 mg S 0 mg CH

FRESH STRAWBERRY PRESERVES

PREP TIME: | 8 MINUTES | COOKING TIME: | 21–25 MINUTES | STANDING TIME: | NONE

MAKES 8 HALF-PINTS

6   cups crushed ripe
    strawberries (about 3
    quarts)

4½ cups sugar

1   package (1¾ ounces)
    powdered "light" fruit
    pectin (for jams and jellies
    with less sugar)

Place berries in 5-quart casserole at least 4" deep. Mix ¼ cup sugar with pectin and stir into berries. Microwave, uncovered, on HIGH (100% power) 10–12 minutes, until boiling, stirring at halftime. Mix in remaining sugar and microwave, uncovered, on HIGH (100% power) 10–12 min-utes, or until mixture reaches full rolling boil that foams up in casserole, stirring every 4 minutes. **Note:** Toward end of cooking, monitor progress through oven door. A small area in center of preserves may be too obscured by foam to show boiling, but balance should roll like ocean waves. Maintain full boil by microwaving 1 minute longer on HIGH (100% power). Using thick potholders, remove to heat-resistant surface. With large metal spoon, quickly skim off foam, stirring

267

preserves occasionally. Ladle preserves at once into hot, sterilized half-pint preserving jars, filling to within ⅛″ of tops. Wipe jar rims and seal jars. Cool, check seals, then label and store in cool, dark, dry place. Allow preserves to mellow several weeks before opening.

PER TABLESPOON: 33 C 0.1 g P 0.1 g F 8.4 g CARB 0.3 mg S 0 mg CH

OLD-FASHIONED APPLE BUTTER

PREP TIME: 20 MINUTES COOKING TIME: 49–57 MINUTES STANDING TIME: NONE

In the old days, giant cauldrons were set outside during apple season, then windfalls were gathered and set to boil for the better part of the day, emerging late afternoon as a butter-smooth spread. This microwave version cooks in less than an hour but has the same buttery texture and intense flavor of the boiled-all-day variety. The best apples to use are extra tart ones such as Greenings.

MAKES 5 HALF-PINTS

4   **pounds tart cooking apples, cored, quartered, and each quarter sliced into 16 pieces**

1   **pint apple cider or water**

2½ cups sugar (about)

1   **teaspoon ground cinnamon**

¼   **teaspoon ground allspice**

¼   **teaspoon ground cloves**

¼   **teaspoon ground ginger**

¼   **teaspoon salt**

Place apples and cider in 5-quart casserole at least 4″ deep, cover with lid or vented plastic food wrap, and microwave on HIGH (100% power) 27–31 minutes, stirring every 10 minutes, until apples are mushy. Put mixture through fine sieve, measure apple pulp, and return to casserole. For each cup pulp, add ½ cup sugar. Stir in all spices and salt, making sure no sugar sticks to sides of casserole. Microwave, uncovered, on HIGH (100 power) 22–26 minutes, until very thick. **Note:** *To test for doneness, spoon a little apple butter onto saucer; if it cools into a firm mass and clings to saucer when turned upside down, it is done.* Using thick potholders, remove to heat-resistant surface. Ladle apple butter at once into hot, sterilized half-pint preserving jars, filling to within ¼" of tops. Wipe jar rims and seal jars, then process 10 minutes in hot-water bath (185°F.).† Cool, check seals, label, and store in cool, dark, dry place. Allow apple butter to mellow several weeks before opening.

PER TABLESPOON: 38C 0gP 0.1gF 9.8gCARB 7mgS 0 mg CH

† About Hot-water Baths:

If you do not have a standard hot-water bath equipped with its own rack, you can improvise one using a 2-to-4 gallon kettle and an 8" or 9" round cake rack. The kettle should be two thirds full of simmering water (185° F.) and the jars to be processed should stand squarely on the rack, not touching one another or the kettle sides. The water should at all times be at least 1" above the tops of the sealed jars, and to prevent boilover there must also be 1" to 2" of airspace above the waterline. During the processing, the kettle should be covered. And one final note: Once the jars are in the kettle, let the water return to 185° F. before you begin timing the processing.

ORANGE AND LEMON MARMALADE

PREP TIME: 15 MINUTES COOKING TIME: 33-39 MINUTES STANDING TIME: NONE

This marmalade is fast on two counts: the food processor chops the rind and fruit in 1 minute; the microwave boils it—with no threat of scorching—to just the right jewel-bright consistency in less than 40 minutes. **Note:** *Because sugar mixtures heat unevenly in the microwave, the surest way to determine doneness is to use the old-fashioned sheeting test.*

MAKES 7 HALF-PINTS

2 large thick-skinned oranges (Valencias are best)

1 large lemon

1 cup water

3 cups sugar (about)

Peel oranges and lemon, trim off inner white rind so outer rind is about ⅜" thick overall; cut rind into ½" pieces. Section fruit, discarding pith and seeds but saving juice. Place rind, juice, and fruit in food processor; add ½ cup water and churn 1 minute until rind is finely chopped. Add remaining water and measure fruit mixture; for each 1 cup, measure out and reserve 1 cup sugar. Place fruit mixture in 5-quart casserole at least 4" deep, cover with lid or vented plastic food wrap, and microwave on HIGH (100% power) 8–9 minutes, stirring at halftime, until mixture boils. Mix in reserved sugar and microwave, uncovered, on HIGH (100% power) 25–30 minutes, stirring every 5 minutes, until thick and glistening. **Note:** *Begin testing for doneness after 20 minutes: spoon a little hot marmalade onto large metal spoon, cool slightly (15–20 seconds), then tilt; if drops slide together in sheet, marmalade is done (if you use microwave thermometer, it will register 218°–220°F.).* Using thick potholders, remove to heat-resistant surface and stir 1 minute. With large metal spoon, quickly skim off foam, stirring marmalade occasionally. Ladle marmalade at once into hot, sterilized half-pint preserving jars, filling to within ⅛″ of tops. Wipe jar rims and seal jars. Cool, check seals, then label and store in cool, dark, dry place. Allow marmalade to mellow several weeks before opening.

PER TABLESPOON: 22 C 0.1 g P 0 g F 6 g CARB 0.2 mg S 0 mg CH

LEMON CURD *(LEMON CHEESE)*

PREP TIME: | 10 MINUTES | COOKING TIME: | 9-10 MINUTES | STANDING TIME: | NONE

Spread this rich ''cheese'' on English muffins or quick breads or use to fill cakes, bite-size cream puffs, or tarts. This modern version of the old English classic proves the microwave's efficiency: you don't need a double boiler and you don't have to stand and stir to make the lemon curd silky.

MAKES ABOUT 4 HALF-PINTS

⅔ **cup lemon juice**

3 **tablespoons finely grated rind**

2 **cups sugar**

1 **cup unsalted butter (no substitute)**

4 **eggs**

Mix lemon juice, rind, and sugar in 2-quart casserole. Add butter, cover with wax paper, and microwave on HIGH (100% power) 4½–5 minutes, whisking after 2 minutes, until sugar dissolves and butter melts; whisk again. Beat eggs until frothy, blend in about ½ cup hot lemon mixture, stir back into casserole, and whisk well. Cover with wax paper and microwave on MEDIUM (50% power) 4½–5 minutes, whisking every 2 minutes, until as thick as mayonnaise. **Note:** *Do not boil mixture or it will curdle. In ovens of 700 watts or more, check edges of mixture each time before whisking; if they begin to bubble at any time, reduce power level to MEDIUM-LOW (30%) for remaining cooking time.* When lemon curd is done, whisk well, ladle into hot, sterilized half-pint preserving jars, cover, cool to room temperature, and store in refrigerator.

PER TABLESPOON: 55 C 0.4 g P 3.2 g F 6.5 g CARB 4.8 mg S 24.9 mg CH

8

CASSEROLES, STEWS, AND ONE-DISH DINNERS

Stews and casseroles, the comfort foods everyone loves, microwave splendidly. But most, instead of cooking zip-quick, utilize a microwave's slow-cooker capability. Then what, pray tell, is the point of microwaving stews and casseroles when they cook perfectly well (and almost as fast) on top of the stove or in the oven? For one thing, they won't burn or boil over in the microwave, so it eliminates messy cleanup. For another, they require very little attention. Best of all, they can often come to table in their microwave casserole. Like conventional stews and casseroles, many microwave versions improve in flavor if made ahead, and some freeze well. For best results, follow these guidelines.

ABOUT CONTAINERS

Choosing the right container is integral to correct timing as well as to developing tenderness and taste. Often a casserole's diameter is as important as its volume—when it's necessary, for example, to arrange meat, poultry, or seafood in a single layer for greater microwave exposure and more even heat distribution. *Note: If container diameter is essential to a recipe's success, the recipe will specify both diameter and volume. To avoid boilovers, always use the container size recipes recommended. And if combination cooking is involved, be sure to use a container that can go from stovetop to microwave or from microwave to conventional oven or broiler (most plastic containers cannot).*

2-, 3-, AND 4-QUART CASSEROLES: Choose straight-sided ones measuring 9"–10" across (large families will find the 5-quart size handy too). Whenever food requires frequent stirring or rearranging, or whenever it is added in stages, lidded casseroles are the best choice (glass lids, of course, let you monitor a recipe's progress).

MULTIPURPOSE CASSEROLES: These can withstand abrupt temperature changes, meaning they can go directly from freezer to microwave, also from microwave to broiler when recipes need a last-minute browning (see Microwave Utensil Chart in Chapter 3).

ABOUT BROWNING SKILLETS AND DISHES

A good idea that needs perfecting. So far, it's quicker to brown meats on top of the stove than to use a browning skillet, which must be preheated before any meat is added. Even if you have no multipurpose casserole that can move from stovetop to microwave, it's quicker and easier to brown meats in a skillet and transfer them to an appropriate casserole than to fiddle with a browning skillet.

SOME GENERAL TIPS FOR MAKING BETTER STEWS AND CASSEROLES

Do not double recipes. Large quantities often take longer to microwave than to cook the old-fashioned way. Their taste and texture, moreover, will suffer.

To halve recipes, see About Doubling and Halving Microwave Recipes in Chapter 1.

To eliminate the need of rotating stews or casseroles, use a turntable. You may _still_ have to stir and rearrange some food, however.

Maple-Glazed Loin of Pork (p.329) with vegetable accompaniments

Roast Turkey (p.352) with Apple-Pecan Stuffing (p.368) and Turkey Cream Gravy (p.156)

Cranberry Sauce (p.173) • Orange Candied Sweet Potatoes (p.481) • Jiffy Succotash (p.451) • Pumpkin Pie (p.543)

Mussels in a Cataplana (p.391)

Poached Pears Cardinal (p.523)

Almond-Apricot Bundt Bread dusted with confectioners' sugar (p.262)
Date Muffins (p.255) topped with cinnamon sugar and Nut Muffins (p.255)

Butterscotch-Glazed Cinnamon-Raisin Coffee Cake (p.262)

Chocolate Chip Bars (p.568) • *Brownies (p.567)* • *Nutty Caramel Apples (p.575)* • *Almond Brittle (p.576)*

The easiest way to tell when a stew or casserole is done is to use an automatic temperature probe, following manufacturer's directions to the letter. For stews and casseroles, submerge the probe's tip in the mixture (never in an individual piece of meat) midway between the container's rim and center. For pot roasts and other large braised cuts, insert the probe in the liquid *beside* the meat, *not in the meat itself.* (Read Automatic Temperature Probes in the Special Features and Optional Extras section of Chapter 2.)

Never microwave biscuits or pastry on top of stews or casseroles—they'll be pale and clammy. Instead, arrange dough or pastry on top of a stew or casserole *after* it comes from the microwave and bake the old-fashioned way. Or add fully baked biscuits or pastry to the stew or casserole just before serving.

SOME SPECIFIC TIPS FOR MAKING BETTER CASSEROLES

If raw rice or other grains are to microwave plump and tender in casseroles, two things are needed: enough moisture and sufficient cooking time. **Note:** *Our recipes are quite specific about whether a grain is to be added raw or cooked; make no substitutions.*

Always cook and drain pasta by package directions *before* adding it to a casserole that's to be microwaved.

To give casseroles crisp and/or brown finishes, run quickly in a preheated broiler *after* microwaving. Just make sure the container can withstand intense broiler heat.

SOME SPECIFIC TIPS FOR MAKING BETTER STEWS

For really succulent stews, use well-marbled meat, but trim off all external fat; it attracts microwaves, meaning the lean next to it may overcook. For the same reason, excess fat should also be removed from poultry.

For even cooking, make sure each meat and vegetable is cut into pieces of uniform size. The precut "stew meat" most supermarkets sell is too irregular to microwave evenly, so you're better off buying a boned shoulder or round and cubing it yourself.

For extra juiciness, some cooks recommend piercing stew meat deeply before it's microwaved so moisture can penetrate. We can't see that piercing makes meat any more succulent and tender. So pierce or not as you like.

For added color and flavor (necessary for certain stews), brown meats on the stove before microwaving. Many stews, however, need only to have the meat juices sealed—a few minutes in the microwave on HIGH (100% power) does it—before they slow-cook at a lower power level. *Note: Our recipes include directions for stovetop browning whenever it's important to the finished dish.*

Because fats melt so completely in a microwave oven, you'll find it necessary to skim stews before they're served, even those made of lean meats.

To prevent meats and vegetables from drying, keep them submerged in the stew liquid. If there's insufficient liquid, stir vegetables and turn meats or poultry often to ensure uniform cooking.

For better flavor, greater tenderness, bring stews to a boil on HIGH (100% power), then simmer on MEDIUM (50% power) or, in ovens of 700 watts or more, MEDIUM-LOW (30% power)—whatever it takes to keep the stew at a *slow* simmer. *Note: If meats are browned on the stovetop, you can save 5 to 6 minutes of microwave time if you add the liquid to the meat and bring it to a boil before transferring all to the microwave oven.*

If a stew contains large amounts of vegetables, it's better to cook them separately on the stovetop (time the cooking carefully so that they're done when the stew is). Microwaving them in the stew will only prolong the cooking time. You can either mix the cooked vegetables into the stew or serve them separately.

ABOUT MAKING STEWS AND CASSEROLES AHEAD OF TIME

Many stews and casseroles—except for those containing potatoes or squash of any kind, cabbage, heavy cream, or sour cream—freeze well. Others actually profit from a stay in the fridge (if so, our recipes tell just how to refrigerate and reheat). Be sure to read in Chapter 4 the information on freezing microwaved foods and to consult the timetables for defrosting and reheating.

CORNED BEEF AND CABBAGE

PREP TIME: | 5 MINUTES | COOKING TIME: | 80-93 MINUTES | STANDING TIME: | 15 MINUTES |

With a microwave, you can trim the cooking time of this St. Patrick's Day classic by at least 50%, *even* when you cook the corned beef and cabbage separately (necessary to keep the cabbage from becoming salty or greasy).

SERVES 6–8

3½–4 **pounds corned brisket of beef, rinsed in cold water**

2 **cups water**

4 **peppercorns**

4 **whole allspice**

1 **large bay leaf**

1 **medium-size yellow onion, peeled and cut into 8 wedges**

1 **medium-size cabbage (about 2 pounds), trimmed of coarse outer leaves, cored, and cut into 12 wedges of equal size**

Place beef flat in 3-quart casserole 2½"–3" deep, add water, peppercorns, allspice, bay leaf and onion, cover with lid or vented plastic food wrap and microwave on HIGH (100% power) 13–15 minutes, rotating casserole 180° at halftime, until water boils. Turn meat over, rotate casserole 90°, re-cover, and microwave on MEDIUM (50% power) 55–65 minutes, again turning meat over and rotating casserole 90° at halftime, until meat is tender. Let stand, still covered, 15 minutes. Meanwhile, arrange cabbage wedges in single layer but slightly overlapping with thickest parts toward outside in 11" × 7" × 2" casserole. Add ¼ cup corned beef cooking liquid (if not salty) or water, cover with lid or vented plastic food wrap, and microwave on HIGH (100% power)

277

12–13 minutes, rotating casserole 180° at half-time, until cabbage is barely crisp-tender. Let stand, still covered, 2 minutes. Lift corned beef to heated deep platter, slice across the grain, and surround with well-drained cabbage. Accompany with boiled potatoes and mustard or horse-radish.

PER SERVING: 263–197 C 18–14 g P 18–13 g F 7–5 g CARB 1077–808 mg S 91–68 mg CH

~~~~~~~~ V A R I A T I O N S

BOILED FRESH BRISKET OF BEEF: Prepare as directed, substituting 3½–4 pounds fresh brisket for corned beef and dissolving 1 teaspoon salt in the 2 cups water before adding. Omit cabbage. If you like, cook Dumplings (see Old-fashioned Chicken and Dumplings) in casserole liquid while beef stands (wrap in foil instead of letting stand in liquid in covered casserole). Serve with broccoli and carrots.

PER SERVING: 787–590 C 46–35 g P 65–49 g F 0 g CARB 305–229 mg S 187–140 mg CH

BARBECUED FRESH BRISKET OF BEEF: Prepare Boiled Fresh Brisket and let stand as directed; lift to large shallow roasting pan, brush generously with All-Purpose Barbecue Sauce or other thick barbecue sauce, and bake, uncovered, in preheated 325° F. oven 20 minutes, basting once or twice with additional barbecue sauce. Serve with coleslaw.

PER SERVING: 848–636 C 47–35 g P 67–50 g F 12–9 CARB 615–461 mg S 187–140 mg CH

BEEF AND VEGETABLE STEW

PREP TIME: [15 MINUTES] COOKING TIME: [64–75 MINUTES] STANDING TIME: [5 MINUTES]

Most stews only cook 30%–50% faster in a microwave than on a stove, but they *won't* stick or scorch and need little attention. If you cook the vegetables while the stew microwaves, you'll save about 10 minutes (see Beef Stew).

¢

SERVES 4–6

2	*pounds boned beef chuck, cut into 1″ cubes*
½	*cup unsifted flour*
1½	*teaspoons salt*
¼	*teaspoon pepper*
2	*cups beef broth or water or a half-and-half mixture*
1	*bay leaf*
1	*cup frozen small white onions (do not thaw)*
½	*pound medium-size carrots, peeled, halved, and cut into 1″ chunks*
¼	*pound small white turnips, peeled and quartered*

Dredge beef in mixture of flour, 1 teaspoon salt, and ⅛ teaspoon pepper; arrange in single layer in 4-quart casserole and microwave, uncovered, on HIGH (100% power) 5 minutes to seal in juices. Add broth, remaining salt and pepper, and bay leaf, cover with lid, and microwave on HIGH (100% power) 9–10 minutes, stirring at halftime, until broth boils. Reduce power to MEDIUM (50%) and microwave, covered, 30 minutes. Stir, scatter onions, carrots, and turnips evenly over stew and push down into liquid. Re-cover and microwave on MEDIUM (50% power) 20–30 minutes, stirring at halftime, until beef and vegetables are tender. Let stand, still covered, 5 minutes. Remove bay leaf and serve.

PER SERVING: 715–477 C 45–30 g P 47–32 g F 25–16 g CARB
1422–948 mg S 157–104 mg CH

V A R I A T I O N S

BEEF STEW: Microwave beef on HIGH (100% power) as directed, adding 1 small peeled and minced onion, 1 teaspoon salt, and ¼ teaspoon pepper along with broth. Omit all vegetables and microwave stew, covered with lid, on MEDIUM (50% power) 40–50 minutes, stirring at halftime, until beef is tender. Let stew stand as directed, then serve.

PER SERVING: 667–445 C 44–29 g P 47–31 g F 13–9 g CARB 1095–730 mg S 157–104 mg CH

279

BEEF STEW WITH DUMPLINGS: Prepare Beef Stew as directed; when beef is tender, lift with slotted spoon to heated deep platter, cover, and keep warm. Prepare and microwave Dumplings in beef gravy as Old-fashioned Chicken and Dumplings recipe directs. Arrange dumplings on platter with beef, ladle gravy on top, and serve.

PER SERVING: 896–597 C   49–33 g P   55–37 g F   48–32 g CARB   1871–1247 mg S   161–107 mg CH

CARBONNADE À LA FLAMANDE
(FLEMISH BEEF AND BEER STEW)

PREP TIME:
| 10 |
| MINUTES |

COOKING TIME:
| 60–72 |
| MINUTES |

STANDING TIME:
| 5 |
| MINUTES |

If this stew is to be properly brown and nutty, you must first brown the beef.

SERVES 4–6

3   tablespoons bacon drippings or butter

2   medium-size yellow onions, peeled and minced

2   large cloves garlic, peeled and minced

2   pounds boned beef chuck, cut into 1" cubes

½   cup unsifted flour

2   teaspoons salt

¼   teaspoon pepper

2   cups beer

¼   teaspoon crumbled dried thyme

⅛   teaspoon ground nutmeg

Microwave 1 tablespoon drippings with onions and garlic in wax-paper-covered 3-quart casserole on HIGH (100% power) 4–5 minutes, until glassy. Meanwhile, dredge beef in mixture of flour, 1 teaspoon salt, and ⅛ teaspoon pepper; brown in 2 batches in remaining drippings in large heavy skillet over moderately high heat, allowing 3 minutes per batch. Add beef to casserole, heat, and stir 1 cup beer in skillet 1 minute to loosen browned bits. Stir into casserole along with remaining beer, salt, and pepper, thyme, and nutmeg. Cover with lid and microwave on HIGH (100% power) 9–10 minutes, stirring at halftime, until boiling. Stir, re-cover, and microwave on MEDIUM (50% power) 40–50 minutes, stirring at halftime, until beef is tender. Let stand, still covererd, 5 minutes. Serve with new potatoes and well-chilled beer.

PER SERVING: 758–505 C 44–30 g P 54–36 g F 20–13 g CARB
1288–859 mg S   164–109 mg CH

BEEF BALLS BOURGUIGNON

PREP TIME: **10 MINUTES** COOKING TIME: **39–46 MINUTES** STANDING TIME: **NONE**

SERVES 6

Sauce

1 **medium-size yellow onion, peeled and minced**

1 **medium-size carrot, peeled and minced**

1 **cup red Burgundy**

1 **cup strong beef broth**

1 **tablespoon tomato paste**

1 **bay leaf, 1 sprig each parsley and thyme, and 4 peppercorns tied in cheesecloth (bouquet garni)**

⅓ **cup water**

2 **tablespoons flour blended with 2 tablespoons water**

Beef Balls

1 **small yellow onion, peeled and minced**

1 **medium-size clove garlic, peeled and minced**

1 **tablespoon olive oil**

1 **pound ground beef**

½ **cup fine dry bread crumbs**

1 **egg, lightly beaten**

2 **tablespoons Worcestershire sauce**

1 **tablespoon cold water**

1 **tablespoon minced parsley**

1 **teaspoon salt**

¼ **teaspoon pepper**

¾ **pound medium-size mushrooms**

1 **tablespoon butter**

For Sauce: Place onion, carrot, wine, broth, tomato paste, and bouquet garni in 2-quart casserole, cover with lid, and microwave on HIGH (100% power) 20–25 minutes, stirring at halftime, until vegetables are mushy. Discard cheesecloth bag and press sauce mixture through fine sieve; return to casserole, mix in water and flour paste, and microwave, uncovered, on HIGH (100% power) 3½–4 minutes, stirring after 2 minutes and again at end, until sauce boils and thickens. Remove from oven and let stand, covered, while you proceed.

For Beef Balls: Microwave onion, garlic, and oil in wax-paper-covered 1½-quart casserole on HIGH (100% power) 2½–3 minutes, until glassy. Mix in remaining beef ball ingredients and shape into 16 (1½") balls; arrange ½" apart on roasting rack (set in casserole if rack has no drip well). Cover with wax paper and microwave on HIGH (100% power) 4½–5 minutes, turning balls over and rearranging at halftime, until firm and no longer pink in center. Add beef balls and drippings to casserole, cover, and let stand while you cook mushrooms.

Spread mushrooms in shallow 1½-quart casserole, dot with butter, cover with paper toweling, and microwave on HIGH (100% power) 4 minutes. Stir mushrooms into beef ball mixture, cover with lid, and microwave on HIGH (100% power) 4–5 minutes to blend flavors. Taste for salt and pepper and adjust, if needed. Serve with boiled new potatoes.

PER SERVING: 369 C   17 g P   26 g F   16 g CARB   824 mg S   116 mg CH

281

BEEF BALLS STROGANOFF: Prepare sauce as directed but use 2 cups strong beef broth and omit wine and tomato paste. Mix, shape, and microwave beef balls as directed and add to sauce along with 2 teaspoons Dijon mustard; omit mushrooms. Cover casserole with lid and microwave to serving temperature as directed; blend in ½ cup room-temperature sour cream and serve over noodles, spaetzle, or bulgur wheat.

PER SERVING: 396 C   17 g P   30 g F   14 g CARB   996 mg S   124 mg CH

GREEN CHILI

PREP TIME: 8 MINUTES   COOKING TIME: 24-27 MINUTES   STANDING TIME: NONE

This mild chili is best if made ahead and reheated.

SERVES 6

2 medium-size yellow onions, peeled and minced

1 sweet green pepper, cored, seeded, and minced

2 large cloves garlic, peeled and minced

1 tablespoon vegetable oil or bacon drippings

1 pound ground lean beef, lamb, or pork shoulder

1 cup tomato purée

1 cup hot water

1 teaspoon salt (about)

½ teaspoon pulverized cuminseed

¼ teaspoon black pepper

1 can (4 ounces) chopped green chili peppers, drained

2 tablespoons minced fresh coriander (cilantro)

Microwave onions, green pepper, garlic, and oil in wax-paper-covered 2-quart casserole on HIGH (100% power) 5–6 minutes, until glassy. Push vegetables to center of casserole and spread beef around edge. Cover with wax paper and microwave on HIGH (100% power) 4–5 minutes, until beef is no longer pink. Break up beef with fork, and stir in tomato purée, water, salt, cumin, and black pepper, cover with wax paper and microwave on HIGH (100% power) 5–6 minutes, until mixture begins to bubble. Reduce power to MEDIUM-HIGH (70%) and microwave, covered, 10 minutes, mixing in chilies at halftime. Adjust salt as needed, mix in coriander, and serve as is or over pinto beans.

To Reheat: Microwave in covered casserole 12–14 minutes on HIGH (100% power), stirring every 4 minutes.

PER SERVING: 257 C   15 g P   18 g F   8 g CARB   702 mg S   57 mg CH

CHILI CON CARNE

PREP TIME: 5 MINUTES   COOKING TIME: 45–49 MINUTES   STANDING TIME: NONE

Best when made ahead and reheated. If you're watching calories and cholesterol, try the variation made with chicken or turkey.

SERVES 6

2	medium-size yellow onions, peeled and minced
1	large clove garlic, peeled and minced
2	tablespoons vegetable oil
1½	pounds lean ground beef
½	teaspoon crumbled dried oregano
1	large bay leaf, crumbled
3	tablespoons chili powder
⅛–¼	teaspoon red pepper flakes
1½	teaspoons salt
1	can (1 pound) tomatoes (do not drain)
2	cans (1 pound, 3 ounces each) red kidney beans (drain 1 can)

Microwave onions, garlic, and oil in wax-paper-covered 4- or 5-quart casserole on HIGH (100% power) 5–5½ minutes, until glassy. Mix in beef, oregano, and bay leaf, then push mixture around edge of casserole. Cover with wax paper and microwave on HIGH (100% power) 5–6 minutes, breaking up beef at halftime, until beef is no longer pink. Add chili powder and red pepper flakes, re-cover, and microwave on MEDIUM-HIGH (70% power) 2 minutes; mix in salt, tomatoes, and beans. Re-cover and microwave on HIGH (100% power) 15 minutes, stirring every 5 minutes, until mixture begins to bubble. Reduce power to MEDIUM-HIGH (70%) and microwave 18–20 minutes, stirring at halftime, to mellow flavors. ***Note:*** *In ovens of 700 watts or more, MEDIUM (50% power) may be enough to keep mixture simmering.* If chili seems thick, thin with a little hot water.

To Reheat: Microwave in covered casserole 12–14 minutes on HIGH (100% power), stirring every 4 minutes.

PER SERVING: 524 C 31 g P 29 g F 35 g CARB 1414 mg S 85 mg CH

V A R I A T I O N S

CHICKEN OR TURKEY CHILI: Prepare as directed, substituting 1¾ pounds coarsely ground raw chicken or turkey breast for beef.

PER SERVING: 370 C   41 g P   8 g F   35 g CARB   1422 mg S   77 mg CH

Mustcohola

PREP TIME: 12 MINUTES COOKING TIME: 39–40 MINUTES STANDING TIME: NONE

In a microwave, this hearty Midwest specialty cooks in half the usual time.

SERVES 6

- 2 tablespoons bacon drippings or vegetable oil
- 2 medium-size yellow onions, peeled and minced
- 2 medium-size sweet green peppers, cored, seeded, and minced
- 1 pound lean ground beef
- 1 tablespoon chili powder
- ½ pound mushrooms, wiped clean and sliced thin
- 1 teaspoon salt
- ¼ teaspoon black pepper
- 2 cups tomato purée
- ½ pound elbow macaroni or small seashell pasta

Mix drippings, onions, and green peppers in 4-quart casserole; cover with wax paper and microwave on HIGH (100% power) 4½–5 minutes, until glassy. Push vegetables to center of casserole, spread beef around edge, re-cover with wax paper, and microwave on HIGH (100% power) 5–6 minutes, until beef is no longer pink. Break up beef with fork, stir in chili powder and mushrooms, re-cover with wax paper, and microwave on HIGH (100% power) 4 minutes. Mix in salt, pepper, and tomato purée, cover with lid, and microwave on HIGH (100% power) 20 minutes. While mixture simmers, cook macaroni by package directions and drain well. Mix macaroni into meat mixture after the mixture has microwaved 20 minutes; re-cover and microwave on MEDIUM (50% power) 5 minutes to mellow flavors.

PER SERVING: 433 C   21 g P   20 g F   43 g CARB   789 mg S   60 mg CH

SWISS STEAK WITH VEGETABLES

PREP TIME: **10 MINUTES** COOKING TIME: **73–80 MINUTES** STANDING TIME: **5 MINUTES**

Don't try to hurry this recipe by using 100% power full time. If the steak is to be succulent, you must cook it slowly—even in the microwave. For best results, choose a steak that is uniformly 1½" thick.

SERVES 6

¼   cup unsifted flour

1   teaspoon salt (about)

¼   teaspoon pepper (about)

2½–3 pounds semi-boneless or boneless chuck steak, cut 1½" thick

1   large yellow onion, peeled and minced

2   medium-size carrots, peeled, halved lengthwise, and sliced ½" thick

2   medium-size stalks celery, sliced ½" thick

1½   cups beef broth or water blended with 3 tablespoons tomato paste

Mix flour, salt, and pepper and pound into both sides of steak, dividing total amount evenly. Lay steak flat in 4-quart casserole, top with vegetables, and pour in broth mixture. Cover with lid and microwave on HIGH (100% power) 18–20 minutes, rotating casserole 180° at halftime, until liquid boils. Reduce power to MEDIUM (50%) and microwave, still covered, 55–60 minutes, turning steak over and rotating casserole 180° at halftime, until steak is tender. *Note: Test for doneness in 2 or 3 places.* Let stand, covered, 5 minutes, lift steak to heated platter and top with vegetables. Skim fat from gravy, then adjust salt; spoon some gravy over meat and vegetables and pass the rest.

PER SERVING: 419 C   30 g P   28 g F   9 g CARB   656 mg S   104 mg CH

V A R I A T I O N

BRAISED STEAK WITH MUSHROOMS: Prepare Swiss steak as directed, omitting carrots and celery. Lift cooked steak to platter and add ¾ pound halved small mushrooms to skimmed gravy in casserole, cover with lid, and microwave on HIGH (100% power) 5–6 minutes, stirring at halftime, until mushrooms are just cooked. Spoon some mushrooms and sauce over meat; pass the balance.

PER SERVING: 420 C   31 g P   29 g F   9 g CARB   638 mg S   104 mg CH

285

VEAL SHANKS WITH CAPERS, CARROTS, AND SOUR CREAM

PREP TIME: | 5 MINUTES | COOKING TIME: | 61–72 MINUTES | STANDING TIME: | 5 MINUTES

This recipe will be more flavorful if made one day and served the next. If the veal shanks are to microwave evenly, they must be of approximately the same diameter and thickness.

¢

SERVES 4

4   **veal shanks (about ¾ pound each), cut 1½″ thick**

1   **medium-size yellow onion, peeled and minced**

1   **cup chicken broth or water**

1   **bay leaf**

⅛   **teaspoon pepper**

2   **large carrots, peeled and sliced tissue-thin**

1   **teaspoon salt**

1   **cup sour cream (at room temperature)**

¼   **cup drained small capers**

Stand veal shanks on cut sides ½″ apart in single layer in 4-quart casserole. Scatter onion evenly on top, add broth, bay leaf, and pepper; cover with lid and microwave on HIGH (100% power) 9–10 minutes, until broth boils. Rotate casserole 180°, reduce power to MEDIUM (50%), and microwave, covered, 30 minutes. Turn veal over, rearrange pieces, spread carrots evenly on top, then push down into liquid. Re-cover and microwave on MEDIUM (50% power) 15–25 minutes, until veal is tender. Stir in salt and let casserole stand, covered, 5 minutes. *Note: You may prepare recipe to this point a day ahead; cool and refrigerate, tightly covered, until about 15 minutes before serving, then microwave, covered with lid, on HIGH (100% power) 7–8 minutes, rotating casserole 180° at halftime, until bubbly.* With slotted spoon lift veal to heated platter, cover, and keep warm. Drain ½ cup liquid from casserole (save for soup or gravy). Stir sour cream and capers into casserole, re-cover, and microwave on MEDIUM (50% power) 4½–5 minutes, stirring at halftime, until hot (don't boil or sauce will curdle). Return veal to casserole, re-cover, and microwave on MEDIUM-HIGH (70% power) 2 minutes. Serve with boiled noodles.

PER SERVING: 338 C   25 g P   22 g F   10 g CARB   1148 mg S   106 mg CH

286

⚖ ¢ OSSO BUCO: Prepare recipe as directed, adding 1 crushed clove garlic and 1 minced carrot along with onion. Also substitute white wine for chicken broth and add 1 tablespoon minced fresh basil (or 1 teaspoon crumbled dried basil) and a pinch thyme along with bay leaf; omit carrots. When veal is tender, lift to platter and keep warm. Purée casserole mixture, pour back into casserole, and add salt to taste. Return veal to casserole, spoon sauce over all, and sprinkle with gremolata (1 tablespoon each parsley and finely grated lemon rind mixed with 1 minced clove garlic). Cover with lid and microwave on HIGH (100% power) 3–4 minutes, until heated through. Serve with Risotto alla Milanese.

PER SERVING: 199 C   23 g P   9 g F   5 g CARB   639 mg S   81 mg CH

VEAL PAPRIKASH

PREP TIME: **5 MINUTES**   COOKING TIME: **45–53 MINUTES**   STANDING TIME: **NONE**

SERVES 4–6

2 **pounds boned veal shoulder, cut into 1″ cubes**

2 **tablespoons butter or margarine**

2 **medium-size yellow onions, peeled and minced**

1 **clove garlic, peeled and minced**

2 **tablespoons paprika (preferably Hungarian sweet rose paprika)**

⅛ **teaspoon pepper**

¾ **cup dry white wine**

¾ **cup hot water mixed with 1½ teaspoons salt**

2 **tablespoons tomato paste**

¾ **cup sour cream (at room temperature)**

Brown veal in 2 batches in butter in 10″ (2½-quart) glass ceramic casserole or large heavy skillet over moderately high heat, allowing 3 minutes per batch; lift to bowl and reserve. Brown onions and garlic in drippings 2 minutes. *Note: Now transfer veal and onion mixture to 10″ (2½-quart) casserole, if you used skillet. Or return veal to micro-fryer.* Mix in paprika, pepper, wine, and salt water; cover with lid and microwave on HIGH (100% power) 10–12 minutes, stirring at halftime, until mixture boils. Reduce power to MEDIUM (50%) and microwave, covered, 25–30 minutes, stirring at halftime, until veal is tender. Blend in tomato paste and sour cream, re-cover, and microwave on MEDIUM (50% power) 2–3 minutes; do not boil or mixture will curdle. Taste for salt and adjust as needed. Serve over wide noodles.

PER SERVING: 569–379 C   47–31 g P   38–25 g F   9–6 g CARB   1128–752 mg S   196–130 mg CH

287

TAGINE

(MOROCCAN LAMB WITH RAISINS AND CHICK-PEAS)

PREP TIME: 5 MINUTES COOKING TIME: 54–68 MINUTES STANDING TIME: NONE

This simple, subtle version of the classic Moroccan lamb stew is a good introduction to Arabic cooking, which often teams meat and fruit.

SERVES 6

2   pounds boned lean lamb shoulder, cut into 1" cubes

1   tablespoon olive oil

1   large Spanish onion, peeled and halved (slice half tissue-thin, mince remaining half)

1½ cups water mixed with 1 teaspoon salt

¼   teaspoon pepper (about)

¼   teaspoon ground cinnamon

¼   teaspoon crumbled saffron threads (optional)

⅛   teaspoon ground ginger

1   tablespoon honey

3   cups cooked or canned chick-peas, well drained

½   cup seedless raisins

2   teaspoons lemon juice

2   tablespoons minced fresh coriander (cilantro) or Italian parsley

Brown lamb in oil in 2 batches in 5-quart glass ceramic casserole at least 10" across or in large heavy skillet, allowing about 3 minutes per batch. Lift lamb to bowl and reserve. Brown all onion 2 minutes in drippings, add salt water, pepper, cinnamon, saffron, if you like, ginger, and honey. Stir, scraping up brown bits, 1–2 minutes, until mixture boils. *Note: Now transfer all to 5-quart casserole if you used skillet.* Return lamb to casserole, spreading evenly, cover with lid, and microwave on HIGH (100% power) 10–11 minutes, stirring at halftime, until mixture boils. Reduce power to MEDIUM (50%) and microwave, covered, 25–35 minutes, stirring at halftime, until lamb is just tender. Purée ⅓ cup casserole liquid with ½ cup chick-peas by buzzing 20 seconds in food processor. Stir back into casserole, add remaining chick-peas, and raisins. Cover with lid and microwave on MEDIUM (50% power) 10–12 minutes, stirring at halftime, until mixture bubbles and lamb is tender. Stir in lemon juice and coriander, then adjust salt and pepper as needed. Serve with pita bread and fresh spinach salad.

PER SERVING: 444 C   36 g P   16 g F   39 g CARB   474 mg S   106 mg CH

IRISH STEW

PREP TIME: [10 MINUTES] COOKING TIME: [66–70 MINUTES] STANDING TIME: [5 MINUTES]

Slow cooking makes this stew richly flavorful and tender; even so, it cooks nearly twice as fast in a microwave.

SERVES 4

3   pounds lean lamb neck (with bones), cut into 2" chunks

2   large yellow onions, peeled, halved, and sliced tissue-thin

¼   teaspoon pepper

2½   cups water mixed with 2 teaspoons salt

5   medium-size all-purpose potatoes, peeled and halved

2   tablespoons minced parsley

Arrange lamb in single layer in 5-quart casserole with smaller pieces in center. Scatter onions evenly over meat, sprinkle with pepper, add salt water, cover with lid, and microwave on HIGH (100% power) 18–20 minutes, rotating casserole 180° at halftime, until liquid boils. Reduce power to MEDIUM (50%) and microwave 30 minutes, turning lamb over and rearranging at halftime. Space potatoes evenly on top of stew, push down into liquid, re-cover, and microwave on MEDIUM (50% power) 18–20 minutes, rearranging potatoes and rotating casserole 180° at halftime, until potatoes and meat are just tender. Let covered casserole stand 5 minutes. *Note: If liquid seems greasy, lift meat and potatoes to heated deep platter with slotted spoon, cover and keep warm, then skim fat from liquid.* Sprinkle stew with parsley, ladle into bowls, and serve with plenty of liquid.

PER SERVING: 448 C   37 g P   14 g F   44 g CARB   1226 mg S   119 mg CH

VARIATION

YORKSHIRE LAMB AND CAPER STEW: Prepare Irish Stew as directed; lift lamb, potatoes, and onions to heated deep platter, cover, and keep warm. Skim casserole liquid of fat and mix in 3 tablespoons flour blended with ¼ cup cold water. Microwave, uncovered, on HIGH (100% power) 4–5 minutes, whisking well after 2 minutes, until gravy thickens and boils. Whisk again, stir in 2 tablespoons lemon juice and 3 tablespoons drained small capers. Pour some sauce over meat and vegetables and pass the rest.

PER SERVING: 471 C   38 g P   14 g F   49 g CARB   1392 mg S   119 mg CH

289

Pastitsio

(GREEK LAMB AND MACARONI CASSEROLE)

PREP TIME: **8 MINUTES** COOKING TIME: **32–36 MINUTES** STANDING TIME: **5 MINUTES**

If you intend to brown the pastitsio before serving, be sure to use a glass ovenware or glass ceramic casserole that can withstand the intense broiler heat.

SERVES 6

¾ **pound ground lean lamb shoulder or ground lean beef**

1 **small yellow onion, peeled and minced**

1 **small clove garlic, peeled and minced**

1 **teaspoon olive oil**

1¼ **cups tomato purée**

1 **teaspoon crumbled dried oregano**

1 **teaspoon salt**

¼ **teaspoon pepper**

Pinch ground cinnamon

⅓ **cup dry white bread crumbs**

½ **pound ziti or elbow macaroni, cooked by package directions, drained, rinsed in cold water, and drained well again**

¼ **cup finely grated Romano or Parmesan cheese**

Cream Sauce:

3 **tablespoons butter or margarine**

4 **tablespoons flour**

Arrange lamb doughnut-fashion around edge of 2-quart casserole, place onion and garlic in center, and sprinkle with oil. Cover with wax paper and microwave on HIGH (100% power) 3½–4 minutes, stirring at halftime, until lamb is no longer pink. Break up lamb with fork, stir in tomato purée, oregano, salt, pepper, and cinnamon, cover with lid, and microwave on HIGH (100% power) 4½–5 minutes, stirring at halftime, until bubbly. Mix in crumbs, set aside.

For Sauce: Melt butter in wax-paper-covered 6-cup measure by microwaving on HIGH (100% power) 45–55 seconds. Blend in flour and microwave, uncovered, on HIGH (100% power) 30 seconds until foamy. Slowly whisk in 1½ cups milk and microwave, uncovered, on HIGH (100% power) 4–5 minutes, whisking every 2 minutes, until sauce boils and thickens; whisk in salt and pepper. Pour ½ cup sauce into bowl and whisk in remaining milk; beat eggs into sauce remaining in measure and set aside.

To Assemble: Layer half of ziti in ungreased 11" × 7" × 2" casserole, spread with lamb mixture, spoon half of thin (eggless) cream sauce evenly on top and sprinkle with 2 tablespoons cheese. Top with remaining ziti and thin cream

2	cups milk
¾	teaspoon salt
⅛	teaspoon white pepper
2	egg yolks, lightly beaten

sauce, cover with wax paper and microwave on HIGH (100% power) 10 minutes, rotating casserole 180° at halftime. Spread egg-cream sauce evenly on top, sprinkle with remaining cheese and microwave, uncovered, on MEDIUM (50% power) 9–11 minutes, rotating casserole 180° every 3 minutes, until top is just set. *Note: A small area in center may still be liquid, but will set on standing or browning.* Cover casserole loosely with foil and let stand 5 minutes. Or broil pastitsio 4" from heat of preheated broiler 2–3 minutes until tipped with brown. Cut into squares and serve with an oil-and-lemon-dressed crisp green salad.

NUTRIENTS PER SERVING: 430 C   22 g P   17 g F   46 g CARB   1069 mg S   161 mg CH

COUNTY CORK SPICED LAMB

PREP TIME: | 6 MINUTES | COOKING TIME: | 29–45 MINUTES | STANDING TIME: | 3 MINUTES

A microwave version of the succulent lamb stew Myrtle Allen (Ireland's Julia Child) serves at Ballymaloe House near Shanagarry.

SERVES 4

- ½ **cup unsifted flour**
- 1 **teaspoon salt (about)**
- ¼ **teaspoon pepper (about)**
- 1½ **pounds boned lean lamb shoulder, cut into ¾" cubes**
- 1 **cup beef broth mixed with ¼ teaspoon salt**
- 1 **medium-size yellow onion, peeled and minced**
- 1 **small clove garlic, peeled and minced**
- ½ **teaspoon pulverized cuminseed**
- ⅛ **teaspoon ground cloves**
- ⅛ **teaspoon ground nutmeg**

Mix flour with salt and pepper, dredge lamb in mixture, then place in 2-quart casserole. Add broth mixture along with remaining ingredients, cover with lid, and microwave on HIGH (100% power) 9–10 minutes, stirring at halftime, until boiling. Reduce power to MEDIUM (50%) and microwave, covered, 20–35 minutes, stirring at halftime, until lamb is tender. *Note: Baby lamb may need 20 minutes only, but older lamb may take as long as 35; test meat at 5-minute intervals after 20 minutes.* Let stew stand, covered, 3 minutes. Adjust salt and pepper as needed and serve with boiled new potatoes.

PER SERVING: 324 C 34 g P 14 g F 14 g CARB 1003 mg S 119 mg CH

FABADA (SPANISH PORK AND BEAN STEW)

PREP TIME: 10 MINUTES COOKING TIME: 38–43 MINUTES STANDING TIME: NONE

If pork butt is encased in netting, soak 5 minutes in warm water to facilitate its removal.

SERVES 6

2 slices lean bacon, cut into small dice

1 large yellow onion, peeled and minced

1 large leek, finely chopped

1 large clove garlic, peeled and minced

1 medium-size carrot, peeled and minced

1½ pounds boneless smoked pork butt

¾ pound chorizo or smoked pork link sausages

2 cups water

1 bay leaf

1 teaspoon paprika

⅛ teaspoon pepper

2 cans (1 pound each) cannellini or white lima beans, drained

Scatter bacon into 4-quart casserole, cover with paper toweling, and microwave on HIGH (100% power) 2–2½ minutes, until beginning to crispen. Mix in onion, leek, garlic, and carrot. Lay pork butt on vegetables to one side of casserole, then place sausages in middle. Add water, bay leaf, paprika and pepper, cover with lid, and microwave on HIGH (100% power) 20 minutes, turning pork and sausages over and rotating casserole 180° at halftime. Rotate casserole 180° again, reduce power level to MEDIUM (50%), and microwave 12–15 minutes, turning butt and sausages over and rotating casserole 180° at halftime, until butt is fork-tender. With slotted spoon, lift out pork and sausages; slice butt about ⅜" thick and sausages ½" thick. Skim fat from casserole liquid, add beans, cover with lid, and microwave on HIGH (100% power) 2 minutes. Gently stir in meats, re-cover, and microwave on HIGH (100% power) 2–3 minutes, until bubbly. Serve in bowls with crusty country bread.

PER SERVING: 744 C 40 g P 54 g F 24 g CARB 1296 mg S 75 mg CH

293

PORK BALLS AND BUTTERNUT SQUASH PORTUGAISE

PREP TIME: | 15 MINUTES | COOKING TIME: | 35–38 MINUTES | STANDING TIME: | NONE

To save time, brown the pork balls on the stovetop while the squash microwaves.

SERVES 6

- 1 **medium-size yellow onion, peeled and minced**
- 2 **large cloves garlic, peeled and minced**
- 2 **tablespoons olive oil**
- 1 **(2-pound) butternut squash, peeled, seeded, and cut into ¾" cubes**
- 1 **cup tomato purée**
- 1¼ **cups water**
- ¾ **teaspoon salt (about)**
- ⅛ **teaspoon pepper**

Pork Balls

- 1¼ **pounds ground lean pork**
- 1½ **cups soft white bread crumbs**
- 1 **tablespoon finely grated yellow onion**
- 1½ **teaspoons rubbed sage**
- 1 **teaspoon salt**
- ¼ **teaspoon pepper**
- 1 **egg, lightly beaten with 2 tablespoons cold water**

Microwave onion, garlic, and 1 tablespoon oil in wax-paper-covered 3-quart casserole on HIGH (100% power) 2½–3 minutes, until glassy. Add squash, tomato purée, water, salt, and pepper; cover with lid and microwave on HIGH (100% power) 18–20 minutes, stirring every 5 minutes, until squash is firm-tender. Meanwhile, mix all pork ball ingredients and shape into 20 balls about 1½" in diameter. Brown balls well in remaining oil in large skillet over moderately high heat, about 5 minutes. Push squash to center of casserole, wreathe pork balls around edge, cover with lid, and microwave on HIGH (100% power) 9–10 minutes, rotating casserole 180° at halftime, until mixture boils and pork balls are cooked through. *Note: To test, halve pork ball and if pink in center, microwave in 1-minute increments until no longer pink.* Taste sauce for salt and adjust as needed. If mixture seems thick, thin with a little hot water. Serve with wedges of crusty bread and a crisp green salad.

PER SERVING: 322 C   22 g P   15 g F   26 g CARB   947 mg S 110 mg CH

SCALLOPED HAM, CORN, RED PEPPER, AND ZUCCHINI

PREP TIME: | 10 MINUTES | COOKING TIME: | 14–16 MINUTES | STANDING TIME: | NONE |

Delicious ladled over split Corn Muffins or Cheese and Green Chili Muffins

SERVES 4–6

- ¾ pound small zucchini, sliced ¼" thick
- 1 medium-size yellow onion, peeled and minced
- 1 medium-size sweet red pepper, cored, seeded, and coarsely chopped
- 2 tablespoons butter or margarine
- 1 can (17 ounces) cream-style corn
- 1 can (8 ounces) whole-kernel corn, drained
- 3 cups ½" cubes leaned cooked ham
- ¼ cup half-and-half cream
- ¼ teaspoon salt (about)
- ¼ teaspoon black pepper

Optional Topping

- 1 cup seasoned bread cubes or poultry stuffing mix tossed with ¼ cup melted butter or margarine

Mix zucchini, onion, and red pepper in 3-quart casserole, dot with butter, cover with wax paper, and microwave on HIGH (100% power) 6–7 minutes, until zucchini is crisp-tender. Stir in all remaining ingredients except topping, cover with lid or vented plastic food wrap, and microwave on HIGH (100% power) 8–9 minutes, stirring after 4 minutes, until bubbly and hot in center. Taste for salt and adjust as needed. If you like, sprinkle evenly with topping and microwave, uncovered, on HIGH (100% power) 3–4 minutes, rotating casserole 180° after 2 minutes, then let stand, uncovered, 1 minute to crisp topping.

PER SERVING: 346–231 C 25–17 g P 14–9 g F 35–23 g CARB 2047–1365 mg S 70–47 mg CH

HAM AND POTATOES AU GRATIN

PREP TIME: `10 MINUTES` **COOKING TIME:** `16–19½ MINUTES` **STANDING TIME:** `NONE`

If you use leftover baked ham, you'll need the full 2⅓ cups milk. Deli boiled ham, on the other hand, exudes liquid as it microwaves, so if that's what you use, you'll need only 2 cups milk.

SERVES 6

3	cups ½" cubes lean cooked ham
4	cups ¾" cubes cooked all-purpose potatoes
3	tablespoons butter or margarine
3	tablespoons flour
2–2⅓	cups milk
2	tablespoons finely grated yellow onion
¼	cup minced parsley
1	cup coarsely grated sharp Cheddar cheese
1	teaspoon prepared spicy brown mustard
¼	teaspoon pepper

Topping

⅓	cup crushed cornflakes tossed with ⅓ cup coarsely grated sharp Cheddar cheese

Mix ham and potatoes in 3-quart glass ceramic casserole and set aside. Melt butter by microwaving in wax-paper-covered 6-cup measure on HIGH (100% power) 45–55 seconds. Blend in flour and microwave, uncovered, on HIGH (100% power) 30 seconds, until foamy. Gradually whisk in milk, add onion and parsley, and microwave, uncovered, on HIGH (100% power) 5–6 minutes, whisking every 2 minutes, until sauce boils and thickens. Mix in cheese, mustard, and pepper and stir until cheese melts. Pour sauce over ham and potatoes and toss gently. *Note: Cheese and ham are probably so salty you won't need salt, but taste to make sure.* Cover casserole with wax paper and microwave on HIGH (100% power) 8–9 minutes, stirring after 4 minutes, until bubbly and hot in center. Stir again, scatter topping evenly over ham mixture, and microwave, uncovered, on HIGH (100% power) 2–3 minutes, until cheese melts. Or broil 3"–4" from heat in preheated broiler 2–3 minutes, until touched with brown.

PER SERVING: 439 C   27 g P   21 g F   35 g CARB   1192 mg S   91 mg CH

LUNCHEON MEAT OR TONGUE AND PO-
TATOES AU GRATIN: Prepare as directed,
substituting cubed luncheon meat or tongue for
ham and using 2 cups milk.

PER SERVING (with Luncheon Meat): 583 C 21 g P 40 g F 35 g CARB 1263 mg S 92 mg CH

MAPLE HAM AND BEAN CASSEROLE

PREP TIME: **2 MINUTES** COOKING TIME: **16–18 MINUTES** STANDING TIME: **NONE**

The secret of this easy New England recipe is the maple syrup. Serve with Boston Brown Bread.

SERVES 4

2   cans (1 pound each) baked beans

1   (1¼–1½ pounds) ham steak, cut ½" thick

1   tablespoon prepared spicy brown mustard

½   cup maple syrup

2   tablespoons ketchup

½   teaspoon dry mustard

½   teaspoon chili powder

¼   teaspoon ground ginger

Dump beans into large, coarse strainer and let drain while you begin recipe. Slash edges of ham to prevent curling, then spread ham with mustard. Place ham in 3-quart casserole large enough for it to lie flat; pour in maple syrup, cover with wax paper, and microwave on HIGH (100% power) 7–8 minutes, turning ham over at halftime, until sizzling. Divide ham into 4 equal pieces. Mix drained beans with all remaining ingredients, spoon over ham, and microwave, uncovered, on HIGH (100% power) 9–10 minutes, stirring at halftime, until bubbly.

PER SERVING: 591 C 37 g P 17 g F 76 g CARB 2972 mg S 95 mg CH

297

CHICKEN OR TURKEY POTPIE

PREP TIME: 15 MINUTES   COOKING TIME: 17½–20 MINUTES   STANDING TIME: NONE

No point in microwaving pastry on a potpie; it'll be soggy. We bake it the usual way *while* the chicken microwaves, then top the pie just before serving.

SERVES 4–6

3 tablespoons butter or margarine

¼ cup unsifted flour

1½ cups chicken broth

½ cup light cream

1 tablespoon minced parsley

¼ teaspoon ground rosemary

¼ teaspoon ground savory

1 teaspoon salt

⅛ teaspoon pepper

3 cups bite-size pieces cooked chicken or turkey

1 package (10 ounces) frozen baby carrots, peas, and pearl onions or 2 cups frozen peas and carrots (do not thaw)

Pastry for 1 (9") pie

1 egg yolk mixed with 1 tablespoon cold water (optional glaze)

Preheat conventional oven to 425° F. Melt butter in wax-paper-covered 2-quart casserole by microwaving on HIGH (100% power) 45–55 seconds. Blend in flour and microwave, uncovered, on HIGH (100% power) 30 seconds, until foamy. Slowly stir in broth and microwave, uncovered, on HIGH (100% power) 3½–4 minutes, whisking briskly at halftime, until mixture boils and thickens; whisk again. Stir in cream, parsley, rosemary, savory, salt, pepper, and chicken. Rap package of vegetables sharply against counter edge to break up frozen block and stir into chicken mixture. Microwave, uncovered, on HIGH (100% power) 13–15 minutes, stirring every 5 minutes, until carrots are tender and mixture boils.

While chicken microwaves, roll pastry into 9" circle, transfer to ungreased baking sheet, crimp edges and, if you like, brush with glaze. Prick well all over and cut into 6 wedges, separating them slightly. Bake in 425° F. oven 10–12 minutes, until lightly browned. When chicken mixture bubbles, lay pastry wedges on top and serve.

PER SERVING: 631–421 C 37–24 g P 38–25 g F 35–23 g CARB 1429–953 mg S 137–91 mg CH

298

OLD-FASHIONED CHICKEN AND DUMPLINGS

PREP TIME: | 5 MINUTES | COOKING TIME: | 34–39 MINUTES | STANDING TIME: | 5 MINUTES

People say you can't cook dumplings by microwave. Non-sense! These dumplings are as light and airy as any cooked on top of the stove. Best of all, this homey dish cooks in a microwave in a third of the *usual* time.

¢

SERVES 4–6

1   **broiler-fryer (3–3½ pounds), disjointed and skinned**

1   **medium-size yellow onion, peeled and quartered**

1   **medium-size carrot, peeled and sliced ½" thick**

1   **medium-size stalk celery, sliced ½" thick**

1   **bay leaf and 1 sprig each parsley and thyme tied in cheesecloth with 6 peppercorns and 4 cloves (bouquet garni)**

1½   **cups water mixed with 1 teaspoon salt**

Sauce

2½   **cups stock from cooking chicken (add chicken broth, if needed, to round out measure)**

¼   **cup unsifted flour**

½   **cup milk**

2   **teaspoons lemon juice**

1   **teaspoon salt**

⅛   **teaspoon white pepper**

Arrange chicken in 4-quart casserole with meatiest parts toward outside and wings in center. Add onion, carrot, celery, bouquet garni, and salt water, cover with lid, and microwave on HIGH (100% power) 22–25 minutes, turning chicken and rearranging at halftime, just until tender. Let stand, still covered, 5 minutes. Lift chicken to heated deep platter, cover, and keep warm.

To make sauce, strain chicken stock, discarding vegetables; skim off all but 2 tablespoons fat; pour 2½ cups stock back into casserole. Cover with lid and microwave on HIGH (100% power) 2 minutes, until hot. Blend flour with milk, whisk slowly into stock, and microwave, uncovered, on HIGH (100% power) 4–5 minutes, whisking hard at halftime, until sauce boils and thickens; whisk again.

For Dumplings: Sift flour, baking powder, and salt into bowl, cut in shortening with pastry blender until texture of coarse meal; add milk all at once and mix lightly just until dough holds together.

Stir lemon juice, salt, and pepper into sauce. Drop dough by rounded *measuring* tablespoonfuls onto sauce, spacing evenly. Microwave,

299

Dumplings

1   cup sifted flour

1½   teaspoons baking powder

½   teaspoon salt

2   tablespoons chilled vegetable shortening

½   cup milk

uncovered, on HIGH (100% power) 6–7 minutes, rotating casserole 180° at halftime, until toothpick inserted in center of dumpling or two comes out clean. When done, dumplings will be puffy and look dry on top. With slotted spoon, lift dumplings to chicken platter. Ladle sauce over chicken and dumplings and serve.

PER SERVING: 457–305 C   44–29 g P   14–10 g F   35–23 g CARB 1717–1145 mg S   132–88 mg CH

—————— V A R I A T I O N

CHICKEN FRICASSEE WITH VEGETABLES (Serves 6): Microwave chicken, strain, skim, and measure stock into casserole as directed. Add 3 cups frozen mixed peas and carrots, cover, and microwave on HIGH (100% power) 5–6 minutes, stirring at halftime, until done. Transfer vegetables to center of chicken platter. Make sauce as directed, pour over chicken, and serve.

PER SERVING: 221 C   29 g P   5 g F   16 g CARB   901 mg S 85 mg CH

COUNTRY CAPTAIN

PREP TIME: | 6 MINUTES | COOKING TIME: | 29–30 MINUTES | STANDING TIME: | NONE |

This mild curry, popular in the South, freezes well.

SERVES 4

1 large sweet green pepper, cored, seeded, and minced

1 large yellow onion, peeled and minced

1 clove garlic, peeled and minced

2 tablespoons vegetable oil

1½ teaspoons curry powder

½ teaspoon salt (about)

¼ teaspoon ground hot red pepper

¼ teaspoon crumbled dried thyme

⅛ teaspoon ground cloves

⅛ teaspoon black pepper

1 tablespoon tomato paste

1 can (1 pound, 12 ounces) tomatoes (do not drain)

3 cups bite-size pieces cooked chicken or turkey

½ cup chicken broth

⅓ cup dried currants or seedless raisins

⅓ cup toasted blanched slivered almonds*

Microwave green pepper, onion, garlic, and oil in uncovered 3-quart casserole on HIGH (100% power) 4–5 minutes, until glassy. Stir in curry powder, salt, red pepper, thyme, cloves, black pepper, tomato paste, and tomatoes, snipping into smaller pieces as you add. Cover casserole with lid and microwave on HIGH (100% power) 10 minutes, stirring at halftime. Mix in chicken and microwave, uncovered, on HIGH (100% power) 10 minutes, stirring at halftime. Add broth and currants, re-cover, and microwave on MEDIUM (50% power) 5 minutes. Adjust salt as needed, scatter almonds on top, and serve over fluffy boiled rice.

PER SERVING: 431 C 36 g P 22 g F 26 g CARB 850 mg S 93 mg CH

CHICKEN VALENCIA

PREP TIME: **6 MINUTES** | COOKING TIME: **34–38 MINUTES** | STANDING TIME: **NONE**

This delicious casserole demonstrates how to use the stove-top and microwave in tandem. Make the recipe ahead, if you like, and refrigerate until ready to reheat.

SERVES 6

- 1 **broiler-fryer (3–3½ pounds), disjointed and breast halved crosswise**
- 2 **tablespoons olive oil**
- 1 **medium-size yellow onion, peeled and minced**
- 1 **medium-size sweet green or red pepper, cored, seeded, and minced**
- 1 **large clove garlic, peeled and minced**
- 1 **cup converted rice**
- 1 **can (1 pound, 12 ounces) chopped tomatoes (do not drain)**
- 2 **teaspoons paprika**
- 1 **teaspoon finely grated orange rind**
- 1 **teaspoon salt**
- ½ **teaspoon pulverized fennel seeds**
- ½ **teaspoon ground coriander**
- ⅛ **teaspoon pepper**
- ½ **pound chorizo or kielbasa, sliced ¼" thick**
- 1½ **cups frozen peas**
- 2 **tablespoons water**
- 1–2 **tablespoons minced fresh coriander (cilantro)**

Brown chicken in oil in 5-quart glass ceramic casserole at least 10" across or large skillet over moderately high heat about 5 minutes. Lift chicken to platter and sauté onion, green pepper, and garlic in drippings 2 minutes. *Note: Now transfer onion mixture to 5-quart casserole if you used skillet.* Stir in rice, tomatoes, paprika, orange rind, salt, fennel, ground coriander and pepper. Arrange chicken on top, largest pieces toward outside and wings in center; scatter chorizo over all. Cover with lid and microwave on HIGH (100% power) 23–26 minutes, turning chicken over, stirring rice and rotating casserole 180° at half-time, until chicken is done and rice firm-tender. *Note: Recipe may be prepared to this point and refrigerated until ready to reheat. To reheat, microwave in covered casserole 12–14 minutes on HIGH (100% power), stirring every 4 minutes.* Let stand, covered, while you cook peas. Micro-wave peas with water in 1-pint casserole, cov-ered with lid or vented plastic food wrap, on HIGH (100% power) 4–5 minutes, stirring at halftime. Drain, gently mix peas into chicken and rice, sprinkle with fresh coriander, and serve.

PER SERVING: 746 C   46 g P   45 g F   38 g CARB   744 mg S 125 mg CH

CHICKEN INDOCHINE

PREP TIME: 5 MINUTES COOKING TIME: 27–30 MINUTES STANDING TIME: NONE

This spicy Indo-Chinese dish represents only one of the awesome variety of cross-cultural cuisines that can be found on the island of Singapore. **Note:** garam masala, a currylike blend integral to Indian cooking, is available in Asian groceries and specialty food shops. You can also improvise your own by combining ½ teaspoon each ground cinnamon, coriander, cumin, and black pepper with ¼ teaspoon each ground cardamom, cloves, and nutmeg; store airtight.

SERVES 4

½	cup unsifted flour
1¼	teaspoons salt (about)
¼	teaspoon pepper
2	teaspoons ground cumin
2–2½	pounds chicken thighs
2	tablespoons clarified butter* or vegetable oil
1	medium-size yellow onion, peeled and minced
¼	teaspoon garam masala
1	teaspoon curry powder
1	teaspoon finely grated fresh ginger or ⅛ teaspoon ground ginger
½	cup chicken broth
½	cup canned coconut milk or 2 tablespoons cream of coconut blended with 5 tablespoons water and 1 tablespoon lemon juice
½	cup plain yogurt (at room temperature)

Combine flour, 1 teaspoon salt, pepper, and cumin and dredge chicken in mixture. Brown chicken in butter in 2-quart glass ceramic casserole at least 10" across or large skillet over moderately high heat 5 minutes. Lift chicken to platter and sauté onion in drippings 2 minutes. Blend in garam masala, curry powder, ginger and remaining salt, and stir over low heat 30 seconds. *Note: Now transfer onion mixture to 2-quart casserole if you used skillet.* Arrange chicken, skin side down, on onion in single layer with thickest parts toward outside; add chicken broth and coconut milk, cover with lid, and microwave on HIGH (100% power) 9–10 minutes, rotating casserole 180° at halftime, until boiling. Reduce power to MEDIUM (50%) and microwave, covered, 5 minutes. Turn chicken over and rearrange pieces, then microwave, uncovered, 4–5 minutes longer at same power. Using slotted spoon, lift chicken to heated platter, skim fat from liquid, and smooth in yogurt. Cover with lid and microwave on HIGH (100% power) 1½–2 minutes, stirring at halftime, until hot (do not boil or mixture will curdle). Taste sauce for salt and adjust, if needed; pour over

303

chicken. Serve with boiled rice (preferably Basmati) tossed with chopped, toasted unsalted cashews and golden seedless raisins. Pass pappadams and chutney.

PER SERVING: 631 C 39 g P 44 g F 17 g CARB 991 mg S 188 mg CH

THAI POACHED CHICKEN WITH GREEN PENNE AND PEANUT SAUCE

PREP TIME: **10 MINUTES**   COOKING TIME: **10-11 MINUTES**   STANDING TIME: **2 MINUTES**

Time the cooking of the pasta carefully so that it is done just as you begin cooking the sauce. **Note: The chicken is equally good over boiled rice.**

SERVES 4

1	**pound boned and skinned chicken breasts**
2	**tablespoons vegetable oil**
4	**large scallions, minced (include green tops)**
2	**medium-size carrots, peeled and cut into 2″ × ¼″ × ¼″ strips**
¾	**pound green penne (pasta)**
¼	**pound snow peas, washed and trimmed**
1	**teaspoon salt**
¼	**teaspoon pepper**
⅓	**cup creamy peanut butter**
¼	**cup chicken broth or coconut milk**
1	**tablespoon lemon juice**

Pound chicken breasts until ¼″ thick, then cut into strips 4″ long and ¼″ wide; set aside. Microwave oil, scallions, and carrots in wax-paper-covered 10″ casserole 2″–2½″ deep on HIGH (100% power) 2¾–3 minutes, until carrots begin to soften. Begin cooking penne by package directions. Arrange chicken around outer edges in casserole, leaving vegetables in center, re-cover with wax paper, and microwave on HIGH (100% power) 5½–6¼ minutes, stirring at half-time and adding snow peas 2 minutes before chicken is done. Season with salt and pepper and let stand, covered, 2 minutes. Transfer chicken and vegetables to bowl with slotted spoon.

Blend peanut butter, chicken broth, lemon juice, ginger, red pepper flakes, and lemongrass into casserole juices, cover with wax paper, and microwave on MEDIUM (50% power) 2 minutes,

304

1   **teaspoon minced fresh ginger**

Pinch red pepper flakes

¼   **cup minced tender green lemongrass blades (optional)**

¼–⅓   **cup finely chopped unsalted dry-roasted peanuts (garnish)**

stirring at halftime. Return chicken and vegetables to sauce, mixing well. The instant pasta is *al dente,* drain well, and mound on heated platter. Spoon chicken mixture on top and sprinkle with peanuts.

PER SERVING: 677 C   46 g P   24 g F   71 g CARB   806 mg S   146 mg CH

V A R I A T I O N

THAI POACHED TURKEY WITH GREEN PENNE AND PEANUT SAUCE: Prepare as directed, substituting 1 pound (¼″ thick) turkey cutlets for chicken and increasing microwave time for turkey to 6½–8 minutes, or until tender.

PER SERVING: 682 C   46 g P   24 g F   71 g CARB   808 mg S   150 mg CH

LASAGNE

PREP TIME: 5 MINUTES   COOKING TIME: 14-17 MINUTES   STANDING TIME: 5 MINUTES

¢ ⌛

SERVES 6

1   **quart Jiffy Tomato Sauce, Bolognese Tomato Sauce, or other pasta sauce**

½   **pound lasagne (9–10 strips), cooked by package directions and drained**

1   **cup ricotta cheese**

⅓   **cup finely grated Parmesan cheese**

½   **cup coarsely grated mozzarella cheese**

Spread 1 cup sauce in 13″ × 8″ × 2″ casserole, lay 3 strips lasagne on top in single layer, and cover with 1 cup sauce. Dot with ½ cup ricotta and one third each of total amount of Parmesan and mozzarella. Repeat layers and top with remaining lasagne and sauce; reserve final one third of Parmesan and mozzarella. Cover with vented plastic food wrap and microwave on MEDIUM-HIGH (70% power) 12–15 minutes, rotating casserole 180° every 4 minutes, until bubbling and heated through in center. Sprinkle with remaining Parmesan and mozzarella and microwave, uncovered, on MEDIUM-HIGH (70% power) 2 minutes, until mozzarella melts. Cover with foil, shiny side in, and let stand 5 minutes. Cut into squares and serve.

PER SERVING: 389 C   16 g P   17 g F   46 g CARB   1191 mg S   24 mg CH

305

CAJUN SHRIMP ÉTOUFFÉE

PREP TIME: | 10 MINUTES | COOKING TIME: | 17½–21 MINUTES | STANDING TIME: | NONE

This recipe demonstrates how quick and easy it is to make a rich brown roux in the microwave.

SERVES 4

- 2 **tablespoons butter or margarine**
- 2 **tablespoons flour**
- 2 **tablespoons vegetable oil**
- 1 **cup minced scallions (include tops)**
- 1 **small sweet green pepper, cored, seeded, and minced**
- 4 **large cloves garlic, peeled and minced**
- ½ **cup tomato purée**
- 1 **tablespoon minced parsley**
- ½ **teaspoon ground hot red pepper (or to taste)**
- ½ **teaspoon salt**
- ¼ **teaspoon black pepper**
- ⅛ **teaspoon liquid hot red pepper seasoning**
- 1 **cup Fish Stock, clam juice, or water**
- 1½ **pounds medium-size shelled and deveined shrimp**

Melt butter in wax-paper-covered 1-pint measure by microwaving on HIGH (100% power) 35–45 seconds. Blend in flour and microwave, uncovered, on HIGH (100% power) 4–4½ minutes, stirring at halftime, until dark brown, not burnt. *Note: Watch carefully; mixture will foam up, obscuring color underneath.* Cool roux while making sauce.

Mix oil, scallions, green pepper, and garlic in 2-quart casserole at least 10" across, cover with wax paper and microwave on HIGH (100% power) 3½–4 minutes, stirring at halftime, until pepper is soft. Add all remaining ingredients except Fish Stock and shrimp. Whisk stock into roux, add to casserole, cover with lid or vented plastic food wrap, and microwave on HIGH (100% power) 5½–6 minutes, stirring at halftime, until mixture boils and thickens. Reduce power level to MEDIUM (50%) and microwave, still covered, 2 minutes.

Arrange shrimp in sauce doughnut fashion with tails in center. Cover with wax paper and microwave on HIGH (100% power) 3–4 minutes, rearranging shrimp and moving cooked ones to center at halftime. When all shrimp are pink, stir, and serve over steamed rice. *Note: For a jiffy fish stock, simmer shrimp shells with 1½ cups hot water in 6-cup measure covered with vented plastic food wrap on HIGH (100% power) 6 minutes; cool 10 minutes and strain.*

PER SERVING: 336 C 37 g P 16 g F 11 g CARB 780 mg S 274 mg CH

XIN-XIM *(PEPPERY BRAZILIAN SHRIMP STEW)*

PREP TIME: | 6 MINUTES | COOKING TIME: | 15½–18 MINUTES | STANDING TIME: | NONE

Dendê (palm) oil can be bought in some Latin American groceries and specialty food shops, as can cans of unsweetened coconut milk (don't substitute the sweet cream of coconut). As for dried shrimp, Oriental groceries carry them.

SERVES 4

⅓ **cup dried shrimp, rinsed and soaked 1 hour in ⅓ cup cold water**

1½ **pounds medium-size shelled and deveined shrimp**

1 **tablespoon lime or lemon juice**

1 **large yellow onion, peeled and minced**

1 **large clove garlic, peeled and minced**

2 **tablespoons dendê oil or 2 tablespoons olive oil mixed with a pinch ground turmeric**

1 **cup tomato purée**

½ **cup canned unsweetened coconut milk**

¼ **teaspoon ground coriander**

¼ **teaspoon ground hot red pepper**

⅛ **teaspoon black pepper**

Pinch ground cinnamon

Pinch ground nutmeg

1 **tablespoon minced fresh coriander (cilantro)**

¼ **cup coarsely chopped roasted blanched unsalted peanuts**

Drain dried shrimp, reserving liquid; mince shrimp fine, and reserve. Toss fresh shrimp with lime juice and reserve. Mix onion, garlic, and oil in 2-quart casserole, cover with wax paper, and microwave on HIGH (100% power) 3½–4 minutes, until glassy. Add dried shrimp and their liquid, tomato purée, coconut milk, coriander, red pepper, black pepper, cinnamon, and nutmeg. Cover with lid or vented plastic food wrap and microwave on HIGH (100% power) 5–6 minutes, stirring at halftime, until mixture boils. Stir again, re-cover, and microwave on MEDIUM (50% power) 4 minutes to mellow flavors. Add fresh shrimp, cover with wax paper, and microwave on HIGH (100% power) 3–4 minutes, stirring every minute, until shrimp are *just* cooked. Sprinkle with fresh coriander and peanuts and serve over rice or, to be completely cross-cultural, over fusilli.

PER SERVING: 376 C   42 g P   17 g F   13 g CARB   707 mg S 295 mg CH

DAY'S CATCH CASSEROLE

PREP TIME: 3 MINUTES COOKING TIME: 16½–18½ MINUTES STANDING TIME: NONE

If you cook the pasta while you microwave the sauce, you can have dinner on the table in less than 20 minutes.

SERVES 4

½	**pound small pasta shells**
3	**tablespoons butter**
3	**tablespoons flour**
1½	**cups half-and-half cream**
1	**tablespoon snipped fresh dill**
2	**tablespoons minced parsley**
1	**cup clam juice**
1	**teaspoon salt**
⅛	**teaspoon pepper**
3	**tablespoons diced pimientos**
1½–2	**cups flaked, cooked delicate fish, well-drained canned tuna or salmon, shelled and deveined, cooked small shrimp**

Optional Topping

1	**cup soft bread crumbs**
⅓	**cup finely grated Parmesan cheese**
2	**tablespoons melted butter**

Cook pasta by package directions until barely *al dente*. Meanwhile, melt butter in wax-paper-covered 2-quart glass ceramic casserole at least 3" deep by microwaving on HIGH (100% power) 45–55 seconds. Whisk in flour and microwave, uncovered, on HIGH (100% power) 30 seconds, until foamy. Gradually whisk in cream, add dill and parsley, and microwave, uncovered, on HIGH (100% power) 4½–5 minutes, whisking every 2 minutes, until sauce boils and thickens. Whisk in clam juice, salt, and pepper; fold in pimientos and fish.

Drain pasta well, rinse with cold water, and drain again. Mix pasta into casserole. Cover with wax paper and microwave on HIGH (100% power) 7–8 minutes, until bubbling, stirring at halftime. *Note: Check temperature in center of casserole; bubbling around edges is no guarantee food is uniformly hot.* Reduce power level to MEDIUM (50%) and microwave, still covered, 4 minutes, stirring at halftime. If you like, mix topping, sprinkle over casserole and broil 4"–5" from heat 2–3 minutes until lightly browned.

PER SERVING: 543 C 37 g P 20 g F 52 g CARB 1120 mg S 93 mg CH

V A R I A T I O N

CHICKEN, TURKEY, OR HAM AND NOODLE CASSEROLE: Prepare recipe as directed, substituting ½ pound cooked thin noodles for shells, chicken broth for clam juice, ½ teaspoon poultry seasoning for dill, and 1½–2 cups bite-size pieces cooked chicken, turkey, or ham for fish.

PER SERVING (with Chicken):

414 C   24 g P   25 g F   23 g CARB   983 mg S   129 mg CH

SEAFOOD GUMBO

PREP TIME:

| 10 MINUTES |

COOKING TIME:

| 26–29 MINUTES |

STANDING TIME:

| 5 MINUTES |

SERVES 6

- **3   tablespoons bacon drippings**
- **3   tablespoons flour**
- **1   cup minced scallions (include tops)**
- **2   cloves garlic, peeled and minced**
- **½   cup minced celery**
- **½   cup minced sweet green pepper**
- **¾   cup hot water**
- **1   can (1 pound, 12 ounces) crushed tomatoes (do not drain)**
- **2   bay leaves**
- **½   teaspoon salt**
- **¼   teaspoon ground hot red pepper**
- **Pinch black pepper**
- **1   package (10 ounces) frozen sliced okra (do not thaw)**
- **½   pound lump crab meat, well picked over**
- **¾   pound shelled and deveined small or medium-size shrimp**
- **⅛   teaspoon filé powder**

Heat drippings in wax-paper-covered 1-pint measure by microwaving on HIGH (100% power) 35–45 seconds. Blend in flour and microwave, uncovered, on HIGH (100% power) 4–4½ minutes, without stirring, until dark brown, not burnt. *Note: Watch carefully; mixture will foam up, obscuring color underneath.* Scrape brown roux into 3-quart casserole, mix in scallions, garlic, celery and green pepper, cover with wax paper and microwave on HIGH (100% power) 4½–5 minutes until vegetables are soft. Stir in hot water and tomatoes, add bay leaves, salt, red and black pepper, cover with lid and microwave on HIGH (100% power) 10 minutes, stirring at halftime. Add okra, re-cover and microwave on HIGH (100% power) 4–5 minutes, breaking up frozen clump at halftime, until okra is crisp-tender. *Note: Don't overcook okra; it'll become gummy.* Gently mix in crab and wreathe shrimp around edge of casserole, pushing down into sauce. Re-cover and microwave on HIGH (100% power) 3–4 minutes, rearranging shrimp every minute and moving cooked ones to center. As soon as all shrimp are pink, let stand 5 minutes. Stir in filé powder and serve over rice.

PER SERVING: 222 C   22 g P   9 g F   15 g CARB   599 mg S 130 mg CH

309

ABOUT STIR-COOKING IN THE MICROWAVE

Stir-*frying,* for which foods must constantly be tossed and turned over high heat, makes no sense for a microwave. But stir-*cooking* does. First of all, stir-cooked dishes don't require nonstop attention. Second, they can be cooked in a minimum of oil—sometimes with no oil at all, and that's good news for dieters. Finally, vegetables, whether cooked solo or in tandem with meats or seafood, remain crisp and colorful with most of their vitamins intact. To make stir-cooking easier, follow these guidelines:

For stir-cooking meats and poultry, large platters work best. Browning skillets can be used if meats *only* are to be browned, but if vegetables are to be added, it simply takes too long to reheat the browning skillet at each recipe stage to be practical. It's more efficient to stir-cook the vegetables first in a casserole, then the meat via the platter method. ***Note:*** *It's important that the platter be microwave-safe, also that it touch neither the oven sides nor door.*

For uniformly cooked foods, always move the more quickly cooked items from the outside toward the center during cooking as recipes direct.

Always use top-quality, tender cuts of meat for stir-cooking—loin, for example, tenderloin, rib, eye, or top round. And be careful not to overcook them lest they toughen. Microwave stir-cooking is *so* fast there's no time for tougher cuts to tenderize.

Resist the temptation to use supermarket meats precut for stir-frying. They're far too irregular in size and shape to cook evenly, so buy a piece of well-marbled rib eye or top round of beef or boned pork loin or boneless, skinless chicken or turkey breast, and cut the strips yourself to the exact size a recipe recommends. ***Note:*** *Freezing the meat 45 to 60 minutes will make it slice cleanly and quickly.*

CHIU CHOW SHRIMP

PREP TIME: | 10 MINUTES | COOKING TIME: | 17-19 MINUTES | STANDING TIME: | NONE |

Chiu Chow, a robust, often complex version of Cantonese cooking, is best known for its imaginative use of seafood, piquant sauces, and humble vegetables.

SERVES 4

1½ **pounds medium-size, shelled, and deveined shrimp**

1 **tablespoon nam pla or nuoc nam (anchovy sauce available in Oriental groceries) or 2 anchovies mashed to paste with ½ teaspoon soy sauce**

1 **tablespoon rice wine vinegar or dry sherry**

4 **slices bacon, cut into julienne strips**

1 **medium-size sweet green pepper, cored, seeded, and cut into julienne strips**

1 **stalk celery, sliced ⅛" thick**

2 **cloves garlic, peeled and minced**

1 **tablespoon minced fresh ginger**

1 **star anise**

Pinch red pepper flakes

6 **cups finely shredded, stemmed kale (about ½ pound)**

2 **tablespoons Oriental sesame oil**

Toss shrimp with *nam pla* and vinegar and set aside to marinate. Sprinkle bacon doughnut fashion around edge of 4–5-quart casserole, cover with paper toweling, and microwave on HIGH (100% power) 3½–4 minutes, stirring at halftime, until brown and crisp; remove with slotted spoon and reserve. Stir green pepper, celery, garlic, ginger, anise, and pepper flakes into drippings, cover with wax paper, and microwave on HIGH (100% power) 4 minutes, stirring at halftime. Remove star anise, add kale, cover with lid or vented plastic food wrap, and microwave on HIGH (100% power) 2½–3 minutes, stirring at halftime, just until crisp-tender. Mix in bacon, cover, and let stand while you cook shrimp.

Heat oil, uncovered, in 1½-quart casserole about 2" deep on HIGH (100% power) 2 minutes. Arrange shrimp in oil, doughnut fashion with tails toward center, cover with wax paper, and microwave on HIGH (100% power) 3–4 minutes, rearranging shrimp and moving cooked ones to center at halftime, just until all shrimp are pink. Toss shrimp mixture and any remaining marinade with kale mixture, cover with lid or vented plastic food wrap, and microwave on MEDIUM (50% power) 2 minutes to blend flavors. Serve at once with steamed rice.

PER SERVING: 410 C   39 g P   23 g F   10 g CARB   558 mg S   275 mg CH

311

GINGERED RAINBOW BEEF

PREP TIME: **12 MINUTES** COOKING TIME: **12½–17 MINUTES** STANDING TIME: **NONE**

SERVES 4

1   **pound boneless sirloin or top round, cut across the grain into 4″ × ¼″ × ¼″ strips**

1   **teaspoon Japanese soy sauce**

2   **teaspoons cornstarch**

1   **clove garlic, peeled and minced**

1½   **teaspoons finely grated fresh ginger**

1   **large yellow onion, peeled and sliced thin**

1   **large carrot, peeled and cut into 3″ × ¼″ × ¼″ strips**

2   **tablespoons Oriental sesame oil or vegetable oil**

1   **medium-size sweet green pepper, cored, seeded, and cut into 3″ × ¼″ × ¼″ strips**

1   **medium-size sweet red pepper, cored, seeded, and cut into 3″ × ¼″ × ¼″ strips**

½   **cup beef broth**

¼   **cup sake or medium dry sherry**

1   **tablespoon dark brown sugar**

1   **tablespoon white wine vinegar**

1   **tablespoon cornstarch blended with 3 tablespoons Japanese soy sauce**

Mix meat with soy sauce, cornstarch, garlic, and ginger and set aside to marinate. Mix onion and carrot with 1 tablespoon oil in 2-quart casserole at least 10″ across, cover with wax paper, and microwave on HIGH (100% power) 2 minutes. Stir in red and green peppers, re-cover with wax paper, and microwave on HIGH (100% power) 3–4 minutes, until vegetables are crisp-tender. Cover and set aside. Add remaining oil to meat, toss well, and arrange doughnut fashion around edge of 10″ or 11″ round or oval platter. Cover with wax paper and microwave on HIGH (100% power) 3½–4 minutes, rearranging strips and moving done ones to center at halftime, until no strips are pink on outside (they should be pink when cut).

With slotted spoon, lift meat to casserole with vegetables; re-cover. With rubber spatula, scrape meat drippings into 1-pint measure and blend in beef broth, sake, sugar, and vinegar. Cover with vented plastic food wrap and microwave on HIGH (100% power) 1 minute. Whisk in cornstarch mixture and microwave, uncovered, on HIGH (100% power) 1–2 minutes, whisking every minute, until sauce boils and thickens. Pour sauce over meat and vegetables, toss, cover with lid or vented plastic food wrap, and microwave on HIGH (100% power) 2–4 minutes, stirring after 2 minutes, until uniformly hot. Serve with steamed rice.

PER SERVING: 487 C   21 g P   37 g F   17 g CARB   1028 mg S   81 mg CH

312

GINGERED RAINBOW CHICKEN OR TUR-KEY: Prepare as directed, substituting 1 pound boned and skinned chicken breasts or turkey cutlets, cut into 4″ × ¼″ × ¼″ strips, for beef and microwave 1–2 minutes longer than for beef.
PER SERVING: 268 C   29 g P   9 g F   17 g CARB   1050 mg S 70 mg CH

GINGERED RAINBOW PORK: Prepare as directed, substituting for beef 1 pound boned lean pork loin, trimmed of fat and cut across the grain in 4″ × ¼″ × ¼″ strips; microwave 5–6 minutes until no strips of pork are pink on the outside or when cut.
PER SERVING: 534 C   20 g P   43 g F   17 g CARB   1032 mg S 81 mg CH

STIR-COOKED SHRIMP AND SWEET PEP-PERS: Prepare as directed, substituting 1½ pounds medium-size shelled and deveined shrimp for beef. Arrange half of shrimp doughnut fashion with tails toward center of platter and microwave 3–4 minutes as recipe directs until shrimp are *just* cooked. Repeat with remaining shrimp, then proceed as recipe directs.
PER SERVING: 520 C   23 g P   32 g F   20 g CARB   1957 mg S 274 mg CH

STIR-COOKED SCALLOPS AND VEGETA-BLES: Prepare as directed, substituting 1½ pounds bay scallops or sea scallops, halved horizontally, for beef and microwaving in two batches *just* until scallops turn milky. Allow 4½–5½ minutes for each batch and gently rearrange scallops at halftime by moving done ones to center. When scallops are done, proceed as recipe directs.
PER SERVING: 407 C   13 g P   32 g F   17 g CARB   1242 mg S 83 mg CH

313

SZECHUAN CHILI PORK WITH BROCCOLI IN BEAN SAUCE

PREP TIME: 10 MINUTES   COOKING TIME: 11½–15 MINUTES   STANDING TIME: NONE

If you're counting calories, substitute chicken broth for sesame oil and proceed as recipe directs.

SERVES 4

1 pound boned lean pork loin, trimmed of fat, and cut across the grain in 4″ × ¼″ × ¼″ strips

¼–½ teaspoon chili oil (sesame oil in which chilies have been steeped)

2 tablespoons Oriental sesame oil or vegetable oil

1 cup celery, sliced ¼″ thick

1 cup broccoli florets

¾ cup minced scallions (include green tops)

1 large clove garlic, peeled and minced

¼ cup chicken broth

3 tablespoons soy sauce

2 tablespoons black bean sauce, soy bean sauce, or bean paste

1 teaspoon sugar

Mix pork with chili oil and 1 tablespoon sesame oil and set aside to marinate. Mix remaining sesame oil with celery, broccoli, scallions, and garlic in 2-quart casserole at least 10″ across, cover with wax paper, and microwave on HIGH (100% power) 4½–5 minutes, stirring at halftime, until broccoli and celery are crisp-tender. Cover casserole and set aside. Toss pork again and arrange, doughnut fashion, around edge of 10″ or 11″ round or oval platter. Cover with wax paper and microwave on HIGH (100% power) 4 minutes, rearranging strips and moving done ones to center at halftime.

In small bowl combine chicken broth, soy sauce, black bean sauce, and sugar; pour evenly over pork, cover with wax paper, and microwave on HIGH (100% power) 1–2 minutes, testing pork for doneness and rotating platter 180° after 1 minute. Stir pork mixture into vegetables, cover with casserole lid or vented plastic food wrap, and microwave on HIGH (100% power) 2–4 minutes, stirring after 2 minutes. Serve with Chinese Rice.

PER SERVING: 286 C   27 g P   16 g F   8 g CARB   996 mg S   68 mg CH

SZECHUAN CHILI CHICKEN OR TURKEY WITH BROCCOLI IN BEAN SAUCE: Prepare as directed, substituting 1 pound chicken breasts, boned and skinned, or turkey cutlets, cut into 4" × ¼" × ¼" strips, for pork.

PER SERVING: 233 C   29 g P   9 g F   8 g CARB   997 mg S   66 mg CH

SZECHUAN CHILI PORK AND PEPPERS IN BLACK BEAN SAUCE: Omit broccoli and use instead 1 small sweet green pepper and 1 small sweet red pepper, each cored, seeded and cut in strips 4" long and ½" wide. Otherwise, prepare recipe as directed. When you stir vegetables at halftime, test peppers for doneness. They should be crisp-tender, not limp. If peppers are nearing doneness, microwave in 30-second increments and remove from oven the instant they are done.

PER SERVING: 290 C   26 g P   16 g F   8 g CARB   992 mg S   68 mg CH

SZECHUAN CHILI BEEF AND PEPPERS IN BLACK BEAN SAUCE: Prepare as directed for Szechuan Chili Pork and Peppers, substituting 1 pound lean top round, cut into 4" × ¼" × ¼" strips, for pork and beef broth for chicken broth. Also add ¼ teaspoon finely grated orange rind to beef broth, if you like.

PER SERVING: 265 C   23 g P   14 g F   8 g CARB   986 mg S   107 mg CH

9

MEATS AND POULTRY

When it comes to meats, the microwave both shines and bombs. And causes considerable contention. As a rule, it performs best when the cut of meat is a tough one that requires slow cooking or simmering. Still, the microwave performs beautifully with poultry. All kinds of poultry. It's even possible to "roast" the Thanksgiving turkey by microwave provided it's not a whopper.

ABOUT "ROASTING" BEEF, VEAL, AND LAMB IN THE MICROWAVE

There's been plenty of controversy as to whether meats roast properly in a microwave. Indeed, the two of us are of two minds. Purists shriek that the worst crime perpetrated against a pricey prime rib or choice leg of lamb is subjecting it to microwaves. Converts, on the other hand, insist that microwaved roasts cook twice as fast as conventional ones, yet if begun on HIGH (100% power) and finished on MEDIUM (50% power), remain succulent with negligible shrinkage or nutrient loss. They insist that despite complaints to the contrary, roasts do brown in a microwave (but not, perhaps, as much as you'd like, so you may need to heighten the color with liquid gravy browner or other browning agent), and, finally, that they cook uniformly throughout if meticulously timed and tended (truer for roasts in the medium-rare to well-done category than for those cooked really rare). We'd be less than honest if we didn't tell you that the roast you pull from the microwave will neither look nor taste just like the one you take from the regular oven. And we'd be less than helpful if we didn't share the tips and techniques, then let you judge for yourself.

MOST SUITABLE CUTS: Think small, first of all. Roasts weighing more than 6 pounds won't cook evenly nor will irregularly shaped ones. So, choose compact, evenly shaped cuts 4"–6" in diameter, preferably those with thin coverings of fat that will brown lightly after about 15 minutes. Also choose tender cuts (rib, loin, top round, etc.) of top grade, which are well enough marbled with fat to remain juicily tender. Finally, opt for boneless cuts; bones absorb microwaves poorly, thus most—but not all—bone-in roasts cook less than perfectly (see cuts recommended in Microwave Roast Chart).

AMOUNT NEEDED PER SERVING: Allow ⅓–½ pound boneless meat, and for those few bone-in cuts that do microwave well, ½–¾ pound.

GENERAL PREPARATION:

〜〜〜 Trim away all but ¼" fat (excess fat heats rapidly, so meat directly underneath it may overcook).

〜〜〜 Let meat stand 1½–2 hours at room temperature before microwaving; refrigerator-cold meats are less likely to cook evenly.

〜〜〜 Do not salt meat; salt accelerates heating and can toughen meat.

〜〜〜 Rub meat with pepper and compatible herbs (see Microwave Roast Chart) and, if you like, brush with a browning agent such as soy, steak or Worcestershire sauce, a half-and-half mixture of liquid gravy browner and water, or a commercial browner.

〜〜〜 Measure diameter of roast (also weigh, if necessary) to calculate precise microwave time.

〜〜〜 If roast is irregularly shaped, tuck thin ends underneath or shield them with foil (see About Shielding Roasts).

〜〜〜 Place roast fat side down on rack in shallow bake/roast pan (rack keeps meat out of fatty drippings, which heat rapidly and may cause meat touching them to overcook).

Insert microwave-safe meat thermometer in center of the largest muscle, touching neither fat nor bone as shown. Or use an automatic temperature probe as manufacturer directs; it's the surest way to tell when a roast is done although it's not recommended for roasts of less than 2 pounds. Or use an instant-register thermometer when roast nears doneness.

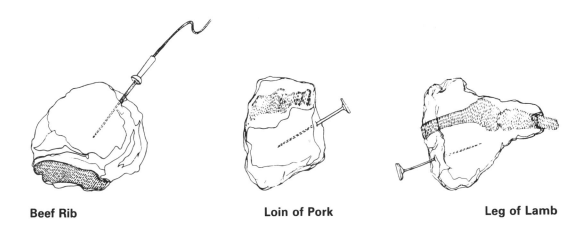

Beef Rib   **Loin of Pork**   **Leg of Lamb**

Do not cover meat (surface won't dry), do not add liquid and don't baste (basting can make the roast's surface overcook). **Note:** *If your microwave oven doesn't cook evenly (maybe it's an old model), the U.S. Department of Agriculture Food Safety and Inspection Service says that you can make meats cook more uniformly simply by covering their container with a lid or vented plastic food wrap.*

Using Microwave Roast Chart, cook meat to desired doneness, turning roast fat side up and rotating pan 180° at halftime—or if your oven cooks unevenly, several times during microwaving. **Note:** *If any parts of roast seem to be overcooking at halftime, shield them with foil (see About Shielding Roasts).*

Remove roast from oven, tent with foil, and let stand on heat-resistant surface 10–15 minutes to complete cooking and firm up meat for carving. Use standing time, if you like, to make Au Jus, Pan or Wine Gravy.

MICROWAVE ROAST CHART

Note: *To complete the cooking, let all roasts stand 10–15 minutes after they come from the microwave oven.*

Cut and Weight	Total Minutes on HIGH (100% power)	Minutes per Pound on MEDIUM (50% power)	Internal Meat Temperature (before standing)
BEEF			
Boned and Rolled Rib (4–6 lbs.)	5	8–11	115° F. Rare
Standing Rib (from small end; 5–6 lbs.)	5	7–10	120° F. Medium-Rare
Rib Eye or Delmonico (3–6 lbs.)	5	10–13	135° F. Medium
Boneless Sirloin, Top Round, Boned and Rolled Rump (3–6 lbs.)	5	12–15	145° F. Well Done

Preparation and Seasoning Tips for Beef

Tie roasts crosswise with string to secure fat; for roasts 5½–6″ in diameter, increase time on HIGH (100% power) to 8 minutes. *Compatible Seasonings* (rub with any of these before microwaving): garlic, dry mustard, marjoram, oregano, rosemary, thyme.

Cut and Weight	Total Minutes on HIGH (100% power)	Minutes per Pound on MEDIUM (50% power)	Internal Meat Temperature (before standing)
VEAL			
Boneless Sirloin (3–4 lbs.)	5	12–14	135° F. Medium
Boned and Rolled Rump, Boned and Rolled Leg (3–5 lbs.)	5	12–14	135° F. Medium

Cut and Weight	Total Minutes on HIGH (100% power)	Minutes per Pound on MEDIUM (50% power)	Internal Meat Temperature (before standing)
VEAL (continued)			
Center Leg, Shank Half Leg (3–6 lbs.)	5	10–12	135° F. Medium

Preparation and Seasoning Tips for Veal

Have butcher remove last 2″–3″ leg bone and save for making soup. Shield shank end with 1″–2″ foil. *Compatible Seasonings* (rub with any of these before microwaving): dill, lemon, marjoram, oregano, paprika, rosemary, thyme.

Cut and Weight	Total Minutes on HIGH (100% power)	Minutes per Pound on MEDIUM (50% power)	Internal Meat Temperature (before standing)
LAMB			
Boned and Rolled Leg,	5	7–9	120° F. Rare
		9–11	130° F. Medium-Rare
Boned and Rolled		11–13	140° F. Medium
Shoulder (3–4 lbs.)	5	13–15	150° F. Well Done
Full Leg (5–6 lbs.),	5	6–8	120° F. Rare
Half Leg: Sirloin,	5	8–10	130° F. Medium-Rare
Shank, or Center	5	10–12	140° F. Medium
Cut (3–5 lbs.)	5	12–14	150° F. Well Done

Preparation and Seasoning Tips for Lamb

Have butcher remove last 2″–3″ leg bone and save for making soup. Shield shank end with 1″–2″ foil. *Compatible Seasonings* (rub with any of these before microwaving): basil, curry powder, dill, garlic, lemon, marjoram, mint, oregano, paprika, rosemary, thyme.

321

ABOUT SHIELDING ROASTS: Inevitably, some roasts—leg of lamb, sirloin tip—will taper at one end or even both. But there's an easy way to keep these slimmer portions from overcooking. Simply smooth 1"–2" foil around them, pressing it to fit and anchoring, if needed, with wooden picks. Make sure foil doesn't touch the oven walls, meat thermometer, or temperature probe. If you use a turntable, check from time to time; the pan may have shifted position and the foil moved closer to the oven walls. Remove foil shields from lamb and veal roasts after half the cooking time has elapsed, and from beef after two thirds. Always check roasts at halftime and occasionally thereafter to see if any spots are beginning to overcook. If so, shield them with 1" strips or small pieces of foil, again anchoring as needed with wooden picks.

ABOUT TESTING FOR DONENESS AND STANDING TIME: The internal temperature of roasts will rise as they stand, so take them from the microwave when meat thermometer or automatic temperature probe is 10°–15° short of the desired reading. *Note: The ultracautious USDA Food Safety and Inspection Service still insists that to be absolutely wholesome, all red meats—whether microwaved or roasted the conventional way—must be brought to an internal temperature of 160° F. Very well done, indeed. Most chefs—and certainly lovers of rare beef and lamb—scoff at the notion.* Always test roasts for doneness after minimum cooking time (see Microwave Roast Chart), then continue roasting at the same power level in 3-minute increments for roasts of 4 pounds or less and 5-minute increments for larger ones, checking temperature after each. If you like well-done meat, remember that any pink traces visible at either end of the roast will disappear on standing. To honor all preferences, slice off rare portions after roast has cooked minimum amount of time and stood 10 minutes. Cover the cut end with wax paper and continue microwaving in 3- or 5-minute increments until roast reaches each desired degree of doneness. *Note: If necessary to bring rarer portions back to serving temperature, microwave, uncovered, on individual plates on MEDIUM (50% power) 30–50 seconds. Roasts should always be reheated in portions, never by the hunk or chunk.*

BRAISED SHORT RIBS

PREP TIME: **5 MINUTES** COOKING TIME: **61–69 MINUTES** STANDING TIME: **NONE**

You can microwave budget-priced short ribs to uncommon tenderness in a microwave *provided* the ribs are uniformly thick—1″ ribs are best.

SERVES 4

3½–4	pounds beef short ribs, about 1″ thick and cut in 3″–5″ lengths
1	medium-size yellow onion, peeled and minced
½	teaspoon celery seeds
1	tablespoon Worcestershire sauce
1½	cups beef broth or water
1	tablespoon tomato paste
1	teaspoon salt (about)
¼	teaspoon pepper
2	tablespoons flour and ½ teaspoon dry mustard blended with 2 tablespoons cold water

Stand ribs on their sides in single layer in 4-quart casserole with meaty parts facing out. Sprinkle with onion and celery seeds; combine all remaining ingredients except flour paste, pour into casserole, cover with lid, and microwave on HIGH (100% power) 13–15 minutes, rotating casserole 180° at halftime, until liquid boils. Reduce power to MEDIUM (50%) and microwave, covered, 45–50 minutes, turning ribs over and rearranging at halftime but keeping meaty sides facing out, until fork-tender. *Note: Ribs vary in tenderness, so begin testing for doneness after 40 minutes.* Lift ribs to heated platter, cover and keep warm. Skim fat from casserole liquid, whisk in flour paste, and microwave, uncovered, on HIGH (100% power) 3½–4 minutes, whisking after 2 minutes, until gravy boils and thickens. Whisk again and adjust salt as needed. Pour some gravy over ribs and pass the balance.

PER SERVING: 380 C   38 g P   22 g F   7 g CARB   1001 mg S 108 mg CH

323

POT ROAST

For richer color and flavor, brown the pot roast before it goes into the microwave—3–4 minutes well spent. To save on dishwashing, use a glass ceramic casserole that can go from stovetop to microwave.

SERVES 6

1	**(3–3½-pound) boned and rolled rump, chuck, or bottom round roast**
2	**tablespoons vegetable oil**
1	**small yellow onion, peeled and minced**
¼	**teaspoon pepper**
1–1½	**teaspoon salt**
2½	**cups beef broth or water (about)**
¼	**cup unsifted flour blended with ⅓ cup cold water**
1	**tablespoon liquid gravy browner (optional)**

Brown roast 3–4 minutes on all sides in oil in 3- or 4-quart glass ceramic casserole at least 10" across or in heavy skillet over moderately high heat. *Note: Now transfer roast to 3- or 4-quart casserole if you used skillet.* Add onion, pepper, and 1 teaspoon salt dissolved in 1½ cups broth. Cover with lid and microwave on HIGH (100% power) 13–15 minutes, rotating casserole 180° at halftime, until broth boils. Rotate casserole 180° again, reduce power to MEDIUM (50%), and microwave 50–60 minutes, turning meat over and rotating casserole 180° at halftime, until fork-tender. Lift meat to heated platter, cover with foil, and let stand while you prepare gravy.

Skim all but 1–2 tablespoons fat from casserole liquid, measure liquid, and add enough broth to total 2½ cups; return to casserole and whisk in flour paste. Microwave, uncovered, on HIGH (100% power) 4–5 minutes, whisking vigorously after 2 minutes, until gravy boils and thickens. Whisk again, taste for salt, and add remaining ½ teaspoon, if needed; also, if you like, deepen color by blending in gravy browner. Slice pot roast, not too thin, and serve with gravy and mashed potatoes, noodles, or Dumplings.

PER SERVING: 468 C 46 g P 28 g F 5 g CARB 876 mg S 145 mg CH

BEEF À LA MODE (French Pot Roast): Brown pot roast as directed. Omit minced onion and broth, substitute 2½ cups dry red wine mixed with 1 teaspoon salt. Add 1 peeled and quartered medium-size yellow onion, 1 peeled carrot cut in 1" chunks, 1 stalk celery cut in ½" chunks, 1 minced clove garlic, 1 bouquet garni (1 bay leaf and 1 sprig each parsley and thyme) tied in cheesecloth with 6 cloves, and ¼ teaspoon pepper; cover and microwave as directed. Strain casserole liquid, skim off all fat, and return liquid to casserole. Add ¼ cup brandy and microwave, uncovered, on HIGH (100% power) 3–4 minutes to blend flavors. Slice pot roast and pass gravy. *Note: If you prefer thickened gravy (not traditional for Beef à la Mode), thicken casserole liquid with flour paste as directed for Pot Roast.*
PER SERVING: 458 C   45 g P   27 g F   5 g CARB   458 mg S 145 mg CH

BAVARIAN POT ROAST: Microwave pot roast as directed. For gravy: Drain casserole of liquid, skim off fat, and return liquid to casserole. Add ¼ cup red wine vinegar and 8 crushed gingersnaps; reduce flour to 3 tablespoons and thicken gravy as directed.
PER SERVING: 465 C   46 g P   28 g F   6 g CARB   880 mg S 145 mg CH

BARBECUE-STYLE POT ROAST: Before microwaving, rub beef with 1 clove garlic and 1 teaspoon each paprika and chili powder. Proceed as directed, adding 1 crushed clove garlic along with onion and using ½ cup tomato juice and 2 cups beef broth instead of all broth.
PER SERVING: 468 C   46 g P   28 g F   5 g CARB   876 mg S 145 mg CH

Sauerbraten

For proper flavor, begin this recipe three days ahead.

SERVES 6

- 1 (3–3½ pounds) boned and rolled bottom round of beef, rump or chuck
- 1 small yellow onion, peeled and minced
- 1 small carrot, peeled and coarsely chopped
- 1 small stalk celery, coarsely chopped
- 4 peppercorns
- 2 cloves
- 2 bay leaves
- 1 cup dry red wine or red wine vinegar
- 2 cups water
- 1 teaspoon salt
- ¼ teaspoon pepper
- ¼ cup unsifted flour blended with ⅓ cup cold water
- ½ teaspoon sugar
- 8 gingersnaps, crushed
- 1 tablespoon liquid gravy browner

Place beef, onion, carrot, celery, peppercorns, cloves, and bay leaves in 4-quart casserole. Mix wine, water, salt, and pepper in 1-quart measure, cover with vented plastic food wrap, and microwave on HIGH (100% power) 8–9 minutes until boiling. Pour over meat, cover, and refrigerate 3 days, turning beef in marinade twice a day. About 1½ hours before you're ready to serve, drain off marinade and measure; return 1½ cups marinade to casserole and reserve balance. Cover casserole with lid and microwave on HIGH (100% power) 13–15 minutes, rotating casserole 180° at halftime, until liquid boils. Rotate casserole 180° again, reduce power level to MEDIUM (50%), and microwave 50–60 minutes, turning beef over and rotating casserole 180° at halftime, until beef is fork-tender.

Lift beef to heated platter, cover with foil, and keep warm while you prepare gravy. Strain casserole liquid, measure, and add enough reserved marinade to total 3 cups. Return to casserole, cover with lid, and microwave on HIGH (100% power) 3–4 minutes until hot but not boiling. Mix in flour paste, sugar, and gingersnaps and microwave, uncovered, on HIGH (100% power) 4–5 minutes, whisking briskly after 2 minutes and making sure to scrape up gingersnaps from casserole bottom, until gravy boils and thickens. Whisk in gravy browner. Slice beef about ¼" thick and serve with gravy, steamed potatoes, spaetzle, or Dumplings.

PER SERVING: 633 C 50 g P 40 g F 15 g CARB 585 mg S 163 mg CH

326

ABOUT MICROWAVING PORK ROASTS AND FRESH HAM

In the beginning, we were told not to microwave pork roasts, that they failed to cook evenly or fully and might cause trichinosis, a serious, sometimes fatal illness caused by microscopic parasites present in pork. According to the most recent research, however, *pork can be safely microwaved, if:*

⁓ The container is tightly closed—with a lid, *not with vented plastic food wrap.* Cooking pork covered means more thorough, even cooking.

⁓ The roast is begun briefly on HIGH (100% power), then finished on MEDIUM (50% power), which ensures slow, even cooking.

⁓ The roast is inverted and rotated 180° at halftime.

⁓ The roast reaches an internal temperature of 170° F., and is then allowed to stand 10 minutes. Always spot-check temperature in several areas before removing a pork roast from the microwave, then again after standing. At 170° F. the meal will be ivory-hued, succulent, and utterly safe.

MOST SUITABLE CUTS: Top-quality loins about 4″ in diameter, either bone-in or boned and rolled, in the 3-to-4-pound category are best although fresh half hams up to 6 pounds microwave well, too.

AMOUNT NEEDED PER SERVING: Allow ⅓–½ pound boneless pork and ½–¾ pound bone-in.

GENERAL PREPARATION:

⁓ Trim away all but ¼″ fat, then score lightly, sprinkle with ¼ teaspoon pepper, and rub with garlic, sage, thyme, dill weed, marjoram or oregano.

⁓ Let meat stand 1½–2 hours at room temperature before microwaving; refrigerator-cold meats are less likely to cook evenly.

⁓ Do not salt meat; salt accelerates heating and can toughen meat.

⁓ Measure diameter of roast (also weigh, if necessary) to determine precise microwave time.

ROAST LOIN OF PORK
(BASIC METHOD)

Prepare roast for cooking as directed above. Place fat side down on rack in deep casserole, insert microwave-safe meat thermometer in center of the largest muscle, touching neither fat nor bone as shown. Or use anautomatic temperature probe as manufacturer directs; it's the surest way to tell when pork is done although it's not recommended for roasts of less than 2 pounds. Cover casserole with tight lid and microwave on HIGH (100% power) 5 minutes. Reduce power to MEDIUM (50% power) and microwave as follows:

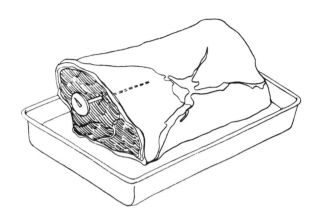

Bone-in Pork Loin (Sirloin, Center, or Blade Loin)	14–16 minutes per pound
Boned and Rolled Loin	15–17 minutes per pound

At halftime, turn pork fat side up and rotate casserole 180°. Continue microwaving on MEDIUM (50% power) until internal temperature reaches 170° F. Let roast stand, covered, 10 minutes. Test temperature in several places; if not at least 170° F. throughout, re-cover pork and continue microwaving on MEDIUM (50% power) in 5-minute increments.

OVEN COOKING BAG METHOD: Shake 1 tablespoon flour into 20" × 14" oven cooking bag (to help keep it from bursting). *Note: Never use supermarket vegetable bags in place of oven cooking bags; they're flimsy and unsafe.* Place pork in bag, close loosely with string or nylon tie, place bag in shallow bake/roast pan so fat side is up and bag touches neither oven floor nor walls. Cut 6 small (½") slits in top of bag to vent steam and, if using meat thermometer or automatic temperature probe, insert through slit into meat as above. Microwave as directed (no cover needed). When pork reaches 170° F., remove from oven, cover with foil, bag and all, and let stand 10 minutes. *Note: In oven bag, pork may cook 1–2 minutes per pound faster.*

PINEAPPLE SWEET-SOUR PORK: Microwave bone-in or boned and rolled loin in casserole to 170° F. as directed. Drain off drippings and spread ½ cup Pineapple Sweet-Sour Sauce over pork. Microwave, uncovered, on MEDIUM (50% power) 5 minutes, basting with additional sauce at halftime. Let stand, covered, 10 minutes. Transfer to platter and top with sauce.

Recipe too flexible for a meaningful nutritive count.

MAPLE-GLAZED LOIN OF PORK (SERVES 4–6): Microwave 3–4-pound bone-in or boned and rolled loin in casserole to 170° F. as directed. Drain off drippings and spread with ½ cup maple sugar mixed with 1 tablespoon dry sherry, Madeira, or orange juice and 1 tablespoon Dijon mustard. Microwave, uncovered, on MEDIUM (50% power) 5 minutes, spooning glaze over pork at halftime. Let roast stand, covered, 10 minutes. Transfer to hot platter, spoon glaze on top.

PER SERVING: 809–539 C 59–39 g P 51–34 g F 26–17 g CARB 261–174 mg S 211–140 mg CH

329

BARBECUED SPARERIBS

PREP TIME: | 3 MINUTES | COOKING TIME: | 60–68 MINUTES | STANDING TIME: | NONE

Barbecue spareribs in a microwave? You bet—and in half the usual time. If you like them brown, try the Crusty-Brown or Outdoor variation.

SERVES 4

3–3½ pounds lean spareribs, cut in 1- or 2-rib widths

1   cup All-Purpose Barbecue Sauce

Place ribs, meatiest side down and overlapping as needed, in 12″ × 8″ × 2″ casserole. Cover with vented plastic food wrap and microwave on HIGH (100% power) 5 minutes. Reduce power to MEDIUM (50%) and microwave 15 minutes per pound, turning ribs over at halftime, rearranging by moving undercooked ones to edge of casserole, and re-covering with wax paper. Drain off all drippings, pour sauce evenly over ribs, cover with wax paper, and microwave on MEDIUM (50% power) 10 minutes.

PER SERVING: 617 C   42 g P   45 g F   9 g CARB   503 mg S   174 mg CH

VARIATIONS

CHINESE BARBECUED SPARERIBS: Prepare as directed but substitute Chinese Barbecue Sauce for All-Purpose Barbecue Sauce.

PER SERVING: 715 C   42 g P   44 g F   37 g CARB   659 mg S   174 mg CH

CRUSTY-BROWN BARBECUED SPARERIBS: Prepare ribs as directed above, then lift from sauce and arrange in single layer in large roasting pan; brush with additional barbecue sauce. Set in preheated broiler and broil 4″–5″ from heat 4–6 minutes until nicely browned.

PER SERVING: 617 C   42 g P   45 g F   9 g CARB   503 mg S   174 mg CH

OUTDOOR BARBECUED SPARERIBS: Microwave ribs as directed, then drain but omit sauce. Instead, marinate ribs 1 hour at room temperature in All-Purpose Barbecue Sauce (or, if you prefer, the Chinese). Grill 4″ from coals of moderate fire about 15 minutes, turning ribs often and basting with sauce until richly browned.

PER SERVING: 639 C   42 g P   45 g F   13 g CARB   688 mg S   174 mg CH

CAJUN COUNTRY SPARERIBS: Prepare 3½–4 pounds country spareribs (from upper part of back) as directed, substituting Cajun Hot Barbecue Sauce for the All-Purpose and microwaving on MEDIUM (50% power) 15 minutes after sauce is added.

PER SERVING: 630 C   31 g P   51 g F   9 g CARB   465 mg S   146 mg CH

*R*OAST FRESH HAM *(BASIC METHOD)*

Cut skin from butt or shank half ham and trim fat evenly to ¼". Score fat lightly and rub with pepper, and, if you like, garlic and a compatible herb such as sage or thyme. Wrap shank end with 1"–2" foil strip, pressing snugly around ham, then mold 1" foil strip smoothly over upper edge of cut side of ham (either butt or shank end), securing as needed with wooden picks.

Place ham fat side down on rack in deep casserole, insert microwave-safe meat thermometer in center of the largest muscle, touching neither fat nor bone as shown. Or use an automatic temperature probe as manufacturer directs; it's the surest way to tell when pork is done. Cover casserole with tight lid and microwave on HIGH (100% power) 10 minutes. Reduce power to MEDIUM (50% power) and microwave 14–16 minutes per pound.

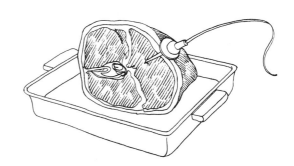

At halftime, remove foil shields, turn ham fat side up, and rotate casserole 180°. Continue microwaving on MEDIUM (50% power) until internal temperature reaches 170° F. Let roast stand, covered, 10 minutes. Test temperature in several places; if not at least 170° throughout, re-cover ham and continue microwaving on MEDIUM (50% power) in 5-minute increments.

ABOUT MICROWAVING SMOKED AND CANNED HAMS
(See Chapter 7, also recipes that follow.)

331

GLAZED HAM

PREP TIME: 5 MINUTES **COOKING TIME:** 38–70 MINUTES **STANDING TIME:** 10 MINUTES

SERVES 6–10

4–6-pound bone-in butt or shank portion ham, or semiboneless ready-to-eat ham, or fully cooked smoked picnic shoulder

½ cup light brown sugar

2 tablespoons prepared spicy brown mustard

1 tablespoon cider vinegar

Trim fat on ham to ⅛″, tie ham with string (to keep fat from separating), and lay on rack in shallow bake/roast pan; if wobbly, prop with ball of wax paper. Smooth sheet of plastic food wrap against cut surface of ham, then mold 1″–2″ foil strip smoothly over upper edge where fat joins lean to shield and prevent overcooking. If cooking shank-portion ham, also foil-wrap shank end. Insert microwave-safe meat thermometer through plastic in center of largest muscle, not touching fat or bone. (Or use automatic temperature probe as manufacturer directs or test with instant-register thermometer as ham

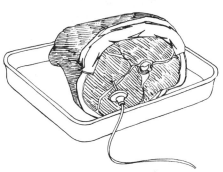

nears doneness.) Microwave, uncovered, on HIGH (100% power) 5 minutes, reduce power to MEDIUM (50%), and microwave 7–10 minutes per pound. At halftime, invert ham, rotate pan 180° and remove foil shields (not plastic). Continue microwaving until thermometer registers 130° F. If you like, score fat, crisscross fashion, 10 minutes before ham is done. Drain off drippings and remove plastic wrap. Combine remaining ingredients, spread on ham, and microwave, uncovered, on MEDIUM (50% power) 5 minutes. Tent ham with foil and let stand 10 minutes.

PER SERVING: 365 C 47 g P 11 g F 18 g CARB 2516 mg S 102 mg CH

Baked boneless ham (Serves 6–15): Substitute 2–5-pound ready-to-eat boneless ham (or canned ham scraped free of loose fat and jelly) for bone-in ham. Microwave as directed, but increase time on MEDIUM (50% power) to 10–12 minutes per pound or until meat thermometer reads 130° F. *Note: Canned hams should be loosely covered with wax paper during cooking.* Omit glaze (it won't stick) but let ham stand as directed. Serve with Raisin Sauce, Hot Mustard Mayonnaise, or Horseradish Sour Cream Sauce.

PER SERVING: 556 C   47 g P   28 g F   26 g CARB   3543 mg S   151 mg CH

Honey-glazed smoked boneless shoulder butt (Serves 4–8): Place 2–4-pound fully cooked, smoked boneless shoulder butt in casserole, add ⅓ cup water, cover with lid or vented plastic food wrap, and microwave on HIGH (100% power) 5 minutes; reduce power to MEDIUM (50%) and microwave 9–11 minutes per pound, turning butt over and rotating casserole 180° at halftime, until fork-tender. Drain, pour ¼ cup honey over butt, and let stand, covered, 10 minutes.

PER SERVING: 876 C   49 g P   66 g F   18 g CARB   2751 mg S   189 mg CH

ABOUT MICROWAVING STEAKS

The microwave just doesn't do them justice, so stick with grilling and broiling. But here's an idea for barbecue buffs. Sear steaks on the grill in summer and freeze them. You need only thaw them, then cook quickly by microwave. You'll have to experiment with the timing. But once you get it right, you'll be able to enjoy steaks with outdoor-grill flavor in the dead of winter.

ABOUT MICROWAVING CHOPS

With the exception of pork chops, which must be cooked well done, only such less tender cuts as shoulder chops should be microwaved. Like pork chops, they profit from the *moist* cooking at which microwaves excel. For best results:

Choose chops of similar size and thickness (those measuring ½"–¾" will microwave the most evenly). Pork chops as thick as 1¼" microwave successfully, but large veal chops will loose flavor and succulence.

Trim exterior fat to ⅛" and remove any nuggets of fat in the lean.

Do not bread chops (the breading will never crispen or brown).

Let chops stand at room temperature ½ hour before microwaving.

Arrange chops—without crowding—in single layer in casserole, then add 1 tablespoon liquid (water, broth, tomato juice, etc.) for each chop.

Salt chops only after they're done; salting raw meat can toughen it.

334

~~~ To help chops cook evenly, turn them over and rearrange at halftime.

~~~ Don't hurry the cooking of chops by keeping the power level at HIGH (100%); you'll only toughen and dry them. For supremely tender chops, cook briefly on HIGH, then simmer slowly on MEDIUM (50% power).

~~~ Test chops for doneness after minimum cooking time, removing any that are done. Be especially meticulous about pork chops. They should be cooked until the meat, slit near the bone, shows no pink.

ABOUT BROWNING CHOPS

By definition, *to braise* means "to brown a meat, then to cook it in the company of liquid" and this is hands down the best way to microwave chops. The browning can be done on top of the stove in a skillet, but you'll have to transfer the chops to a casserole for microwaving. Or you can use a glass ceramic casserole which can move from stovetop to microwave. The third option is to brown the chops by microwave, using a browning skillet or dish as its manufacturer directs. Just make sure these are also deep enough to accommodate the braising liquid. (For more details on microwave containers, see Chapter 3.)

ABOUT MICROWAVING HAMBURGERS

People do cook hamburgers in the microwave, but they're so anemic of color and flavor we can't imagine why anyone would bother. It takes little more time (and less attention) to broil, panbroil, or grill hamburgers the old-fashioned way and the results, certainly, are far superior.

VEAL CHOPS FORESTIÈRE

PREP TIME: [3 MINUTES] COOKING TIME: [30–35 MINUTES] STANDING TIME: [NONE]

SERVES 4

4 **veal shoulder chops, cut ¾"
    thick (about 1¾ pounds)**

1 **tablespoon vegetable oil**

1 **tablespoon butter or
    margarine**

6 **large mushrooms, wiped
    clean and sliced ¼" thick**

¼ **teaspoon crumbled dried
    rosemary**

⅛ **teaspoon pepper**

2 **tablespoons dry white wine**

¼ **cup tomato purée**

1 **teaspoon salt**

2 **tablespoons Worcestershire
    sauce**

Brown chops in oil and butter in 2½-quart glass ceramic casserole at least 10" across or in large heavy skillet over moderately high heat 2 minutes on each side. Lift out chops and set aside; add mushrooms to casserole and sauté lightly 1 minute. Return chops to casserole, thin parts toward center (transfer to 2½-quart casserole if you used skillet), sprinkle with rosemary and pepper, add wine, cover with lid or vented plastic food wrap, and microwave on MEDIUM (50% power) 20–25 minutes, turning chops over and rearranging at halftime, until fork-tender. Lift chops and mushrooms to bowl; blend remaining ingredients into casserole, return chops and mushrooms, re-cover, and microwave on MEDIUM-LOW (30% power) 5 minutes. Serve with buttered wide noodles.

PER SERVING: 353 C   32 g P   22 g F   5 g CARB   833 mg S   119 mg CH

V A R I A T I O N S

VIENNESE VEAL CHOPS: Brown chops and mushrooms as directed; omit rosemary and substitute 2 tablespoons beef broth for wine. When chops and mushrooms are tender, lift to hot platter, cover, and keep warm. Combine ⅓ cup casserole liquid, ¼ cup heavy cream, 1 tablespoon Dijon mustard, 1 teaspoon prepared horseradish, and ½ teaspoon salt; omit tomato purée, remaining salt, and Worcestershire sauce. Microwave, uncovered, on HIGH (100% power) 2–3 minutes, stirring every minute. Top chops and mushrooms with sauce and serve.
PER SERVING: 395 C   32 g P   28 g F   3 g CARB   556 mg S   139 mg CH

VEAL CHOPS PICCATA: Brown veal as directed; omit mushrooms and rosemary and use ¼ cup white wine to microwave chops. When tender, lift chops to hot platter, sprinkle lightly with salt, cover, and keep warm. Mix ⅓ cup casserole liquid with 2 tablespoons each lemon juice, capers, and minced parsley and ½ teaspoon finely grated lemon rind. Microwave, uncovered, on HIGH (100% power) 2–3 minutes. Spoon sauce over chops and serve.

PER SERVING: 329 C   30 g P   22 g F   1 g CARB   249 mg S   119 mg CH

VEAL AND PEPPERS: Brown 4 (½") slices veal shoulder (about 1½ pounds) in 2 tablespoons olive oil as directed. Omit mushrooms and sauté ½ cup minced yellow onion with 1 minced clove garlic and 2 cored and seeded large sweet green peppers, cut lengthwise in ½" strips, in 1 tablespoon olive oil 3–4 minutes. Omit rosemary and use 2 tablespoons dry white wine to microwave veal and vegetables as directed. Sprinkle all with salt and serve with Risotto or Rice Pilaf.

PER SERVING: 405 C   34 g P   27 g F   4 g CARB   118 mg S   121 mg CH

SALTIMBOCCA ALLA ROMANA

PREP TIME: 10 MINUTES   COOKING TIME: 15–17 MINUTES   STANDING TIME: NONE

SERVES 4

1½ **pounds veal scaloppine, cut in 6" × 3" × ¼" pieces and pounded ⅛" thick**

1½ **tablespoons minced fresh sage or ¾ teaspoon rubbed sage**

⅛ **teaspoon pepper**

¼ **pound prosciutto, sliced tissue-thin**

1 **tablespoon olive oil**

1 **tablespoon butter or margarine**

½ **cup dry white wine**

Sprinkle 1 side of each piece of scaloppine with sage and pepper, top with prosciutto, cutting as needed to fit; roll up jelly-roll style and fasten with toothpicks. Brown veal rolls 3 minutes in oil and butter in 10" (2-quart) glass ceramic casserole or large skillet over moderate heat. *Note: If you used skillet, transfer browned rolls and pan drippings to 2-quart casserole.* Arrange rolls in single layer with smaller ones in center; pour in wine, cover with lid, and microwave on HIGH (100% power) 6–7 minutes, rotating casserole 180° at halftime, until wine bubbles. Reduce power to MEDIUM (50%) and microwave, covered, 6–7 minutes, turning rolls over and rearranging at halftime, until tender. Remove toothpicks and serve with generous ladlings of casserole juices.

PER SERVING: 374 C   39 g P   23 g F   1 g CARB   522 mg S   145 mg CH

LAMB CHOPS BRAISED WITH WINE AND HERBS

PREP TIME: [2 MINUTES] COOKING TIME: [19–21 MINUTES] STANDING TIME: [3 MINUTES]

SERVES 4

4 **lamb shoulder (blade) chops, cut ¾" thick (about 1¾ pounds)**

1 **large clove garlic, peeled and halved**

1 **teaspoon minced fresh or ¼ teaspoon crumbled dried rosemary**

1 **teaspoon minced fresh or ¼ teaspoon crumbled dried marjoram**

⅛ **teaspoon pepper**

¼ **cup dry red wine, beef broth, or water**

½ **teaspoon salt**

Rub chops on both sides with garlic and arrange in 2- or 3-quart casserole at least 10" across. Sprinkle evenly with herbs and pepper, add wine, cover with lid or vented plastic food wrap, and microwave on HIGH (100% power) 5 minutes. Reduce power to MEDIUM (50%) and microwave 14–16 minutes, turning chops over and rearranging at halftime, until fork-tender. Let stand, covered, 3 minutes. Lift chops to hot platter, sprinkle with salt, and top with some casserole liquid, skimmed of fat. *Note: If you prefer gravy, strain skimmed casserole liquid into 1-quart measure and microwave, uncovered, on HIGH (100% power) 2–2½ minutes until almost boiling. Slowly whisk in 2 tablespoons flour blended with 2 tablespoons cold water and microwave, uncovered, on HIGH (100% power) 1–1½ minutes, whisking after 30 seconds, until gravy boils and thickens. Whisk again, add 2–3 drops liquid gravy browner and season to taste.*

For 1 Serving: Prepare ¼ recipe. Microwave as directed, using pie plate and allowing 2 minutes on HIGH (100% power), then 5–7 minutes on MEDIUM (50% power).

For 2 Servings: Prepare ½ recipe. Microwave as directed, allowing 3 minutes on HIGH (100% power), then 8–10 minutes on MEDIUM (50% power).

For 6 Servings: Prepare 1½ times the recipe using 6 chops, the same amount of garlic, 1½ teaspoons each fresh herb (or ½ teaspoon dried), ¼ teaspoon pepper, and ⅓ cup wine. Microwave in 12" × 8" × 2" bake/roast pan as directed, allowing 5 minutes on HIGH (100% power), then 16–18 minutes on MEDIUM (50% power).

PER SERVING: 182 C   24 g P   9 g F   1 g CARB   332 mg S   88 mg CH

⚖ BOMBAY LAMB CHOPS: Arrange garlic-rubbed chops in casserole as directed, omit herbs, and top chops with 1 cup thinly sliced yellow onion and the garlic, minced. Mix pepper with ½ teaspoon curry powder, ⅛ teaspoon each cinnamon and ginger, and ¼ cup water; pour evenly over chops, cover, and microwave as directed. Lift chops and onion to hot platter, sprinkle with salt, and keep warm. Skim casserole liquid of fat, pour ½ cup liquid into 1-pint measure, whisk in ½ cup yogurt, and microwave, uncovered, on MEDIUM (50% power) 1 minute (do not boil). Pour over chops, sprinkle with minced fresh coriander or parsley, and serve with fluffy boiled rice, Mutter Pilau, or Basmati Rice with Apricots and Cashews.

PER SERVING: 214 C   25 g P   9 g F   5 g CARB   352 mg S   89 mg CH

CREOLE-STYLE PORK CHOPS

PREP TIME: | 7 MINUTES | COOKING TIME: | 30–35 MINUTES | STANDING TIME: | NONE

SERVES 4

4   **pork loin or rib chops, cut ½"–¾" thick (1½–1¾ pounds), trimmed of all but ⅛" fat**

1   **small yellow onion, peeled, sliced tissue thin, and separated into rings**

1   **small sweet green pepper, cored, seeded, and cut lengthwise in ⅛" strips**

1   **clove garlic, peeled and minced**

⅛–¼   **teaspoon ground hot red pepper**

1   **cup tomato sauce**

Arrange chops in 2-quart casserole at least 10" across with thickest parts toward outside. Cover with wax paper and microwave on HIGH (100% power) 5 minutes. Scatter onion, green pepper, garlic, and red pepper over chops, pour in tomato sauce, cover with lid or vented plastic food wrap, and microwave on MEDIUM (50% power) 25–30 minutes, turning chops over and rearranging them at halftime, until fork-tender and no pink traces remain near bone. Serve with rice.

PER SERVING: 335 C   29 g P   21 g F   6 g CARB   454 mg S   93 mg CH

BARBECUED PORK CHOPS: Prepare as directed, omitting green pepper, garlic, and red pepper and substituting All-Purpose Barbecue Sauce for tomato sauce.

PER SERVING: 403 C   29 g P   23 g F   18 g CARB   822 mg S   93 mg CH

BRAISED PORK CHOPS

PREP TIME: [2 MINUTES] COOKING TIME: [16–19 MINUTES] STANDING TIME: [3 MINUTES]

One great advantage of cooking pork chops by microwave is that they cook done without toughening or drying. Not so on top of the stove. **Note:** *If you like 1"-thick chops, increase microwave time 50%.*

SERVES 4

- **4 loin or rib pork chops, cut ½"–¾" thick (1½–1¾ pounds), trimmed of all but ⅛" fat**
- **1 teaspoon vegetable oil**
- **¼ cup water, apple juice or cider, dry white wine or vermouth**
- **1 sprig (4") fresh rosemary or ¼ teaspoon crumbled dried rosemary**
- **⅛ teaspoon pepper**
- **¾ teaspoon salt**

Brown chops in oil in 2½-quart glass ceramic casserole at least 10" across or in large heavy skillet over moderately high heat 2 minutes on each side. Rearrange chops in casserole with thickest parts toward outside (or transfer them to casserole if you used skillet along with browned bits scraped up with a little of the water). If chops released more than 1 tablespoon drippings during browning, drain off excess. Add water, rosemary, and pepper, cover with lid or vented plastic food wrap, and microwave on MEDIUM (50% power) 12–15 minutes, turning chops over and rearranging at halftime, until fork-tender. *Note: Cut chop near bone; meat should not be pink. If so, continue microwaving in 3-minute increments.* Sprinkle with salt and let stand, covered, 3 minutes. Or, if you prefer, transfer chops to hot platter, cover with foil, and let stand while you make Pan or Herb Gravy using skimmed casserole drippings.

For 1 Serving: Prepare ¼ recipe. Microwave as directed, using pie plate and allowing 5–7 minutes on MEDIUM (50% power).

For 2 Servings: Prepare ½ recipe. Microwave as directed, allowing 7–9 minutes on MEDIUM (50% power).

For 6 Servings: Brown 6 chops in 2 batches, adding more oil, if needed. Arrange in 12" × 8" × 2" bake/roast pan, increase liquid to ⅓ cup and rosemary to 2 sprigs or a scant ½ teaspoon dried rosemary. Cover and microwave as directed, allowing 14–17 minutes on MEDIUM (50% power).

PER SERVING: 319 C   28 g P   22 g F   0 g CARB   496 mg S 93 mg CH

V A R I A T I O N S

 BRAISED BONELESS PORK LOIN CUTLETS: Brown 1 pound cutlets (3 ounces each) as directed, then season and microwave as directed, allowing 7–9 minutes on MEDIUM (50% power).

PER SERVING: 191 C   25 g P   9 g F   0 g CARB   487 mg S   72 mg CH

BRAISED PORK CHOPS WITH ORANGE AND GINGER: Prepare as directed, substituting ¼ cup orange juice blended with 2 tablespoons Dijon mustard and 1 tablespoon each minced fresh ginger and dark brown sugar for water and rosemary.

PER SERVING: 348 C   28 g P   23 g F   6 g CARB   722 mg S   93 mg CH

BERMUDA PORK CHOPS BRAISED WITH ONION, SAGE AND THYME: Brown chops in oil as directed. After rearranging, top with 1 cup thinly sliced Bermuda onion, separated into rings, and 1 minced clove garlic. Use ¼ cup dry white wine as the liquid and substitute ⅛ teaspoon each crumbled dried sage and thyme for rosemary. Proceed as recipe directs.

PER SERVING: 330 C   28 g P   22 g F   3 g CARB   506 mg S   93 mg CH

ABOUT MICROWAVING MEAT LOAVES

Of all the ways we've microwaved meat loaves, the recipes and methods that follow produce the most evenly cooked, lightly browned loaves in the least amount of time. For best results, follow these guidelines:

Use reasonably lean meat; fatty drippings heat rapidly, making outer layer of meat loaf overcook. For the same reason, always remove drippings with bulb baster as they collect.

Shape loaves exactly as recipes direct. Taller or wider loaves may overcook outside before the middle is done.

To speed cooking, pack meat into a ring. Ring-shaped loaves cook more evenly, too. They may crack a bit, but sauces make handy cover-ups.

Always microwave meat loaves in the containers specified. If loaf is block-shaped, there must be enough space around it to baste off drippings. Traditional loaf pans trap liquid and produce soggy meat loaves. Bake/roast pans with built-in trivets raise loaves well above drippings, but those with deep ridges may anchor loaves so securely they're difficult to remove.

To test meat loaves for doneness, make small cut near center; if meat is pink (but done outside), cover ends smoothly with 2" foil strips and microwave in 3-minute intervals, testing after each. **Note:** *It's all right for beef or veal loaves to be pinkish in middle—this will disappear during standing period. But pork loaves must be cooked until no pink remains.* Instant-register meat thermometers aren't reliable for testing meat loaves, but automatic temperature probes usually work well.

To make sure meat loaves containing pork cook thoroughly, shape them into rings. Good practice, too, if your microwave has "hot" or "cold" spots.

HAM AND VEAL LOAF

PREP TIME: 5 MINUTES **COOKING TIME:** 19–22 MINUTES **STANDING TIME:** 5 MINUTES

SERVES 4–6

1   *pound ground cooked ham*

½   *pound ground lean veal shoulder*

1½ *cups soft white bread crumbs*

1   *tablespoon grated yellow onion*

1   *egg, lightly beaten*

⅓   *cup milk*

½   *teaspoon dry mustard*

¼   *teaspoon pepper*

⅛   *teaspoon ground nutmeg*

¼   *cup firmly packed dark brown sugar*

Mix all ingredients but sugar well, shape into 8″ × 4½″ × 1½″ loaf and center in 2- or 3-quart casserole at least 9″ across. Cover with wax paper and microwave on HIGH (100% power) 15 minutes, rotating casserole 180° at halftime. Sprinkle sugar evenly on loaf and drizzle with a little pan drippings. Microwave, uncovered, on HIGH (100% power) 4–7 minutes until sugar melts and loaf, when pressed lightly in center, is slightly resilient. Cover with foil and let stand 5 minutes. Serve hot or cold with a nippy mustard sauce.

PER SERVING: 434–289 C 41–28 g P 18–12 g F 23–15 g CARB 1838–1225 mg S 182–121 mg CH

VARIATION

PINEAPPLE-GLAZED HAM AND VEAL LOAF: Prepare as directed but glaze with ⅓ cup Pineapple Sweet-Sour Sauce instead of brown sugar. Pass extra sauce.

PER SERVING: 415–276 C 41–28 g P 18–12 g F 18–12 g CARB 1870–1247 mg S 182–121 mg CH

SAVORY MEAT LOAF

PREP TIME: [10 MINUTES] **COOKING TIME:** [17–21 MINUTES] **STANDING TIME:** [5 MINUTES]

¢

SERVES 6–8

- **2   pounds ground lean beef**
- **1   medium-size yellow onion, peeled and finely grated**
- **1   clove garlic, peeled and crushed**
- **1¼ cups fine dry bread crumbs**
- **2   tablespoons steak sauce**
- **1   tablespoon prepared spicy brown mustard**
- **1   tablespoon minced parsley**
- **1   teaspoon crumbled dried basil**
- **2   teaspoons salt**
- **¼   teaspoon pepper**
- **½   cup cold water mixed with ½ teaspoon liquid gravy browner**
- **⅓   cup milk**

Mix all ingredients well, shape into 9″ × 5″ × 1½″ loaf, and center in 11″ × 7″ × 2″ casserole or bake/roast pan so loaf doesn't touch pan sides. With wet hands, smooth surface of loaf. Insert automatic temperature probe, if you like, so tip rests in center of loaf, then set temperature to 150° F., or use as manufacturer directs. Microwave, uncovered, on HIGH (100% power) 17–21 minutes, rotating casserole 180° and removing drippings at halftime. Also smooth out any cracks in loaf; these will widen as microwaving continues. When loaf tests done, transfer to hot platter, cover with foil, and let stand 5 minutes. Use this time, if you like, to make Pan or Mushroom Gravy.

To Bake Meat Loaf as a Ring: In 2- or 3-quart casserole at least 10″ across, shape meat mixture into 8″ ring with 3″ hole in center. Smooth surface and microwave as directed, but reduce time to 13–15 minutes or until meat tests done. Baste off drippings before letting loaf stand. Serve ring loaf in casserole—it's too fragile to transfer to a platter.

PER SERVING: 403–303 C 30–23 g P 22–17 g F 19–14 g CARB 1077–808 mg S 90–68 mg CH

V A R I A T I O N S

Sᴡᴇᴇᴛ-sᴏᴜʀ ɢʟᴀᴢᴇᴅ ᴍᴇᴀᴛ ʟᴏᴀғ: Prepare meat loaf as directed, using 1 pound ground lean beef and ½ pound each ground lean pork and veal instead of all beef; reduce crumbs to

344

1 cup, omit basil, and add ⅓ cup minced dill pickles (not too sour). Five minutes before meat loaf is done, baste off all drippings. Spoon 1 cup Pineapple Sweet-Sour Sauce evenly over loaf and finish microwaving as directed. Baste with sauce before standing time; serve with extra sauce.

PER SERVING: 440–330 C 31–24 g P 20–15 g F 32–24 g CARB 1243–932 mg S 103–77 mg CH

Barbecued Meat Loaf: Prepare meat loaf as directed, substituting 1 teaspoon chili powder for basil. Five minutes before meat loaf is done, baste off drippings, spoon 1 cup All-Purpose Barbecue Sauce evenly over loaf, and finish microwaving as directed. Baste with sauce before standing time; serve with extra sauce.

PER SERVING: 467–349 C 30–23 g P 23–18 g F 31–23 g CARB 1569–1177 mg S 90–68 mg CH

¢ Beef and Pork Loaf (Serves 4): Mix 1 pound ground lean beef, ½ pound ground lean pork, ¼ cup minced yellow onion, ¾ cup fine dry bread crumbs, 1 tablespoon Worcestershire sauce, 1 teaspoon prepared horseradish, ½ teaspoon each crumbled dried savory and sage, 1½ teaspoons salt, ⅛ teaspoon pepper, and ⅓ cup cold water mixed with ¼ teaspoon liquid gravy browner. Shape into 6½" ring in 9" pie plate, smooth surface, and microwave, uncovered, 14–18 minutes on HIGH (100% power) as basic recipe directs. *Note: Automatic temperature probe should register 170° F. and there should be no pink traces in meat.*

PER SERVING: 416 C 33 g P 23 g F 16 g CARB 1085 mg S 108 mg CH

345

CHILES RELLENOS
(MEXICAN STUFFED PEPPERS)

PREP TIME: 5 MINUTES **COOKING TIME:** 19–21 MINUTES **STANDING TIME:** 3 MINUTES

¢

For real *chiles rellenos* poblano chilies are stuffed, batter-dipped, and fried. This easy, steamed microwave version uses an authentic *picadillo* (spicy minced meat) stuffing and sweet green peppers. Choose ones that can stand upright without wobbling and leave space between them so that they'll cook evenly.

SERVES 4

4	large sweet green peppers
1	tablespoon vegetable oil
1	large yellow onion, peeled and minced
1	clove garlic, peeled and minced
1	pound lean ground beef
⅓	cup tomato paste
⅛–¼	teaspoon red pepper flakes
¼	teaspoon crumbled dried oregano
3	tablespoons minced seedless raisins
2	tablespoons minced blanched almonds*
1	teaspoon salt
	Pinch black pepper
	Pinch ground cloves
1	tablespoon water

Cut wide circle around stem of each pepper, lift out, then remove cores and seeds and set peppers aside. In wax-paper-covered 2-quart casserole large enough to hold peppers upright with ½" space between them, microwave oil, onion, and garlic on HIGH (100% power) 3½–4 minutes, stirring at halftime, until glassy. Mix in beef and push into doughnut shape around edge of casserole. Re-cover with wax paper and microwave on HIGH (100% power) 4½–5¼ minutes, breaking up beef clumps and stirring at halftime, until no pink remains. Mix in all remaining ingredients except water, re-cover with wax paper, and microwave on MEDIUM-HIGH (70% power) 4 minutes, stirring at halftime. Fill peppers with meat mixture and stand ½" apart in same casserole. Add water, cover with lid, and microwave on HIGH (100% power) 7–8¼ minutes, rotating casserole 180° at halftime, until peppers are *barely* tender (they'll finish cooking on standing). Let stand, covered, 3 minutes. Ladle casserole juices over peppers and serve.

PER SERVING: 435 C   23 g P   30 g F   19 g CARB   805 mg S   85 mg CH

SOME OTHER STUFFINGS FOR PEPPERS

Stuff each pepper with scant ⅔ cup of any of the following, then microwave as directed above.

~~~ Macaroni and Cheese

~~~ Risotto alla Milanese

~~~ Curried Rice

~~~ Ratatouille

~~~ Chili con Carne

ABOUT MICROWAVING POULTRY

Except for tiny whole game birds (which toughen and dry), geese (too big and fat to cook evenly), and breaded or fried chicken that goes limp, poultry microwaves like a dream. Indeed, the boned and the bony, the whole and the cut-up can be baked, braised, "roasted," poached, stewed, or stir-cooked to supreme succulence in a microwave. Here's what you must know to do each job properly.

WHOLE BIRDS

MOST SUITABLE BIRDS: Plump, compact fowl of no more than 12 pounds. Best weights: 6–12 pounds for turkeys, 6–9 for capons, 5–8 for roasting chickens, and 1–2 Cornish hens. Always allow at least 2" between bird and oven walls and ceiling; with less clearance, microwaves will bounce back into the bird and overcook outer portions. Because of their uneven shape, whole birds require special care throughout microwaving.

AMOUNT NEEDED PER SERVING: ¾–1 pound ready-to-cook bird.

GENERAL PREPARATION:

~~~ Remove body cavity fat, giblets, or gravy packets and weigh bird carefully so you can compute microwave time accurately.

~~~ If stuffing bird, pack lightly into body cavity just before bird goes into the microwave, allowing about ½ cup stuffing per pound for turkey or chicken and ⅓ cup per Cornish hen. Close neck and body cavities securely so stuffing doesn't fall out when bird is inverted or turned (see Suggested Microwave Poultry Stuffings). *Note: Because some microwave ovens, and especially older models, cook unevenly, neither the USDA Food Safety and Inspection Service nor the National Turkey Federation recommends microwaving STUFFED turkeys. However, the International Microwave Power Institute considers it safe IF the turkey and stuffing are properly handled throughout and good recipe procedures are followed. Our carefully developed guidelines for microwaving stuffed birds, which include cooking the stuffing until it reaches a temperature of 160° F.–165° F. IN THE MIDDLE as well as testing the bird for doneness IN SEVERAL SPOTS, will ensure wholesomeness. Should you have any qualms, however, by all means bake any suggested stuffing separately in a conventional oven.*

~~~ Truss bird with wooden *(never metal)* skewers. "Tucked" birds or those with plastic leg clamps need not be trussed. Remove any metal clamps.

~~~ Begin large bird (6 pounds or more) breast down in bake/roast pan, preferably on rack that will lift it above drippings (smaller birds can be microwaved breast up but big ones won't cook evenly unless begun breast down and turned over at halftime). If bird wobbles, prop with wax paper crumples. *Note: Avoid deeply ridged racks that may scar skin. If not using rack, baste off drippings as they accumulate; they not only overcook whatever portions of the bird they touch but also slow cooking.*

~~~ Do not salt poultry before microwaving; it will toughen and dry.

~~~ To ensure even cooking, use turntable, then check often to see that bird hasn't inched closer to oven walls. Without turntable, you must rotate bird manually several times during microwaving.

After turning bird breast side up, insert microwave-safe meat thermometer in large inside thigh muscle of bird of 6 pounds or more, making sure it doesn't touch bone. Or use instant-register thermometer as bird nears doneness (for an accurate reading, you must leave thermometer in bird 1 full minute). **Note:** *Do not use automatic temperature probe because drippings may pool around tip causing false, elevated readings. Never rely on "pop-up" thermometers; few work properly in the microwave. If larger birds are stuffed, you can insert thermometer in middle of stuffing instead of in largest thigh muscle.*

To heighten browning of large birds, baste with melted unsalted butter or margarine (this also helps keep skin wrinkle-free). Small birds cook too fast to brown, so you may want to brush with a *browning agent** (see About Browning Agents) or glaze (see Suggested Glazes for Poultry).

Never hurry cooking of large birds by microwaving at power levels higher than those recommended; birds will dry in some spots and undercook in others. At MEDIUM (50% power) turkeys, capons, and large roasters cook uniformly with minimal nutrient and moisture loss.

If necessary, shield breastbone, drumsticks, and other thin or protruding areas with 1"–2" foil strips as shown to deflect microwaves and keep them from drying or overbrowning.

Test birds for doneness after minimum microwave time *and in several spots*—thighs, breast, etc. Thermometer should register 175°–180° F. in thigh, 170° F. in thickest part of breast and 160°–165° F. in middle of stuffing. In small birds, test for doneness by wiggling drumstick; it should move freely at hip joint. Also make tiny slit near bone; juices should run clear. If bird is not done, continue microwaving in 10-minute intervals. Never undercook fowl; their internal temperature will rise only 5° F. during standing.

~~~~~ Always let birds stand, tented with foil, as directed; that's when they finish cooking.

SPECIAL TIPS FOR ROCK CORNISH HENS

If cooking more than one hen, arrange at least 1″ apart with drumsticks toward center of bake/roast pan (crowded birds won't cook evenly). If cooking four hens at once, place two on oven rack, two on oven floor, staggering them and reversing their positions at halftime. Microwave breast up as Microwave Poultry Chart directs, rotating pan 180° at halftime and also brushing, if desired, with a sweet glaze. **Note:** *Shield drumsticks with foil as needed. Also, when cooking more than one hen, test each for doneness; some may cook faster than others. Remove any that test done and continue microwaving the rest in 3-minute increments.*

POULTRY HALVES, QUARTERS, AND PARTS

Small turkey breasts, both bone-in and boneless, "roast" splendidly in the microwave. Drumsticks and thighs are better braised. As for chicken parts, you'll find plenty of recipes for them elsewhere in this book. Here, then, are the best ways to microwave the various poultry halves, quarters, and parts.

ROAST BONE-IN TURKEY BREAST (4–6 pounds): Pat dry and brush, if you like, with browning agent* (see About Browning Agents), or instead, glaze later. Microwave, covered with buttered wax paper, breast down, then breast up, as Microwave Poultry Chart directs. Rotate pan 180° at halftime, insert meat thermometer, and if you like, brush with melted unsalted butter or appropriate glaze (see Suggested Glazes for Poultry). When done, tent with foil, and let stand as directed. **Note:** *Don't try to crisp skin; meat will dry out.*

ROAST BONELESS TURKEY BREAST (2–4 pounds): Microwave as for bone-in breast, but increase time as Microwave Poultry Chart directs. **Note:** *Loosely pack any stuffing into breast, then tie with string to keep shape compact.*

ROAST HALVED, QUARTERED, OR DISJOINTED CHICKEN (1 broiler-fryer [3–3½ pounds]): Rub, if you like, with browning agent* (see About Browning Agents, or instead, glaze later. Lay skin side down in single layer on rack in bake/roast pan with meatiest pieces or portions toward outside (always place wings and drumstick ends in center). ***Note:*** *If you must overlap pieces, do so with thinnest ones in center.* Cover with wax paper and time as Microwave Poultry Chart directs, turning pieces over and rearranging at halftime and brushing, if you like, with suitable glaze. Uncover and continue microwaving as directed. *To test for doneness:* Make slit near bone; juices should run clean and meat show no traces of pink. Cover with foil and let stand 5 minutes.

CHICKEN LIVERS: Never microwave liver with bird—it will explode. Instead, microwave separately while chicken stands. Halve liver at natural separation and prick well with fork. Place in custard cup, cover with wax paper, and microwave on MEDIUM (50% power) 1½–2 minutes until just firm and no longer pink. ***Note:*** *Use gizzard, heart, neck, and back later for making stock.*

ABOUT BROWNING AGENTS

Mix equal quantities water and liquid gravy browner, soy sauce, or Worcestershire sauce and brush on poultry at outset, again after microwaving on HIGH (100% power), and once again midway through microwaving on MEDIUM (50% power).

SUGGESTED GLAZES FOR POULTRY

Use one of the following in place of browning agent, brushing over birds at halftime. Small fowl gain most from sweet glazes, which add color and sheen to otherwise pale birds. Browning agents add color only and butter bastings mostly calories—little birds cook too fast for the butter to brown.

Melted marmalade (orange, ginger, lemon), jelly (apple, grape, or red currant), or preserves (apricot, peach, plum, or cherry)

Finely minced chutney

Jiffy Garlic or Herb Butter, Curry or Chili Butter Sauce

All-Purpose Barbecue Sauce or Chinese Barbecue Sauce

Orange, apple, or pineapple juice or dry red or white wine mixed with dark brown sugar (allow 2 tablespoons sugar for each ⅓ cup liquid)

ABOUT CRISPING POULTRY SKIN

Omit browning agent* or glaze. Also skip standing time. Brush cooked bird with melted unsalted butter or margarine and roast, uncovered, on rack in roasting pan in preheated 500° F. oven, allowing 8–10 minutes for large birds, 5–8 minutes for chickens in the 3-to-6-pound range, and 4–5 minutes for Cornish hens.

SUGGESTED MICROWAVE POULTRY STUFFINGS

FOR TURKEY, CHICKEN, AND CORNISH HENS: Herb Bread Stuffing, Corn Bread and Sausage Stuffing, Mushroom-Pecan-Bulgur Stuffing

FOR CHICKEN AND CORNISH HENS: Herbed Wild Rice and Walnut Stuffing, Onion-Mushroom Rice, Herbed Rice, Saffron Rice, or Mandarin Orange Rice

FOR CORNISH HENS ONLY: Bulgur Pilaf, Basmati Rice with Apricots and Cashews

MICROWAVE POULTRY CHART

Note: All times are for refrigerator-cold birds, either stuffed or unstuffed.

Bird	Time and Power Level	Internal Temp. before Standing	Minutes Standing	Internal Temp. after Standing
TURKEY				
Whole (6–12 lbs.)	10 min. on HIGH *plus* 11–13 min. per lb. on MEDIUM	175°–180° F.	20	180°–185° F.
Breast (bone-in; 4–6 lbs.)	13–15 min. per lb. on MEDIUM	170° F.	15	175°–180° F.
Breast (boneless; 2–4 lbs.)	13–15 min. per lb. on MEDIUM	170° F.	10	175°–180° F.

Bird	Time and Power Level	Internal Temp. before Standing	Minutes Standing	Internal Temp. after Standing
CAPON				
Whole (6–9 lbs.)	10 min. on HIGH *plus* 10–12 min. per lb. on MEDIUM	175°–180° F.	10	180°–185° F.
CHICKEN				
Roaster (4–8 lbs.)	10 min. on HIGH *plus* 10–12 min. per lb. on MEDIUM	175°–180° F.	10	180°–185° F.
Broiler-Fryer (whole; 3–4 lbs.)	7–9 min. per lb. on HIGH	—	10	—
Halved Broiler-Fryer	6–7 min. per lb. on HIGH	—	5	—
Quartered Broiler-Fryer	5–6 min. per lb. on HIGH	—	5	—
Chicken Parts:				
Drumsticks, Wings† Breasts, Thighs	5–6 min. per lb. on HIGH	—	5	—
	†If cooking wings only, reduce time by 1 min. per lb.			
ROCK CORNISH HENS (1–2 lbs.)	6–8 min. per lb. on HIGH	—	5	—

Power Levels: HIGH (100%); MEDIUM (50%).

Note: *Internal temperatures are not reliable tests of doneness for small birds. When birds are done legs will move easily in hip sockets and juices will run clear.*

Coq au vin

PREP TIME: 8 MINUTES | COOKING TIME: 39–42 MINUTES | STANDING TIME: 5 MINUTES

Browning the chicken and vegetables takes about 15 minutes but is essential for the rich flavor and color we expect of this French classic.

SERVES 4–6

- **2** ounces lean salt pork, cut in 1/8" dice
- **2** tablespoons butter or margarine
- **1** broiler-fryer (3–3½ pounds), disjointed
- **1⅔** cups frozen small whole white onions (do not thaw)
- **1** clove garlic, peeled and minced
- **½** pound button mushrooms, wiped clean
- **1** bay leaf and 1 sprig each parsley and thyme tied in cheesecloth (bouquet garni)
- **¼** teaspoon pepper
- **1¼** cups dry red wine mixed with 1 teaspoon salt
- **2** tablespoons flour blended with ¼ cup cold water

Lightly brown salt pork 2 minutes in 4-quart glass ceramic casserole at least 10" across or large heavy skillet over moderate heat; remove with slotted spoon to paper toweling to drain. Add butter to drippings and brown chicken in 2 batches, allowing 3 minutes for each; remove and reserve. Add onions to drippings and turn 2 minutes to glaze lightly. Push onions to side of casserole, add garlic and mushrooms, and stir-fry 2 minutes until lightly browned. *Note: Now transfer garlic, mushrooms, and onions to 4-quart casserole if you used skillet.* Mix salt pork into casserole vegetables and arrange chicken on top with meatiest parts toward outside and wings in center. Add bouquet garni, pepper, and wine mixture. Cover with lid and microwave on HIGH (100% power) 22–25 minutes, turning chicken over and rearranging at halftime, until tender. Let casserole stand, covered, 5 minutes. With slotted spoon lift chicken and vegetables to heated deep platter. Blend flour paste into casserole liquid and microwave, uncovered, on HIGH (100% power) 4½–5 minutes, whisking briskly every 2 minutes, until sauce boils and thickens. Taste for salt and adjust as needed. Strain sauce over chicken and serve with boiled new potatoes or steamed rice.

PER SERVING: 761–507 C 50–33 g P 55–37 g F 14–9 g CARB 1000–667 mg S 216–144 mg CH

OVEN-BARBECUED CHICKEN

PREP TIME: 2 MINUTES **COOKING TIME:** 25–29 MINUTES **STANDING TIME:** NONE

SERVES 4

1 **broiler-fryer (3–3½ pounds), disjointed**

1½ **cups All-Purpose Barbecue Sauce or Cajun Barbecue Sauce**

Lay chicken skin side down in single layer on rack in 11″ × 8″ × 2″ bake/roast pan with meatiest parts toward outside and wings in center. Cover with wax paper and microwave on HIGH (100% power) 15–17 minutes, rearranging at halftime. Drain off drippings, remove rack, turn chicken skin side up with meatiest parts still to outside. Pour barbecue sauce evenly over chicken, cover with paper toweling, and microwave on MEDIUM (50% power) 10–12 minutes, basting with sauce and rotating pan 180° at halftime, until chicken is fork-tender and lightly glazed. If you like crisp skin, broil chicken (minus sauce) 6″–7″ from heat in preheated broiler 3–4 minutes. Or transfer to outdoor grill and cook 6″–8″ from moderately hot coals 5–10 minutes, basting with extra barbecue sauce and turning chicken frequently.

PER SERVING: 457 C   45 g P   24 g F   13 g CARB   687 mg S 143 mg CH

————————— V A R I A T I O N

PINEAPPLE SWEET-SOUR CHICKEN: Microwave chicken as directed, drain off drippings, remove rack, turn chicken skin side up with meatiest parts to outside. Proceed as directed, substituting Pineapple Sweet-Sour Sauce for barbecue sauce. *Note: Do not broil chicken to crisp skin because sauce may burn.*

PER SERVING: 501 C   41 g P   20 g F   36 g CARB   284 mg S 132 mg CH

POACHED CHICKEN

PREP TIME: 6 MINUTES   COOKING TIME: 22–25 MINUTES   STANDING TIME: NONE

Chicken meat is integral to everything from salads to sand-wiches to casseroles. If you need white meat only, use recipe for Poached Whole Chicken Breast.

YIELDS 3–3½ CUPS MEAT

- 1 broiler-fryer (3–3½ pounds), disjointed
- 1 small yellow onion, peeled and quartered
- 1 small carrot, peeled and sliced ½" thick
- 1 small stalk celery, sliced ½" thick
- 1 bay leaf and 1 sprig each parsley and thyme tied in cheesecloth (bouquet garni)
- 1 cup chicken broth or ½ cup each broth and dry white wine or water blended with ½ teaspoon salt

Arrange chicken in 2- or 3-quart casserole with meatiest parts toward outside, wings in center. Add remaining ingredients, cover with lid, and microwave on HIGH (100% power) 22–25 minutes, turning pieces over and rearranging at halftime, until tender. Cool chicken in broth, skin, cut meat from bones, and use as recipes direct. Strain broth, chill, and skim.

PER CUP: 268 C   41 g P   10 g F   0 g CARB   177 mg S 125 mg CH

V A R I A T I O N

POACHED WHOLE CHICKEN BREAST (About 2 cups meat): Place 1 large unboned chicken breast (about 1 pound) in 1-quart cas-serole, add ¼ cup water, chicken broth, or white wine, 1 teaspoon lemon juice, the bouquet garni, and ¼ teaspoon salt. Cover with lid and micro-wave on HIGH (100% power) 6–8 minutes, rotating casserole 180° at halftime, until just tender. Proceed as directed. *When Doubling Recipe:* Use 11" × 7" × 2" casserole and microwave 11–14 minutes.

PER CUP: 178 C   34 g P   4 g F   0 g CARB   345 mg S   91 mg CH

356

HOT TURKEY- OR CHICKEN-ALMOND MOUSSE

PREP TIME: 10 MINUTES   COOKING TIME: 28–32 MINUTES   STANDING TIME: 10 MINUTES

This Southern party favorite is a nifty way to use leftover turkey or chicken. It steams to perfection in the microwave in *half* the usual time and needs no messy hot water bath.

SERVES 8–10

4	cups ground cooked turkey or chicken
2	hard-cooked eggs, peeled and minced
¾	cup very finely ground blanched almonds*
¼	cup soft white bread crumbs
1	small yellow onion, peeled and minced
1	medium-size stalk celery, minced
4	tablespoons butter or margarine
¼	cup unsifted flour
1½	cups milk
1½	teaspoons salt
¼	teaspoon white pepper
¼	teaspoon rubbed sage
¼	teaspoon crumbled dried thyme
⅛	teaspoon ground nutmeg
¼	cup light cream
1	egg white, beaten to soft peaks

Mix turkey, eggs, almonds, and crumbs and set aside. Microwave onion, celery, and 1 tablespoon butter in wax-paper-covered 1-quart measure on HIGH (100% power) 4½–5 minutes until soft; add to turkey mixture. Melt remaining butter in same measure by microwaving, covered with wax paper, on HIGH (100% power) 45–55 seconds; stir in flour and microwave, uncovered, on HIGH (100% power) 30 seconds until foamy. Blend in milk, salt, pepper, sage, thyme, and nutmeg and microwave, uncovered, on HIGH (100% power) 4½–5 minutes, whisking hard after 2 minutes, until sauce boils and thickens; whisk hard again. Mix sauce into turkey mixture along with light cream; fold in egg white. Spoon into greased 2-quart ring mold, cover with vented plastic food wrap, and microwave on HIGH (100% power) 5 minutes, rotating mold 180° at halftime and again at end.

Reduce power to MEDIUM (50%) and microwave 13–16 minutes, rotating mold 180° every 5 minutes, until mousse starts to pull from sides of mold and is *just* set. **Note:** *Test for doneness by pressing top lightly; it should be just set with a ¼" area midway between edge and center slightly soft; this will set as mold stands.* Cover mold with foil and let stand 10 minutes. Loosen

357

mousse with spatula, invert on heated platter, and ease out. Serve as is or accompany with Sweet Red Pepper Sauce, Mushroom Sauce, or Fresh Tomato Sauce. Or fill center with hot buttered peas, asparagus tips, or butter-browned button mushrooms.

PER SERVING: 332–265 C   26–21 g P   21–17 g F   9–7 g CARB   583–466 mg S   154–123 mg CH

POACHED CHICKEN SUPRÊMES
(BASIC METHOD)

 Few meats are more versatile than suprêmes (boneless, skinless half-breasts of chicken), which average 4–6 ounces. And few microwave more quickly. For best results, choose suprêmes of uniform size and microwave with a wax-paper cover.

Pound suprêmes lightly to flatten and arrange in single layer ½" apart, spoke fashion if microwaving more than 2, with thickest portions to outside, in pie plate or casserole. For each supreme, add 1 tablespoon broth, dry white wine, or water, ¼ teaspoon lemon juice, and a small parsley sprig. Cover with wax paper and microwave on HIGH (100% power) as follows, rotating, pie plate or casserole 180° at halftime, until suprêmes are just tender.

1 suprême (4–5 ounces)	2–3 minutes
2 suprêmes (4–5 ounces each)	3½–5 minutes
4 suprêmes (4–5 ounces each)	7–9 minutes
6 suprêmes (4–5 ounces each)	9–12 minutes

Note: Allow 30 seconds longer for each 6-ounce suprême. The nickel-size pink spots in center of suprêmes will fade on standing. Do not microwave suprêmes until well done; they'll toughen and dry. Let suprêmes stand, covered with foil, 2–3 minutes. Salt and pepper to taste and serve hot with Hollandaise, Sweet Red Pepper Sauce, or gravy (Chicken Cream, Mushroom, and Sour Cream Gravy are superb). Or cool suprêmes in liquid, drain, and serve with a squeeze of lime juice and scattering of minced dill and/or tiny capers.

V A R I A T I O N S

SUPRÊMES AMANDINE (Serves 4): Poach 4 suprêmes as directed, lift from casserole with slotted spoon, season, cover, and keep warm. In casserole combine ⅓ cup cooking liquid, ⅔ cup heavy cream, and 1 tablespoon flour blended with 2 tablespoons cold water. Microwave, uncovered, on HIGH (100% power) 3–4 minutes, whisking at halftime, until sauce boils and thickens. Add ¼ cup toasted blanched almonds,* pour over suprêmes, and serve.

PER SERVING: 356 C   36 g P   21 g F   5 g CARB   172 mg S   137 mg CH

358

SUPRÊMES WITH SOUR CREAM-CHIVE SAUCE (Serves 4): Poach 4 suprêmes as directed, lift from casserole with slotted spoon, season, cover, and keep warm. In casserole combine ¼ cup cooking liquid, 1 cup room-temperature sour cream, and 1 tablespoon minced chives. Microwave, uncovered, on MEDIUM-LOW (30% power) 3½–4½ minutes, stirring every minute, until *warm*. *Note: Sauce heats quickly at end; it mustn't boil, even around edges, or it will curdle.* Pour sauce over suprêmes, sprinkle with 1 tablespoon minced chives, and serve.

PER SERVING: 281 C   35 g P   14 g F   3 g CARB   170 mg S   108 mg CH

SUPRÊMES OF CHICKEN IN MUSTARD CREAM

PREP TIME: | 2 MINUTES | COOKING TIME: | 5½–6 MINUTES | STANDING TIME: | 5 MINUTES

If you should have frozen boned and skinned chicken breasts on hand, you can prepare this elegant recipe in less than 15 minutes. It couldn't be easier.

SERVES 2

- 2 **tablespoons dry vermouth**
- 2 **tablespoons heavy cream**
- 1 **tablespoon Dijon mustard**
- ⅛ **teaspoon dried thyme, crumbled**
- ⅛ **teaspoon pepper**
- 2 **solidly frozen boned and skinned chicken breasts (about 5 ounces each)**

In an 8-inch pie plate, combine vermouth, cream, mustard, thyme, and pepper. Turn frozen chicken breasts in mixture to coat well, arrange 2″ apart in pie plate, and microwave, uncovered, on MEDIUM-LOW (30% power) 3 minutes, rotating pie plate 180° at halftime. *Note: If breasts are frozen together, separate them after 1½ minutes as you rotate pie plate.* Let stand, uncovered, 3 minutes. Turn breasts over, spoon sauce on top, cover with wax paper, and microwave on HIGH (100% power) 2½–3 minutes, again rotating pie plate 180° at halftime, until just cooked. *Note: A circle of pink no bigger than ¾″ may show in center of each breast, but will finish cooking on standing.* Let plate stand, still covered, 2 minutes. Serve at once topped with sauce.

PER SERVING: 224 C   33 g P   8 g F   3 g CARB   324 mg S   103 mg CH

CHICKEN SAN MARINO

PREP TIME: 10 MINUTES **COOKING TIME:** 11–13 MINUTES **STANDING TIME:** NONE

Choose deeply smoky country ham and Marsala, the dessert wine of Italy, for this memorable recipe, which cooks in less than 15 minutes.

SERVES 4

- 4 **boned and skinned chicken breasts (about 1½ pounds)**
- ½ **teaspoon salt**
- ⅛ **teaspoon pepper**
- 2 **tablespoons Dijon mustard**
- 4 **slices lean cooked ham (about 6 ounces)**
- 2 **tablespoons melted butter**
- ½ **cup chicken broth**
- ⅓ **cup Marsala wine**
- 2 **teaspoons cornstarch**
- ¼ **cup heavy cream**
- 2 **tablespoons minced chives**
- 2 **tablespoons finely diced pimiento**

Lay chicken breasts on wax paper and with sharp knife, halve each horizontally, cutting not quite clear through, so it will lie flat like an open book. Cover chicken with sheet of wax paper and pound until uniformly ¼" thick. Dividing total amounts evenly, sprinkle each chicken breast with salt and pepper, then spread with mustard. Top with ham, cut slightly smaller than breast, then roll, jelly-roll fashion, and secure with toothpicks. Arrange rolls around edge of 2-quart casserole at least 10" across, brush with melted butter, and pour in broth. Cover with lid or vented plastic food wrap and microwave on HIGH (100% power) 9–10 minutes, turning rolls over and rearranging at halftime, just until juices run clear when rolls are pricked. Using slotted spoon, lift rolls to bowl, cover, and keep warm. Blend Marsala and cornstarch, whisk into casserole liquid, and microwave, uncovered, on HIGH (100% power) 2–3 minutes, whisking at halftime, until sauce boils and thickens. Whisk in cream, return chicken rolls to casserole, spooning sauce over them. Sprinkle with chives and pimiento and serve with fettuccine.

PER SERVING: 381 C 49 g P 16 g F 6 g CARB 1314 mg S 157 mg CH

LEMON-AND-GINGER-GLAZED CHICKEN BREASTS

PREP TIME: 4 MINUTES COOKING TIME: 10½–14 MINUTES STANDING TIME: NONE

Boned and skinned chicken breasts microwave to perfection in less than 10 minutes. **Note:** *Hoisin sauce can be found in many large supermarkets today.*

SERVES 4

- **4 boned and skinned chicken breasts (about 1½ pounds)**
- **¼ cup lemon juice**
- **2 tablespoons minced fresh ginger**
- **2 scallions, minced (include green tops)**
- **1 clove garlic, peeled and crushed**
- **1 tablespoon Oriental sesame oil or vegetable oil**
- **Pinch red pepper flakes**
- **Optional garnish (see below)**
- **¼ teaspoon salt**
- **1 tablespoon cornstarch**
- **¼ cup chicken broth**
- **2 tablespoons soy sauce**
- **¼ teaspoon chili oil (optional)**
- **1 teaspoon hoisin sauce (fermented bean sauce)**
- **½ teaspoon sugar**

Pound chicken breasts to flatten slightly; set aside. Place lemon juice, ginger, scallions, garlic, sesame oil, and red pepper flakes in 10″ casserole 2″–2½″ deep. Lay chicken on top, spoke fashion, with thickest portions toward outside. Cover with wax paper and microwave on HIGH (100% power) 7–9½ minutes, rotating casserole 180° at halftime, until chicken is just tender. *Note: If using optional garnish, lay carrot and red pepper strips in center on top of chicken at halftime. If breasts are of uniform thickness, turn each 180° at halftime so they'll cook evenly.* With slotted spoon, lift chicken to heated plate, also carrot and red pepper strips, if using, then sprinkle with salt; cover snugly with foil and keep warm. In small bowl, combine cornstarch, chicken broth, soy sauce, chili oil, if you like, hoisin sauce, and sugar. Blend into casserole liquid and microwave, uncovered, on HIGH (100% power) 3½–4½ minutes, stirring at halftime, until sauce boils and thickens. Return chicken to casserole, spoon sauce on top to glaze, then serve.

PER SERVING: 244 C 40 g P 6 g F 6 g CARB 869 mg S 99 mg CH

Optional Garnish:

**2 tablespoons matchstick
   strips carrot**

**2 tablespoons matchstick
   strips sweet red pepper**

~~~~~~~~~~ V A R I A T I O N

 ORANGE-AND-GINGER-GLAZED CHICKEN :
Prepare as directed, substituting orange juice
for lemon juice. Omit sugar and hoisin from
sauce and add 1 tablespoon cream sherry. Garnish with orange slices.

**PER SERVING: 249 C   40 g P   6 g F   6 g CARB   824 mg S
99 mg CH**

CHICKEN BREASTS MOZZARELLA

PREP TIME: [5 MINUTES] COOKING TIME: [12–15 MINUTES] STANDING TIME: [NONE*]

We like to prepare this casserole ahead, then pop it in the
microwave for a final few minutes, knowing that it won't
dry or burn if we're inattentive. You needn't brown the
chicken before you microwave it, but it'll taste better.

SERVES 6

**6 boned and skinned chicken
   breasts (about 1¾ pounds),
   trimmed of fat**

**⅓ cup unsifted flour mixed
   with 1 teaspoon salt and ¼
   teaspoon pepper**

2 tablespoons vegetable oil

**1 tablespoon butter or
   margarine**

**2 cups Jiffy Tomato Sauce or
   marinara sauce**

**1½ cups coarsely grated
   mozzarella cheese**

Dredge chicken in flour mixture, then brown 2
minutes on each side in oil and butter in large
heavy skillet over moderate heat; drain on paper
toweling. Smooth sauce over bottom of 13″ ×
9″ × 2½″ oval glass ceramic casserole and lay
chicken on top with thickest parts to outside.
*Note: You can prepare recipe to this point, then
cover and store in refrigerator until 20 minutes
before serving. Increase microwave time 2 minutes for refrigerator-cold casserole.* Cover with
wax paper and microwave on HIGH (100%
power) 6–8 minutes, rotating casserole 180° at
halftime, until chicken is tender. Sprinkle evenly
with cheese and microwave, uncovered, on
HIGH (100% power) 2 minutes until cheese

melts. Or brown 3"–4" from heat in preheated broiler 2–3 minutes.

For 4 Servings: Brown 4 breasts as directed using 1 tablespoon each oil and butter; reduce sauce to 1½ cups, microwave time to 4–6 minutes, and cheese to 1 cup.

For 2 Servings: Brown 2 breasts as directed using 2 teaspoons each oil and butter; reduce sauce to ¾ cup, microwave time to 2–3 minutes, and cheese to ½ cup.

PER SERVING: 378 C 38 g P 19 g F 13 g CARB 1080 mg S 104 mg CH

V A R I A T I O N

 CHICKEN BREASTS WITH MUSHROOMS AND MARSALA: Arrange browned chicken in casserole as directed. Sauté ½ pound thinly sliced mushrooms in 2 tablespoons butter in same skillet over moderately high heat 3 minutes, add ¼ cup Marsala wine, scrape up brown bits, and pour all over chicken. Cover and microwave as directed but increase time to 8–10 minutes or until chicken is tender. Lift chicken and mushrooms to bowl with slotted spoon, cover, and keep warm. Whisk 1 tablespoon cornstarch blended with ¼ cup beef broth into casserole liquid and microwave, uncovered, on HIGH (100% power) 2–3 minutes, whisking at halftime, until sauce boils and thickens. Return chicken and mushrooms to casserole, spoon sauce on top, and serve.

PER SERVING: 282 C 32 g P 12 g F 9 g CARB 548 mg S 92 mg CH

BRAISED TURKEY PARTS

PREP TIME: | 5 MINUTES | COOKING TIME: | 57–64 MINUTES | STANDING TIME: | NONE

¢

SERVES 4–6

- **3** turkey drumsticks or thighs (about 1½ pounds each)
- **1** medium-size yellow onion, peeled and minced
- **1** medium-size carrot, peeled and minced
- **1** bay leaf and 1 sprig each parsley and thyme tied in cheesecloth (bouquet garni)
- **1** teaspoon salt dissolved in 1 cup warm water
- **¼** teaspoon pepper
- **3** tablespoons flour blended with ¼ cup cold water
- **1** teaspoon liquid gravy browner

Arrange turkey parts ½" apart in 11" × 8" × 2" casserole, thin drumstick ends in center. Scatter onion and carrot on top, add bouquet garni, salt water, and pepper. Cover with lid and microwave on HIGH (100% power) 13–15 minutes until water boils. Reduce power to MEDIUM-HIGH (70%) and microwave 40–45 minutes, turning parts over and rearranging at halftime, until fork-tender. Lift turkey to bowl, cover with foil, and keep warm while making gravy. Skim casserole liquid of fat, strain, measure, and add water or chicken broth to total 2½ cups. Return to casserole, whisk in flour paste, and microwave, uncovered, on HIGH (100% power) 3½–4 minutes, whisking after 2 minutes, until gravy boils and thickens. Blend in gravy browner and adjust salt and pepper to taste. Return turkey parts to gravy and serve.

PER SERVING: 542–362 C 68–46 g P 24–16 g F 9–6 g CARB
1196–797 mg S 242–161 mg CH

VARIATION

TURKEY MARENGO: Prepare as directed but add 1 minced clove garlic with onion and carrot and substitute ½ cup dry white wine and ¾ cup crushed tomatoes for water. When turkey is tender, remove to bowl as directed. Skim fat from casserole mixture and purée; return to casserole, whisk in 2 tablespoons tomato paste, and microwave, uncovered, on HIGH (100% power) 2–3 minutes until hot. Adjust salt and pepper to taste, return turkey parts to casserole, sprinkle with minced parsley, and serve.

PER SERVING: 535–356 C 68–46 g P 24–16 g F 8–5 g CARB 1255–836 mg S 242–161 mg CH

ROCK CORNISH HENS WITH BLACK CHERRY SAUCE

PREP TIME: | 5 MINUTES | COOKING TIME: | 23–29 MINUTES | STANDING TIME: | NONE*

SERVES 4

- **2 Rock Cornish hens (1½–1¾ pounds each), halved lengthwise and wingtips removed**
- **2 tablespoons butter, margarine, or vegetable oil**
- **½ teaspoon salt**
- **1 can (1 pound, 1 ounce) pitted dark sweet cherries (do not drain)**
- **1 teaspoon lemon juice**
- **2 tablespoons cornstarch blended with 2 tablespoons cold water**
- **2 tablespoons dry port or Madeira wine**
- **Pinch pepper**

Brown hens in 2 batches 2 minutes on skin side in butter in large skillet over moderately high heat. Transfer to 11″ × 8″ × 2″ casserole, arranging skin side up with meatiest parts toward outside. Cover with wax paper and microwave on HIGH (100% power) 15–20 minutes, rearranging at halftime, until hens are tender. *Note: Leg joints should move easily and juices run clear.* With slotted spoon, lift hens to serving dish, sprinkle with salt, cover with foil, and let stand while making sauce. Skim fat from casserole, strain liquid through fine sieve, and reserve. Drain cherry liquid into 2-cup measure and add enough reserved liquid to total 1¼ cups. Stir in lemon juice and cornstarch mixture and microwave, uncovered, on HIGH (100% power) 3–3½ minutes, whisking at halftime, until sauce boils and thickens. Stir in wine, pepper, and cherries and microwave, uncovered, on HIGH (100% power) 1 minute. Spoon some sauce over birds and pass the rest.

PER SERVING: 538 C 45 g P 28 g F 25 g CARB 470 mg S 158 mg CH

VARIATION

BURGUNDY-STYLE CORNISH HENS: Transfer browned hens to casserole, add ¼ cup dry red wine, ½ cup each minced yellow onion and carrot, 1 minced clove garlic, 1 sprig fresh thyme (or ¼ teaspoon crumbled dried thyme), and 1 bay leaf. Microwave as directed and when tender, lift hens to platter, sprinkle with salt, cover, and keep warm. Discard bay leaf and thyme, then

365

purée casserole vegetables with skimmed casserole liquid. Pour into 1-quart measure, add ½ cup beef broth, 1 tablespoon flour blended with 1 tablespoon cold water, and 2 teaspoons tomato paste. Microwave, uncovered, on HIGH (100% power) 2–3 minutes, whisking at halftime, until sauce boils and thickens. Taste sauce and adjust salt and pepper as needed. If sauce seems thick, thin with a little red wine. Spoon some sauce over hens and pass the rest.

PER SERVING: 467 C   45 g P   28 g F   6 g CARB   596 mg S 158 mg CH

HONEYED DUCKLING WITH MANDARIN ORANGE SAUCE

PREP TIME: | 10 MINUTES | COOKING TIME: | 45–60 MINUTES | STANDING TIME: | NONE

Combination cooking works best for duckling. The microwave speeds cooking and forces out most of the fat (often as much as 2 cups per bird), then a 500° F. oven crisps and browns the skin to perfection.

SERVES 4

1 **duckling (about 5 pounds), cleaned, dressed, and quartered**

¼ **cup honey blended with ¼ teaspoon liquid gravy browner**

2 **tablespoons finely slivered orange zest (colored part of rind)**

⅓ **cup hot water**

2 **tablespoons sugar mixed with 1 tablespoon cold water**

Prick duckling well all over and arrange in single layer, skin side down, on rack in bake/roast pan with thickest parts to outside. Microwave, uncovered, on HIGH (100% power) 35–45 minutes until leg joints move easily and breast juices run clear. At halftime, remove all drippings, turn duck skin side up, and rearrange; re-prick skin and brush evenly with some of the honey mixture. Also preheat conventional oven to 500° F. As soon as duckling is done, place breast side up on rack in shallow roasting pan, brush well with remaining honey mixture, then roast, uncovered, at 500° F. 10–15 minutes until crisply browned. *Note: Take care bird doesn't burn.*

- ½ **cup orange or mandarin orange juice**
- 1 **tablespoon lemon juice**
- 1 **can (11 ounces) mandarin oranges, drained (reserve liquid)**
- ½ **cup chicken broth or Giblet Stock**
- 2 **tablespoons cornstarch blended with 2 tablespoons cold water**
- ⅛ **teaspoon pepper**

Meanwhile, Prepare Sauce: Place orange zest and hot water in 1-pint measure, cover with vented plastic food wrap, and microwave on HIGH (100% power) 2 minutes; drain zest and reserve. In same measure microwave sugar mixture, uncovered, on HIGH (100% power) 2–2½ minutes until mixture boils and turns pale amber. *Note: Watch carefully last 30 seconds lest syrup burn; it'll darken even more on standing.* Let syrup cool, uncovered, 1 minute, mix in orange and lemon juice, and microwave, uncovered, on HIGH (100% power) 1½–2 minutes, stirring after 1 minute, until caramel dissolves (it will have hardened). Mix in reserved mandarin orange liquid, broth, zest, cornstarch paste, and pepper, then microwave, uncovered, on HIGH (100% power) 2½–3 minutes until sauce boils and thickens; gently stir in mandarin oranges. Lift duckling to hot platter, top with some of the sauce, and pass the rest.

PER SERVING: 660 C 42 g P 35 g F 44 g CARB 262 mg S 158 mg CH

———————— V A R I A T I O N

ORIENTAL BLACK TEA DUCKLING: After pricking duckling, rub well with 2 tablespoons soy sauce mixed with 1 crushed clove garlic. While duckling cooks, steep 1 tablespoon lapsang souchong, orange pekoe, or other black tea leaves and 1 crushed clove garlic in 1⅓ cups boiling water 5 minutes. Strain, add ¼ cup soy sauce, ½ cup firmly packed dark brown sugar, and 2 teaspoons red wine vinegar, stirring until sugar dissolves. Use instead of honey mixture to brush duckling at halftime and again when bird roasts in 500° F. oven (take care it doesn't burn).

PER SERVING: 553 C 42 g P 35 g F 16 g CARB 1165 mg S 101 mg CH

HERB BREAD STUFFING

PREP TIME: | 8 MINUTES | COOKING TIME: | 6 MINUTES | STANDING TIME: | NONE |

Moist stuffings microwave best inside birds. Bake any excess in a foil-wrapped casserole in the regular oven.

MAKES ABOUT 6 CUPS, ENOUGH TO STUFF A 10- OR 11-POUND TURKEY

¼	cup (½ stick) butter, margarine, or bacon drippings
2	medium-size yellow onions, peeled and minced
2	large stalks celery, minced
6	cups ½" cubes stale bread
1½	teaspoons poultry seasoning
2	tablespoons minced parsley
1½	teaspoons salt
¼	teaspoon pepper
1½	cups hot water or chicken broth

Melt butter by microwaving in wax-paper-covered 3-quart casserole on HIGH (100% power) 55–65 seconds. Add onions and celery, re-cover, and microwave on HIGH (100% power) 5 minutes until glassy. Toss with remaining ingredients.

For ½ Recipe (for 1 bird [5–7 pounds] or 4 Rock Cornish hens): Reduce butter-melting time to 35–45 seconds and onion/celery-cooking time to 3 minutes

PER CUP: 162C 3gP 9gF 18gCARB 795mgS 22mgCH

~~~ V A R I A T I O N S

APPLE-PECAN STUFFING: Prepare as directed but reduce bread cubes to 5 cups and add 1½ cups coarsely chopped, peeled tart apples and 1 cup coarsely chopped pecans.

PER CUP: 284C 4gP 21gF 23gCARB 770mgS 21mgCH

BRANDIED FRUIT STUFFING: Plump ½ pound pitted, dried fruit (prunes, figs, apricots, or peaches) by spreading in 9" pie plate, sprinkling with 3 tablespoons brandy, covering with vented plastic food wrap, and microwaving on HIGH (100% power) 2 minutes, stirring at halftime. Let stand, covered, 2 minutes. Drain fruit, saving liquor, then chop. Prepare stuffing as directed, using

368

reserved fruit liquor as part of liquid and mixing fruit in at end.

PER CUP: 252 C   4 g P   9 g F   42 g CARB   797 mg S 22 mg CH

CORN BREAD AND SAUSAGE STUFF-ING: Slice ½ pound bulk sausage ½" thick, arrange on roasting rack, cover with paper toweling, and microwave on HIGH (100% power) 3–5 minutes, rearranging at halftime, until no longer pink. Cool sausage slightly and mince fine. Proceed as recipe directs but use sausage drippings to cook onion and celery instead of butter, substitute 6 cups crumbled corn bread for bread cubes, and reduce liquid to 1 cup. Mix in sausage at end.

PER CUP: 378 C   12 g P   23 g F   32 g CARB   1445 mg S 103 mg CH

CRANBERRY STUFFING: Microwave onion and celery as directed, add 1½ cups stemmed fresh or frozen cranberries and ¼ cup hot water; cover with vented plastic food wrap and microwave on HIGH (100% power) 4–6 minutes, stirring at halftime, until cranberries pop. Proceed as recipe directs, but reduce liquid to 1 cup.

PER CUP: 176 C   3 g P   9 g F   22 g CARB   795 mg S 22 mg CH

BACON AND CHICKEN LIVER STUFF-ING: Microwave 2 finely diced bacon slices in wax-paper-covered 1-quart casserole on HIGH (100% power) 2 minutes, stirring at halftime. Add ¾ pound chicken livers, halved and pricked well all over; re-cover with wax paper and microwave on MEDIUM (50% power) 7–9 minutes, stirring every 3 minutes, until livers are just firm and no longer pink. Cool and drain, reserving liquid; chop livers fine. Proceed as basic recipe directs but use reserved liquid as part of liquid and mix in bacon and livers at end.

PER CUP: 275 C   14 g P   15 g F   20 g CARB   892 mg S 276 mg CH

10

FISH AND SHELLFISH

Whether you want to stir up a fancy crab imperial or steam shrimp or fish simply, your microwave will do the job superbly and in less time than you would have dreamed possible. Its moist method of cooking preserves every ounce of natural succulence and intensifies the sea-sweet flavor of fish and shellfish. You can even use your microwave oven to open clams, oysters, and mussels. Remember how pesky it was to do *that* chore the old-fashioned way—by hand?

ABOUT MICROWAVING FISH

Fillets, thick and thin, steaks, chunks, whole fish, both stuffed and unstuffed, can be steamed or poached to perfection in a microwave. When fresh, fish needs no moisture other than its own. And—dieters take note—no oil or butter either. Quantity, shape, thickness, and, to some extent, variety, all affect microwave times for fish. Pound for pound, oily fish (mackerel, pompano, shad, catfish, bluefish, swordfish, tuna, etc.) usually microwave more slowly than the lean (flounder, cod, red snapper, haddock, striped bass, turbot, etc.). The exception? Salmon, which though "oily" microwaves like lean fish. Fresh-caught fish also microwaves faster than any that's been out of the water 1 to 2 days. To keep fish moist, succulent, and flavorful:

> **A**lways thaw frozen fish completely before microwaving lest it cook unevenly. It will microwave faster than fresh fish.

Choose coverings carefully. *Paper toweling* absorbs excess moisture and is ideal for fast-cooking thin fillets. *Wax paper* holds some moisture in, making it a better choice for thicker pieces. And *plastic food wrap* keeps large chunks or whole fish from drying on the surface as they steam or poach.

Use cooked stuffings only for fish; raw ingredients won't cook done in the time it takes to microwave the fish.

Do not salt fish before microwaving; it will toughen and dry.

Don't brush fish with browning agents;* you'll only muddy the surface. The best way to give fish color is to sprinkle with paprika and/or parsley after it's cooked.

Microwave thin fish fillets (up to ½") on HIGH (100% power), thicker ones on MEDIUM (50% power), so they have time to cook evenly throughout.

Don't bother with browning skillets; they save no time and don't work as well as browning by stovetop or broiler.

Because fish microwaves so fast, vegetable accompaniments should be cooked first. Simple sauces can be made while the fish stands (for richer flavor, use some of the fish liquid), but fancier ones should be prepared ahead and kept warm or reheated while the fish stands.

Remove fish from microwave the instant it turns opaque. Any small (1") translucent area in middle of large fillets, steaks, and chunks will finish cooking as fish stands. Pieces microwaved until they flake at the touch of a fork will overcook, dry, and lose flavor as they stand—no matter how briefly. As for whole fish, always test for doneness as individual recipes direct.

Handle cooked fish with kid-glove care; it's fragile. Whenever possible, microwave fish in a container in which it can be served—microwave-safe ramekins or dinner plates for individual portions, platters for larger amounts.

372

DON'T MICROWAVE THESE!

~~~~~~ **BREADED OR BATTER-DIPPED FISH:** They won't crisp or brown unless microwaved on Active Microwave Cookware (see Chapter 3 [commercial foods are packaged in special materials that promote browning]).

~~~~~~ **DEEP- OR SHALLOW-FRIED FISH:** It's dangerous to fry fish in deep—or even shallow fat—in the microwave because fats can ignite. The flash point ranges from 380°–625° F., depending on the composition of the fat or oil. And the lower of these temperatures can quickly be reached in the microwave.

STEAMED FISH (BASIC METHOD)

You've never tasted lovelier fish than that caught hours earlier, then microwaved in its own vapor with plenty of ''t.l.c.''

Amount Needed per Serving:
Allow ⅓ pound fillets, steaks, or chunks, ½ pound dressed whole fish (head and tail removed), and ¾–1 pound dressed whole fish (head and tail on).

To Give Fish Extra Flavor:
Brush uncooked fillets with Lemon or Herb Butter Sauce, then scatter lean white fish lightly with freshly minced chervil, chives, dill, fennel, or tarragon. Tuck a bay leaf in with oily fish or sprinkle with freshly minced marjoram, savory, or thyme. **Note:** *If you substitute dried herbs for fresh, use sparingly.*

Thin (¼″–½″) Fillets: Arrange ½″ apart in shallow baking dish with thickest portions to outside; overlap thin areas and fold tapering ends envelope fashion in toward center. *Note: For 1 or 2 portions, arrange fish around edge of ramekins, dinner plates, or pie plate.* Brush, if you like, with melted butter, then sprinkle each fillet with ¼ teaspoon lemon or lime juice. Cover with paper toweling and microwave on HIGH (100% power) 3–5 minutes per pound, rotating dish 180° at halftime, just until fish is opaque. *Note: Don't cook more than 3 pounds fillets at once and if microwaving more than 1½ pounds, rearrange pieces at halftime.* Cover with foil and let stand 2 minutes. Probe with fork; fish should just flake. If underdone, continue microwaving (covered with paper toweling) on HIGH (100% power) in 30-second increments, testing between each. Drain liquid from fish

373

(save for Fish Stock or use in making complementary sauce). Sprinkle with salt and pepper and, if you like, paprika and/or minced parsley. Serve with lemon wedges or drizzle with Beurre Noir or Beurre Noisette or serve with Hollandaise, Shrimp, Caper, Sweet Red Pepper, or Warm Rémoulade Sauce.

V A R I A T I O N S

FILLETS OF FISH AMANDINE (Serves 4): Steam 1½ pounds flounder, sole, or other flat fish fillets as directed. While fish stands, melt 1 tablespoon butter in wax-paper-covered 8″ pie plate by microwaving on HIGH (100% power) 25–30 seconds. Mix in ⅓ cup slivered or sliced blanched almonds* and microwave, uncovered, on HIGH (100% power) 2½–3 minutes, stirring after 1½ minutes, until lightly browned. Sprinkle over fish and serve.
PER SERVING: 247 C   34 g P   11 g F   2 g CARB   168 mg S   89 mg CH

FILLETS OF FISH À LA BONNE FEMME (Serves 4): Steam 1½ pounds flounder, sole, or other flat fish fillets as directed, but scatter ¼ cup minced shallots and ½ cup button or thinly sliced mushrooms over fish at outset. While fish stands, make 1 cup Medium White Sauce using fish liquid for part of milk; stir in 1 tablespoon dry white wine, spoon over fish, and serve.
PER SERVING: 269 C   35 g P   10 g F   8 g CARB   363 mg S   106 mg CH

Thick (¾″–1″) Fillets, Chunks, and Steaks: Arrange in baking dish as directed for thin fillets; if unskinned, place skin side down and if steaks have "tails," curl to make compact package. Increase amount of lemon or lime juice to 2 tablespoons per pound fish. Cover with wax paper and microwave on MEDIUM (50% power) 6–9 minutes per pound, rotating dish 180° at halftime and turning 1″ thick fish over at halftime. *Note: Very oily fish like tuna and mackerel will cook more evenly if elevated on rack above their drippings.* Let fish stand as directed for thin fillets, then season, and accompany, if you like, with an assertive Curry Butter, Mustard, or Warm Aioli Sauce or French Mayonnaise.

BAHAMIAN STEAMED RED SNAPPER (Serves 4): Mix ¼ cup tissue-thin yellow onion rings with 1 cup crushed tomatoes, 1 crushed clove garlic, 2 crumbled bay leaves, ½ teaspoon salt, and ⅛ teaspoon pepper in 2½- or 3-quart casserole. Cover with lid or vented plastic food wrap and microwave on HIGH (100% power) 5 minutes, stirring at halftime. Lay 1½ pounds ¾″–1″ thick red snapper, pompano, cod, or haddock fillets on top, folding tapered ends in toward center. Sprinkle with 2 tablespoons minced chives and, if you like, ⅛–¼ teaspoon liquid hot red pepper seasoning. Cover with wax paper and microwave as directed (no need to turn fish at halftime). Let stand as directed, then lift fish to plates; whisk 1 tablespoon butter into casserole sauce and spoon over each portion.

PER SERVING: 211 C   36 g P   5 g F   3 g CARB   416 mg S   71 mg CH

Very Thick (1"–1½") Chunks and Steaks: Prepare as directed for thick fillets but cover with vented plastic food wrap and microwave 9–12 minutes per pound; let stand, covered, 5 minutes.

WHOLE FISH

DRESSED WHOLE FISH **(1 pound or less):** Microwave small trout, herring, mackerel, etc., as directed for thick (¾"–1") fillets.

DRESSED WHOLE FISH **(1½–3 pounds):** Sprinkle cavity with salt and pepper and prick skin lightly on each side three to four times to prevent splitting. Lay fish on rack in baking dish, reversing position of heads and tails if cooking more than one and leaving 1" space between them. *Note: Headless fish lose a lot of liquid during microwaving, yet if fish won't fit in oven whole, you may need to remove heads.* Smooth 2" foil strips over heads and tails, making sure eyes are covered (they'll burst otherwise). Insert automatic temperature probe, if desired, on underside of fish in meatiest area just above gill and parallel to backbone as shown. *Note: To prevent arcing,* make sure foil is ¾" from probe.* Brush lean fish with melted or seasoned butter and oily fish with lemon or lime juice. Cover with vented plastic food wrap, gathering loosely around probe, and microwave on MEDIUM (50% power) 7–9 minutes per pound. At halftime, carefully turn fish over and rotate

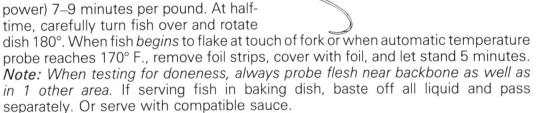

dish 180°. When fish *begins* to flake at touch of fork or when automatic temperature probe reaches 170° F., remove foil strips, cover with foil, and let stand 5 minutes. *Note: When testing for doneness, always probe flesh near backbone as well as in 1 other area.* If serving fish in baking dish, baste off all liquid and pass separately. Or serve with compatible sauce.

375

POACHED FISH

(BASIC METHOD FOR THICK [¾"–1"] FILLETS AND WHOLE FISH)

For each pound fish, microwave 1 cup Fish Stock, white wine, or water mixed with 2 tablespoons lemon juice in measure, covered with vented plastic food wrap, on HIGH (100% power) until boiling (2–3 minutes for 1 cup liquid, 3½–4½ minutes for 2 cups, and 6–8 minutes for 3 cups). Meanwhile, place fish in baking dish as directed for steaming, add hot liquid, and if using water, also add 1 minced scallion, 3–4 peppercorns, and 1 bay leaf. Cover with vented plastic food wrap and microwave on MEDIUM (50% power) 5–8 minutes per pound for thick fillets, chunks, and steaks and 6–8 minutes per pound whole fish, rotating dish 180° at halftime (no need to turn fish). Test often for doneness (liquid speeds cooking). When fish is *barely* done, let stand in liquid, covered, allowing 2 minutes for thick fillets and 5 for whole fish. Lift fish from liquid (save it for soup or sauce) and serve hot with a compatible sauce. Or cover with wax paper, cool to room temperature, then chill well. Serve cold with mayonnaise or cold sauce.

STEAMED GINGER SEA BASS

PREP TIME: | 3 MINUTES | COOKING TIME: | 5¾–7¼ MINUTES | STANDING TIME: | 2¼ MINUTES

A snap to make with fish fillets but equally delicious with small, whole firm-fleshed fish. It's important to prick the skin on both sides of whole fish and to microwave on MEDIUM (50% power) 7–9 minutes per pound *just* until fish flakes at the touch of a fork. You may need to turn the fish halfway through cooking as well as rotate the dish 180° (see Whole Fish in Steamed Fish section).

SERVES 4

1½ pounds sea bass, striped bass, or bluefish fillets, cut in 4 equal portions ½" thick

1 tablespoon minced fresh ginger

1 clove garlic, peeled and minced

1 tablespoon dry sherry

2 tablespoons Oriental sesame oil

2 tablespoons soy sauce

⅛ teaspoon chili oil (optional)

2 teaspoons cornstarch

¼ cup Fish Stock or water (about)

¼ cup minced scallions (include green tops)

Fold any fillets that taper envelope fashion, skinny ends toward center, and arrange ½" apart in shallow 2½–3-quart baking dish, placing thickest pieces around edge and leaving middle empty. Mix ginger, garlic, and sherry and spread evenly over fillets. Mix sesame oil, soy sauce, and if you like, chili oil, and drizzle over fish. Cover with vented plastic food wrap, and if time permits, marinate 1 hour in refrigerator, turning fish after 30 minutes. Microwave, still covered, on HIGH (100% power) 4–5 minutes, rotating dish 180° at halftime just until fish begins to flake when touched with fork. Transfer fish to heated platter, cover with foil, and let stand while you prepare sauce. Blend cornstarch with Fish Stock, stir into casserole liquid (there should be at least ¼ cup; if not add more stock or water to round out measure). Microwave, uncovered, on HIGH (100% power) 1¾–2¼ minutes, stirring at halftime, until sauce boils and thickens. Pour sauce over fish, sprinkle with scallions, and serve at once.

PER SERVING: 241 C   32 g P   10 g F   3 g CARB   647 mg S   70 mg CH

STUFFED WHOLE BLUEFISH

PREP TIME: | 10 MINUTES | COOKING TIME: | 23–28 MINUTES | STANDING TIME: | 5 MINUTES |

For richer flavor and moister texture, leave fish whole, but if you can't look a fish in the eye—or if it won't fit in your oven—behead, reweigh, and recompute microwave time. Salmon, red snapper, striped bass, even four 1-pound trout can be used in place of bluefish. You can also substitute New England Clam and Cracker or Mushroom Stuffing for Fish for this one.

SERVES 4

1 **bluefish (3 pounds), boned and prepared for stuffing**

¼ **teaspoon salt**

⅛ **teaspoon pepper**

Stuffing

1 **small yellow onion, peeled and minced**

1 **stalk celery, minced**

½ **medium-size sweet green pepper, cored, seeded, and minced**

1 **tablespoon butter, margarine, or bacon drippings**

¾ **cup ½" cubes stale bread**

1 **small pimiento, coarsely chopped**

1 **tablespoon well-drained sweet pickle relish**

1 **teaspoon minced parsley**

1 **teaspoon minced fresh or ¼ teaspoon crumbled dried dill or tarragon**

Wipe fish inside and out with damp paper toweling and prick skin lightly 3 to 4 times on each side; sprinkle cavity with salt and pepper. Mix onion, celery, green pepper, and butter in 2-quart casserole, cover with wax paper, and microwave on HIGH (100% power) 2½–3 minutes until vegetables are limp. Mix in remaining stuffing ingredients, spoon loosely into fish, and close with wooden picks. Lay fish on rack in 3-quart baking dish and smooth 2" foil strips over head and tail to shield. Cover with vented plastic food wrap and microwave on MEDIUM (50% power) 20–25 minutes, carefully turning fish over and rotating dish 180° at halftime, until fish just begins to flake when touched with fork near backbone and in one other fleshy spot. Cover with foil and let stand 5 minutes. Remove toothpicks and foil, ease onto hot platter, accompany with lemon wedges, and, if you like, French Mayonnaise, Mustard or Lemon Sauce. *Tip: When serving, first peel skin from head back toward tail; it comes away neatly.*

PER SERVING: 195 C   23 g P   8 g F   6 g CARB   299 mg S 74 mg CH

NEW ENGLAND CLAM & CRACKER STUFFING FOR FISH

PREP TIME: **5 MINUTES** | COOKING TIME: **2–2½ MINUTES** | STANDING TIME: **NONE**

MAKES ABOUT 1 CUP, ENOUGH TO STUFF A 2- OR 3-POUND FISH

- 2 **tablespoons minced yellow onion**
- 1 **stalk celery, minced**
- 1 **tablespoon butter, margarine, or bacon drippings**
- 1 **can (6½ ounces) minced clams, drained (reserve liquid)**
- ⅔ **cup coarsely crushed soda crackers or oyster crackers**
- ¼ **cup clam liquid**
- 1 **teaspoon finely grated lemon rind**
- ¼ **teaspoon salt**
- ⅛ **teaspoon pepper**

Microwave onion and celery with butter in wax-paper-covered 1-quart casserole by microwaving on HIGH (100% power) 2–2½ minutes, stirring at halftime, until glassy. Add remaining ingredients and toss lightly with 2 forks.

PER CUP: 419 C   20 g P   19 g F   42 g CARB   2259 mg S 90 mg CH

VARIATION

MUSHROOM STUFFING FOR FISH (Makes about 1⅓ cups): Prepare as directed, microwaving ½ pound finely chopped mushrooms along with onion mixture and increasing time to 6 minutes. Add remaining ingredients except clams and clam liquid, and toss.

PER CUP: 356 C   18 g P   15 g F   39 g CARB   1701 mg S 68 mg CH

379

SALMON FILLETS EN PAPILLOTE WITH TOASTED ALMOND SAUCE

PREP TIME: 3 MINUTES COOKING TIME: 5¾–7 MINUTES STANDING TIME: NONE

Microwaving this French classic preserves all the delicacy of fresh salmon.

SERVES 4

4   small salmon fillets, cut about ½" thick (1⅓–1½ pounds)

¼   teaspoon salt

⅛   teaspoon pepper

1   teaspoon lemon juice

Toasted Almond Sauce

¼   cup very finely minced toasted blanched almonds*

½   cup heavy cream

2   tablespoons minced chives

Pinch paprika

Pinch salt

Center each salmon fillet on double-thickness wax paper measuring 17" × 12"; sprinkle with salt, pepper, and lemon juice. *Note: Unless fillets taper sharply, there's no need to tuck ends underneath.* Wrap fillets in wax paper, drugstore style, and arrange, not touching, on round or oval platter. Microwave on HIGH (100% power) 4–5 minutes, rearranging at halftime. Test for doneness after 4 minutes; salmon should *just* flake at touch of fork. If not, rewrap and microwave in 30-second increments, testing after each to avoid overcooking. Microwave sauce ingredients in wax-paper-covered 1-pint measure on MEDIUM (50% power) 1¾–2 minutes, stirring at halftime, until hot, not boiling. Partially unwrap fish, top with sauce, dividing total amount evenly, rewrap, and serve.

For 1 Serving: Wrap 1 salmon fillet (5–5½ ounces) in wax paper and microwave as directed 2–2¼ minutes. For sauce, microwave 1 tablespoon minced toasted blanched almonds,* 2 tablespoons heavy cream, 1½ teaspoons minced chives, and pinch each paprika and salt in wax-paper-covered custard cup on MEDIUM (50% power) 50–60 seconds. Unwrap salmon, top with sauce, and serve.

For 2 Servings: Wrap 2 salmon fillets (5–5½ ounces each) in wax paper and microwave as directed 2¾–3 minutes. Halve sauce ingredients and microwave as directed, reducing time to 1–1½ minutes. Unwrap salmon and top with sauce. Rewrap and serve.

PER SERVING: 386 C   34 g P   6 g F   3 g CARB   252 mg S   129 mg CH

V A R I A T I O N

SALMON FILLETS WITH FRESH CORIANDER BÉARNAISE: Prepare 1 recipe Béarnaise Sauce and mix in 2–4 tablespoons minced fresh coriander (cilantro), Italian parsley, or chervil. Cover and keep warm in bowl of warm water. Wrap and microwave salmon as directed. Unwrap salmon, top with sauce, and serve.

PER SERVING: 503 C   35 g P   39 g F   2 g CARB   656 mg S   423 mg CH

KEDGEREE

PREP TIME: | 1 MINUTE | COOKING TIME: | 6–8 MINUTES | STANDING TIME: | 3 MINUTES

¢

SERVES 4

- ¾ **pound cod or haddock fillets, cut ½" thick, or 6 ounces each smoked haddock and cod fillets**
- 1 **tablespoon lemon juice**
- ¼ **cup melted butter or margarine**
- 1¾ **cups hot cooked rice**
- ¾ **teaspoon salt**
- ⅛ **teaspoon white pepper**
- ½ **teaspoon curry powder**
- 3 **hard-cooked eggs, peeled, 2 coarsely chopped and 1 cut in thin wedges**

If fish is in one piece, halve crosswise, then fold each piece envelope fashion, ends toward center, and arrange 1" apart in shallow 2-quart casserole. Sprinkle with lemon juice, cover with vented plastic food wrap, and microwave on HIGH (100% power) 3–4 minutes until fish *just* flakes. Let stand, covered, 3 minutes, then drain fish and flake right in casserole. Add butter, rice, salt, pepper, curry powder, and 2 chopped eggs and toss gently to mix. Cover with wax paper and microwave on MEDIUM-HIGH (70% power) 3–4 minutes, stirring at halftime, until piping hot. Garnish with wedges of hard-cooked egg and serve.

PER SERVING: 330 C   22 g P   16 g F   23 g CARB   628 mg S   273 mg CH

FLOUNDER STUFFED WITH CRAB IMPERIAL

PREP TIME: | 8 MINUTES | COOKING TIME: | 8½–12 MINUTES | STANDING TIME: | NONE

Fish stuffings mustn't contain raw ingredients because they won't cook done in time needed to microwave fish. These flounder rolls can also be cooked unstuffed, then topped with Mushroom Sauce or Medium White Sauce greened with fresh dill.

SERVES 4

1½ **pounds flounder fillets, cut ¼" thick (or use other delicate white fish such as sole, fluke, or turbot)**

Stuffing

6 **ounces cooked crab meat (fresh, thawed frozen, or drained canned), well picked over and chopped fine (or use minced cooked shrimp, lobster, or salmon)**

½ **cup soft white bread crumbs**

2 **tablespoons mayonnaise**

2 **tablespoons half-and-half cream**

¼ **teaspoon prepared horseradish**

⅛ **teaspoon dry mustard**

⅛ **teaspoon paprika**

Spread fillets flat on counter. Mix stuffing, divide evenly among fillets, then roll fillets up from wide ends. Place seam side down ½" apart in shallow 2- or 3-quart casserole, cover with wax paper, and microwave on HIGH (100% power) 4½–7 minutes, rotating dish 180° at halftime, just until fish is opaque. Drain, reserving liquid, cover with foil, and keep warm while making sauce. Melt butter in wax-paper-covered 1-quart measure by microwaving on HIGH (100% power) 35–45 seconds. Blend in flour and microwave, uncovered, on HIGH (100% power) 30 seconds until foamy. Gradually stir in milk, reserved liquid, chili sauce, and salt and microwave, uncovered, on HIGH (100% power) 3–4 minutes, whisking after 2 minutes, until sauce boils and thickens. Ladle a little sauce over fish rolls and pass balance.

PER SERVING: 384 C   44 g P   17 g F   11 g CARB   803 mg S 155 mg CH

V A R I A T I O N S

MUSHROOM-STUFFED FLOUNDER ROLLS: Prepare as directed, using Mushroom Stuffing

Sauce

2 tablespoons butter or margarine

2 tablespoons flour

1 cup milk

Reserved fish cooking liquid

2 tablespoons chili sauce

½ teaspoon salt

for Fish in place of one above.

PER SERVING: 410 C 42 g P 15 g F 26 g CARB 1184 mg S 128 mg CH

CLAM-STUFFED FLOUNDER ROLLS: Prepare as directed, using New England Clam and Cracker Stuffing for Fish in place of one above.

PER SERVING: 396 C 40 g P 15 g F 24 g CARB 1182 mg S 128 mg CH

CHUTNEY-GLAZED FISH STEAKS WITH MANGO SAUCE

PREP TIME: 8 MINUTES COOKING TIME: 14½–18 MINUTES STANDING TIME: NONE

SERVES 4

4 center-cut halibut, swordfish, salmon, or tuna steaks, cut ¾" thick (about 2 pounds)

2 tablespoons chutney, minced fine

2 tablespoons lime juice

1 small clove garlic, peeled and crushed

¼ teaspoon chili powder

Mango Sauce:

1 cup peeled ripe mango chunks, puréed

¼ cup mayonnaise

½ teaspoon lemon or lime juice

¼ teaspoon prepared spicy brown mustard

⅛ teaspoon curry powder

Wipe fish dry. Combine chutney, lime juice, garlic, and chili powder, spread on both sides of fish, and arrange spoke fashion in 10" casserole. Cover with wax paper and microwave on MEDIUM (50% power) 12–15 minutes, rotating casserole 180° at halftime, until fish turns opaque. Cover with foil and keep warm while you make sauce. Blend sauce ingredients well in 1-quart measure and microwave, uncovered, on MEDIUM (50% power) 2½–3 minutes, whisking vigorously at halftime, until warm (don't boil or sauce will separate). Lift fish from casserole liquid to hot platter and pass sauce.

PER SERVING: 352 C 39 g P 15 g F 13 g CARB 201 mg S 67 mg CH

383

ABOUT MICROWAVING CLAMS, MUSSELS, AND OYSTERS

Ever thought of opening mollusks by microwave? You can do it—*without* cooking them—if they're ice cold to start, carefully timed, and tended. In fact, using the steam generated by microwaves is one of the easiest ways we know to open clams and oysters for serving on the half shell or using raw in recipes. Of course you can take the steaming a step further and *cook* them to supreme succulence in the microwave—mussels, too. *For Best Results:* Choose specimens of uniform size and don't crowd them in the dish. It's better to cook two or three batches than to risk overcooking these delicate mollusks by piling too many of them in a single container. But first, a few preliminaries.

TO CLEANSE AND PURGE CLAMS: Scrub clams well, then place in a large, deep enamel kettle, and cover with cold salted water (1 tablespoon salt to each quart water). Toss in a handful of cornmeal, set the uncovered kettle in a cool spot, and let stand about an hour (the cornmeal acts as an irritant, causing the clams to purge themselves of grit). Lift the clams from the water, rinse well, and discard any that are open or don't "clam up" when thumped. If you cannot cook the clams right away, arrange in a large shallow bowl, cover *loosely* with paper toweling, and place in the refrigerator. Do not attempt to store the clams for more than a few hours.

TO CLEAN MUSSELS: Scrub each mussel well with a stiff brush under cool running water, pull or cut off the long beard, scrape any small barnacles from the shell, and rinse the mussel well. Unlike clams, mussels need not be purged. Discard any mussels that are open, cracked, or not tightly shut. If you don't intend to cook the mussels at once, arrange them in a large shallow bowl, cover *loosely* with paper toweling, and set in the refrigerator. The mussels will stay alive for several hours but cook them as soon as possible.

TO CLEAN OYSTERS: These need nothing more than a good scrubbing in cool water. Discard any oysters with broken or cracked shells, also any that are not shut tight. If you must store oysters for a few hours before steaming them, set in the refrigerator as directed for clams and mussels above.

TO OPEN CLAMS AND OYSTERS

If the shellfish are not icy cold, quick-chill 1 hour in the freezer. Working with 6 small clams or 6 medium-size oysters at a time (just the amount for 1 serving), arrange with their hinged edges toward the outside in a circle in a shallow casserole or better yet, a glass ovenware pie plate so you can follow their progress through the oven door and retrieve them the instant you see an almost imperceptible lifting of the top shell. Microwave, uncovered, on HIGH (100% power) using the following times as a guide:

Shellfish	Size	Quantity	Time
Littleneck Clams	1½–2" across	6	50–60 seconds
Cherrystone Clams	2–2½" across	6	1–1½ minutes
Oysters	2–3" long	6	1–2 minutes
Oysters	3–4" long	6	2½–4 minutes, *rotating pan 180° at halftime or rearranging oysters*

Note: Opening times can vary even among clams and oysters of identical size according to their water content (those with more water open faster). Microwaving times may also vary to some extent according to the season. The point is to watch the steaming closely and remove the clams or oysters the instant they *begin* to open. Set them at once in a bed of crushed ice so they don't begin to cook, then microwave the remaining clams or oysters on HIGH (100% power) in 30-second increments, keeping a sharp eye out. Discard any that do not open.

Note: You may need to use a clam or oyster knife to finish the opening, but taking clams and oysters from the microwave when they first show signs of movement is the surest way to have them raw. Besides, the opening is a snap compared to the Herculean task of prying open clams and oysters that haven't had a brief stint in the microwave.

After opening the clams or oysters, discard the top shells and free the "meat" from the bottom shells. Remove any grit or bits of shell, working over a

385

bowl so you don't lose any of the briny juices. Strain the juices through a cheesecloth-lined fine sieve and reserve.

TO SERVE CLAMS OR OYSTERS ON THE HALF SHELL: Return clams or oysters to the bottom shells, top with the reserved juices, then for each portion, bed 6 shells in crushed ice, garnish with lemon wedges and ruffs of cress, fresh coriander (cilantro), or parsley. Set out the pepper mill, and, if you like, cocktail sauce.

TO STEAM CLAMS, MUSSELS, AND OYSTERS

If the clams, mussels, or oysters are not good and cold, quick-chill 1 hour in the freezer. Working with the number of mollusks shown in the chart below and arranging them with their hinged edges toward the outside, place in a circle in a shallow casserole or glass ovenware pie plate and microwave, uncovered, on HIGH (100% power) until shells open fully, using these times as a guide:

Shellfish	Size	Quantity	Time
Hard Clams	1½–2½" across	6	1¼–2 minutes
Hard Clams	3–4" across	6	2½–5 minutes
Soft Clams (steamers)	1½–2" across	12	2–3 minutes (cover *with vented plastic food wrap*)
Oysters	2–4" long	6	2–5 minutes
Mussels	1½–2" across	12	2½–3½ minutes

Note: At halftime, rearrange soft clams and mussels; rotate pan of hard clams or oysters 180°. Shuck mollusks as directed in To Open Clams and Oysters (large clams and oyster shells will be blisteringly hot, so cool until easy to handle). Remove any tag ends of beard from the mussels and snip off any black skin in the steamer clams. Serve the clams, mussels, or oysters hot with melted butter and lemon wedges or use to make chowders, fritters, casseroles, or any recipe calling for any of these three.

SOME QUICK TOPPINGS FOR STEAMED CLAMS, MUSSELS, AND OYSTERS

Always steam mollusks before adding raw toppings. Trying to cook raw toppings on raw mollusks may cause them to explode because they're inevitably done before the toppings are. Piercing the raw mollusks, on the other hand, merely causes savory juices to leak out and microwaving at lower power levels is guaranteed to overcook the shellfish and undercook the topping.

CLAMS OR OYSTERS CASINO (Allow 6 littleneck or cherrystone clams per person or 6 medium-size oysters): Steam and shuck as directed above, then discard top shells and free "meat" from bottom shells. Remove any grit or bits of shell, working over bowl so you don't lose juices. Strain juices through cheesecloth-lined fine sieve and reserve. Return clams or oysters to bottom shells, add reserved juices, then top each with dab of anchovy paste and dot of butter, ½ teaspoon sweet pickle relish, ¼ teaspoon minced pimiento, and sprinkling of crisp bacon crumbles. Arrange 12 mollusks in circle in shallow casserole, anchoring with wax-paper crumples; cover with paper toweling and microwave on MEDIUM (50% power) 1¼–2 minutes, rearranging shells at halftime, until warm.

PER CLAM: 27 C	3 g P	1 g F	1 g CARB	100 mg S	8 mg CH
PER OYSTER: 26 C	2 g P	1 g F	1 g CARB	108 mg S	11 mg CH

CLAMS, MUSSELS, OR OYSTERS RÉMOULADE (Allow 6 littleneck or cherrystone clams per person or 6 medium-size mussels or oysters): Steam and shuck as directed above, then discard top shells and free "meat" from bottom shells. Remove any grit or bits of shell, working over bowl so you don't lose juices; strain juices through cheesecloth-lined fine sieve and reserve. Return clams, mussels, or oysters to bottom shells, add reserved juices, then top each with 1–2 teaspoons Warm Rémoulade Sauce. Arrange 12 mollusks in circle on large platter, anchoring with wax-paper crumples, and microwave, uncovered, on MEDIUM-LOW (30% power) about 2 minutes, rotating platter 180° at halftime, just until warm.

PER CLAM: 52 C	2 g P	5 g F	1 g CARB	59 mg S	8 mg CH
PER MUSSEL: 47 C	1 g P	5 g F	1 g CARB	73 mg S	6 mg CH
PER OYSTER: 50 C	1 g P	5 g F	1 g CARB	66 mg S	11 mg CH

⚖️ CLAMS, MUSSELS, OR OYSTERS MORNAY: Prepare as directed for Rémoulade above, substituting warm Mornay Sauce for Rémoulade.

PER CLAM: 23 C	2 g P	1 g F	1 g CARB	54 mg S	8 mg CH
PER MUSSEL: 19 C	1 g P	1 g F	1 g CARB	69 mg S	5 mg CH
PER OYSTER: 22 C	1 g P	1 g F	1 g CARB	62 mg S	10 mg CH

⚖️ CLAMS, MUSSELS, OR OYSTERS WITH CAPER SAUCE: Prepare as directed for Rémoulade above, substituting warm Caper Sauce for Rémoulade.

PER CLAM: 22 C	2 g P	1 g F	1 g CARB	40 mg S	8 mg CH
PER MUSSEL: 18 C	1 g P	1 g F	1 g CARB	54 mg S	5 mg CH
PER OYSTER: 20 C	1 g P	1 g F	1 g CARB	47 mg S	10 mg CH

SOME OTHER QUICK WAYS TO USE STEAMED CLAMS, MUSSELS, OR OYSTERS

Allowing 1 dozen mollusks per 1 cup of sauce or gravy, mix steamed clams, mussels, or oysters with Medium White Sauce, Mushroom, or Mustard Sauce, or Chicken or Turkey Gravy and serve over boiled rice, hot biscuits, or buttered toast. Or spoon into crisp puff pastry shells.

Allowing 1 dozen mollusks per 1 cup of sauce, mix steamed clams, mussels, or oysters with Jiffy Tomato or Mushroom-Tomato Sauce and serve on pasta.

When making Red Clam Sauce, substitute an equal quantity of whole steamed clams or mussels for minced clams and use to top any pasta.

CLAMS OR OYSTERS REMICK

PREP TIME: | 5 MINUTES | COOKING TIME: | 5¾–6 MINUTES | STANDING TIME: | NONE |

**SERVES 4 AS AN ENTRÉE,
6 AS AN APPETIZER**

2   dozen littleneck or
     cherrystone clams,
     scrubbed and purged* or 2
     dozen medium-size oysters,
     scrubbed

Sauce

¾   cup mayonnaise

3   tablespoons chili sauce

¾   teaspoon Dijon mustard

1   teaspoon lemon juice

2–3 drops liquid hot red pepper
     seasoning

Topping

6   slices crisply cooked bacon,
     crumbled

Steam clams or oysters* as directed, then shuck and return to bottom shells. Combine all sauce ingredients in bowl and microwave, uncovered, on MEDIUM-LOW (30% power) 1¾–2 minutes, stirring at halftime, until lukewarm. Spoon 1 heaping teaspoon sauce onto each clam or oyster and top with bacon. Arrange 12 oysters or clams in circle on each of 2 platters, propping as needed with wax-paper crumples, and microwave, uncovered and 1 at a time, on MEDIUM-LOW (30% power) about 2 minutes, rotating platter 180° at halftime, until lukewarm. Serve at once.

PER SERVING (CLAMS):

432–288 C   15–10 g P   38–26 g F   7–6 g CARB   638–425 mg S
63–42 mg CH

PER SERVING (OYSTERS):

424–282 C   10–6 g P   39–27 g F   7–6 g CARB   682–455 mg S
79–53 mg CH

389

CLAMS AL PESTO

PREP TIME: 10 MINUTES   COOKING TIME: 4 MINUTES   STANDING TIME: NONE

Medium-size mussels or oysters may be used in place of clams, if you like.

**SERVES 4 AS AN ENTRÉE,
6 AS AN APPETIZER**

3 cups tightly packed fresh basil leaves

2 cloves garlic, peeled and crushed

⅓ cup piñon nuts

1 cup olive oil

½ cup finely grated Parmesan cheese

2 dozen littleneck or cherrystone clams, scrubbed and purged*

Prepare pesto sauce ahead so flavors mellow: Churn basil, garlic, piñon nuts, olive oil, and cheese in food processor 1 minute until uniformly smooth. Let sauce mellow at room temperature at least 1 hour. When ready to proceed, steam clams* as directed, then shuck and return to bottom shells. Spoon 1 heaping teaspoon sauce onto each clam and arrange 12 of them in circle on each of two platters, propping as needed with wax-paper crumples. Microwave, uncovered, and one platter at a time, on MEDIUM-LOW (30% power) about 2 minutes, rotating platter 180° at halftime, until lukewarm. Serve at once. *Note: Any leftover pesto sauce can be reserved and used to dress pasta.*

PER SERVING: 708–472 C   22–15 g P   65–44 g F
16–11 g CARB   284–190 mg S   40–27 mg CH

MUSSELS IN A CATAPLANA

PREP TIME: [15 MINUTES] COOKING TIME: [34–40 MINUTES] STANDING TIME: [NONE]

''Cataplana'' is both the name of this Portuguese classic and of the container traditionally used to cook it (it looks like a huge copper clam shell). This microwave version is perfect for a small dinner because the tomato base can be prepared ahead of time and the mussels added shortly before serving.

SERVES 4

- 2 **tablespoons olive oil**
- 2 **ounces prosciutto (in one piece), trimmed of fat and cut into ¼" cubes**
- 2 **ounces chouriço, chorizo, or pepperoni, sliced very thin**
- 1 **medium-size yellow onion, peeled and minced**
- 1 **small Spanish onion, peeled and minced**
- 1 **large clove garlic, peeled and minced**
- ½ **small sweet green pepper, cored, seeded, and cut in thin slivers**
- 1 **large bay leaf (do not crumble)**
- 1 **teaspoon paprika**
- ⅛ **teaspoon red pepper flakes**
- ⅛ **teaspoon black pepper**
- 1 **can (1 pound) tomatoes (do not drain), coarsely chopped**
- 6 **tablespoons dry white wine (preferably a Portuguese Dão or vinho verde)**

Mix 1 tablespoon oil, prosciutto, and chouriço in shallow 3-quart casserole and microwave, uncovered, on HIGH (100% power) 2 minutes; with slotted spoon lift to paper toweling to drain. Add remaining oil to casserole, mix in onions, garlic, and green pepper; add bay leaf and microwave, uncovered, on HIGH (100% power) 6–7 minutes, stirring at halftime, until onions are glassy. Mix in paprika, red pepper flakes, black pepper, tomatoes, and 2 tablespoons wine.

Cover with vented plastic food wrap and microwave on HIGH (100% power) 9–10 minutes until bubbling at edges; stir in reserved prosciutto and chouriço, re-cover, and microwave on ME-DIUM-HIGH (70% power) 13–15 minutes, stirring once or twice. *Note: You can prepare recipe to this point a day or two in advance, cool, cover, and refrigerate until ready to proceed, then microwave, covered, on HIGH (100% power) 9–10 minutes until bubbling at edges.*

Remove bay leaf, arrange mussels in casserole in a single layer, spoon some sauce over them, splash in remaining wine, and sprinkle with half the parsley and coriander. Cover with vented plastic food wrap (this will enable you to watch mussels closely through oven door) and microwave on HIGH (100% power) 4–6 minutes,

391

2 **dozen medium-size mussels in the shell, scrubbed and bearded**

4 **teaspoons minced Italian parsley**

4 **teaspoons minced fresh coriander (cilantro)**

rearranging mussels at halftime, until mussels *just* open. Discard any unopened ones. Sprinkle with remaining parsley and coriander, ladle into soup plates, and serve with rough country bread. *Note: Don't forget to put out a bowl to catch the empty mussel shells.*

PER SERVING: 235 C 13 g P 15 g F 12 g CARB 512 mg S 22 mg CH

~~~~~~~ V A R I A T I O N

 Cₗₐₘₛ ᵢₙ ₐ Cₐₜₐₚₗₐₙₐ: Prepare as directed, substituting soft-shell clams (steamers) or cherrystones for mussels.

PER SERVING: 260 C 19 g P 15 g F 13 g CARB 425 mg S 39 mg CH

Mussels marinière

PREP TIME: | 7 MINUTES | COOKING TIME: | 9¾–12½ MINUTES | STANDING TIME: | NONE |

SERVES 4

¼ cup (½ stick) butter or margarine, at room temperature

2 tablespoons minced shallots or scallions (white part only)

2 sprigs parsley

1 sprig fresh thyme or ¼ teaspoon crumbled dried thyme

1 small bay leaf (do not crumble)

1 cup dry white wine

2 dozen mussels in the shell, scrubbed and bearded

1 tablespoon minced parsley

Mix 3 tablespoons butter and shallots in shallow 3-quart casserole and microwave, uncovered, on HIGH (100% power) 1¼–1½ minutes until shallots are glassy. Add parsley, thyme, bay leaf, and wine, cover with wax paper, and microwave on HIGH (100% power) 3½–4 minutes until mixture boils. Arrange mussels in casserole in single layer, cover with vented plastic food wrap, and microwave on HIGH (100% power) 4–6 minutes, rearranging mussels at halftime, until mussels *just* open. Discard any unopened ones. Transfer mussels to individual serving dishes, cover, and keep warm. Strain cooking liquid through double thickness of cheesecloth, return to casserole, add remaining butter and minced parsley and microwave, uncovered, on HIGH (100% power) 1 minute. Taste liquid for salt, add if needed, and pour over mussels. Serve hot with French bread. ***Note:*** *Do not double this recipe—mussels will overcook and be rubbery. Prepare two batches instead.*

PER SERVING: 150 C   6 g P   13 g F   3 g CARB   259 mg S   44 mg CH

~~~ V A R I A T I O N

 CLAMS MARINIÈRE: Prepare as directed, substituting soft-shell clams (steamers) or cherrystones for mussels.

PER SERVING: 175 C   12 g P   12 g F   4 g CARB   172 mg S   62 mg CH

POACHED SEA SCALLOPS IN SWEET RED PEPPER SAUCE

PREP TIME: 8 MINUTES COOKING TIME: 15½–18½ MINUTES STANDING TIME: NONE

SERVES 4

2   large sweet red peppers
1   large clove garlic (do not peel)
1   tablespoon butter or margarine
1   small carrot, peeled and minced
2   tablespoons minced shallots
1   tablespoon minced fresh or 1 teaspoon crumbled dried tarragon
1½   pounds sea scallops, halved horizontally
2   tablespoons dry vermouth
1   tablespoon orange juice
1   tablespoon lemon juice
½   teaspoon salt
⅛   teaspoon white pepper
3–4 tablespoons crème fraîche or sour cream
4   sprigs fresh tarragon or parsley

Place red peppers in plastic bag, twist ends and knot, place on oven floor, and microwave on HIGH (100% power) 3 minutes. Turn bag over and rotate 180°. Wrap garlic in paper toweling and place in oven beside peppers. Microwave on HIGH (100% power) 2–3 minutes until peppers and garlic are soft. Cool peppers under cold running water, peel, seed, pat dry on paper toweling, then quarter and purée with garlic pulp until smooth.

Microwave butter, carrot, shallots, and minced tarragon in wax-paper-covered shallow 2-quart casserole on HIGH (100% power) 4½–5¼ minutes, stirring at halftime, until carrots are tender. Arrange scallops, slightly overlapping, in single layer on carrots; combine vermouth, orange and lemon juice, salt, and pepper and pour over scallops. Cover with vented plastic food wrap and microwave on HIGH (100% power) 4½–5½ minutes, gently rearranging scallops at halftime, *just* until scallops turn milky. Blend ⅓ cup casserole liquid and crème fraîche into pepper purée; transfer to 1-pint measure, cover with wax paper, and microwave on MEDIUM (50% power) 1½–2 minutes until warm, not boiling. Pool red pepper sauce on heated plates, drain scallops and arrange on top, then sprig with tarragon.

PER SERVING: 234 C 30 g P 7 g F 12 g CARB 593 mg S 69 mg CH

COQUILLES ST. JACQUES

PREP TIME: [6 MINUTES] COOKING TIME: [15½–20 MINUTES] STANDING TIME: [NONE]

If you don't want to go to the trouble of browning these stuffed scallop shells under the broiler, you can give the crumb topping a browner look by including some of the crust in the bread crumbs.

SERVES 6

½ cup dry white wine

2 tablespoons minced shallots or scallions (white part only)

1 small bay leaf (do not crumble)

1 sprig parsley

1 pound bay scallops, rinsed well

6 ounces mushrooms, wiped clean and sliced thin (include stems)

3 tablespoons butter or margarine

4 tablespoons flour

¾ cup scallops cooking liquid

1¼ cups half-and-half cream

¼ teaspoon salt (about)

Pinch white pepper

1 egg yolk, lightly beaten

Topping

1 cup soft white bread crumbs

¼ cup melted butter or margarine

⅓ cup finely grated Gruyère cheese

Place wine, shallots, bay leaf, and parsley in 2-quart casserole, cover with vented plastic food wrap, and microwave on HIGH (100% power) 2 minutes. Add scallops and mushrooms, re-cover, and microwave on HIGH (100% power) 4½–5½ minutes, stirring every 2 minutes, just until scallops turn milky. *Note: Do not overcook or scallops will be rubbery.* Strain, measure out, and reserve ¾ cup scallops liquid; set scallops and mushrooms aside.

Melt butter in same casserole by microwaving, covered with wax paper, on HIGH (100% power) 45–55 seconds. Blend in flour and microwave, uncovered, on HIGH (100% power) 30 seconds until foamy. Gradually stir in reserved scallops liquid, cream, salt, and pepper and microwave, uncovered, on HIGH (100% power) 4½–5½ minutes, beating well every 2 minutes, until sauce boils and thickens. Mix a little hot sauce with egg yolk, stir back into casserole, then microwave, uncovered, on LOW (10% power) 30 seconds, stirring well at halftime. Mix in reserved scallops and mushrooms, taste for salt, and adjust as needed. Spoon into 6 buttered large scallop shells (natural or ceramic) or individual au gratin dishes. Combine topping ingredients and sprinkle over each shell. *Note: Recipe may be prepared to this point ahead of time, covered, and chilled.*

395

Microwave coquilles, uncovered, on MEDIUM (50% power) 3–5 minutes, rearranging shells at halftime, just until bubbly. *Note: Chilled, made-ahead coquilles will take 9–11 minutes and should be rearranged every 3 minutes; test centers frequently toward end of cooking and as soon as coquilles are heated through, remove from oven.* If you like, transfer coquilles to baking sheet, set 4" from the heat in preheated broiler, and broil about 1 minute until crumbs are touched with brown—no longer or scallops may toughen.

PER SERVING: 337 C 19 g P 23 g F 14 g CARB 431 mg S 132 mg CH

CRAB MORNAY

PREP TIME: | 5 MINUTES | COOKING TIME: | 4–5 MINUTES | STANDING TIME: | NONE |

SERVES 4

1   **pound lump crab meat, well picked over**

1   **recipe Mornay Sauce**

¼   **cup finely grated Parmesan cheese**

2   **tablespoons toasted bread crumbs (include crusts for color)**

Mix crab and hot Mornay Sauce, spoon into shallow 1½-quart casserole and microwave, uncovered, on MEDIUM (50% power) 4–5 minutes, stirring at halftime, until steaming. Mix cheese and crumbs and sprinkle evenly over crab and serve. If you prefer lightly browned crust, transfer casserole to preheated broiler and broil 4" from heat about 1 minute until touched with brown.

PER SERVING: 394 C   34 g P   22 g F   12 g CARB 1354 mg S   171 mg CH

V A R I A T I O N

FLOUNDER FLORENTINE: Microwave 1½ pounds flounder, sole or other flat fish fillets as directed for Steamed Thin Fillets. Also prepare

1 recipe Mornay Sauce and keep hot. Spread 1½ cups chopped hot buttered spinach in shallow oval 2½-quart casserole or au gratin dish, arrange fish on top in single layer with larger fillets around edge and smaller ones in center. Pour 1½ cups Mornay Sauce evenly over fish, sprinkle lightly with paprika, cover with wax paper and microwave on MEDIUM (50% power) 4–5 minutes, rotating casserole 180° at halftime, until steaming. Serve at once. Pass remaining sauce.

PER SERVING: 431 C 43 g P 23 g F 12 g CARB 1126 mg S 141 mg CH

STEAMED ALASKA KING CRAB LEGS

PREP TIME: **5 MINUTES** COOKING TIME: **4–5 MINUTES** STANDING TIME: **5 MINUTES**

Like lobsters, whole crabs do not microwave well. Crab legs, on the other hand, steam moist and tender in the microwave.

SERVES 4 AS AN ENTRÉE,
6 AS AN APPETIZER,
YIELDS ABOUT 2⅔ CUPS CRAB MEAT

2 packages (8–10 ounces each) frozen ready-split Alaska king crab legs, thawed

¼ cup Lemon Butter Sauce

Bend crab legs at "knees" into V-shapes, arrange shell side up, spoke fashion, on 12" round platter with thickest portions toward outside; brush with sauce. Cover with vented plastic food wrap and microwave on HIGH (100% power) 4–5 minutes, rotating platter 180° and brushing crab with sauce at halftime, until flesh is opaque. Let stand, covered, 5 minutes. Remove meat from shells, cut in bite-size pieces, and serve with any appropriate cocktail sauce (these make elegant hors d'oeuvre). Or use in any recipe calling for cooked crab meat.

PER SERVING: 166–110 C 13–8 g P 13–8 g F 0–0 g CARB 815–544 mg S 66–44 mg CH

Hot seafood-stuffed avocados

PREP TIME: **3 MINUTES** · COOKING TIME: **7¾–9¾ MINUTES** · STANDING TIME: **NONE**

SERVES 4

- **2 tablespoons butter or margarine**
- **2 tablespoons flour**
- **½ cup milk**
- **½ cup light cream**
- **½ teaspoon salt (about)**
- **⅛ teaspoon white pepper**
- **1 tablespoon small capers**
- **1 tablespoon minced chives**
- **½ pound well picked over, flaked lump crab meat, or cooked shrimp or lobster meat cut in ½" cubes or 1⅓ cups flaked, cooked white fish, salmon, or tuna**
- **2 large (12 ounces each) firm-ripe avocados, at room temperature**
- **2 tablespoons lemon juice**

Melt butter in wax-paper-covered 1-quart measure by microwaving on HIGH (100% power) 35–45 seconds; blend in flour and microwave, uncovered, on HIGH (100% power) 30 seconds until foamy. Gradually stir in milk and cream, add salt and pepper, and microwave, uncovered, on HIGH (100% power) 2¾–3½ minutes, beating well every 1½ minutes, until sauce boils and thickens. Stir in capers and chives; lightly fold in seafood, and adjust salt as needed. Halve, peel, and pit avocados and brush well with lemon juice. Arrange with pointed ends toward center in shallow round 1½–2-quart casserole and fill with seafood mixture. *Note: If avocado hollows are small, enlarge them a bit; save trimmings for salad or sandwich spread.* Cover with wax paper and microwave on MEDIUM-HIGH (70% power) 4–5 minutes, rotating casserole 180° at halftime, until avocados are hot. Serve at once.

PER SERVING: 405 C 16 g P 33 g F 15 g CARB 586 mg S 96 mg CH

V A R I A T I O N

HOT CHICKEN- OR TURKEY-STUFFED AVOCADOS: Prepare as directed, substituting 1⅓ cups diced cooked chicken or turkey for seafood and 2 tablespoons diced pimiento for capers.

PER SERVING: 437 C 18 g P 35 g F 16 g CARB 415 mg S 81 mg CH

CHESAPEAKE CRAB IMPERIAL

PREP TIME: 10 MINUTES **COOKING TIME:** 8½–11 MINUTES **STANDING TIME:** NONE

SERVES 4–6

½ cup minced sweet green pepper

½ cup minced sweet red pepper

2 scallions, minced (white part only)

1 tablespoon butter or margarine

1 tablespoon Worcestershire sauce

1½ teaspoons dry mustard

½ teaspoon salt

¼ teaspoon pepper

1 cup mayonnaise

1 egg white, beaten until foamy

1 pound lump crab meat, well picked over

2 tablespoons light cream

Paprika

Microwave green and red peppers, scallions, and butter in wax-paper-covered 1½-quart casserole on HIGH (100% power) 3½–4¼ minutes, stirring at halftime, until peppers are tender. Mix in Worcestershire sauce, mustard, salt, pepper, ½ cup mayonnaise, and egg white; fold gently into crab and pile in 4–6 crab or scallop shells or shallow ramekins. Combine remaining mayonnaise and cream, spread evenly over crab, and sprinkle with paprika. Microwave, uncovered, on HIGH (100% power) 5–7 minutes, rearranging shells every 2 minutes, until mixture begins to puff and is hot. Serve at once.

PER SERVING: 570–380 C 25–17 g P 50–34 g F 5–3 g CARB 990–660 mg S 159–106 mg CH

CRAB NORFOLK

PREP TIME: | 3 MINUTES | COOKING TIME: | 4½–5¼ MINUTES | STANDING TIME: | NONE

SERVES 4

- **1 pound lump crab meat, well picked over**
- **4 teaspoons white wine vinegar**
- **½ teaspoon salt**
- **⅛ teaspoon ground hot red pepper**
- **Pinch black pepper**
- **⅓ cup butter (no substitute)**

Mix crab lightly with vinegar, salt, red and black pepper, spoon into shallow 1½-quart casserole, and dot evenly with butter. Cover with wax paper and microwave on MEDIUM-HIGH (70% power) 4½–5¼ minutes, stirring gently at half-time, until steaming. Serve as is or on buttered toast points.

PER SERVING: 251 C 23 g P 17 g F 0 g CARB 745 mg S 154 mg CH

STEAMED ROCK LOBSTER TAILS

PREP TIME: | 4 MINUTES | COOKING TIME: | 12–16 MINUTES | STANDING TIME: | 5 MINUTES

It's not practical to microwave whole lobsters because they must be cooked one by one. Their irregular shape, moreover, makes it impossible to cook them evenly—the claws inevitably overcook before the body meat is done. Rock and slipper lobster tails, however, can be steamed successfully in the microwave.

SERVES 2

- **2 frozen rock lobster tails (8–10 ounces each), thawed**
- **2 tablespoons water or dry vermouth**

Using scissors or sharp knife, slit underside of each lobster shell lengthwise, then bend tail to expose meat. Arrange tails, cut side up, in shallow rectangular casserole. *Note: Tails will cook more evenly if arranged facing one another*

**1 tablespoon lime or lemon
juice**

6 black peppercorns

with tail ends in center and meatiest portions toward outside. Add water and remaining ingredients, cover with vented plastic food wrap, and microwave on MEDIUM (50% power) 12–16 minutes, rotating casserole 180° at halftime, until shells turn red and meat becomes opaque. Let casserole stand, covered, 5 minutes. Serve lobster tails warm with Herb or Lemon Butter Sauce, chilled with tartar sauce, mayonnaise, or Warm Aioli Sauce. Or remove meat from shells and use in any recipe calling for cooked lobster meat.

PER SERVING: 134 C   28 g P   1 g F   2 g CARB   515 mg S 97 mg CH

V A R I A T I O N

 STEAMED SLIPPER LOBSTER TAILS: Far smaller than rock lobster tails, these often weigh no more than 4 ounces apiece. Slit undersides of 4 thawed, frozen slipper lobster tails of uniform size as directed for rock lobster, arrange spoke fashion in casserole with tail ends toward center. Add water and remaining ingredients, cover with vented plastic food wrap, and microwave on MEDIUM (50% power) 12 minutes, rotating casserole 180° at halftime. Continue cooking in 1-minute intervals, *just* until shells turn red and meat becomes opaque. Remove from oven and let stand as directed for rock lobster tails.

PER SERVING: 134 C   28 g P   1 g F   2 g CARB   515 mg S 97 mg CH

SHRIMP STEAMED IN THE SHELL

PREP TIME: | 2 MINUTES | COOKING TIME: | 2½–10 MINUTES | STANDING TIME: | 1–2 MINUTES

You won't save much time steaming shrimp in a microwave, but you'll preserve the shrimps' sea-sweet flavor. Overall cooking time will vary according to the size of the shrimp, and to some extent, the variety (for some reason gray-green shrimp take longer to cook than their pink Gulf Coast cousins). Choose shrimp of uniform size to ensure even cooking—miniature or small for canapés, soups, salads, and casseroles; medium-size for cocktails and casseroles where you want the shrimp to show, and jumbo or colossal for stuffing.

SERVES 2–4

1 *pound unshelled raw shrimp*

2 *tablespoons water*

1 *tablespoon lemon juice*

1 *bay leaf, crumbled*

6 *black peppercorns*

Arrange shrimp in single layer, spoke fashion with tail ends toward center, in shallow 10"–12" round casserole. Add remaining ingredients, cover with vented plastic food wrap, and microwave on HIGH (100% power) 2½–3 minutes for miniature and small shrimp, 3–5 minutes for medium-size, 6–8 minutes for jumbo, and 8–10 minutes for colossal, rotating casserole at half-time, and cooking shrimp *just* until pink. Check for doneness after minimum microwaving time and remove any shrimp that are cooked. Remove casserole from oven and let stand, covered, allowing 1 minute for miniature-to-medium-size shrimp, 2 minutes for larger ones. Drain shrimp and serve hot with Lemon, Garlic, or Herb Butter Sauce (let each person shell his own shrimp—be sure to set out a bowl to catch the empty shells). Or cool shrimp, shell and devein, and use for shrimp cocktail or in any recipe calling for cooked shrimp.

PER SERVING: 195–97 C   37–19 g P   3–2 g F   2–1 g CARB
272–136 mg S   279–140 mg CH

CRAYFISH TAILS STEAMED IN THE SHELL: Substitute 1 pound unshelled crayfish tails for shrimp, add 1 sprig fresh dill to other ingredients, and microwave as directed 8–10 minutes or *just* until shells turn scarlet; test for doneness after 8 minutes and at 1-minute intervals thereafter. Serve hot with melted butter.

PER SERVING: 147–74 C   39–20 g P   2–1 g F   0–0 g CARB   88–44 mg S   230–115 mg CH

STEAMED SHELLED SHRIMP

PREP TIME: | 5 MINUTES | COOKING TIME: | 3-10 MINUTES | STANDING TIME: | 1-2 MINUTES

SERVES 2–4

1   **pound shelled and deveined shrimp**

¼   **cup water**

1   **tablespoon lemon juice**

2–3 **sprigs parsley or 1 bay leaf and 1 sprig each parsley and thyme, tied in cheesecloth (bouquet garni)**

Arrange shrimp in single layer, spoke fashion, in shallow 10"–12" round casserole with tail ends toward center. Add remaining ingredients, cover with vented plastic food wrap, and microwave on HIGH (100% power) 2 minutes. Turn casserole 180°, re-cover, and microwave on MEDIUM (50% power) *just* until pink—1–1½ minutes for miniature and small shrimp, 2–3 minutes for medium-size, 3–5 minutes for jumbo, and 6–8 minutes for colossal. Check frequently and remove any shrimp that are done. Remove casserole from oven and let stand, covered, 1–2 minutes. Drain shrimp and serve with Lemon, Garlic, or Herb Butter Sauce. Or chill and use for shrimp cocktail or in any recipe calling for cooked shrimp.

**PER SERVING: 241–120 C   46–23 g P   4–2 g F   2–1 g CARB
336–168 mg S   345–173 mg CH**

STEAMED SHRIMP À LA MEUNIÈRE: Arrange shrimp in casserole as directed, omit water and seasonings, and add ¼ cup melted butter or margarine, 1 tablespoon each Worcestershire sauce, lemon juice, and minced parsley, ½

403

teaspoon snipped dill, and ⅛ teaspoon pepper. Cover and microwave as directed, basting shrimp with casserole liquid at halftime. Serve warm in liquid with bite-size chunks of French bread or ladle over rice or toss with angel hair pasta.

PER SERVING: 454–227 C   47–23 g P   27–13 g F   4–2 g CARB   655–328 mg S   407–204 mg CH

 STEAMED BAY SCALLOPS: Arrange 1 pound bay scallops in single layer, doughnut fashion, in shallow 2-quart casserole. Add no water or other ingredients, cover with vented plastic food wrap, and microwave on MEDIUM (50% power) 5½–6½ minutes, rotating casserole 180° at halftime, until *just* opaque. Transfer scallops and cooking liquid at once to chilled bowl to stop cooking. Cover, cool to room temperature, and serve with lemon wedges or appropriate dipping sauce (tartar, Aioli, etc.) and toothpicks as an hors d'oeuvre. Or use in any recipe calling for cooked scallops.

PER SERVING: 200–100 C   38–19 g P   2–1 g F   5–3 g CARB   365–183 mg S   75–37 mg CH

 SCAMPI

PREP TIME: [5 MINUTES]   COOKING TIME: [3–10 MINUTES]   STANDING TIME: [1–2 MINUTES]

SERVES 2–4

1 **cup olive oil**

3 **tablespoons dry vermouth**

2 **tablespoons minced parsley**

1 **clove garlic, peeled and minced**

⅛ **teaspoon pepper**

1 **pound shelled and deveined shrimp**

Mix oil, vermouth, parsley, garlic, and pepper in large bowl; add shrimp, toss well, cover, and marinate in refrigerator 2–3 hours. Drain shrimp, reserving ¼ cup marinade. Arrange shrimp in single layer, spoke fashion, in shallow 10"–12" round casserole with tail ends toward center. Add reserved marinade, cover with vented plastic food wrap, and microwave on HIGH (100% power) 2 minutes. Turn casserole 180°, re-cover and microwave on MEDIUM (50% power) *just* until pink—1–1½ minutes for miniature and small shrimp, 2–3 minutes for medium-size, 3–5 minutes for jumbo, and 6–8 minutes for colossal. Check frequently and remove any shrimp that are done. Remove casserole from oven and let stand, covered, 1–2 minutes. Serve shrimp warm or at room temperature with a little marinade.

PER SERVING: 561–280 C   46–23 g P   40–20 g F   3–2 g CARB 337–169 mg S   345–173 mg CH

SHRIMP NEWBURG

PREP TIME: 10 MINUTES COOKING TIME: 13¾–16 MINUTES STANDING TIME: 1–2 MINUTES

Classic Newburgs call for 1 egg yolk, at least, but this one is plenty rich without it.

SERVES 4

1   pound medium-size shelled and deveined shrimp

3   tablespoons butter or margarine

3   tablespoons flour

1½ cups light cream

¼   cup shrimp cooking liquid

½   teaspoon salt

⅛   teaspoon ground hot red pepper

Pinch ground nutmeg

1   tablespoon tomato paste

2   tablespoons dry sherry

4   slices hot buttered toast, halved diagonally

Microwave shrimp as directed for Steamed Shelled Shrimp and save cooking liquid. Melt butter in wax-paper-covered 2-quart casserole by microwaving on HIGH (100% power) 45–55 seconds; blend in flour and microwave, uncovered, on HIGH (100% power) 30 seconds until foamy. Gradually stir in cream and shrimp cooking liquid. Smooth in salt, hot red pepper, nutmeg, and tomato paste and microwave, uncovered, on HIGH (100% power) 4½–5½ minutes, beating well every 2 minutes, until sauce boils and thickens. Mix in shrimp and sherry, adjust salt as needed, then microwave, uncovered, on MEDIUM (50% power) 3–4 minutes, stirring every 2 minutes, until mixture steams. Serve over toast.

To Make Ahead and Reheat: Place circle of wax paper flat on Newburg and cool to room temperature; refrigerate until ready to proceed. Remove wax paper, cover with vented plastic food wrap; and microwave on MEDIUM (50% power) 9–11 minutes, stirring every 3 minutes, until mixture steams.

PER SERVING: 501 C   29 g P   33 g F   23 g CARB   761 mg S   266 mg CH

～～～～～～～～～ V A R I A T I O N

SEAFOOD NEWBURG (Serves 6): Prepare as directed, using mixture of flaked lump crab meat, diced cooked lobster meat, shrimp and/or bay scallops; also

405

increase flour to 4 tablespoons, cream to 1¾ cups, and seafood cooking liquid to ⅔ cup. Adjust salt and nutmeg as needed. Microwave as directed but increase final warming time on MEDIUM (50% power) to 5–6 minutes. Serve over steamed rice.

PER SERVING: 355 C   19 g P   24 g F   16 g CARB   611 mg S   145 g CH

Shrimp and corn custard

PREP TIME: **6 MINUTES**   COOKING TIME: **13–14½ MINUTES**   STANDING TIME: **5 MINUTES**

SERVES 4

2   **cups fresh whole-kernel corn or 1 package (10 ounces) frozen whole-kernel corn (do not thaw)**

2   **tablespoons finely grated yellow onion**

2   **tablespoons finely minced celery**

1   **cup (5–5½ ounces) coarsely chopped, cooked, shelled and deveined shrimp**

2   **teaspoons minced parsley**

¼   **teaspoon ground hot red pepper**

⅛   **teaspoon black pepper**

½   **teaspoon Worcestershire sauce**

½   **cup light cream**

1   **tablespoon unsalted butter or margarine, at room temperature**

2   **eggs, lightly beaten**

Mix corn, onion, and celery in 1½-quart round casserole at least 8½" across, cover with vented plastic food wrap, and microwave on HIGH (100% power) 2¾–3 minutes until corn is slightly softened. Transfer all to food processor and churn 5 seconds; return to casserole and mix in shrimp, parsley, red and black pepper, and Worcestershire sauce; set aside. Microwave cream in uncovered 1-pint measure on HIGH (100% power) 1¼–1½ minutes until it steams but does not boil. Add butter, stirring until melted. Mix slowly into eggs, then stir into corn mixture. Cover with wax paper and microwave on MEDIUM (50% power) 9–10¼ minutes, rotating casserole 90° every 3 minutes, until set like custard. *Note: Small moist area in center will set on standing.* Cover with foil and let stand 5 minutes to complete cooking. Serve at once.

For Individual Corn Custards: Prepare custard mixture as directed and divide evenly among 4 lightly greased 6-ounce custard cups. Arrange cups ½" apart on platter, cover with wax paper, and microwave on MEDIUM (50% power) 11–12½ minutes, rearranging cups at halftime, until outer 1" of custard in each cup is set. *Note: Remove any custards from oven that cook faster than others.* Let custards stand as directed and return any that do not firm up to oven, cover with wax paper, and microwave on MEDIUM (50% power) in 1-minute increments until *just* firm. Carefully loosen custards with spatula and turn out on serving plates. *Note: Custard cups retain heat, so use pot holders when unmolding custards.*

PER SERVING: 230 C   14 g P   13 g F   17 g CARB   152 mg S   237 mg CH

V A R I A T I O N

 CRAB OR LOBSTER AND CORN CUSTARD: Prepare as directed, substituting flaked lump crab meat or chopped cooked lobster meat for shrimp.

PER SERVING: 231 C   14 g P   13 g F   17 g CARB   173 mg S   202 mg CH

$=$ *11*

VEGETABLES, GRAINS, AND OTHER SIDE DISHES

The microwave excels at cooking fresh vegetables because it heightens their color, intensifies their flavor, preserves their original texture, and, not least, leaves most of their vitamins intact. There's good reason for this. Vegetables contain considerable water, which the microwave converts to steam. So they cook in an aromatic cloud of their own, requiring little or no additional liquid that can leach out vitamins or water down flavor. Many vegetables cook twice as fast in a microwave as they do on top of the stove and starchy ones (potatoes, sweet potatoes, etc.) can cook four to eight times as fast, depending, of course, on quantity. Yet despite the microwave's speed, you needn't worry about a vegetable's scorching. Or about rice and other grains sticking or gumming. They plump to perfection in the microwave.

ABOUT CONTAINERS AND COVERINGS

Always use the container and covering each recipe specifies—both affect timing and texture. Often, for example, a container's diameter is as critical to a recipe's success as its volume; in such cases, our recipes specify both measurements. Whenever a vegetable is to be browned on the stovetop (we find browning skillets impractical) or in the broiler, choose a container that's both microwave-safe and able to take intense direct heat.

As for coverings, you'll note that some recipes call for casserole lids, plastic food wrap, or wax paper (all trap moisture, speed and equalize the cooking) and others for paper toweling (it absorbs moisture and keeps vegetables from going soggy). In some instances—when vegetables are unusually moist and you want that moisture to evaporate—no covering at all is needed.

SOME GENERAL MICROWAVING TIPS FOR FRESH VEGETABLES

Never double recipes. A vegetable's taste and texture will suffer. Moreover, microwaving a double load of vegetables may take as long to cook as cooking them on top of the stove. Most of our vegetable recipes serve six, *maximum,* because it's impractical to microwave larger quantities. If you're feeding a crowd, do two batches or cook the vegetables the conventional way.

Never microwave two different vegetables at the same time; they'll cook at different speeds and require almost constant testing for doneness. In addition, the increased volume of food will slow overall cooking. There are exceptions: acorn and butternut squash are so similar they can be microwaved in tandem. Many of our recipes combine dissimilar vegetables, but we've carefully engineered each so that all vegetables cook evenly to just the right degree of doneness.

Use common sense about timing vegetables in the microwave. *Weight and quantity determine overall cooking time* (small loads cook faster than big ones) *as do freshness* (garden-fresh vegetables cook faster than over-the-hill ones), *moisture content* (the moister the vegetable, the quicker it will cook), and *shape* (uniformly shaped pieces cook more evenly than irregular ones, small pieces faster than large ones). Temperature, obviously, must be considered, too. Refrigerator-cold vegetables, especially carrots, turnips, and other root vegetables, may take 10–20% longer to cook than room-temperature ones.

Always cut vegetables as recipes direct, making the cubes, dice, or slices of uniform size so they'll cook more evenly or quickly. And when arranging vegetables in a casserole, always place the thicker, coarser pieces (stems, for example) toward the outside and the tender tops or tips in the center. Finally, never crowd the vegetables.

Always pierce potatoes or other unpeeled vegetables so they don't burst during microwaving.

Add only the amount of liquid specified. The point is to keep vegetables moist, not to drown them (excess liquid also slows the cooking). Microwaving, remember, is a moist method of cooking.

Don't salt vegetables until after they're cooked because the salt may spot them or cake. It can actually toughen some vegetables.

To ensure even cooking, always stir, rearrange, and/or rotate vegetables as recipes direct. Using a turntable can eliminate much of this.

Check vegetables frequently for doneness and remove from microwave the instant they're *barely* tender. They'll finish cooking during the standing period.

Underseason vegetables; the microwave accentuates flavors. Taste the vegetables again just before serving, then adjust seasoning as needed.

ABOUT COOKING VEGETABLES AHEAD OF TIME

If properly timed and tended, microwaved vegetables can taste just as fresh the second time around as the first. And here's a handy trick: Parboil vegetables ahead of time, then finish them off in the microwave shortly before serving (they can finish cooking while the microwaved entrée stands).

411

DON'T MICROWAVE THESE!

VEGETABLE SOUFFLÉS: They're so moist they never firm up properly.

BREADED OR BATTER-DIPPED VEGETABLES: They won't crisp or brown unless microwaved on active microwave cookware (see Chapter 3); commercial foods are packaged in special materials that promote browning. For the same reason, frozen french fries fare poorly in the microwave.

DEEP- OR SHALLOW-FRIED VEGETABLES: It's dangerous to fry in deep—or even shallow fat—in the microwave because fats can ignite. The flash point ranges from 380°–625° F., depending on the composition of the fat or oil. And the lower of these temperatures can quickly be reached in the microwave.

ABOUT BLANCHING VEGETABLES IN THE MICROWAVE

If you freeze your own vegetables, you'll be pleased to know that you can blanch them in the microwave. You won't save much time, but you will spare yourself steamy cauldrons of water. There are other advantages, too: Microwaving destroys less vitamin C than the conventional method of blanching and also sets the color, flavor, and aroma more vividly. Use only the plastic storage bags recommended for microwave use and follow the manufacturer's instructions to the letter. *Note: For best results, use an automatic temperature probe and blanch vegetables just until they reach 190° F. Also, blanch no more than one bag of vegetables at a time.*

ABOUT MICROWAVING FROZEN VEGETABLES

Almost all frozen vegetables now include microwaving instructions on the package, so the best plan is to follow them (for crisper vegetables with richer flavor, however, we like to give them 30 seconds less time). *And a word of advice:* Never microwave frozen vegetables in their paper carton; they'll taste terrible and be messy to remove from the carton. It's far better and simpler to microwave them in a casserole that can come to the table.

For those of you who freeze your own vegetables, we provide this handy chart that shows how to microwave those gardener's favorites that freeze well.

Vegetable (1 Pint)	Servings	Water	Minutes on HIGH (100% power)	Minutes Standing Time
Asparagus Spears	2–4	2 T	6–8	2
Beans (Green, Wax)				
Whole	3–4	1 T	8–9	2
Cut	3–4	1 T	6–7	2
Lima Beans				
Baby	3–4	2 T	6–7	2
Fordhook	3–4	2 T	10–11†	2

†Fordhooks cooked on MEDIUM-HIGH (70% power) are less apt to burst.

Vegetable (1 Pint)	Servings	Water	Minutes on HIGH (100% power)	Minutes Standing Time
Broccoli				
Spears	3–4	None	6–8	2
Chopped	3–4	None	5–7	2
Corn				
Whole-Kernel	3–4	None	5–6	2
On-the-Cob	2 Ears	None	3–4	2
	4 Ears	None	5–6	2
	6 Ears	None	8–9	2
	8 Ears	None	9–10	2
Peas				
Green	2–4	None	5–6	2
Sugar Snaps	3–4	1 T	3–4	None
Spinach				
Leaf	2–3	None	7–8	2
Chopped	2	None	5–7	2
Winter Squash	2–3	None	5–7	1

TO MICROWAVE LOOSE-PACK FROZEN VEGETABLES: Place in casserole (1-pint size for 1 cup, 1-quart for 2 cups, 1½-quart for 3 cups, and 2-quart for 4 cups; do not try to cook more—larger quantities cook better and faster the old-timey way). Add 1 tablespoon water per cup frozen vegetables, cover with lid or vented plastic food wrap, and microwave on HIGH (100% power) as follows: 3–4 minutes for 1 cup, 6–8 for 2 cups, 9–11 for 3 cups, and 11–13 for 4 cups. Stir or rearrange vegetables at halftime and test frequently for doneness. Let stand 2 minutes, drain and season (winter squash should stand 1 minute only and snow peas not at all).

TO MICROWAVE FROZEN VEGETABLES IN A POUCH (9- or 10-ounce): Flex pouch and slit on one side; lay bag slit side up in casserole big enough to allow it to lie flat. Microwave, uncovered, as manufacturer directs, rotating casserole 180° and flexing pouch at halftime. Let stand 2 minutes, empty vegetable into serving dish, stir well, season, and serve. ***Note:*** *Handle pouch carefully; it will be very hot.*

TO MICROWAVE 1 SERVING FROZEN VEGETABLES: Place ½–⅔ cup frozen vegetable in 6-ounce ramekin, add 2 teaspoons water, cover with vented plastic food wrap, and microwave on HIGH (100% power) 1½–2½ minutes until crisp-tender. Stir, drain, season, and serve (no standing time needed).

5 QUICK WAYS TO JAZZ UP FROZEN VEGETABLES

⌛ **C**ORN WITH SWEET RED PEPPER AND MUSTARD **SERVES 3-4** Combine 1 tablespoon heavy cream, 1 teaspoon Dijon mustard, and ⅛ teaspoon pepper in 1-quart casserole. Scatter 1 package (10 ounces) frozen whole-kernel corn into casserole, top with ½ cup finely diced sweet red pepper and 1 tablespoon butter or margarine. Tuck in 4 small sprigs fresh rosemary or sprinkle with ¼ teaspoon crumbled dried rosemary, cover with lid or vented plastic food wrap, and microwave by package directions. Remove rosemary sprigs and serve.
PER SERVING: 141–106 C 3–2 g P 7–5 g F 21–16 g CARB 94–71 mg S 17–13 mg CH

⌛ **G**REEN PEAS WITH ROSEMARY AND ORANGE **SERVES 3-4** Spread 2 cups frozen green peas in 1-quart casserole, dot with 1 tablespoon butter or margarine, drizzle with 1 tablespoon heavy cream, tuck in 4 strips (each 2″ × ½″) orange rind and 4 sprigs fresh rosemary or sprinkle with ¼ teaspoon crumbled dried rosemary. Cover and microwave by package directions. Remove rosemary sprigs and orange strips, season to taste with salt and pepper, and serve.
PER SERVING: 190–127 C 8–5 g P 9–6 g F 21–14 g CARB 223–149 mg S 26–17 mg CH

⌛ **B**EANS WITH OIL AND VINEGAR **SERVES 3-4** Cook a package (10 ounces) green, wax, or Italian beans as package directs but add 1 minced clove garlic, 2 tablespoons olive oil, and 1 tablespoon tarragon vinegar in place of water.
PER SERVING: 113–95 C 2–1 g P 9–7 g F 8–6 g CARB 3–2 mg S 0–0 mg CH

⚖ ⌛ **C**ARROTS WITH FRESH GINGER **SERVES 3-4** Microwave 1 package (10 ounces) frozen small whole carrots as package directs but substitute 1 tablespoon butter or margarine for water and add 1 teaspoon finely minced fresh ginger. Sprinkle with 1 tablespoon minced chives before serving.
PER SERVING: 74–56 C 1–1 g P 4–3 g F 9–7 g CARB 87–66 mg S 10–8 mg CH

⌛ **L**IMAS WITH SOUR CREAM AND BACON **SERVES 4** Microwave 2 julienned slices bacon in wax-paper-covered 1-quart casserole on HIGH (100% power) 2½–3 minutes until nearly crisp. Add 1 package (10 ounces) frozen baby limas, cover, and microwave as package directs. Stir in ½ cup room-temperature sour cream and serve.
PER SERVING: 218 C 7 g P 13 g F 19 g CARB 130 mg S 20 mg CH

415

GLOBE ARTICHOKES

Cut stems flush with bottoms, snip off prickly petal tips, and rub cut edges with lemon. Wrap each artichoke in plastic food wrap, lay 1" apart on oven floor (three in a triangle, four or more in a circle), and microwave as follows, turning over at halftime and if cooking more than two, rearranging as well. Test for doneness after minimum time: Pierce through plastic with sharp fork; if tender, unwrap carefully (artichokes will be *hot*) and pull off leaf—it should come away easily. Rewrap any "undone" artichokes and microwave in 1-minute increments. When done, let stand, still wrapped, as chart directs; unwrap and drain upside down. Serve with dipping sauce or melted butter.

No. of 6–8-oz. Artichokes	Servings	Minutes on HIGH (100% power)	Minutes Standing Time
1	1	3–5	3
2	2	5–7	3
4	4	10–13	4
6	6	16–20	4

Note: *Artichokes weighing 10–12 ounces will need about a minute longer per artichoke.*

Suggested Dips: Lemon or Herb Butter Sauce, Hollandaise, French Mayonnaise.

VARIATIONS

STEAMED ARTICHOKE HEARTS: Remove all but inner cone of petals from cooked artichokes; snip off prickly tips and scrape out choke with teaspoon. Season to taste with salt and pepper, drizzle with lemon butter, and serve. Or cool, halve, and marinate in a tart vinaigrette.

STEAMED ARTICHOKE BOTTOMS: Remove all petals and choke from cooked artichokes (flesh at base of petals can be scraped off and mixed into cheese dips). Serve warm bottoms filled with small bright vegetables or Creamed Spinach.

416

STUFFED ARTICHOKES À LA DIABLE

PREP TIME: [5 MINUTES]   COOKING TIME: [14½–17½ MINUTES]   STANDING TIME: [NONE]

An elegant first course or side dish.

SERVES 4

4   globe artichokes (6–8 ounces each), microwaved until just tender*

Stuffing

3   slices lean bacon, cut crosswise in julienne strips

1   tablespoon butter or margarine

1   small clove garlic, peeled and minced

3   shallots, peeled and minced

1½   cups soft white bread crumbs

1   tablespoon coarsely chopped capers

1   tablespoon minced parsley

¼   teaspoon salt

⅛   teaspoon pepper

Dressing

¼   cup dry white wine

2   tablespoons olive oil

Drain artichokes well and cool until easy to handle. Stand upside down on counter and press down firmly to spread leaves and expose chokes. With teaspoon, scrape out chokes and discard. Stand artichokes right side up, ½" apart, in 10" casserole and set aside while you prepare stuffing.

For stuffing, arrange bacon doughnut fashion in 1-quart casserole, cover with paper toweling, and microwave on HIGH (100% power) 4½–5 minutes, stirring at halftime, until crisp. Lift with slotted spoon to paper toweling, crumble, and reserve. Pour off all but 1 tablespoon bacon drippings, add butter, garlic, and shallots, cover with wax paper, and microwave on HIGH (100% power) 3–3½ minutes until soft. Mix in all remaining stuffing ingredients including bacon. Using a teaspoon and dividing total amount equally, spoon stuffing into artichokes where chokes were, mounding it slightly.

Beat wine and oil together, pour around artichokes, cover with lid or vented plastic food wrap, and microwave on HIGH (100% power) 7–9 minutes, rotating casserole 180° at halftime, until artichokes and stuffing are hot. Drizzle with a little casserole liquid and serve.

PER SERVING: 229 C   5 g P   15 g F   19 g CARB   460 mg S   15 mg CH

417

Asparagus

Snap off tough stem ends and peel asparagus if woody. Arrange spears spoke fashion in single layer on plate, tips toward center. Add water, cover with vented plastic food wrap, and microwave as follows, rotating plate 180° at halftime, *just* until crisp-tender. Let stand, covered; drain and season.

Trimmed Weight	Servings	Container	Water	Minutes on HIGH (100% power)	Minutes Standing Time
⅓ lb. (6–7 spears)	1	10" plate	1 T	2½–3	3
⅔ lb. (12–14 spears)	2	10" plate	1 T	3–4	3
1⅓ lbs. (27–31 spears)	4	11" platter	2 T	5–7	3
2 lbs. (36–42 spears)	6	11"–12" platter	2 T	8–10	3

Seasoning Suggestions: Seasoned Butter, Lemon Butter Sauce, Hollandaise, Mustard Sauce, toasted buttered bread crumbs, minced toasted nuts* (any kind), soy sauce and toasted sesame seeds,* crisp bacon crumbles.

VARIATIONS

STEAMED ASPARAGUS TIPS: Use 2" tips only and microwave as directed, reducing times to 2 minutes for 1 serving, 2½–3 for 2, 4–5 for 4, and 6–7 for 6. Season and serve or use in salads, casseroles, omelets, quiches.

ASPARAGUS VINAIGRETTE: Quick-chill cooked asparagus 15 minutes in ice water and drain. Add 2 tablespoons French dressing or vinaigrette per serving, cover, and chill several hours, turning now and then. Drain and serve.

STIR-COOKED ASPARAGUS, RED PEPPER, AND WATER CHESTNUTS

PREP TIME: | 8 MINUTES | COOKING TIME: | 5-6 MINUTES | STANDING TIME: | 2 MINUTES

SERVES 4–6

- 1½ **pounds asparagus, tough stem ends removed**
- 1 **medium-size sweet red pepper, cored, seeded, and cut in ⅛″ strips 2″ long**
- 2 **tablespoons Oriental sesame oil or vegetable oil**
- ¼ **cup thinly sliced water chestnuts or bamboo shoots**
- ¼ **teaspoon salt**
- ⅛ **teaspoon pepper**

Snap tips off asparagus and set aside; slice stems slantwise ½″ thick. Arrange asparagus tips in center of 11″ round platter, cover with red pepper strips, and wreathe asparagus stems around edge. Sprinkle all evenly with oil, cover with vented plastic food wrap, and microwave on HIGH (100% power) 4 minutes. Toss vegetables well, re-cover, and microwave 1–2 minutes longer until jus t crisp-tender. Mix in water chestnuts, salt, and pepper, re-cover, and let stand 2 minutes.

PER SERVING: 93–62 C   3–2 g P   7–5 g F   6–4 g CARB
139–92 mg S   0–0 mg CH

VARIATION

CHINESE ASPARAGUS: Prepare as directed, omitting salt. In 1-quart measure blend 1½ teaspoons cornstarch, 1 tablespoon soy sauce, ¼ teaspoon cider vinegar, ⅛ teaspoon sugar, and liquid drained from vegetables plus enough chicken broth to total ½ cup. Microwave, uncovered, on HIGH (100% power) 2–2½ minutes, whisking after 1 minute, until sauce boils and thickens. Pour over vegetables, toss well, and serve.

PER SERVING: 102–68 C   3–2 g P   7–5 g F   8–5 g CARB
323–216 mg S   0–0 mg CH

419

GREEN OR WAX BEANS

Tip beans and if longer than 4″, snap in 2″ lengths or french. Place in casserole, add water, cover with lid or vented plastic food wrap, and microwave as follows, stirring at halftime (every 4 minutes for 1½ pounds beans), until crisp-tender. *Note: Cooking times are more erratic than for most vegetables; fresh-picked beans cook fastest. To be safe, test beans after minimum cooking time.* Let beans stand, covered, as chart directs; drain and season.

Trimmed Weight	Servings	Container	Water	Minutes on HIGH (100% power)	Minutes Standing Time
¼ lb.	1	8″–9″ pie plate	¼ C	5–6	2
½ lb.	2	1-quart	⅓ C	7–10	2
1 lb.	4	2-quart	½ C	10–15	3
1½ lbs.	6	2½-quart	½ C	15–20	3

Note: Beans of 4″ or less can be cooked whole; increase microwave time in each category 1 minute.

Seasoning Suggestions: Seasoned Butter, Lemon or Garlic Butter Sauce, Mushroom, Mornay, Onion, Béchamel, or Mustard-Sour Cream Sauce; any minced toasted nuts,* soy sauce and toasted sesame seeds,* crisp bacon crumbles; grated Parmesan.

VARIATIONS

PARBOILED GREEN OR WAX BEANS: Reduce microwave chart times by 50%; drain at once (no standing), quick-chill 5 minutes in ice water; drain again.

STEAMED POLE BEANS: Tip, cut on bias ¼″ wide, and cook as directed, increasing microwave times in each category by 1 minute; let stand as directed.

STEAMED WING BEANS: Tip, slice ½″ wide, then microwave as directed for Steamed Pole Beans.

TUSCAN BEANS

PREP TIME: **3 MINUTES** | COOKING TIME: **7¾–9½ MINUTES** | STANDING TIME: **NONE**

SERVES 4

½ **pound green beans, snapped in 2″ lengths or 1 package (10 ounces) frozen cut green beans, cooked and drained**

1 **can (1 pound, 3 ounces) cannellini, drained**

Sauce

3 **tablespoons butter or margarine**

3 **tablespoons flour**

1¾ **cups milk**

⅛ **teaspoon pepper**

2 **tablespoons minced chives**

2 **tablespoons minced Italian parsley**

2 **tablespoons finely grated Parmesan cheese**

½ **teaspoon salt (about)**

Mix green beans and cannellini gently in 2-quart casserole; set aside. Melt butter by microwaving in wax-paper-covered 6-cup measure on HIGH (100% power) 45–55 seconds. Blend in flour and microwave, uncovered, on HIGH (100% power) 30 seconds until foamy. Gradually whisk in milk and microwave, uncovered, on HIGH (100% power) 3½–4 minutes, whisking at half-time, until sauce boils and thickens. Whisk in remaining ingredients and adjust salt as needed. Mix sauce with beans, cover with wax paper, and microwave on MEDIUM (50% power) 3–4 minutes, stirring gently at halftime, until beans are hot and flavors blended.

PER SERVING: 305 C   14 g P   14 g F   34 g CARB   943 mg S 41 mg CH

421

MALAY WARM GREEN BEAN AND CUCUMBER SALAD WITH LEMON-COCONUT DRESSING

PREP TIME: 8 MINUTES   COOKING TIME: 7-8 MINUTES   STANDING TIME: NONE

In Kuala Lumpur this unusual salad, a palette of greens, is made with the foot-long snake beans so popular in the Orient. Snap beans work just as well.

SERVES 4–6

½ *pound green beans, cut slantwise in 2" lengths, parboiled* and drained well*

1 *medium-size cucumber (about ¾ pound), peeled, seeded, and cut in 2" × ¼" × ¼" strips*

½ *medium-size sweet green pepper, cored, seeded, and cut in ⅛" strips 2" long*

1 *bunch scallions, trimmed and cut slantwise in ½" lengths*

1 *clove garlic, peeled and minced*

1 *tablespoon vegetable oil*

¼ *teaspoon salt*

Lemon-Coconut Dressing

½ *cup canned coconut cream*

3 *tablespoons lemon juice*

2 *tablespoons minced fresh mint*

Place beans in center of casserole at least 10" in diameter and 2" deep. Arrange cucumber and green pepper around edge and scatter scallions and garlic on beans. Sprinkle vegetables with oil, cover with lid or vented plastic food wrap, and microwave on HIGH (100% power) 7–8 minutes, rotating casserole 180° at halftime until vegetables are barely tender. Drain well and mix in salt. Blend coconut cream and lemon juice until smooth, stir in mint, pour over vegetables, and toss gently. Serve at once.

PER SERVING: 146–97 C   3–2 g P   10–7 g F   13–9 g CARB   166–111 mg S   0–0 mg CH

LIMA BEANS

Shell baby limas (starchy Fordhooks and favas cook best on the stovetop), arrange in casserole, add water, cover with lid or vented plastic food wrap, and microwave as follows, stirring at halftime, until just tender. Let stand, still covered; drain and season. *Note: 1 pound limas = 1 cup shelled.*

Amount Shelled Beans	Servings	Container	Water	Minutes on HIGH (100% power)	Minutes Standing Time
½ C	1	1-pint	¼ C	5–7	3
1 C	2	1-quart	¼ C	7–10	3
2 C	4	2-quart	½ C	10–16	3
3 C	6	2½-quart	½ C	17–20	3

Seasoning Suggestions: Melted butter and minced pecans; crisp crumbled bacon, bacon drippings and minced chives; sour cream and minced scallions; Parsley or Onion Sauce.

VARIATIONS

PARBOILED LIMA BEANS: Reduce microwave chart times by 2 minutes for 1 serving, 3 minutes for 2, and 4–5 minutes for 4–6 servings; drain at once (no standing), quick-chill 5 minutes in ice water; drain again.

423

PORTUGUESE LIMAS WITH FRESH CORIANDER

PREP TIME: | 10 MINUTES | COOKING TIME: | 25–28 MINUTES | STANDING TIME: | 3 MINUTES |

SERVES 6

3 slices lean bacon, cut crosswise in julienne strips

1 small yellow onion, peeled and minced

3 cups shelled fresh lima beans or 2 packages (10 ounces each) frozen baby limas

¼ cup water

½ teaspoon salt (about)

⅛ teaspoon pepper

¼ cup minced fresh coriander (cilantro) or Italian parsley

Wreathe bacon around edge of 2-quart casserole at least 10″ in diameter. Cover with paper toweling and microwave on HIGH (100% power) 4½–5 minutes, stirring at halftime, until crisp. Lift bacon with slotted spoon to paper toweling and reserve. Add onion to casserole drippings, cover with wax paper, and microwave on HIGH (100% power) 3 minutes until glassy. Stir in limas and water. Cover with lid or vented plastic food wrap and microwave on HIGH (100% power) 17–20 minutes for fresh limas, 9–10 for frozen ones, stirring at halftime, until beans are tender. Let stand, covered, 3 minutes. Drain well, add salt to taste, pepper, coriander, and bacon. Toss well and serve.

PER SERVING: 154 C   6 g P   7 g F   16 g CARB   266 mg S 8 mg CH

Although the microwave can't cook dried beans zip-quick, it does beat conventional cooking times about 50%. It also reduces the risk of boilovers and scorched pots and means a cool kitchen no matter how torrid the weather. For best results, follow these guidelines:

Always use a casserole at least twice the volume of the ingredients put into it to avoid boilovers. Adding a little drippings, margarine, bacon, salt pork, or a ham bone also helps keep beans from bubbling over.

Always use bean soaking water for part of the cooking liquid—it's loaded with vitamins and minerals.

Always cover beans with a tight lid to keep them from cooking dry—not plastic food wrap, which will split during long cooking.

Never salt beans until after they're cooked; it can toughen them.

Never try to hurry the beans along by keeping the power on HIGH (100%); you'll merely toughen and dry them. Once the bean liquid has come to a boil, reduce the power to MEDIUM (50%) for the duration of cooking so the beans will absorb the liquid slowly and soften.

Make sure the beans are good and tender before you take them from the microwave. Although they'll continue to absorb liquid as they stand, they won't become any more tender. ***Note:*** *If beans aren't tender at end of recommended microwaving time, continue to microwave in 5-minute increments, stirring after each (old, superdehydrated beans often take longer to cook).*

425

BASIC BOILED DRIED BEANS

PREP TIME: [2 MINUTES] COOKING TIME: [42–65 MINUTES] STANDING TIME: [5 MINUTES]

This method works equally well for the whole family of dried beans with the exception of chick-peas, which are too hard to microwave well, and dried whole peas, which tend to burst their skins.

SERVES 6

1 pound dried beans, rinsed, sorted, and soaked overnight in 1 quart cold water†

Soaking water plus enough hot water to total 3 cups

1 tablespoon bacon drippings, margarine, or vegetable oil

Salt and pepper to taste

Place beans, soaking water mixture, and drippings in 4- or 5-quart casserole, cover with tight lid, and microwave on HIGH (100% power) 7–10 minutes until boiling. Stir, re-cover, and microwave on MEDIUM (50% power) 35–55 minutes, stirring gently every 15 minutes, until beans are tender. *Note: Cannellini and kidney beans cook the fastest; navy, pea, Great Northern, marrowfat, pinto, and black beans the slowest.* Let stand, covered, 5 minutes. Drain (save liquid for soup or stew), season to taste with salt and pepper, and use in any recipe calling for cooked beans. Or serve with any of these sauces: Garlic, Herb Butter, Cheese, Parsley, Onion, or Jiffy Tomato. Black beans may simply be topped with sour cream, chopped onion, and minced fresh coriander (cilantro). *Note: When halving recipe, use 2-quart casserole. Microwave 5–8 minutes on HIGH (100% power) until boiling, then on MEDIUM (50% power) 25–45 minutes.*

PER SERVING: 269 C   17 g P   3 g F   46 g CARB   21 mg S   2 mg CH

†Instead of soaking beans overnight, you can use this quick stovetop method: Add 1 pound dried beans to 1 quart boiling water, cover and boil 2 minutes. Let stand, covered, off heat 1 hour. For ½ pound beans, use 2 cups water.

¢ SAVORY DRIED BEANS: Add a small ham bone, leftover beef or lamb bone (or ¼ pound diced bacon or salt pork) to beans along with ½ cup minced yellow onion and 1 minced clove garlic. Microwave as directed, allowing an extra 5 minutes on MEDIUM (50% power).
PER SERVING: 293 C   20 g P   3 g F   48 g CARB   260 mg S 11 mg CH

NAVY BEAN SALAD: In large bowl mix 1 pound drained, cooked, unseasoned navy beans with ⅓ cup each minced sweet green and red pepper, ⅔ cup minced celery, and 2 tablespoons minced parsley. In 1-quart casserole mix ⅔ cup minced Spanish onion, 1 minced clove garlic, and 1 tablespoon olive oil. Cover with wax paper and microwave on HIGH (100% power) 3½–4 minutes until glassy. Add ¼ cup cider vinegar and microwave, on HIGH (100% power) 1 minute longer, then add to beans along with ⅓ cup olive oil, 1½ teaspoons salt, and ¼ teaspoon pepper. Toss gently, cover, and chill several hours. Taste for salt and adjust as needed, then let stand at room temperature 30 minutes before serving. *Note: When halving recipe, reduce microwave time for onion and garlic to 2–2½ minutes.*
PER SERVING: 392 C   17 g P   15 g F   49 g CARB   573 mg S 0 mg CH

OLD-TIMEY BAKED BEANS

PREP TIME: 10 MINUTES | COOKING TIME: 43–49 MINUTES | STANDING TIME: 10 MINUTES

Steam buildup can cause tightly covered dried beans to burst during microwaving as can boiling them too hard, so cover loosely and simmer gently. **Note:** *Halve this recipe or its variation, if you like, preparing as directed but allowing 7–9 minutes on HIGH (100% power) to bring beans to a boil, then 20–25 minutes on MEDIUM (50% power) to mellow flavors.*

SERVES 6

1	**medium-size yellow onion, peeled and minced**
¼	**pound lean salt pork, cut in ¼" dice**
5–5½	**cups cooked or canned navy, pea, or other white beans, drained (reserve liquid)**

Bean liquid plus enough water to total ¾–1 cup

⅓	**cup firmly packed dark brown sugar**
¼	**cup dark molasses**
2	**tablespoons Worcestershire sauce**
1	**teaspoon dry mustard**
¼	**teaspoon pepper**

Salt to taste

Mix onion and salt pork in 4- or 5-quart casserole, cover with paper toweling, and microwave on HIGH (100% power) 4 minutes, stirring at halftime. Stir in beans, ¾ cup bean liquid, brown sugar, molasses, Worcestershire sauce, mustard, and pepper. Cover with wax paper and microwave on HIGH (100% power) 9–10 minutes, stirring at halftime, until gently bubbling. Reduce power level to MEDIUM (50%) and microwave, still covered, 30–35 minutes, stirring carefully at halftime, until flavors mellow. Also check liquid at halftime and add ¼ cup more if beans seem dry. When beans are done, stir again, then let stand, covered, 10 minutes. Salt to taste and serve.

PER SERVING: 453 C 15 g P 16 g F 63 g CARB 343 mg S 16 mg CH

¢ **B**ARBECUED BEANS: Substitute drained cooked or canned marrowfat beans for navy beans, omit salt pork, and microwave 2 minced cloves garlic along with onion. Reduce liquid to ½ cup, increase brown sugar to ½ cup, add ½ cup tomato purée and ¼ cup cider vinegar along with all remaining ingredients. Microwave as directed, mixing in 1 tablespoon cornstarch blended with 2 tablespoons water for last 15 minutes of microwaving.

PER SERVING: 277 C   14 g P   1 g F   56 g CARB   147 mg S   0 mg CH

*F*RIJOLES MEXICANOS

PREP TIME: | 5 MINUTES | **COOKING TIME:** | 28–29 MINUTES | **STANDING TIME:** | 5 MINUTES |

¢

SERVES 4–6

1 **medium-size yellow onion, peeled and minced**

2 **tablespoons lard or bacon drippings**

4 **cups cooked or canned pinto or red kidney beans, drained (reserve liquid)**

Salt to taste

Microwave onion and lard in wax-paper-covered 2-quart casserole on HIGH (100% power) 3½–4 minutes until glassy. Meanwhile, purée ½ cup beans with ½ cup bean liquid by pulsing 4–6 times in food processor. Mix purée into onion along with remaining beans and bean liquid. Cover with wax paper and microwave on HIGH (100% power) 4–5 minutes until bubbly. Stir, re-cover, and microwave on MEDIUM (50% power) 20 minutes, stirring at halftime and cooking uncovered for final 10 minutes. *Note: In ovens of 700 watts or more, MEDIUM-LOW (30% power) may be enough to keep beans simmering; they may shatter if they boil constantly.* Let stand, covered, 5 minutes. Season with salt and serve.

PER SERVING: 299 C   14 g P   7 g F   45 g CARB   4 mg S 6 mg CH

429

Beets

¢ Choose beets 2" or less in diameter. Remove all but 1" of the tops, leave roots on, and scrub (avoid breaking skin). Arrange 1" apart in casserole (three in a triangle, four or more in circle), add water, cover with lid or vented plastic wrap, and microwave as follows, rotating casserole with one or two beets 180° at halftime, rearranging more than two beets, until *just* fork-tender. Let stand, covered.

Trimmed Weight	Servings	Container	Water	Minutes on HIGH (100% power)	Minutes Standing Time
⅓ lb. (2 small)	1	1-pint	¼ C	6–8	3
¾ lb. (3 medium)	2	1-quart	¼ C	12–14	3
1½ lbs. (6 medium)	4	2-quart	¼ C	16–20	3
2¼ lbs. (8 medium)	6	2½-quart	⅓ C	21–25	3

Drain beets, quick-chill 1–2 minutes in ice water, and peel. Slice, cube, or julienne. Return to casserole, season to taste, cover with wax paper, and microwave on HIGH (100% power) 1–3 minutes, stirring at halftime.

To Microwave Small Whole Beets: Beets of 1" or less can be served whole. Microwave as directed, allowing 9–12 minutes for ¾ pound trimmed beets, 12–16 for 1½ pounds, and 16–20 for 2¼. Drain, peel, season, and serve.

Seasoning Suggestions: Allowing ¼ cup sour cream and ½ teaspoon prepared horseradish or ⅛ teaspoon each nutmeg and caraway seeds per serving, toss with whole, sliced, cubed, or julienned beets.

CITRUS-GINGER-GLAZED BEETS (Serves 4): Mix 2 tablespoons butter, ¼ cup lemon or orange marmalade, and 2 teaspoons finely grated fresh ginger into 1½ pounds sliced, cubed, or julienned cooked beets. Microwave, uncovered, on HIGH (100% power) 2–3 minutes, stirring at halftime.

PER SERVING: 156 C 2 g P 6 g F 26 g CARB 145 mg S 16 mg CH

¢ HARVARD BEETS (Serves 4): Place 1½ pounds sliced cooked beets in 2-quart casserole and keep warm. Combine ¼ cup sugar, 1 tablespoon cornstarch, ¼ teaspoon salt, ⅛ teaspoon pepper, ⅓ cup cider vinegar, and 3 tablespoons water in 1-quart measure. Micro-wave, uncovered, on HIGH (100% power) 2–2½ minutes, whisking every minute, until sauce boils and thickens. Stir in 2 tablespoons butter or margarine, pour over beets, and mix gently.

PER SERVING: 162 C 2 g P 6 g F 27 g CARB 277 mg S 16 mg CH

SWEDISH BEETS WITH SOUR CREAM AND DILL (Serves 4): Place 1½ pounds sliced, cubed, or julienned cooked beets in 2-quart casserole and keep warm. Mix 1 cup sour cream, 1 tablespoon each grated onion and lemon juice, and 3 tablespoons finely snipped fresh dill (or ¾ teaspoon dill weed). Stir into beets and microwave, uncovered, on MEDIUM (50% power) 3–4 minutes, stirring at half-time, until hot, not boiling. Serve hot or at room temperature.

PER SERVING: 178 C 4 g P 12 g F 14 g CARB 115 mg S 25 mg CH

POLISH BEETS

The Polish way to present the beets is wreathed with whipped potatoes and sprinkled with freshly grated horseradish.

SERVES 6

- 2 tablespoons butter or margarine
- 1 medium-size yellow onion, peeled and minced
- 2 teaspoons sugar
- 2 teaspoons red wine vinegar
- 2 teaspoons prepared horseradish
- 2 pounds beets, cooked and peeled or 2 cans (1 pound each) whole beets, drained
- ¼ cup heavy cream, at room temperature

Microwave butter and onion in wax-paper-covered 2-quart casserole on HIGH (100% power) 3½–4 minutes until glassy. Meanwhile, cut beets in ½" cubes. When onion is glassy, mix in sugar, vinegar, and horseradish, then beets. Cover with lid or vented plastic food wrap and microwave on HIGH (100% power) 4–5 minutes, stirring at halftime, until hot. Mix in cream and serve in small bowls.

PER SERVING: 125 C   2 g P   8 g F   13 g CARB   121 mg S   24 mg CH

BROCCOLI

 Trim off coarse stalks and leaves; divide into florets 3″ long and 2″ wide. Arrange in single layer in container (spoke fashion in pie plate), stems toward outside. Add water, cover with vented plastic food wrap, and microwave as follows, rotating plate 180° at halftime or rearranging florets, *just* until crisp-tender. Let stand, covered; drain and season.

Trimmed Weight	Servings	Container	Water	Minutes on HIGH (100% power)	Minutes Standing Time
¼ lb.	1	9″ pie plate	¼ C	3–4	2
½ lb.	2	10″ pie plate	¼ C	5–7	2
1 lb.	4	11″ × 7″ × 2″	¼ C	8–10	2
1½ lbs.	6	11″ × 7″ × 2″	¼ C	10–15	3

Seasoning Suggestions: Seasoned Butter, Jiffy Garlic Butter, Cheese or Lemon Butter Sauce, Hollandaise, Mornay, Warm Aioli or Blue Cheese-Sour Cream Sauce, Hot Mustard Mayonnaise, toasted buttered bread crumbs and grated Parmesan, butter-sautéed almonds and lemon juice, soy sauce and toasted sesame seeds.*

 VARIATIONS

 PARBOILED BROCCOLI: Reduce microwave chart times by 1 minute for 1 serving, 2 minutes for 2, and 3 minutes for 4–6 servings; drain at once (no standing), quick-chill 5 minutes in ice water, drain again.

433

BROCCOLI PARMIGIANA

PREP TIME: [4 MINUTES] COOKING TIME: [8¾–10¾ MINUTES] STANDING TIME: [NONE]

Artichoke hearts, cauliflower florets, asparagus tips, green, wax or lima beans, whole white onions, leeks, or summer squash can all be cooked this way. Simply substitute an equal amount of the hot, cooked, well-drained vegetable of your choice for broccoli and prepare as follows.

SERVES 4–6

3–4½	**cups hot cooked broccoli florets, well drained**
2	**tablespoons butter or margarine**
2	**tablespoons flour**
1	**cup milk**
½	**cup chicken broth**
⅓	**cup finely grated Parmesan cheese**
½	**teaspoon salt**
⅛	**teaspoon pepper**

Pinch ground nutmeg

Topping

½	**cup soft white bread crumbs (leave crust on bread for color)**
2	**tablespoons finely grated Parmesan cheese**

Arrange broccoli in shallow 1½–2-quart glass ceramic casserole at least 9" across; set aside. Melt butter in wax-paper-covered 1-quart measure by microwaving on HIGH (100% power) 35–45 seconds. Blend in flour and microwave, uncovered, on HIGH (100% power) 30 seconds until foamy. Gradually whisk in milk and microwave, uncovered, on HIGH (100% power) 2¾–3½ minutes, whisking every 1½ minutes, until sauce boils and thickens. Whisk in chicken broth, cheese, salt, pepper, and nutmeg. Spoon evenly over broccoli, cover with lid or vented plastic food wrap, and microwave on HIGH (100% power) 3 minutes, rotating casserole 180° at halftime. Meanwhile, combine topping ingredients. Uncover and sprinkle evenly with topping. Transfer to preheated broiler and broil 4"–5" from heat 2–3 minutes until lightly browned.

PER SERVING: 209–139 C 12–8 g P 12–8 g F 16–11 g CARB 750–500 mg S 33–22 mg CH

V A R I A T I O N

BROCCOLI WITH MOZZARELLA: Prepare as directed but substitute 1–1½ cups coarsely grated mozzarella cheese for crumb topping.

PER SERVING: 279–186 C 17–11 g P 18–12 g F 14–9 g CARB 798–532 mg S 58–39 mg CH

434

THAI BROCCOLI WITH BLACK BEAN SAUCE

PREP TIME: 8 MINUTES COOKING TIME: 12½–15 MINUTES STANDING TIME: NONE*

SERVES 4–6

2 **pounds broccoli, trimmed and cut into florets about 3" long and 2" wide**

¼ **cup water**

2 **slices lean bacon, cut crosswise in julienne strips**

1 **tablespoon vegetable oil**

1 **clove garlic, peeled and crushed**

2 **tablespoons cornstarch blended with 1 cup cold water**

1 **tablespoon nuoc nam or nam pla (anchovy sauce available in Oriental groceries) or 2 anchovies mashed to paste with ½ teaspoon soy sauce**

1 **tablespoon black bean sauce**

Arrange broccoli in single layer in 13" × 8" × 2" casserole with stems toward outside. Add water, cover with lid and microwave on HIGH (100% power) 5 minutes. Let stand, covered, while you prepare sauce. Wreathe bacon around edge of shallow 1½-quart casserole, cover with paper toweling, and microwave on HIGH (100% power) 2½–3½ minutes until almost crisp. With slotted spoon, lift bacon to paper toweling and reserve. Add oil and garlic to drippings, cover with paper toweling, and microwave on HIGH (100% power) 30 seconds. Blend in cornstarch mixture, *nuoc nam,* and black bean sauce and microwave, uncovered, on HIGH (100% power) 1½–2 minutes, stirring at halftime, until sauce boils and thickens. Drain liquid from broccoli into sauce, mix well, then pour over broccoli. Re-cover with lid and microwave on HIGH (100% power) 3–4 minutes until broccoli is hot and crisp-tender. Sprinkle with bacon and serve.

PER SERVING: 155–103 C   6–4 g P   11–7 g F   11–7 g CARB
245–163 mg S   9–6 mg CH

435

*B*RUSSELS SPROUTS

Choose sprouts about 1″ in diameter, trim of withered leaves and stems, and cut an X in base of each. Arrange in single layer in casserole, smaller sprouts in center. Add water, cover with lid or vented plastic food wrap, and microwave as follows, stirring at halftime but keeping small sprouts in center, *just* until crisp-tender. Let stand, covered; drain and season.

Trimmed Weight	Servings	Container	Water	Minutes on HIGH (100% power)	Minutes Standing Time
¼ lb.	1	1-pint	2 T	3–4	3
½ lb.	2	1-quart	2 T	4–6	3
¾–1 lb.	4	1½-quart	3 T	6–8	3
1¼–1½ lbs.	6	2-quart	4 T	7–10	3

Seasoning Suggestions: Seasoned Butter or Lemon Butter Sauce; Mustard-Sour Cream Sauce, Onion, Cheese or Mustard Sauce; sour cream and freshly snipped dill; coarsely chopped cooked chestnuts.

BRAISED BRUSSELS SPROUTS LOUVAIN

PREP TIME: | 6 MINUTES | COOKING TIME: | 8–10 MINUTES | STANDING TIME: | NONE |

SERVES 4

1 **pound Brussels sprouts, trimmed and sliced crosswise 1/16" thick (discard hard cores)**

1/2 **clove garlic, peeled and minced**

2 **tablespoons chicken broth**

1/4 **cup heavy cream**

1/2 **teaspoon salt (about)**

1/8 **teaspoon ground nutmeg**

Pinch pepper

Mix sprouts, garlic, and broth in 2-quart casserole. Cover with lid and microwave on HIGH (100% power) 6–8 minutes, stirring at halftime, until crisp-tender. Mix in remaining ingredients, re-cover, and microwave on MEDIUM (50% power) 2 minutes to blend flavors. Toss sprouts, adjust salt as needed, then serve.

PER SERVING: 97 C   4 g P   6 g F   10 g CARB   336 mg S 20 mg CH

CABBAGE (GREEN, RED, SAVOY)

⚖ Remove outer leaves, quarter, remove cores at point of each quarter, then:

¢ *For Shredded Cabbage:* Shred or slice moderately fine (1½ pounds trimmed cabbage yields about 6 cups). Add water, cover with lid or vented plastic food wrap, and microwave as follows, stirring at halftime, *just* until crisp-tender. Let stand, covered; drain and season.

Amount	Servings	Container	Water	Minutes on HIGH (100% power)	Minutes Standing Time
1½ C	1	1-quart	¼ C	3–5	3
3 C	2	1½-quart	¼ C	5–6	3
6 C	4	3-quart	¼ C	7–10	3
9 C	6	4-quart	⅓ C	9–12	3

VARIATION

⚖¢ STEAMED CHINESE CABBAGE: Slice thin and microwave minimum time; then microwave in 1-minute intervals until crisp-tender; let stand as directed.

438

For Steamed Wedges: Cut in 2½–3-ounce wedges. Arrange in casserole in single layer, overlapping slightly, with points toward center. Add water, cover with lid or vented plastic food wrap, and microwave as follows, rotating 180° at halftime, *just* until crisp-tender. Let stand, covered, drain and season.

Amount	Servings	Container	Water	Minutes on HIGH (100% power)	Minutes Standing Time
2 wedges	1	1-quart	¼ C	5–7	2–3
4 wedges	2	1½-quart	¼ C	8–10	2–3
8 wedges	4	2-3-quart	¼ C	10–12	2–3
12 wedges	6	11″ × 7″ × 2″	¼ C	12–14	2–3

Seasoning Suggestions: Seasoned Butter, Lemon Butter Sauce, sour cream and freshly snipped dill or caraway seeds, chopped chestnuts or crisp bacon crumbles and bacon drippings. For green cabbage only: Onion Sauce or light cream and freshly grated Parmesan. Best with Chinese cabbage: Toasted sesame seeds,* minced fresh ginger, Oriental sesame oil, and soy sauce.

 V A R I A T I O N

¢ SWEET-SOUR RED CABBAGE (Serves 4): Toss 4 servings cooked cabbage with 2 tablespoons each melted butter and light brown sugar, ¼ cup red wine vinegar, and ⅛ teaspoon ground nutmeg.
PER SERVING: 120 C 2 g P 6 g F 16 g CARB 91 mg S 16 mg CH

SPICY INDIAN CABBAGE

PREP TIME: **10 MINUTES** COOKING TIME: **12–14 MINUTES** STANDING TIME: **3 MINUTES**

Ghee or clarified butter is nothing more than melted butter from which the milk solids have been removed. Its flavor is mellow, pure, and golden.

SERVES 6

- 9 **cups moderately finely shredded cabbage**
- 1 **large Spanish onion (about ½ pound), peeled and minced**
- 1 **clove garlic, peeled and minced**
- 1 **teaspoon chili powder**
- 1 **teaspoon ground coriander**
- ¼ **teaspoon mustard seeds, bruised**
- ¼ **teaspoon cumin seeds, bruised**
- ¼ **teaspoon red pepper flakes**
- ⅓ **cup water**
- 2 **tablespoons ghee**
- 1 **teaspoon salt (about)**
- ⅓ **cup toasted flaked coconut* (optional)**

In 4- or 5-quart casserole, toss cabbage with onion, garlic, chili powder, coriander, mustard and cumin seeds, and red pepper flakes. Add water, cover with lid, and microwave on HIGH (100% power) 12–14 minutes, stirring well at halftime, until cabbage is tender. Let stand, covered, 3 minutes. Drain well, add ghee and salt, toss well, and adjust salt as needed. Sprinkle, if desired, with coconut and serve.

PER SERVING: 94 C   3 g P   5 g F   12 g CARB   403 mg S   11 mg CH

GASPÉ COLESLAW

PREP TIME: | 10 MINUTES | COOKING TIME: | 2–3 MINUTES | STANDING TIME: | NONE |

This slaw tastes best when made several hours ahead of time and will remain crisp for two to three days.

SERVES 6–8

1 **small cabbage (about 2 pounds), trimmed, cored, and shredded moderately fine**

2 **medium-size yellow onions, peeled, sliced tissue-thin, and separated into rings**

Dressing

½ **cup sugar**

½ **cup white vinegar**

⅓ **cup vegetable oil**

1 **teaspoon salt**

1 **teaspoon dry mustard**

1½ **teaspoons celery or caraway seeds**

Layer cabbage alternately into large bowl with onions. Place all dressing ingredients except celery seeds in 6-cup measure and microwave, uncovered, on HIGH (100% power) 2–3 minutes, stirring at halftime, until mixture boils. Stir again, mix in celery seeds, pour over cabbage, and toss well. Cover and chill several hours, tossing now and then.

PER SERVING: 214–161 C   2–1 g P   12–9 g F   26–20 g CARB 390–293 mg S 0–0 mg CH

Carrots

For small whole carrots (12–14 per pound): Trim and peel; arrange in single layer in casserole, tips toward center. Add water, cover with lid or vented plastic food wrap, and microwave as follows, rotating casserole 180° at halftime, *just* until crisp-tender. Let stand, covered; drain and season.

Amount	Servings	Container	Water	Minutes on HIGH (100% power)	Minutes Standing Time
⅓ lb.	1	1-pint	2 T	4–5	2
⅔ lb.	2	1-quart	2 T	6–8	2
1⅓ lbs.	4	2-quart	4 T	8–10	2
2 lbs.	6	11″ × 7″ × 2″	4 T	10–15	2

For 1″ chunks (5–6 carrots per pound): Trim and peel, halve carrots crosswise, quarter chunky parts lengthwise, and cut all in 1″ lengths. Place in casserole, add water, cover with lid or vented plastic food wrap, and microwave as follows, stirring at halftime, until crisp-tender. Let stand, covered; drain and season.

Amount	Servings	Container	Water	Minutes on HIGH (100% power)	Minutes Standing Time
⅔ C	1	1-pint	2 T	5–6	3
1⅓ C	2	1-quart	2 T	6–8	3
2⅔ C	4	2-quart	2 T	9–11	3
4 C	6	11″ × 7″ × 2″	3 T	12–14	3

For sliced, diced, or julienned carrots (5–6 per pound): Trim and peel; slice ¼″ thick, or cut in ¼″ dice, or in 2″ × ¼″ × ¼″ strips. Place in casserole, add water, cover with lid or vented plastic food wrap, and microwave as directed for carrot chunks but reduce each time given by 2 minutes, stirring at halftime, until crisp-tender. Reduce standing time to 2 minutes.

Seasoning Suggestions: Seasoned Butter; Lemon or Herb Butter Sauce; Onion or Parsley Sauce, Béchamel or Horseradish Sour Cream Sauce.

PARBOILED CARROTS: Cook whole or cut-up carrots as directed, but reduce cooking times 1 minute for 1–2 servings, 2 minutes for 4–6. Drain at once (no standing), quick-chill 5 minutes in ice water, and drain again.

STEAMED BABY CARROTS (about 40 per pound) (Serves 4–6): Trim, scrub, and arrange in single layer in 2-quart casserole, tips toward center and smallest carrots in middle. Add ¼ cup water, cover with lid or vented plastic food wrap, and microwave on HIGH (100% power) 8–10 minutes, rotating casserole 180° at halftime, until carrots are *barely* tender. Let stand, covered, 3 minutes. Drain and season. *Note: Freshly pulled carrots microwave best; skin on older ones shrivels, but piercing carrots of doubtful age with a sharp fork helps.*

LEMON-GLAZED CARROTS: (Serves 4): Place 2⅔ cups cooked 1" carrot chunks in 2-quart casserole; mix in 2 tablespoons each brown sugar and butter, 2 teaspoons lemon juice, and ¼ teaspoon finely grated lemon rind. Cover with wax paper and microwave on HIGH (100% power) 2–3 minutes, stirring every minute.
PER SERVING: 124 C 1 g P 6 g F 18 g CARB 130 mg S 16 mg CH

MASHED CARROTS (Serves 4): Mash 2⅔ cups cooked cut-up carrots; blend in 2 tablespoons each butter and heavy cream and a pinch ground nutmeg.
PER SERVING: 123 C 1 g P 9 g F 11 g CARB 130 mg S 26 mg CH

443

Carrots provençal

PREP TIME: 7 MINUTES | COOKING TIME: 16–18 MINUTES | STANDING TIME: 2 MINUTES

If vine-ripened tomatoes are unavailable, use the canned, but drain them well.

SERVES 4

1 tablespoon olive oil

1 medium-size yellow onion, peeled and minced

1 clove garlic, peeled and minced

1 pound carrots, peeled and cut in 1" × ½" × ½" pieces

1 cup coarsely chopped, peeled, and seeded red-ripe tomatoes

1 teaspoon salt

⅛ teaspoon pepper

Mix oil, onion, garlic, carrots, and tomatoes in 2-quart casserole about 10" across. Cover with lid or vented plastic food wrap and microwave on HIGH (100% power) 11 minutes, stirring at halftime. Mix in salt and pepper, then microwave, uncovered, on MEDIUM (50% power) 5–7 minutes, stirring at halftime, until almost all liquid evaporates and carrots are just tender. Let stand, covered, 2 minutes. Serve hot or at room temperature.

PER SERVING: 90 C   2 g P   4 g F   14 g CARB   590 mg S   0 mg CH

CAROTE ALL' ACETO
(CARROTS WITH VINEGAR)

PREP TIME: | 10 MINUTES | COOKING TIME: | 15–18 MINUTES | STANDING TIME: | 3 MINUTES

SERVES 4

1¼ pounds carrots, peeled and cut in ½" cubes

¼ cup minced yellow onion

3 tablespoons red wine vinegar

1 bay leaf (do not crumble)

2 juniper berries, crushed

½ teaspoon salt

Pinch pepper

Mix carrots and onion in 2-quart casserole, add vinegar, bay leaf, and juniper berries. Cover with lid or vented plastic food wrap and microwave on HIGH (100% power) 10 minutes, stirring at halftime. Stir, cover with paper toweling, then microwave on HIGH (100% power) 5–8 minutes, stirring at halftime, until almost all liquid evaporates and carrots are tender. Let stand, covered, 3 minutes. Remove bay leaf, season with salt and pepper, and serve.

PER SERVING: 60 C 1 g P 0 g F 14 g CARB 318 mg S 0 mg CH

CAULIFLOWER

Florets: Trim off leaves and coarse stems; divide into florets 2" long and 1" wide. Arrange in casserole, stems outward, add water, cover with lid or vented plastic food wrap, and microwave as follows, rotating casserole 180° at halftime, *just* until crisp-tender. Let stand, covered; drain and season.

Trimmed Weight	Servings	Container	Water	Minutes on HIGH (100% power)	Minutes Standing Time
¼ lb. (1 C)	1	1-quart	2 T	3–4	2
½ lb. (2 C)	2	1½-quart	2 T	4–6	2
1 lb. (4 C)	4	2-quart	4 T	8–10	3
1½ lbs. (6 C)	6	3-quart	4 T	12–15	3

VARIATIONS

 PARBOILED CAULIFLOWER FLORETS: Microwave as directed but reduce time by 1 minute for 1 serving, 2 minutes for 2, and 3 minutes for 4–6. Drain at once (no standing), quick-chill 5 minutes in ice water, and drain again.

 WHOLE CAULIFLOWER: Remove leaves and hollow out as much core as possible. Place in casserole, add water, cover with lid or vented plastic food wrap, and microwave as follows, rotating casserole 180° at halftime, *just* until crisp-tender. Let stand, covered; drain and season.

Trimmed Weight	Servings	Container	Water	Minutes on HIGH (100% power)	Minutes Standing Time
1½ lbs.	4	2-quart	2 T	7–10	3
2 lbs.	6	2-quart	2 T	12–15	3

Seasoning Suggestions: Mornay, Béchamel, or Lemon Butter Sauce; Hollandaise or Chantilly Sauce; Hot Mustard Mayonnaise; Warm Aioli; toasted buttered bread crumbs; minced toasted nuts* (any kind); chopped hard-cooked egg yolk mixed with minced fresh coriander (cilantro) or parsley, Beurre Noir.

SICILIAN CAULIFLOWER

PREP TIME: 10 MINUTES | COOKING TIME: 22–23 MINUTES | STANDING TIME: NONE*

SERVES 6

1   **cauliflower (about 2 pounds), trimmed and separated into florets 2″ long and 1″ wide**

¼   **cup water**

2   **tablespoons olive oil**

1   **medium-size yellow onion, peeled and minced**

1   **medium-size sweet red pepper, cored, seeded, and cut in fine dice**

1   **clove garlic, peeled and minced**

4   **anchovy fillets, minced**

6–7 **pitted large ripe olives, sliced thin**

¼   **teaspoon salt**

⅛   **teaspoon pepper**

1   **cup coarsely grated fontina cheese**

Place cauliflower in 3-quart casserole at least 10″ across with stalks toward outside. Add water, cover with lid, and microwave on HIGH (100% power) 10 minutes, rotating casserole 180° at halftime. Remove from oven and let stand, covered, while you proceed. Mix oil, onion, red pepper, and garlic in 2-quart casserole, cover with wax paper, and microwave on HIGH (100% power) 4 minutes until glassy. Add onion mixture, anchovies, and olives to cauliflower and toss gently. Cover with lid and microwave on HIGH (100% power) 6–7 minutes, tossing gently at halftime, until cauliflower is crisp-tender. Sprinkle with salt and pepper and toss again. Sprinkle cheese evenly over cauliflower and microwave, uncovered, on MEDIUM (50% power) 2 minutes, until cheese melts.

PER SERVING: 149 C   7 g P   12 g F   5 g CARB   227 mg S 23 mg CH

447

CELERY

Trim root end and tops from celery (a 1½-pound bunch yields about 1 pound trimmed celery, 3 cups 1½" chunks). Separate stalks and cut in 1½" chunks. Place in casserole, add water, cover with lid or vented plastic food wrap, and microwave as follows, stirring at halftime, until crisp-tender. Let stand, covered; drain and season.

Trimmed Weight	Servings	Container	Water	Minutes on HIGH (100% power)	Minutes Standing Time
¼ lb.	1	1-pint	1 T	4–6	2
½ lb.	2	1-quart	2 T	6–8	2
1 lb.	4	2-quart	2 T	9–10	3
1½ lbs.	6	2½-quart	2 T	10–12	3

Seasoning Suggestions: Jiffy Herb Butter or Beurre Noir; toasted buttered bread crumbs; minced toasted nuts* (any kind).

VARIATIONS

STEAMED CELERY HEARTS (Serves 4): Cut root ends from 2 large bunches celery and remove all but 4–5 inner stalks; trim hearts so each is 5" long; quarter lengthwise, and remove any feathery inner leaves (they'll turn brown). Lay hearts in single layer, 1" apart with bases outward, in 11" × 7" × 2" casserole. Add 2 tablespoons water or chicken broth, cover with vented plastic food wrap, and microwave on HIGH (100% power) 9–12 minutes, rotating casserole 180° at halftime, until crisp-tender. Let stand, covered, 3 minutes, drain, season, and serve. Or marinate in tart dressing and serve cold.

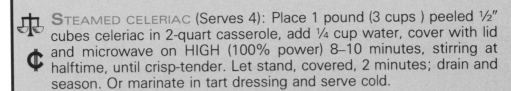

STEAMED CELERIAC (Serves 4): Place 1 pound (3 cups) peeled ½″ cubes celeriac in 2-quart casserole, add ¼ cup water, cover with lid and microwave on HIGH (100% power) 8–10 minutes, stirring at halftime, until crisp-tender. Let stand, covered, 2 minutes; drain and season. Or marinate in tart dressing and serve cold.

PARBOILED CELERY HEARTS OR CELERIAC: Microwave as directed but reduce time 50%. Drain at once (no standing), quick-chill 5 minutes in ice water, and drain again.

STEAMED CELERIAC WITH WARM TOMATO MAYONNAISE

PREP TIME: 5 MINUTES COOKING TIME: 10–12 MINUTES STANDING TIME: 2 MINUTES

Serve as an appetizer, salad or accompaniment to grilled fish.

SERVES 6

3 cups peeled ½″ cubes celeriac

¼ cup water

Tomato Mayonnaise

½ cup mayonnaise

4 teaspoons red wine vinegar

2 teaspoons tomato paste

2 teaspoons celeriac cooking liquid

½ teaspoon Dijon mustard

½ teaspoon sugar

Pinch ground hot red pepper

Microwave celeriac and water in covered 2-quart casserole at least 10″ across on HIGH (100% power) 8–10 minutes, stirring at halftime, until crisp-tender; let stand, covered, 2 minutes. Drain well, reserving 2 teaspoons liquid; set celeriac aside, uncovered. Microwave all mayonnaise ingredients in uncovered 1-quart measure on MEDIUM (50% power) 2 minutes, whisking at halftime, until warm, not boiling. *Note: Mixture will separate a little at edges, so whisk to smooth.* Mix with celeriac and serve.
PER SERVING: 175 C   1 g P   15 g F   9 g CARB   215 mg S 11 mg CH

CORN

On the Cob: No husking needed! And the silks magically come away with the husks after microwaving. If ears are dry, rinse briefly in cool water. Arrange up to 4 ears, 1" apart, on oven floor (an extra 2 ears can go on oven shelf but *no more* or corn won't cook evenly). Microwave, uncovered, as follows, turning ears over and rearranging at halftime. After corn has cooked minimum time and stood, peel husk back slightly and check for doneness. If not done, microwave each ear in 30-second increments. ***Note:*** *Some ears may cook faster than others (age and freshness determine).* Allow 1–4 ears per person and microwave in batches. ***Note:*** *To keep cooked ears hot 15 minutes, wrap individually in foil.*

No. of Ears	Minutes on HIGH (100% power)	Minutes Standing Time
1	2–3	3
2	3–4	3
4	5–6	3
6	7–8	3

Seasoning Suggestions: Seasoned Butter, Jiffy Garlic, or Herb Butter, Curry Butter Sauce.

Fresh Whole-Kernel Corn: Spread kernels evenly in casserole. Add water, cover with lid or vented plastic food wrap, and microwave as follows, stirring at halftime, until tender. Drain and season (no standing needed).

Amount	Servings	Container	Water	Minutes on HIGH (100% power)	Standing Time
¾ C	1	1-pint	1 T	3–4	None
1½ C	2	1-quart	2 T	4–5	None
3 C	4	2-quart	2 T	7–8	None
4½ C	6	2½-quart	2 T	9–10	None

Seasoning Suggestions: Bacon drippings, grated onion, crumbled dried rosemary, and crisp bacon crumbles; sautéed sweet green or red pepper; minced fresh coriander (cilantro) and sour cream.

 V A R I A T I O N S

 JIFFY SUCCOTASH (Serves 4): Mix 1½ cups each hot cooked whole-kernel corn and baby limas, ½ cup light cream, and salt and pepper to taste.
PER SERVING: 206 C 8 g P 7 g F 32 g CARB 54 mg S 20 mg CH

CONFETTI CORN (Serves 4): Mix 3 cups raw whole-kernel corn with ¼ cup each diced sweet red and green pepper; microwave as directed and season to taste with margarine, salt, and pepper.
PER SERVING: 102 C 4 g P 1 g F 23 g CARB 18 mg S 0 mg CH

CREAMED CORN (Serves 4): Microwave as directed, substituting heavy cream for water. Season with salt and pepper, sprinkle with minced chives, and serve.
PER SERVING: 125 C 4 g P 4 g F 22 g CARB 20 mg S 10 mg CH

VEGETABLES, GRAINS, PASTAS, AND OTHER SIDE DISHES

OLD-FASHIONED CORN PUDDING

PREP TIME: `5 MINUTES` COOKING TIME: `24–26 MINUTES` STANDING TIME: `5 MINUTES`

Position the foil collar carefully so the pudding doesn't overcook around the edges.

SERVES 6

3   **eggs**

¼   **cup unsifted flour**

1   **tablespoon sugar**

1   **teaspoon salt**

¼   **teaspoon baking powder**

⅛   **teaspoon ground nutmeg**

1   **can (12 ounces) evaporated milk**

3   **cups whole-kernel corn (fresh, thawed frozen, or drained canned)**

⅛   **teaspoon pepper**

Beat eggs until foamy in large bowl. Combine flour, sugar, salt, baking powder, and nutmeg; add to eggs, and beat until smooth. Stir in evaporated milk, corn, and pepper, pour into 9" casserole at least 2" deep. Center casserole on microwave oven shelf or elevate on upside-down shallow bowl and microwave, uncovered, on HIGH (100% power) 3½–4 minutes until edges of pudding begin to set. Wrap edges all round with foil strips 2" wide and rotate casserole 90°. Microwave on MEDIUM (50% power) 20–22 minutes, rotating casserole 90° every 5 minutes, until pudding is set except for 1" circle in center (this will set as pudding stands). Remove foil collar, cover pudding with foil, shiny side down, and let stand 5 minutes before serving.

PER SERVING: 218 C   10 g P   9 g F   27 g CARB   497 mg S 155 mg CH

EGGPLANT

Some people recommend microwaving eggplants whole. We don't because they won't cook evenly unless turned every minute—a lot of bother. Here's our method:

Prick a 1¼–1½-pound, uniformly plump eggplant (no skinny end) in five or six places with a sharp fork to prevent skin from splitting, halve lengthwise, and place halves side by side, cut sides up and 1" apart, in a shallow casserole. Cover with lid or vented plastic food wrap and microwave on HIGH (100% power) 8–10 minutes, rotating casserole 180° at halftime, until eggplant is very soft. Cool until easy to handle and scrape out flesh (1 medium-size eggplant yields about 2 cups flesh). Use eggplant as recipes direct.

VARIATION

PARBOILED EGGPLANT: Microwave as directed but reduce time to 5 minutes; flesh should be *barely* tender. Transfer eggplant at once to large cold bowl (to stop cooking); use at once in recipes or chill and use later.

_R_ATATOUILLE
(PROVENÇAL EGGPLANT, ZUCCHINI, AND TOMATO STEW)

PREP TIME: 12 MINUTES COOKING TIME: 45–50 MINUTES STANDING TIME: 10 MINUTES

This tastes best if made ahead and reheated. For the ratatouille to develop proper flavor and consistency, the final slow microwaving is essential.

SERVES 6–8

1 **large yellow onion, peeled and minced**

2 **large cloves garlic, peeled and minced**

¼ **cup olive oil**

1 **medium-size eggplant (1¼ pounds), peeled, sliced ¼" thick, and each slice quartered**

2 **medium-size sweet green peppers, cored, seeded, and cut in ⅛" strips 2" long**

2 **medium-size zucchini (about ¾ pound), sliced ¼" thick**

2 **cups peeled, seeded, coarsely chopped red-ripe tomatoes or canned crushed tomatoes**

2 **tablespoons minced parsley**

1 **teaspoon salt**

¼ **teaspoon pepper**

Mix onion, garlic, and oil in 5-quart casserole at least 10" across, cover with wax paper, and microwave on HIGH (100% power) 4 minutes until glassy. Add all remaining ingredients, cover with lid, and microwave on HIGH (100% power) 18–21 minutes, stirring at halftime, until zucchini is barely tender. Stir again, re-cover, and microwave on MEDIUM (50% power) 10 minutes. Stir, cover with paper toweling, and microwave on MEDIUM (50% power) 13–15 minutes, stirring at halftime, until almost all juices have evaporated. Cover with lid and let stand 10 minutes. Serve hot, at room temperature, or cold.

PER SERVING: 139–104 C   3–2 g P   9–7 g F   13–10 g CARB 379–284 mg S   0–0 mg CH

To Reheat Refrigerated Ratatouille: Cover with lid or vented plastic food wrap and microwave on HIGH (100% power) 9–11 minutes, stirring every 3 minutes, until uniformly hot.

~~~~~~ V A R I A T I O N

RATATOUILLE NIÇOISE: Prepare as directed, but mix in ½ cup sliced, pitted ripe olives before final 15 minutes of cooking. Remove from microwave, mix in 3 minced anchovy fillets, if you like, cover, and chill 24 hours. Serve cold as an appetizer with crusty chunks of bread.

PER SERVING: 160–120 C   3–2 g P   12–9 g F   13–10 g CARB 463–347 mg S   0–0 mg CH

PERSIAN EGGPLANT KUKU

PREP TIME: | 3 MINUTES | COOKING TIME: | 19–20 MINUTES | STANDING TIME: | 10 MINUTES |

This Persian ''omelet'' can be served as a vegetable or first course.

SERVES 6

2   **large yellow onions, peeled and minced**

2   **tablespoons olive oil**

2   **cups cooked eggplant***

3   **eggs**

2   **tablespoons flour**

1   **teaspoon salt**

1   **teaspoon lemon juice**

1/8   **teaspoon pepper**

1/8   **teaspoon ground coriander**

1   **tablespoon butter or margarine**

Brown onions slowly in oil in skillet over moderate heat until color of caramel—about 5 minutes. Meanwhile, purée eggplant in food processor by churning 5–10 seconds or on HIGH in the electric blender. Add eggs and churn 5 seconds; sift in flour, add salt, lemon juice, pepper, and coriander, and churn 10 seconds. Add onions and churn 5 seconds. Spoon into 1½-quart glass ceramic casserole 8½" across and smooth top lightly. Cover with wax paper and microwave on HIGH (100% power) 3 minutes. Rotate casserole 90°, reduce power level to MEDIUM (50% power), and microwave 9–10 minutes, rotating casserole 90° every 3 minutes, until just firm. *Note: A dime-size area in middle may be soft, but this will set on standing.* Cover with foil, shiny side down, and let stand 10 minutes. Dot with butter, set 4" from heat in preheated broiler, and broil 2 minutes until speckly. Cut in diamonds or wedges and top, if desired, with yogurt.

PER SERVING: 133 C   4 g P   9 g F   8 g CARB   423 mg S 142 mg CH

455

ENDIVES

Trim medium-size (5-ounce) endives of root ends and brown or wilted leaves, halve lengthwise, and dip in ½ cup water mixed with 2 tablespoons lemon juice. Arrange in single layer, cut sides up and ½" apart, placing 2 halves side by side, more than two in a ring, spoke fashion. Add broth or water, cover with lid or vented plastic food wrap, and microwave as follows, rotating casserole 180° at halftime, until crisp-tender. Let stand, covered; drain and season.

Amount of Endives	Servings	Container	Chicken Broth or Water	Minutes on HIGH (100% power)	Minutes Standing Time
1	1	9" pie plate	2 T	4–5	2
2	2	10" pie plate	2 T	6–8	2
4	4	11" platter	4 T	9–10	3
6	6	11" platter	4 T	10–12	3

Seasoning Suggestions: Butter browned bread crumbs mixed with grated Parmesan cheese; Herb or Garlic Butter Sauce; Mornay, Hollandaise, or Warm Aioli Sauce; French Mayonnaise.

FENNEL

Trim medium-size (8-ounce) fennel bulbs of outer stalks, feathery tops, and tough bases. Lay bulbs on sides and trim each until 4″ long, then quarter lengthwise, and arrange 1″ apart in single layer in casserole with thinner ends toward center. Add broth or water, cover with lid or vented plastic food wrap, and microwave as follows, rotating casserole 180° at halftime, *just* until crisp-tender. Let stand, covered; drain and season.

Amount	Servings	Container	Chicken Broth or Water	Minutes on HIGH (100% power)	Minutes Standing Time
½ bulb	1	1-pint	2 T	4–6	2
1 bulb	2	1-quart	4 T	6–8	2
2 bulbs	4	2-quart	4 T	9–10	3
4 bulbs	6–8	11″ × 7″ × 2″	4 T	12–13	3

Seasoning Suggestions: Seasoned Butter or Lemon Butter Sauce; Warm Aioli Sauce or French Mayonnaise. Or marinate in refrigerator in a tart vinaigrette and serve cold.

VARIATIONS

PARBOILED FENNEL: Microwave as directed but reduce time 50% for 1, 2, and 4 servings, by 4 minutes for 6 servings. Drain at once (no standing), quick-chill 5 minutes in ice water, and drain again.

STEAMED FENNEL CHUNKS: Trim 1 pound fennel as directed, separate stalks, and cut in 1½″ chunks. Arrange in 2-quart casserole, add 2 tablespoons water, cover with lid, and microwave on HIGH (100% power) 9–10 minutes, stirring at halftime, until barely tender. Let stand, covered, 3 minutes. Drain well and serve with any suggested seasoning.

GREENS

Trim off roots, withered leaves, coarse stems, and leaf mid-ribs. *Note: Separate Swiss chard stalks and cook separately like Steamed Fennel Chunks.* Wash greens well, shake lightly but do not dry; slice large leaves ¼" thick, leave small ones whole. Place greens in casserole, add 1–2 peeled and bruised cloves garlic, if you like, cover with lid or vented plastic food wrap, and microwave as follows, stirring at halftime, until tender. Drain at once and season.

Broccoli di Rapa, Kale (1 pound, as purchased, serves 4):

Weight (as purchased)	Servings	Container	Water	Minutes on HIGH (100% power)	Standing Time
¼ lb.	1	1-pint	None	4–5	None
½ lb.	2	1-quart	None	5–7	None
1 lb.	4	2-quart	None	7–9	None
1½ lbs	6	3-quart	None	9–10	None

Beet Greens, Collards, Mustard Greens, Sorrel, Spinach, Swiss Chard, Turnip Greens (2 pounds, as purchased, serves 4):

Weight (as purchased)	Servings	Container	Water	Minutes on HIGH (100% power)	Standing Time
½ lb.	1	1-quart	None	2½–3½	None
1 lb. or 1 (10-oz.) cello bag	2	2-quart	None	4–6	None
2 lbs. or 2 (10-oz.) cello bags	4	3-quart	None	7–9	None
3 lbs.	6	5-quart	None	10–12	None

Seasoning Suggestions: Olive oil and vinegar (especially good on greens cooked with garlic), bacon drippings and crisp bacon crumbles.

V A R I A T I O N S

PURÉED GREENS (Serves 4): Purée 4 servings undrained cooked greens, add 4 teaspoons butter and ¼ teaspoon nutmeg. Return to casserole and microwave, uncovered, on HIGH (100% power) 2–4 minutes until hot. Stir well and serve.
PER SERVING: 78 C 4 g P 4 g F 9 g CARB 495 mg S 10 mg CH

ESPARREGADO (PORTUGUESE GREENS) (Serves 4): Cook 4 servings any greens with 2 cloves garlic as directed, drain well, then purée; mix in 1 robust tablespoon olive oil, ¾ teaspoon salt, and ¼ teaspoon freshly ground black pepper. Return to casserole and microwave, uncovered, on HIGH (100% power) 2–4 minutes until hot.
PER SERVING: 83 C 4 g P 4 g F 10 g CARB 868 mg S 0 mg CH

CREAMED SPINACH (Serves 2): Purée 1 pound undrained, cooked spinach, spoon into 1-quart casserole; blend 2 tablespoons flour, ¼ cup milk, ¼ teaspoon salt, and ⅛ teaspoon each pepper and nutmeg and mix into spinach. Dot with 2 tablespoons butter and microwave, uncovered, on HIGH (100% power) 3–4 minutes, stirring at halftime, until bubbly. *Note: You can substitute 1 (10-ounce) package frozen chopped spinach for the fresh.*
PER SERVING: 202 C 9 g P 13 g F 16 g CARB 561 mg S 35 mg CH

SPINACH BALLS WITH TOMATO SAUCE

PREP TIME: | 8 MINUTES | COOKING TIME: | 10–11 MINUTES | STANDING TIME: | 5 MINUTES |

SERVES 6

- **4 packages (10 ounces each) frozen chopped spinach, cooked and drained**
- **1 medium-size yellow onion, peeled and minced**
- **1 clove garlic, peeled and minced**
- **1 tablespoon butter or margarine**
- **⅓ cup fine dry bread crumbs**
- **¼ cup finely grated Parmesan cheese**
- **1 egg white, lightly beaten**
- **½ teaspoon salt**
- **⅛ teaspoon pepper**
- **2 cups hot Jiffy Tomato Sauce or marinara sauce**

Squeeze spinach as dry as possible and set aside. Mix onion, garlic, and butter in 1-pint casserole, cover with wax paper, and microwave on HIGH (100% power) 4–5 minutes until glassy. Mix into spinach along with all but last ingredient. Shape into 1″ balls and arrange ½″ apart on 11″ round platter. Cover with wax paper and microwave on HIGH (100% power) 6 minutes, rotating platter 180° at halftime. Let stand, covered, 5 minutes. Top with sauce and serve hot as a vegetable or vegetarian entrée.

PER SERVING: 181 C   10 g P   9 g F   20 g CARB   968 mg S 9 mg CH

KOHLRABI

Peel and cut medium-size (6-ounce) bulbs in ½" cubes. Place in casserole, add water, cover with lid or vented plastic food wrap, and microwave as follows, rotating casserole 180° at halftime, *just* until crisp-tender. Let stand, covered; drain and season.

Amount	Servings	Container	Water	Minutes on HIGH (100% power)	Minutes Standing Time
⅔ C	1	1-pint	2 T	4–5	3
1¼ C	2	1-quart	2 T	6–7	3
2½ C	4	1½-quart	4 T	8–9	3
4 C	6	2-quart	4 T	9–11	3

Seasoning Suggestions: Mash and mix with a little melted butter or heavy cream; mix cubes with Cheese Sauce, Mornay, Béchamel, or Medium White Sauce, allowing ¼–⅓ cup per serving.

 V A R I A T I O N S

PARBOILED KOHLRABI: Microwave as directed but reduce time 50%. Drain at once (no standing), quick-chill 5 minutes in ice water, and drain again.

LEEKS

Choose leeks about 1" in diameter, remove roots, tough green tops, and coarse outer layers; wash carefully to remove grit, drain, and slice 1" thick. *Note: Whole leeks won't cook evenly.* Place in casserole, add water, cover with lid or vented plastic food wrap, and microwave as follows, stirring at halftime, until crisp-tender. Let stand, covered; drain and season.

Weight (as purchased)	Servings	Container	Water	Minutes on HIGH (100% power)	Minutes Standing Time
½ lb.	1	1-pint	1 T	5–7	2
1 lb.	2	1-quart	2 T	7–9	2
2 lbs.	4	2-quart	2 T	9–12	2
3 lbs.	6	3-quart	3 T	12–15	2

Seasoning Suggestions: Mornay, Béchamel, Sweet Red Pepper Sauce, Warm Aioli or Cheese Sauce; Beurre Noir.

 V A R I A T I O N S

PARBOILED LEEKS: Microwave as directed but reduce time 50%. Drain at once (no standing), quick-chill 5 minutes in ice water, and drain again.

STEAMED SCALLIONS (Serves 4): Trim 1 pound (about 4 bunches medium-size) scallions of root ends and all but 2" tops. Arrange in shallow casserole with bulbs outward, add 2 tablespoons water, cover with lid or vented plastic food wrap, and microwave on HIGH (100% power) 3–4 minutes, rotating 180° at halftime, until *barely* tender. Let stand, covered, 2 minutes. Drain, season with salt, pepper, and 4 teaspoons butter. Or serve with Béchamel or Cheese Sauce.
PER SERVING: 58 C 2 g P 4 g F 5 g CARB 43 mg S 10 mg CH

MUSHROOMS

For best results, choose commercially grown white mushrooms about 1½" in diameter. Discard woody stem ends, wipe clean, then:

For Whole Mushrooms: Arrange, not touching, in circle in round container, preferably in ring around edge. Cover with paper toweling and microwave as follows, rotating container 180° at halftime. Season and serve at once.

Weight (as purchased)	Servings	Container	Water	Minutes on HIGH (100% power)	Standing Time
¼ lb.	1	8" pie plate	None	2	None
½ lb.	2	10" pie plate	None	2–3	None
1 lb.	4	11" platter	None	4–5	None
1½ lbs.†	6	12" platter	None	6–7	None

†Cook in 2 batches, rearranging mushrooms at halftime.

For Mushroom Caps: Arrange and microwave as directed for whole mushrooms, but reduce times 30–40 seconds.

For Sliced Mushrooms: Slice mushrooms ¼" thick, arrange in casserole, cover with paper toweling, and microwave as directed for whole mushrooms, stirring at halftime, until crisp-tender.

Seasoning Suggestions: Seasoned Butter, Beurre Noir, or Garlic Butter Sauce; Mornay, Béchamel, Chantilly, or Medium White Sauce; melted butter and Madeira.

 V A R I A T I O N

 MUSHROOMS WITH ONION (Serves 4): Mix 1 pound sliced mushrooms, ⅓ cup minced yellow onion, and 2 tablespoons butter in 2-quart casserole; cover with paper toweling and microwave on HIGH (100% power) 5–7 minutes, stirring at halftime, until crisp-tender. Mix in 1 teaspoon steak sauce, salt and pepper to taste. Serve with grilled steaks or chops.

PER SERVING: 85 C 3 g P 6 g F 6 g CARB 86 mg S 16 mg CH

FINNISH MUSHROOMS WITH SOUR CREAM AND DILL

PREP TIME: 5 MINUTES   COOKING TIME: 5½–7 MINUTES   STANDING TIME: NONE

SERVES 4

1   pound medium-size mushrooms, wiped clean and quartered

3   scallions, minced (white part only)

1   cup sour cream, at room temperature

1–2 tablespoons snipped fresh dill or ½ teaspoon dill weed

¼   teaspoon salt

Pinch pepper

Mix mushrooms and scallions in 2-quart casserole at least 9" across. Cover with wax paper and microwave on HIGH (100% power) 4–5 minutes, stirring at halftime. Mix in all remaining ingredients, re-cover, and microwave on MEDIUM (50% power) 1½–2 minutes. Do not boil or sour cream may curdle. Serve at once.

PER SERVING: 155 C   4 g P   13 g F   8 g CARB   171 mg S   25 mg CH

PECAN-STUFFED MUSHROOMS

PREP TIME: | 5 MINUTES | COOKING TIME: | 5½–7½ MINUTES | STANDING TIME: | NONE

These mushrooms can be stuffed ahead of time and refrigerated until shortly before serving. Microwave as directed, but increase cooking time by about 2 minutes.

SERVES 4

16 medium-size mushrooms (about ¾ pound), wiped clean

½ cup minced pecans

2 tablespoons unsalted butter

2 tablespoons minced parsley

2 tablespoons minced chives

2 tablespoons toasted bread crumbs

½ teaspoon salt

⅛ teaspoon pepper

Carefully remove mushroom stems, chop fine, and place in 1½-quart casserole with pecans, butter, parsley, and chives. Cover with wax paper and microwave on HIGH (100% power) 2 minutes. Mix in crumbs, salt, and pepper; stuff mixture into mushroom caps, mounding it in center. Arrange caps on 11"–12" round platter with smaller ones in center. Microwave, uncovered, 3½–5½ minutes until stuffing is hot, rotating platter 180° at halftime and rearranging mushrooms around rim that may cook faster. Serve at once as a vegetable or use to garnish a meat or poultry platter.

PER SERVING: 176 C   3 g P   15 g F   9 g CARB   302 mg S 16 mg CH

465

OKRA

The good news: Microwaved okra *isn't* slimy! Stem pods (without rupturing) and if small, leave whole. Otherwise, slice 1" thick. Arrange in casserole, add water, cover with lid or vented plastic food wrap, and microwave as follows, stirring at halftime, until *barely* tender. Let stand, covered; drain and season to taste.

Weight (as purchased)	Servings	Container	Water	Minutes on HIGH (100% power)	Minutes Standing Time
¼ lb.	1	1-quart	1 T	2–3	1
½ lb.	2	1½-quart	1 T	3½–4	1
1 lb.	4	2-quart	1 T	5–6	1
1½ lbs.	6	2½-quart	1 T	6–8	1

Seasoning Suggestions: Seasoned Butter, Lemon or Garlic Butter Sauce; or toss with minced cooked scallions and hot stewed tomatoes.

 VARIATION

PARBOILED OKRA: Cook as directed but reduce time 1 minute for 1–2 servings, 2 minutes for 4–6. Drain at once (no standing), quick-chill 5 minutes in ice water, and drain again.

═ ONIONS

 Small White Onions (16–18 per pound): Peel, arrange in casserole, add beef or chicken broth, dry white wine or water, cover with lid or vented plastic food wrap, and microwave as follows, stirring at halftime, until crisp-tender. Let stand, covered; drain, and season.

Weight (as purchased)	Servings	Container	Broth, Wine, or Water	Minutes on HIGH (100% power)	Minutes Standing Time
¼ lb.	1	1-pint	2 T	4–5	3
½ lb.	2	1-quart	2 T	5–7	3
1 lb.	4	1½-quart	2 T	7–10	3
1½ lbs.	6	2-quart	2 T	10–12	3

Seasoning Suggestions: Medium White or Cheese Sauce, Béchamel or Mornay Sauce; Seasoned Butter, Beurre Noir, or Jiffy Herb Butter.

 V A R I A T I O N

PARBOILED WHITE ONIONS: Microwave as directed but reduce time 50%. Drain at once (no standing), quick-chill 5 minutes in ice water, and drain again.

YELLOW ONIONS: Peel; slice tissue-thin, or mince. Place in casserole with or without butter or oil, cover with wax paper, and microwave as follows, stirring at halftime, until crisp-tender or glassy. Let *sliced onions* stand, covered.

Amount	Servings	Container	Butter or Oil	Minutes on HIGH (100% power)	Minutes Standing Time
½ C (1 medium)	1	1-pint	1–2 t	3½–4	2
1 C (2 medium)	2	1-pint	1 T	5–6	2
2 C (4 medium)	4	1-quart	2 T	6–8	2
3 C (6 medium)	6	1½-quart	3 T	9–11	2

Seasoning Suggestions: Crumbled dried thyme or rosemary; freshly grated nutmeg.

ONION TIAN

This Provençal gratin owes its name to the shallow earthenware dish in which it's cooked.

SERVES 6

- 2 **pounds Spanish onions, peeled, sliced ⅛" thick, and separated into rings**
- 1 **medium-size carrot, peeled, and grated moderately fine**
- 1 **clove garlic, peeled and bruised**
- 1 **tablespoon olive oil**
- 1 **tablespoon butter**
- 2 **tablespoons flour**
- 1 **cup milk**
- 1 **bay leaf tied in cheesecloth with 1 sprig each parsley and thyme (bouquet garni)**
- ½ **teaspoon salt**
- ⅛ **teaspoon pepper**
- ¼ **cup heavy cream**

Topping:

- ½ **cup soft white bread crumbs**
- 2 **tablespoons finely grated Parmesan cheese**
- 1 **tablespoon olive oil**

Spread onions in 3-quart glass ceramic casserole at least 10" across, cover with lid or vented plastic food wrap, and microwave on HIGH (100% power) 11–12 minutes, stirring at halftime, until onions are just tender. Let stand, covered, while you proceed. Place carrot, garlic, oil, and butter in 6-cup measure, cover with plastic food wrap, and microwave on HIGH (100% power) 3–4 minutes until carrot is soft. Blend in flour and microwave, uncovered, 30 seconds until foamy. Whisk in milk, add bouquet garni, salt, and pepper and microwave, uncovered, on HIGH (100% power) 3½–4 minutes, whisking at halftime, until sauce boils and thickens. Drain liquid from onions into sauce, stir in cream, and strain sauce over onions. Mix well and microwave, uncovered, on HIGH (100% power) 4 minutes, stirring at halftime, until uniformly hot. Mix topping, scatter evenly over onions, set 4" from heat in preheated broiler, and broil 2–3 minutes until lightly browned.

PER SERVING: 198 C   5 g P   13 g F   18 g CARB   289 g S 26 mg CH

469

Parsnips

Trim medium-size (4 per pound) parsnips of root ends and tops and peel. Cut in 3"–4" chunks, halve slim ends lengthwise, quarter thick ones. Arrange in casserole with slimmer pieces in center, add water, and, if desired, a peeled ½"–1" cube fresh ginger; cover with lid or vented plastic food wrap and microwave as follows, stirring at halftime but keeping smaller pieces in middle, until tender. Let stand, covered; drain and season.

Weight (as purchased)	Servings	Container	Water or Broth	Minutes on HIGH (100% power)	Minutes Standing Time
6 ounces	1	1-quart	2 T	3–4	2
¾ lb.	2	1½-quart	4 T	4–6	3
1½ lbs.	4	2-quart	4 T	7–9	3
2 lb.	6	2½-quart	4 T	9–12	3

Seasoning Suggestions: Lemon or Herb Butter; Medium White Sauce or Béchamel.

————————————————————————— V A R I A T I O N S

PARBOILED PARSNIPS: Microwave as directed but reduce cooking time 1 minute for 1 serving, 2 minutes for 2, and 3 minutes for 4–6. Drain at once (no standing), quick-chill 5 minutes in ice water, and drain again.

MASHED PARSNIPS (Serves 4): Mash 1½ pounds drained, cooked parsnips with 2 tablespoons each butter and heavy cream, salt and pepper to taste.
PER SERVING: 204 C 2 g P 9 g F 31 g CARB 78 mg S 26 mg CH

LEMON-GLAZED PARSNIPS (Serves 4): Microwave 1½ pounds parsnips as directed, but do not let stand. Drain, add 2 tablespoons each butter and dark brown sugar and 1 tablespoon lemon juice (or orange or pineapple), cover with wax paper, and microwave on HIGH (100% power) 4 minutes, stirring at halftime, until nicely glazed.
PER SERVING: 205 C 2 g P 6 g F 37 g CARB 78 mg S 16 mg CH

PEAS

Shell peas (1 pound = about 1 cup shelled peas), place in container; add water, a sprig or two of mint, rosemary, or chervil, if you like. Cover with lid or vented plastic food wrap and microwave as follows, stirring at halftime, until barely tender. Season and serve.

Amount	Servings	Container	Water or Butter	Minutes on HIGH (100% power)	Standing Time
⅔ C	1	6-ounce	1 T	2–2½	None
1⅓ C	2	1-quart	2 T	3–5	None
2⅔ C	4	1½-quart	2 T	5–7	None
4 C	6	2-quart	2 T	8–10	None

Seasoning Suggestions: Finely slivered orange rind, chopped mint and melted butter; heavy cream and nutmeg; Curry, Lemon, or Herb Butter Sauce; Medium White Sauce, Béchamel, or Mornay.

VARIATION

PARBOILED PEAS: Microwave as directed but reduce cooking time 1 minute for 1–2 servings, 2 minutes for 4–6. Drain at once (no standing), quick-chill 5 minutes in ice water, and drain again.

≈ PEPPERS

Core, seed, and cut in ½" strips. Place in shallow casserole, add water, cover with lid or vented plastic food wrap, and microwave as follows, stirring at halftime, until crisp-tender. Season at once and serve. *Note: Red and yellow peppers cook faster than green, so check after minimum cooking time.*

No. of 6-ounce Peppers	Servings	Container	Water	Minutes on HIGH (100% power)	Standing Time
1	1	1-pint	1 T	2–3	None
2	2	1-quart	2 T	4–6	None
4	4	2-quart	2 T	6–8	None
6	6	3-quart	2 T	8–10	None

Seasoning Suggestions: Seasoned or Garlic Butter.

VARIATIONS

DICED PEPPERS: Core peppers, seed, and cut in ¼" dice. Microwave as directed, substituting butter, olive, or vegetable oil for water and reducing cooking time 1 minute for 1–2 servings, 2–3 minutes for 4–6.

STEAMED, PEELED WHOLE PEPPERS: Place 2 peppers in plastic bag, twist neck and knot, set bag on oven floor, and microwave red or yellow peppers on HIGH (100% power) 5–6 minutes, green peppers 6–8, turning bag over and rotating 180° at halftime, until peppers are soft. Let green peppers stand in bag 5 minutes; red and yellow peppers need no standing time. Cool peppers under cold running water; core, peel, seed, and pat dry.

ITALIAN PEPPERS AND ONIONS (Serves 6): Core 1 pound green Italian peppers, seed, and cut in ½" strips. Mix with 2 thinly sliced medium-size yellow onions, 1 minced clove garlic, 2 tablespoons olive oil, and ½ teaspoon each crumbled dried basil and oregano or marjoram in 3-quart casserole. Cover with lid or vented plastic food wrap and microwave on HIGH (100% power) 7–9 minutes, stirring at halftime, until vegetables are crisp-tender. Let stand, covered, 3 minutes. If you like, brown 3"–4" from heat in preheated broiler 2–3 minutes. Serve as a vegetable or steak garnish or use in hero sandwiches.

PER SERVING: 66 C   1 g P   5 g F   6 g CARB   3 mg S   0 mg CH

SWEET RED PEPPER CONFIT

PREP TIME: [5 MINUTES] COOKING TIME: [23–25 MINUTES] STANDING TIME: [NONE]

MAKES ABOUT 2½ CUPS

4 **large sweet red peppers (about 2 pounds)**

½ **medium-size Spanish onion, peeled and minced**

1 **tablespoon butter or margarine**

1 **tablespoon vegetable oil**

1 **tablespoon red wine vinegar**

1 **tablespoon sugar**

Place 2 peppers in each of 2 plastic bags, twist ends and knot, place on oven floor 1" apart, and microwave on HIGH (100% power) 9–10 minutes, turning bags over and rotating 180° at halftime, until peppers are soft. Cool peppers under running cold water; pat dry, peel, seed, chop coarsely, and reserve. Mix onion with butter and oil in 1½-quart casserole, cover with wax paper, and microwave on HIGH (100% power) 4–5 minutes until soft. Mix in peppers, vinegar, and sugar, cover with paper toweling, and microwave on HIGH (100% power) 10 minutes, stirring at halftime. Cool slightly, then purée in food processor by churning 10–15 seconds. Serve warm with scallops or other delicate seafood. Also delicious with grilled pork or lamb chops.

PER CUP: 197 C   3 g P   11 g F   24 g CARB   57 mg S   12 mg CH

473

POTATOES

¢ *Baked Potatoes:* Scrub evenly shaped baking potatoes (no pointed ends) of uniform size, pierce deeply in several places, arrange 1″ apart on double-thickness paper toweling on oven floor (use shelf, too, if baking more than 6 potatoes), arranging 3 potatoes in a triangle, 4 or more in a circle. Microwave, uncovered, as follows, turning potatoes over and if baking more than 2, rearranging at halftime, until fork-tender. Let stand, uncovered. Season and serve. *Note: To crisp skin, omit standing time; prick potatoes again, set on rack of preheated 500° F. conventional oven, and bake 5–10 minutes.*

No. of 8–9-ounce Potatoes	Servings	Container	Water	Minutes on HIGH (100% power)	Minutes Standing Time
1	1	None	None	4–5	3
2	2	None	None	7–9	3
4	4	None	None	11–13	3
6	6	None	None	15–18	3
8†	8	None	None	20–24	3

†Do not microwave more than 8 potatoes at one time; do in batches.

Seasoning Suggestions: Minced dill pickle and crisp crumbled bacon; melted butter and minced chives, scallions, fresh mint, or coriander (cilantro).

V A R I A T I O N

¢ MASHED POTATOES: (Serves 4): Microwave 4 cups ½″ cubes baking potatoes with ¼ cup water in covered 2-quart casserole on HIGH (100% power) 10–11 minutes, stirring at halftime; let stand 3 minutes, drain, cover with paper toweling, and microwave on HIGH (100% power) 1 minute. Mash and beat in ¼ cup each melted butter and warm milk, salt and pepper to taste. If dinner must wait, cover casserole with wax paper and reheat by microwaving on HIGH (100% power) 2–3 minutes, stirring at halftime.
PER SERVING: 245 C 4 g P 12 g F 31 g CARB 135 mg S 33 mg CH

¢ *Steamed All-Purpose Potatoes:* Scrub potatoes of even shape and size, peel or not, halve, arrange in single layer in casserole, add water, cover with lid or vented plastic food wrap, and microwave as follows, rearranging at halftime, until fork-tender. Let stand, covered; drain, season, and serve.

No. of 5-ounce Potatoes	Servings	Container	Water	Minutes on HIGH (100% power)	Minutes Standing Time
1	1	1-pint	¼ C	3–4	2–3
2	2	1-quart	¼ C	4–6	2–3
4	4	2-quart	½ C	7–9	3
6	6	3-quart	½ C	9–11	3

Seasoning Suggestions: Melted butter and minced chives, scallions, fresh mint or coriander (cilantro).

V A R I A T I O N

¢ PARBOILED HALVED POTATOES: Microwave as directed but reduce time 50%. Drain at once (no standing), quick-chill 5 minutes in ice water, drain again, and pat dry on paper toweling.

¢ *Steamed Cubed All-Purpose Potatoes:* Peel potatoes and cut in ½" cubes. Place in casserole, add water, cover with lid or vented plastic food wrap, and microwave as follows, stirring at halftime, until crisp-tender. Let stand, covered; drain, season, and serve.

Amount	Servings	Container	Water	Minutes on HIGH (100% power)	Minutes Standing Time
1 C	1	1-pint	2 T	4–5	3
2 C	2	1-quart	4 T	6–8	3
4 C	4	2-quart	4 T	9–10	3
6 C	6	3-quart	4 T	11–13	3

Seasoning Suggestions: Cheese, Onion, or Medium White Sauce; Warm Aioli or Hot Mustard Mayonnaise.

¢ **PARBOILED CUBED POTATOES**: Microwave as directed but reduce time 50%. Drain at once (no standing), quick-chill 5 minutes in ice water, drain again, and pat dry on paper toweling.

¢ *Steamed Whole New Potatoes:* Scrub and prick small (8–9 per pound) new potatoes, or peel thin strip around center of each. Arrange in single layer in casserole with smaller potatoes in middle, add water, and, if desired, a bay leaf or mint sprig. Cover with lid or vented plastic food wrap and microwave as follows, rearranging at halftime, until *barely* tender. Let stand, covered; drain, season, and serve.

Weight (as purchased)	Servings	Container	Water	Minutes on HIGH (100% power)	Minutes Standing Time
6 oz.	1	1-pint	2 T	4–5	2
¾ lb.	2	1-quart	4 T	5–6	3
1½ lbs.	4	2-quart	4 T	7–9	3
2¼ lbs.	6	3-quart	4 T	10–12	3

Seasoning Suggestions: Seasoned Butter, Beurre Noisette; any of the following butter sauces: Lemon, Chili, Curry, or Garlic.

¢ **DANISH GLAZED NEW POTATOES**: (Serves 4): Peel 1½ pounds cooked small new potatoes, place in 2-quart casserole with ¼ cup firmly packed brown sugar, 2 tablespoons butter, cut in pieces, 1 tablespoon each water and freshly snipped dill, and ½ teaspoon salt. Cover with wax paper and microwave on HIGH (100% power) 4 minutes, stirring at halftime. Uncover, turn potatoes over, and microwave on HIGH (100% power) 4 minutes, again turning at halftime. Cool 1 minute, spoon glaze over potatoes, and serve.

PER SERVING: 226 C   3 g P   6 g F   42 g CARB   346 mg S   16 mg CH

POTATOES À LA DAUPHINOISE

PREP TIME: **10 MINUTES**   COOKING TIME: **35–39 MINUTES**   STANDING TIME: **NONE***

In a microwave you can scallop potatoes the classic French way in half the time. The final simmering on MEDIUM (50% power) prevents boilover and thickens the sauce.

SERVES 6

- **5 cups very thin slices all-purpose potatoes of uniform thickness**
- **1 cup heavy cream**
- **2 tablespoons butter (no substitute)**
- **1 clove garlic, peeled and bruised**
- **1 teaspoon flour blended with 1 teaspoon cold water**
- **1 teaspoon salt**
- **⅛ teaspoon white pepper**
- **Pinch ground nutmeg**

Arrange potatoes in 2½- or 3-quart glass ceramic casserole at least 10" across. Cover with lid and microwave on HIGH (100% power) 5 minutes, stirring at halftime. Remove casserole from oven. Pour cream into 6-cup measure, add butter and garlic, and heat, uncovered, on HIGH (100% power) 1½–2 minutes until steaming, not boiling. Discard garlic. Mix in remaining ingredients, pour over potatoes, cover with wax paper, and microwave on MEDIUM (50% power) 23–27 minutes. After 15 minutes stir gently, lightly press potatoes flat, and rotate casserole 180°. When potatoes are tender, cover and let stand while broiler preheats. Set 4" from heat in preheated broiler and broil 5 minutes until richly browned.

PER SERVING: 272 C   4 g P   19 g F   24 g CARB   428 mg S   65 mg CH

POTATOES HANNA
(POTATO AND ONION PIE)

PREP TIME: | 10 MINUTES | COOKING TIME: | 16–18 MINUTES | STANDING TIME: | NONE

The classic Potatoes Anna is tedious to make. This version tastes and looks almost as good and, thanks to the microwave, cooks three times as fast.

SERVES 4

- 4 cups very thin slices all-purpose potatoes of uniform thickness
- 1 medium-size yellow onion, peeled and minced
- ¼ teaspoon pepper
- 3 tablespoons butter or margarine
- 1 teaspoon salt
- ¼ cup heavy cream

Layer potatoes, onion, and pepper in glass ceramic casserole 10" across and 2" deep. Dot with butter, cover with lid, and microwave on HIGH (100% power) 9–10 minutes, stirring gently at halftime, until just tender. Press potatoes down compactly with pancake turner. Mix salt with cream and pour on top. Set 5"–6" from heat in preheated broiler and broil 7–8 minutes until top is crispy-brown. Cut in 4 wedges and serve with grilled steaks or chops.

For 2 Servings: Prepare as directed in 9" glass ceramic pie plate, halving each ingredient and covering with vented plastic food wrap. Microwave on HIGH (100% power) 6–7 minutes and broil as directed to brown.

PER SERVING: 253 C 4 g P 14 g F 30 g CARB 653 mg S 44 mg CH

〜〜〜〜〜 V A R I A T I O N

SCALLOPED POTATOES: Layer potatoes, onion, and pepper in casserole as directed. Dot with 2 tablespoons butter, mix salt with ¼ cup each milk and water, and pour over potatoes. Cover with lid and microwave on HIGH (100%

power) 4 minutes. Stir, re-cover, and microwave on MEDIUM (50% power) 20–23 minutes, stirring gently at halftime, until tender. Let stand, covered, 3 minutes. Sprinkle with paprika and serve.

For 2 Servings: Prepare as directed, halving each ingredient and using casserole 6½" across and 2" deep. Microwave on HIGH (100% power) 2 minutes, then on MEDIUM (50% power) 9–10 minutes as recipe directs.

PER SERVING: 186 C   4 g P   6 g F   29 g CARB   626 mg S 18 mg CH

HOT CURRIED POTATOES

PREP TIME: 10 MINUTES   COOKING TIME: 15–18 MINUTES   STANDING TIME: 3 MINUTES

¢

SERVES 6

6	cups all-purpose potatoes, peeled and cut in ½" cubes
1	large yellow onion, peeled and minced
¼	teaspoon mustard seeds
½	cup chicken broth
2	teaspoons curry powder
1	tablespoon lime or lemon juice
1¼	teaspoons salt
⅛	teaspoon black pepper
⅛	teaspoon red pepper flakes
2	tablespoons butter, margarine, or vegetable oil

Toss potatoes with onion and mustard seeds in 2½- or 3-quart casserole at least 10" across. Mix broth, curry powder, lime juice, salt, black pepper, and red pepper flakes, pour over potatoes, dot with butter, cover with lid, and microwave on HIGH (100% power) 13–15 minutes, stirring at halftime, until potatoes are almost tender. Stir again, cover with wax paper, and microwave on HIGH (100% power) 2–3 minutes until very little liquid remains. Cover and let stand 3 minutes. Toss again and serve.

PER SERVING: 168 C   4 g P   4 g F   30 g CARB   590 mg S 10 mg CH

SWEET POTATOES AND YAMS

Scrub evenly shaped potatoes of uniform size, pierce deeply in several places, arrange 1" apart on double-thickness paper toweling on oven floor (use shelf, too, if baking more than 6 potatoes), arranging 3 potatoes in a triangle, 4 or more in a circle. Microwave, uncovered, as follows, turning potatoes over and if baking more than 2, rearranging at halftime, until fork-tender. Let stand, uncovered. Season and serve.

No. of 8–10-ounce Potatoes	Servings	Container	Water	Minutes on HIGH (100% power)	Minutes Standing Time
1	1	None	None	4–5	3
2	2	None	None	6–8	3
4	4	None	None	10–12	3
6	6	None	None	14–17	3
8†	8	None	None	18–22	3

†Do not microwave more than 8 potatoes at one time; do in batches.

Seasoning Suggestions: Maple syrup, honey, dark or light brown sugar; rum or Madeira wine; orange juice and rind; ginger, cinnamon, and mace.

SPICED KUMARA (SWEET POTATOES)

PREP TIME: 8 MINUTES | COOKING TIME: 19-22 MINUTES | STANDING TIME: 2 MINUTES

In the Orient, sweet potatoes (*kumara*) are glazed and spiced.

SERVES 6

- **4 large sweet potatoes or yams (2–2½ pounds), peeled and sliced ½" thick**
- **⅓ cup water**
- **¼ cup firmly packed dark brown sugar**
- **2 tablespoons butter or margarine**
- **1 clove garlic, peeled and crushed**
- **1 tablespoon lemon juice**
- **1 teaspoon chili powder**
- **1 teaspoon salt**
- **1" piece fresh ginger, peeled and minced**
- **¼ teaspoon pepper**
- **⅛ teaspoon ground cinnamon**

Arrange sweet potatoes in 13" × 8" × 2" casserole, add water, cover with lid, and microwave on HIGH (100% power) 13–15 minutes, rearranging slices at halftime, until barely tender; drain in colander. In same casserole combine remaining ingredients, cover with lid, and microwave on HIGH (100% power) 1 minute. Return sweet potatoes to casserole and mix gently to coat. Re-cover and microwave on HIGH (100% power) 5–6 minutes, turning potatoes in glaze at halftime, until very tender. Let stand, covered, 2 minutes.

PER SERVING: 200 C   2 g P   4 g F   39 g CARB   429 mg S   10 mg CH

VARIATION

ORANGE CANDIED SWEET POTATOES OR YAMS: Microwave and drain sweet potatoes as directed. In same casserole, place ¼ cup each firmly packed dark brown sugar and butter or margarine, 2 tablespoons orange juice, and 2 teaspoons finely grated orange rind; cover with lid and microwave on HIGH (100% power) 1 minute. Return sweet potatoes to casserole and proceed as directed.

PER SERVING: 234 C   2 g P   8 g F   39 g CARB   97 mg S   21 mg CH

PUMPKIN

Halve a 4–5-pound pumpkin, cover cut sides with plastic food wrap, and place cut-side up at least 1" apart on paper toweling on oven floor, allowing at least 2" around edge, or use oven shelf, staggering position of pumpkin halves and repositioning them at halftime. Microwave on HIGH (100% power) 18–22 minutes, rotating halves 180° at halftime, until fork-tender. Wrap each half in foil and let stand 10 minutes. Discard seeds, remove pumpkin from skin, and cut into cubes (4–5 pounds pumpkin = 4–5 cups cubed pumpkin) or mash (4–5 pounds pumpkin = 3–4 cups mashed pumpkin). Season and serve or use as recipes direct.

Seasoning Suggestions: Maple syrup or sugar, honey, or brown sugar plus a pinch ground ginger, cinnamon, or mace.

V A R I A T I O N

PUMPKIN PURÉE: (Makes 3–4 cups): Microwave 4–5-pound pumpkin as directed until very soft, 20–25 minutes. Let stand, discard seeds, scrape pulp into food processor, and purée by buzzing 10–15 seconds. Use in any recipe calling for pumpkin purée.

RUTABAGA

Peel rutabaga and cut in ½" cubes. Place in casserole, add water, cover with lid or vented plastic food wrap, and microwave as follows, stirring at halftime, until fork-tender. Let stand, covered; drain, season, and serve.

Amount	Servings	Container	Water	Minutes on HIGH (100% power)	Minutes Standing Time
1 C	1	1-pint	4 T	5–7	3
2 C	2	1-quart	4 T	9–11	3
4 C	4	2-quart	4 T	12–14	3
6 C	6	3-quart	4 T	15–18	3

Seasoning Suggestions: Sour cream and crumbled crisp bacon; Herb Butter Sauce. Combine with an equal part cooked diced carrots and season to taste with butter, salt, and pepper.

VARIATION

¢ **MASHED RUTABAGA:** Cook as directed, but increase cooking times 1–2 minutes until rutabaga is soft. Mash and microwave, uncovered, on HIGH (100% power) 2–3 minutes to drive off excess moisture. Season to taste with butter, salt, and pepper, adding, if you like, a pinch each ground ginger, cinnamon, and nutmeg or mace.

SCOTTISH NEEPS

PREP TIME: 8 MINUTES   COOKING TIME: 21–24 MINUTES   STANDING TIME: 3 MINUTES

''Turn-NEEP'' is what Scots call rutabaga and here's how they like it best.

SERVES 6

1   rutabaga (about 2½ pounds), peeled and cut in ½" cubes

1   large Idaho potato, peeled and cut in 1" cubes

¼   cup water

2   tablespoons melted butter or margarine

2   tablespoons Scotch whisky

1   teaspoon salt

⅛   teaspoon ground cinnamon

⅛   teaspoon ground nutmeg

⅛   teaspoon ground ginger

Place rutabaga, potato, and water in 3-quart casserole, cover with lid, and microwave on HIGH (100% power) 17–20 minutes, stirring at halftime, until vegetables are fork-tender. Let stand, covered, 3 minutes, then drain well and mash. Beat in remaining ingredients, return to casserole, cover with wax paper, and microwave on MEDIUM (50% power) 4 minutes to warm and blend flavors.

PER SERVING: 117 C   3 g P   4 g F   19 g CARB   440 mg S   10 mg CH

483

VEGETABLES, GRAINS, PASTAS, AND OTHER SIDE DISHES

SNOW PEAS AND SUGAR SNAPS

Remove stem ends and "strings," arrange in casserole (add no water; rinse water clinging to pods is sufficient), cover with lid or vented plastic food wrap, and microwave as follows, stirring at halftime, until crisp-tender. Let stand, covered; drain and season.

Weight (as purchased)	Servings	Container	Water	Minutes on HIGH (100% power)	Minutes Standing Time
2 oz.	1	1-pint	None	1	2
¼ lb.	2	1-quart	None	1½–1¾	2
½ lb.	4	1½-quart	None	2½–3½	2
¾–1 lb.	6	2-quart	None	4–5	2

Seasoning Suggestions: Seasoned Butter, Beurre Noisette, Jiffy Garlic Butter; soy sauce, rice wine vinegar, and minced fresh ginger; toasted sesame seeds,* Oriental sesame oil, minced garlic, and soy sauce.

VARIATION

PARBOILED SNOW PEAS OR SUGAR SNAPS: Microwave as directed but reduce time 50%. Drain at once (no standing), quick-chill 5 minutes in ice water, and drain again.

SPINACH (See Greens)

INDONESIAN SNOW PEAS AND RED PEPPER IN PEANUT SAUCE

PREP TIME: **8 MINUTES** COOKING TIME: **7-8 MINUTES** STANDING TIME: **NONE***

SERVES 4

- 1 **large sweet red pepper, cored, seeded, and cut in ⅛" strips 2" long**

- 4 **scallions, cut slantwise in ½" pieces (include some tops)**

- 1 **clove garlic, peeled and minced**

- 2 **tablespoons Oriental sesame oil or vegetable oil**

- ½ **pound snow peas, stems and "strings" removed**

- 1 **teaspoon finely minced fresh ginger**

- 2 **tablespoons chunky peanut butter**

- 2 **tablespoons soy sauce**

Mix red pepper, scallions, garlic, and oil in 2-quart casserole at least 9" across. Cover with wax paper and microwave on HIGH (100% power) 3 minutes. Stir, add snow peas and ginger, cover with lid or vented plastic food wrap, and microwave on HIGH (100% power) 3–4 minutes, stirring at halftime, until snow peas are barely tender. Let stand, covered, 2 minutes. Meanwhile, spoon peanut butter into 1-cup measure, add soy sauce, cover with wax paper, and microwave on HIGH (100% power) 1 minute. Drain vegetable liquid into sauce, whisk until smooth, pour over vegetables, and toss lightly.

PER SERVING: 148 C 5 g P 11 g F 9 g CARB 551 mg S 0 mg CH

VARIATION

WARM SUGAR SNAP, MUSHROOM, AND RED PEPPER SALAD WITH GINGER-HONEY DRESSING: Cook red pepper, scallions, and garlic in oil as directed, then toss with 1 cup halved button mushrooms, set aside. Microwave ½ pound sugar snaps without any seasoning; drain and keep separate. For dressing, beat 3 tablespoons vegetable oil with 1 tablespoon white vinegar, 2 teaspoons honey, ½ teaspoon each crushed fresh ginger and garlic, ¼ teaspoon salt, and a pinch red pepper flakes. Spoon half of dressing over red pepper mixture and toss; use rest to dress sugar snaps. Mound red pepper mixture in center of round platter and wreathe with sugar snaps. Serve warm.

PER SERVING: 202 C 2 g P 17 g F 11 g CARB 140 mg S 0 mg CH

Summer squash
(YELLOW SQUASH, ZUCCHINI, AND PATTYPAN)

Slices and Cubes: Trim medium-size (5–6 ounce) yellow squash or zucchini and slice ¼" thick. If larger, halve lengthwise and slice or cut in ½" cubes. Or peel, quarter, and seed pattypan squash, then slice each quarter ¼" thick or cut each pattypan in ½" cubes. Place squash in casserole, add water, cover with lid or vented plastic food wrap, and microwave as follows, stirring at halftime, until crisp-tender. Let stand, covered; drain and season.

Amount	Servings	Container	Water	Minutes on HIGH (100% power)	Minutes Standing Time
1 C	1	1-quart	1 T	2–3	1
2 C	2	1½-quart	2 T	3–5	1
4 C	4	2-quart	2 T	6–8	2
6 C	6	3-quart	2 T	9–11	2

Seasoning Suggestions: Sour cream and crumbled crisp bacon; Herb Butter Sauce, Warm Aioli, or Rémoulade Sauce; grated Parmesan and butter-browned crumbs.

— V A R I A T I O N

PARBOILED SUMMER SQUASH: Microwave as directed but reduce time 50%. Drain at once (no standing), quick-chill 5 minutes in ice water, and drain again.

Halves: Prick zucchini or yellow squash in several places, trim, and halve lengthwise; seed or not, and arrange side by side, ½" apart and cut sides up, in shallow casserole. Add water, cover with lid or vented plastic food wrap, and microwave as chart directs, rotating casserole 180° at halftime, and if cooking more than 2 halves, rearranging them as well, until *barely* tender. Let stand, drain, and season.

No. of 5"–6" Halves	Servings	Container	Water	Minutes on HIGH (100% power)	Minutes Standing Time
2	1	8" × 8" × 2"	2 T	3–3½	2–3
4	2	8" × 8" × 2"	2 T	4–5	2–3
6	4	9" × 9" × 2"	2 T	5–6	2–3
8	6	13" × 9" × 2"	2 T	7–8	2–3

Seasoning Suggestions: Herb Butter Sauce, Warm Aioli, or Rémoulade Sauce; grated Parmesan and butter-browned crumbs. Or top with cooked whole-kernel corn, sautéed onions, or crumbled, browned Italian sausage.

487

*P*LANTATION SQUASH PUDDING

PREP TIME: [8 MINUTES] COOKING TIME: [23–29 MINUTES] STANDING TIME: [NONE]

SERVES 6

2½ pounds zucchini or yellow
   squash, sliced ¼" thick

1   medium-size yellow onion,
    peeled and minced

2   tablespoons water

¼   teaspoon crumbled dried
    marjoram

¼   teaspoon crumbled dried
    rosemary

3   tablespoons butter or
    margarine

1   teaspoon salt

¼   teaspoon pepper

Topping

1   cup soft white bread
    crumbs

2   tablespoons melted butter
    or margarine

¼   cup finely chopped pecans
    or walnuts

Place squash, onion, and water in 2-quart glass ceramic casserole, cover with lid, and microwave on HIGH (100% power) 15–20 minutes, stirring at halftime, until squash is soft. Drain well, mash, and drain again, pressing out all liquid. Mix in herbs, butter, salt, and pepper, and return to casserole. Cover with wax paper and microwave on HIGH (100% power) 6 minutes. Mix topping, scatter over squash, set 4" from heat in preheated broiler, and broil 2–3 minutes to brown.

PER SERVING: 167 C   3 g P   13 g F   11 g CARB   508 mg S
26 mg CH

V A R I A T I O N

SQUASH PUDDING WITH CHEESE TOPPING: Prepare as directed, but in topping substitute 2 tablespoons finely grated Parmesan or Romano cheese for nuts.

PER SERVING: 146 C   4 g P   11 g F   10 g CARB   545 mg S
28 mg CH

ITALIAN SWEET-SOUR SUMMER SQUASH

PREP TIME: | 5 MINUTES | COOKING TIME: | 20–22 MINUTES | STANDING TIME: | NONE

¢

SERVES 6

2½ **pounds zucchini or yellow squash, cut in 2″ × ½″ × ½″ strips**

1 **large clove garlic, peeled and minced**

2 **tablespoons olive oil**

2 **tablespoons red wine vinegar mixed with 1 teaspoon salt**

2 **tablespoons sugar**

⅓ **cup golden seedless raisins**

⅛ **teaspoon pepper**

Mix squash, garlic, and oil in 13″ × 8″ × 2″ casserole, cover with lid, and microwave on HIGH (100% power) 5 minutes. Mix in all but last ingredient, re-cover, and microwave on HIGH (100% power) 12–14 minutes, stirring gently at halftime, until squash is crisp-tender. With slotted spoon, lift squash and raisins to serving dish, mix in pepper, cover, and keep warm. Microwave casserole liquid, uncovered, on HIGH (100% power) 3 minutes until syrupy. Pour evenly over squash and serve.

PER SERVING: 108 C   3 g P   5 g F   16 g CARB   374 mg S 0 mg CH

WINTER SQUASH

¢ **A***corn and Butternut:* Choose a 1–1¼-pound squash, halve and seed, arrange cut sides up, 1" apart (3 halves in a triangle, 4 or more in a circle) on double-thickness paper toweling on oven floor. Cover with wax paper and microwave as follows, rotating squash 180° at halftime, and if cooking more than 2 halves, rearranging as well, until fork-tender. Let stand, covered; season and serve. *Note: Unless you have an oven shelf, don't cook more than 5 butternut or 6 acorn squash halves at a time.*

No. of Halves	Servings	Container	Water	Minutes on HIGH (100% power)	Minutes Standing Time
1	1	None	None	4–5	3
2	2	None	None	5–7	3
4	4	None	None	7–9	3
6	6	None	None	10–12	3

Seasoning Suggestions: Honey, maple syrup, brown sugar, orange or ginger marmalade, or quince jelly; cinnamon, nutmeg, and melted butter. Or fill squash hollows with creamed chicken, turkey, or ham, pilaf, green peas, or wild rice.

VARIATION

¢ **M**ASHED SQUASH: (1 pound = 2 cups cooked squash): Mash cooked squash with a little Seasoned Butter and heavy cream, return to squash shells, cover with wax paper, and microwave on HIGH (100% power) 1–2 minutes per serving. Or spoon into casserole and reheat. *Note: Hubbard squash is also delicious mashed.*

490

¢ *Hubbard Squash:* Halve, seed, and cut in 4″ squares. Arrange in single layer (don't crowd!) in bake/roast pan, cover with lid or vented plastic food wrap, and microwave as follows, rearranging pieces every 4 minutes, until fork-tender. Let stand, covered; season with salt, pepper, and butter.

No. of 4″ Squares	Servings	Container	Water	Minutes on HIGH (100% power)	Minutes Standing Time
2	1	None	None	8–10	5
4	2	None	None	10–14	5
8	4	None	None	14–18	5
12	6	None	None	20–24	5

Spaghetti Squash (Serves 4): Halve a 2½–3-pound spaghetti squash, seed, and arrange cut sides up, side by side but not touching, in shallow casserole. Add ¼ cup water, cover with lid or vented plastic food wrap, and microwave on HIGH (100% power) 9–12 minutes, rotating casserole 180° at halftime, until fork-tender. Let stand, covered, 5 minutes. With fork, scrape strands of flesh into serving dish. Toss with melted butter, salt, and pepper. Or top with Cheese Sauce, Jiffy Tomato Sauce, or any favorite spaghetti sauce.

WINTER SQUASH WITH MAPLE AND APPLES

PREP TIME: 8 MINUTES COOKING TIME: 23–27 MINUTES STANDING TIME: NONE*

SERVES 4

1 **large acorn squash (about 1½ pounds), halved and seeded**

1 **medium-size butternut squash (about 1½ pounds), halved and seeded**

2 **tart green apples, peeled, cored, and quartered**

2 **tablespoons apple or orange juice**

1 **tablespoon maple syrup or maple sugar**

Pinch ground mace

Pinch ground cinnamon

1 **teaspoon salt**

¼ **teaspoon pepper**

2 **tablespoons melted butter or margarine**

Place squash, cut sides up and 1" apart, in circle on double-thickness paper toweling on oven floor. Cover with wax paper and microwave on HIGH (100% power) 16–19 minutes, rotating 180° and rearranging at halftime, until tender. Let stand, covered, 6 minutes. Meanwhile, place apples, apple juice, and maple syrup in 9" pie plate, sprinkle with mace and cinnamon, cover with vented plastic food wrap, and microwave on HIGH (100% power) 5–6 minutes, stirring and uncovering at halftime, until apples are soft. Scoop squash flesh into food processor, add apples, lifting them with slotted spoon, salt, pepper, butter, and 1 tablespoon apple cooking liquid. Purée in short bursts, adding more apple liquid, if needed, for consistency of mashed potatoes. Spoon into 1½-quart casserole, cover with paper toweling, and microwave on HIGH (100% power) 2 minutes, stirring at halftime, until uniformly hot. Serve with pork, ham, or poultry.

PER SERVING: 220 C   3 g P   6 g F   44 g CARB   619 mg S   16 mg CH

TOMATOES

Choose medium-size (6-ounce), firm-ripe tomatoes. Halve crosswise and arrange cut sides up, not touching, 3 halves in a triangle, 4 or more in a circle, on plate or platter. Cover with vented plastic food wrap and microwave as follows, rotating plate 180° at halftime if cooking more than 2 halves, until slightly softened. Season and serve at once. *Note: Don't cook more than 8 halves at a time; they won't cook evenly; cook instead in batches.*

No. of Halves	Servings	Container	Water	Minutes on HIGH (100% power)	Standing Time
2	1	6" plate	None	1–2	None
4	2	9" pie plate	None	2–3	None
6	4	10" platter	None	3–4	None
8	6	12" platter	None	4–5	None

Beefsteak Tomatoes: Microwave as directed, but allow 30 seconds longer for 1–2 servings, 1 minute longer for 4–6.

Seasoning Suggestions: Butter-browned crumbs; olive oil, crumbled dried basil or oregano, and grated Parmesan cheese.

V A R I A T I O N

TOMATOES AU GRATIN (Serves 4): Microwave 8 tomato halves as directed, top each with a thin (⅛") slice sharp Cheddar, Swiss, or Gruyère cheese, cut slightly smaller than tomato. Microwave, uncovered, on MEDIUM-HIGH (70% power) 1½–2 minutes until cheese melts.

PER SERVING: 147 C   9 g P   10 g F   8 g CARB   189 mg S   30 mg CH

STEWED TOMATOES

PREP TIME: | 8 MINUTES | COOKING TIME: | 3–6 MINUTES | STANDING TIME: | NONE

The success of this recipe depends on fresh vine-ripened tomatoes. For richer flavor, add 1–2 teaspoons grated onion, 1 crushed clove garlic, and/or ¼ cup minced sweet red pepper or celery.

SERVES 4

1½ **pounds medium-size, firm-ripe tomatoes, peeled, cored, and quartered**

1 **teaspoon minced fresh basil or oregano or ¼ teaspoon crumbled dried**

¼ **teaspoon sugar**

1 **bay leaf (do not crumble)**

¼ **teaspoon celery salt**

⅛ **teaspoon pepper**

Mix tomatoes, basil, and sugar in 2-quart casserole; add bay leaf, cover with tight-fitting lid (wax paper between dish and lid works well), and microwave on HIGH (100% power) 3–6 minutes, stirring after 2 minutes, until *just* soft—don't overcook. *Note: Time will vary according to variety and ripeness of tomatoes; check often.* Discard bay leaf, sprinkle tomatoes with celery salt and pepper, and serve warm, at room temperature, or chilled.

PER SERVING: 32 C   1 g P   0 g F   7 g CARB   101 mg S   0 mg CH

V A R I A T I O N

TOMATO COULIS: Mix ¼ cup each minced yellow onion and celery, 1 crushed clove garlic, and 2 teaspoons olive oil in 2-quart casserole. Cover with wax paper and microwave on HIGH (100% power) 3 minutes until soft. Add tomatoes, herb, sugar, bay leaf, and proceed as directed. When tomatoes are soft, discard bay leaf, drain, and purée. Serve with poached scallops or delicate white fish.

PER SERVING: 57 C   2 g P   3 g F   9 g CARB   108 mg S   0 mg CH

TURNIPS

Choose medium-size turnips (3–4 per pound), remove tops and root ends, peel and cut in ½" cubes (1¼ pounds = 3½ cups cubes). Place in casserole, add water, cover with lid or vented plastic food wrap, and microwave as follows, stirring at halftime, until tender. Let stand, covered; drain and season.

Weight (as purchased)	Servings	Container	Water or Broth	Minutes on HIGH (100% power)	Minutes Standing Time
5 oz.	1	1-pint	2 T	4–5	3
¾ lb.	2	1-quart	4 T	5–7	3
1¼ lbs.	4	1½-quart	4 T	7–9	3
2 lbs.	6	2-quart	4 T	9–11	3

Seasoning Suggestions: Seasoned Butter, Beurre Noisette, Jiffy Herb Butter; Medium White Sauce, Béchamel, or Cheese Sauce.

VARIATIONS

MASHED TURNIPS: Mash cooked turnips with a little butter or heavy cream, salt, pepper, and nutmeg or mace.

PARBOILED TURNIPS: Microwave as directed but reduce time 50%. Drain at once (no standing), quick-chill 5 minutes in ice water, and drain again.

495

GINGERED TURNIP TIMBALES

PREP TIME: | 5 MINUTES | COOKING TIME: | 13–15 MINUTES | STANDING TIME: | 5 MINUTES

¢

SERVES 6

1   tablespoon butter or margarine

¾" piece fresh ginger, peeled and minced

1   tablespoon flour

½   cup milk

1   teaspoon finely grated yellow onion

2   eggs, lightly beaten

¾   teaspoon salt

⅛   teaspoon pepper

1   tablespoon minced parsley

3½ cups cooked cubed turnips* (about 1¼ pounds), puréed

Melt butter with ginger in wax-paper-covered 1-pint measure by microwaving on HIGH (100% power) 25–30 seconds. Blend in flour and microwave, uncovered, on HIGH (100% power) 30 seconds until foamy. Gradually whisk in milk, add onion, and microwave, uncovered, on HIGH (100% power) 2–3 minutes, whisking at 1-minute intervals, until sauce boils and thickens. Mix eggs with salt, pepper, and parsley, then blend in turnip purée and sauce. Divide among 6 (6-ounce) custard cups, arrange ½" apart in circle on large platter, and microwave, uncovered, on HIGH (100% power) 5 minutes, rotating platter 180° at halftime. Reduce power to MEDIUM (50%) and microwave, uncovered, 5–6 minutes, rotating platter 180° at halftime, until 1" is set around edges; start testing for doneness at minimum time, removing timbales that test done; microwave rest in 30-second increments. *Note: The soft quarter-size areas in centers will set on standing.* Let timbales stand, covered with wax paper, 5 minutes. Unmold carefully and serve.

PER SERVING: 87 C   4 g P   5 g F   8 g CARB   391 mg S   99 mg CH

ABOUT MICROWAVING RICE

Since rice takes as long to microwave as to cook the old-fashioned way, you may wonder, "Why bother?" Three good reasons: The rice needn't be started in boiling water, it won't stick to the pan or scorch, and it *will* steam to perfection in a microwave. Follow these guidelines, however:

~~~ To prevent boilover, use a casserole three times the volume of the rice and water put into it (with glass ovenware, you can monitor the cooking). If the rice is to be browned first, the casserole's diameter is also important (our recipes specify diameter wherever necessary). To brown the rice evenly, push it into a doughnut shape.

~~~ To hasten cooking, use the hottest tap water available.

~~~ To reduce evaporation and keep rice fluffy-moist, use a tight lid.

~~~ If rice is to cook evenly, don't add salt until after the rice is done *unless* you dissolve it completely in the cooking liquid *before* adding the rice.

~~~ To avoid breaking the individual grains of rice, stir rice once only.

~~~ So that the rice will absorb all casserole liquid, let it stand, fully covered, as individual recipes specify.

~~~ To hold microwaved rice 10–15 minutes before you serve it, keep it tightly covered.

BASIC STEAMED RICE

Type of Rice	Amount Uncooked Rice	Amount Hot Water or Broth	Minutes on HIGH (100% power)	Minutes on MEDIUM (50% power)	Minutes Stand- ing Time	Yield
Long-Grain, Converted	½ C	1 C	2–3	6–7	5	1½ C
	¾ C	1½ C	3–4	7–8	5	2 C
	1 C	2 C	4–6	9–10	5	3 C
	1½ C	2¾ C	6–8	12–13	5	4½ C
	2 C	3⅔ C	8–10	14–16	5	6 C
Basmati, Patna	1 C	1¾ C	4–5	7–8	5	3⅔ C
Short-Grain (Arborio, Oriental)	1 C	2 C	4–6	9–10	5	3 C
Brown, Long- or Short-Grain	1 C	2¼ C	4–6	28–30	5	3½ C
Brown, Converted	1 C	2 C	4–6	22–25	5	3½ C
Brown, Basmati	1 C	2 C	4–6	26–28	5	3¾ C

Mix rice and liquid in casserole three times volume of combined ingredients, cover with tight lid, and microwave on HIGH (100% power) as chart directs until small bubbles appear around edge; stir once, re-cover, and microwave on MEDIUM (50% power) without stirring until rice is *al dente*. **Note:** *Rice will seem dry on surface but some liquid will remain in bottom of casserole; this will be absorbed as rice stands.* Let rice stand, tightly covered, as chart directs. Add salt to taste and fluff lightly with fork.

> **To Reheat Rice from Room Temperature:** Cover with lid or vented plastic food wrap and microwave on HIGH (100% power), allowing 1 minute per cup of cooked rice. Stir and serve.
>
> **To Reheat Refrigerated Rice:** Microwave as directed for room-temperature rice, increasing time to 1¼–1½ minutes per cup of cooked rice.
>
> **To Reheat Frozen Rice:** See Chapter 4, Microwave Chart for Reheating Frozen Cooked Food.

10 QUICK WAYS TO JAZZ UP RICE

(All amounts based on 1 cup uncooked rice [any kind]; always adjust salt to taste)

⧖ ONION-MUSHROOM RICE: Microwave ½ cup minced yellow onion in 1 tablespoon butter or margarine in wax-paper-covered casserole on HIGH (100% power) 3 minutes before adding rice and liquid. Proceed as directed, adding 1 cup thinly sliced or coarsely chopped mushrooms before microwaving on MEDIUM (50% power).

⧖ CURRIED RICE: Add 1 tablespoon butter or margarine and 2 teaspoons curry powder to chicken broth and uncooked rice, then microwave as directed.

⧖ SAFFRON RICE: Blend ⅛ teaspoon powdered saffron with cooking liquid before adding rice, then microwave as directed.

⧖ GARLIC-SOUR CREAM RICE: Microwave 1 minced clove garlic along with rice. After standing time, fork in ¾ cup room-temperature sour cream and 2 tablespoons minced chives, cover with lid, and microwave on MEDIUM (50% power) 2 minutes to warm and blend flavors.

⧗ **GREEN RICE:** Add ½ cup minced scallions (include some green tops) and 1 tablespoon butter to chicken broth and uncooked rice; microwave as directed, then fork in 1 cup minced parsley just before serving.

⧗ **HERBED RICE:** Mix 2 tablespoons minced fresh basil, dill, chives, or parsley, or 1 tablespoon minced fresh sage or thyme with 2 tablespoons melted butter or margarine and fork into cooked rice before standing. Stir again lightly and serve. *Note: If fresh herbs are unavailable, substitute 1 teaspoon of the dried.*

⧗ **CHEDDAR RICE:** Before rice stands, add (but do not mix in) ½–⅔ cup grated sharp Cheddar (or Swiss, mozzarella, or Monterey Jack) cheese; fork in lightly just before serving.

⧗ **MANDARIN ORANGE RICE:** Microwave rice in half-and-half mixture of orange juice and chicken broth. Before serving, fork in 1 tablespoon butter or margarine, 2 teaspoons finely grated orange rind, and 2 tablespoons minced parsley; garnish with mandarin orange segments.

⧗ **FRUIT RICE:** Toss seasoned, cooked rice with ⅓ cup seedless raisins or dried currants, diced dried apricots, prunes, figs, dates, or apples.

⧗ **NUT RICE:** Toss ⅓ cup coarsely chopped nuts (any kind) and 2 tablespoons melted butter with cooked rice.

BRAZILIAN RICE

PREP TIME: 4 MINUTES
¢
COOKING TIME: 18–21 MINUTES
STANDING TIME: 5 MINUTES

SERVES 4

- 1 **small Spanish onion, peeled and minced**
- 2 **tablespoons lard, bacon drippings, or vegetable oil**
- 1 **cup converted rice**
- 2 **tablespoons tomato paste**
- 2 **cups hot water or chicken or beef broth**
- ⅛ **teaspoon pepper**
- ½ **teaspoon salt (about)**

Microwave onion and lard in wax-paper-covered 2½-quart casserole on HIGH (100% power) 4 minutes until glassy. Add rice, blend tomato paste with water, and stir into rice. Cover with lid and microwave on HIGH (100% power) 5–7 minutes until small bubbles appear at edge. Stir once, re-cover, and microwave on MEDIUM (50% power) 9–10 minutes until almost all liquid is absorbed. Let stand, covered, 5 minutes. Add pepper, salt to taste, and fluff with fork.

PER SERVING: 245 C   4 g P   7 g F   41 g CARB   343 mg S   6 mg CH

BASMATI RICE WITH APRICOTS AND CASHEWS

PREP TIME: 8 MINUTES   COOKING TIME: 15½–19 MINUTES   STANDING TIME: 5 MINUTES

Basmati, an Indian rice of exceptionally fine texture and flavor, is available in many supermarkets and specialty groceries.

SERVES 6

1   medium-size yellow onion, peeled and minced

1   clove garlic, peeled and minced

2   tablespoons butter or margarine

1   teaspoon cumin seeds

1   teaspoon caraway seeds

¼   teaspoon ground cardamom

¼   teaspoon ground cinnamon

⅛   teaspoon ground turmeric

1   cup Basmati rice, washed in cold running water and drained well

2   cups chicken broth or water

½   cup finely slivered dried apricots

½   cup golden seedless raisins

½   cup toasted cashews*

⅛   teaspoon pepper

½   teaspoon salt (about)

Place onion, garlic, and butter in 3-quart casserole, cover with wax paper, and microwave on HIGH (100% power) 3½–4 minutes until glassy. Mix in spices, rice, and chicken broth, cover with tight lid, and microwave on HIGH (100% power) 5–7 minutes until boiling. Stir, re-cover, and microwave on MEDIUM (50% power) 7–8 minutes until almost all liquid is absorbed. Add apricots and raisins, re-cover, and let stand 5 minutes. Add cashews, pepper, and salt to taste. Toss well and serve with curried lamb or chicken, Chicken Indochine, Country Captain, or as a potato substitute.

PER SERVING: 293 C   6 g P   10 g F   47 g CARB   563 mg S   10 mg CH

Note: Long-grain rice may be prepared this way, too, but increase cooking time on MEDIUM (50% power) to 9–10 minutes.

RISOTTO MILANESE

PREP TIME: [5 MINUTES] COOKING TIME: [17½–21 MINUTES] STANDING TIME: [5 MINUTES]

Risotto, the creamy rices of northern Italy, require short-grain rice, either Arborio or Oriental (the brown and the white work equally well). Our microwave risotto is neat, fast, and fail-safe. **Note:** *Saffron threads can be used instead of powdered saffron but you must first make an infusion. Mix saffron with ¼ cup chicken broth in 1-cup measure; microwave, uncovered, on HIGH (100% power) 1 minute, let stand 2 minutes, then strain. Add infusion to risotto along with broth.*

SERVES 4

- 1 **small yellow onion, peeled and minced**
- 3 **tablespoons butter (no substitute)**
- 1 **cup short-grain rice**
- 1 **cup each chicken broth and dry white wine or 2 cups chicken broth**

Pinch powdered saffron

- ⅓ **cup finely grated Parmesan cheese**
- ⅛ **teaspoon pepper**
- ½ **teaspoon salt (about)**

Microwave onion and butter in wax-paper-covered 2½-quart casserole on HIGH (100% power) 2½–3 minutes until glassy. Mix in rice, cover with wax paper, and microwave on HIGH (100% power) 1 minute. Add broth and saffron, cover with tight lid, and microwave on HIGH (100% power) 5–7 minutes until boiling. Stir, re-cover, and microwave on MEDIUM (50% power) 9–10 minutes until almost all liquid is absorbed and rice is *al dente.* Let stand, covered, 5 minutes. Fork in cheese, pepper, and salt to taste.

PER SERVING: 308 C   7 g P   12 g F   42 g CARB   768 mg S   30 mg CH

V A R I A T I O N

RISOTTO CON FUNGHI (RISOTTO WITH MUSHROOMS): Cook ½ pound coarsely chopped mushrooms (either wild or commercial) along with onion, then proceed as directed. If you like, substitute ¼ cup piñon nuts for Parmesan.

PER SERVING: 323 C   9 g P   12 g F   45 g CARB   770 mg S   30 mg CH

Note: *If using short-grain brown rice, increase microwave time on MEDIUM (50% power) to 28–30 minutes.*

RICE PILAF

Rice browns nicely in the microwave if carefully timed and tended. Use untinted glass ovenware so you can monitor the browning at a glance.

SERVES 4

3 **tablespoons butter or margarine**

1 **cup long-grain or converted rice**

2 **cups chicken or beef broth or water**

⅛ **teaspoon pepper**

½ **teaspoon salt (about)**

Melt butter in wax-paper-covered 2½-quart casserole at least 9″ across by microwaving on HIGH (100% power) 45–55 seconds. Mix in rice, push into doughnut shape, cover with wax paper, and microwave on HIGH (100% power) 3½–4 minutes, stirring at halftime, until color of straw. *Note: Watch carefully toward end to avoid burning; stop microwave the instant browning starts and stir rice to "even" the color.* Add broth, cover with tight lid, and microwave on HIGH (100% power) 4–6 minutes, until boiling. Stir, re-cover, and microwave on MEDIUM (50% power) 8–10 minutes until almost all liquid is absorbed. Let stand, covered, 5 minutes. Add pepper, salt to taste, and fluff with fork.

PER SERVING: 261 C   4 g P   10 g F   38 g CARB   866 mg S   23 mg CH

VARIATIONS

MUTTER PILAU (INDIAN PEAS AND RICE): Add ¼ cup minced yellow onion, ¼ teaspoon each ground cinnamon and cardamom, and ⅛ teaspoon ground cloves to browned rice and proceed as directed. Toss cooked rice with 1½ cups drained, cooked peas.

PER SERVING: 316 C   8 g P   10 g F   49 g CARB   868 mg S   23 mg CH

BULGUR PILAF: Substitute 1 cup bulgur wheat for rice, then microwave in butter on HIGH (100% power) 2 minutes only. Proceed as directed, reducing broth to 1¾ cups.

PER SERVING: 248 C   5 g P   10 g F   36 g CARB   802 mg S   23 mg CH

503

CHINESE RICE

PREP TIME: | 5 MINUTES | COOKING TIME: | 7½–9 MINUTES | STANDING TIME: | NONE

SERVES 4

2　tablespoons peanut or vegetable oil

¾　cup julienne strips lean cooked pork or ham

3　cups cold cooked rice

⅓　cup minced scallions (include some tops)

2　tablespoons chicken broth or water

3　tablespoons soy sauce

Pinch sugar

⅛　teaspoon pepper

Mix oil with pork and spread doughnut fashion in 2-quart casserole about 9″ across. Cover with wax paper and microwave on HIGH (100% power) 2½–3 minutes, stirring at halftime. Add all remaining ingredients, pressing out lumps in rice, re-cover, and microwave on HIGH (100% power) 5–6 minutes, stirring at halftime, until uniformly hot.

PER SERVING: 251 C   10 g P   10 g F   28 g CARB   822 mg S   25 mg CH

RICE AND CHEDDAR-STUFFED TOMATOES

PREP TIME: | 10 MINUTES | COOKING TIME: | 9½–12 MINUTES | STANDING TIME: | NONE

Because tomatoes microwave fast, cooked stuffings that require only reheating work best. **Note:** *In microwave ovens of 700 watts or more vine-ripened tomatoes may cook more evenly on MEDIUM (50% power), but you may need to increase microwave time 1–2 minutes.*

¢

SERVES 4

4　medium-size (2½″–3″ diameter) firm-ripe tomatoes

Slice ¼″ off stem ends of tomatoes and discard. Scoop seeds and pulp into bowl; drain tomatoes upside down on several thicknesses paper tow-

1 **small yellow onion, peeled and minced**

1 **tablespoon butter or margarine**

1 **cup cooked rice**

¾ **cup coarsely grated sharp Cheddar cheese**

2 **tablespoons minced canned green chili peppers**

¼ **teaspoon salt (about)**

⅛ **teaspoon pepper**

eling. Discard tomato seeds, drain pulp, and coarsely chop; set aside. Microwave onion and butter in wax-paper-covered 1-quart casserole on HIGH (100% power) 2½–3 minutes until glassy. Mix in tomato pulp and all remaining ingredients; adjust salt as needed. Stuff tomatoes with rice mixture, dividing total amount evenly, then arrange 1″ apart in 9″ pie plate, leaving empty space in center. Microwave, uncovered, on MEDIUM-HIGH (70% power) 7–9 minutes, rotating pie plate 180° at halftime, until tomatoes are *just* soft. Check for doneness after 7 minutes (don't prick tomatoes; they'll lose juice and shape). Serve at once.

PER SERVING: 195 C   8 g P   10 g F   19 g CARB   332 mg S   30 mg CH

~~~~~~ V A R I A T I O N S

SHRIMP- OR CRAB-STUFFED TOMATOES: Prepare as directed, but substitute ¾ cup minced cooked shrimp or flaked, well-picked-over lump crab meat for Cheddar; omit chili peppers and add 2 tablespoons freshly minced dill or 1 teaspoon dill weed.
PER SERVING: 135 C   8 g P   3 g F   19 g CARB   234 mg S   60 mg CH

CHICKEN- OR TURKEY-STUFFED TOMATOES: Prepare as directed, but substitute ¾ cup minced cooked chicken or turkey for Cheddar; add 1 teaspoon each rubbed sage and chili powder to rice mixture.
PER SERVING: 162 C   10 g P   5 g F   19 g CARB   229 mg S   31 mg CH

HAM-AND-RICE-STUFFED TOMATOES: Prepare as directed, but microwave 1 teaspoon curry powder along with onion. Substitute ¾ cup minced cooked ham for Cheddar; add 2 tablespoons finely minced chutney and 1 tablespoon minced parsley to rice mixture.
PER SERVING: 180 C   9 g P   6 g F   24 g CARB   623 mg S   24 mg CH

STUFFED TOMATOES AL PESTO: Prepare as directed, but cook 1 peeled and minced clove garlic along with onion. Omit Cheddar and chili peppers and add ¼ cup finely chopped piñon nuts, ¼ cup finely grated Parmesan cheese, and 1 tablespoon each minced parsley and fresh basil to rice.
PER SERVING: 184 C   7 g P   10 g F   20 g CARB   289 mg S   13 mg CH

505

SOME OTHER STUFFINGS FOR TOMATOES

Use a scant ½ cup of any of the following for each tomato and microwave as directed above:

 Macaroni and Cheese

Risotto alla Milanese

Curried Rice

WILD RICE

PREP TIME: 2 MINUTES   COOKING TIME: 25–28 MINUTES   STANDING TIME: 8 MINUTES

Wild rice costs the earth, but it can be mixed half and half with white or brown rice, even bulgur wheat.

SERVES 4–6

1   cup wild rice
2   cups hot water
1   teaspoon salt
⅛   teaspoon pepper
2–3 tablespoons melted butter
    or margarine

Mix rice and water in 2½-quart casserole, cover with lid or vented plastic food wrap, and microwave on HIGH (100% power) 5–6 minutes until boiling. Reduce power level to MEDIUM (50%) and microwave without stirring 18–20 minutes, rotating casserole 180° at halftime, until a few grains begin to burst. Let stand, covered, 8 minutes, then drain well. Return rice to casserole and microwave, uncovered, on HIGH (100% power) 2 minutes to dry. Mix in salt, pepper, and butter and serve.

PER SERVING: 205–137 C   6–4 g P   7–5 g F   30–20 g CARB
626–417 mg S   19–13 mg CH

WILD RICE WITH HAM AND MUSHROOMS: Mix ¼ pound finely diced lean cooked ham, ½ pound thinly sliced mushrooms, and ¼ cup minced scallions with 2 tablespoons butter or margarine in 2½-quart casserole, cover with wax paper, and microwave on HIGH (100% power) 4 minutes. Mix in wild rice, substitute chicken or beef broth for water, then proceed as recipe directs, reducing salt to ½ teaspoon and omitting butter at end.

PER SERVING: 215–143 C   14–9 g P   3–2 g F   35–23 g CARB   1122–748 mg S   15–10 mg CH

HERBED WILD RICE AND WALNUT STUFFING (About 1 quart): Microwave ½ cup minced yellow onion and ⅓ cup minced celery in 2 tablespoons bacon drippings in wax-paper-covered 2½-quart casserole on HIGH (100% power) 4 minutes. Add wild rice, 2 cups chicken or beef broth, 2 tablespoons each minced chives and parsley, ¼ teaspoon each crumbled dried sage, marjoram, and thyme. Proceed as recipe directs but omit butter at end. Fork in ¾ cup coarsely chopped walnuts or pecans and serve as is or use to stuff poultry, veal, or pork. *Note: To increase amount of stuffing inexpensively, mix ½–1 cup cooked brown rice into cooked stuffing and adjust seasonings to taste.*

PER CUP: 358 C   10 g P   20 g F   37 g CARB   1100 mg S   5 mg CH

*B*ULGUR WHEAT

PREP TIME: [1 MINUTE] COOKING TIME: [13–16 MINUTES] STANDING TIME: [5 MINUTES]

SERVES 4–6

1 **cup bulgur wheat**

1¾ **cups water or chicken or beef broth**

1 **teaspoon salt**

⅛ **teaspoon pepper**

2 **tablespoons butter or margarine (optional)**

Mix bulgur and liquid in 2½-quart casserole, cover with lid or vented plastic food wrap, and microwave on HIGH (100% power) 4–6 minutes until small bubbles appear at edge. Stir lightly, re-cover, and microwave on MEDIUM (50% power) 9–10 minutes without stirring until almost all liquid is absorbed. Let stand, covered, 5 minutes. Mix in salt, pepper, and butter, if desired; fluff with fork and serve in place of potatoes.

PER SERVING: 157–105 C   4–3 g P   1–0 g F   35–23 g CARB
552–368 mg S   0–0 mg CH

507

Tabbouleh: (Serves 6): Cook bulgur with chicken broth as directed, cool to room temperature, and fork in ½ cup minced yellow onion, ¾ cup minced parsley, 3 tablespoons minced mint, and 2–3 coarsely chopped, peeled large ripe tomatoes. Whisk together ¼ cup each lemon juice and olive oil, ½ teaspoon salt, and ⅛ teaspoon pepper, drizzle over bulgur mixture, toss well, cover, and let stand 1 hour at room temperature. Mound on romaine leaves and serve as a salad.

PER SERVING: 215 C   4 g P   10 g F   29 g CARB   487 mg S   0 mg CH

Mushroom-Pecan-Bulgur Stuffing (About 3½ cups): Microwave 1 cup coarsely chopped mushrooms in 2 tablespoons butter or margarine in paper-toweling-covered 2½-quart casserole on HIGH (100% power) 2 minutes; add bulgur and chicken or beef broth and proceed as directed. Mix ⅓ cup coarsely chopped pecans with seasoned, cooked bulgur. Serve as is or use to stuff poultry, lamb, or veal.

PER CUP: 311 C   6 g P   14 g F   43 g CARB   699 mg S   18 mg CH

Kasha Varnishkas (Serves 6): Substitute kasha (buckwheat groats) for bulgur and prepare as directed; while it cooks, brown ½ cup minced yellow onion in 2 tablespoons butter on stovetop; also cook ½ pound medium-wide noodles by package directions. Mix drained noodles, browned onion, and 1 tablespoon poppy seeds into kasha, transfer to 3-quart casserole, cover with lid or vented plastic food wrap, and microwave on MEDIUM (50% power) 5 minutes, stirring at halftime.

PER SERVING: 247 C   7 g P   7 g F   40 g CARB   409 mg S   46 mg CH

MISSISSIPPI GRITS AND CHEDDAR CASSEROLE

PREP TIME: | 5 MINUTES | COOKING TIME: | 18½–21 MINUTES | STANDING TIME: | NONE

¢

SERVES 4

1   **cup grits**

3½   **cups hot water**

1   **teaspoon salt**

⅛   **teaspoon pepper**

6   **tablespoons butter or margarine**

¼   **cup finely grated Parmesan cheese**

1⅓   **cups coarsely grated sharp Cheddar cheese**

Paprika

Combine grits, water, and salt in 3-quart casserole, cover with vented plastic food wrap, and microwave on HIGH (100% power) 9–10 minutes, stirring at halftime, until all liquid is absorbed and mixture thickens. Mix in pepper and 2 tablespoons butter, stirring until butter melts. Spoon into 1-quart measure and cool, uncovered, 30 minutes. Cover and chill until firm. Turn grits out, slice crosswise ½" thick, then cut each slice in 4 wedges *(to facilitate cutting, dip knife in tepid water)*. Arrange wedges, slightly overlapping, points down and with smaller pieces in middle, in rows in 10" casserole at least 2" deep. Melt remaining butter and drizzle evenly over grits. Cover with vented plastic food wrap and microwave on HIGH (100% power) 7–8 minutes, rotating casserole 180° at halftime and basting grits with casserole butter. Sprinkle evenly with Parmesan and Cheddar and microwave, uncovered, on MEDIUM (50% power) 2½–3 minutes until cheese melts. Dust with paprika and serve as a main course. Or broil 4" from heat of preheated broiler 3–4 minutes to brown.

PER SERVING: 477 C   16 g P   32 g F   32 g CARB   1074 mg S 91 mg CH

POLENTA

In northern Italy, polenta (cornmeal mush) is more popular than pasta. It's the traditional accompaniment to rabbit, but is equally compatible with chicken or fish stews. Leftovers can be browned in olive oil or baked with cheese much the way American Southerners handle an excess of grits. Prepared the old-fashioned way, polenta takes about 45 minutes of constant stirring, and even then there's no guarantee the mixture won't scorch. With a microwave, polenta-making is virtually fail-safe. Best of all, you needn't stand and stir the whole enduring time.

SERVES 6–8

1   **cup yellow cornmeal (not stone-ground)**

3½ **cups hot water**

1   **teaspoon salt**

Combine all ingredients in 3-quart casserole, cover with lid or vented plastic food wrap, and microwave on HIGH (100% power) 10 minutes until bubbling gently, stirring at halftime. Remove lid or food wrap, cover with paper toweling (to allow evaporation), and microwave on HIGH (100% power) 9–10 minutes, stirring every 3 minutes, until very thick and a slight crust begins to form around edge. Serve polenta as is or scrape onto hot buttered platter and cool 10 minutes until firm. Slice as you would bread or cut in squares. *Note: Dipping knife in cool water makes slicing easier.*

PER SERVING: 84–63 C   2–1 g P   0–0 g F   18–14 g CARB
367–275 mg S   0–0 mg CH

¢ **P**OLENTA PARMIGIANA (Serves 4 as an entrée, 6 as a side dish): Prepare polenta as directed, mix in 1 tablespoon olive oil, and spoon into buttered 8″ × 8″ × 2″ baking dish. Smooth surface and cool, uncovered, until firm. Cut into 2″ squares and arrange, slightly overlapping, in rows in 8″–9″ glass ceramic casserole that is 2″ deep. Cover with vented plastic food wrap and warm by microwaving on HIGH (100% power) 5½–6 minutes, rotating casserole 180° at half-time. Pour 1 cup any favorite tomato or pasta sauce over polenta, re-cover, and microwave on HIGH (100% power) 2 minutes until bubbly. Sprinkle evenly with ¼ cup grated Parmesan and 1 cup coarsely grated mozzarella or Gruyère cheese and microwave, uncovered, on MEDIUM (50% power) 2½–3 minutes until cheese melts. If you like, transfer to preheated broiler and broil 4″ from heat 2–3 minutes to brown lightly.

PER SERVING: 316–211 C 12–8 g P 15–10 g F 34–22 g CARB 1146–764 mg S 27–18 mg CH

It's quicker and easier to cook pasta and noodles on top of the stove because large quantities of water take even longer to boil in the microwave than they do over direct heat. Once cooked the conventional way, however, pasta and noodles can be slipped into scores of casseroles that microwave to perfection. They can also be topped or tossed with sauces that microwave zip-quick. Best of all, many of these recipes can be made well ahead of time, then whisked into the microwave for a last-minute reheating.

NOODLES FLORENTINE

PREP TIME: | 3 MINUTES | COOKING TIME: | 8 MINUTES | STANDING TIME: | NONE |

SERVES 6

¾ **pound hot cooked medium egg noodles, drained well**

2 **packages (10 ounces each) frozen chopped spinach, cooked and drained well**

⅓ **cup melted butter or margarine or sour cream**

¼ **cup milk**

1 **teaspoon salt**

¼ **teaspoon ground nutmeg**

⅛ **teaspoon pepper**

Mix all ingredients in 3-quart casserole, cover with lid or vented plastic food wrap, and microwave on HIGH (100% power) 4 minutes. Stir, re-cover, and microwave on MEDIUM (50% power) 4 minutes. Serve hot.

PER SERVING: 339 C   10 g P   13 g F   45 g CARB   548 mg S   82 mg CH

To Reheat Refrigerated Casserole: Cover with lid or vented plastic food wrap and microwave on HIGH (100% power) 5–6 minutes, stirring at halftime, until uniformly hot. *Note: A room-temperature casserole will take 3–5 minutes.*

CHEDDAR-NOODLE RING

PREP TIME: 4 MINUTES COOKING TIME: 8–9 MINUTES STANDING TIME: 3 MINUTES

¢

SERVES 6

- ¾ **pound hot cooked medium egg noodles, drained well**
- ¼ **pound sharp Cheddar cheese, coarsely grated**
- 1 **egg plus 1 egg white, beaten lightly**
- ¼ **cup milk**
- ¼ **cup light cream**
- 1¼ **teaspoons salt**
- ⅛ **teaspoon pepper**

Mix all ingredients, spoon into well-oiled 2-quart ring mold, cover with vented plastic food wrap, and microwave on MEDIUM (50% power) 8–9 minutes, rotating 180° at halftime, until just firm. Cover with foil and let stand 3 minutes. Invert ring on hot platter and ease out. Serve in place of potatoes or fill center with creamed spinach or broccoli, creamed chicken, turkey, or ham and serve as a light entrée.

To Reheat Refrigerated Ring: If ring is in mold or on microwave-safe platter, cover with vented plastic food wrap and microwave on MEDIUM (50% power) 6–7 minutes, rotating 180° at halftime. A room-temperature ring will take 1–2 minutes less.

PER SERVING: 338 C   14 g P   12 g F   42 g CARB   606 mg S   127 mg CH

~~~~~~ V A R I A T I O N

NOODLE RING: Prepare as directed but omit cheese and add ¼ cup minced chives or 2 tablespoons poppy seeds or ⅓ cup minced, toasted blanched almonds* (or pecan, piñon, or pistachio nuts) along with milk and cream.

PER SERVING: 262 C   9 g P   6 g F   42 g CARB   489 mg S   107 mg CH

513

LOKSHYNA
(UKRAINIAN NOODLES WITH COTTAGE CHEESE)

PREP TIME: 3 MINUTES   COOKING TIME: 12½–13 MINUTES   STANDING TIME: NONE

SERVES 6

- **4 slices lean bacon, cut crosswise in julienne strips**
- **¾ pound hot cooked medium egg noodles, drained well**
- **1 pound small-curd cottage cheese**
- **⅔ cup light cream**
- **1 teaspoon salt**
- **⅛ teaspoon pepper**
- **2 tablespoons minced parsley**

Arrange bacon doughnut-fashion in 3-quart casserole, cover with paper toweling and microwave on HIGH (100% power) 4½–5 minutes, stirring at halftime, until crisp. Drain on paper toweling; discard drippings. Return bacon to casserole, mix in all but last ingredient, cover with lid or vented plastic food wrap and microwave on HIGH (100% power) 4 minutes. Stir, re-cover and microwave on MEDIUM (50% power) 4 minutes until uniformly hot. Sprinkle with parsley and serve as a light entrée or potato substitute.

PER SERVING: 375 C   19 g P   13 g F   44 g CARB   755 mg S   86 mg CH

To Reheat Refrigerated Casserole: Cover with lid or vented plastic food wrap and microwave on HIGH (100% power) 5–6 minutes, stirring at halftime, until uniformly hot. *Note: A room-temperature casserole will take 3–5 minutes.*

SZECHUAN COLD SPICY NOODLES

PREP TIME: [4 MINUTES] COOKING TIME: [3 MINUTES] STANDING TIME: [1 MINUTE*]

Double or triple this recipe, if you like, adjusting amount of chili oil to taste. The dressing is superb with cooked broccoli, snow peas, or sugar snaps.

SERVES 4–6

½ **pound cooked fine egg noodles**

Dressing

1 **tea bag**

¼ **cup water**

4 **scallions, minced (white part only)**

1 **small clove garlic, peeled and minced**

2 **tablespoons Oriental sesame oil**

3 **tablespoons soy sauce**

2 **tablespoons tahini (sesame seed paste available in specialty groceries)**

1 **tablespoon red rice vinegar or red wine vinegar**

1 **teaspoon sugar**

¼ **teaspoon chili oil (peppery Oriental oil available in specialty groceries)**

Rinse noodles in colander under cold running water 1 minute; drain well and transfer to serving bowl. Place tea bag and water in small measuring cup and microwave, uncovered, on HIGH (100% power) 1 minute. Let stand 1 minute; discard tea bag. In 1-pint measure, mix tea with remaining dressing ingredients and microwave, uncovered, on HIGH (100% power) 2 minutes, whisking well at halftime. Add dressing to noodles, toss well, and serve at room temperature as a first course or as an accompaniment to barbecued meat, poultry, or seafood. *Note: If you make recipe ahead and refrigerate, let stand 30 minutes at room temperature before serving.*

PER SERVING: 344–229 C 10–6 g P 14–9 g F 46–31 g CARB
785–524 mg S 53–36 mg CH

515

12

SWEETS

In a microwave oven, fragile custards cook to unparalleled smoothness, puddings steam to feathery heights, dessert sauces bubble to perfection. And that's just the beginning. The microwave "bakes" Bundt cakes and bar cookies better and faster than you would have dreamed possible, it turns out silkiest-ever cheesecakes and mousses, and is even a whiz at making crumb crusts and certain kinds of candy.

But it does have its limits and can never replace the conventional oven for all-round baking versatility. The point is to use each oven for what it does best.

DON'T MICROWAVE THESE!

FLAKY PASTRIES: Because microwaving is a moist method of cookery, it can never brown, crisp, or dry pastries properly. And this holds true for puff and choux pastes, phyllo pastry, and, alas, your favorite piecrust.

CRÊPES: They come from the microwave clammy and limp.

ANGEL, CHIFFON, AND SPONGE CAKES: With so much steam in the microwave oven, crusts never form to seal in the air bubbles that leaven these cakes. And the egg and flour proteins, which form their framework, coagulate before the cakes can rise.

MACAROONS AND HARD MERINGUES: They need dry heat to crispen and brown.

INDIVIDUAL COOKIES: The dropped, shaped, and pressed microwave poorly.

SHORTCAKES: When microwaved, they remain dense and doughy inside.

HOT SOUFFLÉS: Although savory soufflés microwave successfully, sweet ones cook unevenly.

And now for our collection of desserts that microwave superbly, trim cooking times to fractions, and simplify preparation and cleanup.

ABOUT MICROWAVING FRESH FRUIT

With the exception of berries, which are so fragile and full of juice they're reduced to mush in seconds, fruits microwave superbly. Most brim with just-picked flavor. And *look* garden-fresh, too—bright and plump with rich fruity bouquet. But you must time and tend fruits carefully in the microwave oven. And choose varieties that are "naturals"—apples, apricots, pears, peaches, plums, and other firm fruits, also rhubarb, which though not a fruit, botanically speaking, is nonetheless cooked and served like one.

In addition to variety, a fruit's freshness determines how well it will microwave (the fresher the better). So does its moisture content. Generally speaking, drier fruits microwave better than wet, pulpy ones, which tend to liquefy. That's why we suggest that you continue to cook berries and cherries as you always have—by stovetop or oven. Unless, of course, you want to make berry jams or preserves. *These* the microwave does do to perfection and we've just the recipes to prove it (see Index for page numbers).

APPLESAUCE

PREP TIME: | 10 MINUTES | COOKING TIME: | 8-9 MINUTES | STANDING TIME: | NONE |

The best homemade applesauce you will ever eat. And how fast it cooks!

SERVES 4–6

3	pounds greenings or other tart cooking apples, peeled, cored, and sliced ¼″ thick
¼	cup water
⅓–½	cup sugar (depending on tartness of apples)
⅛	teaspoon ground cinnamon
⅛	teaspoon ground nutmeg
1	teaspoon finely grated orange or lemon rind (optional)

Place apples and water in 3-quart casserole, cover with lid or vented plastic food wrap, and microwave on HIGH (100% power) 8–9 minutes, stirring every 3 minutes. Mix in sugar, spices, and if you like, rind; stir until sugar dissolves. If you like silky applesauce, purée. Serve warm or cold.

PER SERVING: 246–164 C 0–0 g P 1–1 g F 64–43 g CARB 0–0 mg S 0–0 mg CH

— V A R I A T I O N

¢ SPICY APPLESAUCE: Omit water, sugar, ground cinnamon, nutmeg, and grated rind and microwave sliced apples with ⅓ cup orange juice, 2 (2″ × ½″) strips lemon zest, 1 cinnamon stick, and 2 blades mace. When apples are mushy, stir in 3–4 tablespoons granulated maple sugar or light brown sugar and 1 tablespoon unsalted butter. Remove cinnamon, mace, and lemon zest, purée if desired, then serve as is or top with yogurt, heavy cream, Crème Anglaise, or crème fraîche.

PER SERVING: 328–218 C 1–0 g P 4–3 g F 78–52 g CARB 5–3 mg S 8–5 mg CH

519

SWEETS

BAKED APPLES

PREP TIME: 4 MINUTES COOKING TIME: 7-9 MINUTES STANDING TIME: 2 MINUTES

In ovens of 700 watts or more, apples will bake more evenly on MEDIUM-HIGH (70% power) than on full power.

SERVES 4

4 large Rome Beauties or other baking apples (about ½ pound each)

4 tablespoons granulated or light brown sugar

Pinch ground cinnamon or nutmeg

4 teaspoons water or apple or orange juice

Core apples to within ½" of bottoms and peel one third of way down from stem end. Stand each apple in 10-ounce glass ovenware dish or in circle 1" apart in shallow casserole at least 9" across. Combine sugar and cinnamon and spoon 1 tablespoon into each apple along with 1 teaspoon water. Cover with vented plastic food wrap and microwave on HIGH (100% power) 7–9 minutes, repositioning individual dishes or rotating casserole 180° at halftime. When apples are crisp-tender, let stand, covered, 2 minutes. Serve hot or cold, with or without Crème Anglaise, whipped cream, or crème fraîche.

For 1 Baked Apple: Quarter ingredients and microwave as directed, reducing time to 2½–3½ minutes.

For 2 Baked Apples: Halve ingredients and microwave as directed, reducing time to 5–6 minutes.

PER SERVING: 171 C   0 g P   1 g F   44 g CARB   0 mg S   0 mg CH

⚖ BAKED STUFFED APPLES: Peel and core apples as directed. Mix ¼ cup each light brown sugar, minced walnuts or pecans, and seedless raisins, minced pitted dates, prunes, or other dried fruit and stuff into apples, dividing total amount evenly. Drizzle stuffing in each apple with 2 teaspoons orange or lemon juice, brandy, or fruit liqueur. Proceed as recipe directs.

PER SERVING: 238 C   2 g P   5 g F   51 g CARB   6 mg S   0 mg CH

⚖ BAKED PEARS: Substitute 4 (7-ounce) sweet, firm-ripe pears for apples and microwave as directed for Baked Apples, but reduce time to 6–8 minutes.

PER SERVING: 156 C   1 g P   1 g F   40 g CARB   0 mg S   0 mg CH

⚖ BAKED CAMEMBERT-STUFFED PEARS: Substitute tart pears for sweet, prepare as directed but omit sugar. Just before pears stand, stuff each with 1½ tablespoons ripe Camembert cheese. Cover and let stand as directed.

PER SERVING: 171 C   5 g P   6 g F   28 g CARB   179 mg S   15 mg CH

APPLE CRISP

PREP TIME: 10 MINUTES   COOKING TIME: 12-14 MINUTES   STANDING TIME: NONE

¢

SERVES 6

6 cups peeled, cored, and thinly sliced (¼") greenings or other tart cooking apples

¼ cup sugar

1 tablespoon lemon juice

⅔ cup unsifted flour

½ cup firmly packed light brown sugar

½ teaspoon ground cinnamon

¼ teaspoon ground nutmeg

⅓ cup butter or margarine

¼ cup wheat germ

Toss apples with sugar and lemon juice and spread flat in 9" glass ceramic casserole at least 2" deep. Mix flour, brown sugar, and spices, cut in butter with pastry blender until texture of coarse meal, then mix in wheat germ. Spread evenly over apples and microwave, uncovered, on HIGH (100% power) 9–10 minutes until apples are done (stick fork through topping to test). Transfer at once to preheated broiler, setting 4" from heat, and brown 3–4 minutes. Top, if desired, with whipped cream, or vanilla ice cream.

PER SERVING: 333 C   3 g P   11 g F   59 g CARB   111 mg S   27 mg CH

VARIATIONS

BERRY-APPLE CRISP: Prepare as directed, using a half-and-half mix of blueberries or blackberries and sliced apples.

PER SERVING: 342 C   3 g P   11 g F   61 g CARB   116 mg S   27 mg CH

PEACH OR APRICOT CRISP: Substitute 5 cups thinly sliced peeled firm-ripe peaches or apricots for apples, and reduce sugar to 2 tablespoons if they are sweet. Proceed as directed.

PER SERVING: 331 C   4 g P   11 g F   58 g CARB   111 mg S   27 mg CH

POACHED PEARS CARDINAL

PREP TIME: [10 MINUTES] COOKING TIME: [8–11 MINUTES] STANDING TIME: [NONE]

The best pears to poach are Bartlett, Bosc, Anjou, or Seckel. Leftover poaching syrup can be used to macerate any fresh fruits.

SERVES 4

4 *large firm-ripe pears (about 1¾ pounds)*

3 *tablespoons lemon juice*

1 *cup sugar*

½ *cup dry white or red wine*

1 *teaspoon vanilla*

1 *recipe Melba Sauce made with raspberries and 2 tablespoons kirsch instead of liqueur called for*

Carefully core pears from bottom leaving stems intact, then peel smoothly and roll in 2 tablespoons lemon juice. Combine remaining lemon juice, sugar, wine, and vanilla in casserole 8"–9" across and 2" deep, cover with wax paper, and microwave on HIGH (100% power) 2–3 minutes, stirring at halftime, until mixture boils and sugar dissolves. Stir again, lay pears on sides in casserole, spoke fashion and not touching with stems toward center. Cover with vented plastic food wrap or lid and microwave on HIGH (100% power) 6–8 minutes until crisp-tender. At halftime, turn pears over and rotate casserole 180°. Don't overcook; pears will continue cooking as they cool. Cool, covered, in syrup, turning pears now and then; chill well. To serve, stand pears in individual goblets, drizzle with a little Melba Sauce, and pass the balance.

PER SERVING: 272 C 1 g P 1 g F 66 g CARB 1 mg S 0 mg CH

~~~~~~~~ V A R I A T I O N

WINE-POACHED PEARS: Poach pears as directed; omit Melba Sauce, and top with a little poaching liquid and heavy cream.

PER SERVING: 134 C 1 g P 1 g F 34 g CARB 1 mg S 0 mg CH

523

STEWED RHUBARB

PREP TIME: 3 MINUTES   COOKING TIME: 6-7 MINUTES   STANDING TIME: 5 MINUTES

SERVES 4

- **1 quart 1" chunks rhubarb (about 1 pound trimmed rhubarb)**
- **⅔ cup sugar**
- **¼ cup water**
- **1 teaspoon finely grated orange or lemon rind**

Mix all ingredients in 2-quart casserole at least 9" across, cover with vented plastic food wrap, and microwave on HIGH (100% power) 6–7 minutes, stirring at halftime, until crisp-tender. Let stand, covered, 5 minutes. Serve warm or cold with or without Crème Anglaise or heavy cream.

PER SERVING: 153 C   1 g P   0 g F   39 g CARB   5 mg S   0 mg CH

V A R I A T I O N S

STEWED APRICOTS OR PLUMS: Prick 1½ pounds firm-ripe apricots or plums in 2–3 places and arrange in 1½-quart casserole at least 9" across. Mix in ⅔ cup sugar and 1 cup hot water, cover, and microwave as directed, reducing time to 4–5 minutes; rearrange and turn fruit over at halftime. When fruit is barely soft, let stand as directed; cool in syrup and serve warm or cold.

PER SERVING: 205 C   2 g P   1 g F   51 g CARB   2 mg S   0 mg CH

STEWED APPLES: Peel and core 2 pounds Rome Beauty or Golden Delicious apples, cut into eighths, and spread over bottom of 11" × 7" × 2" casserole. Mix in 1 tablespoon lemon juice, ½ cup sugar, and 1½ cups apple juice or water. Cover and microwave as directed, reducing time to 5–6 minutes. Let stand, covered, 2 minutes. Cool in syrup and serve warm or cold.

PER SERVING: 251 C   0 g P   1 g F   65 g CARB   4 mg S   0 mg CH

STEWED PEACHES: Peel, pit, and halve 4 firm-ripe peaches, dip in lemon juice, and arrange in single layer in 2-quart casserole. Mix in ½ cup sugar and 1 cup hot water, cover, and microwave as directed, reducing time to 3–3½ minutes and rearranging after 2 minutes. When peaches are barely soft, let stand, covered, 1 minute. Cool in syrup and serve warm or cold.

PER SERVING: 153 C 1 g P 0 g F 40 g CARB 1 mg S 0 mg CH

Note: Apricots, peaches, and plums will be more richly flavored if you substitute ¼ cup fruit liqueur, brandy, rum, port, or Madeira for ¼ cup cooking water.

STEWED DRIED FRUITS WITH HONEY AND SPICE

PREP TIME: | 1 MINUTE | COOKING TIME: | 6–7 MINUTES | STANDING TIME: | NONE

SERVES 6

1 **pound mixed dried fruits (apples, peaches, pears, apricots, prunes, figs)**

1½ **cups water, apple juice, or semisweet white wine**

2 **tablespoons honey**

2 **thin slices lemon**

1 **stick cinnamon**

Mix all ingredients in 2-quart casserole, cover with lid, and microwave on HIGH (100% power) 6–7 minutes, stirring at halftime, until fruit plumps. Cool, covered, to room temperature.

For 3 Servings: Halve all ingredients and microwave in covered 1-quart casserole on HIGH (100% power) 3½–4 minutes, stirring at halftime. Cool as directed.

PER SERVING: 207 C 2 g P 0 g F 55 g CARB 14 mg S 0 mg CH

525

BAVARIAN TOP HAT BERRY SOUFFLÉ

PREP TIME: 10 MINUTES   COOKING TIME: 1–1½ MINUTES   STANDING TIME: NONE

SERVES 6

1   envelope unflavored gelatin

⅓   cup sugar

¼   cup cold water

1⅓   cups puréed fresh or thawed, frozen strawberries or raspberries

¾   cup heavy cream

2   egg whites

Wrap double-thick 4″ foil strip around outside of 1-quart soufflé dish so it extends 2″ above rim and fasten with tape. Mix gelatin, sugar, and water in 1½-quart casserole and microwave, uncovered, on HIGH (100% power) 1–1½ minutes until gelatin dissolves; mix in berry purée. Cool to room temperature, stirring occasionally, then chill until mixture mounds softly. Whip cream to soft peaks and fold in; then beat egg whites to stiff peaks and fold in also. Spoon into prepared soufflé dish and chill until firm. Decorate, if you like, with fresh berries and rosettes of whipped cream.

PER SERVING: 166 C   3 g P   11 g F   15 g CARB   30 mg S   41 mg CH

— V A R I A T I O N S

COLD FRUIT SOUFFLÉ: Prepare as directed substituting 1⅓ cups apricot, mango, papaya, peach, blackberry, or loganberry purée for strawberry and increase sugar as needed. Spoon into 1½-quart glass serving bowl or stemmed goblets and chill until firm.

PER SERVING: 173 C   3 g P   11 g F   16 g CARB   30 mg S   41 mg CH

CHARLOTTE RUSSE (Serves 12): Line bottom and sides of 9″ springform pan with lady fingers and sprinkle with 3–4 tablespoons framboise or Curaçao. Chill while you prepare double recipe Bavarian Top Hat Berry Soufflé (it'll take 30 seconds longer for gelatin to dissolve in microwave). Spoon into prepared pan and chill 6 hours or overnight. Remove springform sides, decorate top of Charlotte Russe with strawberries, and serve.

PER SERVING: 258 C   5 g P   13 g F   30 g CARB   45 mg S   119 mg CH

ABOUT MICROWAVING EGG- AND STARCH-THICKENED DESSERTS

Say good-bye to scorched milk, lumpy puddings, water baths, and double boilers. Also to sticky, eggy pans that are a nuisance to scrub. The microwave cooks custards and puddings with stunning speed and ease. For best results, however, follow these guidelines:

～～～ Use large eggs only in recipes that follow unless directed otherwise, never bigger or smaller ones that can affect cooking time and degree of thickening.

～～～ Never double recipes; they may curdle or boil over. Whenever you need double amounts, prepare two batches.

～～～ Space custard cups or ramekins 1" apart in circle on microwave-safe tray or platter that eliminates bother of turning each individually. Or better yet, on a turntable that equalizes cooking—no hand-turning needed.

～～～ So that custards cook uniformly without curdling, use low power levels each recipe specifies. Never try to hurry cooking of egg-thickened desserts by upping power level to HIGH (100%). **Note:** *In ovens of 700 watts or more, egg mixtures may cook more evenly on LOW (10% power) or perhaps at 20% power. Whenever mixture seems in danger of curdling, reduce power level at once.*

～～～ Always watch egg mixtures carefully as they microwave and check for doneness after minimum cooking time—microwave times will vary according to oven's power. When it comes to delicate egg-thickened mixtures, seconds, *not minutes,* can spell the difference between success and failure.

～～～ Remember that egg-thickened mixtures continue to cook as they stand, so remove from microwave the instant they test done (each of our recipes tells how to test for doneness).

～～～ To stop cooking of egg mixtures cold, quick-chill in an ice bath. Or whisk briskly for several seconds.

527

CRÈME ANGLAISE (STIRRED CUSTARD)

PREP TIME: [3 MINUTES] COOKING TIME: [8-10 MINUTES] STANDING TIME: [NONE]

⚖ ¢

SERVES 6

1¾ cups milk
¼ cup sugar
4 egg yolks, lightly beaten
1 teaspoon vanilla

Combine milk and sugar in 6-cup measure and microwave, uncovered, on HIGH (100% power) 4–5 minutes until small bubbles appear around edge (don't boil). Blend a little hot mixture into yolks, return to measure, and whisk briskly. Microwave, uncovered, on MEDIUM-LOW (30% power) 4–5 minutes, whisking every minute, until custard thickens and no eggy taste remains. *Note: Watch carefully during final 1–2 minutes— mixture mustn't boil or it will curdle. In ovens of 700 watts or more, you may need to microwave custard on LOW (10% power or perhaps at 20% power). If, despite all precautions, custard threatens to curdle, quickly drop in an ice cube and whisk vigorously.* Stir in vanilla and serve warm over cake, fruit, or pudding. Or quick-chill custard by setting container in ice water; whisk often to prevent lumping.

PER SERVING: 120 C 4 g P 6 g F 12 g CARB 41 mg S 192 mg CH

VARIATIONS

⚖ CRÈME ANGLAISE WITH SOUR CREAM: Prepare and chill as directed, then blend in 1 cup sour cream, a little bit at a time.
PER SERVING: 202 C 5 g P 14 g F 14 g CARB 61 mg S 208 mg CH

⚖ ¢ ORANGE CRÈME ANGLAISE: Prepare as directed, heating 2 teaspoons finely grated orange rind along with milk and sugar. Omit vanilla, strain finished custard through fine sieve, and mix in 2 tablespoons Cointreau or Grand Marnier.
PER SERVING: 132 C 4 g P 6 g F 13 g CARB 41 mg S 192 mg CH

FLOATING ISLAND: Prepare custard as directed and quickly cool to lukewarm by setting container in ice water. Divide custard among 4 (6-ounce) ramekins and arrange 1" apart in circle on tray. Beat 2 egg whites until frothy, gradually beat in ¼ cup sugar, and continue beating to stiff peaks. Using serving spoon dipped in cold water, float meringue puff on each custard; smooth tops lightly. Microwave, uncovered, on MEDIUM (50% power) 2½–3 minutes, rotating platter 90° every minute, until meringues are just firm. Serve at once.

PER SERVING: 157 C   5 g P   6 g F   20 g CARB   57 mg S   192 mg CH

"BAKED" CUSTARD

PREP TIME: | 3 MINUTES | COOKING TIME: | 11–13½ MINUTES | STANDING TIME: | NONE |

If you've never had luck with custard, try this foolproof microwave version, which needs no water bath.

SERVES 4

1¾ cups milk
4   eggs
3   tablespoons sugar
1   teaspoon vanilla
Ground nutmeg or mace

Microwave milk in uncovered 6-cup measure on HIGH (100% power) 4–5 minutes until small bubbles appear around edge (don't boil). Meanwhile, beat eggs with sugar and vanilla. Gradually whisk milk into egg mixture, pour into 4 (6-ounce) ramekins, sprinkle lightly with nutmeg, arrange 1" apart in circle on platter, and microwave, uncovered, on MEDIUM (50% power) 7–8½ minutes, rotating platter 90° after 3 and 6 minutes. Check for doneness at minimum time—custard should be set 1" in from edge; centers will be consistency of softly set gelatin. Remove done custards and microwave rest in 30-second increments. Cool custards, uncovered, to room temperature, then chill, if you like. Serve in ramekins or unmold. Delicious with fresh berries.

PER SERVING: 184 C   10 g P   9 g F   15 g CARB   121 mg S   289 mg CH

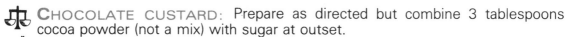
CHOCOLATE CUSTARD: Prepare as directed but combine 3 tablespoons cocoa powder (not a mix) with sugar at outset.

¢ PER SERVING: 195 C   10 g P   9 g F   17 g CARB   122 mg S   289 mg CH

BUTTERSCOTCH CUSTARD: Prepare as directed but substitute dark brown sugar for granulated and, if you like, maple flavoring for vanilla.

¢ PER SERVING: 187 C   10 g P   9 g F   16 g CARB   124 mg S   289 mg CH

COCONUT CUSTARD: Prepared as directed, but spoon 1 tablespoon flaked or toasted coconut* into each ramekin before adding custard.

¢ PER SERVING: 206 C   10 g P   11 g F   17 g CARB   133 mg S   289 mg CH

*C*RÈME BRÛLÉE

PREP TIME: 3 MINUTES   **COOKING TIME:** 15–19 MINUTES   **STANDING TIME:** NONE

¢

SERVES 4

1   **cup milk mixed with ¾ cup light cream, or 1¾ cups milk**

4   **eggs**

3   **tablespoons sugar**

1   **teaspoon vanilla**

¾   **cup loosely packed dark brown sugar**

Microwave milk in uncovered 6-cup measure on HIGH (100% power) 4–5 minutes; don't boil. Beat eggs, sugar, and vanilla, whisk in milk, pour into 8″ round glass ceramic casserole 2″ deep, and microwave, uncovered, on turntable on MEDIUM (50% power) 5–6 minutes, until set 1″ around edge. Microwave, uncovered, on MEDIUM-LOW (30% power) 3–4 minutes until set 3″ around edge. Cool uncovered, and chill 1–2 hours. Sprinkle brown sugar evenly over custard, set in pan of ice and broil 6″–8″ from heat 3–4 minutes until bubbly—watch carefully. Remove from ice, chill 10–15 minutes, and serve.

PER SERVING: 398 C   9 g P   16 g F   55 g CARB   129 mg S   312 mg CH

CHOCOLATE MOUSSE

PREP TIME: | 5 MINUTES | COOKING TIME: | 3½–5 MINUTES | STANDING TIME: | NONE |

The easiest chocolate mousse ever, and, oh, is it good.

SERVES 6

4 ounces semisweet chocolate

2 tablespoons water

3 eggs, separated

1 teaspoon vanilla

1 cup heavy cream

2 tablespoons confectioners' sugar

Melt chocolate with water in uncovered 1-quart bowl by microwaving on MEDIUM (50% power) 2½–3 minutes. Beat until smooth, whisk a little chocolate into egg yolks, mix back into bowl, and microwave, uncovered, on MEDIUM-LOW (30% power) 1–2 minutes. Whisk again and transfer to cold 2-quart bowl; mix in vanilla and cool to lukewarm. Beat cream with confectioners' sugar until it mounds softly and fold into chocolate mixture. Beat egg whites to soft peaks and fold in, a little bit at a time, until no white streaks show. Spoon into serving dish, cover, and chill 6–8 hours or overnight. Decorate, if you like, with chocolate curls or shaved blanched almonds.

PER SERVING: 284 C   5 g P   24 g F   15 g CARB   50 mg S   191 mg CH

V A R I A T I O N

FROZEN CHOCOLATE MOUSSE: Prepare mousse as directed, chill, spoon into parfait glasses, cover, and freeze until firm. Let stand 10–15 minutes at room temperature before serving.

PER SERVING: 284 C   5 g P   24 g F   15 g CARB   50 mg S   191 mg CH

ORANGE YOGURT MOUSSE

PREP TIME: [5 MINUTES] **COOKING TIME:** [1–1½ MINUTES] **STANDING TIME:** [NONE]

A delicious low-cholesterol recipe. And no need to worry about the gelatin's scorching as it dissolves. It won't in a microwave oven.

SERVES 4–6

1 **envelope unflavored gelatin**

¼ **cup sugar**

¼ **cup cold water**

1 **cup orange juice**

1 **teaspoon finely grated orange rind**

1 **cup plain low-fat yogurt**

3 **egg whites**

Mix gelatin, sugar, and water in 2-quart bowl and microwave, uncovered, on HIGH (100% power) 1–1½ minutes until gelatin dissolves. Add orange juice and rind, cool to room temperature, and chill until thick and syrupy. Mix in yogurt. Beat egg whites to stiff peaks and fold in. Spoon into serving dish or parfait glasses, cover and chill at least 6 hours before serving.

PER SERVING: 130–87 C   7–5 g P   1–1 g F   24–16 g CARB   80–53 mg S   3–2 mg CH

V A R I A T I O N

CAFÉ AU LAIT MOUSSE: Dissolve gelatin with sugar and water as directed, then blend in 2 teaspoons instant coffee powder. Substitute 1 cup milk or half-and-half cream for orange juice and proceed as directed. If you like, stir 2 tablespoons coffee liqueur into mousse just before chilling.

PER SERVING: 141–94 C   9–6 g P   3–2 g F   20–13 g CARB   109–73 mg S   12–8 mg CH

CREAMY RICE AND RAISIN PUDDING

PREP TIME: [2 MINUTES] COOKING TIME: [25–29 MINUTES] STANDING TIME: [5 MINUTES]

Remember old-timey rice pudding? The kind you had to stand and stir for hours? This easy microwave version cooks five times as fast and needs very little stirring. For truly creamy pudding, use short-grain rice.

SERVES 4–6

⅔ **cup short-grain rice**

½ **cup hot water**

2½ **cups milk**

⅓ **cup sugar**

⅓ **cup seedless raisins**

Pinch ground nutmeg

1 **tablespoon butter or margarine**

Mix rice and water in 2-quart casserole, cover with lid, and microwave on HIGH (100% power) 3 minutes; stir, re-cover, and let stand while you proceed. Microwave milk in uncovered 6-cup measure on HIGH (100% power) 4–5 minutes until small bubbles appear around edge (don't boil). Mix milk into rice along with sugar and raisins; sprinkle with nutmeg, and dot with butter. Cover with lid and microwave on MEDIUM (50% power) 18–21 minutes, stirring every 5 minutes, and uncovering after 10 minutes. When rice is just tender, let stand, covered with lid, 5 minutes. Serve warm, topped, if you like, with cream.

PER SERVING: 340–226 C   8–5 g P   8–5 g F   60–40 g CARB 107–71 mg S   29–19 mg CH

IRISH BREAD AND BUTTER PUDDING

PREP TIME: 5 MINUTES   COOKING TIME: 13–14½ MINUTES   STANDING TIME: 10 MINUTES

To make something elegant of a humble dessert, the Irish prepare this recipe with stale *barmbrack* (a sweet fruit loaf) and mix in raisins that have been plumped in Irish whiskey. Our easy microwave version uses stale raisin bread. *Note: To "stale" fresh bread, arrange slices on paper toweling flat on oven floor and microwave, uncovered, on HIGH (100% power) 2 minutes, then cool.*

SERVES 6

⅓	**cup golden seedless raisins**
2	**tablespoons Irish whiskey, dark rum, or brandy**
2	**tablespoons butter or margarine**
6	**slices stale raisin bread**
¼	**cup finely chopped candied citron**
1¾	**cups milk**
¼	**cup heavy cream**
3	**eggs**
⅓	**cup sugar**
1	**teaspoon vanilla**
⅛	**teaspoon ground nutmeg**
⅛	**teaspoon ground cinnamon**

Confectioners' sugar (optional topping)

Soak raisins in whiskey 1 hour. Butter each bread slice on one side, quarter, then arrange half of bread in 1½-quart casserole 9" across. Sprinkle with half the raisins and citron. Top with remaining bread, raisins, unabsorbed whiskey, and citron. Pour 1 cup milk over all and let soak 10 minutes; microwave remaining milk and cream, uncovered, in 1-quart measure on HIGH (100% power) 2–2½ minutes, until small bubbles appear around edge (do not boil). Meanwhile, beat eggs and sugar until cream-colored; mix in vanilla, nutmeg, and cinnamon. Gradually stir hot milk into egg mixture, pour over bread, pushing pieces underneath liquid. Microwave, uncovered, on MEDIUM (50% power) 11–12 minutes, rotating casserole 90° every 3 minutes if you have no turntable, until 1" border is set around edges; pudding in center will set on standing. *Note: In ovens of 700 watts or more, MEDIUM-LOW (30% power) may be sufficient to cook pudding.*

Cover cooked pudding with foil and let stand 10 minutes. Dust with confectioners' sugar or transfer casserole (if flameproof) to preheated broiler and brown 3″ from heat about 2 minutes. Top, if desired, with whipped cream.

PER SERVING: 319 C   8 g P   13 g F   43 g CARB   235 mg S   172 mg CH

Vanilla pudding

PREP TIME: [2 MINUTES]   COOKING TIME: [5½–6½ MINUTES]   STANDING TIME: [NONE]

SERVES 4

- 1¾ **cups milk**
- 2 **tablespoons cornstarch**
- ⅓ **cup sugar**
- 1 **egg, lightly beaten**
- 1 **teaspoon vanilla**
- 1 **tablespoon butter or margarine**

Pour 1½ cups milk into 6-cup measure and microwave, uncovered, on HIGH (100% power) 3 minutes. Blend cornstarch and sugar with remaining ¼ cup milk, whisk into hot milk, and microwave, uncovered, on HIGH (100% power) 2½–3½ minutes, whisking at halftime, until mixture boils and thickens. Blend a little hot mixture into egg, stir back into measure, and whisk vigorously; whisk in vanilla and butter and beat 5 seconds. Pour into dessert dishes and serve warm. Or place circle of wax paper flat on pudding, chill, and serve cold.

PER SERVING: 192 C   5 g P   8 g F   25 g CARB   99 mg S   91 mg CH

~~~~~~~~~~ V A R I A T I O N S

CHOCOLATE PUDDING: Prepare as directed but beat in 1 envelope (1 ounce) unsweetened no-melt chocolate after adding egg; omit butter.

PER SERVING: 212 C   6 g P   9 g F   27 g CARB   70 mg S   83 mg CH

535

⚖ CARAMEL PUDDING: Prepare as directed substituting brown sugar for white.

¢ **PER SERVING: 196 C   5 g P   8 g F   26 g CARB   104 mg S 91 mg CH**

⚖ LOW-CHOLESTEROL VANILLA PUDDING: Prepare as directed substituting skim milk for regular; increase cornstarch to 3 tablespoons; omit egg and butter.

¢ **PER SERVING: 127 C   4 g P   0 g F   27 g CARB   56 mg S 2 mg CH**

⚖ TAPIOCA PUDDING: Omit cornstarch and instead mix 3 tablespoons quick-cooking tapioca with sugar and ¼ cup milk; let stand while remaining milk heats. Proceed as directed but omit egg.

¢ **PER SERVING: 183 C   4 g P   6 g F   28 g CARB   82 mg S 23 mg CH**

STEAMED SULTANA SPONGE WITH HOT TREACLE SAUCE

PREP TIME: [10 MINUTE]   COOKING TIME: [8¾–11 MINUTES]   STANDING TIME: [NONE*]

It takes 1½ hours—at least!—to steam pudding the old-fashioned way. The microwave does the job in less than 15 minutes.

¢

SERVES 4–6

1   **cup sifted flour**
½   **teaspoon baking powder**
¼   **cup butter or margarine**
⅓   **cup sugar**

Sift flour with baking powder and set aside. Cream butter and sugar until light, then beat in egg. Combine milk and vanilla and add alternately with flour, beginning and ending with flour and beating well after each addition. Stir in raisins and spoon into well-greased 1-quart glass ovenware measure lined on bottom with 2 circles

536

1 egg

¼ cup milk

1 teaspoon vanilla

⅓ cup golden seedless (sultana) raisins

Hot Treacle Sauce

½ cup dark molasses

¾ cup hot water

1 tablespoon arrowroot blended with 2 tablespoons lemon juice

wax paper. Smooth top of batter and rap measure lightly on counter to expel air bubbles. Cover with vented plastic food wrap and microwave on MEDIUM (50% power) 6–8 minutes, rotating bowl 180° at halftime. When pudding is springy and cake tester inserted in center comes out clean, pudding is done. **Note:** *Small moist circle in center of pudding will dry on standing.* Let pudding stand, covered, 5 minutes.

Meanwhile, make sauce: Microwave molasses and water in uncovered 1-quart measure on HIGH (100% power) 2 minutes until hot, not boiling. Whisk in arrowroot mixture and microwave, uncovered, ¾–1¼ minutes until sauce boils and thickens; pour into sauceboat. Invert pudding on plate and carefully ease out of measure. Peel off wax paper and serve.

PER SERVING: 435–290 C 6–4 g P 14–9 g F 74–49 g CARB 238–159 mg S 102–68 mg CH

—————— V A R I A T I O N

¢ STEAMED CHOCOLATE PUDDING: Prepare pudding as directed but add 1 extra tablespoon sugar. Also beat in 1 envelope (1 ounce) unsweetened no-melt chocolate after adding egg and reduce milk to 3 tablespoons. Top with Hot Fudge or Chocolate-Cream Sauce, Crème Anglaise, or softly whipped cream.

PER SERVING: 394–263 C 6–4 g P 17–12 g F 54–36 g CARB 195–130 mg S 101–67 mg CH

ENGLISH CHRISTMAS PUDDING

PREP TIME: 8 MINUTES **COOKING TIME:** 11–12 MINUTES **STANDING TIME:** 15 MINUTES

This raisin-studded plum pudding, England's Christmas dessert for nearly 300 years, once contained silver charms and coins to forecast the new year's fortunes. The original recipe steamed 4–5 hours. Our microwave pudding needs just 12 minutes—or less. Make it ahead, wrap in brandy-soaked cloth, and store airtight for a week or two in a very cool (50° F.) dry spot.

SERVES 8

1 **tablespoon brandy or dark rum**

2 **cups seedless raisins**

¼ **cup sifted flour**

½ **teaspoon baking powder**

½ **teaspoon ground allspice**

¼ **teaspoon ground ginger**

¼ **teaspoon ground nutmeg**

Pinch salt

1 **cup soft white bread crumbs**

¼ **cup dark molasses**

1 **egg**

1 **teaspoon finely grated lemon rind**

1 **teaspoon finely grated orange rind**

¼ **teaspoon almond extract**

½ **cup prepared mincemeat**

1 **tablespoon minced candied citron**

Sprinkle brandy over raisins and let stand 30 minutes. Sift flour with baking powder, spices, and salt; add crumbs, molasses, egg, lemon and orange rind, and almond extract, and beat hard 30 seconds. Stir in remaining ingredients and pack lightly into greased 1-quart measure lined on bottom with 2 circles wax paper. Cover with vented plastic food wrap and microwave on MEDIUM (50% power) 11–12 minutes, rotating measure 90° every 3 minutes. When pudding is springy and cake tester inserted near center comes out clean, pudding is done. *Note: Small moist circle in center of pudding will dry on standing.* Remove plastic wrap, cover with foil, shiny side down, and let pudding stand 15 minutes. Loosen sides of pudding with spatula all the way to bottom, invert pudding on plate, and carefully ease out of measure. Peel off wax paper, cool pudding 5 minutes, and serve with hard sauce, whipped cream, Crème Anglaise, or Rum Sauce.

PER SERVING: 219 C   3 g P   2 g F   51 g CARB   150 mg S   35 g CH

To Reheat Pudding: Wrap loosely in plastic food wrap and microwave on HIGH (100% power) 1 minute. Turn pudding over, rotate 180° and microwave on MEDIUM (50% power) 1–2 minutes until warm, *not* steaming hot or pudding will be hard to slice. Let stand, still wrapped, 1 minute, then unwrap and serve.

To Flame Pudding: Warm ¼ cup brandy or dark rum in uncovered 1-cup measure by microwaving on HIGH (100% power) 15–20 seconds. Pour into large metal ladle, blaze with match, and pour flaming liquor over pudding. Also spoon a little liquor over each portion.

GRAHAM CRACKER CRUST

PREP TIME: | 3 MINUTES | COOKING TIME: | 3½–4 MINUTES | STANDING TIME: | NONE |

Because of their sugar and butter content, crumb crusts can burn in a microwave oven, even if you use a turntable. So check often, especially the center.

¢

(MAKES A 9″ PIE SHELL— 6–8 SERVINGS)

¼ *cup butter or margarine*

¼ *cup sugar*

1 *cup graham cracker crumbs*

Melt butter in wax-paper-covered 9″ pie plate by microwaving on HIGH (100% power) 45–55 seconds. Mix in remaining ingredients with hands and press over bottom and up sides of pie plate. Microwave, uncovered, on MEDIUM-HIGH (70% power) 2½–3 minutes, rotating plate 180° every minute. Cool before filling.

PER SERVING: 180–135 C 1–1 g P 9–7 g F 23–17 g CARB 198–149 mg S 21–16 mg CH

V A R I A T I O N S

¢ VANILLA WAFER CRUST: Prepare as directed but substitute vanilla wafer crumbs for cracker crumbs and reduce sugar to 1 tablespoon.

PER SERVING: 163–122 C 1–1 g P 11–8 g F 16–12 g CARB 126–94 mg S 28–21 mg CH

539

NUT-CRUMB CRUST: Prepare as directed using ¾ cup graham cracker or vanilla wafer crumbs and ⅓ cup finely minced nuts (any kind).

PER SERVING: 202–152 C   2–1 g P   13–10 g F   20–15 g CARB   169–127 mg S   21–16 mg CH

¢ **CHOCOLATE CRUMB CRUST:** Prepare as directed but substitute chocolate wafer crumbs for cracker crumbs and reduce sugar to 1 tablespoon.

PER SERVING: 162–122 C   1–1 g P   10–8 g F   16–12 g CARB   211–159 mg S   21–16 mg CH

¢ **GINGERSNAP CRUST:** Prepare as directed but substitute gingersnap crumbs for cracker crumbs, omit sugar, and reduce microwave time to 1½–2 minutes.

PER SERVING: 147–110 C   1–1 g P   9–7 g F   15–11 g CARB   186–139 mg S   28–21 mg CH

LEMON MERINGUE PIE

PREP TIME: [10 MINUTES]   COOKING TIME: [14–16 MINUTES]   STANDING TIME: [NONE]

¢

SERVES 6–8

Filling

½ **cup unsifted cornstarch**

1¼ **cups sugar**

Pinch salt

1⅔ **cups water**

½ **cup lemon juice**

1½ **teaspoons finely grated lemon rind**

3 **egg yolks, lightly beaten**

1 **tablespoon butter or margarine**

Pie Shell

1 **(9″) Graham Cracker Crust**

Mix cornstarch, sugar, and salt in 2-quart casserole; gradually whisk in water and lemon juice. Cover with wax paper and microwave on HIGH (100% power) 5–6 minutes, whisking briskly every 2 minutes, until clear, thick, and smooth; mix in lemon rind. Blend a little hot mixture into yolks, stir back into casserole, add butter, and microwave, uncovered, on MEDIUM-LOW (30% power) 3½–4 minutes, stirring at halftime, until no raw egg taste remains (don't boil or mixture will curdle). Cool 2–3 minutes, stirring often, and spoon into crust.

For meringue: Beat egg whites, cream of tartar, and salt until frothy, then beat sugar in, 1 tablespoon at a time; continue beating to stiff peaks. Spoon meringue onto warm filling so it touches crust all around, then smooth and swirl gently (tall peaks dry out). Microwave, uncovered, on MEDIUM (50% power) 5½–6 minutes,

540

Meringue

**3   egg whites, at room
      temperature**

½   teaspoon cream of tartar

Pinch salt

⅓   cup sugar

rotating pie plate 90° every 2 minutes, until meringue tests done. *To test meringue for doneness, touch with finger; a little meringue will cling to finger; if that underneath is set and dry, meringue is done. It won't brown.* To brown meringue, broil 5" from heat in preheated broiler 1½–2 minutes. ***Note:*** *To fake brown top, sprinkle cooked meringue with graham cracker crumbs.* Chill pie 2 hours before cutting.

PER SERVING: 482–362 C 5–3 g P 14–10 g F 86–65 g CARB 296–222 mg S 162–122 mg CH

━━━━━∿∿∿∿∿━━ V A R I A T I O N

¢ **LIME MERINGUE PIE:** Prepare as directed, substituting ⅓ cup lime juice and 1 teaspoon finely grated lime rind for lemon juice and rind; if you like, add 2–3 drops green food coloring.

PER SERVING: 480–360 C 5–3 g P 14–10 g F 86–65 g CARB 294–220 mg S 162–122 mg CH

GEORGIA SWEET POTATO PIE

PREP TIME: | 3 MINUTES | COOKING TIME: | 13–16 MINUTES | STANDING TIME: | NONE

¢

SERVES 6–8

Filling

1¼ cups puréed cooked sweet potatoes

¾ cup milk

⅔ cup sugar

1 teaspoon vanilla

¼ teaspoon ground nutmeg

3 eggs, lightly beaten

Pie Shell

1 (9″) Graham Cracker Crust

Topping

⅔ cup coarsely chopped pecans

¼ cup firmly packed light brown sugar

2 tablespoons butter, at room temperature

1 teaspoon flour

Mix all filling ingredients except eggs in 2-quart casserole, cover with wax paper, and microwave on HIGH (100% power) 3 minutes, stirring at halftime. Blend a little hot mixture into eggs, stir back into casserole, and microwave, uncovered, on MEDIUM (50% power) 2 minutes, whisking well at halftime. Pour into crust, smooth top, center pie on oven shelf or shallow bowl, and microwave, uncovered, on MEDIUM (50% power) 10 minutes, rotating 180° at halftime. Mix topping, scatter evenly over filling, and microwave, uncovered, on MEDIUM (50% power) 3–6 minutes until all but 1″ circle in center of filling is set. Cool and serve.

PER SERVING: 549–412 C 8–6 g P 25–19 g F 75–56 g CARB 299–224 mg S 172–129 mg CH

PUMPKIN PIE

PREP TIME: `3 MINUTES` **COOKING TIME:** `19–22 MINUTES` **STANDING TIME:** `NONE`

¢

SERVES 6–8

Filling

2 **cups unsweetened pumpkin purée**

¾ **cup evaporated milk**

½ **cup firmly packed light brown sugar**

½ **teaspoon ground cinnamon**

¼ **teaspoon ground ginger**

⅛ **teaspoon ground allspice**

3 **eggs, lightly beaten**

Pie Shell

1 **(9″) Graham Cracker Crust**

Mix all filling ingredients except eggs in 2-quart casserole, cover with wax paper, and microwave on HIGH (100% power) 4 minutes, stirring at halftime. Blend a little hot mixture into eggs, stir back into casserole, and microwave, uncovered, on MEDIUM (50% power) 2 minutes, whisking well at halftime. Pour into crust, smooth top, center pie on oven shelf or shallow bowl and microwave, uncovered, on MEDIUM (50% power) 13–16 minutes, rotating pie plate 180° every 5 minutes, until all but 1″ circle in center of filling is set. Cool to room temperature and serve.

PER SERVING: 347–260 C   7–5 g P   14–11 g F   48–36 g CARB   272–204 mg S   167–125 mg CH

~~~~~~~~ V A R I A T I O N

¢ SQUASH PIE: Prepare as directed, substituting puréed cooked acorn, butternut, or Hubbard squash for pumpkin and using a half-and-half mixture of granulated and brown sugar. Also increase ginger to ½ teaspoon.

PER SERVING: 355–267 C   7–5 g P   14–11 g F   50–37 g CARB   270–202 mg S   167–125 mg CH

PEACH CHIFFON PIE

PREP TIME: 8 MINUTES   COOKING TIME: 5–5½ MINUTES   STANDING TIME: NONE

SERVES 6–8

Filling

½	**cup sugar**
1	**envelope unflavored gelatin**
1⅓	**cups puréed peaches**
2	**egg yolks, lightly beaten**
¼	**teaspoon finely grated lemon rind**
⅓	**cup heavy cream, softly whipped (optional)**
3	**egg whites**
1	**large ripe peach, peeled, pitted, sliced thin, and brushed with lemon juice**

Pie Shell

1	**(9") Graham Cracker or Gingersnap Crust**

Mix sugar, gelatin, and purée in 1-quart measure and microwave, uncovered, on HIGH (100% power) 3–3½ minutes until mixture foams up and sugar dissolves. Mix yolks and lemon rind, blend in a little hot mixture, stir back into measure, and microwave, uncovered, on MEDIUM-LOW (30% power) 2 minutes, stirring at halftime, until mixture thickens slightly and no raw egg taste remains (don't boil or mixture may curdle). Transfer at once to 2-quart bowl and cool, stirring occasionally, until mixture mounds slightly, or quick-chill in ice bath. Fold in whipped cream, if you like. Beat egg whites to soft peaks, stir about ¼ cup into peach mixture, then fold in balance. Cover bottom of pie shell with peach slices, top with filling, and chill several hours until firm.

PER SERVING: 352–264 C   6–4 g P   16–12 g F   48–36 g CARB 232–174 mg S   129–97 mg CH

V A R I A T I O N S

ORANGE CHIFFON PIE: Prepare as directed substituting ¾ cup orange juice for puréed peaches and 2 tablespoons finely grated orange rind for lemon rind. Also increase egg yolks to 3; omit sliced peach and decorate, if you like, with well-drained mandarin orange segments.

PER SERVING: 341–255 C   4–3 g P   17–13 g F   44–33 g CARB   209–157 mg S   175–131 mg CH

LEMON OR LIME CHIFFON PIE: Add enough water to ⅓ cup lemon or lime juice to total ¾ cup and use in place of puréed peaches. Increase sugar to ⅔ cup, egg yolks to 3, and lemon rind to 1 teaspoon (or use lime rind). Omit sliced peach but otherwise prepare as directed.

PER SERVING: 349–262 C   4–3 g P   17–13 g F   46–35 g CARB   211–159 mg S   175–131 mg CH

CHERRY CHEESECAKE

PREP TIME: [8 MINUTES] COOKING TIME: [11–12½ MINUTES] STANDING TIME: [NONE]

Make a day ahead so the cheesecake will slice easily. Also use a turntable, if you have one. The cheesecake will cook and rise more evenly.

SERVES 8

Filling

2   **packages (8 ounces each) cream cheese**

2   **eggs**

6   **tablespoons sugar**

1½ **teaspoons vanilla**

Pie Shell

1   **(9") Graham Cracker Crust**

Cherry Topping

½   **cup sugar**

2   **tablespoons cornstarch**

1   **can (1 pound) pitted sour red cherries, drained (reserve liquid)**

Cherry liquid plus enough water to total ⅔ cup

1   **teaspoon lemon juice**

2–3 **drops red food coloring (optional)**

Soften cream cheese by microwaving in wax-paper-covered 1-quart casserole on MEDIUM (50% power) 2 minutes. Meanwhile, beat eggs until foamy, gradually add sugar, and beat until thick. Blend eggs into cheese and stir in vanilla. Pour into crust, set on turntable if you have one, and microwave, uncovered, on MEDIUM (50% power) 9–10½ minutes until filling just sets. *Note: The moist dime-size area in center of cheesecake will set on cooling. If you have no turntable, rotate cheesecake 90° every 3 minutes. Cool to lukewarm. Filling will sink slightly, but this is normal and accommodates topping nicely.*

For Topping: Mix sugar, cornstarch, and cherry liquid in 1-quart measure and microwave, uncovered, on HIGH (100% power) 2½–3 minutes, whisking every minute, until mixture boils and thickens. Mix in cherries, lemon juice, and if desired, food coloring; cool 10 minutes, stirring occasionally. Spread topping evenly over lukewarm cheesecake. Chill 8–10 hours or overnight before cutting.

PER SERVING: 489 C 7 g P 28 g F 54 g CARB 338 mg S 146 mg CH

WALNUT-LEMON CHEESECAKE: Prepare filling as directed, but reduce vanilla to ½ teaspoon and add 1 teaspoon finely grated lemon rind. Spoon filling into 9″ Nut-Crumb Crust made with walnuts and microwave as directed. Omit cherry topping; instead combine 1 cup sour cream, 2 tablespoons sugar, and 1 teaspoon vanilla and spread evenly over filling. Mix ⅓ cup finely minced walnuts with 2 tablespoons finely slivered candied lemon rind and scatter evenly on top. Chill cheesecake as directed before serving.

PER SERVING: 522 C   9 g P   40 g F   34 g CARB   328 mg S   159 mg CH

*M*ELBA *SAUCE*

PREP TIME: 5 MINUTES   **COOKING TIME:** 4½–5 MINUTES   **STANDING TIME:** NONE

To be authentic, this sauce should be made only with raspberries. But we like it with other fruits, too.

MAKES 2 CUPS

2   *cups puréed raspberries, strawberries, or loganberries*

⅓   *cup sugar (about)*

1   *tablespoon cornstarch blended with 2 tablespoons cold water*

1   *teaspoon lemon juice*

2   *tablespoons framboise, Chambord, or red currant jelly*

Mix purée and sugar in 6-cup measure, cover with wax paper, and microwave on HIGH (100% power) 3 minutes. Whisk in cornstarch mixture and lemon juice and microwave, uncovered, on HIGH (100% power) 1½–2 minutes until sauce boils and thickens slightly. Stir in framboise; cool, taste for sweetness, and add more sugar, if needed. Also thin, if needed, with a little water. Use to sauce fruit desserts or ladle over ice cream.

PER TABLESPOON: 16 C   0 g P   0 g F   3.7 g CARB   0 mg S   0 mg CH

APRICOT OR PEACH SAUCE: Prepare as directed substituting puréed apricots or peaches for berries and peach brandy for framboise.

PER TABLESPOON: 17 C   0.2 g P   0 g F   3.9 g CARB   0.2 mg S   0 mg CH

RUM SAUCE

PREP TIME: [1 MINUTE]   COOKING TIME: [5–5½ MINUTES]   STANDING TIME: [NONE]

Delicious with English Christmas Pudding and Steamed Sultana Sponge.

MAKES 2 CUPS

⅓ **cup sugar**

2 **tablespoons cornstarch**

1⅔ **cups milk**

¼ **cup dark rum**

½ **teaspoon vanilla**

Mix sugar and cornstarch in 6-cup measure, whisk in milk, and microwave, uncovered, on HIGH (100% power) 5–5½ minutes, whisking every 2 minutes, until sauce boils and thickens. Mix in rum and vanilla and serve warm.

PER TABLESPOON: 22 C   0.4 g P   0.4 g F   3 g CARB   6.3 mg S   1.8 mg CH

VARIATIONS

BRANDY SAUCE: Prepare as directed, substituting brandy for rum.

PER TABLESPOON: 22 C   0.4 g P   0.4 g F   3 g CARB   6.3 mg S   1.8 mg CH

RUM-RAISIN SAUCE: Prepare as directed but mix in ⅓ cup seedless raisins along with rum and vanilla. Delicious over pound cake or yellow cake.

PER TABLESPOON: 26 C   0.5 g P   0.4 g F   4.3 g CARB   6.4 mg S   1.8 mg CH

CHOCOLATE-CREAM SAUCE: Mix 4 tablespoons cocoa powder (not a mix) with sugar and cornstarch and proceed as directed, substituting ¼ cup heavy cream for rum and increasing vanilla to 1½ teaspoons. Serve warm with Steamed Chocolate Pudding, chocolate or vanilla ice cream.

PER TABLESPOON: 26 C   0.5 g P   1.2 g F   3.5 g CARB   7 mg S   4.3 mg CH

HOT FUDGE SAUCE

PREP TIME: [1 MINUTE] COOKING TIME: [2–2½ MINUTES] STANDING TIME: [NONE]

MAKES ABOUT 1⅔ CUPS

- 1 cup sugar
- 1 can (5 ounces) evaporated milk
- 1 teaspoon freeze-dried coffee crystals
- Pinch salt
- 2 envelopes (1 ounce each) unsweetened no-melt chocolate
- 2 tablespoons butter or margarine, at room temperature
- 2 teaspoons vanilla

Mix sugar, milk, coffee, and salt in 6-cup measure and microwave, uncovered, on HIGH (100% power) 2–2½ minutes, stirring at halftime, until bubbling. Whisk in remaining ingredients, beating until smooth. Serve warm or at room temperature with cake or ice cream.

PER TABLESPOON: 61 C   0.7 g P   2.5 g F   9 g CARB 20.6 mg S 4.1 mg CH

BUTTERSCOTCH SAUCE

PREP TIME: [1 MINUTE] COOKING TIME: [4½–5 MINUTES] STANDING TIME: [NONE]

MAKES ABOUT 2½ CUPS

- 1 cup firmly packed dark brown sugar
- 1 cup maple syrup or pancake syrup
- ¼ cup butter or margarine
- ¾ cup light cream or evaporated milk
- 2 teaspoons vanilla

Mix sugar and syrup in 6-cup measure and microwave, uncovered, on MEDIUM (50% power) 4½–5 minutes until bubbling. Drop in butter, *do not stir,* but let cool, uncovered and undisturbed, until butter melts completely. Whisk in cream and vanilla and beat until smooth. Serve warm or at room temperature with cake or ice cream.

PER TABLESPOON: 60 C   0.1 g P   2 g F   10.6 g CARB 15.9 mg S 6 mg CH

ABOUT MICROWAVING CAKES

Although there are certainly exceptions to the rule, the cakes most apt to microwave well are those made with butter and egg yolks. Angel food, chiffon, and sponge cakes are microwave disasters for two reasons. First, they never develop the crust that's needed to seal in the steam and air that leaven them, and second, they set before they can rise, thanks to the protein-rich egg whites folded into them. We concentrate here on cakes tailor-made for the microwave, but you can learn to adapt old family recipes, too (see How to Convert Favorite Recipes for Microwave Use in Chapter 1). *Note: Many oven manufacturers offer valuable cake-baking tips in their user's manuals; read these carefully. When microwaving cake mixes, follow package directions precisely.* Because the microwave is such a revolutionary new way of cooking, it presents special problems when it comes to "baking" cakes. Here's how to solve them.

PROBLEMS, PREVENTIVES, AND SOLUTIONS:

FAILURE TO BROWN AND DEVELOP A CRUST: Because most cakes are frosted, it really doesn't matter if they don't develop the nice brown finish that they do in conventional ovens. But there are also ways to add or build in color. You can stir brown sugar or chocolate into the batter, as some of our recipes do. You can bake on a crust by coating a well-greased pan with graham cracker or gingersnap crumbs (never use minced nuts, which turn rubbery, or flour, which produces an ugly scum, and always grease the pan with vegetable shortening, unsalted butter, or margarine; crumbs don't stick to oiled pans).

FRUITS AND/OR NUTS SINKING TO THE BOTTOM: Only finely minced fruits or nuts will stay afloat during the first critical stages of microwaving when batters are apt to thin.

FAILURE TO COOK EVENLY: Most important, perhaps, is using the proper pan. Most cakes microwave best in round pans, tubes, or fluted rings although a few, like our Gingerbread, microwave perfectly in a square pan without any shielding* about the corners with aluminum foil. Although there are many made-for-microwave layer-cake pans, some of them with nonstick finishes, we find that glass ovenware casseroles of the right size and shape work just as well. **Note:** *Always use the pan or mold our recipes specify.* To help cakes bake more uniformly in a microwave oven, you should also:

~~~~~ No more than half-fill cake pans and spread batter as smoothly and evenly as possible. Also cut through batter with a spatula to break air bubbles and/or rap the pan lightly on the counter.

~~~~~ Use a turntable and center it on oven shelf or elevate on shallow bowl; if you have no turntable, rotate cake pan as recipes direct. Cakes should bake as near the middle of the microwave oven as possible.

~~~~~ Always begin cakes on MEDIUM (50% power) to allow slow, even rising, then finish on HIGH (100% power) to firm them. Always microwave cakes uncovered.

~~~~~ **STICKINESS OR MOISTNESS:** Because they're crustless, micro-waved cakes are unusually tender. Always let them stand and/or cool as recipes direct. When turning cakes out, loosen carefully around edges and center tube; also clear to bottom of pan or mold, easing them away from pan in several places to allow steam to escape. Finally, invert on serving plate to cool (moist tops will stick to cake racks). If cake doesn't unmold, loosen once again, and invert.

~~~~~ **FAILURE TO REMAIN MOIST:** Paradoxically, the lack of crust, which makes cakes sticky at first, also means they'll dry faster on cooling. To minimize, loosely cover with dish towel or paper toweling *before* cooling. Then wrap or store cakes airtight—and this applies to filled and frosted layers as well as to plain cakes.

~~~~~ **FAILURE TO FROST EVENLY:** Microwaved cakes crumb—and crumble—easily, so first apply a thin wash of frosting to seal in crumbs, thinning frosting, if necessary, with a little water so it spreads evenly, then let dry at room temperature at least 10 minutes before proceeding. If cooled cake is too soft to frost, refrigerate, uncovered, 15–20 minutes.

SOME GENERAL TIPS FOR MAKING BETTER MICROWAVE CAKES

~~~~~~~ Use only the shortening called for by a recipe. Vegetable shortenings and oils are not interchangeable with butter or margarine.

~~~~~~~ Never substitute brown sugar for granulated, baking soda and cream of tartar for baking powder, cake flour for all-purpose flour. You can, however, substitute one flavoring for another.

~~~~~~~ Use little or no salt. In our opinion, saltless cake batters microwave more evenly than salted ones.

~~~~~~~ When greasing pans, always use vegetable shortening, unsalted butter, or margarine, never oil or nonstick vegetable cooking sprays, which can leave splotches or greasy films. As for lining pans with wax paper, a single circle works well, but a double thickness is foolproof (anchor to pan with dab of butter before adding batter).

~~~~~~~ If you must use the same pan to microwave two cake layers, wash, cool in cold water, then wipe dry before refilling. Also wipe moisture from microwave oven walls, floor, and door before cooking second layer.

~~~~~~~ Monitor cakes through oven door; those cooked in ovens of 700 watts or more will need only 1–2 minutes on HIGH (100% power) to finish cooking and will dry rapidly if overcooked.

~~~~~~~ Always test cakes for doneness after minimum cooking time has elapsed.

HOW TO TEST CAKES FOR DONENESS

~~~~~~~ Insert toothpick or cake tester in center of cake and/or in 1 or 2 other areas; when cake is done it will come out clean.

~~~~ Touch cake gently. Despite its few moist spots, it should feel springy. It may or may not have pulled slightly from sides of pan. Touch moist spots; cake underneath should look dry and cooked. **Note:** *These few moist spots will disappear as cake stands or cools.*

~~~~ If cake is not done after maximum cooking time, continuing microwaving at same power level in 30-second increments, testing for doneness after each.

CUPCAKES

PREP TIME: | 8 MINUTES | COOKING TIME: | 2–3 MINUTES | STANDING TIME: | 1 MINUTE |

To give cupcakes extra support and ensure even rising, use two crinkly paper liners for each and fill only one third. To hide pale tops, frost or sprinkle with confectioners' sugar, chopped nuts, toasted flaked coconut,* or cookie crumbs.

MAKES 1 DOZEN

1   **cup sifted flour**
¾ **teaspoon baking powder**
⅓ **cup butter or margarine**
⅔ **cup sugar**
2   **eggs**
⅓ **cup milk mixed with 1 teaspoon vanilla**

Sift flour with baking powder and set aside. Cream butter until light, beat sugar in gradually, and cream until fluffy. Beat eggs in, one by one, then add dry ingredients alternately with milk mixture, beginning and ending with dry. Beat just until smooth. Line each cup of 6-cup cupcaker or muffin pan with two crinkly paper liners and fill each one third with batter. Set on turntable and microwave, uncovered, on HIGH (100% power) 2–3 minutes. **Note:** *If you have no turntable, rotate pan 180° at halftime.* After 2 minutes, insert toothpick in center of each muffin; it should come out clean. **Note:** *Small moist spots will dry on standing.* Let cupcakes stand

1 minute, remove outer liners, and transfer cupcakes in single liners to wire rack to cool. Microwave remaining batter the same way. Frost or decorate as desired.

PER CUPCAKE: 141 C   2 g P   6 g F   19 g CARB   93 mg S   60 mg CH

V A R I A T I O N S

DOUBLE CHOCOLATE CUPCAKES: Prepare as directed but add 1 envelope (1 ounce) unsweetened no-melt chocolate along with eggs and fold ½ cup semisweet chocolate bits into batter at end.

PER CUPCAKE: 192 C   3 g P   10 g F   24 g CARB   93 mg S   60 mg CH

LEMON CUPCAKES: Prepare as directed but add 1 teaspoon finely grated lemon rind after eggs and substitute ⅛ teaspoon lemon extract for vanilla.

PER CUPCAKE: 140 C   2 g P   6 g F   19 g CARB   93 mg S   60 mg CH

COCONUT CUPCAKES (Makes 15): Prepare as directed but substitute almond extract for vanilla and fold ½ cup flaked coconut into batter. Sprinkle each cupcake with ½ tablespoon toasted flaked coconut* and microwave as directed.

PER CUPCAKE: 137 C   2 g P   7 g F   17 g CARB   82 mg S   48 mg CH

ORANGE CUPCAKES: Prepare 1 recipe Orange Cake batter, spoon into cupcaker, and microwave as directed for cupcakes.

PER CUPCAKE: 140 C   2 g P   6 g F   19 g CARB   99 mg S   59 mg CH

BASIC YELLOW CAKE

PREP TIME: [10 MINUTES] COOKING TIME: [7-8 MINUTES] STANDING TIME: [10 MINUTES]

If you want a layer cake, double the recipe and microwave layers one at a time.

MAKES A 9" ROUND CAKE—8 SERVINGS

1   **cup sifted flour**

1   **teaspoon baking powder**

⅓   **cup butter or margarine**

⅔   **cup sugar**

2   **eggs**

⅓   **cup milk mixed with 1 teaspoon vanilla**

Sift flour with baking powder and set aside. Cream butter until light, beat sugar in gradually, and cream until fluffy. Beat eggs in, one by one, then add dry ingredients in thirds alternately with milk mixture, beginning and ending with dry. Beat just until smooth. Spread batter evenly in ungreased 9" round microwave-safe cake pan lined with wax paper. Center pan on oven rack or elevate on shallow bowl and microwave, uncovered, on MEDIUM (50% power) 6 minutes, rotating pan 180° at halftime. Again rotate 180° and microwave on HIGH (100% power) 1–2 minutes until toothpick, inserted in 2 areas other than center, comes out clean. *Note: Small moist area in center will dry on standing.* Let cake stand, uncovered, 10 minutes; loosen edges, invert pan on plate, tap bottom, and ease cake out; remove wax paper. Cool cake and frost, if you like.

PER SERVING: 212 C   3 g P   9 g F   28 g CARB   153 mg S   90 mg CH

V A R I A T I O N S

ORANGE CAKE: Prepare as directed, substituting orange juice for milk and 1 tablespoon finely grated orange rind for vanilla.

PER SERVING: 209 C   3 g P   9 g F   29 g CARB   148 mg S   89 mg CH

NUT CAKE: Prepare as directed, mixing ½ cup finely chopped walnuts or pecans into batter and microwaving cake 1 minute longer on HIGH (100% power).

PER SERVING: 259 C   4 g P   14 g F   30 g CARB   149 mg S   89 mg CH

PINEAPPLE-COCONUT UPSIDE-DOWN CAKE

PREP TIME: 10 MINUTES   COOKING TIME: 13–14 MINUTES   STANDING TIME: 5 MINUTES

SERVES 6–8

- ¼ cup (½ stick) plus ⅓ cup butter or margarine
- ½ cup firmly packed dark brown sugar
- 1 can (8 ounces) sliced pineapple, drained and slices patted dry on paper toweling
- 2 maraschino cherries, halved and drained well
- 1 cup sifted flour
- 1 teaspoon baking powder
- ⅔ cup sugar
- 2 eggs
- 2 tablespoons cream of coconut
- 1 teaspoon finely grated lemon rind
- ¼ cup milk
- ⅓ cup toasted flaked coconut*

Melt ¼ cup butter in wax-paper-covered 9″ microwave layer cake pan by microwaving on HIGH (100% power) 55–65 seconds. Mix in brown sugar and spread evenly over pan bottom. Arrange pineapple artfully on top and stud centers with cherries. Sift flour with baking powder and set aside. Cream ⅓ cup butter until light, beat sugar in gradually, and cream until fluffy. Beat eggs in, one by one, then mix in cream of coconut and lemon rind. Add dry ingredients alternately with milk, beginning and ending with dry. Spread batter evenly over fruit and scatter coconut on top. Center pan on oven rack or elevate on shallow bowl and microwave, uncovered, on MEDIUM (50% power) 8 minutes, rotating pan 180° at halftime. Again rotate 180° and microwave on HIGH (100% power) 4–5 minutes until toothpick, inserted near center, comes out clean. *Note: Small moist area in center will dry on standing.* Let cake stand, uncovered, 5 minutes; loosen edges, invert on plate, and serve warm or cold with or without whipped cream or crème fraîche.

PER SERVING: 472–354 C   5–4 g P   23–17 g F   64–48 g CARB   291–218 mg S   141–106 mg CH

555

WALNUT-GLAZED BROWN SUGAR POUND CAKE

PREP TIME: [10 MINUTES] COOKING TIME: [13½–15 MINUTES] STANDING TIME: [10 MINUTES]

This feathery pound cake bakes more evenly in a ring than in a loaf pan.

MAKES A 9" TUBE CAKE—16 SERVINGS

2   *cups sifted flour*

¾   *teaspoon baking powder*

⅛   *teaspoon ground nutmeg*

1   *cup (2 sticks) butter or margarine*

1   *cup firmly packed dark brown sugar*

4   *eggs*

Glaze

2   *cups sifted confectioners' sugar*

2   *tablespoons light corn syrup*

1–2 *tablespoons water*

½   *teaspoon vanilla*

⅓   *cup walnut halves or pieces*

Sift flour with baking powder and nutmeg and set aside. Cream butter until light, beat sugar in gradually, and cream until fluffy. Beat eggs in, one by one, then mix in dry ingredients and beat just until smooth. Spread batter evenly in greased 9" (8-cup) ring mold and rap lightly on counter to expel air bubbles. Center mold on oven rack or elevate on shallow bowl and microwave, uncovered, on MEDIUM (50% power) 10 minutes, rotating mold 180° at halftime. Again rotate 180° and microwave on HIGH (100% power) 2–3 minutes until toothpick, inserted midway between rim and center, comes out clean. *Note: Small moist areas will dry on standing.* Let cake stand in upright mold, uncovered, 10 minutes. Loosen cake all the way to bottom of mold, invert on plate, ease out, and cool completely.

Meanwhile, prepare glaze: Microwave sugar, syrup, and 1 tablespoon water in uncovered 1-quart measure on HIGH (100% power) 1 minute. Mix well and microwave, uncovered, on MEDIUM (50% power) ½–1 minute until sugar dissolves and mixture is smooth. *Note: Don't allow glaze to boil.* Mix in vanilla and additional water as needed to make glaze pouring consistency. Spoon glaze evenly over cooled cake, letting it run down sides, then quickly arrange nuts on top. Cool until glaze hardens.

PER SERVING: 295 C 3 g P 14 g F 39 g CARB 161 mg S 100 mg CH

PINEAPPLE-CARROT CAKE

PREP TIME: [10 MINUTES] COOKING TIME: [14½–15 MINUTES] STANDING TIME: [NONE]

This cake will taste better and cut more easily if you make it a day ahead of time. Wrapped airtight, it will keep moist and tender for about a week.

MAKES A 9″ TUBE CAKE—16 SERVINGS

1	**cup sifted all-purpose flour**
1	**tablespoon baking powder**
¼	**teaspoon salt**
1	**cup unsifted whole wheat flour (not stone-ground)**
1	**cup firmly packed light brown sugar**
2	**eggs, lightly beaten**
⅓	**cup vegetable oil**
1	**teaspoon vanilla**
1	**can (8 ounces) crushed pineapple, drained (reserve ¼ cup liquid)**
1½	**cups coarsely grated carrots**

Sift all-purpose flour, baking powder, and salt together into mixing bowl; stir in whole wheat flour. Add sugar and rub between fingers to break up lumps. Combine eggs, oil, vanilla, and ¼ cup pineapple liquid and mix into dry ingredients. Add pineapple and carrots and mix thoroughly. Spoon into well-greased 9″ (8-cup) ring mold, spreading batter evenly. Center mold on oven shelf or elevate on upside-down shallow bowl. Microwave, uncovered, on MEDIUM (50% power) 10 minutes, rotating mold 180° at halftime. Raise power to MEDIUM-HIGH (70% power) and microwave 4½–5¼ minutes, again rotating mold 180° at halftime, until cake pulls slightly from sides of mold, is springy to touch, and toothpick inserted in cake comes out clean. *Note: If you use turntable, there's no need to rotate mold.* Cool cake 20 minutes. Loosen carefully, invert on wire rack, and immediately turn right side up on serving plate. Cover loosely with clean dish towel and cool to room temperature. *Note: To facilitate cutting, use knife dipped in very hot water (shake off excess water).*

PER SERVING: 166 C   3 g P   5 g F   28 g CARB   130 mg S   34 mg CH

GINGERBREAD

PREP TIME: 2 MINUTES · COOKING TIME: 7½-8 MINUTES · STANDING TIME: NONE

Although it microwaves in a square container, this gingerbread needs no shielding* at the corners. For best results, use a turntable.

⚖ ¢ ⧖

MAKES AN 8″ × 8″ × 2″ CAKE— 16 SERVINGS

1¼ **cups sifted flour**

½ **teaspoon baking soda**

1 **teaspoon ground ginger**

½ **teaspoon ground cinnamon**

¼ **teaspoon ground cloves**

¼ **cup vegetable oil**

¼ **cup sugar**

1 **egg**

⅓ **cup dark molasses**

3 **tablespoons hot water**

Sift flour, soda, and spices into mixing bowl. Add remaining ingredients and beat 1 minute at moderate electric mixer speed. Spread batter evenly in well-greased 8″ × 8″ × 2″ baking dish and rap lightly on counter to expel air bubbles. Set on turntable centered on oven rack or elevate on shallow bowl and microwave, uncovered, on MEDIUM (50% power) 6 minutes. *Note: If you have no turntable, rotate dish 180° at halftime and again after 6 minutes.* Microwave, uncovered, on HIGH (100% power) 1½–2 minutes until toothpick, inserted in two places other than center, comes out clean. *Note: Small moist area in center will dry on cooling.* Cool in dish flat on heat-resistant surface, cut in squares, and serve as is or top with vanilla ice cream and finely slivered candied ginger.

PER SERVING: 95 C   1 g P   4 g F   14 g CARB   37 mg S   17 mg CH

MARBLE BUNDT CAKE

PREP TIME: [10 MINUTES] COOKING TIME: [12–13 MINUTES] STANDING TIME: [10 MINUTES]

⚖ ¢

MAKES A 9″ BUNDT CAKE—12 SERVINGS

2   *cups sifted flour*

1½   *teaspoons baking powder*

⅔   *cup butter or margarine*

1¼   *cups sugar*

3   *eggs*

½   *cup milk mixed with 1 teaspoon vanilla*

⅓   *cup unsifted cocoa powder (not a mix)*

1   *teaspoon freeze-dried coffee crystals dissolved in 1 teaspoon water*

Grease 9″ (10–12-cup) Bundt pan well. Sift flour with baking powder and set aside. Cream butter until light, beat sugar in gradually, and cream until fluffy. Beat eggs in, one by one, then add dry ingredients in thirds alternately with milk mixture, beginning and ending with dry. Beat just until smooth. Spoon 2 cups batter into bowl and mix in cocoa and coffee. Alternately spoon plain and chocolate batters into pan; zigzag knife through batter to marbleize. Spread batter evenly and rap pan lightly on counter to expel air bubbles. Center pan on oven rack or elevate on shallow bowl and microwave, uncovered, on MEDIUM (50% power) 10 minutes, rotating pan 180° at halftime. Again rotate 180° and microwave on HIGH (100% power) 2–3 minutes until toothpick, inserted midway between rim and center, comes out clean. *Note: The few moist spots on surface will dry on standing.* Let cake stand, uncovered, 10 minutes; loosen edges, all the way to bottom of pan, invert pan on plate, and ease cake out. Cool cake and frost, if you like.

PER SERVING: 275 C   4 g P   13 g F   37 g CARB   181 mg S   98 mg CH

DOUBLE FROSTED DEVIL'S FOOD CAKE

PREP TIME: 10 MINUTES   COOKING TIME: 15½–18 MINUTES   STANDING TIME: 20 MINUTES

Don't microwave both layers at the same time—they'll cook unevenly. Instead, microwave second layer while first one stands.

MAKES A 9" TWO-LAYER CAKE—16 SERVINGS

2	cups sifted flour
2	teaspoons baking powder
⅔	cup butter or margarine
1⅓	cups sugar
3	eggs
3	envelopes (1 ounce each) unsweetened no-melt chocolate
½	cup milk mixed with 1½ teaspoons vanilla

Filling

2½	tablespoons butter or margarine
2¼	cups sifted confectioners' sugar
¼	cup sifted cocoa powder (not a mix)
1	teaspoon vanilla
⅛	teaspoon salt
2–3	tablespoons light cream

Sift flour with baking powder and set aside. Cream butter until light, beat sugar in gradually, and cream until fluffy. Beat eggs in, one by one, then mix in chocolate. Add dry ingredients in thirds alternately with milk mixture, beginning and ending with dry. Beat just until smooth. Spread batter evenly in 2 ungreased 9" round microwave-safe cake pans lined with wax paper. Center 1 pan on oven rack or elevate on shallow bowl and microwave, uncovered, on MEDIUM (50% power) 6 minutes, rotating pan 180° at halftime. Again rotate 180° and microwave on HIGH (100% power) 1–2 minutes until toothpick, inserted in 2 areas other than center, comes out clean. *Note: Small moist area in center will dry on standing.* Let cake stand, uncovered, 10 minutes. Meanwhile, microwave second layer the same way and let stand. Loosen 1 layer around edge, invert pan on plate, tap bottom, and ease cake out; remove wax paper. Invert second layer on wax paper dusted with cocoa and peel off wax paper. Cool layers to room temperature.

Glaze

2   **cups sifted confectioners'
     sugar**

2   **tablespoons light corn
     syrup**

1–2 **tablespoons water**

1   **envelope (1 ounce)
     unsweetened no-melt
     chocolate**

Meanwhile, prepare filling: Cream butter, sugar, cocoa, vanilla, and salt until light. Mix in enough cream for good spreading consistency. Spread ⅔ filling on first layer, top with second layer, cocoa-dusted side up, and spread with remaining filling; chill while you prepare glaze.

For glaze: microwave sugar, corn syrup, and 1 tablespoon water in uncovered 1-quart measure on HIGH (100% power) 1 minute. Stir and microwave on MEDIUM (50% power) ½–1 minute until sugar dissolves. Add chocolate and beat until smooth. ***Note:*** *Do not boil or glaze will not dry to glossy finish.* Stir again, and, if necessary, add 1–3 teaspoons warm water to thin to pouring consistency. Spoon evenly over cake, smoothing edges with metal spatula dipped in hot water. Cool until glaze hardens.

**PER SERVING: 385 C   4 g P   15 g F   59 g CARB   187 mg S
80 mg CH**

PECAN TORTE WITH MOCHA CREAM

PREP TIME: 15 MINUTES   COOKING TIME: 15–17 MINUTES   STANDING TIME: 20 MINUTES

As impressive as anything produced in a fancy French pâtisserie, yet it microwaves in less than 20 minutes. Only the assembly requires a bit of ''t.l.c.''

MAKES A 9″ TWO-LAYER CAKE— 16 SERVINGS

44 vanilla wafers

1 cup finely minced or ground pecans

1 teaspoon baking powder

1 teaspoon finely grated lemon rind

3 eggs, separated

⅓ cup plus 2 tablespoons sugar

2 tablespoons light rum mixed with 1 tablespoon water

1 cup apricot preserves

Mocha Cream

1 cup heavy cream

½ cup sifted confectioners' sugar

¼ cup sifted cocoa powder (not a mix)

1½ teaspoons instant coffee dissolved in 1 teaspoon warm water

Chocolate Glaze

⅓ cup heavy cream

6 squares (1 ounce each) semisweet chocolate

Churn wafers to fine crumbs in the food processor or on HIGH in the electric blender; transfer to bowl and mix in pecans, baking powder, and lemon rind. In separate bowl beat egg yolks until thick, gradually beat in ⅓ cup sugar, and continue beating until very thick. Beat egg whites until frothy, gradually beat in 2 tablespoons sugar, and whip to soft peaks. Stir ¼ cup whites into yolk mixture, then fold in balance. Also fold in dry ingredients, ½ cup at a time, blending lightly. Dividing batter equally, spread smoothly in 2 wax-paper-lined 9″ layer cake dishes; rap lightly on counter to expel air bubbles. Cover one dish with wax paper and refrigerate. Center other on oven rack or on shallow bowl and microwave, uncovered, on MEDIUM (50% power) 5 minutes, rotating dish 180° after 3 minutes. Again rotate 180° and microwave on HIGH (100% power) ½–1 minute just until springy (there should be no moist spots). Let stand, uncovered, 10 minutes. Meanwhile, microwave second layer the same way and let stand. Loosen layers around edges, then slip spatula underneath wax paper on pan bottoms, and lift layers gently to free them. Invert pans on wire racks, gently ease layers out, and peel off wax paper. Cover loosely with clean dish towel and cool completely. Brush tops with rum mixture. Microwave preserves in uncovered 2-cup measure on HIGH (100% power) 1½–2 minutes, sieve, and spread on rum-soaked layers.

For mocha cream: Using chilled bowl and beaters, whip cream until frothy. Gradually add sugar, cocoa, and coffee and beat until stiff. Spread evenly on one layer and top with second layer. Refrigerate while preparing glaze.

For chocolate glaze: Microwave cream in uncovered 1-quart measure on HIGH (100% power) 1 minute. Add chocolate and microwave, uncovered, on MEDIUM (50% power) 1½–2 minutes until chocolate melts. Stir until smooth and cool to spreading consistency, stirring occasionally. Spread glaze over top of cake, just to edge. Chill torte at least 2 hours before serving.

PER SERVING: 313 C   3 g P   18 g F   38 g CARB   71 mg S 82 mg CH

*B*UTTERSCOTCH-MAPLE *FROSTING*

PREP TIME: | 2 MINUTES | COOKING TIME: | 3½–4 MINUTES | STANDING TIME: | NONE

MAKES ABOUT ½ CUP, ENOUGH TO FROST AN 8″ OR 9″ QUICK BREAD OR CAKE, 1 DOZEN MUFFINS OR CUPCAKES

- ¼ *cup (½ stick) butter (no substitute)*
- 1 *cup sifted confectioners' sugar*
- 1 *tablespoon milk*
- ½ *teaspoon maple flavoring*

Microwave butter in wax-paper-covered 1-quart measure on HIGH (100% power) 3½–4 minutes until amber in color. ***Note:*** *Do not overbrown butter.* Cool 2 minutes, then blend in sugar, a little at a time, alternately with milk. When smooth, mix in maple flavoring.

PER TABLESPOON: 100 C   0.1 g P   5.8 g F   12.6 g CARB 59.6 mg S   15.8 mg CH

CREAMY VANILLA FILLING

PREP TIME: 1 MINUTE   COOKING TIME: 3½–4 MINUTES   STANDING TIME: NONE

For extra creaminess, fold in ¼ cup cream, softly whipped, just before using.

MAKES ENOUGH TO FILL AN 8" OR 9" TWO-LAYER CAKE—16 SERVINGS

3   **tablespoons cornstarch**

¼   **cup sugar**

1   **cup milk**

1   **egg yolk lightly beaten with 2 tablespoons milk**

1   **teaspoon vanilla**

Mix cornstarch, sugar, and milk in 1-quart measure and microwave, uncovered, on HIGH (100% power) 2½–3 minutes, whisking every minute, until mixture boils and thickens (it will be very thick). Gradually whisk egg yolk into hot mixture and microwave, uncovered, on MEDIUM (50% power) 1 minute, whisking vigorously at halftime and again at end. Stir in vanilla and cool to room temperature, whisking now and then. Cover, chill well, then use to fill cake.

PER SERVING: 33 C   1 g P   1 g F   5 g CARB   9 mg S   19 mg CH

VARIATIONS

¢ CREAMY CHOCOLATE FILLING: Mix 2 ounces melted semisweet chocolate into finished filling.

PER SERVING: 101 C   2 g P   4 g F   15 g CARB   18 mg S   39 mg CH

¢ CREAMY COCONUT FILLING: Mix ½ cup flaked coconut into finished filling.

PER SERVING: 87 C   2 g P   3 g F   13 g CARB   30 mg S   39 mg CH

¢ CREAMY COFFEE FILLING: Prepare as directed but add 1½ teaspoons instant coffee along with cornstarch.

PER SERVING: 66 C   1 g P   2 g F   11 g CARB   18 mg S 39 mg CH

¢ CREAMY BUTTERSCOTCH FILLING: Prepare as directed, substituting ⅓ cup brown sugar for white and, if you like, maple flavoring for vanilla.

PER SERVING: 75 C   1 g P   2 g F   13 g CARB   21 mg S 39 mg CH

¢ CREAMY LEMON FILLING: Prepare as directed adding 1 teaspoon finely grated lemon rind with egg yolk; substitute ⅛ teaspoon lemon extract for vanilla.

PER SERVING: 64 C   1 g P   2 g F   10 g CARB   18 mg S 39 mg CH

¢ CREAMY ORANGE FILLING: Prepare as directed for Creamy Lemon Filling, substituting 2 teaspoons orange rind for lemon rind and orange extract for lemon extract.

PER SERVING: 65 C   1 g P   2 g F   11 g CARB   18 mg S 39 mg CH

ABOUT MICROWAVING COOKIES

Although carefully adapted cookie recipes do microwave successfully, you can "bake" so few at a time it hardly seems worthwhile. For that reason, we prefer the conventional oven for most cookies and certainly for any that should be crisp (the microwave fails dismally here as it also does with commercial slice-and-bake cookies that haven't been especially formulated for the microwave). But bar cookies are another story. We've adapted some of our particular favorites for the microwave and they've been a huge hit with family, friends, and neighbors. Imagine brownies cooling on the counter in just 10 minutes! And that, of course, is the big microwave advantage.

FOR BEST RESULTS WITH BAR COOKIES:

Always use the size and shape pan or container recipes recommend.

Always microwave uncovered so steam can escape.

Always cool before cutting. The first bar may be tricky to get out of the pan, so pry up—gently—with flexible metal spatula. The rest will be a snap to remove.

Store tightly covered either in baking pan or airtight canister. Being crustless, microwaved bars dry out almost as fast as they cook.

Note: Because it's unlikely you'll be able to eat just one brownie or bar cookie and because nutritional fractions do add up, the figures given here are precise rather than being rounded off to the nearest whole number.

BROWNIES

PREP TIME: | 4 MINUTES | COOKING TIME: | 9¼–10½ MINUTES | STANDING TIME: | NONE

MAKES 16

- ½ cup (1 stick) butter or margarine
- 1 cup sugar
- ⅓ cup unsifted cocoa powder (not a mix)
- 2 eggs
- 1 cup sifted flour
- ½ teaspoon baking powder
- 1 teaspoon vanilla
- ½ cup moderately finely chopped pecans or walnuts

Soften butter by microwaving in wax-paper-covered mixing bowl on HIGH (100% power) 20–30 seconds (do not melt). Add sugar and cocoa and beat at high mixer speed 5 seconds. Beat in eggs, one at a time. Sift flour with baking powder and beat in gradually at lowest speed. Add vanilla and beat at high speed 15 seconds. Stir in nuts, spread batter evenly in greased 8″ × 8″ × 2″ glass ovenware dish. Wrap corners smoothly with 2″ foil strips, center dish on oven rack or elevate on shallow bowl, and microwave, uncovered, on MEDIUM (50% power) 6 minutes, rotating dish 180° at halftime. Remove foil and microwave on HIGH (100% power) 3–4 minutes, again rotating 180° at halftime, until toothpick inserted in center of brownies comes out clean and top is springy. *Note: The few moist spots will dry as brownies cool.* Cool brownies in dish flat on heat-resistant surface to room temperature, then cut into squares.

PER BROWNIE: 163 C 2.1 g P 9.1 g F 19.6 g CARB 80.8 mg S 49.8 mg CH

CHOCOLATE CHIP BARS

PREP TIME: 7 MINUTES COOKING TIME: 6-7 MINUTES STANDING TIME: NONE

¢

MAKES 2 DOZEN

- 1⅓ **cups sifted flour**
- ½ **teaspoon baking powder**
- ½ **cup (1 stick) butter or margarine**
- ⅓ **cup granulated sugar**
- ⅓ **cup firmly packed dark brown sugar**
- 1 **egg**
- 1 **tablespoon milk mixed with ½ teaspoon vanilla**
- 1 **cup semisweet or milk chocolate bits**
- ½ **cup moderately finely chopped walnuts or pecans (optional)**

Sift flour with baking powder and set aside. Cream butter until light, beat sugars in gradually, and cream until fluffy. Beat egg in, then add dry ingredients in two batches alternately with milk mixture, beginning and ending with dry. Beat just until smooth; stir in half of chocolate bits and, if desired, nuts. Spread batter evenly in greased 11" × 7" × 2" baking dish and scatter remaining bits evenly on top. Center on oven rack or elevate on shallow bowl and microwave, uncovered, on HIGH (100% power) 6–7 minutes, rotating dish 180° after 3 minutes, until slightly firm. *Note: Small damp spots will dry on cooling.* Let cool, uncovered, 1 hour; cut in bars and cool completely in dish before removing.

PER BAR: 119 C   1.3 g P   6.7 g F   14.6 g CARB   52.2 mg S   21.8 mg CH

———————— V A R I A T I O N

BUTTERSCOTCH BARS: Prepare as directed, substituting butterscotch bits for chocolate.

PER BAR: 120 C   1 g P   6.3 g F   14.8 g CARB   52 mg S   21.8 mg CH

PEANUT BUTTER BARS

PREP TIME: | 5 MINUTES | COOKING TIME: | 5½–6 MINUTES | STANDING TIME: | 5 MINUTES

MAKES 2 DOZEN

⅓ **cup creamy peanut butter**

⅓ **cup firmly packed light brown sugar**

1 **egg**

1 **teaspoon vanilla**

2 **tablespoons milk**

⅔ **cup sifted flour**

¼ **teaspoon baking soda**

¼ **cup moderately finely chopped toasted blanched peanuts**

Beat peanut butter with sugar, egg, vanilla, and milk to combine. Sift flour with baking soda, add to mixture, and beat just until smooth. Mix in peanuts. Spread evenly in greased 8″ × 8″ × 2″ glass ovenware dish, center dish on oven rack or elevate on shallow bowl, and microwave, uncovered, on MEDIUM-HIGH (70% power) 5½–6 minutes, rotating dish 180° after 3 minutes, until just firm to the touch. Let stand, uncovered, in dish 5 minutes, then transfer dish to wire rack and cool completely. Cut into bars and serve.

PER BAR: 51 C   1.7 g P   2.3 g F   6.2 g CARB   34.4 mg S 11.6 mg CH

569

DATE CHEWS

PREP TIME: 5 MINUTES   COOKING TIME: 7–8 MINUTES   STANDING TIME: NONE

Even better the second day. To speed-chop dates, pop in freezer for 20 minutes, then snip with scissors.

MAKES 2½ DOZEN BARS

- ¾ **cup sifted flour**
- ¾ **cup sugar**
- ¾ **teaspoon baking powder**
- 1 **cup moderately finely chopped dates**
- ¾ **cup moderately finely chopped walnuts or pecans**
- 2 **eggs**
- ½ **teaspoon vanilla**
- 2–3 **tablespoons confectioners' sugar**

Sift flour, sugar, and baking powder into bowl; add dates and nuts and toss well. Beat eggs until frothy, add vanilla, pour into dry ingredients, and mix well. Spread evenly in greased 10″ × 10″ × 2″ baking dish, center on oven rack or elevate on shallow bowl, and microwave, uncovered, on HIGH (100% power) 7–8 minutes, turning dish 180° after 4 minutes, until springy. *Note:* Small damp spots will dry on cooling. Let cool in uncovered dish, flat on heat-resistant surface, until lukewarm; cut in bars and cool completely in dish before removing. Recut bars and dust with confectioners' sugar.

PER BAR: 73 C   1.2 g P   2.3 g F   12.8 g CARB   15.8 mg S   18.3 mg CH

GRANOLA BARS

PREP TIME: 5 MINUTES COOKING TIME: 5-6 MINUTES STANDING TIME: 10 MINUTES

These bars brown like conventionally baked ones, yet cook four times as fast.

MAKES 32

- **1 cup rolled oats (quick-cooking or regular)**
- **½ cup wheat germ**
- **⅓ cup sifted flour**
- **¾ cup unsweetened flaked coconut**
- **¾ cup moderately finely chopped blanched peanuts**
- **¾ cup coarsely chopped pitted dates or prunes, seedless raisins, dried apples, apricots and/or figs (use any combination)**
- **½ cup firmly packed light brown sugar**
- **½ cup (1 stick) butter or margarine, melted**
- **2 tablespoons dark molasses**
- **1 teaspoon vanilla**

In large bowl mix oats, wheat germ, flour, coconut, nuts, dried fruit, and sugar. Combine butter, molasses, and vanilla, dump into dry ingredients, and mix well. Spread mixture evenly in well-greased 11″ × 7″ × 2″ baking dish, then pat firmly with wet hands. Center on oven rack or elevate on shallow bowl and microwave, uncovered, on HIGH (100% power) 5–6 minutes, turning dish 180° after 3 minutes, until lightly browned. *Note: Remove at once from oven even though center may be less brown than edges; it will brown further on standing.* Let stand in uncovered dish, 10 minutes, set dish on wire rack, and cool 20 minutes. Score surface, marking off 32 bars, then cool completely in dish before serving.

PER BAR: 88 C   1.4 g P   4.5 g F   11.2 g CARB   43.5 mg S   7.8 mg CH

HAZELNUT SHORTBREAD

PREP TIME: **5 MINUTES** — COOKING TIME: **5½–6 MINUTES** — STANDING TIME: **NONE**

This delicious shortbread will microwave more evenly if you use a turntable.

MAKES 12 WEDGES

- **1 cup sifted flour**
- **½ cup blanched hazelnuts, almonds, or peanuts***
- **⅓ cup sugar**
- **⅓ cup very soft butter or margarine (not melted)**
- **1 teaspoon vanilla**

Churn flour, nuts, and sugar in food processor 20 seconds until uniformly fine. Add butter and vanilla and pulse 5–6 times just to blend. Turn mixture onto board and knead 30 seconds; pat firmly and smoothly into greased 9" pie plate, prick well with fork, and cut into 12 wedges of equal size. Center pie plate on turntable on oven rack or elevate on shallow bowl and microwave, uncovered, on MEDIUM (50% power) 5½–6 minutes, until slightly firm. *Note: If you do not use turntable, rotate pie plate 180° at halftime. Watch center of shortbread closely for last minute and remove instant it begins browning; otherwise shortbread will overcook as it cools.* Cool shortbread, uncovered, in pie plate on wire rack 5 minutes; carefully recut and separate wedges. Sprinkle, if you like, with granulated sugar; cool to room temperature before serving.

PER WEDGE: 132 C 1.7 g P 8.1 g F 13.6 g CARB 51.9 mg S 13.7 mg CH

ABOUT MICROWAVING CANDY

There's no point in trying to microwave fudge or fondant, caramels or taffy, which must be cooked to just the right temperature because you'll be opening the oven door constantly to check on their progress. These old-fashioned candies, moreover, don't really cook much faster by microwave and they bubble and boil so furiously they can be dangerous to move, especially if your oven is a high-level one set above your range or counter. So reserve these family favorites for the stovetop.

The microwave does excel, however, at short-cut candies that involve little more than melting chocolate or caramel. It can even be used to boil up a terrific nut brittle—and from scratch, at that.

The recipes that follow have all been developed especially for the microwave oven and if you follow them to the letter, you should succeed every time.

Note: Because it's unlikely you'll be able to eat just one piece of candy, and also because nutritional fractions add up fast (not to mention alarmingly), the figures given here are precise rather than being rounded off to the nearest whole number.

ROCKY ROAD CANDY

PREP TIME: | 5 MINUTES | COOKING TIME: | 3-4 MINUTES | STANDING TIME: | NONE

¢ ⧖

MAKES 64 (1") SQUARES

- **1 package (12 ounces) semisweet or milk chocolate bits**
- **3 tablespoons milk**
- **1 cup miniature marshmallows**
- **1 cup coarsely chopped walnuts or pecans**

Arrange chocolate bits in doughnut shape in 1½-quart casserole and microwave, uncovered, on MEDIUM (50% power) 3–4 minutes, rotating casserole 180° and adding milk at halftime. Mix until smooth, stir in marshmallows and nuts, and spread in well-buttered 8" × 8" × 2" pan. Cool, chill until firm, then cut in 1" squares.

PER PIECE: 42 C   0.5 g P   3.1 g F   4 g CARB   0.9 mg S   0.1 mg CH

6-MINUTE CHOCOLATE CHIP-PECAN FUDGE

PREP TIME: | 4 MINUTES | **COOKING TIME:** | 2–2½ MINUTES | **STANDING TIME:** | NONE

MAKES 64 (1″) SQUARES

- **1 box (1 pound) confectioners' sugar, sifted**
- **½ cup unsifted cocoa powder (not a mix)**
- **½ cup (1 stick) butter or margarine, cut in small pieces**
- **¼ cup light cream**
- **1 tablespoon vanilla**
- **Pinch salt**
- **¾ cup semisweet chocolate bits**
- **¾ cup coarsely chopped pecans or walnuts**

Mix sugar, cocoa, butter, cream, vanilla, and salt in 2-quart casserole and microwave, uncovered, on HIGH (100% power) 2–2½ minutes, stirring after 1 minute, until bubbling. Beat until smooth, mix in chocolate bits and nuts, and spread evenly in well-buttered 8″ × 8″ × 2″ pan. Cool, chill until firm, then cut in 1″ squares. For better flavor, ripen 24 hours in airtight container.

PER PIECE: 63 C   0.3 g P   3.3 g F   8.9 g CARB   17.2 mg S   4.5 mg CH

V A R I A T I O N

 Coconut Fudge: Prepare as directed, substituting 1¼ cups flaked coconut for chocolate bits and nuts.

PER PIECE: 51 C   0.2 g P   2.2 g F   8.2 g CARB   20.9 mg S   4.5 mg CH

CHOCOLATE-RAISIN-NUT BARK

PREP TIME: | 3 MINUTES
COOKING TIME: | 2½–3½ MINUTES
STANDING TIME: | NONE

¢ ⧖

MAKES ABOUT 1 POUND

1 **package (12 ounces) semisweet chocolate bits**

⅔ **cup toasted blanched (or unblanched) whole almonds or filberts***

⅓ **cup seedless raisins**

Arrange chocolate bits in doughnut shape in 9″ pie plate and microwave, uncovered, on MEDIUM (50% power) 2½–3½ minutes, stirring after 2 minutes, until glossy. Stir until smooth, mix in nuts and raisins, and spread thin over wax-paper-lined 15″ × 10″ baking sheet. Chill until firm and break in pieces.

PER OUNCE: 170 C 2.8 g P 12.4 g F 16.1 g CARB 1.7 mg S 0 mg CH

NUTTY CARAMEL APPLES

PREP TIME: | 3 MINUTES
COOKING TIME: | 3–3½ MINUTES
STANDING TIME: | NONE

¢ ⧖

MAKES 4

1 **package (14 ounces) vanilla caramels**

2 **tablespoons water**

4 **wooden skewers**

4 **medium-size red apples, washed, dried, and stemmed**

⅓ **cup moderately finely chopped walnuts, pecans, or toasted blanched almonds or peanuts***

Melt caramels with water in uncovered 1-quart measure by microwaving on HIGH (100% power) 3–3½ minutes, stirring every minute. Meanwhile, insert skewers in stem ends of apples. When caramels are melted, stir until smooth. Dip apples into melted caramels to coat evenly, then roll in nuts. Cool on wax paper until caramel hardens.

PER APPLE: 541 C 6 g P 17 g F 99 g CARB 225 mg S 2 mg CH

575

ALMOND BRITTLE

PREP TIME: [4 MINUTES] COOKING TIME: [7½–8 MINUTES] STANDING TIME: [NONE]

MAKES ABOUT ¾ POUND

1   **cup sugar**

⅓   **cup light corn syrup**

1¼ **cups sliced unblanched almonds or slivered blanched almonds***

1   **tablespoon butter or margarine**

½   **teaspoon vanilla**

½   **teaspoon baking soda**

Mix sugar and corn syrup in 2-quart measure or casserole and microwave, uncovered, on HIGH (100% power) 4 minutes, stirring at half-time. Mix in almonds and butter and microwave, uncovered, on HIGH (100% power) 3½–4 minutes until pale brown. Quickly stir in vanilla and soda, pour onto buttered baking sheet, and spread as thin as possible with buttered metal spatula. For extra thin brittle, cool 4–5 minutes, then pull and stretch with buttered fingers (mixture should be pliable). When cold, crack into pieces and ripen 24 hours in airtight canister.

PER OUNCE: 157 C   1.9 g P   6 g F   25.4 g CARB   51.2 mg S   2.6 mg CH

V A R I A T I O N

¢ PEANUT BRITTLE: Prepare as directed, substituting roasted, blanched peanuts for almonds.

PER OUNCE: 120 C   0.9 g P   2.4 g F   24.8 g CARB   99.4 mg S   2.6 mg CH

Glazed Nuts

PREP TIME: | 1 MINUTE | COOKING TIME: | 4–5¼ MINUTES | STANDING TIME: | NONE

MAKES ABOUT 1 POUND

¼ cup (½ stick) butter or
margarine

½ cup firmly packed light
brown sugar

⅓ cup unsifted confectioners'
sugar

2½ cups pecan or walnut halves
or toasted blanched whole
almonds or filberts*

Melt butter in wax-paper-covered 9" casserole by microwaving on HIGH (100% power) 55–65 seconds. Mix in remaining ingredients and microwave, uncovered, on HIGH (100% power) 3–4 minutes, stirring at halftime, until mixture bubbles vigorously. Cool and stir 1 minute, then spread on wax-paper-lined baking sheet, and cool completely. Store airtight.

**PER OUNCE: 173 C   1.3 g P   14.3 g F   12.2 g CARB
31.5 mg S 7.8 mg CH**

V A R I A T I O N

SPICED NUTS: Prepare as directed, mix in 1 teaspoon ground cinnamon, ¼ teaspoon ground nutmeg, and ⅛ teaspoon ground ginger along with sugar and nuts.

**PER OUNCE: 174 C   1.3 g P   14.3 g F   12.3 g CARB
31.5 mg S 7.8 mg CH**

INDEX

587

589

INDEX

BOOK MARK

The text of this book was composed in
various fonts of the Univers family of typefaces,
predominantly that of Univers 55.
The display typography was set in Baur Topic Medium Italic
by Monotype Composition Company, Inc.,
Baltimore, Maryland

This book was printed in two colors
with four color inserts
by Arcata Graphics • Fairfield,
Fairfield, Pennsylvania

BOOK DESIGN BY
CAROL MALCOLM

(Continued on Front End Papers)

CONTAINERS AND COVERINGS

〰〰〰 Use only microwave-safe containers.

〰〰〰 Use only the specific container sizes and shapes recipes recommended; for example, a casserole at least 9″ across (diameter) or 13″ × 9″ × 2″ baking dish or 9″ (12-cup) Bundt pan or ring mold. Whenever volume and depth are essential to a recipe's success as well as the container's diameter or length and width, those dimensions are also included.

〰〰〰 Never grease containers unless recipes direct you to do so. Microwaved foods rarely stick.

〰〰〰 Use only the coverings recipes specify—wax paper, for example, paper toweling, a casserole lid or vented plastic food wrap. They are essential to the recipe's success.

〰〰〰 Whenever covering containers with plastic food wrap, always vent by turning the wrap back at one corner to allow steam to escape.

INGREDIENTS: UNLESS RECIPES SPECIFY OTHERWISE

〰〰〰 Flour called for is all-purpose flour, sifted before measuring.

〰〰〰 Baking powder is double-acting.

〰〰〰 Sugar is granulated.

〰〰〰 Butter is salted.

〰〰〰 Brown sugar is measured firmly packed.

〰〰〰 Eggs are large.

〰〰〰 Garlic cloves are of medium size.

〰〰〰 Ground hot red pepper is what was previously known as cayenne.

〰〰〰 *Never substitute one ingredient for another unless the recipe specifies alternative ingredients* (margarine for butter, for example; oil for shortening; honey for sugar; yogurt for sour cream).

〰〰〰 All recipes call for brand-name products by their generic (general descriptive) names (liquid hot red pepper seasoning, for example, is Tabasco or other hot pepper sauce, converted rice is the processed or parboiled variety [Uncle Ben's], not quick-cooking [Minute] rice).

〰〰〰 *All measures are standard, all measurements level.*

MAKE-AHEAD RECIPES

〰〰〰 Whenever a recipe may be wholly or partially made ahead, instructions indicate at which point it may be refrigerated or frozen.

〰〰〰 Whenever a recipe may be made ahead, reheating times are also included.

RECIPE YIELDS

〰〰〰 All yields are given in average-size servings or portions.

〰〰〰 Recipe variations yield the same number of servings as the basic recipes unless otherwise indicated.